T0202797

Lecture Notes in Computer Science   11094

Commenced Publication in 1973
Founding and Former Series Editors:
Gerhard Goos, Juris Hartmanis, and Jan van Leeuwen

Editorial Board

David Hutchison
  Lancaster University, Lancaster, UK
Takeo Kanade
  Carnegie Mellon University, Pittsburgh, PA, USA
Josef Kittler
  University of Surrey, Guildford, UK
Jon M. Kleinberg
  Cornell University, Ithaca, NY, USA
Friedemann Mattern
  ETH Zurich, Zurich, Switzerland
John C. Mitchell
  Stanford University, Stanford, CA, USA
Moni Naor
  Weizmann Institute of Science, Rehovot, Israel
C. Pandu Rangan
  Indian Institute of Technology Madras, Chennai, India
Bernhard Steffen
  TU Dortmund University, Dortmund, Germany
Demetri Terzopoulos
  University of California, Los Angeles, CA, USA
Doug Tygar
  University of California, Berkeley, CA, USA
Gerhard Weikum
  Max Planck Institute for Informatics, Saarbrücken, Germany

More information about this series at http://www.springer.com/series/7408

Barbara Gallina · Amund Skavhaug
Erwin Schoitsch · Friedemann Bitsch (Eds.)

Computer Safety, Reliability, and Security

SAFECOMP 2018 Workshops
ASSURE, DECSoS, SASSUR, STRIVE, and WAISE
Västerås, Sweden, September 18, 2018
Proceedings

 Springer

Editors
Barbara Gallina 🆔
Mälardalen University
Västerås
Sweden

Amund Skavhaug
Norwegian University of Science
and Technology
Trondheim
Norway

Erwin Schoitsch 🆔
AIT Austrian Institute of Technology
Vienna
Austria

Friedemann Bitsch 🆔
Thales Deutschland GmbH
Ditzingen
Germany

ISSN 0302-9743   ISSN 1611-3349 (electronic)
Lecture Notes in Computer Science
ISBN 978-3-319-99228-0   ISBN 978-3-319-99229-7 (eBook)
https://doi.org/10.1007/978-3-319-99229-7

Library of Congress Control Number: 2018950937

LNCS Sublibrary: SL2 – Programming and Software Engineering

© Springer Nature Switzerland AG 2018
This work is subject to copyright. All rights are reserved by the Publisher, whether the whole or part of the material is concerned, specifically the rights of translation, reprinting, reuse of illustrations, recitation, broadcasting, reproduction on microfilms or in any other physical way, and transmission or information storage and retrieval, electronic adaptation, computer software, or by similar or dissimilar methodology now known or hereafter developed.
The use of general descriptive names, registered names, trademarks, service marks, etc. in this publication does not imply, even in the absence of a specific statement, that such names are exempt from the relevant protective laws and regulations and therefore free for general use.
The publisher, the authors and the editors are safe to assume that the advice and information in this book are believed to be true and accurate at the date of publication. Neither the publisher nor the authors or the editors give a warranty, express or implied, with respect to the material contained herein or for any errors or omissions that may have been made. The publisher remains neutral with regard to jurisdictional claims in published maps and institutional affiliations.

This Springer imprint is published by the registered company Springer Nature Switzerland AG
The registered company address is: Gewerbestrasse 11, 6330 Cham, Switzerland

Preface

The SAFECOMP Workshop Day has for many years preceded the SAFECOMP Conference, attracting additional participants. The SAFECOMP Workshops have become more attractive since they started generating their own proceedings in the Springer LNCS series (Springer LNCS vol. 11094, the book in your hands; the main conference proceedings are LNCS 11093). This meant adhering to Springer's guidelines, i.e., the respective international Program Committee of each workshop had to make sure that at least three independent reviewers reviewed the papers carefully. The selection criteria were different from those for the main conference since authors were encouraged to submit workshop papers, i.e., on work in progress and potentially controversial topics. In total, 49 regular papers (out of 73) were accepted.

Three of the five workshops are sequels to earlier workshops, which shows continuity of their relevance to the scientific and industrial community:

- ASSURE 2018 – 6th International Workshop on Assurance Cases for Software-Intensive Systems, chaired by Ewen Denney, Ibrahim Habli, Ganesh Pai, and Richard Hawkins
- DECSoS 2018 – 13th ERCIM/EWICS/ARTEMIS Workshop on Dependable Smart Embedded and Cyber-Physical Systems and Systems-of-Systems, chaired by Erwin Schoitsch and Amund Skavhaug
- SASSUR 2018 – 7th International Workshop on Next Generation of System Assurance Approaches for Safety-Critical Systems, chaired by Alejandra Ruiz, Jose Luis de la Vara, and Tim Kelly

Finally, two new workshops were part of Safecomp for the first time (a third new proposal was withdrawn in the end):

- STRIVE 2018 – First International Workshop on Safety, securiTy, and pRivacy In automotiVe systEms, chaired by Gianpiero Costantino and Ilaria Matteucci
- WAISE 2018 – First International Workshop on Artificial Intelligence Safety Engineering, chaired by Huascar Espinoza, Orlando Avila-García, Rob Alexander, and Andreas Theodorou;

The workshops provide a truly international platform for academia and industry.

It has been a pleasure to work with the Safecomp chair, Barbara Gallina, and with the publication chair, Friedemann Bitsch, the workshop chairs, Program Committees, and the authors. Thank you all for your good cooperation and excellent work!

September 2018

Erwin Schoitsch

Organization

Committee

EWICS TC7 Chair

Francesca Saglietti — University of Erlangen-Nuremberg, Germany

General Chair

Barbara Gallina — Mälardalen University, Sweden

Program Co-chairs

Barbara Gallina — Mälardalen University, Sweden
Amund Skavhaug — The Norwegian University of Science and Technology, Norway

Workshop Chair

Erwin Schoitsch — AIT Austrian Institute of Technology, Austria

Publication Chair

Friedemann Bitsch — Thales Deutschland GmbH, Germany

Local Organizing Committee

Irfan Sljivo — Mälardalen University, Sweden
Lena Jonsson — Mälardalen University, Sweden
Martina Pettersson — Mälardalen University, Sweden
Elena Rivani — Mälardalen University, Sweden
Linda Claesson — Mälardalen University, Sweden
Gunnar Widforss — Mälardalen University, Sweden

Publicity Chair

Alexander Romanovsky — Newcastle University, UK

Workshop Chairs

ASSURE 2018

Ewen Denney — SGT/NASA Ames Research Center, USA
Ibrahim Habli — University of York, UK
Richard Hawkins — University of York, UK
Ganesh Pai — SGT/NASA Ames Research Center, USA

DECSoS 2018

Erwin Schoitsch	AIT Austrian Institute of Technology, Austria
Amund Skavhaug	NTNU, Norway

SASSUR 2018

Alejandra Ruiz Lopez	Tecnalia, Spain
Jose Luis de La Vara	Carlos III University of Madrid, Spain
Tim Kelly	University of York, UK

STRIVE 2018

Gianpiero Costantino	IIT-CNR, Italy
Ilaria Matteucci	IIT-CNR, Italy

WAISE 2018

Huascar Espinoza	CEA LIST, France
Orlando Avila-García	Atos, Spain
Rob Alexander	University of York, UK
Andreas Theodorou	University of Bath, UK

Supporting Institutions

European Workshop on Industrial
Computer Systems Reliability, Safety
and Security

Mälardalen University, Sweden

Norwegian University of Science and
Technology

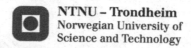

AIT Austrian Institute of Technology

Thales Deutschland GmbH

Lecture Notes in Computer Science
(LNCS), Springer Science + Business
Media

Austrian Computer Society

ARTEMIS Industry Association

European Network of Clubs for
Reliability and Safety of
Software-Intensive Systems

German Computer Society

Electronic Components and Systems
for European Leadership - Austria

Verband österreichischer Software
Industrie

European Research Consortium for
Informatics and Mathematics

IEEE SMC Technical Committee on
Homeland Security (TCHS)

Contents

**7th International Workshop on Next Generation of System
Assurance Approaches for Safety-Critical Systems (SASSUR 2018)**

**1st International Workshop on Safety, securiTy,
and pRivacy In automotiVe systEms (STRIVE 2018)**

6th International Workshop on Assurance Cases for Software-Intensive Systems (ASSURE 2018)

6th International Workshop on Assurance Cases for Software-Intensive Systems (ASSURE 2018)

Ewen Denney[1], Ibrahim Habli[2], Richard Hawkins[2], and Ganesh Pai[1]

[1] SGT/NASA Ames Research Center, Moffett Field, CA 94035, USA
{ewen.denney,ganesh.pai}@nasa.gov
[2] Department of Computer Science, University of York, York YO10 5DD, UK
{ibrahim.habli,richard.hawkins}@york.ac.uk

1 Introduction

This volume contains the papers presented at the 6th International Workshop on Assurance Cases for Software-intensive Systems (ASSURE 2018), collocated this year with the 37th International Conference on Computer Safety, Reliability, and Security (SAFECOMP 2018), in Västerås, Sweden.

As with the previous five editions of ASSURE, this year's workshop aims to provide an international forum for presenting emerging research, novel contributions, tool development efforts, and position papers on the foundations and applications of assurance case principles and techniques. The workshop goals are to: (i) explore techniques to create and assess assurance cases for software-intensive systems; (ii) examine the role of assurance cases in the engineering lifecycle of critical systems; (iii) identify the dimensions of effective practice in the development/evaluation of assurance cases; (iv) investigate the relationship between dependability techniques and assurance cases; and, (v) identify critical research challenges towards defining a roadmap for future development.

2 Program

ASSURE 2018 kicked off with an invited keynote talk by Robin Bloomfield, Founding Partner of the engineering consultancy Adelard LLP, and Professor of System and Software Dependability, Centre for Software Reliability, City University London. Eight papers were accepted this year covering three assurance case themes: *confidence assessment, patterns and processes, and tools and automation*.

Papers under the theme of assurance case confidence assessment frameworks examined issues such as the relationship between argumentation elements at the same layer, and the challenges associated with assurance of machine learning-based systems. The theme of assurance case patterns and processes included papers that dealt with a new notion of *assurance recipe*, attack modeling to address safety and security assurance jointly, and the interoperability of medical systems. Finally, the theme concerning assurance case tools and automation comprised papers providing a survey of assurance case tools developed over the past two decades, addressing change impact management in assurance cases, and additional methodological steps in authoring assurance cases.

3 Acknowledgments

We thank all those who submitted papers to ASSURE 2018 and congratulate the authors whose papers were selected for inclusion into the workshop program and proceedings. For reviewing the submissions and providing useful feedback to the authors, we especially thank our distinguished Program Committee members:

- Simon Burton, Bosch Research, Germany
- Isabelle Conway, ESA/ESTEC, The Netherlands
- Martin Feather, NASA Jet Propulsion Laboratory, USA
- Alwyn Goodleo, NASA Langley Research Center, USA
- Jérémie Guiochet, LAAS-CNRS, France
- Joshua Kaizer, Nuclear Regulatory Commission, USA
- Tim Kelly, University of York, UK
- Yoshiki Kinoshita, Kanagawa University, Japan
- Andrew Rae, Griffith University, Australia
- Philippa Ryan, Adelard LLP, UK
- Mark-Alexander Sujan, University of Warwick, UK
- Kenji Taguchi, CAV Technologies Co. Ltd., Japan
- Sean White, NHS Digital, UK

Their efforts have resulted in an exciting workshop program and, in turn, a successful sixth edition of the ASSURE workshop series. Finally, we thank the organizers of SAFECOMP 2018 for their support of ASSURE 2018.

Research on the Classification of the Relationships Among the Same Layer Elements in Assurance Case Structure for Evaluation

Biao Xu[1(✉)], Minyan Lu[1], Tingyang Gu[1], and Dajian Zhang[2]

[1] The Key Laboratory on Reliability and Environmental Engineering Technology, Beihang University, Beijing, China
{xubiaorms,lmy}@buaa.edu.cn, gutingyang@126.com
[2] China Financial Certification Authority, Beijing, China
greatdjz@163.com

Abstract. The use of assurance cases in certification raises the question of assurance argument sufficiency and the issue of confidence (or uncertainty) in the argument's claims. Some researchers propose to model confidence quantitatively and to calculate confidence in argument conclusions. However, most of the existing assurance evaluation techniques focus on top-bottom decomposition and assume that the elements of the same level are independent of each other. The lack of information on the relationships among supporting elements of the same level may easily lead to deviations from estimation expectations. In this paper, a modified approach for evaluation of confidence in assurance cases is proposed. Firstly, in order to eliminate the deviation from the independence hypothesis, we discuss the relationships of the supporting elements for confidence evaluation and propose a simple classification. Then we compare the different confidence results under the independence assumption and the correlation assumption using the same confidence evaluation method, and discuss the causes of differences. Finally, we discuss several future work.

Keywords: Assurance case · Quantified confidence · Informal logic
Toulmin Model · Bayesian Belief Network

1 Introduction

Assurance case has been deeply studied in safety domain for decades, and its applications in reliability domain and security domain have also made some progress [1]. As arguments and evidences are practically imperfect, it is difficult to determine that the claim is true with 100% certainty. The question that "how should the assessor determine whether the argument and its evidence are sufficient?" leads to the concepts of confidence (uncertainty) in the argument's claims [2].

There have been many studies on the evaluation of confidence in assurance case. These studies can be roughly divided into two types according to their calculation methods. One kind is based on Bayesian Belief Networks (BBNs) [3–6]. The other kind is based on Dempster-Shafer theory (D-S theory) [7–10], Jøsang's opinion triangle [11],

© Springer Nature Switzerland AG 2018
B. Gallina et al. (Eds.): SAFECOMP 2018 Workshops, LNCS 11094, pp. 5–13, 2018.
https://doi.org/10.1007/978-3-319-99229-7_1

or Evidential Reasoning [12]. However, most of these approaches pay more attention to the tree structure for calculation, while ignoring the relationships among the supporting elements of the same level. In [6], if the key evidence of confidence "coverage of hazard classifications" assigns from 1 to 0, the system safety confidence result changes from 90% to 86%, which is illogical. Key evidence should have a decisive influence on the system's overall confidence [13]. Aiming at this problem, this paper proposes a modified confidence assessment approach for assurance case based on the existing research [6].

In the next section, the related work and supporting theory are briefly introduced. After that, we modify the assumption that the same level elements in case structure for confidence evaluation are independent of each other, discuss the relationships of the elements and give a relationship classification. In Sect. 4, we compare the results under the independence assumption or the correlation assumption using the same confidence evaluation approach, and discuss the causes of differences. The conclusion and future work to improve this approach are presented in Sect. 5.

2   Related Work

Assurance cases are generally developed to support claims in areas such as safety, reliability, maintainability, human factors, operability, and security. The assurance case has one or more top level claims in which confidence is needed and has supporting arguments connecting the top-level claims with multiple levels of sub-claims. The sub-claims are in turn supported by evidences or assumptions.

As both arguments and evidences are practically imperfect, we could never say the claims in our assurance case are 100% true. So we consider the confidence of each claim in the case should be provided as other elements (e.g. assumptions, context) to facilitate the decision making.

The studies on the evaluation of confidence in assurance case can be roughly divided into two types according to their calculation methods. One kind is based on Bayesian Belief Networks (BBNs). The researchers transform assurance case into BBN [3, 6], or directly use BBN tools to construct network [4, 5]. The analyst assign probability value (confidence) for leaf nodes, and The BBN tool could compute the confidence of the non-leaf nodes, including the root-node representing the top goal. The other kind is based on D-S theory, Jøsang's opinion triangle, or Evidential Reasoning. Approaches based on D-S theory [7–10], differ from Bayesian approaches in that they reason about both the strength of belief in opinions and the plausibility of those opinions, which means another dimension of the assessment of each claim in an assurance case. Jøsang's opinion triangle [11] reimagines the two dimensional space as three dimensions: belief, disbelief, or uncertainty. As one of the dimensions grows, the other two dimensions shrink accordingly. Evidential reasoning [12] is a method to using the D-S theory in multi-attribute decision problems.

We proposed our previous work [6] to calculate confidence using BBNs. However, when we re-examined this approach, we found that it produced unreasonable system safety confidence results when critical evidence was extremely assigned. In other words, if the confidence of a critical evidence is extremely low (or high), there is no significant change in the calculation result of the system's confidence. This approach needs to be improved to accommodate this kind of extreme assignment. A similar problem occurs in [8], which amplifies small doubts about each hazard's mitigation into large doubt about system safety. This effect is the result of multiplying together the assessor's beliefs in the adequacy of the mitigation of each hazard and will worsen as the number of hazards increases [13].

3 Research on the Classification of the Relationships Among the Same Layer Elements in Assurance Case Structure

Assurance case evaluation approaches based on BBN usually assume that the same level elements in case structure or case-like structure are independent of each other to simplify the calculation - in fact this assumption is not always true. In this section, we revise the independence hypothesis, discuss the classification of relationships among elements with correlation, and give some suggestions on improving the case structure and leaf node value assignment.

This section takes GSN [14] as an example. GSN has a typical top-down assurance case structure, and the confidence of the top-level goal depends on the rationality of the argument from sub-goal (solution) to top-level goal. Therefore, the first step to determine the confidence (sufficiency) is to establish the correlations between each isolated sub-goal and the top-level goal.

A solution (which represents the sub-goal or solution in GSN) can either fully support the goal or partially support the goal. The support of the solution to the goal can usually be divided into three types.

Type A represents a solution that supports one goal, and type B represents multiple solutions that support the same goal. These two types are the main types of assurance case argument. Type C means that N solutions can support the same goal independently. Type C and type A are actually the same pattern. Type A can be regarded as a special case of type C (i.e., (solution) $N = 1$), or the solutions of type C are coincident which are completely equivalent for supported goal. Therefore, according to Fig. 1, we get the solution classification as shown in Fig. 2.

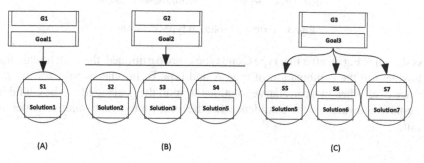

(A)   (B)   (C)

Fig. 1. The types of supports that the solution provides to the goal

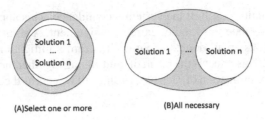

Fig. 2. Solution types diagram

All supporting elements of a goal/sub-goal can be regarded as a universal set, and each solution contains some supporting elements and is a subset of the universal set. The process of constructing assurance case is to attach solutions to the goal. However, according to Set Theory, the types of solutions in Fig. 2 are not complete, set intersection is not taken into account. The absence of intersection is likely to produce counterintuitive results in the confidence calculation. In [8], if we have high confidence or better in the mitigation of twenty hazards—very high confidence or certainty in the mitigation of all but three—we still have very low confidence in system safety. This effect is the result of multiplying together the assessor's beliefs in the adequacy of the mitigation of each hazard and will worsen as the number of hazards increases [13]. More evidences lead to lower confidence, which is not plausible.

So we extend the solution types diagram as shown in Fig. 3. In Fig. 3, solutions of type C and type D are overlapping. The confidence degree of the goal of those assurance cases with the two types of solutions shall not only consider the degree to which each solution supports the goal, but also the degree to which each overlapping part of solutions supports the goal.

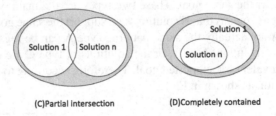

Fig. 3. Extended solution types diagram

As shown in Fig. 4, after that type C and type D are partitioned, they can be calculated as equivalent to the combination of type A and type B. In other words, for the same assurance case, when two correlative solutions support the goal together, the confidence of the goal is equivalent to the confidence that the three (or two) sub-solutions offer after the split.

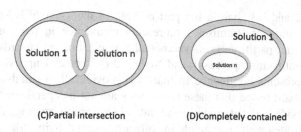

(C)Partial intersection   (D)Completely contained

Fig. 4. Segmentation diagram of extended solution types

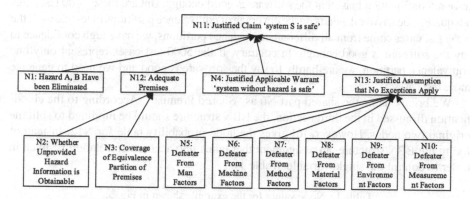

Fig. 5. An example "basic BBN for the typical safety argument", taken from [6]. For compactness, we represent BBNs nodes as rectangles.

4 Case Study

We use these examples taken from [6] to illustrate that the proposed modified approach is more sensitive to the critical factors. Thus, we can obtain results that are relatively more reliable.

We created four variants of the original example, namely Independence 1, 2 and Correlation 1, 2. Independences represent extreme assessments of confidence in the completeness of hazard identification classification. Correlations modify assessments of confidence in the completeness of hazard information according to the relationship that a large part of the node N2 and N3 are shared (Fig. 6).

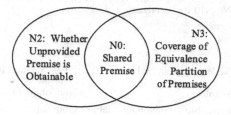

Fig. 6. Relationship between N2 and N3

The node N2 and N3 share a big part of both of them. Node N3 ("Coverage of Equivalence Partition of Premises") represents confidence in the completeness of different equivalence partitions (i.e., whether all classifications of hazards were covered in the hazard identification process), and Node N2 ("Whether Unprovided Premise is Obtainable") represents confidence in that "we provide all obtainable premises we could". It is not hard to see that these two claims are not independent, "all obtainable premises are provided" is not credible without "classification coverage is sufficient".

We grasp this idea with an example in software testing activity [6]. Assume that we have tested the target software with 5000 test cases without any failure, so the tester may have a 'confirmation bias' that the software is good enough. But are these 5000 test cases adequate? The answer depends on the coverage of equivalence partitions of test cases. If the 5000 test cases come from all different equivalence partitions, we have high confidence to say the software is good enough. In contrary, if the 5000 test cases represent only one equivalence partition, we are hardly to say the software is good and we need to generate more test cases.

We briefly name the shared part N0 as "Shared Premise". According to the classification discussed in the third section, the BBN structure should be modified to split the original two nodes. However, [6] gives the node probability table for N12. Instead of fixing the BBN structure, an assignment that takes into account correlation is given in order to control the single variable (Table 1).

Table 1. Node values for the example shown in Fig. 5.

Node	Value	Original	Independence 1	Correlation 1	Independence 2	Correlation 2
N1	Present	90%	90%	90%	90%	90%
	NotPresent	10%	10%	10%	10%	10%
N2	NotObtainable	85%	85%	**15%**	85%	**95%**
	Obtainable	15%	15%	**85%**	15%	**5%**
N3	Complete	85%	**0.1%**	**0.1%**	**99.9%**	**99.9%**
	NotComplete	15%	**99.9%**	**99.9%**	**0.1%**	**0.1%**
N4	Present	100%	100%	100%	100%	100%
	NotPresent	0%	0%	0%	0%	0%
N5–	Present	0%	0%	0%	0%	0%
10	NotPresent	100%	100%	100%	100%	100%
N11	Present	If N1, N12, N4, and N13 are Present				
	NotPresent	Otherwise				
N12	See Table 2					
N13	Present	If N6–N10 are NotPresent				
	NotPresent	Otherwise				

Table 2. Node probability table for N12 in Fig. 5, taken from [6].

N3	Complete		NotComplete	
N2	Obtainable	NotObtainable	Obtainable	NotObtainable
Present	1	1	0.8	1
NotPresent	0	0	0.2	0

Independence 1 Example. Node N3 ("Coverage of Equivalence Partition of Premises") represents confidence in the completeness of the hazard classification in hazard analysis (i.e., whether all kinds of hazards were identified). While the original example shows 85% confidence in N3, our Independence 1 Example variant uses 0.1%, leaving all other inputs and CPTs unchanged. This represents extreme pessimism in the completeness of the hazard classification coverage.

Correlation 1 Example. The Correlation 1 example is identical to the Independence 1 example except that we assess the confidence in N2 as 15%. This represents the relationship that a large part of the node N2 and N3 are shared. Incomplete hazard classification coverage of hazard identification shall seriously impairs the confidence of hazard identification.

Independence 2 Example. This optimistic example assesses the confidence in N3 as 99.9%. This represents extreme optimism in the completeness of the hazard classification coverage.

Correlation 2 Example. The Correlation 2 example is identical to the Independence 2 example except that we assess the confidence in N2 as 95%. Complete hazard classification coverage of hazard identification shall enhance the confidence of hazard identification.

Analysis of Examples. Table 3 gives the calculated confidence in safety for all five examples. It is not plausible that extreme negative changes in confidence in hazard classification coverage would produce as small a change in confidence in safety as the difference between 89% and 86% indicates. After we revise the values, it is somehow plausible that anyone who completely distrusted a hazard analysis would only have 67% confidence that the analyzed system is safe. The two optimistic examples do not make any differences, because the original value is optimistic enough.

Table 3. Calculated value of N11 ("Justified Claim 'system S is safe'") for the original version presented in [6] and our Independence and Correlation variants.

Case	Present	NotPresent
Original	89%	11%
Independence 1	86%	14%
Correlation 1	67%	33%
Independence 2	90%	10%
Correlation 2	90%	10%

5   Conclusion

In this article, we discuss the classification of relationships among elements (solutions and sub-goals) to eliminate the deviation from the absence of correlative relationships among case elements of the same level, and modify the approach [6] for assessment of confidence in assurance cases. The case study shows that the modified evaluation method is more sensitive to the change of key solution and can better reflect the influence of key evidence in assurance case.

In practice, the relationships among elements are not limited to the same level. There may be a cross-layer or cross-block relationship. The approach presented in this article does not apply to this situation. To improve the approach, database of elements needs to be developed for different domains. This database contains goals, sub-goals, solutions, and relationships among these elements within each domain. An assurance case construction tool with patterns and elements database could also be developed. The database that stores the potential relationships among different types of elements will help the developers to build and decompose assurance case for confidence evaluation.

References

1. Weinstock, C.B., Goodenough, J.B.: Towards an Assurance Case Practice for Medical Devices. CMU/SEI-2009-TN-018 (2009)
2. Bloomfield, R., Littlewood, B., Wright, D.: Confidence: its role in dependability cases for risk assessment. In: International Conference on Dependable Systems and Networks, Edinburgh, pp. 338–346 (2007)
3. Denney, E., Pai, G., Habli, I.: Towards measurement of confidence in safety cases. In: 2011 International Symposium on Empirical Software Engineering and Measurement, vol. 9337, pp. 380–383 (2011)
4. Guo, B.: Knowledge representation and uncertainty management: applying Bayesian Belief Networks to a safety assessment expert system. In: Proceedings of the 2003 International Conference on Natural Language Processing and Knowledge Engineering, NLP-KE 2003, pp. 114–119 (2003)
5. Hobbs, C., Lloyd, M.: The application of Bayesian Belief Networks to assurance case preparation. In: Dale, C., Anderson, T. (eds.) Achieving Systems Safety, pp. 159–176. Springer, London (2012). https://doi.org/10.1007/978-1-4471-2494-8_12
6. Zhao, X., Zhang, D., Lu, M., Zeng, F.: A new approach to assessment of confidence in assurance cases. In: Ortmeier, F., Daniel, P. (eds.) SAFECOMP 2012. LNCS, vol. 7613, pp. 79–91. Springer, Heidelberg (2012). https://doi.org/10.1007/978-3-642-33675-1_7
7. Ayoub, A., Chang, J., Sokolsky, O., Lee, I.: Assessing the overall sufficiency of safety arguments. In: SSS 2013 21st Safety-Critical Systems Symposium (2013)
8. Cyra, L., Gorski, J.: Support for argument structures review and assessment. Reliab. Eng. Syst. Saf. **96**, 26–37 (2011)
9. Guiochet, J., Do Hoang, Q.A., Kaaniche, M.: A model for safety case confidence assessment. In: Koornneef, F., van Gulijk, C. (eds.) SAFECOMP 2014. LNCS, vol. 9337, pp. 313–327. Springer, Cham (2015). https://doi.org/10.1007/978-3-319-24255-2_23
10. Zeng, F., Lu, M., Zhong, D.: Using D-S evidence theory to evaluation of confidence in safety case. J. Theor. Appl. Inf. Technol. **47**, 184–189 (2013)
11. Duan, L., Rayadurgam, S., Heimdahl, M.P.E., Sokolsky, O., Lee, I.: Representing confidence in assurance case evidence. In: Koornneef, F., van Gulijk, C. (eds.) SAFECOMP 2015. LNCS, vol. 9338, pp. 15–26. Springer, Cham (2015). https://doi.org/10.1007/978-3-319-24249-1_2
12. Nair, S., Walkinshaw, N., Kelly, T.: Quantifying uncertainty in safety cases using evidential reasoning. In: Bondavalli, A., Ceccarelli, A., Ortmeier, F. (eds.) SAFECOMP 2014. LNCS, vol. 8696, pp. 413–418. Springer, Cham (2014). https://doi.org/10.1007/978-3-319-10557-4_45

13. Graydon, P.J., Holloway, C.M.: An investigation of proposed techniques for quantifying confidence in assurance arguments. Saf. Sci. **92**, 53–65 (2017)
14. Kelly, T.: The goal structuring notation-a safety argument notation. In: Workshop on Proceedings of the Dependable Systems and Networks (2004)

Continuous Argument Engineering: Tackling Uncertainty in Machine Learning Based Systems

Fuyuki Ishikawa[1]([⊠]) [iD] and Yutaka Matsuno[2]

[1] National Institute of Informatics, Tokyo, Japan
f-ishikawa@nii.ac.jp
[2] Nihon University, Funabashi, Japan
matsuno.yutaka@nihon-u.ac.jp

Abstract. Components or systems implemented by using machine learning techniques have intrinsic difficulties caused by uncertainty. Specifically, it is impossible to logically or deductively conclude what they can(not) do or how they behave for untested inputs. In addition, such systems are often applied to the real world, which has uncertain requirements and environments. In this paper, we discuss what becomes difficult or even impossible in the use of arguments or assurance cases for machine learning based systems. We then propose an approach for continuously analyzing, managing, and updating arguments while accepting uncertainty as intrinsic in nature.

Keywords: Assurance cases · Arguments · Machine learning
Artificial intelligence · Cyber-physical systems

1 Introduction

Software systems play an increasingly critical role in the real world, as further investigated in emerging paradigms such as cyber-physical systems (CPSs) and artificial intelligence (AI). A representative example is an autonomous driving support system that deals with safety-critical operations in the real world. Assuring the dependability of such systems is highly demanded as the systems have more direct effects on society and people.

For these emerging systems, there is a notably active effort to apply machine learning (ML) techniques given their recent advance, specifically in deep learning. Implementations of advanced functions, such as image recognition, are obtained in an inductive way from training data sets. This is quite different from classical software systems where implementations are obtained in a deductive way by writing down processing rules as programs. The resulting implementations contain intrinsic uncertainty. We cannot grasp what an implementation can do exactly, nor can we logically explain the obtained results [6,7,14,15].

Clearly, arguments or assurance cases [9] play a significant role in assuring the dependability of emerging ML-based systems. On one side, arguments describe

© Springer Nature Switzerland AG 2018
B. Gallina et al. (Eds.): SAFECOMP 2018 Workshops, LNCS 11094, pp. 14–21, 2018.
https://doi.org/10.1007/978-3-319-99229-7_2

goals and how top-level abstract goals are decomposed into concrete goals that are objectively measurable. On the other side, arguments describe how the satisfaction of the goals is supported by evidences. Arguments can serve as the foundation for analysis, discussion, and tracing done by development teams as well as third parties.

However, uncertainty in ML imposes fundamental obstacles against the use of arguments. It is more difficult or even impossible to be confident of completeness in arguments. Development teams may still claim completeness to account for their products in the best way currently known. Nevertheless, it will be increasingly more significant not to stop at releasing arguments (and products) but to continuously resolve uncertainty and react to expected or unexpected changes. The development process also has such an incremental nature as the trial-and-error style is required for uncertainty. For example, ML systems usually require proof-of-concept (POC) development and evaluation. We believe arguments can play an essential role in such incremental and continuous activities in addition to the currently typical role in assurance for release.

In this paper, we discuss the significance of *continuous argument engineering* in tackling the uncertainty of emerging systems, specifically ML-based systems that contain intrinsic uncertainty even in an implementation. Our contributions are as follows.

- Discussion on the impacts by different kinds of uncertainty on arguments with concrete examples
- Concepts and principles as well as potential support through GSN extensions, patterns, and tools as countermeasures to the impacts.

In the remainder of this paper, we discuss related work in Sect. 2. We present the proposed principles of continuous argument engineering for machine learning in Sect. 3. We give concluding remarks in Sect. 4.

2 Background and Related Work

2.1 Difficulties of ML

With ML, the behavior of a component (e.g., neural net model) is inductively derived from training data and uncertain (black-box and unexplainable). This uncertainty has been actively discussed.

One direction under active discussion in the ML/AI community is explainable AI (XAI) [7]. For example, in [12], an area of images is chosen that explains the result of image classification. Such a technique only works to explain one output result, and the lack of deductive or logical conclusions still remains the same.

The existence of adversarial examples has been also discussed intensively [6]. Slight perturbations in input that are not even recognizable by humans can radically change the output when using the most sophisticated image classifiers. This is investigated in the testing community too, e.g., by white-box testing with "neuron coverage" [11] and formal verification [8].

Even though this problem with small perturbations could be resolved, achieving high accuracy is difficult in general. Engineers may face unexpected difficulties or limitations, e.g., the problem of socially inappropriate tagging in Google Photos could not be essentially fixed[1].

There have been engineering guidelines, such as on what kinds of checks are necessary in ML and how to avoid unique technical debts in ML [3,14,17]. These guidelines present more focus on continuous activities, especially monitoring. This is due to the uncertainty of an implementation as well as external factors such as the distribution of input data.

In this paper, we also put focus on continuous engineering but targets arguments rather than specific points of monitoring.

2.2   Uncertainty and Continuous Engineering

Increased uncertainty in requirements and environments has already been long discussed in the software engineering community. Intrinsic incompleteness at development time suggests that continuous engineering in the form of runtime monitoring and reasoning by using a system are important [1,2,13].

In this paper, we also put focus on continuous engineering but target ML, which causes uncertainty in implementation, as well as arguments for human activities rather than automated system reactions to changes.

2.3   Continuous Activities on Arguments

The primary use of arguments has been to account for the dependability of a system product to be released. Thus, incremental or continuous updates of arguments have not been discussed that intensively. In some studies, continuously enhancing the evidence part by accumulating operation data has been considered [4,16].

In this paper, we focus on the continuous engineering of arguments that is necessary due to uncertainty and consider updates in the argument structure, not only the addition of evidences.

2.4   Arguments for Machine Learning

In [5], the use of arguments was discussed for autonomous driving systems that use machine learning. The imperfectness of obtained functions, e.g., image recognition, was primarily handled, i.e., accuracy cannot be 100%. Typical goals and evidences were discussed that are used to show that the risks of imperfection are mitigated.

In this paper, we focus on incompleteness or uncertainty in the sense that it is impossible to deductively or logically conclude some claims. We focus on the

---

[1] https://www.theguardian.com/technology/2018/jan/12/google-racism-ban-gorilla-black-people.

higher possibility of future updates, and thus, discuss the continuous engineering of arguments even after we do the current best as suggested in [5].

Note that this does not deny the use of arguments in the typical way. For example, it is essential to construct arguments, deductively, for safety mechanisms used for autonomous driving in the case that an image recognition function fails to detect a pedestrian. Our position is to *extend* the use of assurance cases for the case in which we want to account for how well an image recognition function works, which cannot be perfect or deductively reasoned.

3 Continuous Argument Engineering

Below, we discuss the impacts of uncertainty and countermeasures for different aspects of arguments. We use examples from driving support systems that use an image recognition function constructed by ML.

3.1 Uncertainty of Goal Decomposition

One key aspect of arguments is the completeness of goal decomposition; it is explicitly argued what sub-goals are said to be exhaustive or whether there is a missing sub-goal. Sometimes, deductive reasoning is applicable for the decomposition of a concrete goal. For example, we may support a goal, "a train will not hit the preceding one," by using the sub-goals "the distance to the preceding train is precisely measured" and "the velocity is controlled to allow the train to stop within the distance"[2].

Goals regarding ML often deal with infinite possibilities in the real world or fuzzy human perceptions. We try to define more concrete, measurable sub-goals for such goals, but it is intrinsically difficult to claim that they are exhaustive and sufficient. New sub-goals may be discovered, or the significance of sub-goals may be more precisely recognized only after a system is faced with a variety of users and environments during the test phase or even the operation phase. In addition, decomposition can be invalidated by changes in external elements (user requirements and environments).

Example. Suppose we want to decompose goals such as "reliability of the image recognition function is shown for the expected operation environments" or "reliability is shown for the weaknesses of the image recognition function." One potential sub-goal of these goals is "reliability is shown for images of foggy situations." This sub-goal may be noticed only after test results or operation data are inspected. The significance and necessity of a goal can be assessed and justified also only by inspecting data. In addition, after updating an implementation, foggy situations may no longer be a weakness. It is necessary to explicitly plan and conduct continuous inspections to uncover uncertainty for goal decomposition.

---

[2] From an example of goal-oriented requirements analysis [10].

Principles and Supports. We propose the following concepts and principles as well as potential support through GSN extensions, patterns, and tools.

- Explicitly distinguish *open goals* whose decomposition has high uncertainty intrinsically and is thus likely to be incomplete or volatile. An additional notation for this kind of goal should be introduced to GSN extensions.
- For open goals, a *continuous decomposition sub-goal (CD sub-goal)* should be considered to ensure that acceptably sufficient effort is taken to discover new sub-goals and validate existing ones. This will make a new GSN pattern.
- Empirical data obtained as solutions or evidences for continuous decomposition goals should be continuously updated and linked to arguments. This is already supported by some tools (Sect. 2.3).
- For sub-goals of an open goal, except for a CD sub-goal, justification should be given by using empirical data requested by the CD sub-goal. Tools should support the easy tracing of data that justify each sub-goal.

3.2   Uncertainty of Contributions by Evidences

Another key aspect of arguments is the attachment of evidences for each goal. It can be determined that the satisfaction of each leaf goal (the most concrete goals obtained by decomposition) is supported by evidences.

For goals regarding ML, the attachment of evidences often cannot provide strong confidence regarding the satisfaction of goals. Evidences are basically based on test result data for ML rather than deductive reasoning. It is more difficult or even impossible to reason about the satisfaction of a goal for untested input data. For example, it is not possible to base reasoning on an equivalence class, i.e., we cannot expect that testing one piece of input data will provide confidence regarding the behavior with another piece of input data in the same class. There is also the issue of adversarial examples (Sect. 2.1).

Example. Let us consider a goal, "reliability is shown for images of foggy situations." Suppose we had tests using 5,000 images collected by test driving and 10,000 images obtained by synthesizing fog on those images taken in non-foggy situations. It is intrinsically not possible to deductively say that test results using these test data can be sufficient evidences for the goal. It is significant for various stakeholders to understand and validate concerns regarding the test data amount or use of artificially created data, e.g., maintenance developers in the future, third parties for quality assurance, or customers. In addition, it is necessary to continuously monitor and validate evidences, e.g., by analyzing images that caused wrong recognition during operation and comparing them with current test data.

Principles and Supports. We propose the following concepts and principles as well as potential support through GSN extensions, patterns, and tools.

- Explicitly distinguish a *soft contribution (isSupportedBy* relationship) that denotes that an evidence can contribute to increasing confidence regarding goal satisfaction but cannot ensure it. An additional notation for this kind of relationship should be introduced to GSN extensions.
- Goals and evidences should explicitly mention the attributes of test data, e.g., foggy situations, so that stakeholders can understand and validate in what sense and how sufficiently tests are done. Arguments should be linked to a tool for test data management to allow for continuous checks between test requirements and used test data sets. This requires good integration with tools for test data management, which have not been sufficiently investigated for ML yet, to the authors' knowledge.

3.3   Uncertainty of Feasible Goals

It is desirable for goals, especially in nodes at the bottom (leaf) side, to be concrete so that their satisfaction can be objectively judged. For example, defining a specific value in a goal regarding accuracy is desirable to allow for clear evaluation of it satisfaction as well as discussion for its validity. However, uncertainty in defining such concrete values is much larger for ML. It is difficult to assess feasible values before implementation and experimentation. The feasibility may collapse at runtime given changes in distributions of inputs from the external world.

Example. Suppose a goal, "sufficiently high accuracy is achieved for a real data set collected in the driving operation" for image recognition used in a driving support system. This goal can be decomposed into a sub-goal to define a specific value to be satisfied and the other one to show its validity. At the beginning, the customer may mention "accuracy is more than 95%" but this goal may be nothing more than a desire. This goal may turn out to be too ideal and unfeasible. Then exploration starts for goals that are both feasible and useful. For example, we may decide to focus more on accuracy only for objects within a certain distance, which matter the safety more.

Suppose a good set of goals is identified and supported well by intensive testing. Even so, the goal of accuracy can be violated at runtime. For example, the operation environment may contain images that are not contained in the training or test data, e.g., those under exceptionally heavy snow and those of vehicles of a new type suddenly that got hot. Gaps between the development-time data and the runtime data can easily invalidate assurance of goals.

Principles and Supports. We propose the following concepts and principles as well as potential support through GSN extensions, patterns, and tools.

- Explicitly distinguish *fragile goals* whose validity and satisfaction depend on changeable assumptions or justifications, typically regarding the real world.

– Empirical data obtained as solutions or evidences for fragile goals should be continuously updated and linked to arguments. This is already discussed for CD sub-goals (Sect. 3.1). In the case of fragile goals, monitoring of satisfaction is much more significant as satisfaction of a goal, ensured well at the design-time, may be broken at runtime.

4   Concluding Remarks

In this paper, we discussed the uncertainty introduced by ML techniques and its impacts on arguments. We proposed extending the use of arguments by considering the potential incompleteness or volatility of arguments. We presented concepts and principles as well as potential support through GSN extensions, patterns, and tools for continuous argument engineering.

Our next step is to conduct industrial case studies and to provide concrete implementations of the proposed support in the form of notations and tools.

Acknowledgments. This work is partially supported by ERATO HASUO Meta-mathematics for Systems Design Project (No. JPMJER1603), JST. We are thankful to the industry researchers and engineers who gave deep insight into the difficulties of engineering for cyber-physical systems and machine learning systems.

References

1. Baresi, L., Ghezzi, C.: The disappearing boundary between development-time and run-time. In: FSE/SDP Workshop on Future of Software Engineering Research, pp. 17–22, November 2010
2. Blair, G., Bencomo, N., France, R.B.: Models@ run.time. IEEE Comput. **42**(10), 22–27 (2009)
3. Breck, E., Cai, S., Nielsen, E., Salib, M., Sculley, D.: What's your ML test score? a rubric for ML production systems. In: NIPS 2016 Workshop on Reliable Machine Learning in the Wild, December 2017
4. Fujita, H., Matsuno, Y., Hanawa, T., Sato, M., Kato, S., Ishikawa, Y.: DS-Bench Toolset: Tools for dependability benchmarking with simulation and assurance. In: IEEE/IFIP International Conference on Dependable Systems and Networks (DSN 2012), pp. 1–8, June 2012
5. Burton, S., Gauerhof, L., Heinzemann, C.: Making the case for safety of machine learning in highly automated driving. In: Tonetta, S., Schoitsch, E., Bitsch, F. (eds.) SAFECOMP 2017. LNCS, vol. 10489, pp. 5–16. Springer, Cham (2017). https://doi.org/10.1007/978-3-319-66284-8_1
6. Goodfellow, I., Shlens, J., Szegedy, C.: Explaining and harnessing adversarial examples. In: International Conference on Learning Representations (ICLR), May 2015
7. Gunning, D.: Explainable artificial intelligence (XAI). In: IJCAI 2016 Workshop on Deep Learning for Artificial Intelligence (DLAI), July 2016
8. Huang, X., Kwiatkowska, M., Wang, S., Wu, M.: Safety verification of deep neural networks. In: Majumdar, R., Kunčak, V. (eds.) CAV 2017. LNCS, vol. 10426, pp. 3–29. Springer, Cham (2017). https://doi.org/10.1007/978-3-319-63387-9_1

9. Kelly, T., Weaver, R.: The Goal Structuring Notation - a safety argument notation. In: Dependable Systems and Networks 2004 Workshop on Assurance Cases, July 2004
10. van Lamsweerde, A.: Requirements Engineering: From System Goals to UML Models to Software Specifications. Wiley, January 2009
11. Pei, K., Cao, Y., Yang, J., Jana, S.: Deepxplore: automated whitebox testing of deep learning systems. In: The 26th Symposium on Operating Systems Principles (SOSP 2017), pp. 1–18, October 2017
12. Ribeiro, M.T., Singh, S., Guestrin, C.: "why should i trust you?" explaining the predictions of any classifier. In: The 22nd ACM SIGKDD International Conference on Knowledge Discovery and Data Mining (KDD 2016), pp. 1135–1144, August 2016
13. Sawyer, P., Bencomo, N., Whittle, J., Letier, E., Finkelstein, A.: Requirements-aware systems: A research agenda for re for self-adaptive systems. In: The 18th IEEE International Requirements Engineering Conference (RE 2010), pp. 95–103, September 2010
14. Sculley, D., Holt, G., Golovin, D., Davydov, E., Phillips, T., Ebner, D., Chaudhary, V., Young, M.: Machine learning: the high interest credit card of technical debt. In: NIPS 2014 Workshop on Software Engineering for Machine Learning (SE4ML), December 2014
15. Seshia, S.A., Sadigh, D., Sastry, S.S.: Towards verified artificial intelligence (v3), October 2017. https://arxiv.org/abs/1606.08514
16. Tokuda, H., Yonezawa, T., Nakazawa, J.: Monitoring dependability of city-scale iot using d-case. In: 2014 IEEE World Forum on Internet of Things (WF-IoT), pp. 371–372, March 2014
17. Zinkevich, M.: Rules for reliable machine learning: Best practices for ML engineering. NIPS 2016 Workshop on Reliable Machine Learning in the Wild, December 2017

The Assurance Recipe: Facilitating Assurance Patterns

Justin Firestone[✉] and Myra B. Cohen

Department of Computer Science and Engineering, University of Nebraska - Lincoln,
Lincoln, NE 68588-0115, USA
{jfiresto,myra}@cse.unl.edu

Abstract. As assurance cases have grown in popularity for safety-critical systems, so too has their complexity and thus the need for methods to systematically build them. Assurance cases can grow too large and too abstract for anyone but the original builders to understand, making reuse difficult. Reuse is important because different systems might have identical or similar components, and a good solution for one system should be applicable to similar systems. Prior research has shown engineers can alleviate some of the complexity issues through modularity and identifying common patterns which are more easily understood for reuse across different systems. However, we believe these patterns are too complicated for users who lack expertise in software engineering or assurance cases. This paper suggests the concept of lower-level patterns which we call recipes. We use the safety-critical field of synthetic biology, as an example discipline to demonstrate how a recipe can be built and applied.

Keywords: Assurance case · Assurance pattern · Synthetic biology
iGEM

1 Introduction

Assurance cases have grown in popularity to reason about safety-critical systems. They are commonly used in domains such as aviation, nuclear energy, railways, and offshore drilling [6]. Recent work has proposed using assurance cases in non-traditional domains where engineering safety is also paramount, such as in synthetic biology and medical devices [1,5]. However, complex systems may lead to complex assurance cases that are hard to understand and build for novice users. One way to make assurance cases easier to share and use across domains has been to abstract similarities for reuse via *patterns* [3]. Patterns are meta-models of common argument structures and can be described and catalogued for retrieval and reuse. While useful for an expert in building assurance cases, these patterns may not be usable by the novice who may have too many degrees of freedom to concretize the abstraction.

Instead we propose to provide better guidance through a new abstraction, a template-like model that we call an *assurance recipe*. The user is provided a

B. Gallina et al. (Eds.): SAFECOMP 2018 Workshops, LNCS 11094, pp. 22–30, 2018.
https://doi.org/10.1007/978-3-319-99229-7_3

structure/pattern for the assurance case and is guided to select *ingredients* for a set of options. Although, not as general as a pattern, recipes can be customized for a domain and then parameterized for easy user instantiation.

In this paper we focus on a non-traditional domain (synthetic biology) where users will be non-experts in building assurance cases. We first perform a pre-study to understand if there is sufficient commonality across solutions. We examine projects submitted to the International Genetically Engineered Machine (iGEM) competition between 2015 and 2017 and examine their approaches to safety. We use this data to develop common recipes. We then present a feasibility study to demonstrate how we can apply the recipes in practice. Although the recipes shown only apply to synthetic biology and are small in size, we believe that recipes can be useful for other disciplines and be a starting point for further research, development, and discussion.

2   Background and Related Work

Researchers have recognized a need for modularity and reuse of patterns which can facilitate design and understanding of assurance cases. To address the difficulty of assuring and certifying electronics systems in the aerospace industry, Ruiz et al. [9] suggest combining Case-Based Reasoning (CBR) as a way to represent, retrieve, and reuse previously assured safety cases. For the general safety-critical domains Conmy and Bate [2] propose a method to understand reuse of software components in different contexts, such as when a software module needs to be verified on new hardware. Evidence used to verify a software module in one context is not necessarily sufficient or appropriate in another. They combine Component-Based Software Engineering (CBSE) concepts with argument fragments to guide the user.

Hawkins and Kelly [4] propose a catalog of argument patterns to describe claims that could apply to *any* software assurance case. Similar to software design, argument patterns are abstractions of common strategies (or best practices). This concept was expanded by Szczygielska and Jarzebowicz [10] who proposed an online repository for assurance patterns with a focus on universal application and uniformity across different industry domains.

The *recipes* in this work are influenced heavily by the work of Denney and Pai, who developed a foundation for a theory of assurance patterns, or a *pattern for patterns* [3]. Their work formalizes definitions of argument structures and argument patterns, and provides an algorithm for instantiating their patterns. We use the Claim Formalization Pattern developed by them (shown in Fig. 1) for this work. The field of synthetic biology has been growing rapidly, and uses engineering design techniques to develop models to then program living organisms (*chassis*), such as *Escherichia coli* (*E. coli*), to perform modified or novel functionality [7]. Given that synthetic biology is designing and programming a safety-critical system (these are living organisms that may be released eventually into the environment or used for medicinal purposes), the need to assure their safety is important. Recent work has suggested that assurance cases can be

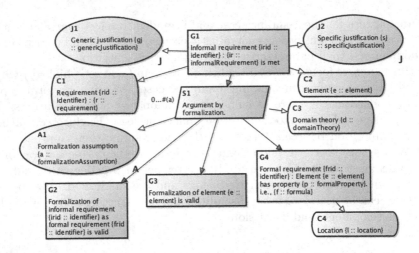

Fig. 1. A high-level pattern based on [3].

used for this purpose [1]. We use the acronym *SEBO* to represent synthetically engineered biological organism.

3   Pre-study

We examined three years of projects from the iGEM competition, held yearly for teams of students from high school through to graduate school. This competition has grown rapidly in popularity, with 314 teams from over 40 countries in 2017 [11]. The iGEM competition provides a plentiful source of real-world projects because teams are encouraged to share information in an open-source database. Teams must also explicitly discuss safety of their projects.

Teams can attempt to earn a bronze, silver, or gold medal for satisfying increasingly stringent criteria. Gold-medal teams must accomplish Integrated Human Practices, which asks teams to "consider whether their projects are safe, responsible, and good for the world" [13]. We thus limited our investigation to gold-medal teams from 2015–2017, assuming they addressed safety.

The most common chassis for iGEM projects is the K-12 strain of *E. coli*, a bacterium which does not inherently produce toxins and can be handled in a Safety Level One lab. By far, most experiments are performed in a Safety Level One lab using organisms which are *generally regarded as safe* (GRAS) [17]. However, even the relatively safe K-12 *E. coli* could pose safety-critical risks outside the lab, since SEBOs have added functionality and behavior.

3.1   Categorization Methodology

We manually investigated the safety pages of every gold-medal iGEM team from 2015–2017. There were 334 projects which we grouped into the following categories of safety features.

- **Containment (Con)**: the organisms and their products are safely contained in the lab and the SEBOs are not intended for release into the environment.
- **Kill-switch (KS)**: upon unwanted evolution or mutation, a process is triggered to actively kill the SEBOs, often through lysis of cell membranes.
- **Auxotrophy (Aux)**: the organisms cannot survive without the presence of a specific chemical or food source.
- **Degradation (Deg)**: the organisms or their products degrade naturally over time when exposed to certain environmental conditions.
- **Sterility (Ster)**: the organisms' offspring are engineered to be sterile.
- **GRAS**: the organisms and their products are in Risk Group 1 as defined by the FDA or the NIH.

Some of the categorization required making subjective determinations about which safety features were used. Also, some teams used terminology inconsistently. These subjective decisions represent a threat to the validity of our categories and statistics, but we nevertheless believe them to be a fair representation.

Table 1. Most-common safety features from recent iGEM competitions.

Year	# Gold medals	KS	Con	GRAS	Aux	Deg	Ster
2015	114	7.02%	14.04%	50.00%	3.51%	1.75%	0.88%
2016	111	12.61%	20.72%	43.24%	2.70%	5.41%	0.00%
2017	109	13.76%	16.51%	44.04%	6.42%	0.00%	0.00%

Most teams base the safety of their projects on the mere fact their organisms are GRAS (43–50%), but some teams add safety features into their projects. Table 1 shows usage of safety features. The percentages do not add up to 100% for a few reasons. First, many teams did not complete their webpage stubs for the Safety category, or it was otherwise unclear what their approach for safety was. It is likely those teams were relying on GRAS *Only* as their safety feature, meaning the percentages from Table 1 for GRAS *Only* are probably under-reported. Second, some of the teams considered more than one safety feature. We list all that they use. Finally, some teams entered projects which were *in silico*, such as software or hardware improvements. Table 1 demonstrates that we can group safety techniques into a small number of categories, with a Kill-switch (7–14%) and Containment (14–17%) being the most popular mechanisms. We show in the next section how we developed recipes for these.

4 Assurance Recipes

To build an assurance recipe we begin with a pattern. We use the Claim Formalization Pattern from [3] for our recipes. We use goal structuring notation [6] and leave the evaluation compared to alternative modeling languages as future work.

We build recipes for the two most-common safety features in Table 1. The first, the *Containment Recipe*, assumes SEBOs are not intended for release into the environment. The second, the *Safety Mechanism Recipe*, assumes SEBOs will be applied outside of the laboratory.

4.1 Containment Recipe

For this recipe we focus on the safety levels and risks. We show this recipe in Fig. 2(a). It is intended to address the four lab safety levels and the risks associated with organisms requiring those safety levels. The assumption is that a competent government agency has declared the organisms to be from a specific risk group. The evidence needed will mostly be documentation of adequate training and physical measures to certify the lab. Table 2 suggests ingredients for the recipe from which the user can select the appropriate choices.

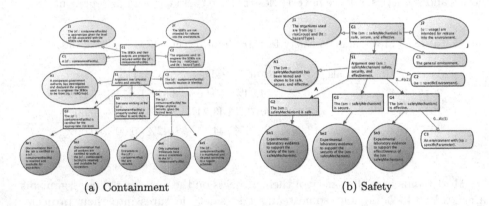

(a) Containment   (b) Safety

Fig. 2. Recipes for (a) Containment and (b) Safety.

4.2 Safety Mechanism Recipe

The recipe in Fig. 2(b) addresses the most-common SEBO safety mechanisms. The assumption is that the SEBOs will be released into the environment and they pose some risk of harm. The evidence will heavily rely on wet-lab experimental data. The safety and security of the SEBOs are included as sub-goals, but there may not be sufficient experimental evidence to support them. Table 3 suggests ingredients for the recipe.

5 Feasibility

We used these recipes on four real projects. The first is the 2017 University of Nebraska - Lincoln team. They thoroughly documented the safety training each member completed before working in the lab, therefore we used the Containment

Table 2. Suggested ingredients for the Containment Recipe.

Variable	Ingredients
cf :: containmentFacility	1. Safety Level One Lab
	2. Safety Level Two Lab
	3. Safety Level Three Lab
	4. Safety Level Four Lab
rg :: riskGroup	1. Risk Group One
	2. Risk Group Two
	3. Risk Group Three
	4. Risk Group Four
ht :: hazardType	1. Cannot cause disease in healthy adults;
	2. Can cause treatable or preventable disease in humans;
	3. Can cause serious disease in humans which might not have a treatment or vaccine;
	4. Can cause serious disease in humans which has no known treatment or vaccine

Table 3. Suggested ingredients for the Safety Mechanism Recipe.

Variable	Ingredients
sm :: safetyMechanism	1. Kill-switch
	2. Auxotrophy
	3. Degradation
	4. Sterility
u :: usage	1. The SEBOs
	2. Only the SEBOs' outputs
se :: specificEnvironment	1. Soil
	2. Water table
	3. [Specific species habitat]
	4. Atmosphere
	5. Rivers
	6. Freshwater rivers or lakes
	7. Saltwater lakes or oceans
	8. Human body
	9. [Non-human] body
sp :: specificParameter	1. [Temperature Range]
	2. [pH Range]
	3. [Aerobic/Anaerobic] environment
	5. [Natural/Specific frequencies/Absence] of light
	7. [Presence/Absence] of nutrients
	8. [Altitude range]

Recipe. They listed themselves as a Safety Level 1 lab, in Risk Group 1, and were thus the first hazardType. For evidence we need to demonstrate that the students followed protocols for containment. We were able to use their documentation to fill in evidence such as Sn2 (of the recipe). They wrote: "We took a total of 6 safety modules including a Biosafety Level 1 course before we were allowed to work in the lab. All modules that required a quiz to be taken had to be completed with 80% proficiency" [15]. The assurance case is shown in Fig. 3(a).

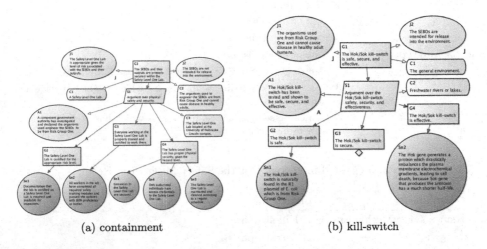

(a) containment   (b) kill-switch

Fig. 3. Assurance case fragments for (a) Containment and (b) Kill-switch.

Since kill-switches are one of the most common approaches to non-containment safety we built a recipe for the Hok/Sok kill-switch from a University of Maryland team, one of the most commonly implemented kill-switches [14]. The key feature is the evidence based on wet-lab experiments showing that the kill-switch will trigger within 30 s of mutation. This is shown in Fig. 3(b).

We also implemented an auxotrophy assurance case based on the 2016 Wageningen team [16] (see Fig. 4(a)). They implemented the auxotrophic system developed in [8]. They designed SEBOs to produce a chemical which helps bees defend against mites. The SEBOs need a synthetic amino acid, BipA, to survive, which beekeepers add to the sugar water feeding the bee colony. If the SEBOs escape the beehive, they will die within 72 h without BipA.

Last, we built a degradation assurance case based on the 2016 Formosa team which developed a pesticide called Pantide [12]. Because it was a novel toxin, the team performed experiments to determine it sufficiently degrades within two hours of exposure to natural light at 36.8C. This is shown in Fig. 4(b).

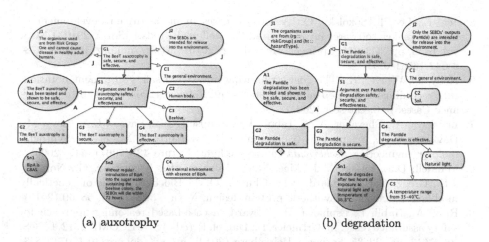

(a) auxotrophy   (b) degradation

Fig. 4. Assurance case fragments for (a) Auxotrophy and (b) Degradation.

6 Conclusions and Future Work

In this paper we have presented the idea of an assurance recipe and demonstrated how it can be applied in the non-traditional domain of synthetic biology. Although our recipes are based on the most common safety features of SEBOs from iGEM projects, they are intended for general application to any SEBOs, and should be helpful for other safety-critical disciplines. Assurance recipes and ingredients can facilitate use and reuse by domain experts who lack expertise with building assurance cases. In future work we will apply these more generally and are working on an interactive software system to help iGEM users build assurance cases using recipes.

Acknowledgments. This work was supported in part by the National Institute of Justice grant 2016-R2-CX-0023 and the National Science Foundation Grant CCF-1745775.

References

1. Cohen, M.B., Firestone, J., Pierobon, M.: The assurance timeline: building assurance cases for synthetic biology. In: Skavhaug, A., Guiochet, J., Schoitsch, E., Bitsch, F. (eds.) SAFECOMP 2016. LNCS, vol. 9923, pp. 75–86. Springer, Cham (2016). https://doi.org/10.1007/978-3-319-45480-1_7
2. Conmy, P., Bate, I.: Assuring safety for component based software engineering. In: 2014 IEEE 15th International Symposium on High-Assurance Systems Engineering (HASE), pp. 121–128. IEEE (2014)
3. Denney, E.W., Pai, G.J.: Safety case patterns: theory and applications (2015)
4. Hawkins, R., Kelly, T.: A Software Safety Argument Pattern Catalogue. The University of York, York (2013)

5. Jee, E., Lee, I., Sokolsky, O.: Assurance cases in model-driven development of the pacemaker software. In: Margaria, T., Steffen, B. (eds.) ISoLA 2010. LNCS, vol. 6416, pp. 343–356. Springer, Heidelberg (2010). https://doi.org/10.1007/978-3-642-16561-0_33

6. Kelly, T., Weaver, R.: The goal structuring notation-a safety argument notation. In: Proceedings of the Dependable Systems and Networks 2004 Workshop on Assurance Cases, p. 6. Citeseer (2004)

7. Levskaya, A., Chevalier, A.A., Tabor, J.J., Simpson, Z.B., Lavery, L.A., Levy, M., Davidson, E.A., Scouras, A., Ellington, A.D., Marcotte, E.M., et al.: Synthetic biology: engineering *Escherichia coli* to see light. Nature **438**(7067), 441 (2005)

8. Mandell, D.J., Lajoie, M.J., Mee, M.T., Takeuchi, R., Kuznetsov, G., Norville, J.E., Gregg, C.J., Stoddard, B.L., Church, G.M.: Biocontainment of genetically modified organisms by synthetic protein design. Nature **518**(7537), 55–60 (2015)

9. Ruiz, A., Habli, I., Espinoza, H.: Towards a case-based reasoning approach for safety assurance reuse. In: Ortmeier, F., Daniel, P. (eds.) SAFECOMP 2012. LNCS, vol. 7613, pp. 22–35. Springer, Heidelberg (2012). https://doi.org/10.1007/978-3-642-33675-1_3

10. Szczygielska, M., Jarzębowicz, A.: Assurance case patterns on-line catalogue. In: Zamojski, W., Mazurkiewicz, J., Sugier, J., Walkowiak, T., Kacprzyk, J. (eds.) DepCoS-RELCOMEX 2017. AISC, vol. 582, pp. 407–417. Springer, Cham (2018). https://doi.org/10.1007/978-3-319-59415-6_39

11. igem.org

12. http://2016.igem.org/Team:NCTU_Formosa/Safety

13. http://2017.igem.org/Human_Practices

14. 2015.igem.org/Team:UMaryland/HokSok

15. 2017.igem.org/Team:UNebraska-Lincoln/Safety

16. http://2016.igem.org/Team:Wageningen_UR/Safety

17. http://osp.od.nih.gov/wp-content/uploads/NIH_Guidelines.html

Incorporating Attacks Modeling into Safety Process

Amer Šurković[1], Džana Hanić[1], Elena Lisova[1]([✉]), Aida Čaušević[1],
Kristina Lundqvist[1], David Wenslandt[2], and Carl Falk[2]

[1] Mälardalen University, Västerås, Sweden
{asc17003,dhc17002}@student.mdh.se,
{elena.lisova,aida.causevic,kristina.lundqvist}@mdh.se
[2] Knightec AB, Västerås, Sweden
{david.wenslandt,carl.falk}@knightec.se

Abstract. Systems of systems (SoS) are built as a collection of systems capable of fulfilling their own function, as well as contributing to other functionalities. They are expected to increase production efficiency and possibly decrease human involvement in harmful environments, and in many cases such systems are safety-critical. For SoS it is a paramount to provide both safety and security assurance. It is not sufficient to analyze and provide assurance of these properties independently due to their mutual connection. Hence, a joint effort addressing safety and security that provides joint guarantees on both properties, is required. In this paper we provide a safety and security assurance argument by incorporating an adversary point of view, and identify potential failures coming from the security domain that might lead to an already identified set of hazards. In this way system assets, vulnerabilities and ways to exploit them can be assessed. As an outcome mitigation strategies coming from security considerations can be captured by the safety requirements. The approach is illustrated on an autonomous quarry.

1 Introduction

Advances in operational and industrial technologies accelerate progress in the area of autonomous system of systems (SoS). SoS are built as a collection of interconnecting systems with cooperation capabilities and sharing resources allowing to extend its collective functionality, increase efficiency compared to traditional systems and provide better performance. SoS are applicable in different domains such as nuclear power plants, automotive, automation, construction works, etc. Many of such systems are safety-critical, i.e., their failure can bring harm to humans, environment or a significant money loss. Given the complexity level of SoS, their analysis with respect to safety and security arises as a paramount challenge to address.

Traditionally safety and security analyses have been conducted independently, resulting in their own techniques, terminologies, standards and practices. The need for their joint consideration due to openness and interconnections of

© Springer Nature Switzerland AG 2018
B. Gallina et al. (Eds.): SAFECOMP 2018 Workshops, LNCS 11094, pp. 31–41, 2018.
https://doi.org/10.1007/978-3-319-99229-7_4

modern systems has already been recognized for more than 25 years [5] and based on the current state-of-the-art it is widely accepted in these communities. However, the state-of-the-practice on joint consideration of these properties does not have the same level of maturity yet. SoS might have external and inter-connections via modern communication infrastructures, e.g., cloud, which represent an attack surface potentially affecting system safety. Thus, to be able to guarantee such critical system properties as safety and security they need to be addressed in a joint effort.

Safety-critical systems are usually developed according to domain specific safety standards which are required to be followed for assurance purposes, as a product has to be sufficiently safe to be accepted at the market. A security breach can lead to an already identified or a new hazard, and therefore security causes leading to hazards need to be considered in order to claim a specific system safety level. A system certified to be acceptably safe without considering security related failures, can be still unsafe due to attacks potentially leading to hazards [10]. Hence, we advocate security informed safety process for autonomous SoS as for systems prone to attacks.

Consideration of safety and security in a joint effort facilitates their joint assurance. First, in Sect. 2 we present necessary definitions and background information related to this topic. We also recognize the necessity to identify attack models relevant for SoS, as surveyed in Sect. 3, and propose to connect them with a set of safety requirements in Sect. 4, in order to capture safety relevant security aspects as well. Thus, this paper contribution is an approach of incorporating attack models into existing safety process. As it is shown in Sect. 5, we complement the process with corresponding arguments presented using a goal-structuring notation (GSN) over the example of an autonomous quarry being acceptable safe, given existing threats that can jeopardize system safety. Finally, Sect. 6 concludes the paper.

2   Background

This section presents security terminology used in the proposed approach. **Security** can be defined as a system property allowing it *"to perform its mission or critical functions despite risks posed by threats"* [16], where a **threat** can be defined as *"the potential source of an adverse event"* [16].

Each system has a set of **assets**, i.e., values that need to be protected against an adversary. A **vulnerability** is a flaw in the system that enables a threat targeting one of the system assets. An **attack** realizes a threat by exploiting a vulnerability in an attempt to break a system asset as it is demonstrated in Fig. 1. **Countermeasures** are *"actions, devices, procedures, or techniques that meet or oppose (i.e., counters) a threat, a vulnerability, or an attack by eliminating or preventing it"* [16]. They can be classified as (*i*) preventive, e.g., encryption, (*ii*) detective, e.g., intrusion detection systems, (*iii*) responsive, e.g., forensics [22]. An **attack model** can be defined as an instantiation of an adversary model in a specific scenario [28], where the latter implies adversary capabilities, constraints and possible interactions with the system. Thus, an attack model demonstrates how an adversary can achieve his or her goal by different techniques and methods for launching an attack, which threats are realized, which vulnerabilities are exploited and which assets are targeted [27].

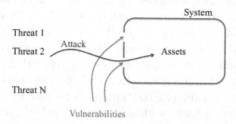

Fig. 1. Security terminology [19]

3   An Overview of Existing Attack Models

In this section we present a summary of the literature survey on attack models [9]. The survey papers from 2010–2018 in the following databases: IEEE Explore Digital Library, Springer Link, Web of Science and ACM. The identified papers have been grouped according to the application domain. The majority of selected papers, (10) are originated from control systems domain followed by vehicular and recommended systems domain, (6) and (5) papers correspondingly, whereas IoT and cloud computing is the least represented. The latter can be justified by the relative novelty of the domains.

Control systems can be categorized into Process Control Systems, Supervisory Control and Data Acquisition (SCADA) Systems, Distributed Control Systems and Cyber Physical Systems (CPSs). They are becoming increasingly vulnerable as they are more exposed and available towards open networks. Existing attack models are focused either on general problems like protocols in SCADA systems, or on specific problems, i.e., smart grid subsystems [27]. The identified attack models are a general sensor attack model from which Denial of Service (DoS) and integrity attacks can be launched [4], attack models in CPSs that can be summarized into DoS and deception attacks [17], aspect-oriented models for CPSs [33], an attack model for CPSs instantiated for a Secure Water Treatment (SWaT) system [1], a smart grid attack model [21], attack models tackling the sparsity of attacks in a distributed smart grid framework [26], and data injection attack models that target integrity of sensor measurements for power grid systems [23].

Attack models related to vehicular domain are exploiting in-vehicle control area network (CAN) vulnerabilities, vulnerabilities in on-board units (OBU) [31], an electric vehicle infrastructure [24]. They might also provide a specific attack, e.g., an attack on a vehicle position forging attacks [8], or specific vehicle type, e.g., resource-constrained Unmanned Aerial Vehicle (UAV) [14]. In IoT attack models can be related to its middleware [7] or be focused on a particular attacks, e.g., the command disaggregation attack [35]. In the context of cloud services, attack models might be connected with an issue of service providers getting access to sensitive client information [36], or aligned with stages of using cloud services, i.e., registration, data gathering about the infrastructure and finally creation of virtual machines for accessing data from other clients [3].

Attack models targeting communication part of systems might be categorized as attack models based on targeted functionalities in different network layers [29], or grouped based on an attack goal as DoS and deception attacks [6]. Further, they could aim for specific protocols, e.g., HTTP/2 Internet service [2], or a specific attack, e.g., jamming attacks for wireless networks [34]. Considering radio-frequency identification (RFID) applications the following attack models have been identified: a forgery attack, a replay attack, a man-in-the-middle attack, a tracking attack [20], DoS, an eavesdropping and scanning [15] and, finally, those attacks focusing on air interfaces [25]. The last identified area for attack models is recommender systems, systems that try to predict a user preference based on the previous behavior of the user, where a large number of new web-services makes it difficult to maintain quality of service for clients [18]. The majority of publications in this area are focused on shilling attacks [13,32,37], i.e., an attack with the goal to manipulate the output of a recommender system. However, other types of attacks, e.g., injection attacks [11], are also used for attack models in recommended systems.

4   Attack Models and Safety Process

4.1   Inclusion of Attack Models into Safety Process

This work that combines attack models with functional safety requirements is an extension of our initial idea of incorporating security concerns into safety process [30]. Figure 2 depicts a reference structure of a safety process, where based on a given system definition, hazard analysis and risk assessment are conducted followed by formulation of safety goals and elicitation of corresponding functional and technical safety requirements (FSRs and TSRs). By executing the system development process artifacts are collected and used as an input into a security analysis. We propose to engage the attack modeling process once there is enough artifacts collected, i.e., hazards and safety goals are formulated. The approach allows engaging the attack modeling process on demand, e.g., if there is an update in the system and correspondingly during the artifacts collection, addressing the dynamic nature of security. The attack modeling process starts with identification of system assets and iterates later on for each identified asset. Each iteration includes identification of related system vulnerabilities, risk assessment of potential threats and finally identification of possible attacks targeting the considered asset. The output of the process is a set of mitigation techniques or countermeasures that is forwarded as an input to the FSRs elicitation step.

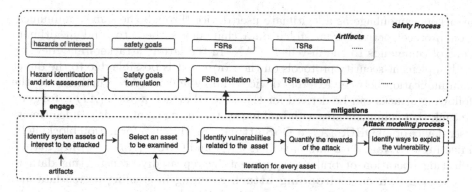

Fig. 2. An approach of incorporating attack modeling into safety process

4.2 Use Case: An Autonomous Quarry

We illustrate our approach on an example of an autonomous quarry. The quarry is equipped with a battery-powered electric load carriers capable to cooperate with other machines such as wheel loader. They are expected to follow a path, load/unload, transport, avoid waiting and carrying load over longer distances than needed, as well as any unnecessary movement, including rework. The goal is that a fleet of these unmanned carriers is jointly able to move the same amount of load as one large haul truck and in case any of these carriers would go down, the loss to the overall quarry production should be much smaller, compared to the loss of a large haul truck. Assuming the carriers being fully autonomous, all possible processes and scenarios need to be documented and analyzed, taking into consideration all new critical situations, including possible threats coming from the security domain affecting the safety of the system. The described autonomous quarry follows the ISO 17757 standard [12] to document safety requirements and criteria for semi-autonomous and autonomous machines and associated systems, typically used in earth-moving and mining operations. For a given use case we have been provided with a quarry architecture description and a list of hazards, identified based on ISO 17757.

Given our findings in Sect. 3, we have chosen to work with an attack model described by Wang et al. [31] that focuses on the in-vehicle network and ways to compromise it. In general, in-vehicle networks are considered as closed networks and secure from malicious attacks, but with multiple network access (e.g., PC, co-pilot unit), there is a number of threats that might endanger them (e.g., current OBUs used in vehicles fail to protect network due to the lack of awareness of possible attacks). Also, an attacker may perform illegitimate vehicle control through unsecured OBUs and in-vehicle CAN. For the in-vehicle CAN the following vulnerabilities have been identified: *(i)* weak access control mechanism, *(ii)* CAN data frames do not have encryption, and *(iii)* no authentication in data exchange exists.

We have chosen two scenarios, that are **short-range attack** and **long-range attack**. Wang et al. [31] describe two methods for short-range attack. In the first, attackers camouflage as a legitimate user device through the same communication protocol derived from stolen data that allows them to send illegitimate control commands to the in-vehicle CAN. In the latter, attackers may develop and implement security protocols on their own that is possible due to the direct communication between external devices and in-vehicle CAN. Furthermore, the following attacks can be derived for the selected attack model: *(A1)* **a forgery attack** that communicates with braking system using commands as a legitimate user device or an OBU; *(A2)* **a DoS attack** resulting in information blocking by injecting irrelevant data into in-vehicle CAN and OBU; *(A3)* **a replay attack** affecting operation of braking equipment by repeatedly transmitting data to CAN; *(A4)* **an eavesdropping attack** resulting in stealing users' data and compromising privacy. Described attacks might be counter-reacted using the following security measures: *(M1)* the identity authentication or access control; *(M2)* data authentication and filtering false information; *(M3)* blocking a large number of packets; *(M4)* hardware isolation.

4.3   Hazards of Interest for the Presented Attack Model

Based on the provided documentation, we have selected a set of hazards of interest for this work [9]. However, in this paper we present information about only one hazard detailed below to illustrate the approach.

The navigation and collision hazard due to: *(i)* failures to detect in time an object; *(ii)* increased latency caused by other applications or computation loading to the processor being used for the object detection or classification system; *(iii)* material on the transmitter or receiver erroneously detected as objects; *(iv)* erroneous location of a detected object; *(v)* inability to stop the machine remotely or in an emergency state; *(vi)* lack of access to situational awareness information; *(vii)* inaccurate terrain data; *(viii)* lost or delayed command input; *(ix)* inaccurate position (due to loss of GNSS correction); *(x)* inaccurate planning information; *(xi)* incomplete or improper system updates and changes to software; **caused by either a DoS attack or a forgery attack.**

5   Joint Safety and Security Argumentation

5.1   GSN for the Autonomous Quarry

We aim to identify possible attacks provided that an attack model exist and discover which of them can cause already recognized hazards. Due to the space limitation, we choose to present only one hazard. Figure 3 depicts a part of the argument for the chosen hazard *"joint navigation and collision hazard (H_1)"*. In the presented argument, we take into account a possibility that a DoS attack on in-vehicle CAN might occur in the quarry since it has enabled Internet connection, blocking the information transmission on-board the vehicle from the main vehicle processor to sensors and/or ECUs that it communicates to. The communication that is performed through CAN is safety-critical since it occurs

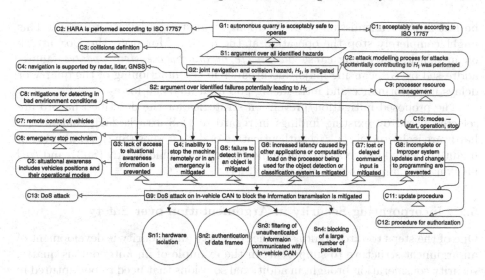

Fig. 3. Argument for the hazard H_1

in real time and failure to obtain an information from an expected ECU might lead to a hazard. Having that in mind, performing a DoS attack on quarry's autonomous vehicles might contribute to failures leading to (H_1) as described in Sect. 4.3. Therefore, we have introduced seven sub-goals, $G2$- to prevent this.

A DoS attack might cause *lack of access to situational awareness information* captured by $G3$, as a vehicle would not be able to gain real time information from its sensors regarding the surrounding environment and its position. This might lead to uncontrolled vehicle movements at the quarry creating and possibly endangering high value equipment at the site, including itself, and even cause a risk to people at the quarry. In case of the *inability to stop machine remotely or in an emergency situation* failure, captured by $G4$, not being prevented and the in-vehicle CAN being flooded with DoS information packets, a vehicle would not be able to perform safety-critical functions such as emergency stop. This is one of the highest degree severity attacks since it may block one of the core safety functions of the vehicle.

The failure *to detect or late detection of an object* addressed by $G5$, that can be caused by communication between modules sending important commands and information within a vehicle, is either limited or completely disabled due the DoS attack. A vehicle would not be able to react to critical situations such as avoiding obstacles. *Increased latency in system functions due to other applications or computation load* failure addressed by $G6$ if not mitigated might reduce the overall system performance. If such event is introduced to the processor used for the object detection, severity of the attack would increase. With the DoS attack, the failure *command inputs can be either lost or delayed* captured by $G7$, can be introduced to the system. Communication channels might be blocked with sufficient amount of irrelevant data packets, causing command inputs to either be lost in the transmission or delayed long enough for a hazard to occur. This might completely stop the operation at the quarry. Moreover, the DoS attack on in-vehicle CAN may cause *incomplete or improper system updates* failure, addressed by $G8$, causing major disturbance in the functioning of the quarry or delays in performance and introducing potential financial losses.

The proposed mitigation/prevention strategies for the described hazard are selected based on existing findings in regard to DoS attacks [31], that are *(i)* hardware isolation (Sn1), *(ii)* authentication of data frames (Sn2), *(i)* filtering of unauthenticated information communicated with in-vehicle CAN (Sn3), and *(iii)* blocking of a large number of packets (Sn4).

5.2   Incorporating Security in Argumentation over Safety

One of the steps towards joint assurance of safety and security is development of an argument structure to support it. In the example of an autonomous quarry, security consideration brought in additional solutions that need to be captured in the corresponding requirements. However, this might require changes in patterns of arguments itself, as it is not enough to argue over system vulnerabilities being mitigated, as security is dynamic and one may also require to argue over system patches being implemented timely in place due to established security process. In this work a security assurance has been introduced at the stage when parts of the safety assurance have been already done (i.e., safety requirements elicited, hazard analysis and risk assessment conducted, etc.). However, a joint assurance assumes security being considered during system development process as different phases of development may require different levels of assurance.

The most important difference between arguing security compared to arguing safety of a system is the presence of an adversary. The behavior of adversaries is not predictable, implying that security threats evolve and adapt with time and therefore an existing case might have its assumptions unexpectedly being violated, or its strength might not be adequate to protect against new attacks. Therefore assurance cases would need to be revisited more frequently than assurance cases covering only safety. Based on this, system assets to be protected change and new vulnerabilities arise. The system evolution of that kind goes against the static structure of an assurance case that in this example would requires (re-)building the case from scratch given any update at run-time. Therefore, it is crucial to enable continuous assurance through the entire life cycle and provide arguments regarding evolving assets and mitigation actions on new vulnerabilities. This process can be seen as a way of enabling run-time assurance of systems that evolve over time (e.g., self-adaptive systems). Run-time assurance case adaptation would not only allow handling of updates in a cost-efficient and effective way, but would be able to facilitate continuous joint assurance of systems that adapt at run-time.

6 Conclusions

Well established methods, techniques and processes within separate communities of safety and security are not sufficient anymore to produce acceptably safe and secure systems, most importantly they should not be isolated one from another. With the growing number of cyber attacks on safety-critical systems, we have identified the need to observe a system from an adversary point of view. In this paper we choose to incorporate an attack that focuses on ways to compromise an in-vehicle network and include the knowledge about preventing/mitigating it while providing argumentation for system safety. We demonstrate parts of the argumentation at example of autonomous quarry using GSN. In the future we plan to investigate ways how this information can be included into security assurance case, similar to one from safety domain, possibly at run-time.

Acknowledgments. This work is supported by the SAFSEC-CPS project funded by KKS, the SeCRA project funded by Vinnova and the Serendipity project funded by SSF.

References

1. Adepu, S., Mathur, A.: An investigation into the response of a water treatment system to cyber attacks. In: 17th IEEE International Symposium on High Assurance Systems Engineering (2016)
2. Adi, E., Baig, Z.A., Hingston, P., Lam, C.P.: Distributed denial-of-service attacks against http/2 services. Clust. Comput. **19**(1), 79–86 (2016)
3. AlJahdali, H., et al.: Multi-tenancy in cloud computing. In: 8th IEEE International Symposium on SOSE (2014)
4. Cárdenas, A.A., et al.: Attacks against process control systems: risk assessment, detection, and response. In: ACM Symposium on Information, Computer and Communications Security (2011)
5. Causevic, A.: A risk and threat assessment approaches overview in autonomous systems of systems. In: The 26th IEEE International Conference on Information, Communication and Automation Technologies (2017)
6. Ding, D., Wang, Z., Wei, G., Alsaadi, F.E.: Event-based security control for discrete-time stochastic systems. IET Control Theory Appl. **10**(15), 1808–1815 (2016)
7. Ferreira, H.G.C., de Sousa Junior, R.T.: Security analysis of a proposed internet of things middleware. Clust. Comput. **20**(1), 651–660 (2017)
8. Grover, J., Laxmi, V., Gaur, M.S.: Attack models and infrastructure supported detection mechanisms for position forging attacks in vehicular ad hoc networks. CSI Trans. ICT **1**(3), 261–279 (2013)
9. Hanić, D., Šurković, A.: An Attack Model of Autonomous Systems of Systems. Master's thesis, Mälardalen University, IDT, June 2018
10. Hänninen, K., Hansson, H., Thane, H., Saadatmand, M.: Inadequate risk analysis might jeopardize the functional safety of modern systems, March 2016
11. Huang, S., Shang, M., Cai, S.: A hybrid decision approach to detect profile injection attacks in collaborative recommender systems. In: Chen, L., Felfernig, A., Liu, J., Raś, Z.W. (eds.) ISMIS 2012. LNCS (LNAI), vol. 7661, pp. 377–386. Springer, Heidelberg (2012). https://doi.org/10.1007/978-3-642-34624-8_43

12. ISO 17757 - International Organization for Standardization: Earth-moving machinery and mining-, and semi-autonomous machine system safety (2017)
13. Jiang, F., Tian, R.: The influence of shilling attacks with different attack cycles. In: 6th IIAI International Congress on Advanced Applied Informatics (2017)
14. Katewa, V., Anguluri, R., Ganlath, A., Pasqualetti, F.: Secure reference-tracking with resource-constrained uavs. In: IEEE CCTA (2017)
15. Khan, G.N., Yu, J., Yuan, F.: XTEA based secure authentication protocol for RFID systems. In: ICCN (2011)
16. Kissel, R.: Glossary of key information security terms. U.S. Dept. of Commerce, National Institute of Standards and Technology (2006)
17. Kwon, C., Liu, W., Hwang, I.: Security analysis for cyber-physical systems against stealthy deception attacks. In: American Control Conference, June 2013
18. Li, X., Gao, M., Rong, W., Xiong, Q., Wen, J.: Shilling attacks analysis in collaborative filtering based web service recommendation systems. In: IEEE International Conference on Web Services (2016)
19. Lisova, E.: Monitoring for Securing Clock Synchronization. Ph.D. thesis, Mälardalen University, April 2018
20. Liu, H., Ning, H.: Zero-knowledge authentication protocol based on alternative mode in RFID systems. IEEE Sens. J. **11**(12), 3235–3245 (2011)
21. Lu, Z., Wang, W., Wang, C.: Camouflage traffic: minimizing message delay for smart grid applications under jamming. IEEE Trans. Dependable Secure Comput. **12**(1), 31–44 (2015)
22. Miede, A., et al.: A generic metamodel for IT security attack modeling for distributed systems. In: International Conference on Availability, Reliability and Security (2010)
23. Mohammadi, A., Plataniotis, K.N.: Secure estimation against complex-valued attacks. In: IEEE Statistical Signal Processing Workshop (2016)
24. Mousavian, S., Erol-Kantarci, M., Wu, L., Ortmeyer, T.: A risk-based optimization model for electric vehicle infrastructure response to cyber attacks. IEEE Trans. Smart Grid (2017)
25. Huansheng, N., Hong, L.I.U., Chen, Y.A.N.G.: Ultralightweight RFID authentication protocol based on random partitions of pseudorandom identifier and pre-shared secret value. Chin. J. Electron. **20**(4), 701–707 (2011)
26. Ozay, M., Esnaola, I., Vural, F.T.Y., Kulkarni, S.R., Poor, H.V.: Distributed models for sparse attack construction and state vector estimation in the smart grid. In: 3rd IEEE International Conference on Smart Grid Communications (2012)
27. Paudel, S., Smith, P., Zseby, T.: Attack models for advanced persistent threats in smart grid wide area monitoring. In: 2nd CPSR-SG. ACM (2017)
28. Rocchetto, M., Tippenhauer, N.O.: On attacker models and profiles for cyber-physical systems. In: Askoxylakis, I., Ioannidis, S., Katsikas, S., Meadows, C. (eds.) ESORICS 2016. LNCS, vol. 9879, pp. 427–449. Springer, Cham (2016). https://doi.org/10.1007/978-3-319-45741-3_22
29. Sunghyuck, H., Sunho, L., Jaeki, S.: Unified modeling language based analysis of security attacks in wireless sensor networks: a survey. KSII Trans. Internet Inf. Syst. **5**(4), 805–821 (2011)
30. Surkovic, A., et al.: Towards attack models in autonomous SoS. In: IEEE SoS Engineering (2018)
31. Wang, L., Liu, X.: NOTSA: novel OBU with three-level security architecture for internet of vehicles. IEEE Internet Things J. (2018)

32. Wang, Y., Wu, Z., Cao, J., Fang, C.: Towards a tricksy group shilling attack model against recommender systems. In: Zhou, S., Zhang, S., Karypis, G. (eds.) ADMA 2012. LNCS (LNAI), vol. 7713, pp. 675–688. Springer, Heidelberg (2012). https://doi.org/10.1007/978-3-642-35527-1_56
33. Wasicek, A., Derler, P., Lee, E.A.: Aspect-oriented modeling of attacks in automotive cyber-physical systems. In: 51st ACM/EDAC/IEEE DAC (2014)
34. Xu, W., Trappe, W., Zhang, Y., Wood, T.: The feasibility of launching and detecting jamming attacks in wireless networks. In: 6th ACM International Symposium on Mobile Ad Hoc Networking and Computing (2005)
35. Xun, P., Zhu, P.D., Hu, Y.F., Cui, P.S., Zhang, Y.: Command disaggregation attack and mitigation in industrial Internet of Things. Sensors 17(10), 2408 (2017)
36. Yiu, M.L., Ghinita, G., Jensen, C.S., Kalnis, P.: Enabling search services on outsourced private spatial data. The VLDB J. 19(3), 363–384 (2010)
37. Zhang, F.: Analysis of bandwagon and average hybrid attack model against trust-based recommender systems. In: 5th ICMeCG (2011)

Assurance Case Considerations
for Interoperable Medical Systems

Yi Zhang[1(✉)], Brian Larson[2], and John Hatcliff[2]

[1] U.S. Food and Drug Administration, Silver Spring, MD 20993, USA
yi.zhang2@fda.hhs.gov
[2] Kansas State University, Manhattan, KS 66506, USA
{brl,hatcliff}@ksu.edu

Abstract. Modern medical devices are increasingly developed by composing a variety of interoperable elements such as medical devices, services, and platform infrastructures. In many scenarios, multi-vendor consortia are organized to support the development and deployment of interoperable medical systems, in which safety-critical element implementations, risk management results, and safety assurance are reused across organizational boundaries. This reality calls for an assurance case approach that supports interfacing, refinement, and composition of distributed, component-level claims and evidences to construct system-level assurance argumentation. We present a collection of objectives and top-level safety claims towards the development of such an approach for interoperable systems built using medical application platforms.

Keywords: Assurance case · Interoperable medical system Ecosystem

1 Introduction

Modern medical devices are increasingly developed as interoperable systems composed with a variety of reusable interoperable components and services from different vendors. One vision of realizing interoperable medical systems is by using medical application platforms (MAPs) [4]. A MAP provides a real-time computing platform for: (a) integrating heterogeneous devices, medical IT systems, and displays via a communication infrastructure, and (b) hosting application programs ('apps') that provide medical utility by coordinating other components in the system.

While a MAP may be used within a single organization, there are scenarios in which multi-vendor consortia (e.g., [6]) are organized to support the development

---

B. Larson—This work is sponsored in part by US National Science Foundation and Food and Drug Administration Scholar-in-Residence program (CNS 1238431, 1355778,1446544,1565544).

B. Gallina et al. (Eds.): SAFECOMP 2018 Workshops, LNCS 11094, pp. 42–48, 2018.
https://doi.org/10.1007/978-3-319-99229-7_5

and deployment of interoperable medical systems. This essentially establishes an ecosystem where a collection of stakeholders share the same interoperability reference architecture, and follow the established processes to develop, assure, market, deploy, and operate interoperable systems [9].

We argue that consortia-supported ecosystems should have management elements to enable cross-vendor coordination on life-cycle activities including quality management, risk management and safety assurance. Thus, it becomes possible to reuse components and infrastructure implementations, risk management information, and safety assurance results. Otherwise, system builders would have to rework all component-level risk management and assurance activities to re-assure components with each new system instance.

These characteristics of MAP-based ecosystems however pose challenges to constructing compelling assurance cases for interoperable medical systems built using the ecosystems' assets. The first challenge is how to phrase and present evidence for component-level assurance claims, so that component assurance can be reused to effectively support system assurance claims. It is therefore important that individual component manufacturers not only have a good approach to presenting assurance and evidence, but also that the approach is compatible with other manufacturers in the consortia and aligned with the reference architecture.

The second challenge is the protection of intellectual properties. Component vendors need to share implementations and supporting risk management and assurance artifacts, so that system builders can acquire sufficient understanding of functional and safety properties of a component and trust that its implementation meets the specifications. However, doing so should not force component vendors to disclose unnecessary proprietary information of their products.

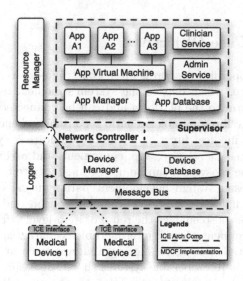

Fig. 1. ICE architecture and its MDCF realization

To address these challenges, we advocate for an assurance case approach that provides structural support for reusing component-level safety assurance efforts while protecting proprietary information. In this paper, we summarize characteristics of medical device interoperability ecosystems, based on which a collection of objectives are defined for the assurance case approach. We also lay down a set of top-level safety claims that need to be considered by assurance cases for interoperable medical systems.

2   MAPs and Interoperable Medical Systems

MAPs can be realized via different architectures. One prominent example is the Integrated Clinical Environment (ICE) defined in the ASTM F2761-2009 standard [1]. As illustrated as dashed-line boxes in Fig. 1, the ICE infrastructure incorporates a set of architectural components to achieve the MAP goals of interoperability and safety.

Two primary components of the ICE architecture are the *Network Controller* and the *Supervisor*, where the Network Controller provides a high-assurance network communication capability to establish virtual information pipes between devices and apps running in the Supervisor. The Supervisor, on the other hand, provides a platform, including application logic and an operator interface, for functional integration between ICE compliant equipments.

The interoperability community has committed significant efforts in developing technologies of implementing the ICE architecture, such as OpenICE [11] and the Medical Device Coordination Framework (MDCF) [10]. For example, the solid-line boxes in Fig. 1 indicate how MDCF components realize the ICE architecture.

3   Assurance Case Objectives

A MAP-based interoperable system is often constructed based on the notion of *interoperable scenario*, which defines the system's medical function and specifies items that conform to the platform and can be connected to the system at interaction points. An interoperable scenario is constrained enough to ensure the delivery of intended medical function with acceptable risks, yet provides flexibility so specific items (i.e., device, app, equipment, and architecture) provided by vendors across the ecosystem can be used to instantiate the scenario.

This platform-based system development paradigm calls for an assurance case approach that not only supports item integration and system composition/instantiation, but also enables the reuse of item-level safety claims and evidences for safety argumentation of interoperable scenarios and their instances. We elaborate the detailed objectives for such an approach in Table 1.

Items to be used in interoperable systems should be assured to be integrated and reused in different system contexts. Thus, the **AssumedClaim-Obj** objective in Table 1 enforces that each item must clearly state its provided services and capabilities, as well as the assumptions on what its context (either other items or operators) must do to ensure its safety and security.

The context assumptions of an item can be viewed as claims that other entities are responsible for justifying. Thus, effective management should be established across the ecosystem, so that participating entities not only have clear understanding of their own roles, but also know the roles or activities responsible for justifying the context assumptions of their products. This requirement is captured by the **AssumedClaimsAllocation-Obj** objective in Table 1. When an item is integrated, explicit traceability should be established between its context assumptions and claims/evidence provided by the responsible roles demonstrating that these assumptions are satisfied (the **Assured-Reconciliation-Obj** objective).

Each item used in the system can be member of a family of products with common capabilities and behaviors, captured in interfaces that hide their implementation details/differences. Thus, a mechanism is needed for (1) defining assurance case templates for a family of products (the **Template-Obj** objective), and (2) instantiating these templates (also called assurance case refinement) to specific items with the common and additional capabilities (the **Refinement-Obj** objective).

The risk management and assurance artifacts of an item should be reused to refine its corresponding template or support other assumed claims it is responsible for justifying. However, such reuse should not unnecessarily disclose proprietary information of the item (the **InfoHiding-Obj** objective). Explicit *conformity* relations should also be established between claims about an item and the assurance case template it refines, to facilitate the assessment of the item's conformity to the expected interfaces (the **Conformance-Obj** objective).

4   Assurance Case Use Cases

The objectives in Sect. 3 articulate the needs for an assurance case approach to effectively construct safety arguments for interoperable medical systems. It would also benefit all stakeholders in the ecosystem to share a consensus pattern of top-level safety claims, which establishes the safety goals of interoperable scenarios and their instances. This can help the stakeholders to better plan and perform development and risk management activities, and to produce artifacts and evidence sufficient enough to support system-level safety claims.

We argue that such a consensus pattern of safety claims should at least cover safety properties regarding item conformance, item placement, and ecosystem management, as listed in Table 2. We envision that these safety claims, when instantiated with specific interoperable scenario designs, can also be used as *use cases* for designing and evaluating the assurance case approach envisioned in this paper.

Table 1. Objectives for an assurance case approach for interoperable medical systems

Item Integration Objectives
AssumedClaim-Obj: To enable composition of assurance cases as an item is integrated, the approach should be able to distinguish (a) claims about the capabilities provided by one item through its interfaces, and (b) claims that capture assumptions about the assurance activities to be realized by other entities in the item's context.
AssumedClaims-Allocation-Obj The approach should be able to indicate the organizational roles responsible for external measure claims of every item in the system.
Assured-Reconciliation-Obj: The approach should be able to specify 'linking argument' that establishes the association between an assumed claim of one item and the provided claims of another item supporting it.
Assurance Case Management Objectives
InfoHiding-Obj The approach should be able to distinguish between (a) claims about the capabilities provided by one item through its interfaces, and (b) claims about its design and implementation.
Templates-Obj: To allow the ecosystem to share component- and system-level safety claims, the approach should have a schematic mechanism for defining assurance case templates of claims and argument structures that subsequently can be instantiated to obtain complete assurance cases for specific items.
Refinement-Obj: The approach should provide the ability to refine an assurance case template for a class of items with additional claims and evidence specific to a particular item in that class.
Conformance-Obj: The approach should be able to specify the *conformity relation* between an assurance case template and its refining template/ template instantiation, to support the conformity assessment of particular items integrated into the system.

Table 2. Top level safety claims for interoperable medical systems

Claims on Item Realization conforms to Item Specification
Claim on unit implementation conforms to specification.
Claim on system implementation conforms to specification.
Claims on Item Placement in Context
Claims on item placement conforms to its use specification
Claims on interfaces are compatible at points of composition
Claims on composition discrepancies being addressed
Claims on Ecosystem Management
Claims on item specification conforms to Architectural Role
Claims on item class conforms to Architectural Role
Claims on item specification conforms to item class
Claims on interoperability architecture conforms to the reference architecture

5   Related Work

The notion of assurance case composition can be dated back to early 2000s [7], when an extension to the GSN notation was proposed to support the composition of multiple assurance cases via *contracts*. Based on this work, Tim Kelly proposed the concept of *modular assurance case* and principles for composing modular assurance cases for complex systems according to a pre-defined assurance case architecture [8]. This thread of research, as it continues to evolve (e.g., [2,12]), provides the theoretical basis for composing item-level assurance cases into a system-level assurance case discussed in this paper.

The need for establishing assurance case patterns for a family of products and refining them to specific items (see Sect. 3) can be addressed using *assurance case template* [3], which allows safety argument patterns to be reused and instantiated with concrete assurance details.

The research closest to the assurance case approach envisioned in this paper is [5], where a set of modular assurance case patterns were automatically instantiated using a model-based process to establish assurance cases for systems developed based on D-MILS, a distributed, safety-assured, and interoperable architecture. However, this research work, as well as others discussed in this section, need to be leveraged and customized to achieve an assurance case approach that supports distributed risk management across MAP ecosystems, reuse of risk management and assurance artifacts, and conformity assessment of interoperable items.

6   Conclusion

We have presented a collection of objectives and top-level safety claims for effective safety argumentation of interoperable medical systems. The presented objectives and safety claims address the needs from different stakeholders and the need for reusing risk management and assurance effort of system components. We are currently developing an assurance case approach towards the objectives laid down in the paper.

References

1. ASTM: F-2761: Medical devices and medical systems - essential safety requirements for equipment comprising the patient-centric integrated clinical environment (ICE) - Part 1: general requirements and conceptual model (2009)
2. Denney, E., Pai, G.: Towards a formal basis for modular safety cases. In: Koornneef, F., van Gulijk, C. (eds.) SAFECOMP 2015. LNCS, vol. 9337, pp. 328–343. Springer, Cham (2015). https://doi.org/10.1007/978-3-319-24255-2_24
3. Gorski, J., Jarzebowicz, A., Miler, J.: Validation of services supporting healthcare standards conformance. Metrol. Meas. Syst. **19**(2), 269–284 (2012)
4. Hatcliff, J., et al.: Rationale and architecture principles for medical application platforms. In: Proceedings of the 2012 International Conference on Cyberphysical Systems, pp. 3–12 (2012)
5. Hawkins, R., Kelly, T., Habli, I.: Developing assurance cases for D-MILS systems. In: International Workshop on MILS: Architecture and Assurance for Secure Systems (2015)
6. ICE Alliance. http://www.icealliance.org

7. Kelly, T.: Concepts and principles of compositional safety case construction. Contract Research Report for QinetiQ COMSA/2001/1/1 34 (2001)
8. Kelly, T.: Using software architecture techniques to support the modular certification of safety-critical systems. In: Proceedings of the 11th Australian Workshop on Safety Critical Systems and Software, vol. 69, pp. 53–65 (2006)
9. Kim, Y.J., Procter, S., Hatcliff, J., Ranganath, V.P., Robby: ecosphere principles for medical application platforms. In: IEEE International Conference on Healthcare Informatics (ICHI) (2015)
10. King, A., et al.: An open test bed for medical device integration and coordination. In: Proceedings of the 31st International Conference on Software Engineering, pp. 141–151 (2009). https://doi.org/10.1109/ICSE-COMPANION.2009.5070972
11. MDPnP Program: OpenICE - open-source integrated clinical environment (2015). https://www.openice.info/
12. Sljivo, I., Gallina, B., Carlson, J., Hansson, H.: Generation of safety case argument-fragments from safety contracts. In: Bondavalli, A., Di Giandomenico, F. (eds.) SAFECOMP 2014. LNCS, vol. 8666, pp. 170–185. Springer, Cham (2014). https://doi.org/10.1007/978-3-319-10506-2_12

Two Decades of Assurance Case Tools: A Survey

Mike Maksimov[1]([⊠]), Nick L. S. Fung[1], Sahar Kokaly[2], and Marsha Chechik[1]

[1] University of Toronto, Toronto, Canada
{maksimov,nlsfung,chechik}@cs.toronto.edu
[2] McMaster University, Hamilton, Canada
kokalys@mcmaster.ca

Abstract. In regulated safety-critical domains, such as the aerospace and nuclear domains, certification bodies often require systems to undergo a stringent safety assessment procedure to show their compliance to one or more safety standards. Assurance cases are an emerging way of communicating safety of a safety-critical system in a structured and comprehensive manner. Due to the significant complexity of the required materials, software tools are often used as a practical way of constructing assurance cases. This paper presents the first, to the best of our knowledge, systematic review of assurance case tools. Specifically, we provide a comprehensive list of assurance case tools developed over the past 20 years and an analysis of their functionalities.

Keywords: Assurance case · Tools · Systematic literature review

1 Introduction

Assurance cases (ACs) can be very complex; e.g., an assurance case for an air traffic control system may comprise over 500 pages and 400 referenced documents [34]. Tools to support safety engineers in creating, maintaining and analysing ACs have been developed. For example, Resolute [23] can automatically generate ACs based on a system's architectural models, while AGSN [35] supports the assessment of an AC's validity. The development of these tools has been enabled by the introduction of formal syntaxes for ACs, such as the Goal Structuring Notation (GSN) [28]. In this paper, we aim to perform a systematic review of the progress made in the development of tools for ACs. To the best of our knowledge, this is the first such study. More specifically, the main contributions of this work are (1) a comprehensive list of AC tools developed over the past 20 years; and (2) an analysis of these tools according to their functionality.

The remainder of this paper is organised as follows. Sect. 2 presents our methodology for finding and comparing AC tools. In Sect. 3, we present and summarise our findings and potential threats to validity. We conclude by discussing the implications of our work in Sect. 4.

© Springer Nature Switzerland AG 2018
B. Gallina et al. (Eds.): SAFECOMP 2018 Workshops, LNCS 11094, pp. 49–59, 2018.
https://doi.org/10.1007/978-3-319-99229-7_6

2   Methodology

We carried out a Systematic Literature Review (SLR) in order to establish a complete list of AC tools and provide a comprehensive assessment of their features. Our SLR followed a simplified version of the guidelines proposed by Kitchenham et al. [8], as well as the search strategy proposed by Zhang et al. [46]. It consists of three stages: **(1)** establishing the *quasi-gold standard* (QGS) through a manual search of different publication venues, **(2)** an automated literature search of digital libraries, e.g., Springer Link and IEEE Xplore, and **(3)** a web-based search for commercial tools and tools that may not have been mentioned in publications. We describe these steps below.

Manual Search and Establishing the QGS. A QGS is a set of high quality studies from the related publication venues on a research topic, e.g., domain-specific conferences and journals recognized by the community in the subject, for a given time span [46]. To create a QGS, relevant publication venues are identified and manually searched in order to retrieve studies that serve as a benchmark for the subsequent automated search. Through consultation with domain experts, we identified six major conferences and journals that published research on ACs: **(1)** SAFECOMP (International Conference on Computer Safety, Reliability, & Security), **(2)** HASE (International Symposium on High Assurance Systems Engineering), **(3)** IMBSA (International Symposium on Model-Based Safety and Assessment), **(4)** ISSRE (International Symposium on Software Reliability Engineering), **(5)** Reliability Engineering & System Safety (journal), and **(6)** COMPSAC (International Conference on Computers, Software & Applications). We performed a manual search through the proceedings of these venues including all associated workshops, for 2015-17 inclusive, yielding 10 relevant AC tool papers which established our QGS.

Defining the Search String and Performing the Automated Search. A careful examination of the papers in our QGS constructed the search string to be *"("Safety Assurance" OR GSN OR SACM OR "Safety Case" OR "Safety Cases" OR "Assurance Case" OR "Assurance Cases" OR "Safety Compliance") AND (Editor OR Tool OR Editors OR Tools OR Toolset OR Toolsets)"*. We used it to conduct an automated literature search on IEEE Xplore, Engineering Village, ACM Digital Library and Spring Link[1], combined with the criterion that the papers were in English and published after 1998.

IEEE Xplore, Engineering Village, ACM Digital Library, and Springer Link returned 112, 739, 21, and 80 papers respectively, for a total of 952 papers. We checked the resulting papers against our QGS which captured 8/10 papers, achieving the recommended 80% sensitivity [46]. After filtering out duplicate papers, papers not accessible in full text, irrelevant papers (based on a manual review of their abstracts or the full text), we identified 82 papers.

Performing the Web-Based Search. To obtain knowledge about commercial AC tools, tools that were published but were not found by our literature search,

---

[1] The literature search was conducted in the dates between 02.02.2018 - 19.02.2018.

or tools that simply were not mentioned in publications, we conducted a web-based search[2] using Google as the search engine. We used the same search string as for the literature search and viewed the first 100 results. This step yielded eight additional tools.

Table 1. Tool functionality categories and the corresponding degrees of support.

Feature category	Level of tool support			
	D (No support)	C (Minimal support)	B (Moderate support)	A (Strong support)
Support for AC creation (Creation).	None	Basic support for the manual creation of ACs.	Partial automation or re-use in creating ACs is available (e.g. argument patterns and templates).	Automatic creation of complete ACs.
Support for maintaining ACs as they evolve (Maintenance).	None	Manual editing with no guidance on affected parts provided.	Tracking of relevant artefacts (e.g. system models and evidence), notifying user of changes and/or indicating their potential impact on the AC.	Automatic updates of ACs to reflect changes in the relevant artefacts (e.g., evidence, system models, requirements specifications).
Support for assessing ACs (Assessment).	None	Support for manual annotations to indicate potential problems.	Support for syntactical checks (e.g., for well-formedness, completeness and/or consistency).	Syntactic and semantic checking (e.g., validity of overall argument given its supporting arguments and evidence).
Support for collaboration between users (Collaboration).	None	A basic concurrent multi-user environment.	Additional features such as user access/permission management.	A complex multi-user environment (e.g., change requests and change reviews).
Support for creating reports from ACs (e.g. for certification purposes or for different stakeholders) (Reporting).	None	Generic reports with no user configurability, limited range of document formats and/or limited content.	Some user configurability, in multiple document formats and/or containing more content.	High user configurability, extensive document formats and/or detailed/interactive content (e.g., generating different reports).
Support for other design/assurance lifecycle processes (e.g. RE specs, hazop, verification) (Integration).	None	Manual integration.	Some support (e.g., bundling with specific third-party tools).	Extensive support for many other design/assurance lifecycle processes.

Evaluating the Tools. Having read all of the publications and the resources gathered by our searches, we established six distinct recurring tool functionalities, using them as the basis for our evaluation. These functionalities are categorized as AC creation, maintenance, assessment, collaboration, reporting and integration (see Table 1). We then defined four levels of tool support for each of the categories, ranging from D (no support) to A (strong support), thus creating our grading criteria. We then graded each tool's degree of support for each

---

[2] Carried out on 25.02.2018.

category, using information from the publications and the web resources. Since information in some of the publications can be out of date, we made an effort to use the newest publications so as to arrive at a more accurate evaluation. Please note that our evaluation is based purely on the information found in the above resources rather than on the hands-on testing of the tools.

3   Results

Our systematic literature review discovered a total of 46 AC tools. Eight of these tools (AssureNote [1], PREEVision [3], SMS Pro [4], Artisan GSN modeler [2], Assure-It [45], SEAS [12], TurboAC [5] and eDependabilityCase [33]) were discovered by our web search; two (MMINT-A [22] and Resolute [23]) were identified with the help of domain experts, and the remainder were found by our literature search. Nine tools (AssureNote [1], DECOS Test Bench [11], e-Safety Case [32], GSN CaseMaker ERA [32], ISIS High Integrity Solutions [32], PREEVision [3], SCAPT [10], SEAS [12] and SMS Pro [4]) did not provide sufficient information allowing us to conduct an educated evaluation, and are thus excluded from further discussion[3].

Out of the 37 AC tools (see Table 2), 32 offer support for GSN [6]. Some exceptions to this are Modus [44] (a plug-in for Enterprise Architect), ACBuilder [27], NOR-STA [24], etc., which have their own notations. Multiple tools (e.g., CertWare [13] and ASCE [40]) also offer support for a variety of different notations, such as the Structured Assurance Case Metamodel (SACM) [7] and the Claims-Arguments-Evidence (CAE) [15] notations, in addition to others. Our findings also show that most of the tools are not domain specific, meaning that they can be used to construct ACs for military, automotive, medical, and nuclear systems, among others. Exceptions to this are tools such as ACBuilder [27] (hardware security analysis) and TurboAC [5] (medical devices). Non domain specific tools (e.g., D-Case Editor [37]) have been marked with a hyphen under the domain column in Table 2.

3.1   Evaluation of the Tools and Discussion

Each tool has been manually evaluated for its support in the previously established categories, with the results shown in Table 3. Figure 1 represents the overall grade distribution for each category. To simplify visualization, all split grades have been rounded up and represented as the higher grade.

Creation. Support for creation of ACs primarily ranges between minimal (43%) and moderate (49%) (see Fig. 1(a)). The notable exceptions, ENTRUST [16] and Resolute [23], offer strong support by providing the automatic generation of

---

[3] A table listing more information about each evaluated tool, such as where it was produced, how it was discovered, a link to the tool, its availability, its supported notations and domain, can be accessed at goo.gl/A4yWs9.

Table 2. General tool information.

Tool name	Supported notations	Domain
ACBuilder [27]	Textual	Hardware security analysis
ACCESS [32]	GSN	-
ACEdit [32] https://github.com/arapost/acedit	GSN, ARM	-
AdvoCATE [20] https://ti.arc.nasa.gov/tech/rse/research/advocate/	GSN, SACM, Bowtie	-
AGSN [35] https://github.com/AGSNeditor/development	GSN	-
ASCE [40] https://www.adelard.com/asce/choosing-asce/index/	CAE, SACM, GSN, Bowtie	-
Assure-It [45]	GSN	-
Astah GSN [32] http://astah.net/download	GSN, ARM, SACM	-
Artisan GSN modeler [2]	GSN	-
AutoFOCUS3 [17] https://af3.fortiss.org/download/	GSN	Distributed, reactive, embedded software systems
CertWare [13] https://nasa.github.io/CertWare/	ARM, CAE, GSN, EUROCONTROL	-
D-Case Communicator [38] https://mlab.ce.cst.nihon-u.ac.jp/dcase/login.html	GSN	-
D-Case Editor [37] http://www.jst.go.jp/crest/crest-os/osddeos/en/tech.html	GSN, SACM	-
D-Case Weaver [21] http://www.jst.go.jp/crest/crest-os/osddeos/en/tech.html	GSN	-
D-MILS [18] https://github.com/phy3rdh/DmilsMBAC	GSN	-
Eclipse & Papyrus extension [26]	GSN	-
eDependabilityCase [33]	GSN	-
ENTRUST [16] https://github.com/gerasimou/ENTRUST	GSN	Self-adaptive software
eSafetyCase Toolkit [41]	GSN	-
ETB (Evidential Tool Bus) [19] https://github.com/SRI-CSL/ETB	Claims table	-
Event-B extension [30]	GSN	-
EviCA [39] Can be acquired by emailing the authors	GSN	-
GAGE [14]	GSN	-
HiP-HOPS extension [43] http://www.hip-hops.eu/	GSN	-
ISCaDE [32] http://www.iscade.co.uk/	GSN, ASCAD, WeFA	-
MMINT-A [22] https://github.com/adisandro/MMINT	GSN	-
Modus [44] http://modelme.simula.no/Modus	KAOS	-
NOR-STA [24] https://www.argevide.com/purchase/assurance-case/	TRUST-IT Argument Representation	-
OpenCERT [31] https://www.polarsys.org/proposals/opencert	GSN	-
Resolute [23] https://github.com/smaccm/smaccm	Unique notation	Distributed real-time embedded systems
SafeEd [25] http://cs-gw.utcluj.ro/~adrian/tools/safed/gsn/gsn.html	GSN	-
Safety.Lab [42]	GSN	-
SAM [29]	GSN	-
SCT: Safety Case Toolkit [9] http://www.dependablecomputing.com/	GSN, MDD (MultiMarkdown doc.)	-
SBVR/GSN Editor [36]	GSN	-
TurboAC [5] http://www.gessnet.com/	Subset of GSN, Tabular, Narrative	Medical devices
Visio add-on [32] http://www-users.cs.york.ac.uk/~tpk/gsn/	GSN	-

Table 3. Evaluation of capabilities of individual tools.

Tool name	Creation	Maintenance	Assessment	Collaboration	Reporting	Integration
ACBuilder [27]	B	D	D	D	D	D
ACCESS [32]	B	C	C	D	C	D
ACEdit [32]	C	C	B	D	D	D
AdvoCATE [20]	B	B	A	D	A/B	B
AGSN [35]	C	C	B	D	C	D
ASCE [40]	C	B	B	B	A/B	C
Assure-It [45]	C	C/D	D	D	D	D
Astah GSN [32]	B	C	B	D	C	D
Artisan GSN modeler [2]	B	C	B	A	D	D
AutoFOCUS3 [17]	B	B	B	D	D	B
CertWare [13]	B	B	A	C	D	B
D-Case Communicator [38]	C	C	D	C	D	D
D-Case Editor [37]	B	B	B	D	D	B
D-Case Weaver [21]	C	C	C	C	C	B
D-MILS [18]	B	B	B	D	D	B
Eclipse & Papyrus Ext. [26]	C	C	A	D	D	D
eDependabilityCase [33]	C	C	B	D	D	D
ENTRUST [16]	A	A	C	D	D	B
eSafetyCase Toolkit [41]	B	C	B	B	B	D
ETB (Evidential Tool Bus) [19]	C	A	D	C	D	B
Event-B extension [30]	B	C	B	D	D	B
EviCA [39]	C	C	B	D	D	D
GAGE [14]	D	B	B	D	D	D
HiP-HOPS extension [43]	B	B	D	D	D	B
ISCaDE [32]	B	C	C	B	A/B	B
MMINT-A [22]	C	B	C	D	D	C
Modus [44]	C	B	A	B	C	C
NOR-STA [24]	B	B	B	A	A/B	C
OpenCERT [31]	B	B	C	B	B	C
Resolute [23]	A	B	A	D	C	B
SafeEd [25]	C	C	A	D	B	C
Safety.Lab [42]	C	B	A/B	D	D	B
SAM [29]	B	B	C	D	B	B
SCT: Safety Case Toolkit [9]	B	C	C	A/B	A	C
SBVR/GSN Editor [36]	C	C	D	D	D	C
TurboAC [5]	B	C	C	D	A/B	B
Visio add-on [32]	C	C	D	D	D	D

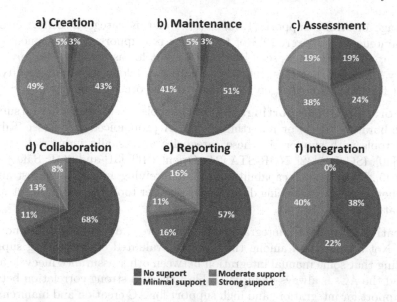

Fig. 1. Overall AC tool support for: (a) creation, (b) maintenance, (c) assessment, (d) collaboration, (e) reporting and (f) integration.

ACs, based on various underlying system and/or behavioral models. As previously mentioned however, these tools are domain specific. Unless modified, their use is confined to the specific underlying architectural languages, models, etc., that they support. To our knowledge, a tool that can automatically generate complete ACs for a broad range of domains is yet to be developed. Based on these observations, it would seem that the benefits obtained by creating a strong dependency between ACs and system models come at the cost of flexibility and generalized usability.

Maintenance. Again, the absolute majority of tools provide either minimal (51%) or moderate (41%) support for maintenance (see Fig. 1(b)). Tools with moderate support for maintenance often allow the linking of evidence, models and other artefacts to the corresponding AC elements, making it easy to notify the user of the impacts of the change. In turn, ENTRUST [16] and ETB [19] offer strong support by automatically reflecting artefact changes on the AC. ETB [19] allows the incorporation of 3rd party tools for the purpose of generating evidence and logs timestamps of their invocations in order to determine which analyses are out of date with respect to the current development artefacts, re-running those that are not synchronized. ENTRUST [16] is tightly coupled with the design-time and runtime models of a system. It has the ability to dynamically verify self-adaptive systems at runtime and update their ACs as necessary.

Assessment. Figure 1(c) shows that the results for AC assessment are fairly distributed among all levels of support as compared to the other functional categories, with the majority offering moderate support (38%). The highest percentage of strong support (19%) is seen in this category. Unlike creation and maintenance however, 19% of tools offer no support for assessment. Furthermore, no correlation is seen between support for assessment and any other category, implying that assessment is a fairly standalone tool functionality, the support for which is not largely dependent on the other categories.

Collaboration and Reporting. Most of the tools we surveyed offer no support for collaboration (68%) or reporting (57%). A pronounced trend (see Table 3) is that tools with support in these categories are usually industrial, such as ASCE [40], ISCaDE [32], NOR-STA [24], OpenCERT [31] and SCT: Safety Case Toolkit [9]. Perhaps such capabilities are not receiving adequate interest among researchers, and thus are being developed only after tools reach significant maturity, if at all.

Integration. Support for integration is split between moderate (40%) and none (38%). Not a single tool among the ones we evaluated offered strong support, indicating that some manual integration between other assurance lifecycle activities and the ACs is always required. Table 3 shows a strong correlation between high support for integration, and high support for AC creation and maintenance. It would appear that a more integrated environment allows tighter coupling between various artefacts, such as system models and evidence, subsequently enabling automation through dependencies. As previously discussed however, the creation of these dependencies might introduce limitations in other aspects.

3.2   Threats to Validity

The main threat to validity in our work is the completeness of our list of tools and tool information. Even though our search methodology is thorough, it is possible that it did not capture all existing AC tools. As discussed in Sect. 2, our evaluation was based only on information found in the corresponding tool's documentation, publications, website and other publically available resources. It is possible that the description of some functionality received a lower grade because it was not adequately described or the relevant resource was unavailable.

4   Summary and Conclusion

In this paper, we reported on a comprehensive identification and a preliminary evaluation of AC tools, comparing them w.r.t. several categories using the available documentation. In the future, we intend to refine our results using deeper analysis, through a systematic evaluation of the tools themselves.

Our experience shows that there is significant room for improvement of the tools in all of the discussed categories. Furthermore, it appears that several categories are interdependent, i.e., high support in one is strongly correlated with high support in another. For example, we expect that improvements in the integration category will significantly benefit other categories such as creation and maintenance. Yet, to the best of our knowledge, there is currently no tool that supports the seamless linking of the various assurance lifecycle processes.

Acknowledgements. The work reported in this paper has been funded by General Motors and NSERC Canada. The authors thank Mark Lawford, Alan Wassyng and Tom Maibaum for many useful discussions about assurance cases.

References

1. AssureNote. https://github.com/AssureNote/AssureNote
2. Impact case study - University of York. https://impact.ref.ac.uk/CaseStudies/CaseStudy.aspx?Id=43445
3. PREEVision. https://vector.com/vi_preevision-iso26262_en.html
4. SMS Pro. https://www.asms-pro.com/Modules/SafetyAssurance/SafetyCaseStudy.aspx
5. TurboAC. http://www.gessnet.com/products
6. Goal Structuring Notation Working Group: GSN Community Standard Version 1, November 2011. http://www.goalstructuringnotation.info/
7. Object Management Group: Structured Assurance Case Metamodel (SACM) version 1.0. Formal, 01 February 2013 (2013)
8. Kitchenham, B.: Guidelines for Performing Systematic Literature Reviews in Software Engineering. Technical rep. EBSE-2007-01, EBSE (2007)
9. Aiello, M.A., Hocking, A.B., Knight, J.C., Rowanhill, J.C.: SCT: a safety case toolkit. In: Proceedings ISSRE 2014 Workshops, pp. 216–219 (2014)
10. Allan, J., Williams, J., Gander-Miller, G., Turner, M., Ballantyne, T., Harvey, J.: Safety case production. WIT Trans. Built Environ. **37** (1998)
11. Althammer, E., Schoitsch, E., Eriksson, H., Vinter, J.: The DECOS concept of generic safety cases - a step towards modular certification. In: Proceedings of SEAA 2009, pp. 537–545 (2009)
12. Ankrum, T.S., Kromholz, A.H.: Structured assurance cases: three common standards (presentation). In: Proceedings of HASE 2005, pp. 99–108 (2005)
13. Barry, M.R.: CertWare: a workbench for safety case production and analysis. In: Proceedings of Aerospace Conference 2011, pp. 1–10 (2011)
14. Bjornander, S., Land, R., Graydon, P., Lundqvist, K., Conmy, P.: A method to formally evaluate safety case arguments against a system architecture model. In: Proceedings of ISSREW 2012, pp. 337–342 (2012)
15. Bloomfield, R., Bishop, P.: Safety and assurance cases: past, present and possible future – an adelard perspective. In: Dale, C., Anderson, T. (eds.) Making Systems Safer, pp. 51–67. Springer, London (2010). https://doi.org/10.1007/978-1-84996-086-1_4
16. Calinescu, R., Weyns, D., Gerasimou, S., Iftikhar, M.U., Habli, I., Kelly, T.: Engineering trustworthy self-adaptive software with dynamic assurance cases. IEEE TSE **PP**(99), 1–30 (2017)
17. Cârlan, C., Barner, S., Diewald, A., Tsalidis, A., Voss, S.: ExplicitCase: integrated model-based development of system and safety cases. In: Tonetta, S., Schoitsch, E., Bitsch, F. (eds.) SAFECOMP 2017. LNCS, vol. 10489, pp. 52–63. Springer, Cham (2017). https://doi.org/10.1007/978-3-319-66284-8_5
18. Cimatti, A., DeLong, R., Marcantonio, D., Tonetta, S.: Combining MILS with contract-based design for safety and security requirements. In: Koornneef, F., van Gulijk, C. (eds.) SAFECOMP 2015. LNCS, vol. 9338, pp. 264–276. Springer, Cham (2015). https://doi.org/10.1007/978-3-319-24249-1_23

19. Cruanes, S., Hamon, G., Owre, S., Shankar, N.: Tool integration with the evidential tool bus. In: Giacobazzi, R., Berdine, J., Mastroeni, I. (eds.) VMCAI 2013. LNCS, vol. 7737, pp. 275–294. Springer, Heidelberg (2013). https://doi.org/10.1007/978-3-642-35873-9_18

20. Denney, E., Pai, G.: Tool support for assurance case development. J. Autom. Softw. Eng. **25**(3), 435–499 (2018)

21. Fujita, H., Matsuno, Y., Hanawa, T., Sato, M., Kato, S., Ishikawa, Y.: DS-bench toolset: tools for dependability benchmarking with simulation and assurance. In: Proceedings of DSN 2012, pp. 1–8 (2012)

22. Fung, N.L.S., Kokaly, S., Di Sandro, A., Salay, R., Chechik, M.: MMINT-A: a tool for automated change impact assessment of assurance cases. In: Proceedings of SAFECOMP 2018 Workshops. Springer (2018, accepted for publication)

23. Gacek, A., Backes, J., Cofer, D., Slind, K., Whalen, M.: Resolute: an assurance case language for architecture models. In: Proceedings HILT 2014, pp. 19–28 (2014)

24. Górski, J., Jarzębowicz, A., Miler, J., Witkowicz, M., Czyżnikiewicz, J., Jar, P.: Supporting assurance by evidence-based argument services. In: Ortmeier, F., Daniel, P. (eds.) SAFECOMP 2012. LNCS, vol. 7613, pp. 417–426. Springer, Heidelberg (2012). https://doi.org/10.1007/978-3-642-33675-1_39

25. Groza, A., Marc, N.: Consistency checking of safety arguments in the goal structuring notation standard. In: Proceedings of ICCP 2014, pp. 59–66 (2014)

26. Huhn, M., Zechner, A.: Analysing dependability case arguments using quality models. In: Buth, B., Rabe, G., Seyfarth, T. (eds.) SAFECOMP 2009. LNCS, vol. 5775, pp. 118–131. Springer, Heidelberg (2009). https://doi.org/10.1007/978-3-642-04468-7_11

27. Kawakami, H., Ott, D., Wong, H.C., Dahab, R., Gallo, R.: ACBuilder: a tool for hardware architecture security evaluation. In: Proceedings of HOST 2016, pp. 97–102 (2016)

28. Kelly, T.P.: Arguing Safety: A Systematic Approach to Managing Safety Cases. Ph.D. thesis, Univ. of York, UK (1998)

29. Kelly, T., McDermid, J.: A systematic approach to safety case maintenance. J. Reliab. Eng. Syst. Saf. **1**(3), 271–284 (2001)

30. Laibinis, L., Troubitsyna, E., Prokhorova, Y., Iliasov, A., Romanovsky, A.: From requirements engineering to safety assurance: refinement approach. In: Li, X., Liu, Z., Yi, W. (eds.) SETTA 2015. LNCS, vol. 9409, pp. 201–216. Springer, Cham (2015). https://doi.org/10.1007/978-3-319-25942-0_13

31. Larrucea, X.: Modelling and certifying safety for cyber-physical systems: an educational experiment. In: Proceedings of SEAA 2016, pp. 198–205 (2016)

32. Larrucea, X., Walker, A., Colomo-Palacios, R.: Supporting the management of reusable automotive software. IEEE Softw. J. **34**(3), 40–47 (2017)

33. Lautieri, S., Cooper, D., Jackson, D., Cockram, T.: Assurance cases: how assured are you? In: Proceedings of DSN 2004 Supplemental Volume (2004)

34. Lewis, R.: Safety case development as an information modelling problem. In: Dale, C., Anderson, T. (eds.) Safety-Critical Systems: Problems, Process and Practice, pp. 183–193. Springer, London (2009). https://doi.org/10.1007/978-1-84882-349-5_12

35. Luo, Y., van den Brand, M., Li, Z., Saberi, A.: A systematic approach and tool support for GSN-based safety case assessment. J. Syst. Archit. **76**(pp), 1–16 (2017)

36. Luo, Y., van den Brand, M., Kiburse, A.: Safety case development with SBVR-based controlled language. In: Desfray, P., Filipe, J., Hammoudi, S., Pires, L.F. (eds.) MODELSWARD 2015. CCIS, vol. 580, pp. 3–17. Springer, Cham (2015). https://doi.org/10.1007/978-3-319-27869-8_1

37. Matsuno, Y., Takamura, H., Ishikawa, Y.: A dependability case editor with pattern library. In: Proceedings of HASE 2010, pp. 170–171 (2010)
38. Matsuno, Y.: D-case communicator: a web based GSN editor for multiple stakeholders. In: Tonetta, S., Schoitsch, E., Bitsch, F. (eds.) SAFECOMP 2017. LNCS, vol. 10489, pp. 64–69. Springer, Cham (2017). https://doi.org/10.1007/978-3-319-66284-8_6
39. Nair, S., Walkinshaw, N., Kelly, T., de la Vara, J.L.: An evidential reasoning approach for assessing confidence in safety evidence. In: Proceedings of ISSRE 2015, pp. 541–552 (2015)
40. Netkachova, K., Netkachov, O., Bloomfield, R.: Tool Support for assurance case building blocks. In: Koornneef, F., van Gulijk, C. (eds.) SAFECOMP 2015. LNCS, vol. 9338, pp. 62–71. Springer, Cham (2015). https://doi.org/10.1007/978-3-319-24249-1_6
41. Newton, A., Vickers, A.: The benefits of electronic safety cases. In: Redmill, F., Anderson, T. (eds.) The Safety of Systems, pp. 69–82. Springer, London (2007). https://doi.org/10.1007/978-1-84628-806-7_5
42. Ratiu, D., Zeller, M., Killian, L.: Safety.Lab: model-based domain specific tooling for safety argumentation. In: Koornneef, F., van Gulijk, C. (eds.) SAFECOMP 2015. LNCS, vol. 9338, pp. 72–82. Springer, Cham (2015). https://doi.org/10.1007/978-3-319-24249-1_7
43. Retouniotis, A., Papadopoulos, Y., Sorokos, I., Parker, D., Matragkas, N., Sharvia, S.: Model-connected safety cases. In: Bozzano, M., Papadopoulos, Y. (eds.) IMBSA 2017. LNCS, vol. 10437, pp. 50–63. Springer, Cham (2017). https://doi.org/10.1007/978-3-319-64119-5_4
44. Sabetzadeh, M., Falessi, D., Briand, L., Di Alesio, S.: A goal-based approach for qualification of new technologies: foundations, tool support, and industrial validation. J. Reliab. Eng. Syst. Saf. 119(C), 52–66 (2013)
45. Shida, S., Uchida, A., Ishii, M., Ide, M., Kuramitsu, K.: Assure-It: a runtime synchronization tool of assurance cases. In: SAFECOMP 2013 FastAbstract (2013)
46. Zhang, H., Babar, M.A., Tell, P.: Identifying relevant studies in software engineering. J. Inf. Soft. Technol. 53(6), 625–637 (2011)

MMINT-A: A Tool for Automated Change Impact Assessment on Assurance Cases

Nick L. S. Fung[1(✉)], Sahar Kokaly[2], Alessio Di Sandro[1], Rick Salay[1], and Marsha Chechik[1]

[1] University of Toronto, Toronto, Canada
{nlsfung,adisandro,rsalay,chechik}@cs.toronto.edu
[2] McMaster University, Hamilton, Canada
kokalys@mcmaster.ca

Abstract. Assurance cases are a means to argue about the safety, security, etc., of software systems in critical domains. As systems evolve, their assurance cases can grow in complexity, making them difficult to maintain. In this paper, we present a tool *MMINT-A* that can, in the context of model-driven development, assess the impact of system changes on their assurance cases. To achieve this, *MMINT-A* implements an impact assessment algorithm from previous work [7,8] and incorporates a graphical assurance case editor, an annotation mechanism, and two summary tables for the assessment results. We demonstrate the usage of *MMINT-A* on a Power Sliding Door example from the automotive domain.

Keywords: Assurance Cases · Change Impact Assessment
Tool support

1 Introduction

Assurance cases (AC) are a means to argue about the safety, security, etc., of software systems in critical domains. Since ACs relate to specific system designs, changes to the design will necessitate the corresponding changes to the AC. However, maintaining ACs can be non-trivial. First, they can be very complex; an AC for an air traffic control system may, e.g., comprise over 500 pages and reference some 400 documents [10]. Second, system changes can occur often (especially for software), thus, maintaining ACs can involve frequent and substantial updates.

To facilitate this process, we developed a collection of extensions to the *MMINT* model management framework [5] to support automated Change Impact Assessment (CIA) on ACs, focusing specifically on the automotive domain. The resulting tool, *MMINT-A* (which is available at https://github.com/nlsfung/MMINT), identifies how different parts of an AC may be impacted by some given changes to the associated system, whether they can be reused in the updated AC or must revised or rechecked for validity. Thus, the engineer can direct her efforts to reviewing and updating the appropriate parts of the AC.

© Springer Nature Switzerland AG 2018
B. Gallina et al. (Eds.): SAFECOMP 2018 Workshops, LNCS 11094, pp. 60–70, 2018.
https://doi.org/10.1007/978-3-319-99229-7_7

In this paper, we present *MMINT-A* and describe its features. We outline the *MMINT* architecture in Sect. 2, describe our extensions to create *MMINT-A* in Sect. 3, and demonstrate its features using an example from the automotive domain in Sect. 4. We discuss related work in Sect. 5 and conclude in Sect. 6.

2 The *MMINT* Architecture

As shown in Fig. 1, *MMINT* (which is available at https://github.com/ adisandro/MMINT) is built on top of the Eclipse platform and is designed for managing megamodels, which are defined as collections of related models and are represented as MIDs (Model Interconnection Diagrams). In particular, *MMINT* supports both the "instance" level, in which models, megamodels and their relations are instantiated and manipulated, as well as the "type" level, in which the necessary metamodels, relation types and model operators are defined.

For example, a metamodel for UML class diagrams can be created on top of the Eclipse platform and plugged into *MMINT* via the type support runtime layer. The Type MID would then be populated with metadata about the new metamodel, allowing UML class diagrams to be created and manipulated inside megamodels using the MID editor and the ModelRel (model relation) editor. With the workflow editor, new operators can be created by connecting predefined model operators into a directed, acyclic network, with the roots being the input models to the workflow and the leaves being the outputs.

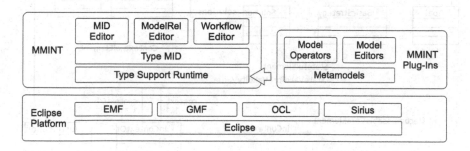

Fig. 1. The architecture of *MMINT*.

3 Extensions for *MMINT-A*

MMINT-A comprises a collection of extensions to *MMINT* for instantiating and operating on ACs. However, since the impact assessment is driven by changes to the system, *MMINT-A* also requires the availability of appropriate metamodels (and editors) for instantiating the desired system models. Availability of operators, viz., slicers [13], for CIA on individual system models is also assumed since they form part of the overall procedure executed by *MMINT-A*. Currently, *MMINT* supports CIA on simplified versions of UML class diagrams

(CD), sequence diagrams (SD) and state machines (SM), which involved: (1) creating the metamodels using EMF (Eclipse Modeling Framework), (2) creating the corresponding editors using Sirius, (3) implementing each slicer as a Java class, and (4) incorporating them into *MMINT* by editing their plug-in files.

3.1 Assurance Case Metamodel

Our metamodel for ACs (Fig. 2) is derived from the Goal Structuring Notation (GSN) version 1 [1] in which an AC is modelled as a directed acyclic network of six types of elements: goals, strategies, solutions, contexts, justifications and assumptions. The former three form the core of an AC and are connected to each other via "supported-by" relations, with a top level goal as the root and the solutions as leaves, while the latter three are connected to the core via "in-context-of" relations. Each of these elements can also be given a unique identifier and description in accordance to the standard, but we extended it by

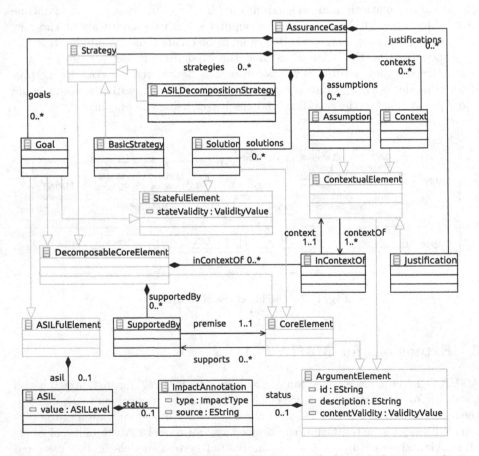

Fig. 2. The AC metamodel in *MMINT-A*. Concrete and abstract classes are distinguished with black and grey borders, respectively.

adding states to goals and solutions which, although unnecessary for CIA in *MMINT-A*, allow the user to indicate, respectively, their truth values and the currentness of their evidence as part of the overall change management process.

Furthermore, to capture the CIA results, we introduced annotations to our metamodel, which we previously modelled as comprising three types [8]: *Reuse*, to indicate that the element is not impacted; *Recheck*, to indicate that the element may no longer be valid and needs a recheck; and *Revise*, to indicate that the element's contents requires changing. However, in *MMINT-A*, we also distinguish between: (1) recheck *content*, which indicates that the element's content may (but not necessarily) require revision, and (2) recheck *state*, which is applicable to goals and solutions only and indicates that the element's content, while reusable, may no longer be supported by the underlying sub-goals or evidence.

Focusing on the automotive domain, certain domain-specific features were also incorporated into our metamodel that can be disregarded in general. Specifically, goals are modelled to contain an optional ASIL (automotive safety integrity level) attribute that captures the inherent safety risk of the associated system component and is annotated separately from its goal for CIA. ASILs of sub-goals are generally inherited from their parent goals, but in accordance to ISO 26262 [6], they can be decomposed following certain conditions, which are captured in *MMINT-A* using a sub-type of strategy (viz., `ASILDecompositionStrategy`).

3.2   Assurance Case Editor

Figure 3 shows a screenshot of the editor that was implemented on top of Sirius and comprises multiple "views" for creating and visualizing ACs. In the main view (left), ACs are visualized in accordance to the GSN standard but with additional decorations for ASILs and annotations. In particular, ASILs are represented as small, rectangular nodes bordering the goal nodes, while annotations are represented as exclamation marks, circular arrows and check marks to denote Revise, Recheck and Reuse, respectively. The subscripts "C" and "S" are used to disambiguate Recheck Content and Recheck State.

Although compliant with the standard, this graphical representation may not always be the most appropriate. The user may wish to, for example, quickly analyse the amount of impact different changes have on an assurance case or review the source of each annotation. Therefore, to address these use cases, we also created two tabular representations to summarise the results of the CIA. The first table (upper right in Fig. 3) displays the number (and percentage) of each type of node that are annotated for revision, rechecking or reuse, while the second table (lower right in Fig. 3) displays the type of impact for each node and the source of the impact. For example, Fig. 3 shows that goal G1.2 must be revised because of a change in the class `Redundant Switch`.

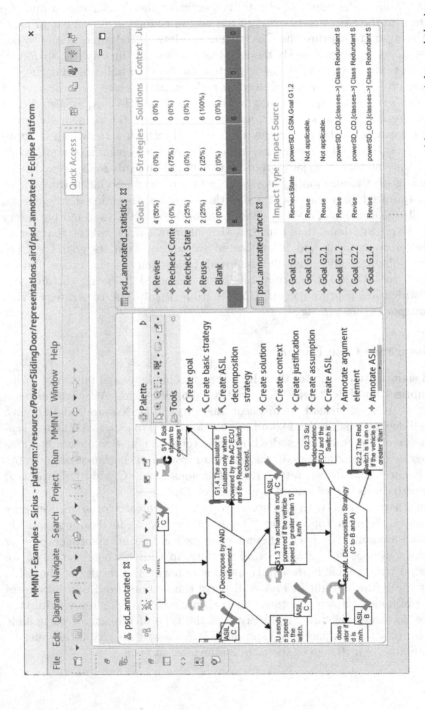

Fig. 3. Screenshot of the AC editor in *MMINT-A*. The main graphical view is on the left, the statistics table upper right, and the impact trace table lower right.

3.3   Assurance Case Slicers

We make use of two AC slicers based on previous work [8] as part of our overall AC CIA. The *Revise Slicer* uses rules V_1 to V_4 in Table 1 to identify elements to be rechecked given an element marked for revision (which applies to the content and not the state of an element). The *Recheck Slicer* uses the rules C_1 and C_2 in Table 1 to identify elements to be rechecked given another element marked for rechecking. Note that the Recheck Slicer applies only to state rechecks and that while the Revise Slicer only performs a one-step slice to find direct dependencies of the revised elements, the Recheck Slicer recursively expands a subset of AC elements to include its dependent elements until closure is reached.

Table 1. The assurance case slicer dependency rules.

Rule	Element	Dependent element(s) (Annotation)
V_1	Goal G	All strategies linked to G on either end of the IsSupportedBy relation (recheck content)
V_2	Strategy S	1. All goals that S supports (recheck state)
		2. All goals or solutions that support S (recheck content)
		3. All justifications that are used to justify S (recheck content)
V_3	Context C	1. All goals, strategies and solutions A that introduce C as the context via the InContextOf relation (recheck content)
		2. All goals, strategies and solutions that inherit C as the context (i.e., all children of A) (recheck content)
V_4	Solution S	All strategies that S supports (recheck content)
C_1	Goal G	All parent goals that are linked to G by the same strategy (recheck content)
C_2	Solution S	All goals that are linked to S by the same strategy (recheck content)

3.4   Change Impact Assessment Algorithm

MMINT-A implements an AC CIA algorithm based on the one developed in [7,8] which accepts as inputs the original and the updated system megamodel, the set of changes made (i.e., additions, deletions and modifications) as well as the AC and its relation to the megamodel. However, the *MMINT-A* implementation assumes that additions can only impact other model elements indirectly via the modifications and deletions required to accommodate them. Thus, the implemented algorithm (see Fig. 4) does not require the added model elements nor the updated system megamodel.

This algorithm is encoded as a *MMINT* workflow with 13 model operators. To ensure that the workflow is independent of any specific model types for the input system megamodel, it utilizes higher-level collection-based operators (particularly, **map** [14]), enabling it to apply the appropriate operators to the appropriate models in the system megamodel at runtime.

1. Perform CIA on the system megamodel itself.
2. Propagate results to the AC to obtain the elements requiring content recheck.
3. Identify AC elements requiring revision from the deleted system model elements.
4. Apply Revise Slicer on results of step 3.
5. Merge and apply Recheck Slicer on results of steps 2 and 4.
6. Annotate the AC. The results of steps 2, 3 and 5 are marked for content recheck, revision, and state recheck, respectively.

Fig. 4. *MMINT-A* impact assessment algorithm.

4   Power Sliding Door Example

As part of our evaluation process, we used *MMINT-A* to recreate a pre-existing case study [8] on the power sliding door (PSD) system presented in ISO 26262 [6] for vehicles. For this case study, the system is modelled using a class diagram (CD) and a sequence diagram (SD) as shown in Fig. 5, and it is associated with

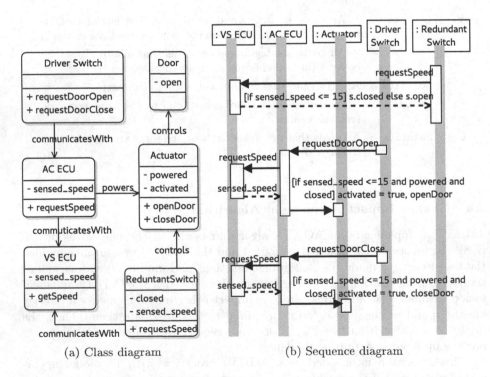

(a) Class diagram   (b) Sequence diagram

Fig. 5. Models for the PSD system. Recreated in *MMINT-A* from [8].

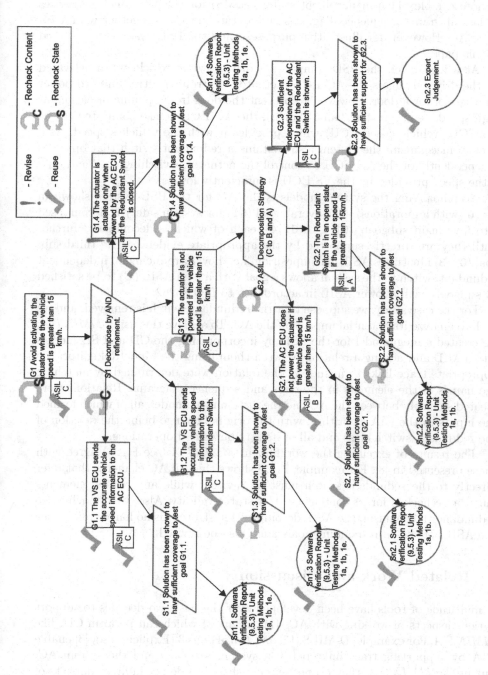

Fig. 6. The PSD AC after change impact assessment in *MMINT-A*.

an AC comprising 22 nodes as shown in Fig. 6. *MMINT-A* was also applied on
a more complex lane management system (LMS) for vehicles which comprises
1 class diagram, 4 sequence diagrams and 4 state machines together with a 74-
node AC. However, for illustrative purposes, only the PSD system is presented
in this paper.

At a high level, the PSD comprises a driver switch which, when activated
by the driver, triggers the AC ECU (actuator electronic control unit) to power
an actuator for a door. However, to prevent the door from opening or closing at
high speeds (e.g., greater than 15 km/h), the AC ECU is also connected to the
VS ECU (vehicle speed ECU) which provides it with the vehicle's speed. As a
backup mechanism, the system also contains a redundant switch that operates
independently of the AC ECU to control the actuator, switching on if and only
if the speed provided by the VS ECU is sufficiently low.

Accompanying the system models is the AC for the PSD system shown in
Fig. 6 (with annotations). The overall goal (G1) for system safety is decomposed
into four main subgoals (G1.1 to G1.4), each of which is decomposed further
until they are directly supported by the appropriate evidence. The third sub-
goal (G1.3) illustrates ASIL decomposition, i.e., how introducing an independent
redundant switch to the system allows a goal with a high ASIL (C) to be satisfied
by subgoals with a lower ASIL in accordance to ISO 26262.

For the case study, we suppose that the redundant switch is removed, and we
wish to analyze its potential impact on the AC. To achieve this using *MMINT-A*,
we created a megamodel for the PSD by incorporating the CD and SD models
into a MID and adding a relation between them using the ModelRel editor; the
appropriate trace links to include in the relation were determined by matching
the names of the elements in the class and sequence diagrams. Relations were
created similarly between the AC and the system megamodel, all of which formed
the inputs to the CIA algorithm, with the original change being the deletion of
the redundant switch class and all of its attributes and operations.

The results of executing the workflow in *MMINT-A* (see Fig. 6) agree with
those presented in [8]. For example, Fig. 6 shows that all AC elements that refer
directly to the redundant switch must be revised, while any related elements
must be rechecked for its content (and/or state) validity. Also, by removing the
redundancy mechanism, the ASIL decomposition strategy is no longer valid, thus
the ASILs of the corresponding goals must also be revised.

5   Related Work and Discussion

A multitude of tools have been developed over the past two decades to support
various aspects of working with ACs [11], many of which can perform CIA like
MMINT-A. For example, D-MILS [15] and AutoFocus 3 (ExplicitCase) [3] enable
CIA by supporting trace links between system artefacts and the system AC,
but unlike *MMINT-A*, they do not employ slicers to detect indirect impacts of
change. Other tools, such as ENTRUST [2] and Evidential Tool Bus (ETB) [4],
remove the need for CIA altogether by automatically propagating changes in the

system artefacts to the AC. However, ENTRUST only supports certain changes to the AC, while ECB can only propagate changes to the underlying evidence.

Although the CIA functionality proposed and implemented in *MMINT-A* can be implemented on top of existing AC tools, these tools are generally highly specialized, making it impractical to adapt them for the automotive domain. On the other hand, before *MMINT-A* can become a usable tool itself, it must be extended with many "standard" features such as strong support for AC creation and assessment. In fact, unlike D-MILS and AutoFocus 3, *MMINT-A* can only support trace links to system models; other system artefacts such as natural language documents are not yet incorporated into *MMINT*.

6   Conclusions and Future Work

In this paper, we presented the features of *MMINT-A* and demonstrated how it supports the maintenance of ACs, specifically by performing CIA on them. However, since *MMINT-A* is built on top of the generic *MMINT* model management framework, it can be easily extended beyond CIA to address other scenarios, including those presented in [9] for regulatory compliance management. In fact, with the appropriate changes to the AC metamodel, *MMINT-A* can also be applied to non-automotive domains, but because of the focus on models, *MMINT-A* (and *MMINT*) may be best suited for model-based software systems only.

In the future, we will use larger case studies, such as that for the lane management system, to better evaluate the effectiveness of the implemented CIA algorithm in *MMINT-A*. We also aim to, amongst other things, incorporate the improvements suggested in [8], add support for OMG's Structured Assurance Case Metamodel (SACM [12]) and conduct a usability study with our industrial partner to identify specific barriers in adopting *MMINT-A*. These may include integration with other tools (e.g., for compliance checking) as well as support for assuring product lines.

Acknowledgements. The work reported in this paper has been funded by General Motors and NSERC Canada. The authors thank Mark Lawford, Alan Wassyng and Tom Maibaum for many useful discussions.

References

1. Attwood, K., Chinneck, P., Clarke, M., et. al.: GSN Community Standard Version 1. Technical report, Origin Consulting (York) Limited (2011)
2. Calinescu, R., Weyns, D., Gerasimou, S., Iftikhar, M.U., Habli, I., Kelly, T.: Engineering trustworthy self-adaptive software with dynamic assurance cases. In: IEEE TSE 2017, p. 1 (2017)
3. Cârlan, C., Barner, S., Diewald, A., Tsalidis, A., Voss, S.: ExplicitCase: integrated model-based development of system and safety cases. In: Tonetta, S., Schoitsch, E., Bitsch, F. (eds.) SAFECOMP 2017. LNCS, vol. 10489, pp. 52–63. Springer, Cham (2017). https://doi.org/10.1007/978-3-319-66284-8_5

4. Cruanes, S., Hamon, G., Owre, S., Shankar, N.: Tool integration with the evidential tool bus. In: Giacobazzi, R., Berdine, J., Mastroeni, I. (eds.) VMCAI 2013. LNCS, vol. 7737, pp. 275–294. Springer, Heidelberg (2013). https://doi.org/10.1007/978-3-642-35873-9_18
5. Di Sandro, A., Salay, R., Famelis, M., Kokaly, S., Chechik, M.: MMINT: a graphical tool for interactive model management. In: Proceedings of MoDELS 2015 (demo) (2015)
6. International Organization for Standardization: ISO 26262: Road Vehicles - Functional Safety, 1st version (2011)
7. Kokaly, S., Salay, R., Cassano, V., Maibaum, T., Chechik, M.: A model management approach for assurance case reuse due to system evolution. In: Proceedings of MoDELS 2016, pp. 196–206 (2016)
8. Kokaly, S., Salay, R., Chechik, M., Lawford, M., Maibaum, T.: Safety case impact assessment in automotive software systems: an improved model-based approach. In: Tonetta, S., Schoitsch, E., Bitsch, F. (eds.) SAFECOMP 2017. LNCS, vol. 10488, pp. 69–85. Springer, Cham (2017). https://doi.org/10.1007/978-3-319-66266-4_5
9. Kokaly, S., Salay, R., Sabetzadeh, M., Chechik, M., Maibaum, T.: Model management for regulatory compliance: a position paper. In: Proceedings of MiSE 2016 (2016)
10. Lewis, R.: Safety case development as an information modelling problem. In: Dale, C., Anderson, T. (eds.) Safety-Critical Systems Problems, Process and Practice, pp. 183–193. Springer, London (2009). https://doi.org/10.1007/978-1-84882-349-5_12
11. Maksimov, M., Fung, N.L.S., Kokaly, S., Chechik, M.: Two decades of assurance case tools: a survey. In: Proceedings of SAFECOMP 2018 Workshops. Springer (2018, accepted for publication)
12. Object Management Group (OMG): Structured Assurance Case Metamodel (SACM) Version 2.0 (2018)
13. Salay, R., Kokaly, S., Chechik, M., Maibaum, T.: Heterogeneous megamodel slicing for model evolution. In: Proceedings of ME@MoDELS 2016, pp. 50–59 (2016)
14. Salay, R., Kokaly, S., Di Sandro, A., Chechik, M.: Enriching megamodel management with collection-based operators. In: Proceedings of MODELS 2015 (2015)
15. University of York (UK): D4.2 Compositional Assurance Cases and Arguments for Distributed MILS (2015)

D-Case Steps: New Steps for Writing Assurance Cases

Yuto Onuma[1], Toshinori Takai[2], Tsutomu Koshiyama[1],
and Yutaka Matsuno[1(✉)]

[1] College of Science and Technology, Nihon University, Funabashi, Japan
matsuno.yutaka@nihon-u.ac.jp
[2] Change Vision, Inc., Fukui, Japan
toshinori.takai@change-vision.com

Abstract. This paper presents *D-Case Steps*, new steps for writing assurance cases. Although the concept of assurance cases is simple, writing assurance cases is difficult: stating the top goal, selecting strategies for decomposing goals and setting evidence, etc. are all difficult. For this problem, based on conventional writing steps such as the six steps method by Kelly [8], we incorporate stakeholder analysis step and consensus building step. This paper reports two assurance case workshops using D-Case steps, and evaluates the D-Case steps by the results of questionaries done by the participants.

1 Introduction

System assurance has become important in many industrial areas, and the notion of assurance cases has been getting a lot of attention. The basic structure of assurance cases is simple: contexts, claims, and evidence form a network and as a whole structure, they support the top claim. However, writing assurance cases is difficult. System attributes such as safety and dependability of a system involve almost all aspects of the system, and the argument structure tends to be diverge and huge. Also, as the nature of goal oriented structure, decomposing a goal into sub-goals has essential difficulties.

This paper presents *D-Case Steps*, a new steps for writing assurance cases. The D-Case steps particularly focus on *stakeholders* and define practical evaluation criteria for assurance cases written in GSN (Goal Structuring Notation) [2]. Our observation is as follows. To avoid argument divergence and difficulties of goal decomposition, we restrict the content of a GSN diagram only for particular stakeholders, and the way of goal decomposition is determined by preference of the stakeholders.

We consider the following running example. The example is called "smart room viewing". The system is used for viewing a room when a customer considers renting the room from the real estate company. The functions are as follows.

© Springer Nature Switzerland AG 2018
B. Gallina et al. (Eds.): SAFECOMP 2018 Workshops, LNCS 11094, pp. 71–78, 2018.
https://doi.org/10.1007/978-3-319-99229-7_8

– Unattended viewing by advance reservation. Usually (in Japan) when renting a room, first the customer views the room accompanied with a real estate employee. However, using smart room viewing, the customer can view the room without one of the employees.
– Unlocking the room key is done by user authentication using customer's smart-phone.
– Inside the room, the customer can check information of the room by a smart tablet.
– The customer can freely view the room within the time limits.
– The customer receives a notation of 5 min before the end by the tablet.
– The room is secured by surveillance cameras when customer is viewing the room.
– When finishing room viewing, the customer check that the room key is locked.

The flow of Smart Room Viewing system is shown in Fig. 1.

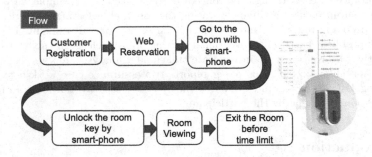

Fig. 1. Flow of Smart Room Viewing system

The rest of the paper is organized as follows. In Sect. 2, we discuss related work. Section 3 defines D-Case steps. Section 4 shows contents of two D-Case workshops held in January and March 2018, Tokyo, Japan, and evaluation results of the workshops. Section 5 concludes the paper.

2 Related Work

There have been several writing steps for assurance cases. Kelly proposed the six steps method for writing GSN diagrams [8]. Using the six step method, a GSN diagram is drawn in a top down manner. There are also several guidebooks on writing assurance cases, specially in GSN such as [1,5,11]. Such guidebooks are basically based on [8], and and/or require knowledges on safety analysis and the system domain. We observe that the six steps method is an abstract method and needed to be elaborated for actual uses. Also, it is difficult for beginners to assume safety analysis and domain knowledge of the system for writing assurance cases. In software engineering, it is common to consider stakeholders, their concerns, and relationships among them such as i^* framework [12] and KAOS [3]. However, in assurance cases, as far as we know, stakeholders analysis has not been well discussed. Recently, the second version of GSN community standard has been published [2]. In [2], "Stakeholder node" (which already appeared in previous papers) is explained as "This is a form of context symbol which is used to indicate one of the stakeholders associated in some way with the goal to which it is attached". However, detailed usage of stakeholder node is not shown.

3   D-Case Steps

D-Case Steps consist of three steps: Stakeholder analysis step, GSN writing step, and consensus building step. Figure 2 depicts the D-Case steps.

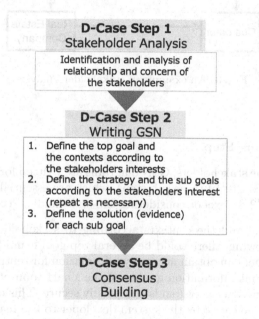

Fig. 2. D-Case steps

3.1   Stakeholder Analysis Step

To write an assurance case, first we need to analyze the stakeholders of the system. An assurance case must be understandable to and concern of the stakeholders. Also, identifying stakeholders helps to limit the content of the GSN diagram. There are various methods for stakeholder analysis. Currently, D-Case steps do not specify which stakeholder analysis to use. However, at least the result of analysis should include the relationship between stakeholders. For example, a result of stakeholder analysis for "Smart Room Viewing" is shown in Fig. 3. From the stakeholder analysis, three stakeholders are identified: system provider, real estate company, and customer. The arrows among them indicate assurance relations. The system developer and real estate company have some claims which are needed to be assured to each other. For example, the system developer needs to assure security of Smart Room Viewing. Both the system developer and real estate company need to assure some claims to the customer.

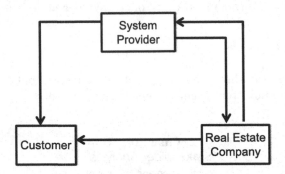

Fig. 3. An example of stakeholder analysis

3.2   GSN Writing Step

After specifying the stakeholders, GSN diagrams are written for the stakeholders. The writing step consist of three sub steps, which are essentially the same steps of the six step in [2,8], except considering the stakeholders' concerns.

1. Set the top goal and the contexts according to stakeholders' concerns. For smart room viewing, there could be several top goal candidates:
   – The customer can obtain necessary information for renting the room. This claim is about information quality of the smart room viewing system.
   – Smart room viewing system is acceptably secure. This claim is assured in possibly three cases: by the system developer to the real estate company, by the system developer to the customer, and by the real estate company to the customer.
   – Smart room viewing system is cost-effective. This claim is assured by the system developer to the real-estate company.
   Dependability of a system involves various aspects of the system: safety, security, information quality, cost-effectiveness, and so on. Each stakeholder has his or her own concerns and they are related to each other, and form the dependability of the system as a whole. D-Case steps specifies how to write a GSN diagram between particular stakeholders. Note that there could be multiple top goals.
2. Set the strategy from stakeholders' interests and divide them into subgoals. This step is repeated until the stakeholders reach detailed evidence that can be accepted.

3. Set each evidence as the final leaf of the GSN.

In order to write a GSN diagram, it is necessary to set evaluation criteria of GSN. There are several criteria proposed in previous work. From such criteria, in D-Case step, we use the following three criteria.

– Context Validity. Context nodes plays crucial rules for GSN, and contexts nodes should be linked to appropriate goals or strategies to describe context information of them. The importance of context is discussed in several previous work, such as [7,10].
– Logicality. The structure of GSN represents a logical argument that the claim in the top goal holds. Therefore it is important to check the logicality of the GSN.
– Relevance of Scale. The stakeholders of a system have their own limited time and knowledge about the system. Thus it is important to limit the scale of the GSN diagram so that the stakeholders can read and understand it. As far as we know, this criteria has not been discussed in the literature.

There are other criteria proposed in the literature such as quantitating confidence [4,6]. Based on our experience, we have set the above three evaluation criteria. In addition, it was adopted as criteria for general engineers to understand easily.

3.3   Consensus Building Step

After writing a GSN diagram, the stakeholders argue that the claim in the top goal is acceptable or not by checking the GSN diagram. From our experience, the number of stakeholders should be within five. Discussions will diverge when it comes to more stakeholders. In this step, the three evaluation criteria (context validity, logicality, and relevance of scale) are also used. Once all participated stakeholders make consensus that the claim is acceptable, then this step finishes. This step can be elaborated as shown in [2] or other methods such as Mind Map or FTA analysis.

4   D-Case Workshops

Using D-Case steps, we had two GSN workshops in January and March 2018. The numbers of participants were 20 and 21, respectively. The contents of the workshops are as follows.

1. Introduction of GSN and simple exercises for GSN syntax.
2. Introduction of D-Case steps.
3. Exercises for D-Case steps by group discussion.

Figure 4 shows a snapshot of D-Case workshop. We used D-Case Communicator [9], a web based GSN editor, by which the participants can freely share GSN diagrams. An example of GSN diagrams drawn by the participants is shown in

Fig. 4. A snapshot of D-Case workshop

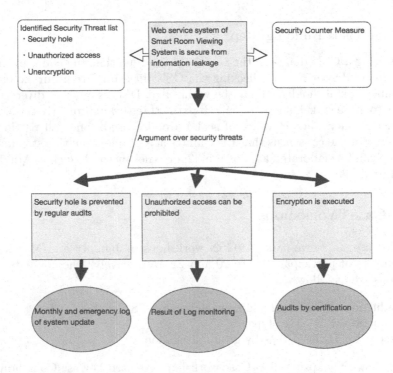

Fig. 5. An example of GSN by workshop participants

Fig. 5. Figure 5 is a GSN diagram assured by the system developer to the real-estate company. The top goal is part of the security of Smart Room Viewing system. Although the scale of the GSN in Fig. 5 is small, it takes about 30 min to write the GSN (by three participants, who are new to GSN, but have some knowledge on security of web system). In this GSN, the top goal is decomposed by three sub goals for threats listed in the left context linked to the top goal, a typical goal decomposition.

4.1 Workshop Evaluation

After the workshops, we ask the participants to fill questionaries. Table 1 shows the result of questionaries by the participants of second workshop. In Table 1, 4 is higher and 1 is lower. For example, for the first question (content of WS), 1 participant marked 2, 7 participants marked 3, and 10 participants marked 4. First we ask the participants about the content of the workshop. Most participants are satisfied with the contents of the workshop. The second question is about the understandability of the workshop. From the result the participants seems to have understood GSN and D-Case steps. From the third to the seventh questions are about the difficulties of GSN nodes: top goal, context, strategy, and evidence (solution). The average of context and strategy nodes are 2.61 and 2.72, respectively. These indicate that context and strategy nodes are not easy to write for beginners. The eighth and ninth questions are about whether GSN and D-Case steps are good or not for consensus building and practical use, respectively. The results were positive, and we observe that the workshops using D-Case steps succeeded as first steps.

Table 1. Result of Questionaries

	1	2	3	4	Average
Content of WS	0	1	7	10	3.5
Understandability	0	1	9	8	3.39
Easy to write top goal?	0	1	13	4	3.17
Easy to write contexts?	0	9	7	2	2.61
Easy to write strategies?	4	1	9	4	2.72
Easy to write sub goals?	1	4	10	3	2.83
Easy to write evidence?	0	6	7	5	2.94
Good for consensus building?	0	4	7	7	3.17
Good for practical use?	1	2	9	6	3.11

5   Concluding Remarks

This paper has presented D-Case steps, a new method for writing assurance cases. D-Case steps focuses on stakeholders, and includes conventional GSN writing steps and consensus building steps. We had two GSN workshops held in Japan, and the feedbacks from the participants were positive. We are planning to use the D-Case steps for writing GSN in conventional use such as of functional safety of automobiles, specially autonomous automobiles, for which various stakeholders are related. We would like to report the results near future.

Acknowledgements. This work has been supported by KAKENHI 17K12664, MEXT, Japan. We thank the participants of the first D-Case Steps workshop for introducing us the Smart Room Viewing example, and of the second workshop for their feedbacks. Also, we are grateful to DEOS D-Case meeting members for valuable discussions.

References

1. Adelard: Adelard Safety Case Development Manual. Adelard (1998)
2. Assurance Case Working Group: Goal structuring notation community standard version 2, January 2018. https://scsc.uk/r141B:1
3. Dardenne, A., van Lamsweerde, A., Fickas, S.: Goal-directed requirements acquisition. Sci. Comput. Program. **20**(1–2), 3–50 (1993)
4. Duan, L., Rayadurgam, S., Heimdahl, M.P.E., Sokolsky, O., Lee, I.: Representation of confidence in assurance cases using the beta distribution. In: 17th IEEE International Symposium on High Assurance Systems Engineering, HASE 2016, Orlando, 7–9 January 2016, pp. 86–93 (2016)
5. European Organisation for the Safety of Air Navigation: Safety case development manual, European Air Traffic Management (2006)
6. Goodenough, J.B., Weinstock, C.B., Klein., A.Z.: Toward a theory of assurance case confidence. Technical report, Carnegie Mellon (2012)
7. Graydon, P.J.: Towards a clearer understanding of context and its role in assurance argument confidence. In: Bondavalli, A., Di Giandomenico, F. (eds.) SAFECOMP 2014. LNCS, vol. 8666, pp. 139–154. Springer, Cham (2014). https://doi.org/10.1007/978-3-319-10506-2_10
8. Kelly, T.: Arguing safety - a systematic approach to safety case management. Ph.D. thesis, Department of Computer Science, University of York (1998)
9. Matsuno, Y.: D-case communicator: a web based GSN editor for multiple stakeholders. In: Tonetta, S., Schoitsch, E., Bitsch, F. (eds.) SAFECOMP 2017. LNCS, vol. 10489, pp. 64–69. Springer, Cham (2017). https://doi.org/10.1007/978-3-319-66284-8_6
10. Spriggs, J.: GSN—The Goal Structuring Notation. Springer, London (2012). https://doi.org/10.1007/978-1-4471-2312-5
11. Weinstock, C.B.: Assurance cases, December 2008. http://www.seas.upenn.edu/~lee/09cis480/lec-AssuranceCasesTutorial.pdf
12. Yu, E.S.: Social modeling and i^*. In: Borgida, A.T., Chaudhri, V.K., Giorgini, P., Yu, E.S. (eds.) Conceptual Modeling: Foundations and Applications. LNCS, vol. 5600, pp. 99–121. Springer, Heidelberg (2009). https://doi.org/10.1007/978-3-642-02463-4_7

13th International ERCIM/EWICS/ARTEMIS Workshop on Dependable Smart Embedded Cyber-Physical Systems and Systems-of-Systems (DECSoS 2018)

13th ERCIM/EWICS/ARTEMIS Workshop on Dependable Smart Cyber-Physical Systems and Systems-of-Systems (DECSoS 2018)

European Research and Innovation Initiatives in the Area of Cyber-Physical Systems and Systems-of-Systems-Systems

Erwin Schoitsch[1] and Amund Skavhaug[2]

[1] Center for Digital Safety & Security,
AIT Austrian Institute of Technology GmbH, Vienna, Austria
Erwin.Schoitsch@ait.ac.at
[2] Department of Mechanical and Industrial Engineering,
NTNU (The Norwegian University of Science
and Technology), Trondheim, Norway
Amund.Skavhaug@ntnu.no

1 Introduction

The DECSoS workshop at SAFECOMP follows already its own tradition since 2006. In the past, it focussed on the conventional type of "dependable embedded systems", covering all dependability aspects as defined by Avizienis, Lapries, Kopetz, Voges and others in IFIP WG 10.4. To put more emphasis on the relationship to physics, mechatronics and the notion of interaction with an unpredictable environment, the terminology changed to "cyber-physical systems" (CPS) and "Systems-of-Systems" (SoS). The new megatrend (and hype?) IoT ("Internet of Things") as super-infrastructure for CPS as things added a new dimension with enormous challenges. Collaboration and co-operation of these systems with each other and humans, and the interplay of safety, cybersecurity and reliability are leading to new challenges in verification, validation and certification/qualification, as these systems operate in an unpredictable environment and are themselves open, adaptive and highly automated or even (partly) autonomous. Examples are e.g. the smart power grid (power plants and power distribution and control), smart transport systems (rail, traffic management with V2V and V2I facilities, air traffic control systems), advanced manufacturing systems ("Industry 4.0"), mobile co-operating autonomous vehicles and robotic systems, smart health care, smart buildings up to smart cities and the like.

Society as a whole strongly depends on CPS and SoS - thus it is important to consider dependability (safety, reliability, availability, security, maintainability, etc.), resilience, robustness and sustainability in a holistic manner. CPS and SoS are a targeted research area in Horizon 2020 and public-private partnerships such as the ECSEL JU (Joint Undertaking) (Electronic Components and Systems for European Leadership), which integrated the former ARTEMIS (Advanced Research and Technology for Embedded Intelligence and Systems), ENIAC and EPoSS efforts. Industry and research ("private") are represented by the industrial associations ARTEMIS-IA, AENEAS (for ENIAC, semiconductor industry) and EPoSS ("Smart Systems Integration"), the public part are the EC and the national public authorities of the member states. Funding comes from the EC and the national public authorities ("tri-partite funding": EC, member states, project partners). Besides ECSEL, other JTIs (Joint Technology Initiatives), who organize their own research & innovation agenda and manage their work programs and calls as separate legal entities according to Article 187 of the Lisbon Treaty, are: Innovative Medicines Initiative (IMI), Fuel Cells and Hydrogen (FCH), Clean Sky, Bio-Based Industries, Shift2Rail, Single European Sky Air Traffic Management Research (SESAR).

Besides these Joint Undertakings there are many other so-called contractual PPPs, where funding is completely from the EC (now Horizon 2020 program only), but the work program and strategy are developed together with a private partner association, e.g. Robotics cPPP SPARC with euRobotics as private partner. Others are Factories of the Future (FoF), Energy-efficient Buildings (EeB), Sustainable Process Industry (SPIRE), European Green Vehicles Initiative (EGVI), Photonics, High Performance Computing (HPC), Advanced 5G Networks for the Future Internet (5G), the Big Data Value PPP and the cPPP for Cybersecurity Industrial Research and Innovation. These PPPs cover highly prioritized areas of European research and innovation.

2 ARTEMIS/ECSEL: The European Cyber-Physical Systems Initiative (Electronic Components and Systems)

The last ARTEMIS JU projects have been finished last year (see reports in last year's Springer Safecomp 2017 Workshop Proceedings). This year, mainly ECSEL projects and a few purely Horizon 2020 or nationally funded projects are "co-hosting" the DECSoS Workshop:

- AMASS (Architecture-driven, Multi-concern and Seamless Assurance and Certification of Cyber-Physical Systems) (https://www.amass-ecsel.eu/),
- AQUAS ("Aggregated Quality Assurance for Systems", (https://aquas-project.eu/),
- IoSENSE ("Flexible FE/BE Sensor Pilot Line for the Internet of Everything"), (http://www.iosense.eu/),
- SemI40 ("Power Semiconductor and Electronics Manufacturing 4.0"), (http://www.semi40.eu/),
- SECREDAS ("Product Security for Cross Domain Reliable Dependable Automated Systems"), (https://www.ecsel.eu/projects/secredas),
- SCOTT ("Secure Connected Trustable Things"), (https://scottproject.eu/),
- ENABLE-S3 ("European Initiative to Enable Validation for Highly Automated Safe and Secure Systems"), (https://www.enable-s3.eu/)
- DEIS ("Dependability Engineering Innovation for Cyber Physical Systems"), (http://www.deis-project.eu/), a Horizon 2020 project, funded only by the EC,
- WADI ("Innovative Airborne Water Leak Detection Surveillance Service"), (http://www.waditech.eu/), a Horizon 2020 project, funded only by the EC,

which means, that results of these projects are partially reported in presentations at the DECSoS-Workshop.

Other most important ECSEL projects in the context of DECSoS are the two large ECSEL "Lighthouse" projects for Mobility.E and for Industry4.E, which aim at providing synergies by cooperation with a group of related European projects in their area of interest, for which each of them has already in the first year organized joint project conferences:

- AutoDrive ("Advancing fail-aware, fail-safe, and fail-operational electronic components, systems, and architectures for fully automated driving to make future mobility safer, affordable, and end-user acceptable"), (https://autodrive-project.eu/), (Mobility.E).
- Productive 4.0 ("Electronics and ICT as enabler for digital industry and optimized supply chain management covering the entire product lifecycle"), (https://productive40.eu/), (Industry4.E).

New projects starting this year, which are expected to report in the next years in this workshop, are iDev40 ("Integrated Development 4.0", https://www.ecsel.eu/projects/idev40) and AfarCloud ("Aggregated Farming in the Cloud", https://www.ecsel.eu/projects/afarcloud). Short descriptions of the projects, partners, structure and technical goals and objectives are described on the project websites and the ECSEL project website (https://www.ecsel.eu/projects). See also the Acknowledgement at the end of this introduction.

3   This Year's Workshop

The workshop DECSoS'18 provides some insight into an interesting set of topics to enable fruitful discussions during the meeting and afterwards. The mixture of topics is hopefully well balanced, with a certain focus on multi-concern assurance issues (cybersecurity & safety co-engineering), and on IoT and collaborative and autonomous systems. Presentations are mainly based on ECSEL, Horizon 2020, and nationally funded projects mentioned above, and on industrial developments of partners' companies and universities.

The session starts with an introduction and overview to the ERCIM/EWICS/ARTEMIS DECSoS Workshop, setting the European Research and Innovation scene. The first session on **Testing for Trusted Safety-Critical Systems** comprises two presentations:

(1) "A Testbed for Trusted Telecommunications Systems in a Safety Critical Environment", describing a testbed environment that can be configured into various telecommunication operator configurations around Network Function Virtualization, Edge Cloud and Internet-of-Things along with trusted computing. A medical application is the motivating case to demonstrate reliability, resiliency, security and safety (projects SECREDAS and SCOTT).

(2) "Constraint-based Testing for Buffer Overflows"; Research of the University of Erlangen-Nuremberg, Germany, work funded by the German Federal Ministry for Economic Affairs and Energy, in the project SMARTEST, about avoidance of security vulnerability through buffer overflow.

The second session covers **Cooperative Systems Safety & Security** by three papers:

(1) "Multi-Layered Approach to Safe Navigation of Swarms of Drones"; this paper proposes a novel multi-layered approach to ensuring safety of drone navigation. It aims at maintaining an optimal ratio between efficiency of mission execution and safety at a hierarchical distributed manner. The approach is formalized in Event-B.
(2) "Dynamic Risk Management for Cooperative Autonomous Medical Cyber-Physical Systems"; This paper reflects the challenges of cooperative medical devices, demonstrated at a patient controlled analgesia (drug infusion and optimization of alarms). During runtime, information regarding the safety properties of the constituent systems, relevant information about the patient, and other relevant context information is utilized to dynamically and continuously optimize the system performance while guaranteeing an acceptable level of safety (Brazilian National Research Council partial funding).
(3) "Towards (semi-)automated synthesis of runtime safety models: A safety-oriented design approach for service architectures of cooperative autonomous systems"; the full potential of autonomous cars requires cooperation between these vehicles and infrastructure. To facilitate safe cooperative autonomous systems at runtime, the Con-Serts approach of previous work, which allows fully automated safety interface compatibility checks in the field based on runtime safety models, is extended, synthesizing these runtime safety models based on design time architecture and safety models, which does not exist today (partially DEIS project).

The session after lunch is dedicated to **Safety & Cybersecurity Systems Engineering**, a general topic nowadays for all areas of CPS and IoT in a connected (smart) world:

(1) The session starts with a presentation on safety and security co-engineering. "Co-Engineering in the Loop" describes the approach of co-engineering with interaction points as taken in the ECSEL project AQUAS, which has been running since May 2017. The methodology is illustrated with first details on how the co-engineering approach for the concept phase is realized in the industrial drive use case provided by Siemens AG Austria.
(2) "STPA Guided Model-Based Systems Engineering"; this paper presents a new design methodology to design systems that can handle the complexity issues of systems by design. The new methodology is based on System-Theoretic Process Analysis (STPA) and standard systems engineering methods. A safe medical ventilator system is chosen as an example to demonstrate the approach.
(3) "A Quantitative Approach for the Likelihood of Exploits of System Vulnerabilities" presents a review of safety & security concern considerations of cyber-physical systems. The safety impact of security compromises is evaluated in a semiquantitative manner because it is a relatively new area so there is not enough

real data available to analyze attack rates quantitatively and the attack-vulnerability scenario is constantly changing. This paper proposes an approach for the quantification of vulnerabilities based on learning from data obtained by concrete pattern implementations in safety critical systems. The SAHARA and the FMVEA method are explained (AMASS project).

(4) The last paper in this session discusses safety and security interdependencies and co-engineering in a smart production environment. It includes tight cooperation of robots and humans, a seamless integration of Information Technology (ICT) and the Operation Technology (OT), wired or wireless interconnection of devices and machinery across the existing manufacturing components plant borders. A data driven product life cycle with secured product configuration and secured data communication and a "digital twin" approach is exemplified (IoSENSE project).

The last session of the day is about **Dependability of Advanced Networks/IoT.** This concerns particularly security of communication, of IACS (Industrial Automation and Control Systems) and IoT respectively sensor networks. This is a topic of increasing interest in industry, automotive and environmental technologies:

(1) Future high throughput and bandwidth requirements should allow applications which are not possible today with 3G or 4G networks – 5G is the hope for a large application landscape! "Survey of Scenarios for Measurement of Reliable Wireless Communication in 5G" studies reliability of different scenarios which need different methods to measure the reliability (e.g., active and passive). This paper selects two scenarios which are suited to measure the reliability of the wireless networks: (1) vehicles transmitting collision warnings at intersections and (2) wireless emergency-stop buttons in factories (national funding in Austria: BMVIT and Salzburg).

(2) "Application of IEC 62443 for IoT Components": IEC 62443 series is the basic IACS security standard, but is it appropriate also for IoT based systems? The basic approach defined in the standard is to break down the system components into zones and conduits based on required security levels. This paper reuses this idea on a small scale to show how the same concept can be used to define zones and conduits between mixed-criticality IoT components to improve the security on component level. The MORETO tool, which supports the security risk analysis process, is discussed (projects AQUAS and SemI40).

(3) "Dependable Outlier Detection in Harsh Environments Monitoring systems" – this paper proposes a novel approach for a framework for dependable detection of failures in harsh environments monitoring systems, aiming to improve the overall sensor data quality in a sensor network. It presents the application of an early framework implementation to an aquatic sensor network dataset, using neural networks to model sensors' behaviors, to correlate data between neighbor sensors, and using a statistical technique to detect the presence of outliers in the datasets (WADI project, national funds).

As chairpersons of the workshop, we want to thank all authors and contributors who submitted their work, Friedemann Bitsch, the SAFECOMP Publication Chair, and the members of the International Program Committee who enabled a fair evaluation through reviews and considerable improvements in many cases. We want to express our thanks to the SAFECOMP organizers, who provided us the opportunity to organize the workshop at SAFECOMP 2018 in Västeras. Particularly we want to thank the EC and national public funding authorities who made the work in the research projects possible. We do not want to forget the continued support of our companies and organizations, of ERCIM, the European Research Consortium for Informatics and Mathematics with its Working Group on Dependable Embedded Software-intensive Systems, and EWICS, the creator and main sponsor of SAFECOMP, with its working groups, who always helped us to learn from their networks.

We hope that all participants will benefit from the workshop, enjoy the conference and accompanying programs and will join us again in the future!

Acknowledgements. Part of the work presented in the workshop received funding from the EC (ARTEMIS/ECSEL Joint Undertaking) and the partners National Funding Authorities ("tripartite") through the projects AMASS (grant agreement 692474), ENABLE-S3 (692455), IoSENSE (692480), SemI40 (692466), ENABLE-S3 (692455), AQUAS (737475), Productive4.0 (737459), AutoDrive (737469), SCOTT (737422) and recently started projects SECREDAS (783119), iDev40 (783163) and AfarCloud (783221). Other EC funded projects are e.g. in Horizon 2020 WADI (689239) or DEIS (732242). Some projects received national funding, e.g. SMARTEST (Germany, BMWi), Brazilian, Portuguese and Austrian authorities, and others (see individual acknowledgements in papers).

4   International Program Committee

Friedemann Bitsch	Thales Deutschland GmbH, Germany
Peter Daniel	EWICS TC7, UK
Wolfgang Ehrenberger	University of Applied Science Fulda, Germany
Francesco Flammini	Linnaeus University, Sweden
Janusz Gorski	Gdansk University of Technology, Poland
Hans Hansson	Mälardalen University, Sweden
Maritta Heisel	University of Duisburg-Essen, Germany
Haris Isakovic	Vienna University of Technology, Austria
Floor Koornneef	TU Delft, The Netherlands
Willibald Krenn	AIT Austrian Institute of Technology, Austria
Peter Ladkin	University of Bielefeld, Germany
Markus Murschitz	AIT Austrian Institute of Technology, Austria
Dejan Nickovic	AIT Austrian Institute of Technology, Austria
Frank Ortmeier	Otto-von-Guericke-University Magdeburg, Germany
Thomas Pfeiffenberger	Salzburg Research, Austria
Francesca Saglietti	University of Erlangen-Nuremberg, Germany
Christoph Schmittner	AIT Austrian Institute of Technology, Austria
Christoph Schmitz	Zühlke Engineering AG, Switzerland
Daniel Schneider	Fraunhofer IESE, Kaiserslautern, Germany

Erwin Schoitsch   AIT Austrian Institute of Technology, Austria
Rolf Schumacher   Schumacher Engineering Office, Germany
Amund Skavhaug   NTNU Trondheim, Norway
Mark-Alexander Sujan   University of Warwick, UK
Stefano Tonetta   Fondazione Bruno Kessler, Trento, Italy

A Testbed for Trusted Telecommunications Systems in a Safety Critical Environment

Ian Oliver[1]($\boxtimes$), Aapo Kalliola[1], Silke Holtmanns[1], Yoan Miche[1], Gabriela Limonta[2], Borger Vigmostad[2], and Kiti Muller[3]

[1] Cybersecurity Research Group, Nokia Bell-Labs, Espoo, Finland
ian.oliver@nokia-bell-labs.com
[2] Mobile Networks: Radio Cloud, Nokia Networks, Espoo, Finland
[3] Medical and Neuroscience Group, Nokia Bell-Labs, Espoo, Finland

Abstract. Telecommunications systems are critical aspects of infrastructure with more safety-critical systems utilising their capabilities. Domains such as medicine and automotive applications are required to be resilient and failure tolerant. We have constructed a testbed environment that can be configured into various telecommunication operator configurations based around Network Function Virtualisation, Edge Cloud and Internet-of-Things along with trusted computing. Utilising a medical application as the motivating case to demonstrate reliability, resiliency and as a compelling demonstration we can investigate the interaction of these security technologies in telecommunications environment while providing a safety-critical use case.

1 Introduction

Telecommunications systems are now firmly established as pieces of critical infrastructure and are indeed designed and constructed to be as resilient to failure as possible. These systems however are extending from their infrastructure role into more diverse and distributed systems encompassing the now increasing reliance on IoT devices beyond that of traditional user equipment such as mobile phones. The forthcoming 5th generation (5G) telecommunication systems explicitly addresses aspects of latency, communication frequency, authorisation and other aspects of Internet-of-Things (IoT), connected cars and of virtualised infrastructures [1].

Given this increased functionality and ubiquitous nature, telecommunications systems are being used as a platform for providing services to safety-critical systems: GSM-R (now LTE-R), Tetra have been used in rail and public safety systems (police, border protection, military etc.). Some governments even consider the usage of commercial networks for their public safety communications[1].

---

[1] https://www.kauppalehti.fi/lehdistotiedotteet/nokia–finnish-state-security-networks-group-and-telia-finland-trial-prioritization-of-public-safety-traffic-over-lte-networks/8JWFyZEX.

© Springer Nature Switzerland AG 2018
B. Gallina et al. (Eds.): SAFECOMP 2018 Workshops, LNCS 11094, pp. 87–98, 2018.
https://doi.org/10.1007/978-3-319-99229-7_9

The ability to provide private services through virtual operators and virtualised infrastructure then lends capabilities to other domains, such as medical and automotive domains. Indeed in the latter case the concept of the connected car with a plethora of sensors, video streaming, data collection, on-board processing and ad hoc networking is a canonical example of this.

This trend of running safety-critical systems, which almost by default now means 'cyber-physical', will continue and is extending into domains such as medicine. In that respect, we have a need to understand how said systems behave under anomalous situations and how the suite of security, privacy and trust technologies can best interact to provide better protections related to overall system integrity and its resilience under duress.

This paper presents our testbed environment [19] for examining the security properties of such systems. We utilise a motivational medical use case for demonstration built upon the telecommunications' "Network Function Virtualisation (NFV) - Edge Cloud - IoT architecture". We are currently exploring aspects of Interconnection Network security - the 'inter-telco operator internet' (SS7/Diameter) protocols affecting 5G/LTE and 3G systems, novel distributed denial of service (DDoS) analysis and protection/mitigation mechanisms especially related to virtualised workload, and the use the trusted computing environments for integrity measurements, identity and attestation.

The rest of this paper will introduce the testbed components and the current set of experiments/proof of concepts.

2   Testbed Components

We have (and are continually) constructing a testbed environment for evaluating and prototyping various security technologies and their interactions. The testbed is primarily focused on the secure provisioning of telecommunications infrastructure in a safety-critical environment - in this case we demonstrate with a medical case based on a remote medic interacting with a local medic. A visualisation of this is presented in Fig. 1, which shows one possible configuration to be used in testing. The testbed - while demonstrating a medical case - can be retargeted towards automotive and rail cases as required - all application domains which require not only security but some degree of real-time performance.

The application for demonstration is relatively straightforward and is based around the idea of remote surgery or some suitable medical procedure [24] to be performed at a remote site. An example of this has been the proposed usage of a robotic device [23] to enable a neurologist working to provide accurate or confirmed diagnosis at a remote location in cases of stroke, for example, a single neurologist can provide service to a number of emergency departments with aid of local medical personnel.

The hardware being used consists of Nokia AirFrame NFV servers with customised Linux based operating system, various base station 5G/LTE and Wifi controller components with 'Edge' functionality. IoT components come in various kinds from small scale sensors - cameras, physiological measurements etc. -

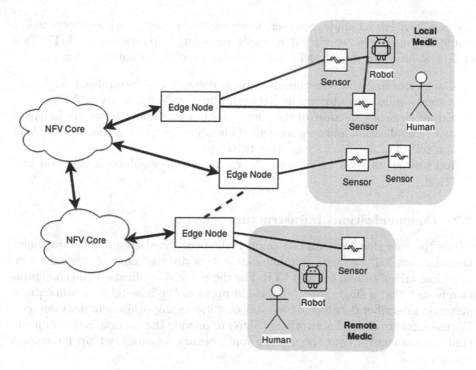

Fig. 1. Example instantiation of testbed

to larger scale independently functioning components such as the 'robot surgeon' played by a Universal Robots UR3 arm[2] and other devices accordingly. Additionally, we take into consideration the role of a human in both the remote and local roles in all scenarios.

The properties being investigated by the testbed come from the provisioning of such applications in a telco/5G environment where service availability and reliability is to be preserved in terms of system integrity and defence when under attack, e.g.: denial of service, specific telco core attacks, system tampering etc.

– Ensuring that the application data and instructions are not tampered with; including the workload elements (hardware, software)
– Ensuring that the application continues to function under network attack
– Ensuring that the application fails or degrades in a known or safe manner if the above characteristics are not met

2.1   High-Level Components

The high-level architecture components are classified into three parts with the distinction being made on overall computing resources and 'interaction' with

---

[2] https://www.universal-robots.com/products/ur3-robot/.

the end-user. For example, a server providing telecommunications functionality would be considered 'core', but a sensor recording temperature as 'IoT'. This classification is not meant to be read as being absolute in nature.

- **Core:** meaning the telecommunications network and centralised workload, servers - collectively known as Network Function Virtualisation (NFV)
- **Edge:** elements 'outside' of the core cloud but providing, relatively independently, application and core services. This might range from base station/Wifi controllers to localised application platforms
- **IoT:** elements such as sensors, direct human or machine interaction etc. [21,29].

2.2 Communications Infrastructure

While the core elements can rely upon high-speed, fixed communications lines, the edge and IoT elements communicate over a diverse range of systems: wifi, fixed line and of course 5G and LTE. For the medical application the configuration is such that a single core, NFV cloud provides the base telecommunications systems: subscriber databases, base stations, messaging equipment/services, etc. We use software defined networking (SDN) to provide the necessary, dynamically configurable control over the routing and network topology set up for certain applications.

2.3 Application Components

The application components are either run as hardware components (e.g.: robot + controller), IoT devices, 'bare-metal' software running as processes on some operating system, microcontroller - Intel NUC, ATMEL and ARM based devices - etc., or on some virtualised environment such as provided by some hypervisor, e.g.: Docker.

In this respect, this allows us effectively to implement any application that requires strong interaction with telecommunication systems. For example, in the medical case certain parts of the application, such as real-time video streaming, require close to core implementation, while data aggregation can be made in the edge nodes before being sent to core. Further, the medical application has security and privacy requirements which require virtualised networking to be set up to ensure these characteristics.

3 Security Test Technologies

In this section, we outline the three areas of active research regarding telecommunications system security, these are:

- Attestation and trusted environments
- Distributed denial of service and network anomaly protection
- Interconnection Network protocol protection

3.1   Attestation

Trusted computing concepts based around the ideas of Trusted Platform Module (TPM), Remote Attestation (RA) and Trusted Execution Environments (TEE) [28,30] are well known. Their application in cloudified environment is limited; however, mechanisms such as the TPM quote, a strong identity of the actual TPM chip (and thus computing element), run-time kernel level integrity measurements and remote attestation provide a reliable mechanism for ensuring that systems confirm to a known configuration [26]. Extending these mechanisms beyond x86 servers to ARM, microcontroller and virtualised components is being prototyped within this testbed [2,3,12].

We have a generic attestation *environment* based around the ability to utilise any number of measurement mechanisms for any given identifiable and attestable element [6,7,27]. We extend this out to a more generic notarisation - ostensibly blockchain based - mechanism which provides longer term identities [4] and known measurements globally for hardware components and particularly virtual images and software components, while at a local level would be supplemented by measurements for that local system's hardware in conjunction with measurements for virtual machines taken at particular points during that machine's life cycle, e.g.: start, suspension, migration etc.

The attestation is made through a combination of policies denoting known or good states with rules over various aspects of the machine's measurement. A TPM quote contains not just a measure but also information about the TPM clock, reboot counts, firmware versions etc. We also utilise the ability to reason over integrity measurements over time giving the opportunity to make correspondence with other system aspects, such as comparing a given machine's TPM reboot count with, for example, reboots triggered by system updates and patching. Figure 2 shows the result of one audit of a given element and the cross-referencing of particular attestation rules against certain policies for machine configuration.

The core of the testbed utilises OpenStack as the virtualisation management environment. Here, we utilise the remote attestation to guide workload placement and add trust to VM life cycle operations. Virtual machines (implementing VNFs) are measured as images using simple cryptographic hashing [32,33]. Life cycle operations, such as instantiation (running), suspension and migration [8] in particular, present further check points. The testbed provides a proof of concept interaction between the virtual machine management and attestation server for the purposes of providing trust over the operation on the virtual machine - this is described later in Sect. 4. Mechanisms for extending this *into* the virtual machine are under investigation [22], for example, virtual trusted platform module (vTPM) [5] being one potential solution.

Two other aspects are under investigation, the first being the distribution of attestation functionality away from a single centralised attestation server. Partially inspired by blockchain style distribution and also to investigate localising trust responsibilities. The second derives from the first which is to form a system-wide graph of who trusts whom, once each element is capable of deciding

Trust Decision Event Details

NUC3 is trusted 🔒

	Basic trust checks	Reset count matches the amount of boot events	Reset count has either increased or not changed	Clock increasing, but clock integrity might be compromised	TPM clock integrity maintained	Clock has increased	Deatiled checks for attested value	Attested value has not changed	Element has been updated	Policy has changed	Correct attested value	Final Result
NUC3's CRTM policy (SHA256)	✓	✓	✓	✓	✓	✓	✓	✓	✗	✗	✓	(13/13)
NUC3's CRTM policy (SHA1)	✓	✓	✓	✓	✓	✓	✓	✓	✗	✗	✓	(12/13)
NUC3's SRTM policy (SHA1)	✓	✓	✓	✓	✓	✓	✓	✓	✗	✗	✓	(13/13)
NUC3's SRTM policy (SHA256)	✓	✓	✓	✓	✓	✓	✓	✓	✗	✗	✓	(13/13)
NUC3's DRTM policy (SHA256)	✓	✓	✓	✓	✓	✓	✓	✓	✗	✗	✓	(13/13)
NUC3's DRTM policy (SHA1)	✓	✓	✓	✓	✓	✓	✓	✓	✗	✗	✓	(13/13)
NUC3's Custom IMA policy (SHA1)	✓	✓	✓	✓	✓	✓	✓	✓	✗	✗	✓	(13/13)
NUC3's Custom IMA policy (SHA256)	✓	✓	✓	✓	✓	✓	✓	✓	✗	✗	✓	(13/13)

Fig. 2. Example result of machine trust audit

which other elements it trusts (and to what degree). This latter *trust graph* also addresses ideas of the degree of trust between nodes and the transitivity of trust [18].

3.2 DDoS Protection

The defence mechanism is implemented on the testbed network as part of the software defined networking (SDN) as an extension of the mechanisms introduced in [20]. Typical functional blocks in the implementation include traffic sampling capabilities in the network either directly from switches or indirectly through an SDN controller, a feature extraction and learning VNF, and, finally, the rule creation and deployment logic in the form of an SDN application running on top of the SDN controller.

In order to effectively mitigate DDoS attacks, the defence logic must have an understanding of the structure of the network within the security control domain, and of the traffic flows and insertion points into the security control domain. This information can be gained from e.g. the SDN controller, which may directly contain capabilities for providing network graphs, or the graphs may be deduced from the overall set of known nodes and the rules deployed on the nodes for traffic routing.

The full testbed is constructed with multiple different networking technologies. In reality, SDN capabilities are unlikely to extend through all traffic forwarding points in the network. Thus, the DDoS protection mechanism must also be capable of reasoning where the edges of the "controllable" security control domain lie within the network. Any rules targeting traffic flowing in from edges would ideally be placed as near to the edge as possible in order to avoid forwarding malicious traffic within the network and incurring the related costs or risking bandwidth exhaustion. An example of this configuration in the context of the testbed is shown in Fig. 3.

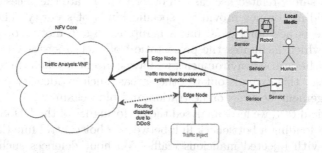

Fig. 3. Example instantiation of networking architecture and protection in the testbed

3.3   Interconnection Network (SS7/Diameter) Protection

The network was considered closed - accessible only by mostly state owned trusted telecoms operators - it has now been opened to facilitate new services and operators. In our testbed, we, effectively, create a private telecom operator for processing medical data and connecting the medics in Fig. 1 together.

We isolate the control and user data related to this application by running it fully on protected and firewalled virtual nodes. In unprotected networks, utilising the commands provided by SS7 [10] and Diameter [11], a large number of potentially serious attacks can be made against individual subscribers or IoT devices, network equipment, including subscriber modification [14], location tracking [16] and password interception [15] over SMS.

In a similar manner to that shown in Fig. 3, we can inject such commands, directly and indirectly, into our network against VNFs existing in the core and also some edge agents and elements providing telecommunications network functionality. As these attacks can be made over a long period of time, detection is difficult. The testbed utilises machine learning over these protocols to attempt to detect the weak signals of such an attack [25].

The virtual network for critical applications has full network functionality. Its security is based on a trust system, dynamic DoS protection and a signalling firewall protection. This allows us to protect against the following attack types:

- Availability attacks (DoS) coming via interconnection, malicious updates, bots.
- Sensitive data extraction using roaming interfaces, remote code execution.

In addition, our testbed allows extensive monitoring and logging of unusual events and, by that, a better possibility to identify a potential attacker and its technique. This monitoring and logging of events is used to identify key features of abnormal and normal traffic on a connection specific or partner specific basis.

4   Scenarios, Results and Future Work

The testbed has been designed to support a number of security experiments with a 'compelling' safety related use case, in order to facilitate the necessity and the effect of providing, or not providing, specific kinds of security. The choice of a medical case is new for Nokia, but a mapping to automotive or rail can be easily made, which facilitates the presentation of such a system. In this short description of the testbed environment, we have concentrated on three particular areas, of course, this extends out to other areas, such as identity provisioning, update management, security orchestration and blockchain.

As a practical test, we have analysed the performance of the DDoS mitigation system by overloading a bottleneck link between robot control functionality and actual robot with injected malicious traffic. Without defences such an attack seriously impairs or completely prevents correct robot operation. With the DDoS mitigation system in place, the normal traffic is protected from overload-induced packet drops, and normal operation is maintained.

The amount of information that is generated through detecting security anomalies is significant, and reacting to these in a meaningful manner is complex. One aspect of this work has been to introduce the concept of security orchestrator [17] as a system-wide component, though implemented as part of the core management and operations functionality.

The use of a *security orchestrator* allows for more coördinateed responses across the system as a whole. For example, if a machine fails an integrity measurement the local response might be to migrate workload away, whereas a wider - system - response would be to additionally isolate that machine at various protocol levels and via SDN, prepare other machines for additional workload by migrating their workload in a coordinated manner, reducing the overall trust relationships in the system and causing additional protection mechanisms to be brought dynamically on-line. We actually aim to move to a more 'graceful' response to system failure than is currently possible.

Two significant results have come from extended analysis of attestation quotes: the first being that trust is fragile due to updates, file changes, configuration changes and, often, due to the misimplementation of TCG standards; the second being that reaction to a trust failure can not be to remove the element (machine, VM or device) from the network but to react in an appropriate manner.

The role of trust beyond boot-time measurement and, in the case of OpenStack, when a virtual machine is instantiated - the attestation server provides information about which physical hardware a VM that requires trust can be started on - are currently the only points where trust is considered. Ignoring the case where measurements can be taken inside a VM and reported by some vTPM mechanism - this has other issues that are not well solved in the current CPU architectures - we are left with the situation of when to take measurements. A basic pattern emerges where an operation on a virtual machine is the trigger for both a pre and post-operation measurement of the hardware environment coupled with a measurement of the virtual machine itself. These measures can then be used (a) to ensure that the underlying hardware has remained in a known state (e.g.: no reboots, or if reboot has occurred, no changes), and (b) that the virtual machine snapshot/instance has not changed [9] under operations, such as suspend and migrate. We can extend this, in the case of suspend operations, to ensure that when the machine is being restarted then it is on the same physical hardware backed up through TPM sealing, for example.

We have developed using root cause analysis (RCA) [13] a set of causal factor trees (CFTs) over the attestation results that identify the possible causes of failures. Each attestation rule can be mapped to its corresponding causal factor tree for analysis, which is then linked to a mitigation procedure. Often, it is the case that a trust failure is an indication of a failed or not yet performed update, system management error, a system crash etc.

Figure 4 shows a common situation in which an element fails its attestation checks due to inconsistencies in the number of reboots reported by the TPM and the amount stored on the attestation server. This kind of failure is common in server class hardware, since they perform a series of self-tests on start up, which are only recorded by the TPM. By using RCA and CFT, we can identify situations in which trust or trustworthiness of an element can be safely recovered. Then, the existing attestation rules can be extended to include this behaviour as normal and avoid a failure in the future.

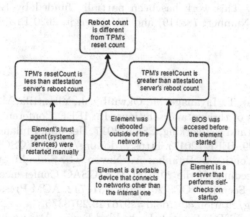

Fig. 4. Causal factor tree for one kind of common trust failure

An investigation is now under way regarding how each of the above interact. One scenario is that DDoS attacks now appear to act as covers for more sophisticated attacks, such as those seen in Interconnection Network. By relating the points of attack and the routing graph [31], we can deliberately reduce the amount of trust between components, or vice versa, if a component fails attestation then the network routing can be directed via additional checks, such as firewalls or sandboxing. The aim here is, primarily, to preserve availability and functionality of the system by increasing the resilience.

Returning to the medical application - this as noted has provided the use case and requirements for the kinds of resilience and mitigations that we are constructing and evaluating within this testbed. For the user of the medical application they can be sure that the data being received is uncorrupted and that the service they are providing over the telecommunications infrastructure is reliable. For example, taking the cases above, we have been able to examine scenarios:

- provisioning of real-time data feeds and interaction under DDoS attack
- dynamic reorganisation of routing to ensure no loss of traffic and minimised network performance loss
- ensuring that the VNFs providing the application are of good integrity
- ensuring that the telco infrastructure remains reliable, and the medical applications isolated, under interconnection attacks
- ensuring the hardware, especially edge and IoT node are untampered

We continue this work with more integration of the above, addressing alternate domains - particularly rail and automotive, applying the lessons learnt in constructing the testbed and experiment into those domains and evaluating automated and proactive, proportionate responses to network/system anomalies/failures.

Acknowledgement. This work has been partially funded by EU ECSEL Project SECREDAS (Grant Number: 783119) and EU Horizon 2020 Project SCOTT (Grant Number: 737422).

References

1. Ahmad, I., Kumar, T., Liyanage, M., Okwuibe, J., Ylianttila, M., Gurtov, A.V.: 5G security: analysis of threats and solutions. In: IEEE Conference on Standards for Communications and Networking, CSCN 2017, Helsinki, Finland, 18–20 September 2017, pp. 193–199. IEEE (2017). https://doi.org/10.1109/CSCN.2017.8088621
2. Ambrosin, M., Conti, M., Ibrahim, A., Neven, G., Sadeghi, A.R., Schunter, M.: SANA. In: Proceedings of the 2016 ACM SIGSAC Conference on Computer and Communications Security - CCS 2016, pp. 731–742. ACM Press, New York (2016). http://dl.acm.org/citation.cfm?doid=2976749.2978335
3. Asokan, N., et al.: SEDA: Scalable Embedded Device Attestation. http://www.ics.uci.edu/~gts/paps/seda-CCS15.pdf
4. Augot, D., Chabanne, H., Chenevier, T., George, W., Lambert, L.: A user-centric system for verified identities on the bitcoin blockchain. In: Garcia-Alfaro, J., Navarro-Arribas, G., Hartenstein, H., Herrera-Joancomartí, J. (eds.) ESORICS/DPM/CBT -2017. LNCS, vol. 10436, pp. 390–407. Springer, Cham (2017). https://doi.org/10.1007/978-3-319-67816-0_22
5. Berger, S., Cáceres, R., Goldman, K.A., Perez, R., Sailer, R., Doorn, L.: vTPM: Virtualizing the trusted platform module. In: USENIX Security, pp. 305–320 (2006)
6. Berger, S., Goldman, K., Pendarakis, D., Safford, D., Valdez, E., Zohar, M.: Scalable attestation: a step toward secure and trusted clouds. In: 2015 IEEE International Conference on Cloud Engineering, pp. 185–194. IEEE (2015). http://ieeexplore.ieee.org/document/7092916/

7. Chen, L., Landfermann, R., Löhr, H., Rohe, M., Sadeghi, A.R., Stüble, C.: A protocol for property-based attestation. In: Proceedings of the First ACM Workshop on Scalable Trusted Computing - STC 2006, p. 7. ACM Press, New York (2006). http://portal.acm.org/citation.cfm?doid=1179474.1179479

8. Danev, B., Masti, R.J., Karame, G.O., Capkun, S.: Enabling secure VM-vTPM migration in private clouds. In: ACSAC 2011, pp. 187–196 (2011)

9. Dewan, P., Durham, D., Khosravi, H., Long, M., Nagabhushan, G.: A hypervisor-based system for protecting software runtime memory and persistent storage. In: Proceedings of the 2008 Spring Simulation Multiconference, SpringSim 2008, pp. 828–835. Society for Computer Simulation International, San Diego, CA, USA (2008). http://dl.acm.org/citation.cfm?id=1400549.1400685

10. Dryburgh, L., Hewett, J.: Signaling System No. 7 (SS7/C7): Protocol, Architecture, and Applications. Cisco Press (2003)

11. Fajardo, V., Arkko, J., Loughney, J., Zorn, G.: Diameter Base Protocol. RFC 6733 (2012). https://rfc-editor.org/rfc/rfc6733.txt

12. Ghosh, A., Sapello, A., Poylisher, A., Chiang, C.J., Kubota, A., Matsunaka, T.: On the feasibility of deploying software attestation in cloud environments. In: 2014 IEEE 7th International Conference on Cloud Computing, pp. 128–135. IEEE (2014). http://ieeexplore.ieee.org/lpdocs/epic03/wrapper.htm?arnumber=6973733

13. Ghosh, M., Varghese, A., Gupta, A., Kherani, A.A., Muthaiah, S.N.: Detecting misbehaviors in VANET with integrated root-cause analysis. Ad Hoc Netw. 8(7), 778–790 (2010). http://www.sciencedirect.com/science/article/pii/S157087051000034X

14. Holtmanns, S., Miche, Y., Oliver, I.: Subscriber profile extraction and modification via diameter interconnection. In: Yan, Z., Molva, R., Mazurczyk, W., Kantola, R. (eds.) NSS 2017. LNCS, vol. 10394, pp. 585–594. Springer, Cham (2017). https://doi.org/10.1007/978-3-319-64701-2_45

15. Holtmanns, S., Oliver, I.: SMS and one-time-password interception in LTE networks. In: IEEE International Conference on Communications, ICC 2017, Paris, France, 21–25 May 2017, pp. 1–6. IEEE (2017). https://doi.org/10.1109/ICC.2017.7997246

16. Holtmanns, S., Rao, S.P., Oliver, I.: User location tracking attacks for LTE networks using the interworking functionality. In: 2016 IFIP Networking Conference, Networking 2016 and Workshops, Vienna, Austria, 17–19 May 2016, pp. 315–322. IEEE (2016). https://doi.org/10.1109/IFIPNetworking.2016.7497239

17. Jäger, B.: Security orchestrator: introducing a security orchestrator in the context of the ETSI NFV reference architecture. In: 2015 IEEE TrustCom/BigDataSE/ISPA, Helsinki, Finland, 20–22 August 2015, vol. 1, pp. 1255–1260. IEEE (2015). https://doi.org/10.1109/Trustcom.2015.514

18. Jøsang, A., Pope, S.: Semantic constraints for trust transitivity. In: Proceedings of the 2nd Asia-Pacific Conference on Conceptual Modelling, APCCM 2005, vol. 43, pp. 59–68. Australian Computer Society Inc., Darlinghurst, Australia, Australia (2005). http://dl.acm.org/citation.cfm?id=1082276.1082284

19. Kalliola, A., Lal, S., Ahola, K., Oliver, I., Miche, Y., Holtmanns, S.: Testbed for security orchestration in a network function virtualization environment. In: 2017 IEEE Conference on Network Function Virtualization and Software Defined Networks, NFV-SDN 2017, Berlin, Germany, 6–8 November 2017, pp. 1–4. IEEE (2017). https://doi.org/10.1109/NFV-SDN.2017.8169857

20. Kalliola, A., Lee, K., Lee, H., Aura, T.: Flooding DDoS mitigation and traffic management with software defined networking. In: 4th IEEE International Conference on Cloud Networking, CloudNet 2015, Niagara Falls, ON, Canada, 5–7 October 2015, pp. 248–254. IEEE (2015). https://doi.org/10.1109/CloudNet.2015.7335317

21. Kennell, R., Jamieson, L.H.: Establishing the genuinity of remote computer systems (2003). https://dl.acm.org/citation.cfm?id=1251374

22. Liu, Q., Weng, C., Li, M., Luo, Y.: An In-VM measuring framework for increasing virtual machine security in clouds. IEEE Secur. Priv. 8(6), 56–62 (2010). https://doi.org/10.1109/MSP.2010.143

23. Lukander, K., Jagadeesan, S., Chi, H., Müller, K.: OMG!: a new robust, wearable and affordable open source mobile gaze tracker. In: Proceedings of the 15th International Conference on Human-computer Interaction with Mobile Devices and Services, MobileHCI 2013, pp. 408–411. ACM, New York (2013). https://doi.org/10.1145/2493190.2493214

24. Marja, S., et al.: Live delivery of neurosurgical operating theater experience in virtual reality. J. Soc. Inf. Disp. 26(2), 98–104 (2018)

25. Miche, Y., et al.: Data anonymization as a vector quantization problem: control over privacy for health data. In: Buccafurri, F., Holzinger, A., Kieseberg, P., Tjoa, A.M., Weippl, E. (eds.) CD-ARES 2016. LNCS, vol. 9817, pp. 193–203. Springer, Cham (2016). https://doi.org/10.1007/978-3-319-45507-5_13

26. Oliver, I., Holtmanns, S., Miche, Y., Lal, S., Hippeläinen, L., Kalliola, A., Ravidas, S.: Experiences in trusted cloud computing. In: Yan, Z., Molva, R., Mazurczyk, W., Kantola, R. (eds.) NSS 2017. LNCS, vol. 10394, pp. 19–30. Springer, Cham (2017). https://doi.org/10.1007/978-3-319-64701-2_2

27. Oliver, I., Lal, S., Ravidas, S., Taleb, T.: Assuring virtual network function image integrity and host sealing in Telco cloud. In: IEEE ICC 2017, Paris, France (2017)

28. Osborn, J.D., Challener, D.C.: Trusted Platform Module Evolution. Johns Hopkins APL Tech. Dig. 32(2), 536–543 (2013)

29. Seshadri, A., Luk, M., Perrig, A.: SAKE: software attestation for key establishment in sensor networks. In: Nikoletseas, S.E., Chlebus, B.S., Johnson, D.B., Krishnamachari, B. (eds.) DCOSS 2008. LNCS, vol. 5067, pp. 372–385. Springer, Heidelberg (2008). https://doi.org/10.1007/978-3-540-69170-9_25

30. TCG: Trusted Platform Module Library, Part 1: Architecture. Trusted Platform Module Library Specification, Family 2.0 Level 00, Revision 01.38, The Trusted Computing Group, September 2016

31. Thottan, M., et al.: The network OS: carrier-grade SDN control of multi-domain, multi-layer networks. Bell Labs Tech. J. 21, 1–29 (2017)

32. Yeluri, R., Castro-Leon, E.: Trusted virtual machines: ensuring the integrity of virtual machines in the cloud, pp. 161–178. Apress, Berkeley, CA (2014)

33. Yu, A., Qin, Y., Wang, D.: Obtaining the integrity of your virtual machine in the cloud. In: Lambrinoudakis, C., Rizomiliotis, P., Wlodarczyk, T.W. (eds.) IEEE 3rd International Conference on Cloud Computing Technology and Science, CloudCom 2011, Athens, Greece, November 29–December 1 2011, pp. 213–222. IEEE Computer Society (2011). https://doi.org/10.1109/CloudCom.2011.37

Constraint-Based Testing for Buffer Overflows

Loui Al Sardy[✉], Francesca Saglietti[✉], Tong Tang,
and Heiko Sonnenberg

Software Engineering (Informatik 11), University of Erlangen-Nuremberg,
Martensstr. 3, 91058 Erlangen, Germany
{loui.alsardy, francesca.saglietti, tong.tang,
heiko.sonnenberg}@fau.de

Abstract. This article proposes two heuristic approaches targeted at the optimized generation of test cases capable of triggering buffer overflows
resp. underflows. Both testing techniques are based on guiding conditions
statically derived by Integer Constraint Analysis. First experimental evaluations
confirmed the superiority of local optimization algorithms over global ones.

Keywords: Software vulnerability · Buffer overflow
Integer Constraint Analysis · Testing technique · Global optimization
Local optimization

1 Introduction

It is well-known that the safe behaviour of critical cyber-physical systems may be
severely jeopardized by the intentional activation of system vulnerabilities, typically
software weaknesses known to the attacker and exploited during operation to trigger
unwarranted effects. A major part of such attacks relies on redirection techniques [1, 2,
15] aimed at shifting the instruction pointer to an illegal memory cell such as to enforce
the execution of an illegal piece of hidden code. For example, the attack described in
[12] and further analysed in [1] assumes a machine code allowing for overlapping
instructions such that shifting the instruction pointer to a cell inside an instruction may
cause the execution of malicious code hidden within a correct binary code. A still
widespread redirection technique consists of provoking buffer overflows
resp. underflows by writing data intended for a buffer into memory space lying outside
of this buffer [9].

Although buffer overflows resp. underflows may be constructively avoided during
development, e.g. by forbidding the use of widespread programming languages [18],
for a considerable part of already operating cyber-physical systems their occurrence
could not be systematically excluded a priori so far. The relevance of these vulnerabilities is confirmed by a recent report [5] ranking stack-based resp. heap-based buffer
overflows among the four most frequent software vulnerabilities. In addition, successful attacks on power plants based on buffer overflows were recently reported [19].

On the whole, this confirms the need for systematic approaches capable of detecting
the potential of buffer overflows resp. underflows before allowing critical systems to
become operational. The design, development and evaluation of such approaches build

© Springer Nature Switzerland AG 2018
B. Gallina et al. (Eds.): SAFECOMP 2018 Workshops, LNCS 11094, pp. 99–111, 2018.
https://doi.org/10.1007/978-3-319-99229-7_10

the goal of the present article which is structured as follows: after an overview on existing related approaches and their limitations (Sect. 2), classical theoretical foundations of Integer Constraint Analysis (ICA) are introduced in Sect. 3. The outcome of such a preliminary static analysis is then exploited to provide systematic guidance during a successive dynamic analysis. Heuristic test techniques are subsequently designed in Sect. 4 to take advantage of the insight gained by ICA such as to optimize the chances to trigger potential overflows or underflow before operation. Section 5 presents a comparative evaluation of two testing approaches on the base of two different examples before the final Sect. 6 summarizes the work proposed and draws some conclusions.

2 Related Work

State-of-the-art approaches address the problem of detecting exploitable buffer overflows in different ways.

Static analyses examine source code listings without requiring code execution. They range from mere search of source code for buffer accesses in order to derive a list of potentially vulnerable instructions to more sophisticated code analyses in order to derive numerical constraints for variable values proven to be necessary and/or sufficient for buffer overflow occurrence. Evidently, for well-known theoretical reasons involving undecidability of program behaviour, in general static analysis alone cannot grant the detection or the exclusion of buffer overflows resp. underflows. In other words, in general the outcome of static analysis is doomed to incompleteness. Among these static approaches are [3, 6, 7, 13, 14, 23].

Dynamic analyses, on the other hand, aim at detecting the occurrence of buffer overflows by executing the program during testing. Hereby, the main challenge concerns the intelligent generation of test data capable of triggering – if possible – a buffer overflow during execution. For this purpose, test data generation may be based on assumptions restricting the search to program patterns reported or experienced to be affected by illegal buffering effects, e.g. [10, 21].

Hybrid approaches combining static and dynamic analyses [4, 17] let dynamic analysis take advantage of the insight preliminarily gained during static analysis. This insight may allow for a justified restriction of the testing scope by targeting only those buffer accesses preliminarily identified as potentially vulnerable while ignoring those already statically verified as being secure with respect to overflow or underflow.

The approach proposed in this article belongs to the latter class of hybrid approaches. Its novelty lies in the implementation of intelligent testing strategies targeted at the fulfilment of predicates derived from existing integer constraint analysis techniques. In more detail, the intention of the suggested testing strategy is to make full use of the static analysis outcome to guide the search for suitable test cases capable of fulfilling conditions guaranteeing the triggering of a buffer overflow.

3 Integer Constraint Analysis (ICA)

In the following, classical Integer Constraint Analysis is illustrated based on [8, 20]. As already mentioned, it aims at extracting information as complete as possible, in particular necessary and sufficient constraints, such as to provide a valuable guide in the search for exploitable vulnerabilities.

3.1 Potential Overflow Statements

Initially, only those program instructions allowing for a modification of buffer variables are selected for further consideration, as only their execution may trigger a buffer over- or underflow. Any such instruction is denoted as Potential Overflow Statement (in the following abbreviated by POS). More precisely, a POS denoted by <instr(k), V> , is a pair consisting of an instruction instr(k) located at code line k with writing access to buffer variables building a variable set V, where the access may be of different type:

- type 1: data may be directly written into buffer elements, e.g. by the assignment list [i-1] = 1 the integer 1 is written into the i-th element of a buffer variable list;
- type 2: alternatively, instr(k) may invoke a function parameterized by a buffer and writing data into this buffer, e.g. the function call *strcpy(des, src)* reading data from string *src* and writing them into the array referenced by *des*.

For any POS = <instr(k),V> , a subprogram results from the original program by slicing, i.e. by deleting all instructions which do not influence the variables from V [25]. By doing so, the search for test cases triggering buffer over- resp. underflows can be reduced to the program slice derived.

3.2 Necessary and Sufficient Constraint Excluding Buffer Overflows

In the following, let C(NBO) (abbreviating "Constraint for No Buffer Overflow") represents a necessary and sufficient condition for buffer accesses at POS causing neither overflows nor underflows.

In other words, fulfillment of C(NBO) upon execution of the POS instruction allows to exclude buffer overflows and underflows, while, on the contrary, violation of C(NBO) guarantees the occurrence of at least one overflow or underflow.

Depending on the type of writing data into buffer elements (s. above), the determination of C(NBO) may vary:

- type 1 (direct writing): absence of buffer overflowing or underflowing requires the index of overwritten elements to lie in the range between 0 and the allocated buffer memory size (in the following denoted as *buf.aSize*); for example, if the POS instruction assigns a new value to the element buf[i] of a buffer buf, then C(NBO) reads $0 \leq i < buf.aSize$.

- type 2 (indirect writing by call): if buffer variable(s) are parameter(s) of a function, constraint C(NBO) can be analogously derived, in particular for the C standard functions modifying buffer variables, as listed in [7, 11]; for example, for a function call *gets(str)* reading a string input from *stdin* and writing this string into the buffer *str*, the C(NBO) reads *str.aSize* $\geq$ *stdin.len*.

3.3   Necessary Condition C(POS) upon Reaching a POS

In the following, let C(POS) (abbreviating "Constraint for reaching POS") represent a predicate on program variables and buffer parameters always fulfilled upon reaching POS, but before executing the given POS instruction. The determination of a C(POS) requires an accurate analysis of the control and data flow of the corresponding program slice. More precisely, analysis of data flow along all control flow paths reaching the POS results in path-specific constraints whose logical disjunction may be taken to provide C(POS).

3.4   Logical Relations Between C(POS) and C(NBO)

Since C(POS) holds upon reaching POS and C(NBO) is sufficient and necessary for the exclusion of buffer overflows and underflows, the ICA focuses on examining whether C(POS) may imply C(NBO) or not (s. Fig. 1), where the outcome can be classified as follows:

- if C(POS) implies C(NBO), absence of buffer overflows at POS is proven;
- if C(POS) implies ¬C(NBO), a buffer over- or underflow is guaranteed to occur whenever POS is reached;
- if C(POS) neither implies C(NBO) nor ¬C(NBO), by executing the POS instruction a buffer over- or underflow might occur. In order to provoke it, test cases must be generated such as to reach POS and to violate C(NBO).

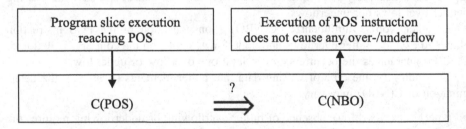

Fig. 1. Overview of integer constraint analysis

These three possibilities are summarized in Table 1.

Table 1. Possible outcomes of Integer Constraint Analysis

Implications	Buffer over-/underflow occurrence	Test need	Test goal
I1: C(POS) $\Rightarrow$ C(NBO)	never	no need	–
I2: C(POS) $\Rightarrow$ ¬ C(NBO)	whenever POS executed	need	reach POS
neither I1 nor I2	if POS executed such that C(NBO) violated	need	reach POS such that ¬ C(NBO)

4 ICA-Guided Dynamic Analysis

4.1 Test Case Generation Based on Guided Evolution

The test goal is to generate test cases triggering a buffer over- or underflow at a given POS, i.e. test cases which upon reaching POS fulfill ¬C(NBO). Evidently, upon reaching POS, C(POS) is fulfilled. In order to enforce coincidentally the validity of ¬C (NBO), the conjunction C(POS) ∧ ¬C(NBO), can provide guidance for the optimization of variables contained both in C(POS) and in ¬C(NBO).

The heuristic test generation technique considered in the following is based on genetic algorithms [16]: in general, it starts with an initial random population which successively evolves into new generations by making use of the classical genetic operators *selection*, *mutation* and *crossover*. The evolution is controlled via fitness evaluation. The process is repeated until one of the following termination conditions is fulfilled:

- a given maximal number of iterations is reached;
- an individual with a given maximum fitness is generated.

4.2 Heuristic Test Case Generation Based on Global Optimization

The first approach developed is based on global optimization. In this case, the fitness of a test case should reflect the degree of fulfilment of the target constraint C(POS) ∧ ¬C (NBO) upon reaching POS. Therefore, for individuals reaching POS the fitness is maximized by minimizing the degree of violation of the same guidance condition which can be captured by a distance metric Θ_P as proposed in [22]. Such a metric depends on the type of the underlying predicate P, as summarized in Table 2 for some typical predicates, where K denotes a positive constant intended to reflect a penalization in case of a predicate violation.

A conjunction $A = \bigwedge_{k=1}^{n} A_k$ of predicates A_k ($1 \leq k \leq n$) has the distance metric

$$\Theta_A = \sum_{i=1}^{n} \Theta_{A_i} \tag{1}$$

Table 2. Atomic predicates and distance metrics as proposed in [22]

Atomic predicate P		Distance metric Θ_P
integer a, b	a = b	if abs(a − b) = 0 then 0 else abs(a − b) + K
	a ≠ b	if abs(a − b) ≠ 0 then 0 else K
	a < b	if a − b < 0 then 0 else (a − b) + K
	a ≤ b	if a − b ≤ 0 then 0 else (a − b) + K
	a > b	if b - a < 0 then 0 else (b − a) + K
	a ≥ b	if b − a ≤ 0 then 0 else (b − a) + K
boolean A, B	A	if A = TRUE then 0 else K
	A ∨ B	min (Θ_A, Θ_B)
	A ∧ B	$(\Theta_A + \Theta_B)$

If the POS instruction is executed more than one time, upon reaching POS the variables may have different values depending on the number of times POS has already been reached in advance. As buffer overflowing resp. underflowing can be critical as soon as it happens, fulfilling the guidance conditions once at any time during execution is enough to trigger a buffer overflow. Therefore, in such cases the distance metric is taken as the minimum distance metric evaluated during execution. Formally, let t denote a test case that reaches POS m times during the whole execution and let $\Theta_A(t, j)$ denote the distance metric w.r.t. a guidance condition A upon reaching POS for the j-th time. The metric capturing the distance of test case t is then evaluated by:

$$\Theta_A(t) = \min_{1 \leq j \leq m} \Theta_A(t,j) \tag{2}$$

4.3   Heuristic Test Case Generation Based on Local Optimization

Although the aforementioned approach based on global optimization revealed as successful in some cases (s. Sect. 5 for an example), it failed to detect a buffer overflow for a particularly complex program. Therefore, this approach was modified by refining the original overall test goal "reach POS while fulfilling the guidance condition" via two different sub-goals addressing control flow and predicate fulfilment separately. To do so, the original program was first transformed into a new program by insertion of an additional branch, as shown in Fig. 2. As both outgoing arcs of the new branching node lead to identical copies of the POS instruction, both programs are behaviourally equivalent.

By this semantics-preserving program transformation the original optimization problem is transformed into a classical test coverage problem demanding to cover all nodes, in particular the POS-node highlighted by a thick border on the right of Fig. 2.

According to previous work carried out in local optimization [16, 24], the following distance metric can be used to reflect the quality of test progress:

$$distance = sub-path\ distance + branch\ distance \tag{3}$$

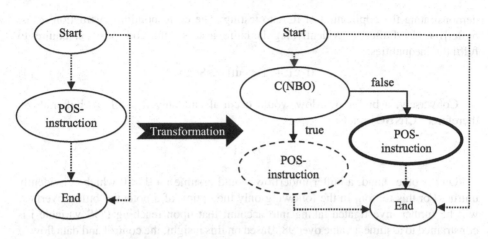

Fig. 2. Original program slice (left); transformed program slice (right).

where

- the sub-path distance captures the number of branching nodes separating the closest node already reached from the target node annotated by C(NBO); by its nature, this metric is a natural number;
- the branch distance captures the degree of violation of the branching condition C (NBO) in terms of the distance metric for the predicate ¬C(NBO); in order to enforce the dominance of the sub-path distance over the branch distance, this metric can be normalized to enforce a range between 0 and 1.

With respect to the examples analyzed, this locally optimized refinement revealed to be superior both in performance and in detection capability, as reported in the next section.

5   Examples

Both testing approaches proposed in Sect. 4 were evaluated by means of different examples. The applicability of ICA is first demonstrated via Example 1 (s. Appendix, Fig. 3) which contains two global variables, namely an integer array *buffer* for 100 integers and an integer variable *nE* indicating the number of elements already inserted in the buffer; *function* is the program under test, invoked by the integer array *values* and its size *valuesNumber*. All instructions of *function* lie within a *for* loop such that any of them might influence any of the buffer variables. Therefore, slicing the program does not help reducing the original program.

Five alternative Potential Overflow Statements were identified; only two of them require further testing. In the following, due to its nesting depth and complexity, the analysis presented focuses on the POS located at code line 10 for the purpose of demonstrating the application of ICA to testing. The corresponding instruction reads: buffer[i + 1] = buffer[i]. Evidently, regular buffer access at this code position requires to fulfil the inequalities:

$$0 \leq i + 1 < buffer.aSize \tag{4}$$

Conversely, a buffer overflow would occur if and only if $i + 1 \geq buffer.aSize$; therefore, ¬C(NBO) reads:

$$99 \leq i \tag{5}$$

On the other hand, a buffer underflow would assume $i + 1 < 0$ which is evidently untrue. For this reason, in the following only the option of a potential buffer overflow will be further investigated taking into account that upon reaching POS variable i is constrained to assume a value over 98. Based on this insight, the control and data flow of the program under test, i.e. *function* is analysed for further variable values on which i depends: among them is evidently nE which provides the initial value of i before i is successively decremented within the internal loop (s. LOC #8); in particular this implies:

$$i \leq nE \tag{6}$$

On the other hand, nE is subject to changes within the external loop (s. LOC #4); more precisely, during each iteration of the external loop nE may remain unchanged or increase by a maximum of 1 (s. LOC #13 and LOC #23); in particular, upon reaching POS in the course of the (v + 1)-th iteration, nE can have incremented at most by v, i.e.

$$nE \leq v \tag{7}$$

On the whole, the guidance provided by the overall constraint C(POS) ∧ ¬C(NBO) reads:

$$99 \leq i \leq nE \leq v \tag{8}$$

As the inequality chain $i \leq nE \leq v$ always holds by semantic analysis for the aforementioned reasons, the guiding constraint A was captured by the conjunction of three atomic conditions with distance metric:

$$\Theta_A(t) = \min_{1 \leq j \leq m} \Theta_A(t, j) \tag{9}$$

where

$$\Theta_A(t, j) = \Theta_{99 \leq v}(t, j) + \Theta_{99 \leq nE}(t, j) + \Theta_{99 \leq i}(t, j) \tag{10}$$

and j denotes the case where execution of t by *function* has just reached POS for the j-th time. Each test cases t = (*values*, *valuesNumber*) consists of an integer array *values* and an integer *valuesNumber* providing its size which in this case is 300 in view of the call in *main*.

In order to evaluate the fitness for any test case t, *function* is instrumented to return the minimum distance value $\Theta(t)$ of t upon reaching POS. For example, when executing a test case with *values* = {150, 151, 149, 152, 148, 153, 147, 154, 146} and *valuesNumber* = 9, POS is accessed 3 times. Table 3 shows the variable values and the distance metric each time POS is reached. Evidently, the minimum distance for this test case is 283.

Table 3. Variable values and distances upon reaching POS

i-th access of POS instruction	Variable values			Distance Θ
	v	nE	i	
1st	6	2	2	287
2nd	8	3	3	283
3rd	8	3	2	284

Similar procedures can be applied to the other four POS alternatives. On the whole, only those located at lines 10 and 20 require further testing (s. Table 4).

Table 4. Results of Integer Constraint Analysis for POS alternatives of Example 1

POS = <instr(k), {buffer}>		C(NBO)	testing required?
k	instr(k)		
10	buffer[i + 1] = buffer[i]	i + 1 < buffer.aSize	Yes
15	buffer[1] = value	1 < buffer.aSize	No
16	buffer[0] = 0	0 < buffer.aSize	No
19	buffer[0] = 1	0 < buffer.aSize	No
20	buffer[nE] = value	nE < buffer.aSize	Yes

Both global and local algorithms were subsequently applied 10 times each with different initial random populations of size 70, where distance metrics were evaluated with a penalty constant K = 1; the minimum distance over all individuals within a population was taken as the fitness value of that population.

All 20 test optimizations were successful in detecting an exploitable buffer over-flow. Performance was evaluated by comparing the number of iterations required to trigger the vulnerability; this allows to exclude the influence of the underlying computer hardware as would be the case if running time was measured instead. Local optimization hereby performed considerably better, the slowest local optimization requiring only ca. 53% of the effort needed by the fastest global one.

The superiority of local optimization was revealed also in the context of a further, more complex example involving higher execution times and including non-monotonic jumps in buffer accesses. For this Example 2, all global approach variants failed to exploit the existing buffer overflow within the affordable time, while the vulnerability was easily detected by all locally optimizing instances, the slowest one demanding only an effort of ca. 12% of the maximum affordable.

A comparison of the experimental results obtained is shown in Table 5.

Table 5. Comparison of global and local optimization techniques for both examples

Examples	Global Optimization (10 executions)		Local Optimization (10 executions)	
	Fastest	Slowest	Fastest	Slowest
Example 1	55869	196389	3846	29781
Example 2	no buffer overflow detection after 10000 iterations		199	1197

6   Conclusions and Future Work

This article presented two testing approaches targeted at the triggering of potential buffer overflows resp. underflows before deployment. Both approaches combine existing static analyses based on Integer Constraints with heuristics guided by the constraints derived.

The applicability was illustrated by an example; a comparative evaluation of this and of a further example showed that the local optimization techniques were superior both in detection capability and in performance.

In view of the promising results it is planned to apply similar guided test concepts to further classes of software vulnerability.

Acknowledgement. The authors gratefully acknowledge that a major part of the work presented was supported by the German Federal Ministry for Economic Affairs and Energy (BMWi), project no. 1501502C (SMARTEST). They also thank Marc Spisländer for his support in providing the code examples considered in this article.

Appendix

```
1:     int buffer[100];
       int nE = 0;
3:     void function(int *values, int valuesNumber) {
           for (int v = 0; v < valuesNumber; v++) {
5:             int value = values[v];
               if (value < buffer[1]) {
7:                 if (buffer[0] == 1) {
                       for (int i = nE; i > 1; i--) {
9:                         if (buffer[i+1] > buffer[i]){
                               buffer[i+1] = buffer[i];
11:                        }
                       }
13:                    nE++;
                   }
15:                buffer[1] = value;
                   buffer[0] = 0;
17:            } else {
                   if (buffer[nE] < value)
19:                    buffer[0] = 1;
                   buffer[nE] = value;
21:            }
               if (nE == 0)
23:                nE++;
           }
25:    }
       int main(void) {
27:        for (int i = 0; i < 100; i++)
               buffer[i] = (i+1)*1000;
29:        int values[300];
           ...
31:        function(values, 300);
           return EXIT_SUCCESS;
33:    }
```

Fig. 3. Code of Example 1

References

1. Al Sardy, L., Tang, T., Spisländer, M., Saglietti, F.: Analysis of potential code vulnerabilities involving overlapping instructions. In: Tonetta, S., Schoitsch, E., Bitsch, F. (eds.) SAFECOMP 2017. LNCS, vol. 10489, pp. 103–113. Springer, Cham (2017). https://doi.org/10.1007/978-3-319-66284-8_10

2. Andriesse, D., Bos, H.: Instruction-level steganography for covert trigger-based malware. In: Dietrich, S. (ed.) DIMVA 2014. LNCS, vol. 8550, pp. 41–50. Springer, Cham (2014). https://doi.org/10.1007/978-3-319-08509-8_3

3. Chess, B., McGraw, G.: Static analysis for security. In: IEEE Security & Privacy, vol. 2, pp. 76–79. IEEE (2004). https://doi.org/10.1109/msp.2004.111

4. Del Grosso, C., Antoniol, G., Merlo, E., Galinier, P.: Detecting buffer overflow via automatic test input data generation. In: Computers & Operations Research, vol. 35, pp. 3125–3143. Elsevier (2008)

5. Department of Homeland Security (U.S.): Annual Vulnerability Coordination Report. National Cybersecurity and Communications Integration Center/Industrial Control Systems Cyber Emergency Response Team (2016)
6. Dor, N., Rodeh, M., Sagiv, M.: Cleanness checking of string manipulations in C programs via integer analysis. In: Cousot, P. (ed.) SAS 2001. LNCS, vol. 2126, pp. 194–212. Springer, Heidelberg (2001). https://doi.org/10.1007/3-540-47764-0_12
7. Dor, N., Rodeh, M., Sagiv, M.: CSSV: towards a realistic tool for statically detecting all buffer overflows. In: Programming Language Design and Implementation (PLDI), vol. 38, pp. 155–167. ACM (2003). https://doi.org/10.1145/780822.781149
8. Evans, D., Larochelle, D.: Improving security using extensible lightweight static analysis. IEEE Softw. **19**, 42–51 (2002). https://doi.org/10.1109/52.976940
9. Foster, J.C., Osipov, V., Bhalla, N., Heinen, N.: Buffer Overflow Attacks: Detect, Exploit, Prevent. Syngress, Rockland (2005)
10. Haugh, E., Bishop, M.: Testing C programs for buffer overflow vulnerabilities. In: Network and Distributed System Security Symposium (2003)
11. International Organization for Standardization (ISO): Programming Languages — C, International Standard ISO/ IEC 9899:TC3 (E). ISO (2007). http://www.open-std.org
12. Jämthagen, C., Lantz, P., Hell, M.: Exploiting trust in deterministic builds. In: Skavhaug, A., Guiochet, J., Bitsch, F. (eds.) SAFECOMP 2016. LNCS, vol. 9922, pp. 238–249. Springer, Cham (2016). https://doi.org/10.1007/978-3-319-45477-1_19
13. Larochelle, D., Evans D.: Statically detecting likely buffer overflow vulnerabilities. In: 10th Conference on USENIX Security Symposium, vol. 10, pp. 177–190. ACM (2001)
14. Le. W., Soffa, M.L.: Marple: a Demand-driven path-sensitive buffer overflow detector. In: 16th ACM SIGSOFT International Symposium on Foundations of Software Engineering. ACM (2008). https://doi.org/10.1145/1453101.1453137
15. Lhee, K., Chapin, S.: Buffer overflow and format string overflow vulnerabilities. J. Softw. Pract. Exp. **33**, 423–460 (2003). https://doi.org/10.1002/spe.515
16. Oster, N., Saglietti, F.: Automatic test data generation by multi-objective optimisation. In: Górski, J. (ed.) SAFECOMP 2006. LNCS, vol. 4166, pp. 426–438. Springer, Heidelberg (2006). https://doi.org/10.1007/11875567_32
17. Padmanabhuni, B.M., Tan, H.B.K.: Auditing buffer overflow vulnerabilities using hybrid static–dynamic analysis. In: 38th Annual International Computers, Software and Applications Conference, vol. 10, pp. 54–61 (2014). https://doi.org/10.1109/compsac.2014.62
18. Saglietti, F., Meitner, M., von Wardenburg, L., Richthammer, V.: Analysis of informed attacks and appropriate countermeasures for cyber-physical systems. In: Skavhaug, A., Guiochet, J., Schoitsch, E., Bitsch, F. (eds.) SAFECOMP 2016. LNCS, vol. 9923, pp. 222–233. Springer, Cham (2016). https://doi.org/10.1007/978-3-319-45480-1_18
19. Schneider Electric Software Security Response Center: InduSoft Web Studio and InTouch Machine Edition – Remote Code Execution Vulnerability, Security Bulletin LFSEC00000125 (2018)
20. Shahriar, H., Zulkernine, M.: Classification of static analysis-based buffer overflow detectors. In: 4th International Conference on Secure Software Integration and Reliability Improvement Companion (SSIRI-C). IEEE (2010). https://doi.org/10.1109/ssiri-c.2010.28
21. Shahriar, H., Zulkernine, M.: Mutation-based testing of buffer overflow vulnerabilities. In: Computer Software and Applications (COMPSAC 2008), pp. 979–984. IEEE (2008)
22. Tracey, N., Clark, J., Mander, K., McDermid, J.: An automated framework for structural test-data generation. In: 13th IEEE International Conference on Automated Software Engineering, pp. 285–288. IEEE (1998). https://doi.org/10.1109/ase.1998.732680

23. Wagner, D., Foster, J.S., Brewer, E.A., Aiken, A.: A first step towards automated detection of buffer overrun vulnerabilities. In: Network and Distributed System Security Symposium (NDSS), pp. 3–17 (2000)
24. Wegener, J., Baresel, A., Sthamer, H.: Evolutionary test environment for automatic structural testing. In: Information and Software Technology, vol. 43, pp. 841–854. Elsevier (2001). https://doi.org/10.1016/s0950-5849(01)00190-2
25. Weiser, M.: Program slicing. In: 5th International Conference on Software Engineering, pp. 439–449. IEEE Press (1981)

Multi-layered Approach to Safe Navigation of Swarms of Drones

Inna Vistbakka[1]([✉]), Amin Majd[1], and Elena Troubitsyna[1,2]

[1] Åbo Akademi University, Turku, Finland
{inna.vistbakka,amin.majd}@abo.fi
[2] KTH, Stockholm, Sweden
elenatro@kth.se

Abstract. Swarms of drones are complex distributed systems that should operate safely, i.e., avoid collisions with each other and unforeseen objects appearing in the flight zones. Ensuring safety of drone navigation is challenging due to unreliability of drones, communication channels and non-determinism of the operating environment. In this paper, we propose a novel multi-layered approach to ensuring safety of drone navigation. It aims at maintaining an optimal ratio between efficiency of mission execution and safety at a hierarchical distributed way. We formalise the proposed approach in Event-B and derive the coordination and reconfig-uration mechanisms ensuring efficiency and safety of mission execution.

1 Introduction

Drones are widely used in a variety of applications such as monitoring and surveillance, search and rescue operations, military missions etc. Due to their mobility, swarms of drones can produce high-quality payload data (e.g., such as images) collected from the geographical area. However, widespread use of the swarm systems is currently hindered by a lack of methods for ensuring their efficient yet safe operation.

To accomplish the required mission, the drones of the swarm should have a high probability to survive throughout the mission, i.e., they should not get damaged or prematurely deplete their batteries. This puts three main require-ments on software navigating a swarm: firstly, position the drones to produce the payload data with the required quality; secondly, ensure resource efficiency, and thirdly, guarantee collision avoidance between the drones, between the drones and static obstacles or objects unpredictably appearing in the flight zone. To achieve these goals, in this paper, we propose a novel multi-layered approach to safe and efficient navigation of swarms of drones.

The top-most layer of our approach contains a decision center. It runs high-performance machine learning and evolutionary algorithms proposed in our pre-vious work [7,8]. They allow us to safely navigate the drones and optimise travel distance, resource consumption and quality of payload data ratio. The algorithms also ensure inter-drone and drone-obstacle collision avoidance. The

© Springer Nature Switzerland AG 2018
B. Gallina et al. (Eds.): SAFECOMP 2018 Workshops, LNCS 11094, pp. 112–125, 2018.
https://doi.org/10.1007/978-3-319-99229-7_11

central navigation is augmented with the drone-local mechanisms for ensuring collision avoidance. This mechanism ensures that whenever the radar of a drone detects an obstacle on its way, it immediately moves away to a safe position.

Our multi-layered approach mimics the self-preservation mechanism of humans. Indeed, our brains navigate us to achieve our functional goals in an efficient way while avoiding "known" dangers. Meanwhile, the reflexes bypass brain signals and get unconditionally deployed when an unforseen danger occurs, which removes or mitigates the incurred hazard.

Due to the highly dynamic nature of swarm systems and their operating environment, the proposed approach requires a complex coordination logic. We need to define the coordination schemes between the different hierarchical layers, analyse the impact of drone failures, define the mechanisms of losing and regaining the coordination and reconfiguration as well as ensure correctness of the interplay between the centralised control and local collision avoidance mechanisms. We use the notion of modes [6] to structure system behaviour, which allows us to define a generic pattern for modelling inter-drone interactions at different architectural layers.

To tackle the complexity associated with deriving such a complex mode-structured coordination scheme, we rely on formal modelling in Event-B. Event-B [1] is a state-based approach to correct-by-construction system development. The main development technique – refinement – supports stepwise construction and verification of complex specifications. We start the development by creating a high-level abstract specification, which is incrementally augmented to unfold the entire multi-layered architecture and represent static and dynamic behaviour of the system. Abstraction, refinement and proofs as well as automated tool support allow us to scale the formal development to such complex systems as swarms of drones.

2 Safe Swarm Navigation

The swarms of drones are increasingly used for surveillance, shipping, rescue etc. A swarm is a group of drones that, in a coordinated manner, provides the required service, i.e., executes a mission. For instance, a mission can be "video surveillance of a certain area". A mission can be defined in terms of *goals* – functional and non-functional objectives that the system should achieve. A video surveillance mission can be represented by a (generic) goal $G1$: "periodically upload to the cloud the images covering certain sectors of the monitored area".

Goals constitute a convenient mechanism for structuring requirements via goal decomposition. For swarm of drones, we can identify the following generic subgoals contributing to achieving the overall goal $G1$: $G2$ – produce the payload data (e.g., images) with the required quality level; and $G3$ – guarantee survivability of drones allowing them to complete the mission.

To achieve the goal $G3$, we have to ensure that the following (sub-)goals are satisfied: $G4$ – the drones do not prematurely deplete their batteries, i.e., they are navigated in an efficient way; $G5$ – the drones do not collide with each other and static obstacles; and finally, $G6$ – the drones do not collide with the unforeseen dynamically appearing objects. The goals are interdependent and might even be seen as conflicting, e.g., the travel distance has to be increased to guarantee safety and produce the payload data of the required quality. Hence, the controlling software should rely on sophisticated coordination mechanisms to ensure that all the goals remain satisfiable throughout mission execution.

In swarm systems, each drone has an individual goal that contributes to achieving the system-level goals. There are two main strategies to defining the individual goals: self-organising and centralised. The self-organising approach assumes full autonomy of drones in defining their own goals. The drones fully rely on their self-awareness facilities to (locally) compute their trajectories and react to the changing operating conditions. The self-organising approach is clearly beneficial for achieving the goal $G6$ – collision avoidance with unexpectedly appearing objects. Indeed, whenever a drone detects an obstacle, it can locally (and hence, promptly) decide to move away. On the other hand, self-organising approach is typically energy-greedy because it requires an extensive inter-drone and drone-to-cloud communication. It quickly depletes the batteries of the drones, i.e., makes the goals $G2$ and $G4$ hard to satisfy.

In the centralised approach, the decision center is responsible for generating the individual goals for drones. Since the decision center has powerful computing resources, it can rely on high-performance evolutionary algorithms and machine learning [7] to navigate the drones in an optimal way with respect to coverage, energy efficiency and inter-drone collision avoidance way. However, while this approach is beneficial for achieving goals $G1$-$G5$, it might be too rigid and slow to address the goal $G6$.

To alleviate this problem, in this paper, we propose a hybrid *multi-layered* approach to safe and efficient navigation of swarms of drones. Our approach aims at mimicking the principles of human autonomic nervous system to optimise the trade-off between efficiency and safety. Humans operate based on the "commands" generated by their brain, which continuously monitors the environment and navigates the body to achieve the desired functional goals while avoiding known hazards. On the other hand, when an unknown or unforeseen hazard occurs, the reflexes (from the spinal cord) supersede the brain commands and get immediately deployed to remove the hazards. Then the information about the occurred danger is "forwarded" to the brain, which registers it and generates further strategies using the extended knowledge about hazards.

Figure 1 presents our approach to implementing the multi-layered architecture of the system. In our approach, the "brain" – the decision center (DC) – is an intelligent component which is responsible for generating the efficient navigation strategies according to the mission goals and preventing unsafe behaviour, i.e., it navigates the drones to avoid collisions with each other and static obstacles.

At each cycle (usually called time frame) DC receives the payload (e.g., imaging) and telemetry data from the swarm, processes this information, and, if required, generates a new routing for the entire swarm. The information obtained from the Dynamic Monitoring component (see Fig. 1) allows DC to detect the

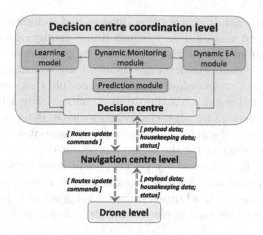

Fig. 1. Overview of system architecture

changes in the swarm and in the flying zone. Such changes may invoke swarm reconfiguration and regeneration of the drone routes.

In addition, the Prediction module uses the runtime monitoring data to predict the movement of drones and moving obstacles in the flying zone. The monitoring data and prediction results are fed to both a Dynamic evolutionary algorithm EA and a Learning Algorithm. Both modules compute the alternative routes. The routes are compared by DC and the best alternative is chosen. In our previous works [7,8], we have developed a number of high performance route planning algorithms (shown as the corresponding modules in Fig. 1), which guarantee that at each cycle the swarm receives the navigation plan optimising path, efficiency, payload data quality and safety.

The Navigation Centre (NC) at ground is able to communicate with the drones. It broadcasts the navigation plan received from DC to them. In their turn, the drones periodically send their payload and telemetry data (current status, position, battery level, etc.) to NC, which packages them, probably preprocesses and forwards to DC.

Drones communicate with NC and each other in order to achieve their individual and common goals. Since communication with NC is typically long range, it consumes significant energy. To alleviate the problem of fast energy depletion, we propose to compose the swarm from the drones of different capabilities. Thus, the swarm can be organised hierarchically and forms a tree-structure depending on different capabilities of the drones: more powerful drones – *the leaders* and less powerful drones – *the slaves* – that communicate with their leaders using less power consuming means. We also distinguish a *sink* drone – a dedicated leader drone – what besides area monitoring tasks establishes communication and transmits data between NC and drones at the leader level.

The drones of the leader level send data to the sink. Each leader has a number of the slave drones and periodically gathers information from its corresponding slaves. Finally, drones of the slave level exchange information with their leaders and receive new commands. Since some drones might change their predefined routes or even fail, to maintain an efficient drone configuration, at each cycle DC assesses the current state of the swarm and might reconfigure the tree.

Moreover, each drone of any level has its own local collision avoidance mechanism – *drone reflexes computation module* – a module that overrides the goals received from DC and commands the drone to move away when a camera or radar of the drone detects an obstacle. When a drone detects a possible collision with an unforeseen obstacle, the drone reflexes computation module quickly computes a reflex movement for the drone to prevent or mitigate the collision.

In our approach, the top-most layer – DC – is responsible for achieving goals *G1-G5*, i.e., it controls the swarm to ensure quality, efficiency and implement *preventive* safety. The on-board drone software is responsible for satisfying goal *G2* and *G6*, in the latter case implementing *defensive* safety.

3   Mode Logic of Coordination

In this paper, we use the notion of modes as a mechanism to structure the behaviour of the system [6]. Modes define coarse-grained representation of system behaviour. Changes in component (drone) states trigger a change of a mode – a mode transition. In our work, we propose to connect the states of the drones with the goals and trigger a mode transition every time when the level of satisfaction of system goals changes.

To derive the mode logic, next we will analyse the factors affecting the goal satisfaction and define the corresponding mode logic that allows the system to achieve the overall system goals despite failures and deviations.

Mode Analysis. In normal situation (called *Nominal* mode), the drones fly according to the routing plan issued by DC. Periodically, upon receiving new commands from DC the drones change their current routes as well as perform *reconfiguration* if it is commanded by DC. In this case, reconfiguration means that the logical relationships between the drones (i.e., *sink-leader* and *leader-slave* relationships) might be changed according to a new update of a drone tree-structure recalculated by DC.

We further distinguish the following modes:

- Appearing an unpredictable obstacle in a drone flying zone might prevent a drone to achieving the goal *G6*. Thus, when a drone detects a possible collision with an unforeseen obstacle, transition into the *Reflection Activation* mode is initiated. The drone reflexes computation module quickly computes a reflex movement for the drone to prevent and mitigate the collision.
- NC is responsible for actual communication between DC and the drone level. In particular, NC distributes the information between the sink drone and DC (both directions). NC is also able to identify the health status of the sink drone. In case of a sink failure, the NC triggers a transition to *Sink Failure* mode and retransmits the DC commands to the predefined candidate for a new sink. A sink failure can have severe consequences and might prevent

a system in achieving all goals *G1-G6*. The reconfiguration is triggered to substitute the failed sink drone by the predefined drone among the leaders. In this case, NC retransmits the DC commands to the predefined candidate for a new sink. Moreover, if a leader drone detect sink failure before NC does it, all healthy leaders should issue the commands to its corresponding slaves to slow down flying speed.

- Every leader tries to re-establish connection with a slave within the time bound period. Slave failure prevents a drone to achieving the goal *G2*. If it fails, then the failed slave "leaves" swarm. In this case, the *Slave Failure* mode is triggered.
- In case of a leader failure, detectable by the sink, the sink should trigger the *Leader Failure* mode. The sink drone tries to re-establish connection with the failed leader drone and, in case of unsuccessful outcome considers this leader as failed. The reconfiguration procedure is triggered to substitute the failed leader drone by the predefined slave drone of the failed leader.
- Every drone is able to identify its local communication failure. When a drone detects such a failure, a transition to *Local Communication Failure* mode is triggered. Upon this transition, every drone should move to reconnect with NC and reunite with the swarm. This is a self-triggered mode transition, i.e., the drones perform it independently upon detection of failure.

Despite the small number of modes, the mode logic is complex due to the highly non-deterministic nature of the conditions triggering mode transitions. Ensuring correctness of coordinated behaviour of collaborative swarm of drone is a challenging engineering task. To approach it in a systematic rigorous way, we choose Event-B and its refinement approach as our modelling framework, which we overview in the next Sect. 4. Further, in the Sect. 5, we will demonstrate how to derive and verify properties of the multi-layered drone coordination in a structured rigorous way using Event-B.

4   Modelling and Refinement in Event-B

Event-B is a state-based formal approach that promotes the correct-by-construction development paradigm and formal verification by theorem proving. In Event-B, a system model is specified using the notion of an *abstract state machine* [1]. An abstract state machine encapsulates the model state, represented as a collection of variables, and defines operations on the state, i.e., it describes the dynamic behaviour of a modelled system. The important system properties to be preserved are defined as model invariants. A machine usually has the accompanying component, called context. A context may include user-defined carrier sets, constants and their properties (defined as model axioms).

The dynamic behaviour of the system is defined by a collection of atomic *events*. Generally, an event has the following form:

$$e \mathrel{\widehat{=}} \textbf{any } a \textbf{ where } G_e \textbf{ then } R_e \textbf{ end}, \tag{1}$$

where e is the event's name, a is the list of local variables, and (the event *guard*) G_e is a predicate over the model state. The body of an event is defined by a *multiple* (possibly nondeterministic) assignment to the system variables. In Event-B, this assignment is semantically defined as the next-state relation R_e. The event guard defines the conditions under which the event is *enabled*, i.e., its body can be executed. If several events are enabled at the same time, any of them can be chosen for execution nondeterministically.

Event-B employs a top-down refinement-based approach to system development. A development starts from an abstract specification that nondeterministically models the most essential functional system behaviour. In a sequence of refinement steps, we gradually reduce nondeterminism and introduce detailed design decisions. In particular, we can add new events, refine old events as well as replace abstract variables by their concrete counterparts.

The consistency of Event-B models – verification of model well-formedness, invariant preservation as well as correctness of refinement steps – is demonstrated by discharging the relevant proof obligations. The Rodin platform [15] provides tool support for modelling and verification. In particular, it automatically generates all required proof obligations and attempts to discharge them. When the proof obligations cannot be discharged automatically, the user can attempt to prove them interactively using a collection of available proof tactics.

5   Formal Development of the Coordination Logic

In this section, we outline the formal Event-B development of the coordination logic in the proposed multi-layered swarm system. We start from specifying the high-level general requirements and unfold the entire coordination logic in the refinement process.

5.1   The Initial Model

The initial model represents the global control cycle spanning over all layers of the architecture shown in Fig. 2. At each cycle, DC analyses the telemetry data and either maintains the previously calculated routing or generates a new one. The routing commands are transmitted from DC to NC and then from NC to the sink. Next, the sink drone broadcasts the received information to all the drones at the leader level. In its turn, upon receiving commands from the sink each leader further distributes the routing commands to its corresponding slaves.

Once per cycle, the collected information about the monitored area – *payload data* – as well as *housekeeping data* (e.g., battery level) and *health check status* are sent by the slaves to their leaders. When all the required information is gathered by all the leaders, they transmit the collected data to the sink. Then the sink drone sends this information to NC and, NC forward it to DC. DC analyses the received data and, if it is needed, issues the new commands to the drones as well as triggers the drone reconfiguration. In this case, reconfiguration

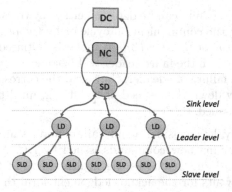

Fig. 2. System layered architecture

might affect (involve) changing the relationships between drones (at every layer) in order to optimise routing, coverage, energy and safety ratio.

Our initial Event-B specification abstractly models the control cycle as a sequence of phase changes: *DC_NC*, *NC_Sink*, *Sink_Leaders*, *Leaders_Slaves*, *Slaves_Leaders*, *Leaders_Sink*, *Sink_NC* and *NC_DC*.

5.2 Introducing Drones and Drone Failures

In our first refinement, we introduce a representation of the behaviour of the system components, in particular, we augment the specification by representation of drones and their failure. We model the impact of failures on the system dynamics and safety.

Slave Drone Failure. Since drones operate in a highly dynamic environment, they can experience different types of failures. We distinguish the permanent (e.g., due to a physical drone damage) and transient drone failure (e.g., due to loss of communication). If a transient failure occurred then after some time a drone can restore the connection with the swarm and continue to function. This behaviour is modelled by the transition to the *Local Communication Failure* mode and then returning back to the *Nominal* mode.

In the case of a permanent slave failure, the corresponding leader drone will detect a failure of its slave and, eventually, DC will be notified about the loss in the swarm. In this case, the transition to the *Slave Failure* mode is triggered. However, such a slave failure will not affect the global system behaviour and the swarm will continue to function. Let us note, that if the failed slave drone was a candidate for the next leader then the new candidate is recalculated.

Leader Drone Failure. Similar to a slave failure, we assume that a leader drone can temporarily or permanently fail. In case of a transient failure, the leader can restore the connection with the swarm and continue to function normally. This behaviour is covered by the transition to the *Local Communication Failure* mode.

A permanent leader failure can be detected either by the sink while sending a new command during the communication cycle or by the other leaders. In both cases, the transition to the *Leader Failure* mode is initiated. Some predefined slave drone associated with the failed leader will become a new leader. When the other leaders detect a failure of a leader, they send the corresponding commands to their slaves to slow down their speed of the flying, until the new commands from the DC will be issued.

Sink Failure. Finally, lets consider a sink failure and its impact on the system behaviour. Upon receiving new commands issued by DC, NC establishes connection with the sink drone. It checks the health status of the sink and sends the data. Then NC awaits for the acknowledgement form the sink drone. Upon receiving the acknowledgement from the sink, the data are considered being transmitted successfully.

However, if the sink has failed and consequently NC has not received an acknowledgement from the sink, NC triggers the transition to *Sink Failure* mode. As a result of this transition the reconfiguration of the system is activated. Namely, the predefined leader node becomes a new sink and the predefined slave drone replaces it by becoming a leader. The impact of the sink failure on the overall system architecture is represented in Fig. 3.

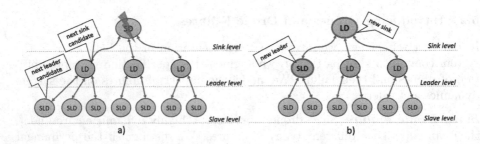

Fig. 3. Sink failure

To model the behaviour described above, we refine our initial model by introducing a number of new variables and events as well as refining some abstract events. We represent the swarm by a finite non-empty set of drones *SWARM*. It can be seen as a set that contains the ids of all drones in the swarm. Then we define variables to specify the set of all drones, sets of leader and slave drones, the sink drone (by corresponding model variables *drones, leaders, slaves, sink*).

The new variables *slaves_of_leaders* and *status* establish the relationship between a leader and slaves it supervises and the health state of every drone from a swarm, respectively:

$$slaves\_of\_leaders \in leaders \rightarrow \mathbb{P}(slaves), status \in drones \rightarrow STATUSES. \quad (2)$$

Here set $STATUSES = \{OK, FAILED, DISCON\}$, while elements of this set represent correspondingly the nominal, failed and disconnected drone status. In the system implementation, the decision about the drone status is made on the basis of the analysis of the currently received telemetry data and the routing plan.

A number of new events are introduced to model possible drone failures as well as system reaction on them (e.g., SINK_Failure, LEADER_Failure, SLAVE_Failure, SINK_discon, etc.). Upon execution of these events, the value of the variable *status* is changed. As soon as a sink failure is detected, as modelled by the new event SINK_Failure_Reconfiguration, the "new" leader chosen from one of its slave drones. In this case, *slaves_of_leaders* variable as well as *leaders*, *slaves* and *leader_alt* variables are updated. Similarly, SLAVE_Failure_Reconfiguration and LEADER_Failure_Reconfiguration events are introduced to model a slave and sink failure reconfiguration, correspondingly. An excerpt from the first refinement step is presented in Fig. 4.

```
Machine SwarmOfDrones_m1 refines SwarmOfDrones_m0 Sees SwarmOfDrones_c1
Variables phase, mode, drones, sink, leaders, slaves, status, slaves_of_leaders, sink_alt, ...
Invariants
mode ⊆ MODES ∧ drones ⊆ SWARM ∧ leaders ⊆ drones ∧ slaves ⊆ drones ∧
sink ∈ drones ∧ sink_alt ∈ drones ∧ slaves_of_leaders ∈ leaders → ℙ(slaves) ∧
∀ sl. sl ∈ slaves  ⇒  (∃ ld. ld ∈ leaders  ∧  sl ∈ slaves_of_leaders(ld)) ∧
status ∈ drones → STATUSES  ∧ ...
Events
SINK_Failure_Reconfiguration ≙
  any  ld_alt, new_ld_alt, sls
  where  ... ∧ status(sink) = FAILED ∧ status(sink_alt) = OK∧
  sls = slaves_of_leader(sink_alt) \ {ld_alt} ∧ ld_alt = leader_alt(sink_alt) ∧ new_ld_alt ∈ sls
  then
    sink := sink_alt
    sink_alt := ld_alt
    leaders := (leaders \ {sink_alt}) ∪ {ld_alt}
    slaves := slaves \ {ld_alt}
    leader_alt(ld_alt) := new_ld_alt
    slaves_of_leader := ({sink_alt} ◁ slaves_of_leader) ∪ {ld_alt ↦ sls}
  end
...
```

Fig. 4. The machine SwarmOfDrones_m1

At this refinement step we formulate and prove the correctness of coordinated reconfiguration involving all the layers of the architecture. For instance, we prove invariant property (3) stating that no slaves become dispatched from some leader:

$$\forall\ sl.\ sl \in slaves\ \Rightarrow\ (\exists\ ld.\ ld \in leaders\ \wedge\ sl \in slaves\_of\_leaders(ld)). \quad (3)$$

5.3 Multi-level Drone Communication Modelling

Now we discus communication between the sink and NC as well as communication between the drones. We present a simple communication scheme that can be instantiated to implement communication between the drones at any level.

Lets consider *Sink-Leader* communication. At every cycle, the sink initiates the communication with a leader. The sink checks status of a leader and if it is *OK*, then the sink sends the data via the inter-drone communication link. Upon delivery of the message, a leader updates its route commands and sends the acknowledgement to the sink. In its turn, the sink waits for the acknowledgement from a leader. Upon receiving the acknowledgement, the sink considers the data transition to be successfully completed. If no acknowledgement is received, the sink triggers the transition to *Leader Failure* mode.

The communication between the leaders and their slaves as well as between NC and the sink can be implemented in the similar way. Here we assume that the communication between drones is reliable, i.e., no sent message is lost. We could also consider communication failures, as we did it in, e.g., [17]. However, since communication failures and recovery are not the main focus of this work, for the sake of simplicity we decided not to include them into the model.

5.4   Data Modelling and Introducing Reflexes Mechanisms

In the further refinement steps, we model data flow between all system components at the different layers presented in Fig. 2 and also specify the local drone safety reflexes mechanisms.

To goal of the mission to produce the payload data. As a part of the mission, the drones periodically send the collected data to DC. Upon receiving these data, DC makes a decision to recalculate the current route commands or restructure drone tree-structure. To reflect the required data flow, we introduce a number of events and variables and refine our model.

Moreover, for each drone, we model possibility to react on particular hazardous situations – an unexpected appearance of an obstacle in the drone flying zone. In our proposed approach, when a drone detects a possible collision with an unforeseen obstacle, the drone safety reflex computation module quickly computes a reflex movement for the drone to prevent the collision.

To model drone safety reflex mechanisms, first we model possibility of appearing an obstacle in a drone flying zone (at any level of hierarchy). Then, upon detection an obstacle, a drone triggers mode transition to *Reflection Activation* mode. Let us note that the drones perform this transition autonomously and independently upon detection of an obstacle. Upon triggering a transition to this "local" mode, a drone computes the best safe position and moves there. The nominal mode is restored after DC receives the update about the current drone positions and calculates the routing for the swarm. We introduce the new events Unpredictable_Obstacle and Reflection_Activation and refine the number of old events, e.g., Update_Local_Routes (omitted here due to the lack of space).

6   Related Work and Conclusions

Nowadays, the problem of motion safety of autonomous robotic systems attracts significant research attention. A comprehensive overview of the problems associated with autonomous mobile robots is given in [16]. The analysis carried out in [19], shows that the most prominent routing schemes do not guarantee motion safety. Our approach resolves this issue and ensures not only safety but also efficiency of routing.

Macek et al. [4] have proposed a layered architectural solution for robot navigation. They focus on a problem of safe navigation of a vehicle in an urban environment. Similarly to our approach, they distinguish between a global route planning and a collision avoidance control. However, in their work, they focus on the safety issues associated with the navigation of a single vehicle and do not consider the problem of route optimization in the context of swarms of robots.

A formal approach that employs formal verification to ensure motion safety has been proposed by Aniculaesei et al. [2]. They employ UPPAAL to verify that a moving robot engages brakes and safely stops upon detection of an obstacle. In our work we employed formal verification to ensure the correctness of the architecture that supports multi-layered distributed approach. Moreover, the solution proposed in our work is more performant and flexible – it allows the system to dynamically recalculate the route to prevent a collision and avoids unnecessary stopping of drones.

Modelling and verification of a system architecture using Event-B in the context of multi-agent and multi-robotic systems has also been investigated in works [10–12]. Moreover, in [13] we verified by proofs correctness and safety of agent interactions. In [5] the interactions between agents have been studied using goal-oriented perspective. In this work, the roles were defined as agent capabilities to perform certain tasks in order to accomplish the entire mission.

In this paper, we have presented a novel multi-layered approach to safe and efficient navigation of swarms of drones and formalised it in Event-B. We have defined and validated the architecture that supports multi-layered distributed approach to ensuring safety and efficiency of swarm navigation.

We have formally defined the requirements that ensure correct coordination of drones using the notion of modes. The Rodin platform was used to automate modelling and verification efforts. The framework has demonstrated a good scalability and provided us with a suitable basis for designing such a complex distributed system as a swarm of drones. We believe that the following aspects were critical for the success of the development. The first aspect is support for refinement and decomposition. It allowed us to start from a centralised succinct system model and derive complex and tangled coordination mechanism gradually in a correctness preserving way. The second aspect, is a support for highly iterative development provided by the Rodin platform. Proofs provided us with an immediate feedback on our models and helped to spot many intricate interdependencies between modes, phases and effects of faults. We believe that our work has offered a promising solution to the problem of ensuring dependability of swarm systems.

As a part of the future work, we are planing to extend our approach and focus on its communication mode. Indeed, communication is a critical aspect in ensuring coordination and safety of the autonomous swarms of drones. The drones of any layer communicate with each other to coordinate their efficient flying and successful mission execution. To extend the communication model of the discussed system we can rely on our approach discussed in [17].

During the presented in this paper refinement process we arrived at a centralised specification of the multi-layered swarm system. Our next goal can also focus on deriving its distributed implementation by refinement. We can employ modularisation facilities of Event-B [3,14] to achieve this. We can further decompose a system-level model and derive the interfaces of the drones and guarantee that their communication supports correct coordination despite unreliability of the communication channel and drones failures. To achieve it our current work can be complemented with our approaches proposed in [9,17].

An important aspect of demonstrating system safety is its quantitative evaluation. This work has been further extended to enable probabilistic assessment of safety and reliability using Event-B specifications [18]. It would be interesting to quantitatively assess the impact of drone and communication failures on overall system safety.

References

1. Abrial, J.R.: Modeling in Event-B. Cambridge University Press, Cambridge (2010)
2. Aniculaesei, A., Arnsberger, D., Howar, F., Rausch, A.: Towards the verification of safety-critical autonomous systems in dynamic environments. In: V2CPS. pp. 79–90 (2016). EPTCS 232
3. Iliasov, A., et al.: Supporting reuse in Event B development: modularisation approach. In: Frappier, M., Glässer, U., Khurshid, S., Laleau, R., Reeves, S. (eds.) ABZ 2010. LNCS, vol. 5977, pp. 174–188. Springer, Heidelberg (2010). https://doi.org/10.1007/978-3-642-11811-1_14
4. Macek, K., Vasquez, D., Fraichard, T., Siegwart, R.: Safe vehicle navigation in dynamic urban scenarios. In: Proceedings of 11th International IEEE Conference on Intelligent Transportation Systems, pp. 482–489. IEEE (2008)
5. Laibinis, L., Pereverzeva, I., Troubitsyna, E.: Formal reasoning about resilient goal-oriented multi-agent systems. Sci. Comput. Program. **148**, 66–87 (2017)
6. Leveson, N., Pinnel, L.D., Sandys, S.D., Koga, S., Reese, J.D.: Analyzing software specifications for mode confusion potential. In: Human Error and System Development, pp. 132–146 (1997)
7. Majd, A., Ashraf, A., Troubitsyna, E., Daneshtalab, M.: Integrating learning, optimization, and prediction for efficient navigation of swarms of drones. In: PDP 2018, pp. 101–108. IEEE Computer Society (2018)
8. Majd, A., Troubitsyna, E., Daneshtalab, M.: Safety-aware control of swarms of drones. In: Tonetta, S., Schoitsch, E., Bitsch, F. (eds.) SAFECOMP 2017. LNCS, vol. 10489, pp. 249–260. Springer, Cham (2017). https://doi.org/10.1007/978-3-319-66284-8_21
9. Pereverzeva, I., Troubitsyna, E.: Formalizing goal-oriented development of resilient cyber-physical systems. In: Romanovsky, A., Ishikawa, F. (eds.) Trustworthy Cyber-Physical Systems Engineering (2017). Chapter 6
10. Pereverzeva, I., Troubitsyna, E., Laibinis, L.: A case study in formal development of a fault tolerant multi-robotic system. In: Avgeriou, P. (ed.) SERENE 2012. LNCS, vol. 7527, pp. 16–31. Springer, Heidelberg (2012). https://doi.org/10.1007/978-3-642-33176-3_2

11. Pereverzeva, I., Troubitsyna, E., Laibinis, L.: Formal development of critical multi-agent systems: a refinement approach. In: EDCC 2012, pp. 156–161. IEEE Computer Society (2012)
12. Pereverzeva, I., Troubitsyna, E., Laibinis, L.: Formal goal-oriented development of resilient MAS in Event-B. In: Brorsson, M., Pinho, L.M. (eds.) Ada-Europe 2012. LNCS, vol. 7308, pp. 147–161. Springer, Heidelberg (2012). https://doi.org/10.1007/978-3-642-30598-6_11
13. Pereverzeva, I., Troubitsyna, E., Laibinis, L.: A refinement-based approach to developing critical multi-agent systems. IJCCBS 4(1), 69–91 (2013)
14. Rodin. Modularisation plug-in. http://wiki.event-b.org/index.php/Modularisation_Plug-in
15. Rodin. Event-B platform. http://www.event-b.org/
16. Siegwart, R., Nourbakhsh, I.R.: Introduction to Autonomous Mobile Robots. MIT Press, Cambridge (2004)
17. Tarasyuk, A., Pereverzeva, I., Troubitsyna, E., Latvala, T.: The formal derivation of mode logic for autonomous satellite flight formation. In: Koornneef, F., van Gulijk, C. (eds.) SAFECOMP 2015. LNCS, vol. 9337, pp. 29–43. Springer, Cham (2015). https://doi.org/10.1007/978-3-319-24255-2_4
18. Tarasyuk, A., Troubitsyna, E., Laibinis, L.: Integrating stochastic reasoning into Event-B development. Form. Asp. Comput. 27(1), 53–77 (2015)
19. Fraichard, Th.: A short paper about motion safety. In: Proceedings of the IEEE International Conference on Robotics and Automation. IEEE (2007)

Dynamic Risk Management for Cooperative Autonomous Medical Cyber-Physical Systems

Fábio L. Leite Jr.[1,2(✉)] (iD), Daniel Schneider[3], and Rasmus Adler[3]

[1] Department Software Engineering: Dependability Kaiserslautern,
University of Kaiserslautern, Kaiserslautern, Germany
[2] Center for Strategic Health Technologies – NUTES, Paraíba State University (UEPB),
Campina Grande, PB, Brazil
fabioleite@cct.uepb.edu.br
[3] Fraunhofer IESE, Kaiserslautern, Germany
{daniel.schneider,rasmus.adler}@iese.fraunhofer.de

Abstract. Medical cyber-physical systems (MCPS) combine independent devices at runtime in order to render new patient monitoring/control functionalities, such as physiological closed loops for controlling drug infusion and optimization of alarms. MCPS and their relevant system contexts are highly variable, which detrimentally affects the application of established safety assurance methodologies. In this paper, we introduce an approach based on dynamic risk assessment and control for MCPS. During runtime, information regarding the safety properties of the constituent systems, relevant information about the patient's characteristics, as well as other relevant context information is utilized to dynamically and continuously optimize the system performance while guaranteeing an acceptable level of safety. We evaluated our approach by means of a patient-controlled analgesia proof-of-concept simulation and sensitivity analysis.

Keywords: Medical cyber-physical systems · System of systems
Adaptive systems · Cooperative system · Autonomous systems
Runtime risk management · Modular safety certification · Risk assessment

1 Introduction

Medical cyber-physical systems (MCPS) are multiple independent systems that share information and cooperate to render higher-level services that cannot be provided by single systems alone.

Patient-controlled analgesia (PCA), for instance, can be realized by a MCPS through the orchestration of independent connected devices to provide a physiological closed loop for patient monitoring and infusion control [1]. However, due to the inherent characteristics of MCPS, such as high degrees of automation, system dynamicity, and openness, challenges have been raised with respect to safety assurance, which complicates certification and thus hinders easy and wide-spread utilization of such systems.

Recent solution ideas such as runtime safety certification (e.g., Conditional Safety Certificates – ConSerts [2]) tackle the challenges of system dynamicity and openness

© Springer Nature Switzerland AG 2018
B. Gallina et al. (Eds.): SAFECOMP 2018 Workshops, LNCS 11094, pp. 126–138, 2018.
https://doi.org/10.1007/978-3-319-99229-7_12

by shifting certain safety checks from development time into runtime. ConSerts are based on predefined guarantees and demands, which are formalized assumptions regarding each constituent system's environment. These assumptions/demands can be evaluated dynamically and, eventually, top-level guarantees can be determined for a dynamically formed system composition.

Once the top-level guarantees have been determined, the question arises whether they are actually sufficient for the current system context. A PCA, for instance, could be utilized in different clinical scenarios, each implying specific top-level safety requirements that need to match with the current system guarantees. Now we could either go with a worst-case assumption, i.e. take the most critical PCA scenario and derive the requirements from that. This would lead to many situations where the current top-level guarantee would not be deemed sufficient and hence certain constraints would be required (e.g., not allowing the application to run at all, only allowing a degraded mode, or demanding the presence of a human in the loop).

Alternatively, MCPS could become context- and risk-aware, meaning they could be enabled to perceive their context and dynamically determine the current risk and corresponding safety requirements of an MCPS application such as PCA.

Therefore, in this work we present a runtime risk assessment approach for autonomous and cooperative MCPS. The main aim of this approach is to assess the current risk for a given situation/clinical scenario. In combination with a runtime certificates approach such as ConSerts, it is then possible to continuously check the matching between current top-level safety guarantees of the MCPS (which might also be subject to dynamic change due to, for instance, an added sensor) on the one hand and the current top-level safety requirements on the other. Based thereon, a sufficient level of safety can be ensured and at the same time performance and availability can be optimized.

The proposed risk assessment approach is based on a wide set of relevant aspects, such as physiological vital signs, treatment details, context dynamicity, and runtime cooperation features, for defining the situational risk. All these aspects are combined by means of a Bayesian belief network, which supports runtime risk reasoning through its structure, and conditional probability tables designed and validated by domain experts.

This paper is organized as follows: analysis of the related work. In the Sect. 3, we present our approach for dynamic risk management for MCPS. In the Sect. 4, we present evaluation of the risk model and the whole approach. Finally, in Sect. 5, we conclude with relevant open issues and overall discussion about the achievements.

2   Related Work

Runtime risk management has already been applied in several domains, such as avionics [3], robotics [4], unmanned underwater vehicles [5], and automotive [6, 7]. The state of the art shows that it has focused more on single autonomous systems. However, dynamic cooperation has become a fundamental aspect for achieving autonomy because such systems require situation awareness because of the cooperation among different systems.

In our previous work [8], we analyzed the limitations of safety certification approaches as well as dynamic risk management strategies for assuring autonomous and collaborative safety systems. Several works have proposed the evolution of safety contract approaches for open and cooperative systems, e.g. [9, 10]; however, such techniques have focused on the assurance of system guarantees at runtime and lack a deep analysis of the context in order to identify the demands of the situation and derive a complete safety concept.

Understanding the manifold situations for the use of patient-controlled analgesia requires reasoning about sensor uncertainty, treatment complexity, and dynamicity. Multisensor data fusion works [11, 12] provide a comparison among the main probabilistic methods for dealing with uncertainty such as Dempster-Shafer-Theory (DST), Hidden Markov models (HMM), or Bayesian networks (BN). The DST models measures of belief based on the idea of mass, as opposed to probability, which is used in the Bayesian approach. In general, both techniques are found to be robust and show comparable performance in the sensor fusion domain. HMM can be used as an extension of a Bayesian network with three time slices or as a dynamic Bayesian network. Our approach utilizes BN and benefits from the natural framework for dealing with uncertainty and easily understanding diverse stakeholder profiles in the probability elicitation process. We also take into account the widespread adoption in several domains [5, 13–15].

3 Dynamic Risk Assessment for MCPS

Patient-controlled analgesia (PCA) enables self-administration of predetermined doses of analgesics (in most cases an opioid). It has been widely used in hospitals as it enhances a patient's comfort in pain relief for postoperative treatment. However, PCA has been associated with accidents such as respiratory depression (or failure) caused by opioid overdoses. Therefore, several works and health associations [16, 17] have urged healthcare professionals to consider the potential safety value of proper monitoring of oxygenation and ventilation in patients receiving IV opioids (e.g., sufentanil, piritramid, morphine, remifentanil, fentanyl) during the postoperative period.

The main aim of the safety interlock[1] scenario is to avoid respiratory depression caused by excessive opioid doses in patient-controlled analgesia treatment. It is based on the concept of continuous monitoring of physiological parameters such as oxygen saturation (SpO_2, which might be measured via pulse oximetry), heart rate, respiration rate, and end-tidal carbon dioxide ($EtCO_2$, which can be measured via capnometry/capnography). In our previous work [8], we analyzed the most common configurations to realize the safety interlock function. Overall, an integrated clinical environment (ICE) controls bolus doses according to the monitoring of a patient's vital signs data from (a) only a pulse oximeter sensor; (b) only a respiration sensor (capnography/capnometry); or (c) both medical devices. Hence, the overall behavior permits bolus doses to be given only when it is considered safe for the patient and stops the infusion as soon as any respiratory depression is identified.

---

[1] Specified according to the standard ASTM F2761-2010.

3.1 Self-adaptive Architecture for Risk Management

Considering the state of the practice for MCPS in hospitals, we shall assume that technicians have a high level of control over the reconfiguration process. Moreover, our approach assumes a predefined set of standardized configurations; however, the system supervisor component must be capable of demanding a new configuration when necessary. In this way, predefined reconfiguration suits most runtime certification solutions, such as ConSerts [2]. Therefore, each standardized abstract configuration must have a ConSert Tree (CST) describing the guarantees and demands for each required system service.

The reference architecture for the Integrated Clinical Environment (ASTM F2761-2010) defines the role for several functional modules. In Fig. 1, we extended the ASTM ICE manager architecture with relevant components for the scenario implementation (components in red frames). The function of each component is described as follows:

- *ICE supervisor* – responsible for processing the risk model (presented in the next subsection) in order to assess and manage the risk at runtime.
- *ICE network controller* – responsible for ensuring that the functional capabilities are in accordance with the non-functional capabilities. Hence, this component holds a set of CSTs that describe all potential configurations that the system might activate and certify at runtime. Once the configuration is selected, it triggers the runtime certification process with the configuration manager.
- *Configuration manager* – this component manages the current configuration, such as the runtime certification process.
- *Device controller* – responsible for dealing with the actuation communication interface of the devices that control the treatment, e.g., the infusion pump.
- *Alarm system* – responsible for managing alarms according to the requirements of the standard IEC 60601-1-8.

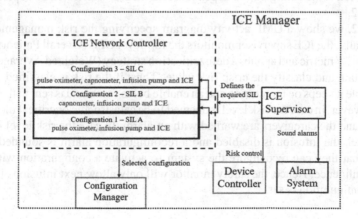

Fig. 1. Functional components of the ICE manager

The runtime certification process can assure the safety of the contracts for the selected configuration. In Fig. 1, there are three different configurations: *configuration 1* SIL-A (lower integrity level); *configuration 2* SIL-B; and *configuration 3* SIL-C (higher integrity level). The hospital staff can switch between any potential configurations. The literature and practical experience show that the most common method for PCA treatment is the configuration 1. However, the configuration manager is responsible for monitoring any changes in the running system and notifies the ICE network controller so that it triggers the recertification process according to the respective CST.

We specify the ICE supervisor component such that it can improve the decision making in terms of (1) changing the configuration in order to better support PCA treatment and pain relief; and (2) deciding when the opioid infusion should be provided to the patient.

The risk control actions must be specified according to their integrity level and the different risk levels measured for the situation. For the safety interlock scenario, we consider three different types of actions:

a. Sounding alarms – Risk alarms are sounded when a new configuration is required; in addition, functional alarms are sounded to warn caregivers about the situation status.
b. Disabling infusion – An intermediate risk control action to disable further required infusion does not require sudden stopping of any ongoing infusion.
c. Stop infusion – Stopping any ongoing infusion is the action with the highest integrity level because it is associated with the most critical risk levels. We assume that taking this action implies disabling any required infusion and sounding an alarm with the highest level of criticality.

The dynamic risk management approach monitors the risk at runtime and then take control actions based on the risk levels and the current configuration. The basis for the risk evaluation is the configuration dependent risk metric, which will be depicted in the Subsect. 3.2.

Figure 2, we show a UML activity diagram specifying the risk management algorithm. Initially, the ICE supervisor monitors the top-level OPC (Overall Patient Context) node of the risk metric and applies a defuzzification strategy (Weighted Average Method [19]) to obtain and classify the crisp risk value. Thus, if the risk is classified as Minor or Negligible it keeps on monitoring and an enable bolus command is sent to the infusion pump. However, in case the risk level is deemed to be catastrophic or critical the infusion is stopped and the caregivers are warned with an alarm. In case the risk level reaches a serious level, the infusion is disabled and a reconfiguration alarm is sounded to caregivers so that they can reconfigure the system to activate a configuration with higher level of confidence. Hence, the safety monitor will only allow next infusions in case of a new reconfiguration is set.

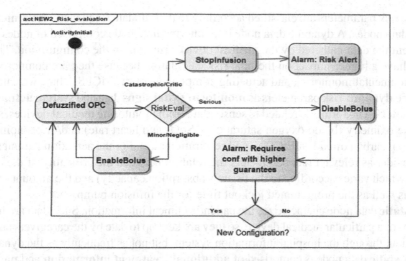

Fig. 2. Algorithm for runtime risk management in the ICE supervisor

3.2 Risk Metrics for PCA

The risk metric was implemented using a Bayesian network based on a tree structure that identifies the probability distribution nodes and relations. We also defined that each abstract configuration must have its own risk metric and that the reconfiguration process defines the transition from one risk metric to another.

The Fig. 3 depicts a logical representation of the risk metric for the configuration 3, which utilizes all possible monitoring medical devices. The top target node (black node) represents an abstraction of the overdosage risk. The intermediate nodes are dark gray and represent the aggregation of different risk parameters defined by medical experts. The bottom-level are the observable risk parameters (light gray) that represent data gathered from sensors and actuators.

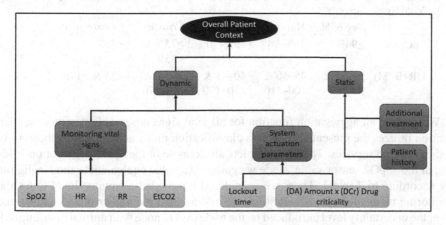

Fig. 3. Logical view of the risk metric for configuration 3

The risk parameters are classified according to their update frequency: **dynamic** and **static** data nodes. A dynamic data node is an intermediate node comprised of nodes that represent the data gathered by the medical devices running in the configuration. These nodes have a higher impact on the final risk calculation because they are composed of the fundamental monitoring and actuating components of the MCPS. Thus, we categorized the **dynamic** risk parameters as **monitoring vital signs** data and **system actuation parameters**. The former is related to sensor data from monitoring medical devices, such as pulse oximetry (blood oxygen saturation – SpO_2 and heart rate) and/or capnometry (end-tidal carbon dioxide – $EtCO_2$ – and respiration rate). For the actuation parameters, we consider as relevant risk parameters the relation between the criticality of the drug types (which varies according to the tissue's absorption capacity) and the amount of the dose, as well as the programmed lockout time for the infusion pump.

A **static** data node characterizes the patient's clinical information. Such data are independent of a particular medical device, so they are kept up to date by the caregivers and/or the patient through the hospital information system, but not as frequently as the dynamic data. A **static** data node is comprised of **additional treatment information** and **patient history**. **Additional treatment** is comprised of risk parameters such as the amount of oxygen supplement the patient is receiving and/or any further relevant medication that might increase the risk of respiration depression, such as diazepam. **Patient history data** that can be relevant for the risk of respiration depression includes age, weight, and some apnea history. In terms of risk calculation, we considered a three-class of risk classification (Negligible, Minor, Serious) for all child nodes of the static data; its impact on the overall risk calculation is lower than the relevance of the dynamic data node.

For the observable nodes, we also classified the whole data range measured by the sensors according to a five-class risk classification (derived from EN ISO 14971:2012 severity classes). For example, for blood oxygen saturation (SpO_2), the range of values is from 0% to 100%. The medical experts assigned the value ranges according to the risk of respiration depression. In Table 1, we present examples for SpO_2 and $EtCO_2$ value range classification.

Table 1. Example of five-class risk classification ranges.

Vital sign	Severity				
	Negligible	Minor	Serious	Critical	Catastrophic
SpO_2 (%)	≥94%	91%–94%	85%–90%	≥75% & <85%	<75%
HR (BPM)	50–55 & 90–100	45–50 & 100–110	40–45 & 110–130	35–40 & 130–170	<35 & >170

We derived an aggregation function for all vital signs observable parameters, such function utilizes the presented five-class classification range and considers uncertainty by the provided services. The Fig. 4 depicts an example of the SpO2 aggregation function, in the "SpO2 sensor value" node we gathered a value equivalent to the Negligible risk according to Table 1. Then, we considered a provided guarantee level C for the monitoring medical device. In addition, we assume that the higher the guarantee, the lower the uncertainty level introduced by the node (SpO2 node with normal distribution). The result for the measurement is actually a normal distribution of the likelihood, with the measured value (Negligible range) being at 63% and the neighbors Minor at 32% and Serious at 5%. We therefore introduce an uncertainty level according to the provided integrity level and then provide a more realistic risk estimation.

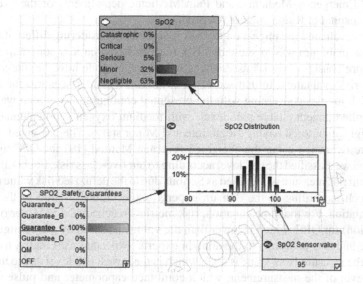

Fig. 4. Excerpt of the observable nodes with sensor value and the safety guarantee utilized to better estimate the distribution of SpO$_2$.

4 Evaluation

To evaluate the proposed approach, we performed simulations in two different environments under the supervision of a medical expert. In the first subsection, we show the BBN evaluations done by means of sensitivity analysis and comparative analysis of the simulation results considering a concrete scenario. In the following subsection, we present a simulation environment integrated with the OpenICE framework to simulate MCPS scenarios and patient profiles.

4.1 Evaluation Based on Configuration Risk

In order to evaluate the Bayesian networks, we applied qualitative and quantitative methods known from the literature [5, 15, 18]. As part of the quantitative and qualitative analysis, we performed a sensitivity analysis to investigate the effects of simulated changes in observable parameters on the output parameters. Therefore, we identified the highly sensitive parameters that have a considerable impact on the reasoning results.

Considering a controlled scenario, we simulated a patient in post-operative PCA treatment and evaluated various respiration rate values measured by the capnometer. Then we identified the most relevant risk parameters of the risk model through sensitive analysis using the tool GeNIe[2]. According to this analysis, the top five most relevant parameters are respiration rate, capnometry, monitoring vital signs, dynamic data, and additional treatment. We validated the results in workshops with the Anesthesia, Intensive Care, Emergency Medicine, and Pain Medicine departments of the Westpfalz-Klinikum hospital in Kaiserslautern, Germany.

We also evaluated the impact on the risk assessment considering different configurations. The main aim was to show that risk metrics based on less confident methods imply a more conservative risk assessment and to demonstrate how the integrity level affects the risk evaluation. In that sense, we evaluated a similar scenario for the three different risk metrics concerning with the presented configurations, which were based on a controlled patient (stable pain level) with medium oxygen supplementation, and the vital signs monitored having Negligible and Minor status. The presented values in Fig. 5 were defuzzied using the Weighted Average Method [19] for OPC and MVS nodes. Then we classified the risk level according to our five-class risk. For configuration 1, the current risk measure is classified as Serious due to the defuzzied risk value reaching 47.15, which, according to the domain experts' expectations, is due to the oxygen supplementation. For the same situation, risk metric 2 reached 42.15 (Minor risk value classification) for OPC, which is lower than the value measured by the configuration 1 risk metric and also conforms to the domain experts' expectations. Finally, for configuration 3, the measured risk value is 40.2, which is the lowest risk level due to the higher integrity level of the measurement, which combined capnometer and pulse oximeter readings. It is worth noting the similar values for the node MVS in the evaluated scenarios; however, these values show the relevance of other contextual information (such as additional treatment nodes and patient history). We can observe the difference between the OPC and MVS in each scenario: In the less confident risk metric

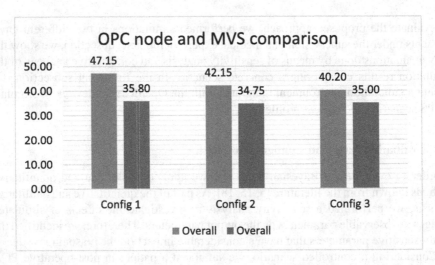

Fig. 5. Comparison of defuzzied values of overall patient context (OPC) and monitored vital signs (MVS) nodes of different risk metrics concerning the corresponding configurations

---

[2] https://www.bayesfusion.com/genie-modeler.

(configuration 1), we gave more relevance to the contextual information, whereas in configuration 3, we considered contextual information less relevant.

4.2 Presenting the Simulation Environment

To support the validation of the approach with the medical staff, we developed a Java simulation environment to evaluate the results from the ICE safety supervisor and the risk assessment model. We intended to evaluate the proposed approach in a realistic simulated environment considering different patient profiles and configuration modes.

For the simulation of the MCPS component systems and the patient variables, we worked with the OpenICE[3]. It defines an integration architecture for healthcare IT ecosystems through a distributed system platform for connecting network nodes with each other. It deals with several technical issues as such node discovery, external interface definition, data publishing, proprietary protocol translation, and so on.

Figure 6 presents an OpenICE GUI for the safety interlock application, which simulates the infusion, defines some alarms and stop infusion interlocks based on respiration rate, heart rate, and blood saturation (SpO_2). In this way, the infusion interlocks are based on fixed thresholds (horizontal configurable sliders in the figure) that we defined together with medical experts. This baseline approach implements a very simple risk metric with a higher level of integrity due to its simplicity and precision on detecting critical situations; however, it does not realize when a situation is heading to a critical status and might thus miss evaluate such situations (emerging risk) as well as constraining the treatment when the patient actually could get an infusion with a more confident configuration. Moreover, the baseline approach does not consider the provided integrity level of the services nor the confidence level of the detection method, meaning that pulse oximetry and capnometry are considered with the same level of confidence. Therefore, there is no reasoning in the risk metric about eventual reconfiguration, which frequently occurs in this kind of treatment.

We developed an external ICE supervisor that is responsible for gathering simulated data from the OpenICE, performing risk evaluation based on the proposed risk assessment model, and showing the risk assessment results in a GUI for evaluation by physicians. In Fig. 7, we can see a screenshot of the current measured risk for the same situation presented in the Fig. 6, but with the proposed risk assessment. Figure 7 shows the defuzzied risk value classified according to the five classes of risk and the time. We can observe that the risk level is classified as Serious, whereas there is no indication of any alarm or measure in Fig. 6 (baseline comparation). The risk metric has a lower integrity level due to the complexity of the risk assessment implementation; however, we improved the identification of risky situations (emerging risk). This fact is due to our risk model considering a wider set of parameters, their relationships, and their weights. Moreover, our risk assessment model considers dynamic adaptation and provided guarantees of the active configuration; thus the risk metric varies according to the reconfiguration, evaluating the current risk and sounding alarms to the caregivers as specified in Sect. 3.

---

[3] https://www.openice.info/.

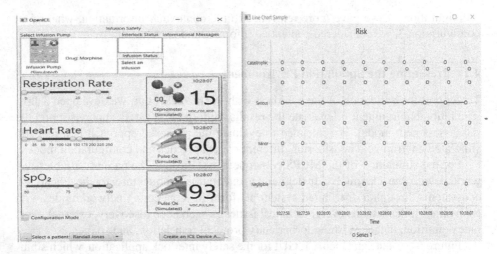

Fig. 6. OpenICE graphical interface of the infusion safety application

Fig. 7. Graphical User Interface of the ICE supervisor indicating a Serious risk level.

5   Conclusions and Future Work

In this work, we proposed a novel runtime risk management approach for autonomous and cooperative MCPS. The approach is composed of a holistic risk assessment model that considers relevant safety parameters with a syntax based on Bayesian probabilistic networks. Such a risk model enables a more complete assessment and classification of the risk of the situations, which enhances both autonomous decisions and the reconfiguration process in terms of runtime safety certification. Therefore, the presented solution considers a configuration's guarantees in the risk assessment, thereby improving the detection of risky situations while the system's availability is enhanced due to the identification of proper system guarantees suitable to the situation's risk.

Currently, we are refining the risk model, taking into account data gathered through simulations, as we are unaware of any available data set with PCA cases considering the data described in the risk model. With the publication of our risk model, we intend to motivate healthcare industry practitioners to create datasets to support statistical tests of ICE monitors. We understand that this is an enabling solution that needs to be refined either in terms of quantitative or qualitative aspects, such as tuning of the probabilities distribution and consideration of new relevant data nodes (e.g., temperature, blood pressure). Furthermore, we also consider expanding the risk model to assess the risk of other hazards such as underdosage and wrong dose configuration, which are strongly related to the risk parameters already modeled.

Acknowledgments. The ongoing research that led to this paper is funded by the Brazilian National Research Council (CNPq) under grant CSF 201715/2014-7 in cooperation with Fraunhofer IESE and TU Kaiserslautern. We would also like to thank Sonnhild Namingha for proofreading.

References

1. Lee, I., Sokolsky, O., et al.: Challenges and research directions in medical cyber-physical systems. Proc. IEEE. **100**, 75–90 (2012)
2. Schneider, D., Trapp, M.: Conditional safety certification of open adaptive systems. ACM Trans. Auton. Adapt. Syst. **8**, 1–20 (2013)
3. Kurd, Z., Kelly, T., McDermid, J., Calinescu, R., Kwiatkowska, M.: Establishing a framework for dynamic risk management in 'intelligent' aero-engine control. In: Buth, B., Rabe, G., Seyfarth, T. (eds.) SAFECOMP 2009. LNCS, vol. 5775, pp. 326–341. Springer, Heidelberg (2009). https://doi.org/10.1007/978-3-642-04468-7_26
4. Machin, M., Guiochet, J., Waeselynck, H., Blanquart, J., Roy, M., Masson, L.: SMOF: A safety monitoring framework for autonomous systems. IEEE Trans. Syst. Man, Cybern. Syst. 1–14 (2016)
5. Thieme, C.A., Utne, I.B.: A risk model for autonomous marine systems and operation focusing on human–autonomy collaboration. Proc. Inst. Mech. Eng. Part O J. Risk Reliab. **231**, 446–464 (2017)
6. Wardziński, A.: Safety assurance strategies for autonomous vehicles. In: Harrison, M.D., Sujan, M.-A. (eds.) SAFECOMP 2008. LNCS, vol. 5219, pp. 277–290. Springer, Heidelberg (2008). https://doi.org/10.1007/978-3-540-87698-4_24
7. Feth, P., Schneider, D., Adler, R.: A conceptual safety supervisor definition and evaluation framework for autonomous systems. In: Tonetta, S., Schoitsch, E., Bitsch, F. (eds.) SAFECOMP 2017. LNCS, vol. 10488, pp. 135–148. Springer, Cham (2017). https://doi.org/10.1007/978-3-319-66266-4_9
8. Leite, F.L., Adler, R., Feth, P.: Safety assurance for autonomous and collaborative medical cyber-physical systems. In: Tonetta, S., Schoitsch, E., Bitsch, F. (eds.) SAFECOMP 2017. LNCS, vol. 10489, pp. 237–248. Springer, Cham (2017). https://doi.org/10.1007/978-3-319-66284-8_20
9. Wei, R., Kelly, T.P., Hawkins, R., Armengaud, E.: DEIS: dependability engineering innovation for cyber-physical systems. In: Seidl, M., Zschaler, S. (eds.) STAF 2017. LNCS, vol. 10748, pp. 409–416. Springer, Cham (2018). https://doi.org/10.1007/978-3-319-74730-9_37
10. Medawar, S., Scholle, D., Sljivo, I.: Cooperative safety critical CPS platooning in SafeCOP. In: 2017 6th Mediterranean Conference on Embedded Computing (MECO)
11. Cremer, F., Den Breejen, E., Schutte, K.: Sensor data fusion for anti-personnel land-mine detection. In: Proceedings of EuroFusion 1998, International Conference on Data Fusion, pp. 55–60 (1998)
12. Challa, S., Koks, D.: Bayesian and Dempster-Shafer fusion. Sadhana **29**, 145–174 (2004)
13. Stevens, N., et al.: Smart alarms: multivariate medical alarm integration for post CABG surgery patients. In: Proceedings of the 2nd ACM SIGHIT - IHI 2012, p. 533. ACM Press, New York (2012)
14. Jiang, Y., Tan, P., Song, H., Wan, B., Hosseini, M., Sha, L.: A self-adaptively evolutionary screening approach for sepsis patient. In: IEEE 29th International Symposium on Computer-Based Medical Systems (CBMS), pp. 60–65, August 2016
15. Brito, M., Griffiths, G.: A bayesian approach for predicting risk of autonomous underwater vehicle loss during their missions. Reliab. Eng. Syst. Saf. **146**, 55–67 (2016)

138   F. L. Leite Jr. et al.

16. Lynn, L.A., Curry, J.P.: Patterns of unexpected in-hospital deaths: a root cause analysis. Patient Saf. Surg. **5**, 3 (2011)
17. Practices institute for safe medication: fatal PCA adverse events continue to happen… Better patient monitoring is essential to prevent harm, **41**, 736–738 (2013)
18. Jensen, F.V.: An introduction to Bayesian networks. Springer, Heidelberg (1996)
19. Ross, T.J. (University of N.M.): Fuzzy logic with engineering applications. Wiley, Chichester (2010)

Towards (Semi-)Automated Synthesis of Runtime Safety Models: A Safety-Oriented Design Approach for Service Architectures of Cooperative Autonomous Systems

Jan Reich[✉] and Daniel Schneider

Fraunhofer IESE, Kaiserslautern, Germany
{jan.reich,daniel.schneider}@iese.fraunhofer.de

Abstract. Future automotive systems will exhibit ever-higher grades of automation up to the point of autonomy. The full potential in automation can only be unlocked when combining it with the capability of cooperation, leading to the vision of comprehensively networked cooperative autonomous systems (CAS). To enable a safe CAS cooperation at runtime, we introduced the ConSert approach in previous work, which allows fully automated safety interface compatibility checks in the field based on runtime safety models. However, a systematic engineering approach for synthesizing these runtime safety models based on design time architecture and safety models does not exist to date. As all safety-engineering activities require the functional description of a system as input, we describe in this paper, how a top-down service-based design approach can look like for CAS, preparing an effective safety analysis and formulation of black-box behavioral deviation bounds in shape of safety guarantees and demands. Thereby, we point out challenges, which especially occur due to the complexity introduced by the distributed development of CAS. These challenges are exemplified for the traffic light assistant system, an example CAS from the automotive domain.

Keywords: Safety interface synthesis · ConSerts · Service architecture

1 Introduction

Cooperative autonomous transportation systems (CAS) are the next evolution step of automotive systems realizing innovative applications, which are subsumed under the term *Smart Mobility* [1]. They aim at advancing the human driving experience with significant improvements to energy consumption, driving comfort or vehicle safety. However, these benefits can only be unlocked by extending the perception and action horizon of traditional systems through cooperation, i.e. both knowledge and capabilities of a system must be made accessible to its vicinity over wireless communication so that other systems can leverage from these capabilities.

The development of CAS is a complex endeavor as cooperative applications are executed on a set of different systems developed by different manufacturers. For CAS it is therefore not possible to completely predict the system structure or behavior already at

© Springer Nature Switzerland AG 2018
B. Gallina et al. (Eds.): SAFECOMP 2018 Workshops, LNCS 11094, pp. 139–150, 2018.
https://doi.org/10.1007/978-3-319-99229-7_13

design time, because environmental conditions such as the weather as well as the capabilities of potential collaboration partners can only be resolved in a concrete runtime situation – when all of these collaboration partners as well as other dynamic context properties of the environment are known. Consequently, mechanisms need to be developed that realize such dynamic context evaluation and system of system integration based on the evaluation results.

Many CAS especially in the automotive sector are safety-critical. Therefore, the assurance of system safety is an obligatory activity before a CAS can be introduced to the market. Due to the fact that safety is a system property and the runtime operational context is at most incompletely known, safety can only be demonstrated for the CAS at runtime, but not through the mere safety certification for each constituent system at design time alone. Consequently, parts of the safety assurance need to be shifted into runtime. One corresponding means are conditional safety certificates (ConSerts) [2] that are a model-based runtime representation of safety guarantees and demands (and mapping functions in between) associated to black-box functional interfaces of a system or to other properties of the relevant environmental context (runtime evidences). By equipping each constituent system with models about its provided and required functional behavior as well as associated safety guarantees and demands, interface compatibility checks can be automatically executed. Dynamic composition hierarchies are formed and at the root nodes of the hierarchies, the top-level safety guarantees for the collaboration at hand can be determined based on the safety guarantees and demands along the branches of the hierarchy. Based on this evaluation, it can be decided, whether a collaboration is safe to run and which constraints or parameterization might be necessary. As safety guarantees and demands specify maximum allowed bounds on externally visible deviations relative to the intended provided or required behavior, a precise specification of the nominal functional behavior is indispensable. Service-oriented approaches are a suitable means to describe black-box behavior interfaces in terms of services.

Even though the ConSerts approach enables the model-based integration of safety interfaces at runtime, the required models and mechanisms have to be synthesized manually already at design time, as the demonstration of sufficient safety with minimum cost needs a certain creativity that machines do not have to date. Moreover, the goal is to shift only those safety decisions to runtime, where design time knowledge is insufficient. Consequently, runtime safety models such as ConSerts should be synthesized out of well-understood traditional safety engineering activities carried out at design time such as fault tree analysis, hazard analysis and safety concept creation.

In this paper, we describe a top-down service-based design approach for CAS, which enables effective safety analysis and formulation of black-box behavioral deviation bounds in shape of safety guarantees and demands. Thereby, we point out challenges, which especially occur due to the complexity introduced by the distributed development of CAS. These challenges are exemplified by means of a traffic light assistant system, an example CAS from the automotive domain.

2   Top-Down Design of Cooperative Autonomous Systems

This section describes a top-down approach for the functional and architectural design of CAS. In order to make the described concepts and challenges in this paper more tangible, a traffic light assistant system (TLA) introduced in [3] shall be used as an example. The TLA's goal is to improve the energy consumption of a vehicle by automatically adjusting the vehicle speed in a way that green traffic light waves can be driven, thus minimizing energy loss due to unnecessary braking at red lights. As the perception capabilities of both driver and vehicle-internal sensors, such as radar or camera, are limited regarding their range, the idea of TLA is to make external knowledge from intersection control systems and/or other vehicles accessible to the ego vehicle.

Connectivity and cooperation are key enablers for intelligent new CAS applications such as the TLA, because intelligent or autonomous behavioral decisions yielding the desired benefits can only be taken based on comprehensive knowledge about the system's environment. This access of knowledge does not only enable intelligent applications, but it does so in a very cost-effective manner, because also systems with limited local sensing capabilities can benefit from rich context knowledge through connectivity.

The remainder of this section will sequentially guide through a top-down design approach for CAS (see Fig. 1) covering the application design of the CAS, the subsequent allocation of functionality to systems and components as well as the implications of the allocation on both vertical and horizontal development interfaces.

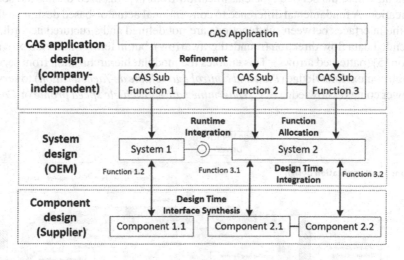

Fig. 1. Top-down approach for cooperative autonomous system development

2.1   Service-Oriented CAS Application Refinement

A cooperative application such as the TLA can only be realized through an interplay of several connected systems, which may be developed in isolation by different companies. Moreover, for the execution of such an application, there are several conceivable system topologies incorporating variations in the provided services of each system and their quality. Therefore, the conceptualization and design of the application itself needs to abstract from concrete systems and thus happen on the functional level, which enables a decoupling of the application's specification from its concrete realization.

More specifically, this means that the derivation of interfaces during the functional refinement of the CAS application into CAS sub-functions is a critical factor for the probability of a successful cooperation at runtime. Depending on its planned capabilities, each constituent system can then implement one or more CAS sub functions (i.e. provides a service) with precisely defined interfaces (e.g. adhering to a standardized service type). If every system manufacturer adheres to the application specification by implementing a subset of the CAS functionality, a successful cooperation can be guaranteed at runtime under the condition that the whole CAS functionality is covered by the systems to be integrated. This means that service types, which represent sub functions of the application, are established as development interface for the system manufacturers. Note that the CAS application abstraction enables successful runtime cooperation without the necessity for case-by-case coordination between system manufacturer companies, because this coordination is replaced by precisely defined interface specifications by means of services during the CAS application design phase.

The functional application design of the TLA is shown in Fig. 2. The TLA's provided service to the ego vehicle driver is the automated control of longitudinal movement to efficiently cross intersections. This is the starting point for the hierarchical service refinement, where the service type classification from [4] was used during the service identification. A fundamental difference to conventional actuator-based design methods is that the interfaces between sub functions are not defined and structured according to the intended data flow direction (rounded gray arrow), but in terms of service provision direction [5] (patterned arrows). This enables the modular hierarchization from services with high context knowledge (*Plan and control ego vehicle de-/acceleration*) to services with lower context knowledge (e.g., *Determine safe ego vehicle speed profile* or *Control*

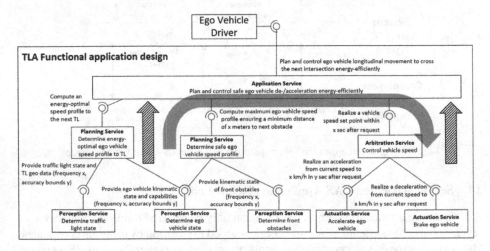

Fig. 2. Functional application design of the "Traffic Light Assistant"

vehicle speed). While the direction of service provision for sensing services (left in Fig. 2) matches the dataflow direction, this is different for the actuation branch (right in Fig. 2), where the provided service of *Control vehicle speed* abstracts from the actual details of how the speed is controlled.

Synthesizing functional interfaces according to service provision has the benefit that the required context knowledge for a function is decreasing in line with the concreteness of the function (i.e. going further down in the hierarchy), which is not the case, if functions are structured according to dataflow (see Fig. 3). For instance, the *Brake ego vehicle* function does not need to know about the context in which braking is required, while *Plan and control ego vehicle de-/acceleration* needs full context for properly fulfilling its responsibility, but does not care of how required information is gathered and concrete vehicle control such as braking is performed. This scheme is analog to the modular-hierarchical allocation of safety responsibilities that is used in conjunction with the ConSerts approach. Each constituent system in the hierarchy has the safety scope of its provided service, including everything below in the hierarchy – i.e. all services rendered by lower level systems that are required for rendering the provided service. For application services, this means that they have the safety scope of the overall application such as, for instance, the TLA (cf. [6] for further information).

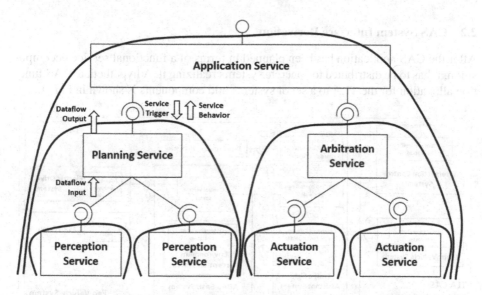

Fig. 3. Hierarchical context knowledge reduction during service decomposition

Another major difference between the dataflow-oriented and the service-oriented description of functions is the perspective, from which the input-output relationship of a function is described. The difference is depicted with arrows at the *Planning* Service in Fig. 3. In the dataflow-oriented case, a function specifies the intended relation between data input and data output. This requires, however, to expose information about the function's realization (i.e. which concrete inputs are needed to produce the output), which detriments modularity and in consequence prevents a strict black-box description of provided functionality. In order to preserve the desired modularity when specifying behavior, it shall be described from the perspective of the service consumer [7]. This means that the service consumer (typically another system or component) can only perceive the external visible behavior through a service interface. For instance, the *Control Vehicle Speed* function in Fig. 2 provides the service *Realize a vehicle speed set point within x sec after request*. This service description does not expose details about how this realization is performed (i.e., by braking or accelerating), as from the service consumer perspective, the service's behavior can only be perceived by the external visible state, which is a change in the vehicle's speed over time after the consumer triggered the service execution.

Thus, in summary, the key trait in using a service concept is that the external visible behavior is described independently from the functional realization rendering it. Due to these characteristics, the service-oriented function refinement has major benefits when it comes to the synthesis and integration of system interfaces across multiple system and company boundaries. In addition, the ability to express black-box service interfaces abstracting from lower-level functions paves the way for a proper identification and description of safety-critical behavioral deviations referring to the externally visible behavior only.

2.2 CAS System Interface Derivation

After the CAS application has been planned in terms of a functional service decomposition, it has to be distributed to concrete systems realizing it. A hypothetical CAS function allocation for the TLA to a set of systems and components is shown in Fig. 4.

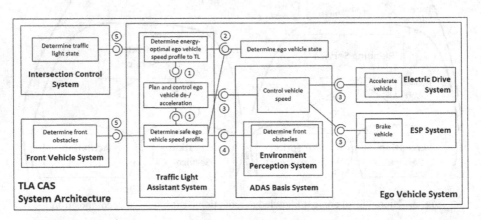

Fig. 4. Establishment of system service interfaces through CAS function allocation

The allocation shows three systems that will execute the cooperative TLA behavior at runtime, the *Ego Vehicle System*, the *Intersection Control System* and the *Front Vehicle System*, which represents a car driving in front of the ego vehicle within the TLA scenario emitting its own position to the ego vehicle via Wi-Fi. Within the *Ego Vehicle*

System, functionality has been further allocated to several components being provided to the ego vehicle OEM by Tier 1 and 2 suppliers.

An important observation is that there exist many different allocation possibilities for the same application. For instance, the function *Determine safe ego vehicle speed profile* along with their required service *Determine front obstacles* could also be executed by an off-the-shelf collision avoidance system, if the ego vehicle was equipped with such a system. The implication would be that the manufacturer of the TLA component could rely on the ego vehicle platform to avoid rear-end collisions leading to a lower development cost. However, this would lead to a lower probability for a successful cooperation, because the TLA component needs to make an additional assumption that needs to be fulfilled by the integration context (i.e. the ego vehicle). Thus, the analysis of multiple allocation variants is of outmost importance to properly resolve the trade-off between cost and availability.

In principle, service interfaces between systems are automatically determined by the mere function allocation to a concrete system and component structure. However, the required level of detail for the development interface contracts varies significantly depending on the relation type of connected systems (CAS constituent system, Tier 1 component, Tier 2 component) and the time when the integration has to be performed (design time vs. runtime). In order to effectively support automated interface synthesis and integration of both functional and safety interfaces, it is important to understand the properties and differences of the interface types.

In general, interface synthesis describes the task, where an interface description is generated that contains sufficient information for the interface consumer to independently perform the intended realization without further coordination with the interface provider. On the other hand, interface integration describes the activity, where one or more concrete realizations of an interface are checked against the interface with respect to consistency and assumption validity in both directions.

For the TLA, we identified five different interface types that can be distinguished with respect to their required properties and challenges for synthesis and integration (numbers in Fig. 4).

1. **Company-Internal:** With interfaces that are generated and realized by the same company, the main challenge lies in making the interface synthesis and integration activities as efficient as possible. Considering for instance that the functions *Determine safe ego vehicle speed profile* and *Determine energy-optimal ego vehicle speed profile* are developed by different business units of the *Traffic Light Assistant System Provider*. These might use different tools and techniques for the function realization, but there are no needs for intellectual property protection within a company. Thus, for an efficient interface synthesis and integration with the high-level control function *Plan and control ego vehicle de-/acceleration*, fully detailed white-box models can serve as a basis.

2. **Tier 1 - OEM:** A fundamental property of this interface relationship is that the OEM generates an interface specification that enables the supplier to deliver a component fitting into the OEM system. This poses serious challenges for the safety mechanisms that have to be implemented by the supplier, as they are dependent on the OEM system context. Nowadays, the safety interfaces between OEM and Tier 1 are often

comprised only of a set of textual safety requirements that shall be fulfilled by the supplied component. However, the resulting requirements do often not contain sufficient information on the integration context to allow an isolated component development. This leads in the best case to correct assumptions about the integration context on supplier side and in the worst case to further information gathering iterations yielding additional effort. After a component has been realized, the OEM needs to check, whether the integrated component satisfies the generated (safety) interface. This includes on the one hand checking validity of assumptions and on the other hand performing system tests, which is problematic especially in early development phases.

In summary, the key challenge of this interface type is to first generate a precise safety development interface containing sufficient contextual information to avoid unnecessary interactions. For the subsequent integration phase, it is deemed desirable to have (semi-)automated integration methods that can check the component's realization against the interface specification. In this step, model-based integration shall ideally be used to detect interface compatibility flaws, which increases confidence in the supplied component before system safety tests can be performed.

3. **Tier 1 – OEM – Tier 2:** This relation type introduces an interface from a supplier 1 over OEM to a supplier 2. The difference to the *Type 2* interface is that the OEM has to generate and maintain two interfaces that are horizontally dependent on each other, because the two components provide a single OEM-level function together. During integration, the integrator has to check the interoperability of different supplied components given the context of the OEM system. This includes checking the validity of assumptions posed by all supplied components together and checking whether the goals of the OEM-level functions with respect to performance, timing and safety are satisfied.

4. **Tier 1.1 – OEM – Tier 1.2 – Tier 2:** This relation type extends *Type 3* interfaces with another lower-level interface, where the *ADAS Basis System Provider* acts as both interface implementer and generator. The complexity arising from this relation is that the interface realization of the OEM interface depends on the interface realization of the *Environment Perception System Provider*, i.e. changes propagate over multiple vertical integration interfaces demanding for proper traceability as first-class objective to minimize efforts for change impact analyses.

5. **Vendor 1 – Vendor 2:** The interface between constituent systems of a CAS such as vehicles from different vendors and the *Intersection Control System* share the property that these systems are developed in complete isolation based on service interfaces derived at the CAS application refinement. Thus, their interoperability can be checked only as soon as they are about to form a CAS at runtime. Since, no humans are involved at runtime; the integration must be carried out fully automated in turn demanding machine-processable interface models. A major challenge for deriving these machine-processable interface models is the required level of precision and unambiguity in describing both intended functionality (i.e., the service) and its deviations (i.e. the safety guarantees/demands) from a black-box perspective.

Note that the identified interface types 1–4 are not new as these are classical interface types that also emerge during the development of closed systems. Nevertheless, they have been added to emphasize the fact that CAS functionality has to be built on top of existing systems, which are developed according to traditional methods and organizational structures. Therefore, the additional engineering activities required for the development and safety assurance of CAS functionality (CAS application design, runtime interface synthesis and integration in Fig. 1) have to be harmonized with the traditional ones by defining clear process and artifact interfaces.

During the isolated development of constituent systems such as a vehicle, this means in particular a continuous model-based synthesis and integration of design time models starting at the CAS application design phase and ending in an integrated design time model of the whole constituent system. Such an integrated design time model consists, for instance, of detailed architecture models, hazard models, failure propagation models and safety concept models. For this context, a conceptual framework (DDI – Digital Dependability Identities) for the synthesis and exchange of dependability-related design time and runtime models is currently developed in the European DEIS project [8]. In order to make a constituent system ready for runtime integration, the integrated design time models need to be transformed into black-box runtime representations of provided and required services as well as their safety guarantees and demands in shape of ConSerts. However, as these transformations will be still carried out at design time, adequate tool support will be necessary to enable engineers to synthesize correct runtime interfaces (*Type 5*) in an effective and efficient way.

3   Related Work

There have been various evaluations and attempts for the application of service-oriented design approaches (SOA) in a cooperative system context.

As part of the EMC^2 project, a state-of-the-art-analysis for the general applicability of SOA in the embedded system domain has been performed [9]. The analysis concludes that a trend towards such architectures can be found but an accepted approach in the automotive context is not presented in the report.

The distribution of sensor fusion across different cars in a cooperative adaptive cruise control scenario (CACC) implemented with SOA has been presented in [10]. One fundamental assumption in this case was that only the environmental situation around the cooperation changed, while the internal systems of the cars stayed static over cooperation time, which is typically not the case for CAS as system topologies can explicitly change.

Wagner et al. proposed a SOA-based middleware solution as well as a development process guiding the creation of service architectures of distributed driver assistance systems in [11]. The approach is derived from IBM's "Service-Oriented Modeling and Architecture" methodology and is called Service-Oriented Driver Assistance (SODA). For the development and documentation of service models, they used the Service Oriented Modeling Language (SoaML). While the SODA approach considers the use of SOA for middleware decoupling, the approach presented in this paper focuses explicitly on the application level, i.e. the decoupling of functionality on the CAS level.

Similar to the distributed nature of CAS having a direct impact on the design process by presuming interface synthesis and integration activities, this is equally true for the safety engineering process. Although the automotive safety standard ISO 26262 describes the *Safety Element out of Context* (SEooC) [12] concept for tackling safety interface abstraction, it cannot be applied as-is to CAS, because it primarily addresses the challenges of distributed development from the perspective of supplier companies providing general-purpose software and hardware components to vehicle vendors. The scope of SEooC is thus not to dynamically monitor safety properties and perform reactions during runtime, but to facilitate reuse of software and hardware components at design time. However, the SEooC recommendation to make safety-related assumptions of a component explicit in a modular way can be used as a starting point for formalizing safety-related assumptions in the context of CAS.

Although the evaluations conclude that future cooperative systems such as Car2X will have to follow service-based design principles for the description of functionality, concrete guidelines are missing on how to systematically embed service-oriented design approaches into state-of-the-art safety engineering processes. This is especially true for the model-based synthesis of runtime service interfaces incorporating safety information.

The service-oriented approach presented in this paper aimed at marking an engineering starting point for the subsequent derivation of ConSert runtime models. ConSerts as described in [2] were used to check during runtime integration of several constituent systems into a CAS, whether the given set of configurations can yield a safe CAS behavior at all. If no safe combination of configurations exists after the ConSert composition and evaluation, the CAS formation is rejected. However, the description of externally visible behavior at the service (and safety) interface as described in this paper paves the way for more dynamic reactions to environmental or structural changes during operation of the CAS (i.e., when the CAS is already collaborating). This first includes the runtime monitoring of the environmental context (e.g. changing weather or road surface conditions) as well as the CAS structure and capabilities (e.g. changing configurations due to system failures or reconfiguration of constituent systems). After a change has been detected, its effect onto the fulfillment of CAS safety goals has to be evaluated. The resulting safety demands, which have to be fulfilled by the CAS, are matched against the currently possible safety guarantees the CAS can currently give (determined via classical ConSert evaluation plus the check of safety-related assumptions fulfillment). If there is a mismatch between required safety demands (for a given environmental context) and given safety guarantees (for a given system topology and capabilities), reconfiguration strategies have to be executed for the CAS to remain fail-operational. The described activities represent the well-known MAPE cycle (Monitor – Analyze – Plan – Execute), applied to dynamic runtime safety assurance. The respective conceptual framework has been introduced under the term *Dynamic Safety Management* (DSM) in [13]. While ConSerts as described in [2] focus mainly on the determination of currently valid safety guarantees of the CAS, DSM embeds the ConSerts approach into a larger context by adding conceptual links to safety-related context monitoring, dynamic risk management and dynamic risk control, which includes the execution of safety-driven adaptation mechanisms.

4   Conclusion and Future Work

To enable a safe cooperation of CAS at runtime based on runtime safety models such as ConSerts, we believe that a continuous model-based approach needs to be established allowing for a (semi-)automated synthesis of runtime safety models from design time safety models emerging from traditional safety engineering activities such as fault tree analysis or safety concept models. As all safety engineering activities focus on malfunctional deviations of the intended functional behavior of a system, the first open question was to examine how the functional behavior of CAS applications has to be modeled to effectively prepare the safety analysis and the formulation of black-box behavioral deviation bounds in shape of safety guarantees and demands.

In this paper, we first gave an overview on the principal activities that have to be carried out during CAS development from CAS application design to the eventual runtime integration. Next, we focused on the service-oriented function refinement of CAS applications and explained the major benefits of service-oriented refinement over data-flow-oriented refinement when aiming for a modular description of functional black-box interfaces. Finally, we described the allocation of functions to a concrete structure of systems and their components leading to a set of system interfaces. We identified five different system interface types leading to different required properties and challenges for their synthesis and integration at both design and runtime.

With a defined CAS functional behavior and its allocation to systems and components as a basis, we plan as future work to perform service-oriented safety analyses to identify safety-critical deviations and consider the impact that the interface types identified in this paper have on this task. Furthermore, we will investigate the degree of how much information about employed safety mechanisms needs to be transferred into runtime to allow a successful and safe integration of CAS runtime interfaces in the field.

Acknowledgements. The work presented in this paper was created in context of the *DEIS Project (Dependability Engineering Innovation for CPS)*, which is funded by the European Commission (Grant Agreement No. 732242).

References

1. Proff, H., Schönharting, J., Schramm, D., Ziegler, J.: Zukünftige Entwicklungen in der Mobilität. Springer, Wiesbaden (2012, in German). https://doi.org/10.1007/978-3-8349-7117-3
2. Schneider, D., Trapp, M.: Engineering conditional safety certificates for open adaptive systems. IFAC Proc. Vol. **46**(22), 139–144 (2013)
3. Kural, E., Jones, S., Parrilla, A., Grauers, A.: Traffic light assistant system for optimized energy consumption in an electric vehicle. In: International Conference on Connected Vehicles and Expo (ICCVE), Vienna, Austria, pp. 604–611 (2014)
4. Back, R.J.R., Sere, K.: Superposition refinement of reactive systems. Formal Aspects Comput. **8**, 324–346 (1996)

5. Feth, P., Adler, R.: Service-based modeling of cyber-physical automotive systems: a classification of services. In: Workshop CARS 2016 – Critical Automotive Applications: Robustness and Safety (2016)
6. Schneider, D.: Conditional Safety Certification for Open Adaptive Systems. Doctoral thesis, Fraunhofer IRB Verlag, Germany (2014). ISBN:383960690X 9783839606902
7. Avizienis, A., Laprie, J.-C., Randell, B., Landwehr, C.: Basic concepts and taxonomy of dependable and secure computing. IEEE Trans. Dependable Secure Comput. **1**(1), 11–33 (2004)
8. Schneider, D., et al.: WAP: digital dependability identities. In: IEEE 26th International Symposium Software Reliability Engineering (ISSRE), pp. 324–329 (2015)
9. Eckel, A., et al.: State of the art and SoA architecture requirements report. Edited by EMC2 Project Consortium (2014)
10. Röckl, M., Gacnik, J., Schomerus, J.: Integration of Car-2-Car communication as a virtual sensor in automotive sensor fusion for advanced driver assistance systems. In: Proceedings of FISITA 2008. Springer Automotive Media (2008)
11. Wagner, M., Zobel, D., Meroth, A.: SODA: service-oriented architecture for runtime adaptive driver assistance systems. In: 2014 IEEE 17th International Symposium on Object/Component/Service-Oriented Real-Time Distributed Computing. Institute of Electrical and Electronics Engineers (IEEE) (2014)
12. International Organization for Standardization: ISO 26262-10 Clause 9: Road Vehicles - Functional Safety – Safety Element out of Context Development (2010)
13. Trapp, M., Weiss, G., Schneider, D.: Towards safety-awareness and dynamic safety management. In: Proceedings of IEEE 14th European Dependable Computing Conference (EDCC) (2018, to be published)

Co-Engineering-in-the-Loop

Thomas Gruber[1(✉)], Christoph Schmittner[1], Martin Matschnig[2],
and Bernhard Fischer[2]

[1] AIT Austrian Institute of Technology GmbH, Giefinggasse 4, 1210 Vienna, Austria
{thomas.gruber,christoph.schmittner}@ait.ac.at
[2] Siemens Aktiengesellschaft Österreich, Siemensstraße 90, 1210 Vienna, Austria
{martin.matschnig,bernhard.bf.fischer}@siemens.com

Abstract. System safety standards have been available for two decades. Remarkably, none of the functional safety standards gave detailed guidance on how to treat potential security risks; security was – if at all – only mentioned in a small remark. However, the way how systems are built has changed; today's safety-critical systems are more and more integrated in networks and, thus, the old paradigm of isolated systems is not any more valid. It has been recognized that safety and security, and since recently also performance, need to be treated in combination: Co-engineering is required. After a short glance at the state of the art in co-engineering methods and in respective standardization, the paper describes the approach of co-engineering with interaction points taken in the ECSEL project AQUAS, which has been running since May 2017. The methodology is illustrated with first details on how the co-engineering approach for the concept phase is realized in the industrial drive use case provided by Siemens AG Austria.

Keywords: Co-engineering · Product lifecycle · Industrial drives · Safety
Security · Performance · Interaction point

1 Introduction

System safety considerations look back on a long tradition; the first edition of the generic Functional Safety standard IEC 61508 [1] was issued in 1998. However, none of the Functional safety standards gave detailed guidance on how to treat potential security risks; security was – if at all – only mentioned in a small remark. Instead, the assumption was that safety-critical systems usually have to be separated from the outside world in a way that attacks that could compromise them were possible only with physical access.

The way how systems are communicating has changed; today's safety-critical systems are more and more integrated in networks and, thus, the old paradigm of isolated systems is not any more valid (e.g. Industry 4.0 [21]). Real events like the steel mill attack in Germany [2] or hackers causing power outages [22] attracted attention even in a wider public. It is therefore increasingly understood that attacks can compromise safety and, therefore, security considerations are inevitably necessary also for safety-critical systems.

© Springer Nature Switzerland AG 2018
B. Gallina et al. (Eds.): SAFECOMP 2018 Workshops, LNCS 11094, pp. 151–163, 2018.
https://doi.org/10.1007/978-3-319-99229-7_14

Several research projects like MERGE [9], AMASS [25] or AQUAS [27] have treated or are currently dealing with co-engineering, i.e. the concurrent treatment of more than one quality attribute in order to address risks of different origin. Primary target of the projects was the interplay between safety and security, but in recent projects like AMASS and AQUAS, the scope has been conceptually extended to cover more quality attributes, in particular performance. The problem the projects are trying to solve is that solutions like for instance risk mitigation measures targeting one quality attribute often have a negative impact on another one [26]. These trade-offs need to be handled properly, and the projects try out different approaches to reach a balanced set of measures addressing the different concerns.

This paper presents the concepts of the interaction-point-based safety-security-performance co-engineering approach that is currently being elaborated in the AQUAS project. It is structured as follows: Sect. 2 describes existing approaches for co-engineering and current guidance given by standards. Section 3 introduces the general AQUAS approach for co-engineering and explains then its application in the industrial drive case study for the concept phase. An outlook on future work is given in Sect. 4.

2   State of the Art

As explained above, the industry relied for a long time on the paradigm that safety-critical systems are separated from the outside world. With today's systems getting more and more networked attacks can compromise system safety. Thorough security analysis and the respective risk prevention and risk mitigation measures must therefore be deployed for safety-critical systems. Safety and security measures require the reservation of performance-related capabilities in order to provide their service when needed. For example, a safely-limited speed function (IEC 61800 - Adjustable speed electrical power drive systems [3]) for e-motors has to take action very quickly, but should not deteriorate the overall system function (e.g. the positioning of a motor axis should still be precise). In the industrial domain one of the most important performance factors is the cycle response time in control loops (hard real-time), which is impacted by both, safety and security measures. State-of-the-art approaches treat the approximation of performance by simulation and experience data and they handle safety and security separately. This means that the design cycle has to be run several times and even then the gained results might differ at a large scope from what was originally intended.

As said in the Introduction, the mutual influence between the measures addressing various quality attributes made a trade-off analysis necessary. This leads to the concept of co-engineering, for which different approaches are under development in several research projects. Also standardization groups from different domains have reacted and they are offering guidance for treating security in safety-critical systems. The following subsections explain some of these developments.

2.1 Co-engineering

Co-engineering means that, in a system development phase, the engineering processes targeting different quality attributes are not anymore performed with high independence, but there are interactions of some kind between them. In the following, three existing co-engineering approaches are outlined shortly. They focus on the mutual influence between safety and security. The interrelation of these two quality attributes has hardly been studied up to now except for performance in the sense of human performance in the context of safety management.

SAHARA (Security Aware Hazard Analysis and Risk Assessment). [8] presents a framework for the security aware identification of safety hazards for the automotive domain. The method enhances the inductive analysis method HARA (Hazard Analysis and Risk Assessment), which is requested by ISO 26262 [6], to cover also threats defined in Microsoft's Threat Model STRIDE (Spoofing identity, Tampering with data, Repudiation, Information disclosure, Denial of service and Elevation of privilege) [7]. The STRIDE approach allows quantifying the probability of occurrence and the impacts of security issues on safety concepts (safety goals). Each system component is analysed for its susceptibility to threats and, subsequently, all identified threats can be mitigated to ensure system security.

FMVEA (Failure Modes, Vulnerabilities and Effects Analysis). The safety and security co-analysis method FMVEA [10] was developed in the context of the Arrowhead [28] project and extends the established FMEA (Failure Mode and Effects Analysis, see for instance [11]) with security related threat modes.

The failure part of the method consists, like in the FMEA, of failure cause, failure mode, and effect. The novelty is that security related parts are added here, including vulnerability, threat agent, threat mode and effect. Depending on the level of analysis, a vulnerability can be an architectural weakness or a known software vulnerability. Compared to safety, security requires not only a weakness but also an element, which is exploiting this weakness. This can be a software or a human attacker.

Different threat modelling concepts can be used for the identification of threat modes such as CIA (confidentiality, integrity, availability) [12], summarizing security properties an attack could exploit, or also STRIDE. Based on the severity of the effect, measured in terms of financial damage, loss of confidentiality or privacy and on the operational or safety impact and, finally, the likelihood of the failure or threat, the criticality is measured. In the likelihood context, the system properties and attacker properties have to be investigated. As a result, the FMVEA yields a semi-quantitative measure for the risk of each individual threat and failure mode, and, accordingly, security controls can be chosen based on the associated risk.

The Communication Approach of SAE J3061. The Automotive security guidebook SAE J3061 [13] provides flexible guidelines for treating security in automotive systems. One of the recommended practices is a safety-security co-engineering process with "potential communication paths" between the yet separate safety- and security-related lifecycles.

These "potential communication paths" activities correspond to the "interaction points", which are defined for the AQUAS approach. AQUAS, however, has also performance in the focus, which increases the complexity of the interactions. Therefore, the project is investigating ways how to shape these interactions and at which points of the PLC (product life cycle) they should take place. There are more approaches for safety-security co-engineering, e.g. STPA-Sec [23] or combined Fault and Attack trees [24]. We restricted our selection to those most closely related to the AQUAS approach.

2.2 Standardization

As mentioned in the Introduction, Functional Safety standards have a 20 years long tradition since IEC 61508 [1] has been issued. IT security standards like the ISO 27000 [5] series or the common criteria [4] appeared slightly later. The development of targeted security standards for IACS (Industrial Automation and Control Systems) started much later. Here, two standards with relevance to the AQUAS methodology or the Industrial domain are shortly outlined.

The security standards for automation and control systems usually provide methods for security analysis and techniques for security controls. Most of them provide also lifecycle models, which, however, consist of separate process flows for safety and security, connected by interactions.

The guidebook **SAE J3061** [13] provides set of high-level guiding principles for Cybersecurity engineering in the automotive industry and establishes a framework reaching from the concept phase through production, operation, and service until the decommissioning.

IEC 62443 "Industrial communication networks -Security for industrial automation and control systems" [14–20] is a series of standards and technical reports with the goal of improving safety, availability, integrity, and confidentiality of IACS (Industrial Automation and Control Systems). The standards define Procedures for implementing electronically secure IACS. Their guidance applies to end-users, system integrators, security practitioners, and control systems manufacturers responsible for manufacturing, designing, implementing, or managing IACS.

Out of these standards, the main concepts relevant for the AQUAS approach and in particular for the Industrial Drive use case are the concept of partitioning the system into zones and conduits, which allows a structured cybersecurity risk analysis with targeted measures for the safety-critical zones, and the concept of security levels, which links the identified risk to security requirements for the IACS components.

3   Co-engineering Approach with Interaction Points

3.1   The General Approach

The AQUAS approach is based on separate activities for the different quality attributes running in parallel and an interaction point which brings together experts for all concern in order to evaluate the compatibility of the results. Figure 1 shows an AQUAS safety/security/performance co-engineering process with an interaction point.

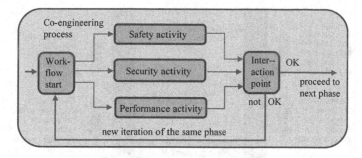

Fig. 1. AQUAS co-engineering process with separate activities and interaction point.

When the workflow starts, activities for all considered quality attributes (here: safety, security and performance) are triggered, ant they run independently in parallel until they yield their results. When all (here: three) activities run for a certain duration, the experts for safety, those for security, and those for performance hold a meeting together in order to verify whether the results of the parallel activities are compatible. This means, they include the mutual influences between the results in an overall evaluation and determine whether the goals of the Co-engineering process w.r.t. all considered quality attributes are met. If they are compatible ("OK"), then the workflow proceeds to the next development lifecycle phase. Otherwise ("not OK") the workflow goes back into a new iteration of the same phase, and all three activities are conducted again.

To illustrate the process, we can think of a safety/security/performance analysis process in the concept phase. They analyze the system model or structure for safety, security and performance properties and yield, as a result, three sets with safety, security and performance requirements. These may be contradictory, and in this case the mitigation measures for the three concerns have to be modified in order to meet all requirements. Therefore, as shown in Fig. 1, a new iteration of the activities is triggered, where the safety, security and performance analyses from the first iteration can be reused but the definition of mitigation measures is different. One of the goals of the AQUAS project is to minimize the necessary count of iterations until the results fulfill all safety, security and performance goals. The better the experts for the concerns understand each other, and the more they already discuss with each other during requirements definition, the easier is it to quickly find a solution compatible with safety, security and performance criteria.

The AQUAS approach is applicable to the entire PLC (Product Life-Cycle). As an example, Fig. 2 shows safety and security co-engineering during the PLC. The approach with parallel engineering processes for safety and security is in line with standards, in particular the guidebook SAE J3061 [13] for the automotive Industry, and the series of IEC 62443 security standards for the Industrial domain, from which several parts are not finished yet.

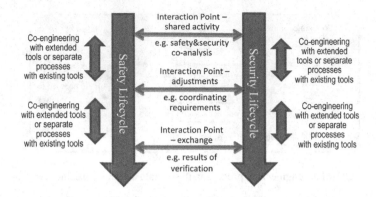

Fig. 2. AQUAS co-engineering process throughout the product lifecycle.

The AQUAS project plans the application of tools for activities. In the above example, a safety, a security and a performance analysis tool could be launched in parallel, and their results checked for compatibility in the interaction point. On the other hand, there are combined methods like for instance the FMVEA, which has been described in the previous section. In this case, the tool implements two activities in one process, in our example safety and security (co-)analysis. Then the interaction verifies only the compatibility between the FMVEA and the performance tool results. By that approach experts may work with their well-known and preferred tools for analysis, while the interaction activities, in this case between FMVEA and performance tool, may apply mediator tools that connect data between the different specialty tools.

The decision whether to use combined co-engineering tools or established tools for single quality attributes is individually possible for all phases. Moreover, the AQUAS approach as such can be deployed for a single phase only while, in the other phases, the company continues using the established legacy technologies, for which the staff is already trained. This flexibility allows a smooth transition from current company practices to the AQUAS framework with low effect on business continuity and low cost for tools and training. The following subsection brings an example for the use of AQUAS concepts in the Industrial Drive use case provided by Siemens AG.

3.2   Detailed Example for Interaction Points in the Concept Phase

Automating workflows across multiple iterations of system development helps to accelerate the development flow while avoiding wrong or incomplete process chains caused by human error in the case of manually managing the activities. The Eclipse RCP-based tool WEFACT (Workflow Engine for Analysis, Certification and Test) support defining the, if applicable too-based, activities in the product lifecycle as well as their sequence (predecessor, successor), and then executing the workflow automatically. The concept allows also forking the process flow and combining the results after completing the parallel activities, as it is needed for the interaction point concept in AQUAS. WEFACT traces moreover whether the executed activities have been accomplished successfully and enables automated iterations in case the overall result of the parallel activities is not satisfactory (e.g. contradictions between resulting safety, security and performance requirements).

In the first step of the Industrial Drive use case, WEFACT is supporting the automated workflow of first performing Safety, Security and Performance Analyses, and finally starting interactions between the quality attribute-specific analysis processes. In case the interactions yield incompatibilities between the quality attribute specific processes, WEFACT leads the workflow back to a second iteration of the analyses. The above explained capabilities of WEFACT allow to instantiate exactly the process flow structure which is needed for the implementation of co-engineering with interaction points. Figure 3 shows an example for a part of a multi-concern assurance process. The process is usually an iterative one, therefore the exemplary interaction points in the figure are traversed more than once.

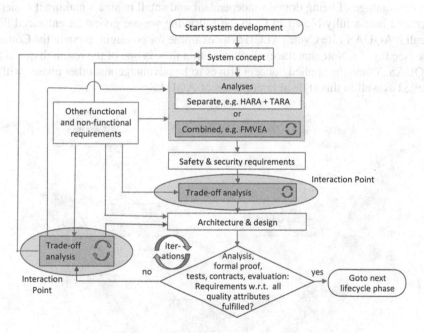

Fig. 3. The iterative lifecycle process modelled in WEFACT

The AQUAS approach allows separate as well combined processes for the individual quality attributes under consideration (e.g. safety, security, performance); at least in the case of separate processes, after performing them, an interaction point is needed to analyze the trade-offs between the potentially contradictory quality attributes treated in the separate parallel processes.

Co-engineering Example in the Industrial Drives Use Case. Within the scope of AQUAS, the shown approach is applied to five very relevant application domains: Air Traffic Management, Medical Devices, Railway, Space and Industrial Drives. Industrial drives are the backbone of many automated industrial processes. Motion control is an essential part for machinery construction and industrial automation. Motion control platforms aim to precisely control electric motors (e-motor) under consideration of safety and security requirements. They are usually realized as Programmable Logic Control applications based on microcontroller, FPGA and ASIC solutions. Typical applications are wood/ceramics/glass/stone processing, handling systems, packaging, plastics and textile machines, milling machines, lathes, handling systems, grinders, laser processing, storage and retrieval machines, extruders, winders, rolling machines, tooling machines and many more. One suitable example out of the domain is an FPGA-based generic motion control platform. This demonstrator acts as a test vehicle for piloting the AQUAS methodology. In particular, a virtual prototype of a motion control system is developed which will enable upfront performance considerations and assessment of safety and security features without having the live system at hand.

The use case follows the generalized product life-cycle (PLC) depicted in Fig. 4. It has the advantage of being domain-independent and small in size – making it easier to integrate it into a fully-blown PLC. In the following we are giving an enhanced flow (we call it AQUAS Life Cycle (ALC)) as an example for co-engineering in the Concept Phase (see Fig. 5). Note that the evaluation of that flow is one of the research questions in AQUAS. When the applied concept proves to be advantageous, other phases will be modelled as well in this style at later phases of AQUAS.

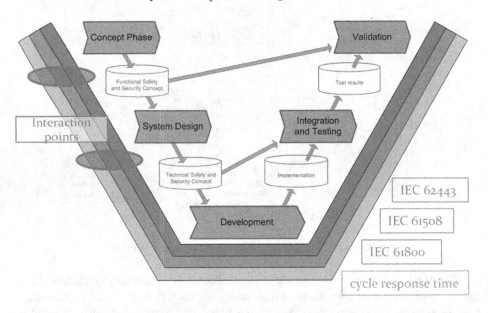

Fig. 4. Generalized PLC in the industrial drives use case for piloting co-engineering

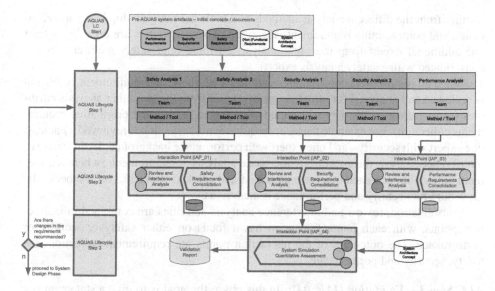

Fig. 5. Co-engineering example with interaction points in the concept phase

Co-engineering with Safety, Security and Performance in the Concept Phase. The major *goal* is to have a well-balanced and stable set of safety-security-performance requirements in place that will hold in subsequent PLC phases.

ALC start:
We start with an initial set of artefacts, including functional, safety, security, other non-functional requirements and a preliminary system architecture.

ALC Step 1 – Safety/Security/Performance Analysis:
The system is analyzed concurrently by analysis activities with specialized methods/ tools with focus set on the system attributes safety, security or performance. Figure 5 depicts such analysis activities paradigmatically: Two for safety analysis, two for security analysis and one performance analysis activities. The number of applied analyses is basically chosen freely under consideration which combination of tools for analysis makes sense. Applying more than one distinct analysis activity for the same system attribute has the advantage of possibly discovering new requirements and contradicting requirements that might have been undetected by applying only a single analysis activity. The goal for each analysis activity is to create a refined set of requirements.

ALC Step 2 – Consolidation, Review, Interference - (IAP_01 to IAP_03):
Results emerging from the various analysis methods with the same attribute focus have to be consolidated and then checked for interference with requirements of other system attributes. In AQUAS we approach that by introducing the concept of *Interaction Points (IAP)*.

The resulting requirements collections that have the same attribute (e.g. safety) from the previous phase are *consolidated*. During the consolidation activities the requirements coming from the different analysis methods and tools are merged, duplicates are eliminated and contradicting requirements identified. These activities are done by at least one additional expert from the same analysis attribute (e.g. safety requirements are consolidated with a safety analysis expert).

When all requirement consolidations are finished, then each requirement collection is reviewed and analyzed for *interference* by expert from the two other analysis attributes (arising discussions may still include the expert(s) from the originating requirements collection). For example the safety requirements collection is reviewed by at least one expert with security-, and one expert with performance background. In this context, interference analysis means a discussion-based analysis of requirements, where requirements that influence each other are identified and marked (linked to each other). The procedure for security and performance is analogous.

Consolidation, review and interference analysis activities are combined in interaction points, with each interaction point has a focus on either safety or security or performance. The outcomes of the interaction points are requirement collections for safety, security and performance.

ALC Step 3 – Validation (IAP_04): In this phase the goal is to give a statement (by quantitative assessment) on the condition and the validation of the current requirements collection and the system architecture concept. The system is modelled based on the currently, preliminary, system architecture concept. Some information on the system is not matured in this early PLC phase. Assumptions have to be made, e.g. timing information for different system components. The better the assumptions are the more accurate simulation results and statements on the validation of the current system architecture against the current collection of requirements will be. That interaction point might be triggered again in later phases of the PLC, when more accurate information is available. Such a re-triggering might reinforce the system architecture concept and requirements when previously taken assumptions were sufficient, or reject the current system architecture with its requirements in the other case.

The output of that interaction point is a validation report that can be used to give recommendations on the current system architecture and requirements. That information is crucial for either a re-iteration of steps 1 to 3 or the advancement to the next PLC phase ("System Design").

ALC – Criteria for Transitioning to the next phase: After ALC step 3, a transition to the next phase and thus leaving the iteration loop of steps one to three, may be done if:

- There are no more changes to the requirements recommended by any ALC step.
- Each analysis method (ALC Step 1) was run at least twice.
- The output of each interaction point is the same as the one from the previous round, i.e. there is no more new knowledge gained.

These conditions might cause some overhead, but with these in place there is a higher confidence for having a contradiction-free and complete set of requirements. Analysis methods have to be re-run after interaction points if the interaction points change the requirement collections, because requirements added, changed or dismissed by a concurring analysis method might be evaluated differently by the other analysis method in place. This means that only after a complete run through steps 1 to 3 without any changes to requirements and system architecture the concept gives better confidence.

4 Conclusions and Outlook

Currently (May 2018) the AQUAS project has just passed the first project year out of three; the consortium is gaining experience and working on the refinement of the inter-action point and co-engineering approach, which has been shortly presented in the previous section. AQUAS goes beyond the scope of SAHARA which addresses only the analysis phase, and it integrates the FMVEA approach as a possible combined co-engineering method. AQUAS contributes evidences to the concept of the security-informed safety case as suggested by Bloomfield et al. [29] and goes even beyond as it takes performance into account.

By using WEFACT, AQUAS provides flexibility w.r.t. manual and tool-based processes in the workflow, without any further requirements for tool adaptation. As co-engineering phases can be adapted to the AQUAS approach individually while the rest of the lifecycle model continues using the established company practices, a transition to the AQUAS approach can be performed step-by-step. This results in the advantage of a smooth transition from legacy to new processes, avoiding risk and cost of a changing to entirely new lifecycle processes.

This distinguishes the AQUAS approach also from the related AMASS project [AMASS], which focuses on multi-concern assurance and develops a model-based, open-source assurance framework with mainly integrated tools and the possibility for external tools to be used via adapters.

In the remaining two years of the project runtime, exemplary processes for the AQUAS approach will be implemented and evaluated, and more development phases will be considered. With experience from the case studies, we expect to have a clearer view on how the interaction points shall be organized and where in the product lifecycle they shall be located. This will enable us to address, apart from Co-engineering and Product Life-Cycle, the third main goal of AQUAS – Influencing Standardization. As mentioned, there are already comparable approaches described in standards, but we expect to contribute with detailed guidance from experience

Acknowledgements. The work published here is based on research in the AQUAS project that has been funded by the ECSEL Joint Undertaking and the Austrian Ministry for Transport, Innovation and Technology (BMVIT) in the program "ICT of the Future" and the Austrian Research Promotion Agency (FFG) under Grant Agreement number 737475.

References

1. IEC_61508-1_Ed.2.0: Functional safety of electrical/electronic/programmable electronic safety-related. Part 1-6 (2010)
2. BBC Report: Hack attack causes 'massive damage' at steel works, http://www.bbc.com/news/technology-30575104. Accessed May 2018
3. IEC 61800: Adjustable speed electrical power drive systems Part 1-7
4. ISO/IEC 15408-1:2009: Information technology – security techniques – evaluation criteria for IT security – Part 1: introduction and general model
5. ISO/IEC 27000:2018: Information technology - security techniques - information security management systems - overview and vocabulary
6. ISO - International Organization for Standardization. ISO 26262 Road vehicles Functional Safety Part 1-10 (2011)
7. Scandariato, R., Wuyts, K., Joosen, W., Microsoft Corporation: A descriptive study of Microsoft's threat modeling technique. http://scholar.google.at/scholar_url?url=https://lirias.kuleuven.be/bitstream/123456789/424554/1/rej-stride.pdf&hl=de&sa=X&scisig=AAGBfm37KabrVfVeveavNgju0SLcmf351w&nossl=1&oi=scholarr. Accessed May 2018
8. Macher, G., Sporer, H., Armengaud, E., Kreiner, C.: SAHARA: a security-aware hazard and risk analysis method (2015)
9. The_MERgE_Project: D3.4.4: Recommendations for Security and Safety Co-engineering (2016). http://www.merge-project.eu/merge-deliverables
10. Schmittner, C., Gruber, T., Puschner, P., Schoitsch, E.: Security application of failure mode and effect analysis (FMEA). In: Bondavalli, A., Di Giandomenico, F. (eds.) SAFECOMP 2014. LNCS, vol. 8666, pp. 310–325. Springer, Cham (2014). https://doi.org/10.1007/978-3-319-10506-2_21
11. IEC 60812: Analysis techniques for system reliability – procedure for failure mode and effects analysis (FMEA), 2nd edn. (2006)
12. https://www.techrepublic.com/blog/it-security/the-cia-triad/. Accessed 26 May 2018
13. SAE J3061: Cybersecurity guidebook for cyber-physical vehicle systems (2016)
14. IEC/TS_62443-1-1: Industrial communication networks – network and system security – Part 1-1: terminology, concepts and models (2009)
15. IEC_62443-2-1: Industrial communication networks – network and system security – Part 2-1: establishing an industrial automation and control system security program (2010)
16. IEC_62443-3-1: Industrial communication networks – network and system security – Part 3-1: system security requirements and security levels, Draft
17. IEC_62443-3-2: Industrial communication networks – network and system security – Part 3-2: security risk assessment and system design, Draft
18. IEC_62443-3-3: Industrial communication networks – network and system security – Part 3-3: system security requirements and security levels (2013)
19. IEC 62443-4-1: Security for industrial automation and control systems - Part 4-1: secure product development lifecycle requirements (2018)
20. IEC 62443-4-2: Industrial communication networks - security for industrial automation and control systems - Part 4-2: technical security requirements for IACS components, Draft (2017)
21. Industry 4.0 – Wikipedia. https://en.wikipedia.org/wiki/Industry_4.0
22. Hackers trigger yet another power outage in Ukraine, ars TECHNICA. https://arstechnica.com/information-technology/2017/01/the-new-normal-yet-another-hacker-caused-power-outage-hits-ukraine/

23. Schmittner, C., Ma, Z., Puschner, P.: Limitation and improvement of STPA-Sec for safety and security co-analysis. In: Skavhaug, A., Guiochet, J., Schoitsch, E., Bitsch, F. (eds.) SAFECOMP 2016. LNCS, vol. 9923, pp. 195–209. Springer, Cham (2016). https://doi.org/10.1007/978-3-319-45480-1_16

24. Fovino, I.N., Masera, M., De Cian, A.: Integrating cyber attacks within fault trees. Reliab. Eng. Syst. Saf. **94**, 1394–1402 (2009)

25. The AMASS Project. https://www.amass-ecsel.eu/

26. Gashi, I., Povyakalo, A., Strigini, L.: Diversity, safety and security in embedded systems: modelling adversary effort and supply chain risks. In: 12th European Dependable Computing Conference (EDCC), Gothenburg, pp. 13–24 (2016)

27. The AQUAS Project. https://aquas-project.eu/

28. The Arrowhead Project. http://www.arrowhead.eu/

29. Bloomfield, R., Netkachova, K., Stroud, R.: Security-informed safety: if it's not secure, it's not safe. In: Gorbenko, A., Romanovsky, A., Kharchenko, V. (eds.) SERENE 2013. LNCS, vol. 8166, pp. 17–32. Springer, Heidelberg (2013). https://doi.org/10.1007/978-3-642-40894-6_2

STPA Guided Systems Engineering

Uwe Becker[✉] [iD]

Draegerwerk AG&Co KGaA, Moislinger Allee 53-55, 23552 Luebeck, Germany
uwe.becker@draeger.com

Abstract. Today systems become more and more complex and networked. This increasing complexity requires new methods for systems engineering. In addition, with the number of internal or external components the probability of faulty components within systems increases. At every point of time, some component may be faulty or does not deliver the desired function. This paper presents a new design methodology to design systems that can handle the mentioned issues of the systems by design. The new methodology is based on System-Theoretic Process Analysis and standard systems engineering methods.

Keywords: Systems engineering · Safety engineering · STPA · STAMP · MBSE
Fault tolerance

1 Introduction

Today we face the situation that previously standalone systems become more and more networked. This is a continuous development. The number of devices in the Internet of Things (IoT) increases rapidly. In addition to be pervasive, systems provide more functionality thereby increasing their complexity. To cope with the ever-increasing complexity, systems are divided into more or less independent sub-systems. The probability of faulty components within the systems increases with the number of their internal or external components. At every point of time there may be some component that is faulty or does not deliver the desired function. The ever-increasing complexity, the increasing risk of failure, and the increasing safety requirements demand for new methods for systems engineering. In this paper, a new way is presented to design systems that can handle the mentioned issues of modern systems by design.

Today, generally, first a system architecture is defined. Based on this architecture a detailed design is developed. Only after that hazard analysis techniques are applied to the design. In consequence, security and safety are designed-in only after all design decisions have already been made. This is too late to result in good designs. Therefore, we propose to apply System-Theoretic Process Analysis (STPA) earlier; before detailed design decisions are made. The early application of STPA will result in better design and increased safety of the designs because safety requirements are considered a priory and not in retrospect as with other approaches.

The paper is organized as follows. Some basics of STPA and MBSE are given in the next section. The general design algorithm is described in Sect. 3. This is followed by the description of a real-world design example in Sect. 4. Section 4 itself is divided into

© Springer Nature Switzerland AG 2018
B. Gallina et al. (Eds.): SAFECOMP 2018 Workshops, LNCS 11094, pp. 164–176, 2018.
https://doi.org/10.1007/978-3-319-99229-7_15

several sub-sections each of which represents a step of the design algorithm proposed such as the definition of the design space, the reduction of the design space, and the optimization of the design. The paper concludes with a summary.

2 STPA and MBSE

2.1 Basics

Both System Theoretic Process Analysis (STPA) and Model-Based Systems Engineering (MBSE) have a system-theoretic background. Therefore, in this paper a method is presented that combines both approaches. Usually designs are optimized for space, for cost, or for another metric. In general, traditional approaches first optimize designs for the metrics described and afterwards try to make the design safe or secure. This design flow poses the risk that design decisions may have been different and even may have led to better designs when safety had been taken into account earlier. Thus, we propose STPA-guided systems engineering.

STPA [1, 2, 5] focuses on analyzing the dynamic behavior of systems. STPA is a top-down method based on systems theory rather than on reliability theory. It uses a model of the system that consists of a functional control diagram instead of a physical component diagram used by other hazard analysis methods. STPA considers safety as a system's control (constraint) problem rather than a component failure problem.

The contemporary world is crowded of large, interdisciplinary, complex systems made of personnel, hardware, software, information, processes, and facilities. An integrated holistic approach is crucial to develop these systems and take proper account of their multifaceted nature and numerous interrelationships [11]. Complexity and the system's extent continually grow. This ever-increasing multidimensional complexity of today's systems demands for adequate design methods. Model-based systems engineering (MBSE) is widely accepted to be a well-suited design methodology for modern systems [12].

2.2 Related Work

There is quite a lot of literature that performs retrospective STPA analysis on accidents or designs e.g. [7, 8]. Even the invention of the approach is based on retrospective analysis [2, 5, 10]. Retrospective analysis can be used as justification to introduce STPA into the development cycle. Many examples can be found in literature that describe success stories of STPA-guided development e.g. [3, 4, 9]. STPA may also help to speed up the certification process [6].

Even though some authors just see MBSE as only an emerging discipline [11] it is already widely used in industry [12]. In the automotive industry as well as in aircraft industry it is seen as the only way to handle the complexity of today's systems. MBSE and STPA both are based on systems theory. Nevertheless, only few literatures exist that combine the two [10]. To our knowledge no literature exists that uses the combination as early in the design cycle as our approach. In our mind, it is too late and may not result in optimal designs when a design alternative is selected first and STPA is applied on it afterwards. Better designs will be achieved when STPA analysis is performed on all design alternatives. A broader design space may show better alternatives and will allow finding synergies between different building blocks. This may lead to different selection of alternatives.

3 The Design Algorithm

A design problem can be mapped to a transformation problem. Let $\mathcal{U}$ be the unit or device to be designed. Let $\mathcal{B}$ be the input alphabet and $\mathcal{A}$ the output alphabet. Furthermore, let $\mathcal{E}$ be the environmental influences on unit $\mathcal{U}$. The function of unit $\mathcal{U}$ can be mapped to a transformation problem such that an input alphabet $\mathcal{B}$ has to be transformed into an output alphabet $\mathcal{A}$. The input alphabet $\mathcal{B}$ denotes the user settings and/or inputs from other devices to a system. In general, the input alphabet $\mathcal{B}$ is accompanied by environmental influences $\mathcal{E}$ on the system. The output alphabet $\mathcal{A}$ is the reaction of the unit $\mathcal{U}$ on the input alphabet $\mathcal{B}$ and the environmental influences $\mathcal{E}$. By restricting the output alphabet $\mathcal{A}$, safety of the design is obtained. Some of the reactions of the unit $\mathcal{U}$ may lead to unstable behavior or are already unstable or dangerous themselves. The output alphabet is restricted in such a way that those reactions are removed from the output alphabet $\mathcal{A}$ and thus the system avoids unstable behavior by design.

Model-based systems engineering is used to find the optimal system architecture for a given design problem. STPA is a safety engineering method that defines safety of a system as the solution of a control problem. The control problem addressed is the avoidance of unstable or uncontrollable states of the system. The transformation problem above views stability of the system as the avoidance of certain dangerous outputs that indicate or result in uncontrollable or unstable behavior. We will use STPA to perform the restriction of the output alphabet $\mathcal{A}$, thus solving the control problem.

At the very beginning of a design project, little information regarding the implementation of a project is available. A first safety analysis is performed to partition the design into (a few) high level blocks. The aim is to identify blocks that allow independent use of the algorithm proposed such that scalability of the methodology is given. With this information, a first coarse system architecture consisting of the (few) high level functional blocks is defined. Even at this level a first partitioning of the design will be performed. Most designs can be partitioned such that there are areas which are more safety relevant than others. The idea of the STPA guided system design is to first find good (if not optimal) solutions for such parts of the design using STPA. Each partition of the design will contain elements of one or more functional blocks. This (only slight) refinement of the high-level architecture will still contain only a few high level blocks. Multiple design solutions will exist for each block. In the next step, hyper-models that contain all design solutions for each of the blocks will be generated. We now continue with the generation of a control structure from the first coarse system architecture and afterwards perform a first STPA analysis. In general, this will result in a few high-level hazards to be identified. With this information, a first optimization of the design is done. Only those realizations of the design (for the respective block) will remain that are able to eliminate or at least mitigate the hazards identified (for the respective block). The optimization step will also lead to a simplification of the hyper-model.

We propose an iterative approach. The pseudo-code description of our algorithm is given below. It may be required to further divide the blocks of the first block diagram into a number of sub-blocks or sub-sub-blocks (steps 5–10). Normally, different options exist when blocks are refined or divided into sub-blocks. Some functions may be realized mechanically or electronically. Other functions may be realized with or without redundancy. In order to perform optimization steps on different levels and to allow for certain trade-offs we need models that hold all of these different realization options. These models will be called hyper-models in this paper. Hyper-models are generated for each of the (sub-) sub-blocks; followed by STPA analysis and optimization as described above. Optimization will lead to a reduction of the design options in the hyper-models. In the next step, we will go one level up and find combinations that eliminate or at least mitigate the hazards found at the respective lower level. In each iterative step, the number of elements in the hyper-model will be reduced thus reducing design complexity.

Pseudo code of the design algorithm
```
1.   generate architecture proposal
2.   define building blocks of architecture proposal
3.   perform STPA on building blocks
4.   incorporate STPA results into building blocks to miti-
     gate possible hazards
5.   while not enough refinement (of building blocks)
6.      refine building blocks and design alternatives
7.      generate hyper-model with all (new and refined)
        design alternatives
8.      perform STPA on building blocks and design alter-
        natives
9.      incorporate STPA results into building blocks and
        design alternatives to mitigate possible hazards
10.     eliminate unfeasible and unsatisfactory design al-
        ternatives
11.     reduce hyper-model
12.  end while
13.  perform design optimization
14.  reduce hyper-model
15.  select final design
```

At the end (after some analysis and optimization loops), there will be a hyper-model that contains all possible solutions for a safe design. As far as possible, hazards have been eliminated by design. In a next step, an optimal solution is found using model-based systems engineering approaches and methods. To find the final (optimal) design solution for the example in this paper the usual and well-known systems engineering tool Pugh matrix will be used. A Pugh matrix will compare all possible design solutions against each other such that an optimal final design alternative can be selected. With this final design solution, again a STPA analysis will be performed. At the end of the process, when more design information is available, the final step is to check whether the whole design meets the safety requirements using STPA. It will be checked whether the design (as a whole) has introduced new hazards and whether the combination of design elements fulfills all design (safety) requirements. The risk associated with the final design shall be acceptable and as low as possible.

4 A Case Study

The algorithm proposed has already successfully been used in several designs. We use the design of a safe ventilator system as an example to demonstrate the STPA guided model-based systems engineering approach. Figure 1 shows the topmost system architecture of a ventilator system. Patient ventilators provide gas with a certain pressure to patients. The pressure lets the gas flow into the lungs of the patients against the forces caused by the thorax and its muscles. As long as the pressure is present at the patient interface the patient inhales. The patient exhales when the pressure is released and the expanded thorax makes the gas flow from the lungs towards the ventilator.

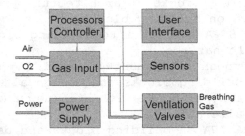

Fig. 1. High-level architecture (and control structure) of a ventilator system.

In a coarse system architecture, a ventilator consists of six building blocks. A power supply to provide power to all other blocks (connections not shown to reduce the number of lines in the graphic). Some processors that control both the user interface and the ventilation functions. Sensors e.g. for pressure and flow provide information on the situation at the patient interface. A gas input block (with inputs for O_2 and Air) is responsible to handle the high pressure (up to 6 bar) gas inputs and to provide the correct oxygen concentration to the patient. The ventilation valves block consists of different valves to control inspiration and expiration of the patient respectively.

Due to space restrictions in this paper, we will concentrate on the gas input section (module) of the ventilator system. The gas input section connects the ventilator device with an external gas supply (e.g. a wall gas outlet in a hospital). In the first step of the design, just this function of the module is known (step 1 of our algorithm). During subsequent steps of development the system architecture of the device and hence the gas input module become more and more refined (steps inside the loop of the algorithm). In the example case, this would mean that in the second step it is known that in the gas input module pressurized Air and O_2 are mixed to obtain a desired oxygen concentration (first iteration loop). In the next step, it is decided to have the valves at the input fill a small volume (tank) with gas (second iteration loop). The gas in the small volume shall have the desired oxygen concentration because it is directly delivered as breathing gas to the patient. It is essential to keep the pressure within a predefined limit in order to increase patient safety and to protect the device itself. In this step, the first restrictions of the output alphabet are applied. The concentration of the gas shall be within a small tolerance band because both high and low oxygen concentrations can be of danger for the patients. In such a way all the input alphabet, the environmental influences, and the output alphabet of the module under consideration become more and more defined with each iterative design step.

4.1 Coarse Architecture

In the ideal case, the sub-blocks are chosen in such a way that they can be optimized independently. In some cases, it might not be possible to find such a partition of the design and the sub-blocks more or less overlap each other. This will require an additional iteration step to find the final system architecture. In our case, the gas input section of the ventilator system is an independent functional block that can be optimized on its own. There is no need for an overlapping with elements of other blocks. As can be seen in Fig. 2 the coarse architecture of the gas input section of the ventilator consists of four logical blocks. There are valves for the high-pressure gases (Air and O_2), Sensors, a small Tank, and a low pressure Valve. The latter is the valve to control patient inspiration of the functional block "Ventilation Valves" of Fig. 1.

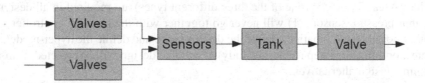

Fig. 2. Input section of a ventilator system - coarse architecture.

4.2 Generation of the Hyper-model

The STPA guided model-based systems engineering approach continues with both the generation of a control structure for the functional block under consideration and a hyper-model for this functional block. This hyper-model includes all options for the design of the functional block. It allows for system simulation during all stages of the design. The hyper-model is partitioned into logical sub-components or sub-blocks.

There are some alternatives in how to design the gas input section. Figure 3 shows all optional components the hyper-model will consider. (1) There can be pressure sensors at the gas input (pressure range up to 15 bar). (2) There may be a pressure controller at the input. This pressure controller will lower the high input pressures to a lower inter-mediate pressure thus equalizing pressure variations at the inputs. Pressure variations are frequent and often have adverse effects on the final product. (3) The input section contains valves both in input paths of oxygen and of pressurized air. These valves are controlled to obtain the desired oxygen concentration. The example design will consider three different types of valves. They differ in the way they can be controlled and in the accuracy with which they can dose small volumes of gas. This has a large influence on the pricing of the respective valves. (4) The less exact the valves can dose small volumes of gas the more desirable it is to have flow sensors to measure current dosage. (5) For device safety and increased patient safety, there may be a tank pressure sensor. (6) The small volume (tank) to pre-mix the breathing gas provides gas for the next breathing cycle of the patient. (7) A valve at the tank outlet is connected to the breathing circuit and delivers the breathing gas to the patient. This is the interface of the gas inlet module to other modules of the ventilator system.

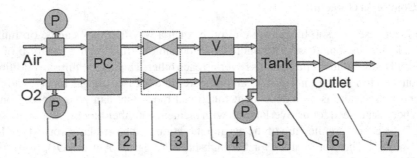

Fig. 3. Input section of a ventilator system – hyper-model.

The valves (7) and (3) (one of the three different types) are required in all designs. The input pressure sensors (1) will never go together with the pressure controller (2). All other possible combinations define the design space and define the hyper-model. In the latest optimization step (trade-off study), a suitable design will be selected from all remaining design alternatives.

4.3   First STPA Analysis and First Design Optimization Step

In our example design, we started with the information to design the gas input section of a ventilator. In such early design phases, only few information regarding the design is available. Nevertheless, two main groups of hazards of the gas input section can be identified: a) the pressure at the patient interface is wrong and b) the oxygen concentration is wrong. Both parameters can deviate in positive or in negative direction from the set value. In general, the risk increases with the deviation of the actual value from the set value. This results in the following three main hazards.

H1: Injury of the patient by too high pressure in the lungs (baro trauma).
(H2: Injury of the patient by not providing breathing gas to the patient[1])
H3: Injury of the patient by too low oxygen concentration (hypoxy)
H4: Injury of the patient by too high oxygen concentration (retinosis)

The design space comprises 33 combinations in total. (One of the three possible valve technologies combined with all permutations of pressure sensors, pressure regulator (only one of the two may be present), flow sensor, and tank pressure sensor.) After the different design possibilities for the gas input block have been identified, an evaluation using STPA is performed. In order to mitigate the hazards the design of the gas input section has to provide sufficient signals to enable the controller to detect faults of the components. Failure modes of valves may be e.g. stuck open or stuck closed. Failure modes of sensors may be e.g. no reading, reading too high, reading too low, and reading beyond the limits. In addition to the failure modes mentioned, STPA also considers failures of the control command. In general, this will include:

activation signal not given,   activation signal given too early,
activation signal given too late,   activation signal given out of sequence
activation signal given not long enough,   activation signal given too long
de-activation signal not given,   de-activation signal given too early,
de-activation signal given too late,   de-activation signal given out of sequence,
de-activation signal given too long   de-activation signal given not long enough

The design vector consists of three different parts: (1) the design description, (2) the cost/performance of the design, and (3) the failure modes covered by the design. Part (3) of the design vector holds the evaluation results of the vector. The evaluation shows hazards still present in the respective combination of elements. It will contain a value of "0" in the respective field in part (3) when the failure can go undetected with the respective design. Otherwise, it will contain a value different from "0". The optimization step will only consider design vectors that have values different from "0" in all fields of part (3). Only such designs are considered "Good designs" because they eliminate all hazards under consideration.

Some combinations are considered undesirable (e.g. because the combination of components does not make sense or is unsafe) and thus these vectors are removed from the design space. Input valves without any sensors are such an undesirable combination. In the case of a valve stuck in an open position, the error could not be detected and input pressure would be in the tank and at the inspiration valve of the patient. This would be

---

[1] Please note that stopping ventilation in case of an error is the defined safe state and thus not considered as a hazard. (Safe states are defined in the respective standards e.g. IEC60601-2-12.) Therefore, it is put in parenthesis. Nevertheless, this situation may be added as hazard in order to improve the design and to increase reliability. In addition, it may be regarded as a business risk because some notified bodies or government institutions (e.g. the German ministry of health) require information regarding interrupted ventilation caused by devices going to their safe states.

an unacceptable risk. The combination of flow sensor, tank pressure sensor and input valve can detect all considered failures. One sensor can be used to monitor the function of the other sensor and the sensors can be used to monitor the function of the valves. E.g. flow without pressure increase detects failure in the pressure sensor reading, and flow where not expected will detect open valves.

The initial phase of STPA (Step 1) is efficient and it does not take much time and effort. According to Asplund [3] in order to achieve the best possible outcome using STPA, the main focus should be put on step 1. We use a similar approach in this design phase. In each iteration loop, we reduce the design space by deleting those input combinations that are not capable to detect at least one hazard. In the final iteration loop only those remaining input combinations that are capable to fulfill the safety requirements are kept. All other input combinations are removed from the design space. In the case study, the design space is reduced from 33 input combinations to 22 combinations. We experienced similar results for other designs. The final trade-off analysis can either be based on the remaining input combinations or on a reduced design space. A reduction of the design space may be obtained based on additional criteria such as pricing, expected precision of control, or a simulation of the performance.

4.4 Hazards Identified

STPA analysis is performed for every design alternative. In addition to the four hazards mentioned, the probability of detection for each hazard is evaluated. For example, if there is no sensor at the input, a valve stuck in the open condition will not be detected. If a flow sensor is added a flow of gas even after the intended closing of the valve will detect the defective valve and thus help to mitigate the hazard. In addition to the defective valve, the flow sensor will also detect failures in the gas supply. If the valve is opened and no gas flows, either the valve is defective and does not open as intended or the respective gas is not supplied at the input of the gas input section.

The combination of a pressure sensor at the input and a tank pressure sensor will detect defective valves and failures of the input gas supply. The combination of flow sensors in each input gas line and a tank pressure sensor is capable of detecting the same failures. Nevertheless, the second option is considered the superior solution because from the flow the volume of gas flowing into the tank may be calculated. This may be used to calculate gas concentration and thus may be used as a second channel for the oxygen sensor. Even though the performance/accuracy of this combination may not be as high as the one of an oxygen sensor, it may be sufficient for use as a second channel and to continue operation during failure of the first oxygen sensor. Knowing the volume of gas flowing into the tank, an expected increase of pressure in the tank may be calculated. For this reason, failures in the tank pressure sensor may be detected also. Hence, the second design alternative is capable to detect two additional failures in the system (independent of the type of input valve) thus increasing safety of the overall design. This example shows why it is important to evaluate all possible design alternatives and select only after applying STPA. Using other approaches, it is very common to select the combination of input pressure sensors and tank pressure sensor (many existing ventilators use this combination at their gas input section). With our approach, it becomes evident that there is a better combination at the input, which is also capable to detect and even mitigate additional failures.

4.5   Overlapping Blocks

As described earlier some functional blocks may more or less overlap each other. For example, a "Pressure Release" block is required for safety reasons. In case a high pressure (depending on the ventilation mode but always below 125 mbar) in the patient circuitry is detected this block will release pressure by opening a path to ambient pressure. Typically, no extra valves are used for this block. Those valves of the ventilation valves that control exhalation are shared with the "Pressure Release" block instead. I.e. both blocks overlap regarding the valves but independently control them.

The overlapping of different blocks may be the result of design optimization also. In the above example, design might at first have required a distinct solution for both functions. For cost, size, and performance reasons one might have come to the solution to share valves between the two blocks.

There are many possibilities to share components between different building blocks. Gas input section and ventilation control section may share different sensors (flow sensors, pressure sensors, oxygen sensors). Processors may be shared between different building blocks. Trade-offs may be required to determine whether elements should be shared or not. In many cases, it might be cheaper to share elements between different building blocks. It may on the other hand not be desirable for safety reasons.

4.6   Hyper-model

We have seen that the ventilator consists of six main parts. Therefore, the model of the ventilator would consist of six sub-models. One for each main part of the ventilator. For each main part there may exist different possibilities to realize it. For example in the gas input section there might be a tank, flow sensors, pressure sensors, a pressure regulation device, and different realizations of input valves and ventilation valves. We found that in total there are 33 different combinations of these elements to realize the gas input section. Thus, the sub-model of the gas input section will be converted to be a hyper-model that holds all 33 different realizations.

It is advantageous to realize models such that they are executable. This means that either the model of the whole ventilator or, in our case, the (sub-) model of gas input section can be executed. Given values for gas input pressure and maximum gas flow provided by the external gas supply, the model will provide values for inspiration pressure, inspiration gas flow, and inspiration oxygen concentration. There is a set of input values and the response is a set of output values. In this case, the set of output values consists of the triple (gas flow, gas pressure, gas (O_2) concentration).

Normally, only one (sometimes idealized) realization or even an abstraction of a realization is used to model a component. In contrast, our hyper-models replace those abstract or idealized realizations with a number of distinct realizations. Thus, the output of a simulation will no longer be a single set of output values. Instead, it will be an assembly of a number of sets of values. E.g. for 33 different possible realizations, the hyper-model will hold all of these 33 realizations. The simulation of the hyper-model will result in 33 triple sets of output values. Therefore, even performance comparison of the different realizations will be possible (to select the final design).

4.7   Selection of the Final Design

The different alternatives of the input Section (1) through (7) form a design vector. This design vector is used to evaluate the design space. Input valves without any additional sensor are undesired because in the case of an error high input pressure will be present at the patient. In addition, the combination of pressure sensor and pressure regulator is considered undesirable because it is a very expensive combination without additional benefits. With the information from above, we know that the initial 33 combinations of input elements can (manually) be reduced to 22 combinations. To select the final design, each of the remaining combinations is attributed with some metrics such as performance (from simulation), accuracy value, and price. The attribute "price" may not only take into account the unit price but also the resulting complexity of the final design. The attribute "accuracy" defines how good small volumes of gas can be dosed. Please note that at this point only a coarse rating such as "better", "much better", or "same" is used. The rating for price is essentially the same. For a given realization, the sum for both values is calculated from the respective values of all input elements in the vector. This simplification is reasonably accurate and fast. Therefore, the evaluation and comparison of the different vectors is fast and efficient.

From the 22 combinations, only nine are on a cost/performance Pareto front. These nine designs identify the designs that eliminate all identified hazards and provide the best accuracy for a given price. Thus, it was possible to reduce the initial input design space by more than a factor of three in this design example. Knowledge from other designs shows that the reduction of the design space is similar or even larger.

In the last step, one design from the remaining nine combinations on the Pareto front is selected for final realization. A reasonably simple and cost-efficient design is selected. The final design of the case study consists of the input valves with the best price/performance ratio, flow sensors, and tank pressure sensor (see Fig. 4).

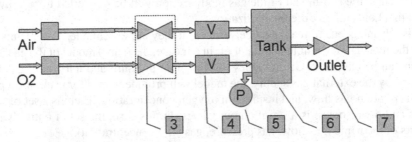

Fig. 4. Input section of a ventilator system - final design.

4.8 Overall STPA Analysis

As shown above, systems design is an iterative activity. At some point of the design, decisions have to be made. Our approach is to use STPA during the whole development cycle and thus also to support the required design decisions. Therefore, after the final design decision for the gas input section is made another STPA analysis is performed. This is to check whether all considered hazards are actually eliminated and whether new hazards have been introduced by the design decisions made.

Hazards H1 and H2 (pressure delivered to the patient is too high or too low) are detected by the flow sensors and the tank pressure sensor. The flow sensors act as second channel for the pressure sensor such that even one of them can fail and still both, the failure and the hazard are detected. In case of too high pressure, the expiration valve can be opened for pressure release or the inspiration valve remains closed.

Hazards H3 and H4 (oxygen concentration too high or too low) can be detected by the flow sensors. The flow sensors can act as a second channel to the oxygen sensor in the "Sensors" block. Users of the ventilator can decide whether to continue ventilation with wrong oxygen concentration or to stop ventilation.

5 Summary

A new STPA-guided model-based systems engineering approach was presented. For the first time an integrated approach, combining systems engineering and STPA has been described. This new and improved method to perform systems engineering for complex designs integrates safety engineering and systems engineering. The approach will ensure safe systems by design. STPA integrates well into model-based systems engineering as both are based on systems theory. The combination of both approaches provides a holistic view both on the design and on safety of the systems and results in better designs. STPA-guided MBSE fits well in the tool box of systems engineers.

An example has been provided to show the application of the new approach to a real-world design. The input section of an existing ventilator system has been used as a design example for this approach. The example shows that the proposed approach is both feasible and ensures safe systems by design. In the current example, we only used design alternatives that eliminated identified hazards from the design. Future work will explore whether it could be beneficial to allow partial elimination of hazards to a certain degree in order to better reach a global optimum of the overall design (when combining multiple blocks of the coarse system architecture).

References

1. Leveson, N.G., Thomas, J., Young, W., Williams, A.: An STPA Primer. Version 1 (2013)
2. Leveson, N.G.: Engineering a Safer World. The MIT Press, Cambridge (2011)
3. Asplund, F., El-khoury, J.: Safety-guided design through system-theoretic process analysis, benefits and difficulties. KTH Royal Institute of Technology, Sweden (2012)
4. Asplund, F.: Safety and Tool Integration, A System-Theoretic Process Analysis. TRITA-MMK 2012:01, ISRN/KTH/MMK-R-12/01-SE (2012)

5. Leveson, N.G.: A new approach to hazard analysis for complex systems. In: Proceedings of the 21st International System Safety Conference, pp. 498–507 (2003)
6. Leveson, N.G.: The Use of Safety Cases in Certification and Regulation. ESD Working Paper Series. MIT (2011)
7. Nelson, P.S.: A STAMP Analysis of the LEX Comair 5191 Accident. Master Thesis, Lund University (2008)
8. Ouyang, M., Hong, L., Yu, M.-H., Fei, Q.: STAMP-based analysis on the railway accident and accident spreading: taking the China-Jiaoji railway accident for example. Saf. Sci. **48**, 544–555 (2010)
9. Pereira, S.J., Grady, L., Jeffrey, H.: A system-theoretic hazard analysis methodology for a non-advocate safety assessment of the ballistic missile defense system. In: Proceedings of the 2006 AIAA Missile Sciences Conference (2006)
10. Ishimatsu, T., Leveson, N.G., Thomas, J., Katahira, M., Miyamoto, Y., Nakao, H.: Modeling and hazard analysis using STPA. In: Proceedings of the 4th IAASS Conference Making Safety Matter, p. 10 (2010)
11. Ramos, A.L., Vasconcelos Ferreira, J., Barceló, J.: Model-Based Systems Engineering: An Emerging Approach for Modern Systems
12. INCOSE SE Vision 2020: INCOSE-TP-2004-004-02, September 2007

A Quantitative Approach
for the Likelihood of Exploits
of System Vulnerabilities

Siddhartha Verma$^{(\boxtimes)}$, Thomas Gruber$^{(\boxtimes)}$, Peter Puschner$^{(\boxtimes)}$,
Christoph Schmittner$^{(\boxtimes)}$, and Erwin Schoitsch$^{(\boxtimes)}$

AIT Austrian Institute of Technology, Giefinggasse 4, 1210 Vienna, Austria
{Siddhartha.Verma,Thomas.Gruber,Christoph.Schmittner,
Erwin.Schoitsch}@ait.ac.at,
peter@vmars.tuwien.ac.at

Abstract. Modern systems' transition towards more connected, information and communication technologies (ICT) has increased the safety, capacity and reliability of systems such as transport systems (railways, automotive) and industrial systems but it has also exposed a big additional surface for cyber attackers which makes it necessary to take in consideration general IT security concerns. Cyber-physical systems need more effort to consider safety critical IT security concerns. The safety impact of security compromises is evaluated in a semiquantitative manner because it is a relatively new area so there is not enough real data available to analyse attack rates quantitatively and the attack-vulnerability scenario is constantly changing because of adversary intelligence. This paper proposes an approach for the quantification of vulnerabilities based on learning from data obtained by concrete pattern implementations in safety-critical systems. This will allow combined analysis of safety and security.

Keywords: Security patterns · Co-analysis · Colored petri nets
Security and dependability

1 Introduction

1.1 Safety and Reliability

System safety has been treated in a systematic manner by Functional Safety standards since the 1990s; the first edition of the generic Functional Safety standard IEC 61508 [34] was issued in 1998. Since then, many domain-specific standards have been elaborated by IEC, ISO and CENELEC, most of them based on the generic concepts of IEC 61508, which relies on process quality for coping with systematic faults and on probabilistic concepts for stochastic hardware faults.

A large amount of work has been done for analysing the reliability and availability of the system e.g. [3,8,9]. In [3] the railway operation is analysed based

© Springer Nature Switzerland AG 2018
B. Gallina et al. (Eds.): SAFECOMP 2018 Workshops, LNCS 11094, pp. 177–189, 2018.
https://doi.org/10.1007/978-3-319-99229-7_16

on the failure and maintenance data obtained from the Swedish infrastructure manager for the automatic train control signalling system. The paper uses a classical state-space Markov chains approach with stochastic transition rates for analysis. Redundancy technique is widely used for increasing the reliability of systems especially in safety-critical systems, which require high reliability and availability. In [8] a hybrid TMR (triple modular redundancy) fault tolerant structure is analysed. A hybrid redundant structure integrates voting scheme, fault detection and reconfiguration together. It uses a partial detection stochastic Petri net model for the system and a state transition Markov chain model for analysis.

There are many approaches for modeling and analysis/simulation of the reliability and availability of systems such as Markov Chains [1–3], eDSPNs (extended deterministic and stochastic Petri nets), colored Petri nets, or Fault-trees. Dependability patterns (e.g. [20]) also exist, which can provide solutions to recurring problems in the design of the system to control faults and their consequences by detection of errors, recovery from errors or by masking the error.

1.2   Security and Security Patterns

Security patterns are best practices to handle recurring security problems. Similar to safety, a large amount of work is available on security patterns e.g. [10–14] which includes a catalog of security patterns and describes the problem (about all the possible attacks) and the solution (how to implement the security strategies efficiently). The availability of a large number of patterns and the consideration of a further increase due to new patterns make it necessary to classify patterns to make the application of patterns easy along the life cycle of software. In [15, 16] classification approaches for design patterns have been explained. In [17–19] classification approaches for security patterns have been described. In [4], a classification of security patterns based on application domains (Enterprise, Network, User, Software, Cryptographic) is presented.

1.3   Security and Safety Interdependence

In former years, Functional Safety standards did not address security-related safety-critical failures in detail because the assumption was that safety-critical systems are separated from externally reachable network areas like the internet, from where attackers could compromise it. In recent years, some standard updates mention at least security, however, without treating the related threats to safety in more detail.

For a few years now, awareness about security threats has been rising, also caused by reports about actual attacks. Currently, new editions of Functional Safety standards which include security concepts at least to some extent are being elaborated. Complementary to them, there are now a couple of domain-specific security standards in elaboration, like, as an example for the industrial control domain, IEC 62443 [30], which gives guidance how to analyze the system for security flaws, how to rate it regarding the necessary security level, and which security controls are appropriate to implement.

The security attacks can affect the dependability of the system. For example consider an industrial drive system with a motor controller and communication networks (this raises a security concern). Figure 1. shows a sequence diagram of the system with communication among three software applications (client, server and motor control). The reliability of the system cannot be ensured unless the given level of security is not provided against security attacks. Therefore the reliability strategy of the system needs to be properly integrated with the security strategy. In [21, 22] a hybrid pattern approach is represented which consists of security and dependability patterns which provide a way for addressing both dependability and security concerns. But the availability of documents containing catalogue of such patterns is not enough and not easily available.

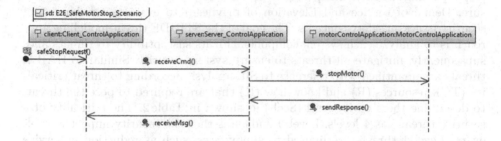

Fig. 1. Industrial drive sequence diagram

2 State of the Art Security and Dependability Co-engineering Approach

2.1 Safety Integrity Level and Tolerable Hazard Rate

According to Functional Safety standards, the maximum tolerable safety-critical failure rate of a component is related to the SIL (safety integrity level) assigned to it based on risk parameters (severity of the hazardous event, exposure time and controllability). The required SIL is determined in a HARA [24] (hazard analysis and risk assessment) in the concept phase of component development, and it is, according to functional safety standards like the generic IEC 61508 [34], directly assigned to a range for the rate of safety-critical failures λ as shown in Table 1.

Since security for information and communication systems in software based control systems in industrial, transport, health and other sector's is a relatively new area, there is not enough real data available to analyse attack rates quantitatively. Some works exist based on data-driven cybersecurity analytics to predict the attack rates, for instance [29] but only corresponding to a specific use case. Therefore, in the state of the art co-engineering approaches, the safety impact of security compromises has been evaluated in a semiquantitative manner, as shown in the next two sections.

Table 1. Maximum tolerable hazard rate (THR) ranges per SIL

SIL	λ [in h^{-1}]
4	$10^{-9} \leq \lambda < 10^{-8}$
3	$10^{-8} \leq \lambda < 10^{-7}$
2	$10^{-7} \leq \lambda < 10^{-6}$
1	$10^{-6} \leq \lambda < 10^{-5}$

2.2 SAHARA (Security Aware Hazard Analysis and Risk Assessment)

SAHARA (Security-Aware HARA) [6]) is an extension of HARA with STRIDE [25] (Spoofing identity, Tampering with data, Repudiation, Information disclosure, Denial of service and Elevation of privilege) to evaluate the impact of security issues on safety concepts. The goal of the STRIDE threat modelling approach is to analyze each system component for its susceptibility to threats and, subsequently, mitigate all threats to ensure system security. Similar to HARA, threats are quantified with reference to SIL analysis according to threat criticality (TC), resources (R) and know-how (K) that are required to pose the threat, to determine the security level (SecL) as shown in Table 2. The criticality of a security threat has 4 levels. Level 0, indicates that the security impact is irrelevant. Level 1 threats are limited to annoyances, such as reduction in service availability of non-safety-critical functions . Level 2 implies damage to products or manipulation of data or services and financial loss. Level 3 threats result in impacts on safety features (impact on human life). In comparison with HARA where the likelihood is expressed in terms of a failure rate, threat models determine likelihood semi-quantitatively in terms of required know-how and tools to launch an attack.

2.3 FMVEA (Failure Mode, Vulnerabilities and Effect Analysis)

FMVEA [1] is an extension of FMEA (Failure Mode and Effect Analysis [26, 27] to include threats and vulnerabilities in addition to accidental or stochastic failures. The system is divided into components, and failure/threat modes for each component are identified. For each failure/threat mode, the severity of the final effect and potential causes are examined. The severity of the effect is determined by the specific industry norms such as ISO 26262 [28]. In safety, the likelihood is expressed in terms of failure rate while, in security, the likelihood of an attack is expressed semi-quantitatively as an Attack Probability matrix (as shown in Table 3) which is determined from two factors: System susceptibility and Threat properties.

Motivation and Capabilities characterize the threat agent and their sum constitutes the Threat Properties. Values for Motivation are

Table 2. SecL Determination Matrix

R	K	TC 0	1	2	3
0	0	0	3	4	4
	1	0	2	3	4
	2	0	1	2	3
1	0	0	3	4	4
	1	0	2	3	4
	2	0	1	2	3
2	0	0	1	2	3
	1	0	0	1	2
	2	0	0	0	1
3	0	0	0	1	2
	1	0	0	0	1
	2	0	0	0	1

1 = opportunity target,
2 = mildly interested,
3 = main target,
and for Capabilities
1 = low,
2 = medium,
3 = high.

The sum of Reachability and Unusualness of the system characterize the System Susceptibility. Reachability is rated 1 = no network,
2 = private network, or
3 = public network,
and Unusualness
1 = restricted,
2 = commercially available, and
3 = standard.

Finally, the sum of System Susceptibility and Threat Properties yields the semi-quantitative value for the Attack Probability, as can be seen in Table 3.

3 Security and Dependability Co-engineering Approach - Proposed

In this section we proposed a co-engineering approach for analysing security and dependability, considering their interdependence. In Sect. 3.1, the Architectural Analysis for Security (AAFS) [3] approach has been illustrated for designing a secure system based on the architecture of the system under consideration. Section 3.2 mentions categories of component failures and explains why

Table 3. Estimation table for attack probability

System susceptibility	Threat-prop.				
	2	3	4	5	6
6	8	9	10	11	12
5	7	8	9	10	11
4	6	7	8	9	10
3	5	6	7	8	9
2	4	5	6	7	8

stochastic HW failures and cyber-attacks are considered for analysis. Section 3.3 discusses the idea of combining stochastic failure rates and attacks (successful exploitation of vulnerabilities) as a co-analysis approach. Section 3.4 discusses in detail a quantitative approach for the likelihood of exploits of vulnerabilities which makes it possible to combine the likelihood of (security-related) attacks with stochastic failure rates, allowing a quantitative safety-security co-analysis. The example presented in Sect. 3.1 will also be used to illustrate how the concrete implementation of security patterns can be used to generate enough data which will be used for learning how vulnerabilities can be quantified at discrete level based on vulnerability factors (system susceptibility and threat property as discussed in Sect. 2.3).

3.1 Architectural Security Analysis

Till recently most of the focus in security has been on secure coding to address the security concerns, which is evident by the presence of diverse static and dynamic code analysis tools. But by focussing only on coding it is not possible to achieve a high level of security. Architectural designs can sometimes overcome most of the complex coding issues very easily. Therefore, architecture has the central role in ensuring security.

We will use the AAFS approach for designing a secure system. AAFS proposes a combination of three approaches to design security. These approaches are Tactic-oriented Architectural Analysis (ToAA), Pattern-oriented Architectural Analysis (PoAA) and Vulnerability-oriented Architectural Analysis (VoAA).

ToAA - Tactic is the realization of design intention; it involves architects' experience and expertise about the system architecture instead of detailed analysis. Depending on the system architecture and requirements, the architect decides if the tactic is applied or not, and, if applied, whether there is any weakness or not. The tactic covers all possible design approaches available to the architect, so they can function as a design checklist.

For example a case study is presented in [3] about the Open Electronic Medical Record (OpenEMR) Project which demonstrates the use of AAFS, in ToAA phase with the architect's expertise it was realised that there is a weakness in the tactic 'verify message integrity'.

PoAA - Patterns are proven solutions to recurring problems. The pattern associated with a weak tactic realised in the ToAA phase is investigated and applied, if already applied evidence for system-wide adoption and proper implementation needs to be checked. Continuing the above example, the 'verify message integrity' tactic mentioned above is commonly associated with the 'intercepting validator' pattern which verifies inputs according to validation rules.

VoAA - Vulnerabilities are weaknesses in a software-intensive system that attackers exploit to breach security. Software vulnerabilities comprise coding errors and design flaws. Vulnerabilities are a measure of software security. Pattern implementation and coverage in PoAA can be checked during VoAA by exposing the architect to well-known software vulnerabilities (such as penetration testing) that can be addressed by the implemented pattern.

The list of known software vulnerabilities can be found at 'CWE (Common Weakness Enumeration) View- Architectural Concepts' [31]. For instance corresponding to the 'validate input' pattern, the list of possible vulnerabilities can be found at 'CWE- Architectural Concepts- Validate Inputs'. For example, some of the listed vulnerabilities associated to the 'validate input' strategy are 'improper neutralization of input during webpage generation (CWE-79)', 'improper neutralization of special elements used in SQL command (CWE-89)', and 'improper neutralization of special elements used in an OS Command (CWE-78)'.

Instances of the vulnerabilities can be found in the CVE list at National Vulnerability Database [33]; this list also evaluates the score of the vulnerability instance based on CVSS (Common Vulnerability Scoring System) which consists of vulnerability factors such as attack complexity, privileges required, user interaction and attack vector (which is the same as the susceptibility factor of FMVEA).

From the list, the vulnerabilities relevant to the system under consideration are identified and, based on the vulnerability scores from FMVEA and CVSS, critical vulnerabilities are identified that need to be checked to provide the required reliability and availability for the system. Availability plays a role for on-demand safety functions, while reliability for continuous-mode safety functions.

3.2 How Components Can Fail

Components can fail (in particular also in a hazardous manner) due to the following causes:

1. safety-related failures, i.e.
    a. software errors (these correspond to systematic failures),
    b. systematic hardware failures (due to faulty construction or manufacturing), and
    c. stochastic hardware failures (due to ageing or wear-out), or
2. successful (security-related) attacks, which cause safety-relevant functions to fail.

All of these four categories, 1.a., 1.b., 1.c and 2., contribute to the overall failure rate. The Functional safety standards, which excluded security aspects until recently, needed to treat only the three above listed categories 1.a., 1.b. and 1.c., i.e. the safety-related faults only.

Regarding category 1.a. (software errors), the standards assume that the rate of failures caused by software faults is sufficiently reduced by Functional Safety standard-compliant development processes and, thus, they need not be further considered in the overall failure rate. For category 1.b. (systematic hardware faults), the assumption is that sufficient hardware testing reduces their contribution to the overall failure rate also to a negligible magnitude. (There are, however, also approaches treating software failures as a random failure rate. For our approach, we excluded them at the current stage from the considerations).

What remains is category 1.c., the stochastic hardware failure rate, which can be treated with statistical methods. This safety issue-related partial failure rate is what Functional Safety standards and also this paper are dealing with, and, in addition, we need to consider security-related failures caused by successful attacks against vulnerabilities. Those can be hardware failures (for example caused by overload like in the Stuxnet attack) or software failures (due to maliciously implanted malware code or tampered data).

3.3 How Can We Bring Together Stochastic Failure Rate and Attacks

As discussed in Sect. 2.1 the severity of impact on safety is one of the main factors for deciding on the SIL, which is directly assigned a maximum tolerable failure rate. So in order to meet a required SIL, the combined failure rate due to security attacks and hardware failures must be less than the maximum tolerable hazardous failure rate. But as discussed in Sects. 2.2 and 2.3 the existing co-engineering approaches use semi-quantitative values for attack probability instead of attack rates, therefore a decision based on experience and expertise is made to decide if the likelihood of critical failures due to attacks is less than the maximum tolerable failure rate. If not, the vulnerability exploited by the attack must be checked by a proper security strategy, in order to ensure the required safety level. The goal of the approach presented in this paper is to get a mapping between

1. the semi-quantitative values for threat probabilities of threat modes of components (in the architecture), which are obtained by applying the FMVEA, and
2. the quantitative tolerable hazardous failure rate values of the components associated to their SIL. This will allow combining the safety and the security analyses of the of the system with a quantitative risk assessment scheme that makes the partial hazard rates related to safety issues and to security-related attacks comparable. The critical vulnerabilities need to be checked to ensure safety requirement of the system is met.

3.4 Approach for Quantification of Threats Related to Vulnerabilities

To be precise by quantification of threats, we can calculate the combined failure rate as sum $\lambda_c = \lambda_{HW} + \lambda_{Attack}$ only under the assumption that there are no common cause failures between stochastic HW failures and cybersecurity attack-induced failures. This assumption seems reasonable for most cases. As for the Stuxnet attack, however, there is some inter-relation by the "normal" λ of the centrifuges and the damage caused by overstress. We consciously neglect this imprecision for now as is seems to apply only for rare cases.

A large collection of security patterns is present as discussed in Sect. 1.2, which addresses several vulnerabilities. If we take into consideration a given concrete implementation of a security pattern for a component in the system architecture (which has a required SIL) then we can assume that those potential security-induced failure modes against which the component is protected by the security pattern will not occur. In this sense, we assume that threats to vulnerabilities which are protected by a given security pattern are critical to the system (which has a certain SIL requirement).

As discussed in the FMVEA, the idea is to analyse the system and provide the required safety integrity level (SIL) based on this analysis by implementing the required safety strategy and checking (implementing security pattern to secure) these vulnerabilities for the exploit, we can deduce that these (neutralized) vulnerabilities are critical for the corresponding SIL. E.g. let's say the system requires SIL 2, so the combined tolerable hazardous failure rate is $10^{-7} \leq \lambda < 10^{-6} \ h^{-1}$. As an example, let's assume that the stochastic failure rate due to hardware faults analysed is sufficiently low (low means as in comparison to the system safety requirement of SIL 2, which requires a tolerable failure rate $10^{-7} \leq \lambda < 10^{-6} \ h^{-1}$ or less), e.g. $10^{-9} \leq \lambda < 10^{-8} \ h^{-1}$, then the security strategy must provide a reliability $\geq 10^6$ h.

We can understand the concept in the above two paragraphs by the Open-EMR Project example as discussed in Sect. 3.1. The openEMR project on analysis found a need for implementation of a validator security pattern for following four vulnerabilities, which the experts found to be of highest priority. And, the security strategy applied initially does not seem to cover these vulnerabilities or it cover them only partially.

Four vulnerabilities of highest priority were:

1. Improper neutralization of special elements used in a SQL command
2. Improper neutralization of input during webpage generation
3. Improper neutralization of script-related HTML tags in a web page
4. Improper neutralization of alternate XSS syntax

The mentioned four vulnerabilities can be scored based on vulnerability factors (susceptibility and threat property as discussed in Sect. 2.3 FMVEA) based on the known potential threats that can exploit these vulnerabilities. Let's assume the required SIL for openEMR system is '2'. Now since these vulnerabilities are critical for system which has required SIL '2' because they have been secured by pattern. We will assume that the tolerable failure rate due to these vulnerabilities are higher than $10^{-6} \ h^{-1}$.

Similarly other security patterns have implementations in different systems which have different SIL requirements and different system conditions (such as system reachability and unusualness), this will allow us to generate a lot of data (tolerable failure rate and vulnerability factor's score). And this data will we used to learn how to map the vulnerability factor (susceptibility and threat property) scores to failure rates due to vulnerability exploits. After the learning algorithm will be realized we will be able to predict in which SIL zone the exploit rate of the vulnerability ranges as shown in Fig. 2. E.g. if it ranges in SIL 3, we will use $10^{-7} \ h^{-1}$ as the exploit rate, considering worst case scenario $(10^{-7} > 10^{-8})$.

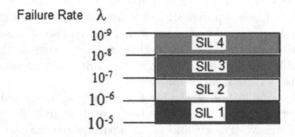

Fig. 2. Discrete Quantification of Vulnerabilities Based on Learning

The quantification will be at discrete level corresponding to the maximum tolerable hazardous failure rate (assigned as SIL requirement).

So the final outcome of this analysis would be, that, based on vulnerability score factors, the range of the rate of exploits can be predicted. E.g. we will be able to predict that, if the given vulnerability (based on its vulnerability factor's score) exploit range is SIL 3 or SIL2. If it is SIL 2, this means that the exploit rate will be greater than $10^{-7} \ h^{-1}$ and less than $10^{-6} \ h^{-1}$. But considering the worst case scenario for the co-analysis, we will take the attack rate = $10^{-6} \ h^{-1}$.

It is important to note and realise that the rate of exploits of vulnerabilities obtained by the above mentioned way is not absolute. All data generated by the concrete implementation of security patterns in safety critical systems, which will be used for the quantification of the likelihood of vulnerability exploits (by a learning algorithm), is based on the expert decision / recommendation that certain vulnerabilities (based on vulnerability factors) are critical for the given system with a certain SIL requirement. This approach will allow us to use all such already established expert decisions in a comprehensive and homogenous way for the quantification of vulnerabilities.

Such a quantification of vulnerability as an exploit rate similar to the failure rate will allow us to consider safety and security under the same umbrella and categorize critical vulnerabilities that need to be checked to ensure the required safety level. The quantitative approaches mentioned in Sect. 1.1 would be possible to use. This will provide more certainty and reliability to our analysis as compared to a semi-quantitative approach for considering attack occurrence (rate), taking into consideration the real existing use cases of the security pattern implementations as a base. The learning algorithm is still to be realised.

The approach described in this paper is still on a conceptual level in that the learning algorithm is still to be realised.

3.5   Data from Security Patterns Implementations

A large collection of security patterns is present as discussed in Sect. 1.2, which addresses several vulnerabilities. If we take into consideration concrete implementation of these security patterns in safety-critical systems (with a required SIL) then we can assume that the specific vulnerabilities checked by these patterns are critical to the system, and that the failure rate due to the exploitation of these vulnerabilities is higher than the one required as discussed in detail in Sect. 3.4. Thus, considering the implementation of patterns in safety-critical systems will provide us with enough data to do a data-driven analysis for the quantification of vulnerabilities based on the score of vulnerability factors.

4   Conclusion and Further Work

In this paper an approach for developing a quantitative metric for the likelihood of exploits of system vulnerabilities has been drafted. The next step will be running a learning algorithm on use cases with concrete implementations of patterns for safety critical systems in order to obtain the quantitative values. After this, the idea is to use architecture based security design as mentioned in detail in Sect. 3.1, in order to to design a secure and safe system. During the VoAA the vulnerabilities will be identified and quantified based on the vulnerability factors as discussed earlier. Then idea is to combine both failure/maintenance and attack/recovery using stochastic colored petri nets where the system's reliability and availability can be analysed or simulated e.g. using tools like TimeNET. A way of modelling and quantitative evaluation of vulnerabilities based on stochastic petri nets is mentioned in [35]. A way of modelling failures/maintenances for reliability and safety evaluation using petri nets is shown in [36]. As a result the critical vulnerabilities can be marked and checked using patterns for providing the required availability and reliability.

Yet another benefit can be obtained from having quantitatively comparable partial hazard rates resulting from stochastic hardware failures and failures induced by cybersecurity attacks: It supports strongly safety-security co-engineering, which strives to achieve a balanced set of measures aiming at security improvements and safety-oriented mitigation measures, which are often contradictory. They can be selected in an optimal way based on a trade-off analysis supported by a quantitative metric.

Acknowledgements. The work published here is based on research in the AMASS project that has been funded by the ECSEL Joint Undertaking under Grant Agreement number 692474.

References

1. Schmittner, C., Gruber, T., Puschner, P., Schoitsch, E.: Security application of failure mode and effect analysis (FMEA). In: Bondavalli, A., Di Giandomenico, F. (eds.) SAFECOMP 2014. LNCS, vol. 8666, pp. 310–325. Springer, Cham (2014). https://doi.org/10.1007/978-3-319-10506-2_21
2. Whitt, W.: Continuous Time Markov Chains, Department of Industrial Engineering and Operations Research, Columbia University (2013)
3. Morant, A., Gustafson, A., Söderholm, P., Larsson-Kråik, P.O., Kumar, U.: Safety and availability evaluation of railway operation based on the state of signaling systems. Proc. Inst. Mech. Eng. Part F J. Rail Rapid Transit **231**, 226–238 (2017)
4. Ryoo, J., Kazman, R., Anand, P.: Architectural analysis for security. IEEE Secur. Priv. **13**(6), 52–59 (2015)
5. Bunke, M., Koschke, R., Sohr, K.: Organizing security patterns related to security and pattern recognition requirements. Int. J. Adv. Secur. **5**, 46–67 (2012)
6. Satty, T.L.: The Analytical Hierarchy and Analytical Network Measurement Process: Applications to Decisions under Risk (2008)
7. Macher, G., Sporer, H., Armengaud, E., Kreiner, C.: SAHARA: A Security-Aware Hazard and Risk Analysis Method (2015)
8. Liu, Z., Liu, Y., Cai, B., Liu, X., Li, J., Tian, X., Ji, R.: RAMS Analysis of Hybrid Redundancy System of Subsea Blowout Preventer Based on Stochastic Petri Nets (2013)
9. Mustafiz, S., Sun, X., Kienzle, J., Vangheluwe, H.: Model-driven assessment of system dependability. Softw. Syst. Model. **7**, 487–502 (2008)
10. Schumacher, M., Fernandez, E.B., Hybertson, D., Buscmann, F., Sommerlad, P.: Security Patterns : Integrating Security and System Engineering. Software Design Patterns. Wiley, Hoboken (2006)
11. Haldikis, S., Chatzigeorigou, A., Stephanides, G.: A practical evaluation of security patterns (2006)
12. Steel, C., Nagappan, R., Lai, R.: Core Security Patterns : Best Practices and strategies for J2EE : Web Services and Identity Management (2014)
13. Kienzle, D.M., Elder, M.C., Tyree, D., Edwards-Hewitt, J.: Security Patterns repository version 1.0 (2002)
14. Dougherty, C., Sayre, K., Seacord, R.C., Svoboda, D., Togashi, K.: Security Design Patterns (2009)
15. Buschmann, F., Meunier, R., Rohnert, H., Sommerlad, P., Stal, M.: Pattern-Oriented Software Architecture: A System of Patterns. Wiley, New York (1996)
16. Shi, N., Olsson, R.A.: Reverse engineering of design patterns from Java source code (2006)
17. Konrad, S., Cheng, B.H., Campbell, L.A., Wasserman, R.: Using security patterns to model and analyse security requirements (2003)
18. Rosado, D.G., Gutierrez, C., Fernandez-Medina, E., Piattini, M.: Security patterns related to security requirements (2006)
19. Washizaki, H., Fernandez, E.B., Maruyama, K., Kubo, A., Yoshioka, N.: Improving the classification of security patterns (2009)
20. Saridakis, T.: A system of patterns for fault tolerance. In: Proceedings of the EuroPLoP Conference (2002)
21. Buckley, I.A., Fernandez, E.B., Larrondo-Petrie, M.M.: Patterns combining reliability and security (2011)

22. Hamid, B.: Modelling of secure and dependable applications based on a repository of patterns : The SEMCO approach
23. Charlwood, M., Turner, S., Worsell, N.: A methodology for the assignment of SILs to safety-related control functions implemented by safety-related electrical, electronic and programmable electronic control system of machines : prepared by Innovation Electronics UK Ltd and Health and Safety Laboratory HSL (2004)
24. Stolte, T., Bagschik, G., Reschka, A., Maurer, M.: Hazard Analysis and Risk Assessment for an Automated Unmanned Protective Vehicle (2017)
25. Microsoft Corporation : The stride threat model (2005)
26. Reifer, D.J.: Software Failure Modes and Effects Analysis (1979)
27. Haapanen, P., Helminen, A.: Failure mode and effect analysis of software-based automation systems (2002)
28. ISO - International Organization for Standarization: ISO 26262 Road vehicles Functional Safety (2011)
29. Zhan, Z., Xu, M., Xu, S.: Predicting cyber attack rates with extreme values (2015)
30. IEC 62443 : Industrial communication networks - Network and system security (2010)
31. cwe.mitre.org: Common weakness enumeration view : Architectural Concepts (2018)
32. TimeNET : A software tool for the performability evaluation with stochastic and colored petri nets. https://timenet.tu-ilmenau.de/template/index
33. Mell, P., Scarfone, K., Romanosky, S.: A Complete Guide to the Common Vulnerability Scoring System (2007)
34. IEC- International Standards and Conformity Assessment for all electrical, electronic and related technologies. http://www.iec.ch/functionalsafety/standards/page3.htm
35. Flammini, F., Marrone, S., Valeria, V.: Petri Net Modelling of Physical Vulnerability (2013)
36. Pinna, B., Babykina, G., Brinzei, N., Petin, J-.F.: Using Coloured Petri Nets for integrated reliability and safety evaluations (2013)

Safety and Security in a Smart Production Environment

Reinhard Kloibhofer[✉], Erwin Kristen, and Stefan Jakšić

AIT Austrian Institute of Technology GmbH, Giefinggasse 4, 1210 Vienna, Austria
{reinhard.kloibhofer,erwin.kristen,stefan.jaksic}@ait.ac.at

Abstract. Industry 4.0 is the term which designates an engineering philosophy of a modern, automated manufacturing technology. It includes tight cooperation of robots and humans and a seamless integration of the Information Technology (IT) and the Operation Technology (OT). Wired or wireless interconnection of devices and machinery across the existing manufacturing components plant borders. A data driven product life cycle starts with product concept ideas, and proceeds with the design, production and testing, commercialization and to end with the decommissioning of the product. Industry 4.0 also defines the smart factory where a smart product guides the production process and issues commands to the machinery about the necessary steps to take to produce the desired product. This paper contains the idea and a solution for a smart factory with a mobile robot, operating with secured product configuration and secured data communication. All production data is stored as a digital copy, named "digital twin".

Keywords: Industry 4.0 · Industrial Automation Control Systems (IACS)
Internet of Things (IoT) · Cyber-physical systems (CPS) · Safety & security

1 Introduction

A main focus of the ongoing international research project IoSense are safety and security (S&S) aspects of an industrial automation control system (IACS). Not only the requirements for today's modern manufacturing plants are under consideration, but also the challenges for S&S in future IACS. In the future, humans and robots will operate in the same working environment which raises new S&S concerns which must be analysed and assessed. The situation gets even more complex with each product becoming an intelligent product with a documented life cycle in form of a so called "digital twin", stored somewhere in the cloud. Security threats are critical more than ever in a strong interconnected world and both human health and production output are vulnerable in the same extent.

In Sect. 2 we provide a brief overview of modern production systems. We proceed with a definition of operation environment of a robot operated production field in Sect. 3. We build such environment as a demonstrator for Trustworthy Systems (TrustworSys) in the project IoSense, and document it in detail. Section 4 introduces the IEC 62443 industrial security standard and deploys this standard to a part of the demonstrator.

© Springer Nature Switzerland AG 2018
B. Gallina et al. (Eds.): SAFECOMP 2018 Workshops, LNCS 11094, pp. 190–201, 2018.
https://doi.org/10.1007/978-3-319-99229-7_17

Section 5 gives an outlook of planned additional future work and a project assessment about safety in the industrial domain.

2 Modern Production State the Art

Industry 4.0 is the synonym for an engineering philosophy for a modern, automated manufacturing technology. The industrial production will be merged intensively with Information and Communication Technology. The base therefore are intelligent and digital networking systems. The production and process is more and more self-organizing, implying there is no engineer to plan each step in detail, but the plant is responsible for organizing the sequences of the production and consequently the use of the production machines and the production resources. Necessary ingredient for such a process is a highly automated facility with assistance from robots and gripper arms to transport the product. But more than only the production, the whole value-added chain should be optimized. All phases of the product circle are under consideration. This begins with the plan of raw material, development of products, production, utilization, service and at the end of the product circle, the decommission of the product.

The Number 4.0 is an expression of the 4th industrial revolution, which will come after the first (mechanization, water and steam power), the second (mass production, assembly lines, electrical current) and the third (computer support and automatization) revolution. The last generation include cyber-physical systems (CPS), Internet of Things (IoT), cloud computing and cognitive systems.

Four design principles support the implementing of Industry 4.0:

- Interoperability: all components like machines, devices, sensors and people are connected and communicating with each other.
- Information transparency: a virtual (digital) copy of the plant is enlarged with sensor data. This means the raw sensor data must be integrated in high level systems.
- Technical assistance: the machines and the interfaces should be understandable to enable the technical support provided by humans.
- Decentralized decisions: most of the decisions should be done by the cyber physical systems itself. In case of exceptions, the decision is delegated to a higher level.

The components of a smart production environment will be more tightly connected one to the other. The complexity of such a system is increasing. A main goal is the communication and data exchange between these components. Many different wired and wireless communication channels are possible for communication. Today, these networks are typically placed in one factory, but in the future also more and more factories will be connected to form a world-wide production plant mesh. However, the data must be secured from malicious manipulation. Therefore, the security of such a network and the interfaces is crucial. Strengthening the system against cyber-attacks is still a very active research topic.

3   Demonstrator for Innovative Manufacturing

In the EU ECSEL (Electronic Components and Systems for European Leadership) project IoSense the focus of the project is to improve the Time-to-Market (TTM) period for sensor-based products and increase the market share with an early market launch. Several demonstrators are planned to demonstrate technologies to fulfill this goal. TrustworSys is one of the demonstrators developed in the project and shall be explained in more detail in this paper.

In the TrustworSys demonstrator we plan the demonstration of an innovative configuration of smart products and their production in a modern factory. A focus will be set to the safety and security process from a product being conceived until its being recycled for decommissioning.

There exist different approaches for configuration management of embedded systems. A direct approach is static configuration by using wire jumpers or zero-ohm resistors directly on the Printed Circuit Board (PCB). A more flexible configuration can be done by deploying simple hardware elements (e.g. pluggable jumpers, DIP-Switches), non-volatile memory (e.g. battery powered SRAM, EEPROM, Flash) contact based command line interfaces (e.g., RS232, USB), remote shells, or even web interfaces (HTTP). However, all these operations need a manual handling and are not simple to use in fully automated processes.

In this demonstrator we use contactless NFC (Near Field Communication) for the wireless configuration of the product in the production process. This technology is well applicable for an automated production line. In an automated factory the (raw) product will be transported by a conveyor belt or more flexible by (autonomous) robots. In our use case the factory layout is flexible, meaning that the production machines i.e. CNC (Computerized Numerical Control) can be replaced or the position of machines can be changed. We do not assume a fixed and inflexible floor plan of the factory. In other words, production process is not static in any aspect. In our approach the raw product is configured the first time and for the production the raw product guides the robot and the machines through the different production steps.

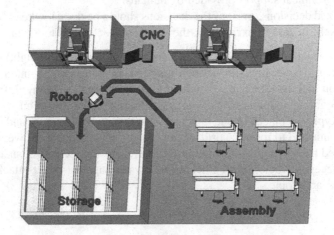

Fig. 1. Example of a manufactory floor plan.

In Fig. 1 a typical floor plan for a manufactory area is show. A robot transports a product from storage to different production machines or to a manual production work benches for assembly. After the production phase, the product instructs the robot to bring it back to storage. The product is now ready to be sold to the consumer.

3.1 Demonstrator Setup for the Demonstration

To demonstrate this new configuration and production approach a set-up in the laboratory will be designed. One central component in this setup is a robot that can navigate autonomous through the factory.

We plan a demonstrator area of about 2 × 2 m (which can be enlarged to a real-scale factory size) where all components are placed. For our demonstration we plan 3 different production machines (PM1, PM2 and PM3) and a storage (STO). These components are placed on the side of the area. In the whole area a mobile robot (ROB) transports a product (PROD) from the storage to the different machines and at the end of manufacturing back to the storage. The robot can navigate on the area and can also detect obstacles and drive around them (Fig. 2).

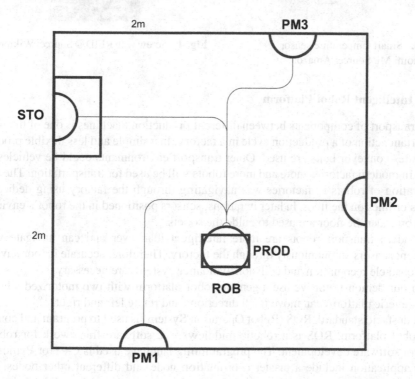

Fig. 2. Demonstrator floor plan (STO: Storage, PMx: Production machinery, ROB: Robot, PROD: Product)

3.2   Smart Product

Smart products are products that are able to communicate with machines, equipment and other systems. They are equipped with embedded systems that can collect, communicate and elaborate data. Similar to configuring of microprocessors and embedded systems, it is possible to store configuration data on the component that speeds up the configuration steps.

Very common types of smart products are (electronic) sensors (e.g. Fig. 3) that communicate in a sensor network or with a high-level machine. In our view not only electronic components are considered as smart products, but also more or less complex mechanical components like a screw (Fig. 4) or an entire car gear box. Typically used passive RFID components have a very low price in mass production.

Fig. 3. Smart temperature sensor   **Fig. 4.** Screw with RFID © Source: Wikipedia.
© Xiaomi Mi, Source: Amazon.

3.3   Intelligent Robot Platform

The transport of components between different production machines is one of the most important action of a production cycle in a factory. In a simple and less flexible production sites conveyor belts are used. Other transport environments could be vehicles on rails. In modern factories more and more robots will be used for transportation. The first generation of robots in factories was navigating through the factory using dedicated tracks or lines on the floor. In later iterations, sensors positioned in the robot's environment or under the floor are used to guide the robots.

Modern transport robots are more intelligent than ever and can navigate with different sensors autonomously through the factory. Therefore, accurate indoor navigation, obstacle recognition and collision avoidance systems are necessary.

In our demonstrator we use a generic robot platform with two motorized wheels. This generic platform can move in all directions and rotate left and right.

A de-facto standard, ROS (Robot Operation System) is used to program and control the robot platform. ROS is a robotic middleware, a software framework for robotic control software development. The programming language used is C++ or Python. A ROS application include a master coordination node and different other nodes, e.g. driving platform, sensor nodes, odometry nodes, navigation node. The nodes are communicating via topics. Nodes can publish to topics and they can subscribe to topics for receiving data. The structure is very flexible and allows simple adding more sensors or actuators.

For the TrustworSys demonstrator a new NFC node will be developed and added to the robot system.

3.4 NFC Communication

A key component in our configuration and production approach is a secure NFC wireless communication [1–5] which is developed by our partner Infineon Austria.

The block diagram for the NFC Enhancement is shown in Fig. 5.

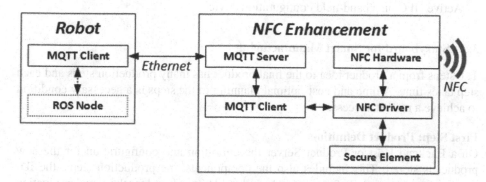

Fig. 5. NFC Enhancement block diagram

The NFC Enhancement is composed of different blocks. One is the NFC Hardware with the antenna for the wireless communication to another NFC device. It must be distinguished between an active and a passive NFC device. An active NFC device needs a power supply and generates an electromagnetic field with the antenna. If there is a passive NFC device in the communication range it will receive power from the electromagnetic field and powers a NFC electronic chip. This passive NFC component will modulate the electromagnetic field and this modulation will be detected from the active NFC device. Such communication with typical small antennas will only work for a few millimeters up to a few centimeters range. This is an important feature against malicious manipulation and therefore an important security aspect.

A second security aspect is the secure element on the NFC chip. This new developed secure element allows an encrypted communication between the passive NFC and the reader. As the secure element is on the same chip it cannot be manipulated without destroying the integrated circuit.

An additional feature is the Message Queue Telemetry Transport (MQTT) server-client approach. It is an ISO standard for a publish-subscribe-based messaging protocol. It works on top of the TCP/IP protocol. It is an extremely simple and lightweight messaging protocol, designed for constrained devices and low-bandwidth, high-latency or unreliable networks. The design principles are to minimize network bandwidth and device resource requirements whilst also attempting to ensure reliability and some degree of assurance of delivery. The publish-subscribe messaging pattern requires a message broker, which is a computer program module that translates the message format from a device (e.g. sensor) to the message format to the receiver (e.g. computer). MQTT can be used for sending and receiving encrypted data and therefore it is very good solution.

The connection of the NFC Enhancement to the robot platform is established via Ethernet cable and it is integrated as a ROS software node with the robot.

In our demonstrator we are using several NFC components:

- Active NFC on the robot
- Passive (or active) NFC on the product
- Passive (or active) NFC on the production machines and storage
- Active NFC on a hand-held configuration device

3.5 Storyboard for Smart Manufacturing

The steps from a product idea to the final product has many production steps and each step takes time. A time and cost-optimal planning of the steps is a necessary condition to achieve a market success.

First Step: Product Definition
On a Backend Host or Product Server the definition and configuration for the new product is stored. This includes also the components, the production steps, the ID-numbers and the number of products which should be produced for the actual production batch.

We demonstrate this for a smart sensor with different alarm levels. The smart sensor is built with the following components:

- Analog to Digital Converter board, including a NFC
- The sensing element (e.g. temperature sensor or humidity sensor)
- Housing

Second Step: Raw Product Configuration
An Operator with a mobile configuration device which is connected to the Backend Server configures the raw product from the storage.

We distinguish between a Trusted Operator and an Untrusted Operator:

- A Trusted Operator has access to the configuration device and can modify some parameter of the smart sensor (e.g. measurement range, resolution, color of the housing). The configuration data is programmed via NFC to the product. Serial Number or other ID numbers are generated automatically and all data which are transferred to the raw product are also stored on the Backend Server.
- An Untrusted Operator has no access to the configuration data. He can only transfer the configuration to the raw product without manipulation.

Third Step: Production Start
After the configuration of the raw product it will be set on the mobile robot by a robot arm (or in a simple form the operator puts the device on the robot). The raw product communicates now via NFC to the robot and instruct the robot for the first production action.

Product Processing Loop
In this phase several steps of the production loop are performed:

- The robot communicates with the Backend Host via WLAN to ask for the coordinates of the first production machine. The robot drives autonomous to the production machine.
- The robot communicates via NFC to the machine what action should be done on the product. The production machine acts according the configuration.
- Production machine confirms that the work is done on the product.
- Robot communicate with product for the next action.

Production Finished
After all production steps are completed, the robot returns the product to the storage. The new smart product is ready to be released for commercial use. The customer product life cycle can start.

3.6 Backend Host

The Backend Host is part of the factory IT-environment. It is assumed that the stored data is safe (periodic backup, …). This server keeps both the product data and the entire factory configuration. This means the Backend Host knows the status of all machines, storage and robots. Every step of the production is also stored. In other words, the Backend Host holds a so called "digital twin" of the product. The digital representation provides both the elements and the dynamics of how the product was produced. Furthermore, also the customization process can be stored on the Backend Host.

An additional important task of the Backend Host is the optimization of the factory. For example, the paths of the robot movements can be optimized by self-learning algorithms.

4 Security Considerations

4.1 IEC 62443 Security Standard

In the industrial sector for products and facilities the IEC 62433 security standard becomes the base for security requirements definitions and security recommendations. The standard series is divided in 14 sub-documents, which are sorted in four main groups,

- **General** – This group includes standard introduction, technical reports, glossary, life cycle definition, and other basic documents.
- **Policies and Procedures** – This group provides documents which focuses on the policies and procedures associated with industrial automation security.
- **System Requirements** – This group lists requirements for the system level.
- **Components Requirements** – This group lists requirements for the components level.

The safety standard IEC 62443 postulate a workflow shown in Fig. 6. The workflow is combined of four ZCR's (Zone and Conduit Requirements) phases.

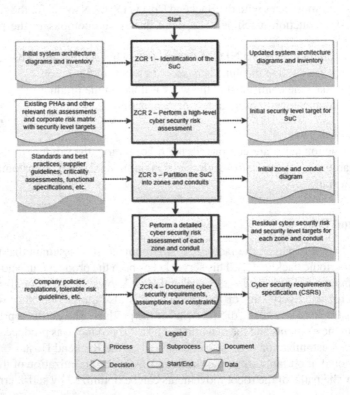

Fig. 6. IEC 62443 workflow to establish zones and conduits and assess risk [5]

On the right-hand side the recommended documents and on the left-hand side the outputted documents are listed. First, in the ZCR1 phase, the System under Consideration (SuC) must be defined by a detailed description of the system architecture and the inventory. With the input of a Process Hazard Analysis (PHA) a high-level cyber security risk assessment determines the target security level (ZCR2). The target security level (Security Level – Target SL-T) stated out the required estimated security level to operate the system in the documented environment.

In general, the security level defines the strength of the security measures, needed to safeguard the system for cyber-attacks.

The five levels are defined as:

SL 0 No protection
SL 1 Protection against casual or coincidental violation
SL 2 Protection against intentional violation using simple means with low resources, generic skills and low motivation
SL 3 Protection against intentional violation using sophisticated means with moderate resources, IACS specific skills and moderate motivation

SL 4 Protection against intentional violation using sophisticated means with extended resources, IACS specific skills and high motivation

The standard provides methods and hints to estimate the suitable security level derived by zone security parameters.

The next step (ZCR 3) in the workflow is to split up the complex overall system in zones and conduits. See Fig. 7 as an example of a possible SuC partitioning in zones and conduits.

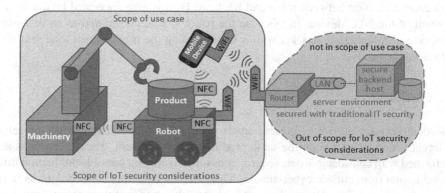

Fig. 7. Demonstrator zones and conduits definition overview

In final step (ZCR 4) a detailed cyber risk assessment for each zone and conduit is performed to estimate the individual target security levels.

The last step is the definition of necessary requirements for security counter-measures to harden the system against all analyzed and assessed cyber threats. The component supplier defines the feasible and cost-optimal archived Security Level (SL-A) for each components of a zone.

In the end of the integration and commissioning phase the system integrator must ensure that all the security measures implemented for the Archived Security Level (SL-A) are efficient, suitable and match the Target Security Levels (SL-T). This reports the final possible Capability Security Level (SL-C) of the system [6].

4.2   Zones and Conduits

The TrustworSys demonstrator has the following zones and conduits figured out in the following Fig. 7.

The zones of the system are:

- Robot
- Product
- Machinery
- Mobile configuration device

And the identified conduits are:

- NFC communication (between different devices)
- WiFi communication

A detailed cyber security risk analysis of the different zones and conduits was performed. The main result of this analysis is that by using the secure element in the NFC communication we have protection against attack to sensitive data and to the software. The robot never gets sensitive data from the product, but only encrypted data. The data communication between robot and Backend Host is also encrypted by the secure element of the NFC device. In this case the robot can be considered as an untrusted component. A malicious attacker who is manipulating the robot cannot read sensitive data from the product.

5 Outlook

The demonstrator allows to present smart production functionalities, like as setup different product variants on the same production environment. These operations are performed with considerable data security measures to prevent possible production flow manipulation from outside cyber-attacks. There are also manipulations or attacks from the inner-side feasible. For such cases, risk analysis and countermeasures must be implemented. In future work a continuous monitoring of the robot operation parameters shall be implemented, a further improvement for preventative maintenance (PM). Monitoring can be also used for anomaly detection and as additional security measure, to prevent manual manipulations of the robot platform.

Acknowledgment. This work has received funding from the IoSense project, under grant agreement No 692480. The project is co-funded by grants from Austria, Germany, Spain, Netherland, Belgium, Slovakia and ECSEL JU.

References

1. Ulz, T., Pieber, T., Höller, A., Haas, S., Steger, C.: Secured and easy-to-use NFC-based device configuration for the Internet of Things. IEEE J. Radio Freq. Identif. **1**(1), 75–84 (2017)
2. Ulz, T., Pieber, T., Steger, C., Lesjak, C., Bock, H., Matischek, R.: SECURECONFIG: NFC and QR-code based hybrid approach for smart sensor configuration. In: 2017 IEEE International Conference on RFID (RFID), pp. 1–6
3. Haas, S., Wallner, A., Toegl, R., Ulz, T., Steger, C.: A secured offline authentication approach for industrial mobile robots. In: 13th IEEE Conference on Automation Science and Engineering (CASE), Xi'an, China, 20–23 August 2017 (2017)
4. Pieber, T.W., Ulz, T., Steger, C., Matischek, R.: Hardware secured, password-based authentication for smart sensors for the industrial Internet of Things. In: Yan, Z., Molva, R., Mazurczyk, W., Kantola, R. (eds.) NSS 2017. LNCS, vol. 10394, pp. 632–642. Springer, Cham (2017). https://doi.org/10.1007/978-3-319-64701-2_50

5. ISA-62443-3-2 Security for industrial automation and control systems (IACS), Security Risk Assessment, System Partitioning and Security Levels, Draft 7, Edit 1, p. 13 (2017)
6. Kobes, P: Protection Levels, an holistic approach based on IEC 62443, VDE Tagung Funktionale Sicherheit und IT-Sicherheit 2017 (2017)

Survey of Scenarios for Measurement of Reliable Wireless Communication in 5G

Matthias Herlich[(✉)], Thomas Pfeiffenberger, Jia Lei Du, and Peter Dorfinger

Salzburg Research, Salzburg, Austria
{matthias.herlich,thomas.pfeiffenberger,jia.du,
peter.dorfinger}@salzburgresearch.at

Abstract. In the future many parts of our lives will increasingly depend on wireless communication. Therefore, wireless communication should be reliable. Different scenarios need different methods to measure the reliability (e.g., active and passive). In this paper, we survey scenarios in which reliable communication is important and select two scenarios which are suited to measure the reliability of the wireless networks.

Based on literature search and interviews with experts in the field we determined two scenarios which demand a wide range of measurement methods: (1) vehicles transmitting collision warnings at intersections and (2) wireless emergency-stop buttons in factories. Both scenarios need wireless communication, but are so different they need different methods to measure the reliability of the wireless system.

Because the selected scenarios have different properties, the methods that can measure the reliability in these scenarios, will also be able to measure the reliability in many other scenarios. To be able to compare methods to measure reliability of wireless networks, researchers should focus on the same scenarios. We propose to use the scenarios described in this paper.

1 Introduction

Wireless communication has become an important technology for many people in their daily lives. Mobile phones and smart phones are used all over the globe. The main advantage of wireless communication is that it reduces the overhead of connecting wires to devices and that it allows devices to communicate that cannot be connected with wires.

The biggest disadvantage of wireless communication is that its operation depends on the environment. When a connection is wired, outside influences have little effect on the communication. In contrast, the environment in which wireless communication is used has a large effect on its performance. There are different metrics for performance, but one of the most important ones is reliability. The reliability of a system describes its probability to successfully handle requests (for the exact definition we use, see Sect. 2).

People have learned to cope with unreliable wireless networks: They do not expect to be able to make phone calls in parking garages and postpone calls

© Springer Nature Switzerland AG 2018
B. Gallina et al. (Eds.): SAFECOMP 2018 Workshops, LNCS 11094, pp. 202–213, 2018.
https://doi.org/10.1007/978-3-319-99229-7_18

when the connection is unreliable. That is, people are flexible and adapt to the reliability of the wireless network. Machines also use wireless communication, but until now this has mostly been limited to communication that is not critical. Therefore, temporary losses of the ability to communicate have not been a major problem.

In the future machines will increasingly use wireless communication for mission-critical communication. For this to be possible, wireless communication must be reliable at each location where machines need it. To describe the reliability, many channel models and characterizations (e.g., [18]) have been developed for wireless communication. However, in other areas where failures of technology can cause death (e.g., medical devices, drugs, mechanical engineering) rigorous protocols are in place to ensure that each product has the desired properties. However, methods to monitor the end-to-end reliability of wireless networks are not yet available.

Because we expect an increased research interest on methods to measure reliability in the future, such research should be comparable (see our definition of reliability in the next section). To achieve this, researchers should focus on the same scenarios. In these scenarios reliable wireless communication should be essential. To cover a wide range of scenarios, the two selected scenarios should need different methods to measure the reliability of the wireless communication.

The contribution of this paper is a survey of scenarios in which reliable wireless communication is essential and a selection of two scenarios which need different methods to determine the reliability. To do this, we describe types of measurements in Sect. 2 and give a broad overview of the areas for wireless communication in Sect. 3. In Sects. 4 and 5 we describe scenarios of automotive and industry in more detail before we compare the selected scenarios in Sect. 6. To ensure a wide range of possible applications and comparability for methods to measure reliability, researchers should focus on these scenarios.

2 Measurement Methods

For a scenario to be included in this survey, it has to depend on reliable wireless communication. For this purpose we define **reliability** as the "packet delivery rate between two end points with a given maximum transmission duration", where the rate is the fraction of delivered error-free packets divided by the number of packets sent. For the receiver to use the packet it is necessary to receive the packet with the correct content. We consider the reliability to be measured at the application level on a per packet basis. That is, the reliability is measured after retransmissions and correction mechanisms (such as Hybrid automatic repeat request, HARQ). However, also the time limit is measured after the application of these mechanisms. While there are many similar definitions of reliability [7,23,29], we consider this the most useful one for our project.

We want the scenarios to be relevant for the sector they appear in. That is, they should have a high technical impact. The value of its application does not have to be available in the near future, but it should have the potential for large changes and have a reasonable chance to be implemented.

2.1 Active and Passive Measurements

Scenarios need different measurements: During **passive** measurements, the measurement system does not generate wireless transmissions, but only monitors wireless traffic that is already transmitted. For this to be possible wireless communication must be used in the scenario already. Ideally the traffic is of high volume to quickly generate measurement data. The advantage of passive measurements is that the effect on the environment is low (only the measurement hardware has to be added, but no additional transmissions are generated).

During **active** measurements, the measurement system generates traffic itself. Thus, it does not depend on a communication system already being in place. However, with active measurements the effect on other wireless transmissions in the area have to be taken into account.

2.2 Periodic and Event-Based Traffic

The traffic that is generated by machine-to-machine communication can be categorized by the regularity of the traffic. **Periodic** traffic consists of packets of the same size that are transmitted in constant intervals. That is, the pattern of the traffic is deterministic. Only the content of the packets cannot be predicted. This type of traffic is usually generated when machines are monitored and the data is archived for later analysis or machines need to coordinate in predefined groups.

In **event-based** traffic the interval between two consecutive transmissions does not follow a regular pattern, but is based on some external event. This type of traffic usually occurs when notifications are generated based on external events.

3 Overview

Many overview papers have been written about the potential of wireless communication for diverse sectors. In contrast to the broad descriptions in most of these, our goal is to determine scenarios which represent the needs for different methods to determine the reliability.

The 5G-PPP document about vertical industries for 5G [5] describes the main verticals for 5G as: Factory of the future, Energy, e-Health, Automotive, and Media & Entertainment. The document provides an overview of the verticals and gives examples for quantified requirements. However, it does not give an in depth analysis of the individual vertical sectors. The 5G-PPP provides more details in the individual documents for each vertical (e.g., for factories [3] and automotive [4]). We will describe the relation to measurements of reliability of these documents in Sects. 4 and 5.

The German position paper "Resiliente Netze mit Funkzugang" ("resilient networks with wireless access") [16] is part of the German initiative industrial radio[1]. It focuses on application perspectives and technological aspects of

---

[1] http://industrialradio.de.

resilient wireless networks. Also, companies (e.g., Siemens [26]) have described their requirements on 5G or wireless communication in general. Such industrial white papers describe what the companies consider important. Yet, they might contain a biased view from the perspective of the company.

The health sector is also considered a vertical sector for 5G by the 5G-PPP [2] and the wireless world research forum [27]. They expect that wireless communication will enable physicians to collect more data and thereby create more effective treatments. This overlaps with the general trend of Internet of Things (IoT) that places sensors and actuators in physical devices.

The railway sector is usually not listed as one of the high priority verticals for 5G. One of the reasons for this is that the railway sector already has a set of standards [22] based on GSM-R in place that allow monitoring and support operation of trains with the The European Rail Traffic Management System ERTMS[2]. Updating ERTMS to a modern communication technology will provide train operators with more data rate and a more reliable communication network. In addition to the passengers on the train benefit from 5G with increased media and entertainment comfort.

To determine which sectors to focus on, we determined which sectors are most in line with strengths in Europe and especially Austria. The European Union [12] and especially Austria [10] see one of their strengths in factories of the future. Another sector of great importance is the automotive sector [9,11].

In the following sections we describe selected scenarios from the automotive and industrial sectors, which focus on reliability. The information is collected from published work as well as interviews with experts in the field (which we were asked to keep confidential).

4   Automotive

The automotive sector is expected to change dramatically in the next decades. Assistance systems are getting more prevalent and autonomous cars are getting closer to production. An important background change is that cars are communicating with each other and with infrastructure. The change is spearheaded by the 5G Automotive Association (5GAA[3]) [6]. For Austria [9,11] and Germany [19] the communication of vehicles is an important area of research.

4.1   Communication

The communication of vehicles can be grouped in three categories: in-vehicle, vehicle-to-vehicle and vehicle-to-infrastructure.

In-vehicle communication allows different parts of the same car to communicate with each other. This has been a standard for many decades and is usually done by wired connections. Only recently have there been efforts to use wireless communication where wired communication is infeasible or expensive.

---

[2] http://www.ertms.net.
[3] http://5gaa.org.

Vehicle-to-vehicle communication allows a car to send messages to other cars. Such a message can, for example, be a collision warning. For most scenarios cars only need to communicate with other cars that are close-by. In contrast to in-vehicle communication, vehicle-to-vehicle cannot be done by wires, because the cars move independently of each other and cannot be interconnected for any individual communication.

Vehicle-to-infrastructure communication is between a car and a stationary unit. This can, for example, be a red light at an intersection. Just as vehicle-to-vehicle communication, it is not feasible to provide vehicle-to-infrastructure communication by wires. There are more types of vehicular communication, which are summarized as vehicle-to-everything.

The European Telecommunications Standards Institute (ETSI) describes the requirements vehicles have when using an LTE network [14]. While these are described for LTE, the general concepts also hold for 5G networks.

4.2 Technologies

The most important wireless communication technologies for the automotive sector are based on next generation cellular mobile networks (5G) and on WiFi.

The 5G-PPP expects **5G** to be an important wireless communication technology in the automotive sector [4]. As 5G aims to be a single interface for all kinds of wireless communication it seems to be the ideal technology to provide vehicles with local communication and connectivity to the Internet using a single technology. However, it is unclear as of now, whether there will be a single interface 5G will provide to the automotive sector or if local and global communication will have different interfaces.

IEEE 802.11p is an adaption of **WiFi** for automotive environments [24]. The most important changes have been made on the physical layer to cope with the speeds at which vehicles move compared to the typical office and home use of other WiFi standards. Built on top of 802.11p are several technologies that provide higher level features for an automotive environment. The most important one (at least for Europe) is ITS-G5 as defined by the ETSI [13]. ITS-G5 is used, for example, in the highway corridor from Rotterdam to Vienna[4].

4.3 Reliability

In the past wireless communication has only been used for non-critical communication such as updating maps of navigation systems. The trend is to transmit information that is time-critical. From traffic-jam warnings, which have acceptable latency in the order of minutes towards collision warnings and control loops for highway platooning, which have acceptable latency of tens or hundreds of milliseconds.

When the acceptable latency is high, a transmission can be made reliable using retransmissions. However, a low acceptable latency limits the number of

---

[4] http://www.eco-at.info.

possible retransmissions and, thus, also the reliability. Hence, high reliability is hard mostly for low latency applications. Other methods to ensure reliability are costly, because they need bandwidth and infrastructure. Hence, providing high reliability is only a focus, when (human) lives are at risk or communication failures are expensive (e.g., damage to vehicles).

4.4 Scenarios

The next step is to determine which automotive scenario is suited best to measure the reliability of wireless communication. We consider only scenarios, which have quantified requirements on reliability and latency.

Automated overtaking [4] on highways is considered relatively easy, because the road is mostly straight, vehicles move in only one direction and there are multiple lanes. However, autonomous vehicles will also have to overtake other vehicles on curvy rural roads, with two-way traffic and one lane per direction. Especially on rural roads an automated vehicle can benefit from communication with other vehicles to safely and comfortably overtake.

Cooperative collision avoidance [4] allows vehicles to communicate to prevent accidents. Autonomous vehicles should be able to handle most situations they encounter using only their built in sensors. However, sometimes situations may arise where the built in sensors are not enough to prevent a collision. In these cases wireless communication can avoid collisions. Human-piloted vehicles can also benefit from collision warnings, if the warnings are implemented such that the driver can react quickly. An example, where cooperative collision avoidance can be used are urban intersections. Collision avoidance can be implemented with trajectory announcements or handshake and status updates.

In **high-density platoons** [4] vehicles follow each other at close distances. This increases efficiency of traffic and reduces fuel consumption [8]. When vehicles use sensors to detect changes in the speed of the vehicle in front, they have to wait for the vehicle in front to change its speed measurably to react. With wireless communication the vehicle in front can inform the vehicle(s) behind it the moment it detects a dangerous situation. Thus, using wireless communication in platoons, reduces the distances and thereby increases efficiency.

Table 1 summarizes the requirements of the scenarios we described in this section. The values presented should not be understood as definitive values, but only provide an estimate for the requirements on this level of aggregation.

4.5 Selection

We select the scenario of cooperative collision avoidance, because: (1) It is possible to measure the reliability of wireless communication at an urban intersection without the need to move at high speeds (such as on highways or rural roads). (2) The wireless environment seems challenging (Non-line-of-sight, many moving objects, many other wireless signals).

208   M. Herlich et al.

Table 1. Requirements of automotive scenarios (data source [4])

Scenario	Latency [ms]	Reliability [%]
Automated overtake	10	99.999
Collision avoidance: handshake	100	99.999
Collision avoidance: status updates	10	99.9
High density platooning	10	99.999

5 Industry

The industrial sector is expected to continue to automate more processes and factories will be more dynamic. That is, they have to change more often instead of producing the same good for a long time. Drivers for this are increased customization of products and the need to reduce the time from design to market of a product. This is part of the general trend towards Industry 4.0 [20,21]. The 5G Alliance for Connected Industries and Automation (5G-ACIA[5]) plans to push the requirements of industry into 5G.

5.1 Communication

The use of wireless communication can be grouped in three categories: within factories, in the supply chain, and during the product life-cycle [3].

To make factories more dynamic, machines **within the factory** need to communicate more. Machines will increasingly communicate by wireless communication, because this reduces the overhead of connecting communication networks when machines are moved. Additionally, wireless communication will allow devices to transmit from locations, where it is impossible to connect them with wires (e.g., inside sealed containers). For communication inside the factory low latency and high reliability are important [28]. However, especially requirements on latency and reliability cannot be fulfilled with todays technologies [17].

Wireless communication can quickly identify parts and connect physical parts with their virtual representation and history. This will improve the way products flow through the **supply chain**. Following each item individually through the supply chain is necessary to customize each product.

Wireless communication will not cease after a product is sold: Monitoring the product will be possible during the complete **product life cycle**. Wireless communication will allow devices to send their usage patterns to the manufacturer to improve the next generation of products. Additionally, it can be used to ensure that each product is correctly disposed of after the end-of-life.

5.2 Technologies

Because wireless communication can be used for different tasks in the industrial sector, different technologies have been developed.

---

[5] https://www.5g-acia.org.

Because **WiFi** is extensively used outside of the industrial sector, it is reused to reduce costs. The biggest drawback of WiFi in the industrial setting is that WiFi was not created for the requirements that industry has. Nevertheless, for much of the non-critical communication it can be used. Standard WiFi has been adapted for industrial applications in proprietary standards.

Wired communication technologies are established in the industrial sector. Some of these have been **adapted for wireless** use. For example, the Highway Addressable Remote Transducer (HART) Protocol can be used wirelessly using WirelessHART. Protocols, which have been adapted from wired protocols, are generally implemented with a specific focus and capability. However, the design and implementation of modern wireless communication systems has become so complex, that implementing a custom system for each use case is expensive.

The target market of **5G** is very broad. This however makes it possible to spread the development cost of the technology over many devices. Thus, technologies that are too expensive to develop for a single-use wireless system can be used by all 5G devices as the development cost is shared. The communication in the supply chain and over the life-cycle of a product can reuse the infrastructure that will be built and can be shared with all other 5G applications. Communication within a factory usually has much higher requirements on the quality of service (see next section) than communication outside the factory. Thus, using a publicly available 5G network will not be enough for in-factory communication. 5G might provide private cells for dedicated operation within factories.

5.3 Reliability

To monitor the life-cycle of a product the most pressing problem is to keep the cost of the communication low. Usually infrequent status updates are enough to gain insights into the usage of the products. When parts of a product are traced in the supply chain, the requirements on the reliability of the wireless communication are higher, because the tracking should be continuous, but it does not require millisecond responsiveness.

The requirements on the wireless system are highest for the in-factory scenarios: Here the reliability and tolerable latency are strictly limited. Because the demands of non-critical monitoring tasks are moderate, these have been approached before 5G already. However, production-critical tasks have rarely been executed over wireless communication. The German industrial Radio Initiative has collected profiles of wireless requirements in industry [30].

5.4 Scenarios

In this section we will summarize industrial scenarios in which reliability is important. From these scenarios we select one that is most suited to demonstrate the use of methods to determine the reliability. Details about the scenarios are available in the corresponding references.

Table 2 shows a summary of the requirements on wireless communication performance from different documents. The requirements on latency are in the

Table 2. Requirements of industrial scenarios

Scenario	Latency [ms]	Reliability [%]
Diagnosis & maintenance [15]	20	99.99
Discrete production [15]	1	99.9999999
Discrete automation [1]	10	99.99
Manufacturing [16]	1	99.9999
Process automation [16]	20	99.9999
Process automation [15]	50	99.999
Process automation (monitoring) [1]	50	99.9
Process automation (remote control) [1]	50	99.9999

range of 1 ms to 50 ms and the reliability in the range of 99.9 % to 99.9999999 %. However, most requirements can be fulfilled with 10 ms latency and a reliability of 99.9999 %.

5.5 Selection

A concrete scenario where reliability is important is a wireless emergency-stop button. An emergency-stop button is a button that an operator of a machine can press to disable a machine. Because this safety feature can be necessary to safe human lives, it has to be highly reliable. Therefore, emergency-stop buttons have until recently always been connected by wired connections to the machines they disable.

In the past each machine had an operator and, thus, each machine had a control panel at which the operator worked. As factories have become more automated, the number of workers was reduced and the control panels have become more complex. Now one operator manages several machines. Hence, it has become cheaper to give each operator a control panel than to attach one to every machine. To be able to work efficiently the machine operator needs to wirelessly connect to the machines.

For an emergency-stop button, which has to reliably shut down a machine, it is a problem when the wirelessly transmitted packets can be lost. Technically, the requirement is that the machines stops at maximum a predetermined time after the button was pressed. Current wireless panels with an emergency-stop button (for example, from Siemens [25] and Sigmatek[6]) implement this by repeatedly sending data packets over the wireless network, which specify that the button has not been pressed ("heartbeat"). In case of a network outage the machine will stop once it has not received a message after a given interval. While this ensures that the machine will reliably stop, a long-enough network outage will erroneously cause the machine to stop. Because this usually results in lost production, having a reliable network is important for the use of wireless emergency-stop buttons.

---

[6] http://www.sigmatek-automation.com/en/products/hmi/mobile-panels/.

The wireless emergency-stop buttons transmit many data packets as the send intervals are low (in the order of 10 ms). They are a good scenario to measure the reliability as they generate packets in regular intervals, which can be passively monitored. That is, no additional traffic needs to be generated in the usually already saturated wireless factory environment.

6   Comparison

In the previous sections we have developed two scenarios (one automotive and one industrial) which are suitable as showcases to demonstrate how to measure the reliability of wireless communication. In this section, we compare both scenarios and determine whether they overlap or need different methods of measurement. Table 3 shows a summary of the properties of the two scenarios.

Table 3. Comparison of scenarios

	Automotive: collision avoidance	Industrial: emergency-stop button
Access-control	None	Strict
Weather susceptibility	High (outdoor)	Low (indoor)
Measurement method	Active	Passive
Traffic profile	Random	Deterministic
Important for 5G	Yes	Yes
WiFi-based operation	Yes	Yes

The automotive scenario of collision avoidance at an urban intersection has no access control as it is located on public land. In contrast to this the wireless emergency-stop button is located within a factory and, thus, is behind access control. These two environments pose different problems for the methods to measure the reliability. Behind access control it is easier to reconstruct events than in an open environment. However, it is also more complex to get access to the measurement system, which then needs to operate with less physical access.

The two scenarios also differ in their susceptibility to weather: The industrial scenario is within a factory and, thus, the effect of weather is limited (both on the measurements and the measurement system). The automotive scenario is situated outside. Therefore, the measurement system has to be able to withstand at least a minimal amount of weather. Additionally, the wireless environment might change with the weather.

Because currently few vehicles use vehicle-to-vehicle communication, it will be necessary to actively generate measurement traffic at the intersection to generate enough data. In contrast, the emergency-stop button will generate large amounts of measurement data simply when passively monitoring the system as it transmits in short intervals. Hence, to measure the reliability of the wireless communication in all scenarios both active and passive methods are needed.

We also expect the profiles of the wireless network traffic to be different. The emergency-stop button generates packets in regular intervals. The collision warnings sent by cars will not be regularly spaced in time. It is unclear which random distribution they follow, but they will likely be different from the pattern of the emergency-stop button.

The scenarios have in common that they are examples for the use of wireless communication in sectors that are important for 5G. Additionally, both have already existing technological variants that are based on WiFi. This allows researchers to run preliminary tests while 5G hardware is not yet available.

In summary, measurement methods which are able to measure the reliability in both of these scenarios are able to measure the reliability in any scenario. Hence, these scenarios are suitable as representative scenarios for all others.

7   Conclusion

The goal of this paper was to survey scenarios in which methods to measure the reliability of wireless networks are essential. We described classes of measurement methods (active vs passive and periodic vs event-based traffic). Based on related work we determined that the most promising scenarios are in the automotive and the industrial sector.

A deeper search in the literature and interviews in these sectors lead us to two scenarios. For the automotive sector the scenario is an intersection in an urban area, where vehicles exchange collision warnings. For the industrial sector the scenario is an emergency-stop button, which regularly transmits its status to cope with outages of the wireless system.

Both scenarios are in important sectors for the future use of 5G systems and need different types of measurement techniques. Because methods, which can measure the reliability in these scenarios, need to use a variety of measurement methods, they should be able to measure the reliability in many scenarios. To make research comparable, we propose that researchers test their methods to determine the reliability of wireless networks on these two scenarios.

Acknowledgment. This research is partly funded by the Austrian Federal Ministry of Transport, Innovation and Technology (BMVIT) and the Austrian state Salzburg.

References

1. 3GPP: TS 22.261 V. 16.1.0: Service requirements for the 5G system (2017)
2. 5G-PPP: 5G and e-Health (2015)
3. 5G-PPP: 5G and the Factories of the Future (2015)
4. 5G-PPP: 5G Automotive Vision (2015)
5. 5G-PPP: 5G Empowering Vertical Industries (2016)
6. 5GAA: The Case for Cellular V2X for Safety and Cooperative Driving (2016)
7. Avizienis, A., Laprie, J.C., Randell, B., Landwehr, C.: Basic concepts and taxonomy of dependable and secure computing. IEEE Trans. Dependable Secur. Comput. **1**(1), 11–33 (2004)
8. Bergenhem, C., Shladover, S., Coelingh, E., Englund, C., Tsugawa, S.: Overview of platooning systems. In: Proceedings of the 19th ITS World Congress, 22–26 October, Vienna, Austria (2012)

9. Bundesministerium für Verkehr, Innovation und Technologie: Automatisiert - Vernetzt - Mobil (2016)
10. Bundesministerium für Verkehr, Innovation und Technologie: Produktion der Zukunft - Forschung und Technologieentwicklung für eine innovative Sachgüterproduktion (2017)
11. ECSEL-Austria: Austrian Research, Development & Innovation Roadmap for Automated Vehicles (2015)
12. European Commission: Factories of the Future - Multi-annual roadmap for the contractual PPP under Horizon 2020 (2013)
13. European Telecommunications Standards Institute: Intelligent Transport Systems (ITS); Access layer specification for Intelligent Transport Systems operating in the 5 GHz frequency band. Technical report EN 302 663 V1.2.0, November 2012
14. European Telecommunications Standards Institute: LTE; Service requirements for V2X services. TS TS 122 185 V14.3.0, March 2017
15. Fachausschuss Funksysteme in der Informationstechnischen Gesellschaft im VDE (ITG): Funktechnologien für Industrie 4.0 - ITG AG FunkTechnologie 4.0 (2017)
16. Fokusgruppe Mobilkommunikation der Informationstechnischen Gesellschaft im VDE (ITG): Resiliente Netze mit Funkzugang (2017)
17. Frotzscher, A., Wetzker, U.: Avoiding down times - monitoring, diagnostics and troubleshooting of industrial wireless systems. In: Proceedings of the Wireless Congress: Systems and Applications (2017)
18. Holfeld, B., et al.: Radio channel characterization at 5.85 GHz for wireless M2M communication of industrial robots. In: Wireless Communications and Networking Conference (WCNC), pp. 1–7. IEEE (2016)
19. IKT für Mobilität: Studie Mobilität 2025: Koexistenz oder Konvergenz von IKT für Automotive? (2016)
20. Industrie 4.0 Working Group: Recommendations for implementing the strategic initiative INDUSTRIE 4.0 (2013)
21. International Eletrotechnical Commision (IEC): Factory of the future (2015)
22. International Union of Railways: UIC Project EIRENE System Requirements Specification (2006)
23. ITU: Minimum requirements related to technical performance for IMT-2020 radio interface(s) (2017)
24. Jiang, D., Delgrossi, L.: IEEE 802.11 p: towards an international standard for wireless access in vehicular environments. In: Vehicular Technology Conference (VTC Spring), pp. 2036–2040. IEEE (2008)
25. Siemens: SIMATIC HMI Mobile Panels wireless - Flexible configuration of effective ranges and zones via the SIMATIC WinCC visualization software (2013)
26. Siemens: 5G communication networks: Vertical industry requirements (2016)
27. Wireless World Research Forum: A new Generation of e-Health Systems Powered by 5G (2016)
28. Yilmaz, O.N., Wang, Y.P.E., Johansson, N.A., Brahmi, N., Ashraf, S.A., Sachs, J.: Analysis of ultra-reliable and low-latency 5G communication for a factory automation use case. In: International Conference Communication Workshop (ICCW), pp. 1190–1195. IEEE (2015)
29. ZDKI Industrial Radio Technical Group 1: Aspects of Dependability Assessment in ZDKI: "Applications, Requirements and Validation" of the Accompanying Research (2017)
30. ZDKI Industrial Radio Technical Group 1: Requirement Profiles in ZDKI: "Applications, Requirements and Validation" of the Accompanying Research (2017)

Application of IEC 62443 for IoT Components

Abdelkader Magdy Shaaban[✉], Erwin Kristen, and Christoph Schmittner

AIT Austrian Institute of Technology, Vienna, Austria
{Abdelkader.Shaaban,Erwin.Kristen,Christoph.Schmittner}@ait.ac.at
https://www.ait.ac.at/

Abstract. Internet technology has changed how people live, work, connect and learn. It connects machines, devices, sensors, and people and enables communication. This enabled a revolution in the industrial perspective, which is named "Industry 4.0." Industry 4.0 is the application of automation and data exchange in manufacturing technologies. This rapid progression of industrial systems towards internet based production networks needs a flexible framework that facilitates addressing current and future vulnerabilities in Industrial Automation Control Systems (IACS). IEC 62443 series provides a standard methodology for building a secure infrastructure, which adapts the security requirements needed by IACS. The basic approach defined in the standard is to break down the system components into zones and conduits based on required security levels. This paper reuses this idea on a small scale to show how the same concept can be used to define zones and conduits between mixed-criticality IoT components to improve the security on component level. The MORETO tool, which is currently under development by AIT, supports the security risk analysis process.

Keywords: Cyber-physical Production Systems
Industrial Automation Control Systems · Internet of Things
Supervisory Control and Data Acquisition

1 Introduction

Cyber-physical Production Systems (CPPS) is one of the technical driving forces. It integrates and builds on a variety of existing technologies and components such as robotics, industrial automation and control, Internet of Things (IoT), big data, and cloud computing [1]. IoT consists of small things, widely distributed, which offer many benefits for industrial systems. IoT is a new enhancement, for Industrial Automation Control Systems (IACS), where billions of devices, with smart data processing capabilities, are networked over the Internet access [2]. In former days the corporate networks for production planning, work scheduling, material ordering and other administrative work was isolated from the Industrial Automation Control Systems (IACS) networks. This top level of enterprise information

© Springer Nature Switzerland AG 2018
B. Gallina et al. (Eds.): SAFECOMP 2018 Workshops, LNCS 11094, pp. 214–223, 2018.
https://doi.org/10.1007/978-3-319-99229-7_19

technology infrastructure was already exposed to external attacks, because of the system related necessary communication links to the outside world.

As corporate networks are covering with IACS networks and the proprietary IACS networks were replaced with commercial off-the-shelf equipment using Ethernet-TCP/IP technology the same cyber vulnerabilities threaten the IACS networks. Additional, the complexity of the overall system is increased dramatically and the controller in the IACS networks are now jeopardize by new threat sources that they were never designed to handle. Replacing them with attack proofed controllers is in many cases not possible or not offered by the machinery supplier. This would also disturb the continuous operation of the production process.

Next generation IACS, which are already existing in various stages of implementation, are more and more open operation architectures which are no longer limited to the plant area. The components of the different operation processes are connected by communication links, wired or wireless, where there is no need to place the components as near as possible for short interconnections. On the contrary, these network interconnection structures allow the totally breakup of conventional enterprise architectures. For the following example, see the well-known Purdue Model of a network layered enterprise architecture, shown in Fig. 1. The name Purdue Model [3] came from the Purdue University, Indiana, U.S, where Theodore J. Williams developed the "Purdue Enterprise Reference Architecture (PERA)" in the 1990's. The Enterprise Resource Planning (ERP), the top levels of the Perdue model, is defined from most of industrial plants. The same will be valid with the next layer, the Manufacturing Execution System (MES).

Level 2, the Supervisory Control and Data Acquisition (SCADA) layer is the next candidate to be moved outside of the plant, partly or complete. In the future the levels 1 and 0 will be connected wireless in a so called ad-hoc network, where the different components connect among each other depending on the product which shall be produced [4]. Especially with increased interconnection and collaboration between manufacturing steps in the supply chain multiple levels will be interconnected.

IACS security goals focus on control system availability, plant protection, plant operations and time-critical system response. There are already standards, which provide the security requirements for the components that make up an IACS, specifically the embedded devices, network components, host components and software applications. One of a most common security standard for IACS is the IEC 62443 standard. The organization of this paper is as follows, Sect. 2 discusses, the main goal of the IEC 62443 security standard in IACS. Section 3 explains, how the MORETO tool can be used to analyze and manage the security requirements, appropriate to the IEC 62443 security standard. Section 4 shows, the concept of Zones and Conduits. The security risk analysis by MORETO is discussed in Sect. 5. Section 6 illustrates how the same idea of Zones and Conduits can be reused on the component-level. Finally, the paper ends with outlook and discussion.

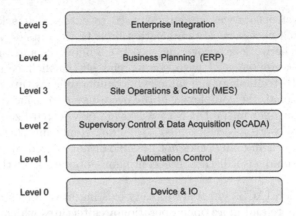

Fig. 1. Network layered architecture (Purdue Model) [4]

2 State of the Art

The primary goal of the IEC 62443 standard series is to present a framework that addresses current and future security vulnerabilities in industrial systems and enables security risk management for the complete life cycle and all layers of industrial networks [5]. This is done by dividing the system into zones, defining security levels for each zone and specifying security capabilities that enable a component to be integrated into a system environment at a given security level (SL). The IEC 62443 standard consists of thirteen documents classified into four main groups: General, Policies and Procedures, System, and Component. The first two groups represent concepts, uses cases, policies and procedures associated with ICS security. The other two groups, System and Component, define the technical requirements for networks and system components [6].

System Requirements. The IEC 62443-3-1 standard part provides an overview of the advantages and limitations of existing network security technologies. IEC 62443-3-2 standard part addresses security risk assessment and network design. Finally, the IEC 62443-3-3 standard part describes general system security requirements such as authentication, data confidentiality and system integrity, emphasizing that performance and availability should not be compromised during the process of addressing these requirements [7].

Component Requirements. The Component group consists of two documents. The IEC 62443-4-1 standard part defines the development process for ICS products, to reduce the number of security vulnerabilities in control system solutions. The IEC 62443-4-2 standard part specifies the technical requirements for securing the individual components of an ICS network. The standard documents are aligned with IACS life-cycle phases. Figure 2 shows, the life-cycle phases of IACS cyber security [7].

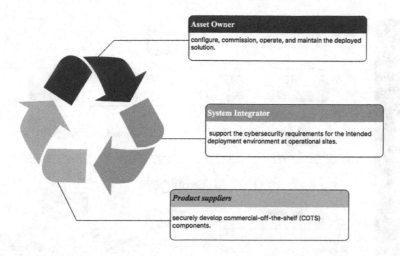

Fig. 2. IACS cyber security life-cycle phases

To be successful in IACS cyber security, all the target audiences (Owner, Integrator, Supplier) have "shared responsibility" for all phases of the IACS cyber security life cycle [8]. The IEC 62443 standard defines rules and methods to operate IACS networks by requirements, controls and best practices recommendations. The following section introduces the MORETO tool. This tool implements a new concept for the modelling process, analysing, and generating security requirements based on the IEC 62443 standard.

3 MORETO

The Model-based Security Requirement Management Tool (MORETO) is a tool for security requirements analysis, allocation, and management using modeling languages as SysML/UML. MORETO is developed by AIT, at the center for Digital Safety and Security. MORETO reuses different features driven by concepts and knowledge of system modelling. It gives the user the flexibility of the modelling process in different SysML diagrams. MORETO is an Enterprise Architect (EA) plugin for managing the IEC 62443 security standard.

EA is a visual modelling software and designing tool based on the UML provided by Sparx Systems [9]. EA gives users the flexibilities to improve its functionalities by defining Model Driven Generation (MDG) Technologies. MDG Technologies allow users to extend EA's modelling capabilities. MDG Technologies seamlessly plug into EA to provide additional toolboxes, UML profiles, patterns, templates and other modelling resources [10]. MORETO is reliable and flexible to model safety & security requirements applied to different components and system architectures.

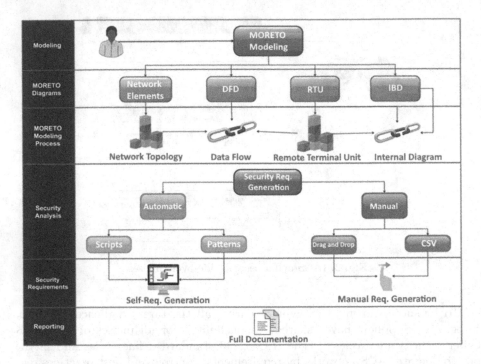

Fig. 3. Workflow of MORETO Tool

Figure 3 shows the workflow for all MORETO phases. The user can define system components, scan the security vulnerabilities in the system, and cover the detected security weaknesses by suitable security measures defined by IEC 62443 standard.

The user chooses the appropriate diagram, which fits the requirements for describing the system components. There are four main diagrams which can be used with the MORETO tool. The Network Components can be used to define a complete network topology. The Dataflow Diagram (DFD) can be used to determine the flow of data through components. Remote-terminal Unit (RTU) diagram has additional elements to describe an operating plant. Finally, the Internal Block Diagram (IBD) can be used to express the internal structure of the components. The security analysis phase constitutes an integral part of MORETO, which is able to scan all elements of the user's model and detect security flaws and risks. Afterwards, MORETO covers these flaws with proper security requirements. Finally, MORETO is collecting all the details of the security analysis and requirements in a final report.

3.1 Security Analysis in MORETO

Security requirements generation features one of the unique services provided by MORETO tool to cover security gaps in the user's model. The security generation process could be manual or automatic as is depicted in Fig. 3 at the "security analysis phase".

Manual Mode. The user uses this mode to create or generate security requirements. This process can be done either by drag and drop or by importing a CSV file.

Drag and Drop. This feature is standard of system modelling software, so the user could specify the security requirements from the toolbox and then drag and drop into the workspace.

Importing CSV files. Importing CSV files is another way to generate security requirements quickly without any efforts from the user side. This feature makes the generating process of security requirements much more comfortable than creating these security requirements one-by-one. This mode supports reusing of security requirements list from former projects.

Automatic Mode. As depicted in Fig. 3, there are two different ways for generating security requirements automatically: either by using Automation (Scripts) or Patterns.

Automation (Scripts). The automated process in MORETO scans the whole system architecture and all components and detect security gaps and needs. Afterwards, MORETO covers the security gaps with security requirements, derived from IEC 62443 security standard. With this feature, MORETO generates automatically a list of security requirements on behalf of the user.

Patterns. Patterns are pre-defined templates implemented and provided by MORETO. This feature generates a list of security requirements with their relationships to the components.

4   Zones and Conduits Concept

The IEC 62443 security standard focuses on the security analysis on the overall manufacturing plant. Based on a security analysis the complete plant is broken into zones which are called security zones. Zones are based on specific characteristics or security needs of the elements. Figure 4 shows an example of an operating plant used in the use case. The operating plant is divided into four security zones (Zone 1, Zone 2, Zone 3, and Zone 4). Three conduits (Conduit 1, Conduit 2, and Conduit 3) define the communication paths between these zones.

The break-down of the above example of an operating plant is performed in the security risk analysis phase. Then the interconnection and communication paths between the zones are defined as "Conduits" , the pipes where secure data and information exchange is performed. The following section explains how this paper will use the concept of the zones and conduits from the IEC 62443 security standard not only for the overall operating plant but also for the single devices from the operating plant.

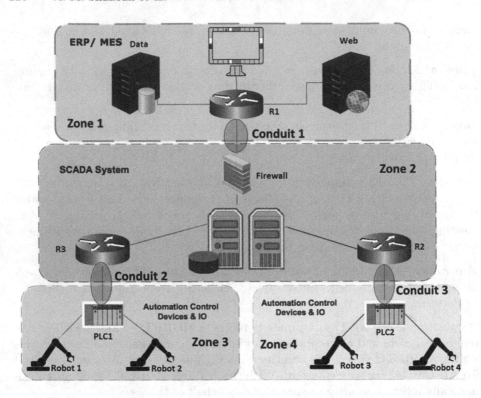

Fig. 4. IEC 62443 zone and conduit concept

5   Security Risk Analysis by MORETO

MORETO tool plays an essential role in generating a list of security requirements for a vast number of different components which are defined in the modelling process. As shown in Fig. 4, there are four zones; each zone has several parts which are connected through communication channels. MORETO scans all of these zones and generates a list of security requirements based on IEC 62443 standard for each modelled component separately. Figure 5 illustrates the list of security requirements, which are generated for the Router device.

Afterwards, MORETO generates a complete report, explaining the security gaps which are detected by MORETO, and which security requirements have been selected to cover these gaps.

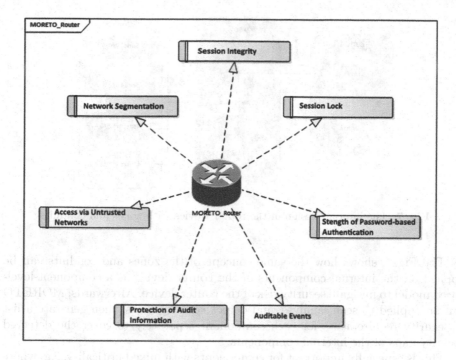

Fig. 5. List of security requirements of the router component

6 Case Study: Router Device

This section shows how we can reuse the concept of the zones and conduits as is described in Sect. 4. However, this will be applied on a small scale on the component level. The proposed component is the router device from the above operating plant example (Fig. 4). Figure 6 shows, the internal block diagram of the router device.

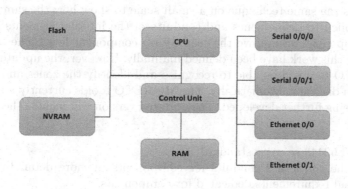

Fig. 6. The internal design of the router device without zones and conduits

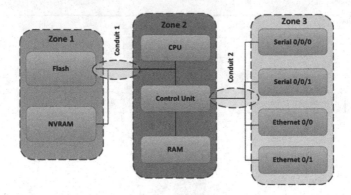

Fig. 7. The internal design of the router device with zones and conduits

The Fig. 7, shows how the same concept of the zones and conduits can be applied on the internal components of the router device as a component-level-based model to mitigate security risk of the router device. Afterwards, MORETO can be applied to scan, analyse, and detect security flaws, then generate a list of security requirements for each component separately to cover the detected security gaps of the internal components.

This is especially important for components with mixed-criticality, e.g. where one part is responsible for the outside communication and the other part is responsible for a timing or safety-critical application. Here this approach allows to divide parts with different criticality, group all interactions between them in conduits and define security requirements based on their needs.

7 Outlook and Discussion

This paper presented how to reuse the basic concept of the IEC 62443 standard on the component level. The standard proposes to break down the system components into zones and conduits based on required security levels. However, this work reuses the same technique on a small scale to show how the same concept can be applied to define zones and conduits of the internal elements of a particular component to improve the security on component level. The zones and conduits in this work have been defined manually. However, the updated version of MORETO tool will be able to recognise and identify the zones and conduits of the given diagram automatically. The MORETO tool is currently a prototype which, is being further developed. The updated version will include the following features:

- The IEC 62443 security standard.
- Adapt the zones and conduits for components in more detail by defining additional requirements dedicated for components.
- Divide the internal structure of components into "Zones" and "Conduits".

- Generate full documentation for the security flaws based on the component-Level.
- Implement additional security standards like as ISO 27000 for information security management systems.

Acknowledgement. This work has received funding from the SemI40 and AQUAS project, under grant agreement No. 692466 and No. 737475. The project is co-funded by grants from Austria, Germany, Italy, France, Portugal and ECSEL JU.

References

1. Ma, Z., Hudic, A., Shaaban, A., Plosz, S.: Security viewpoint in a reference architecture model for cyber-physical production systems. In: 2017 IEEE European Symposium on Security and Privacy Workshops (EuroS&PW), pp. 153–159. IEEE (2017)
2. Shahzad, A., Kim, Y.-G., Elgamoudi, A.: Secure IoT platform for industrial control systems. In: 2017 International Conference on Platform Technology and Service (PlatCon), pp. 1–6. IEEE (2017)
3. Williams, T.J.: The Purdue enterprise reference architecture. Comput. Ind. **24**(2–3), 141–158 (1994)
4. IT/OT Executive Series: What you need to know about - networking. https://www.cogentind.com/it-ot-networking/
5. OVE Osterreichischer Verband fur Elektrotechnik. Industrial communication networks – Security for industrial automation and control systems, Part 4-2: Technical security requirements for IACS components. Technical report, IEC standards, June 2017
6. ISA. The 62443 series of standards: Industrial automation and control systems security, (1–4) (2018)
7. Security Levels in ISA-99 / IEC 62443. ISA 99 security levels proposal. https://www.scribd.com/document/129590220/ISA-99-SecurityLevels-Proposal/
8. Ristaino, A.: Industrial automation cyber security conformity assessments. http://www.isasecure.org/en-US/Articles/Industrial-automation-cybersecurity-conformity-ass
9. Enterprise Architect: Enterprise architect by sparx systems. https://www.sparxsystems.eu/start/home/
10. Enterprise Architect Sparx Systems. Model driven generation (MDG) technologies. http://www.sparxsystems.com/resources/mdg_tech/

Dependable Outlier Detection in Harsh Environments Monitoring Systems

Gonçalo Jesus[1] (ID), António Casimiro[2(✉)] (ID), and Anabela Oliveira[1] (ID)

[1] Hydraulics and Environment Department, LNEC, Lisbon, Portugal
{gjesus,aoliveira}@lnec.pt
[2] LASIGE, Faculdade de Ciências, Universidade de Lisboa, Lisboa, Portugal
casim@ciencias.ulisboa.pt

Abstract. Environmental monitoring systems are composed by sensor networks deployed in uncertain and harsh conditions, vulnerable to external disturbances, posing challenges to the comprehensive system characterization and modelling. When unexpected sensor measurements are produced, there is a need to detect and identify, in a timely manner, if they stem from a failure behavior or if they indeed represent some environment-related process. Existing solutions for fault detection in environmental sensor networks do not portray the required sensitivity for the differentiation of these processes or they are unable to meet the time constraints of the affected cyber-physical systems.

We have been developing a framework for dependable detection of failures in harsh environments monitoring systems, aiming to improve the overall sensor data quality. Herein we present the application of an early framework implementation to an aquatic sensor network dataset, using neural networks to model sensors' behaviors, correlated data between neighbor sensors, and a statistical technique to detect the presence of outliers in the datasets.

Keywords: Dependability · Data quality · Outlier detection · Machine learning
Neural networks · Water monitoring

1 Introduction

Environmental monitoring systems based on wireless sensor networks consist of sensor nodes distributed over the observable areas, which are connected to sink nodes through a wireless network. The sink nodes gather the readings of the sensor nodes, perform sensor fusion and other data processing tasks, and transmit the results to decision-support systems, alert and emergency systems, or actuators in the field. Therefore, environmental monitoring systems can be considered complex cyber-physical systems.

Given the importance of the flux of the gathered data into end systems, it is crucial to recognize, categorize and mitigate sensor faults in environment monitoring networks. As sensor data comprises both correct measurements and noisy or faulty values (either outliers or continuous sets of unreliable data), this error-prone data can lead to the issuing of false warnings or backing wrong decisions.

© Springer Nature Switzerland AG 2018
B. Gallina et al. (Eds.): SAFECOMP 2018 Workshops, LNCS 11094, pp. 224–233, 2018.
https://doi.org/10.1007/978-3-319-99229-7_20

While fault detection in sensor networks has been subject of several studies [1–3], many of the methodologies or techniques used are not appropriate in harsh environments applications. Harsh environments are characterized by extreme or abnormal conditions that can both damage sensor components and create unusual perturbations in environmental conditions, which pose challenges for ensuring the quality and correctness of monitoring. Hence, harsh environments require monitoring solutions that are resilient to these disturbances and uncertainties, in contrast to solutions for controlled and mostly stable settings. And given the criticality of applications, it becomes imperative to meet the requirements on data quality collected from the monitored environment and used in the cyber-physical system.

An important step towards the increase of data quality in sensor networks is the employment of fault detection methodologies [4], starting by a characterization of the possible faulty behaviors affecting the monitored data. However, in harsh environments this characterization is harder than in controlled environments, because unexpected changes in the environmental conditions, such as storms, earthquakes or fires, create abnormal patterns in sensor data which, however, should not be treated as faulty behaviors. For instance, a temperature sensor for weather control affected by a fire incident will output values significantly above the normal one, which, however, do not portray a sensor failure situation.

Furthermore, to improve the monitoring system it is also necessary the definition of strategies to mitigate or, ideally, correct the faulty readings, making it possible to utilize the readings with some level of confidence in the end-systems.

Considering the presented challenges and requirements for monitoring in harsh environments, we have been developing a generic monitoring framework that we briefly describe in this paper. The framework provides: (1) support for the detection of faulty readings in the sensor measurements; (2) quality information associated to every sensor measurement; and (3) a reassessment of a measurement whenever it considered faulty or with insufficient quality. Based on this framework, the main contributions of this paper are the following:

- The application of the framework to an existing sensor network in a river-estuary environment that is subject to severe weather conditions and various hazards affecting sensors;
- An overview of the designed strategy for detecting outliers with high accuracy, along with an approach for the reduction of false positives;
- Experimental results of the application of machine learning techniques in both the framework steps, customized for the scenario of the river-estuary environment using real datasets from sensors deployed in the water, measuring temperature and salinity parameters.

The paper is structured as follows. In Sect. 2 we present an overview of the monitoring framework, with the description of its components and procedures. Section 3 is focused on an application to a river-estuary case study and on the machine learning solution conceived for the detection of outliers. Extensive results comparing the solutions under different customizations are explored in Sect. 4, while Sect. 5 closes the paper with some conclusions and future work considerations.

2 Dependable Monitoring Framework

The dependability of sensor data is directly related with the quality of measurements. Any given framework or fault-tolerant strategy must be able to characterize the possible sources of faults affecting the sensor network, related failure behaviors and corresponding fault models. We presented in [4, 5] a brief overview of the commonly observed failure behaviors, and the strategies based on machine learning technologies, which are proven to be adequate to model the observed system. Furthermore, we proposed and described a generic dependable monitoring framework for harsh environments in [6].

The framework, which we briefly overview, is based on data fusion techniques using machine learning that model each sensor behavior according to all sensors past measurements. Considering that there must be an history of measurements previous to the application of the framework procedures, there is a preliminary step consisting on the creation of such models. For fault-detection purposes, each sensor must be represented by at least two models exploring temporal, spatial and value correlations between either target sensor past measurements or a combination of the sensors existent in the sensor network. Additionally, the framework is composed by the following four main components that are executed in the sink node whenever a new measurement from any sensor is received:

- *Prediction (P)* – in a harsh environment the truthfulness of a measurement can only be assessed by knowing the involved impacting conditions, what is seldomly feasible. Alternatively, to substantiate the truthfulness of a measurement, an attainable method is to employ several prediction methods to estimate the measurement;
- *Failure Detection (FD)* – the objective is to detect and identify failure behaviors affecting measurements of the target sensors. This involves the execution of procedures not only to characterize abnormal measurements but also to distinguish sensor faults from environment-related events. The predictions obtained in the previous component are of great importance in this step;
- *Quality Evaluation (QE)* – the outcome of the previous components enables the quantification of the confidence level on the new received measurement. The component output is a quality coefficient associated to the measurement. When facing a failure behavior, this value is set to 0;
- *Measurement Reassessment (MR)* – if a measurement is faulty it is important for future predictions and for further systems to have access to an estimate of the expected measurement, even if it is not fully reliable (confidence level below standard). This component enables the mitigation of the effects of the failure behavior by producing an estimation of measurement as if it was not affected by any fault.

The flow of information processing through these components is depicted in Fig. 1. Before a measurement can be fully processed, a warm-up stage is necessary to build the histories of past measurements for each sensor. Only then it is possible to employ the prediction methods to obtain an estimate of the expected measurement. Additionally, besides the past measurements it is possible to use other information correlated with the target sensor, such as correlated sensor data or validated numerical models that simulate the dynamics of the monitored system, which work as virtual correlated sensors providing estimated readings.

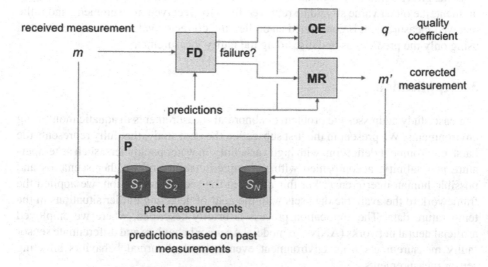

Fig. 1. Flow diagram of the dependable monitoring framework.

The prediction methods consist on the data fusion techniques that correlate sensors past information to build a faithful model of the target sensor. There are no constraints on the used techniques, but some may be more suitable to the conditions and specifics of the sensor network and the environment. Regarding the quantity of predictions, the only requirement is to have at least two predictions, being one of them only based on past measurements of the target sensor. This ensures that either faulty measurements or specific events of other sensors do not propagate to at least one prediction.

In the Failure Detection component, processing is performed to compare the predictions to the newly received measurement. If there are no faults affecting the sensors, or other environmental events, all predictions will be consistent with the measurement. On the other hand, if some prediction is significantly different from the received measurement, this might indicate the presence of faults. It is the comparison strategy that enables the detection of faults and their distinction from real environmental events. As described in the Prediction component, the comparison selection strategy is also part of the application process since there is no specific method to assess the significance of the differences. The method depends on the type of failures, the process dynamics and the type of correlations existent in the predictions. In Sect. 3 we exploit the distribution of square differences to detect outliers, but other statistical or machine learning methods can be also considered.

In the Quality Evaluation component, the confidence level in the received measurement will be quantified as a quality coefficient, between 0 and 1, being 0 the lowest and 1 the highest possible quality. This confidence value can be extracted through an evaluation method that, for example, calculates the significance of the differences among measurement and the predictions.

The Measurement Reassessment component considers the same information, measurement and predictions, and produces an estimated measurement that is expectedly free from the effect of faults. For instance, if an offset failure is affecting the received measurement, the offset value should be removed from the received measurement, and if the received measurement is considered an outlier, the corrected value should be estimated using only the predictions and discarding the faulty measurement.

3   Application

Our case study addresses the problem of abnormal measurements in aquatic monitoring environments. We present in the first subsection the case study, that fully represents the harsh environment definition, with high variability in water parameters, such as temperature and salinity, accompanied with the unpredictability of weather scenarios and possible human interference. For this effect, in the second subsection, we applied the framework to the available data sets with the goal of detecting outlier situations in the temperature data. The application process is briefly described, where we employed artificial neural networks (ANNs) to model the sensor behaviors and differentiate sensor faulty measurements from environment event-related abnormal behaviors affecting sensor measurements.

3.1   Case Study

Although the purpose of the presented framework is to be applied in real-time monitoring, it is also possible to employ the procedures for the analysis of pre-collected data sets. In fact, the results presented in Sect. 4 were obtained using existing data sets from a monitoring network in the Columbia River estuary, situated in the northwest coast of the USA. The sensor network is owned and maintained by CMOP's Science and Technology University Research Network monitoring network (denoted SATURN [7]), and it is comprised of various sensors deployed along the estuary, measuring many water parameters such as water levels, salinity and temperature or biogeochemistry on a 24/7 basis.

From the 27 available stations, each one with many sensors, we selected a few for our experimental evaluations. Jetty A, Lower Sand Island light, Desdemona Sands light and Tansy Point were selected, due to the sensor (temperature, elevation and salinity) and monitoring periods similarity.

In the preliminary stage of the framework application, and given the environment specific characteristics, it was observed that the weather seasons have a clear (and expectable) impact on parameters such as temperature. Another important observation is related to the specific characteristics of the considered aquatic environment, an estuary, where the water parameters are significantly impacted by the tides throughout the day. This influence is represented by tidal harmonic constituents [8], where the largest referring to the principal lunar semi-diurnal is a cycle of 12 h and 25.2 min.

3.2   Prediction Models

The river-estuary system is a good example of the non-linearity present in natural and harsh environments. To successfully model these characteristics and be able to capture the existing correlations in the system, we had to consider machine learning techniques. Among various available techniques, we selected artificial neural networks (ANNs) for their capability to learn patterns using training data and the ability to control the inputs and consequent outputs.

In the preliminary phase, we used the specific knowledge of environment being monitored to better prepare a feature selection step and to define the structure of the input vectors of the ANNs. The objective is to predict the next measurement of a particular sensor based on historic knowledge (past measurements) of that sensor and the neighbors, or a combination of this information. Thus, the feature selection step involves a careful selection of which sensors and which data is used in each model.

Considering the tidal influence (specific to this environment) we designed the input vectors to cover the sensors behavior during the principal lunar semi-diurnal cycle. In the training process, given the weather seasonal patterns, we selected a full year of data from all the sensors involved to form the inputs and target vectors for the models.

3.3   Outlier Detection Strategy

In our outlier detection strategy, we verify the difference between the outputs of prediction models and the received measurements by employing a statistical method of the distribution of square differences. This comparison strategy allows the assessment of the difference with a level of significance based on historical data. This historical knowledge was supported by the fitting of the distributions of the differences between each model (ANN) and the corresponding targets for a period of two months, not included in the training data set of the preliminary phase.

With the fitted distributions, in the Failure Detection component the process is to calculate the probability that the difference between a newly received measurement and the expected value is significant, considering a confidence level. In Sect. 4 we study the impact of selecting different values for the confidence level.

For outlier detection, we verified if all the predictions are significantly different from the received measurement, in which case there is very high probability that it is faulty measurement. As mentioned in the previous section, it is important to use at least one model based only on the target sensor past measurements and another involving just the neighbor sensors. This step verifies if the measurement is part of an expected system behavior or if it is in fact a singular event on the target sensor, due to the existing correlations in the environment.

4   Results

In this section, we present the results obtained when applying the framework to the case study scenario, namely considering the employed prediction models (ANNs) and the outlier detection strategy. We also explore some strategies to implement the

Measurement Reassessment component based on the current application of the framework.

For the results herein, we considered the measurements of temperature sensors in the four selected stations (see Fig. 2). We used a three months data set for this validation processing, different from both training and fitting data sets (a few years after both).

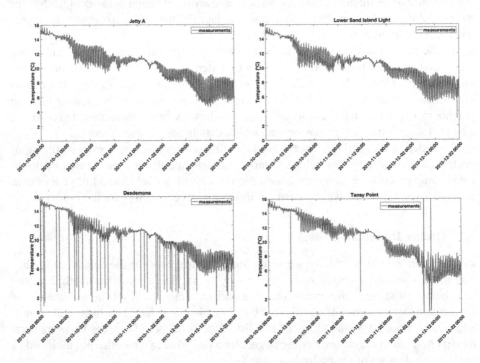

Fig. 2. Sensors measurements for the validation set.

In Fig. 2 it is possible to observe the gradual decrease of the temperature values measured by four different stations from October 2013 to December 2013, and the periodic nature of the "signal", due to the tidal influence. Additionally, we can state from third-party expert validation that in Jetty A (top left graph) there is no presence of outliers, that in Lower Sand Island Light (top right graph) there is 1 outlier, that in Desdemona (bottom left) 43 outliers were identified and, finally, that in Tansy Point (bottom right) 11 outliers were identified, some of which beyond the represented scale.

In the selected outlier detection strategy, for the verification of the conditions, there is a threshold regarding a confidence level that needs to be defined beforehand, associated with the probability that a new measurement is abnormal. Therefore, it is a higher limit threshold that we verified for accuracy by testing four thresholds: 0.997, 0.998, 0.9985 and 0.999. The results for each threshold are presented in Table 1, where it is possible to observe how important it is the selection of the confidence threshold for the employed comparison strategy.

Table 1. Number of detected outliers and number of expert-identified outliers (Real).

Threshold	Jetty A	Lower Sd	Desdemona	Tansy
0.997	2	7	71	24
0.998	2	7	55	24
0.9985	1	4	41	21
0.999	1	2	28	15
Real	**0**	**1**	**43**	**11**

We can observe that while increasing the threshold, the number of detected outliers decreases. For instance, when using a 0.997 threshold, there is a large amount of false positive outliers, contrasting to when setting it to 0.999, in which case number of outliers is lower. In Fig. 3 we highlight the existing trade-off for the Desdemona data set, where it is clear the existence of false positives on the two top graphs and some outliers not detected on the two bottom graphs.

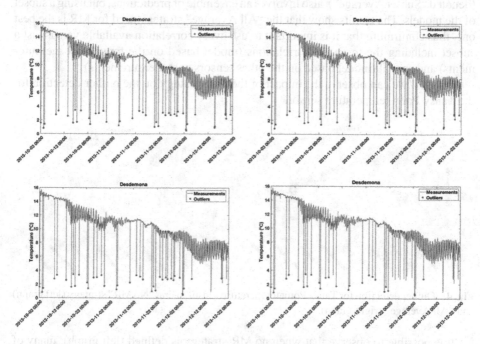

Fig. 3. Outlier detection for Desdemona temperature sensor, with confidence threshold of 0.997, 0.998, 0.9985 and 0.999, from left to right and top to bottom.

Considering both Table 1 and Fig. 3, the best candidate threshold for this application setup is 0.9985, as it provides an overall better outlier detection completeness and at the same time a lower number of false positives.

In addition to failure detection (in this case, outlier detection), there is another important aspect of the framework, namely the Measurement Reassessment (MR). We propose a simple strategy consisting on an ensemble of all the available predictions for the specific case of outliers. This procedure, which involves the replacement of the detected outliers with an average of all the predictions provided by the Prediction component, was used to achieve the results presented in Table 1.

To validate this simple strategy, we tested it against two other strategies using the same candidate threshold (0.9985) and we present the results in Table 2.

Table 2. Number of detected outliers for all sensors according to the MR strategy.

Strategy	Jetty A	Lower Sd	Desdemona	Tansy
No MR	1	3	73	29
Subset Average	16	18	41	24
All Average	1	4	41	21

The first strategy (denoted "No MR"), consists in keeping the original data set intact, allowing the use of erroneous data by the prediction models. The second strategy (denoted "Subset Average"), also involves an ensemble of predictions, but using a subset of the models. The results show that the "All Average" strategy used for MR is the best one, thus confirming that it is important to use every correlation available versus just a subset including the temporal correlations (model based on the target past measurements) and spatial (model based on the other sensors past measurements).

In Fig. 4 we can observe the impact of the MR strategy on the outlier detection for the Tansy Point temperature sensor.

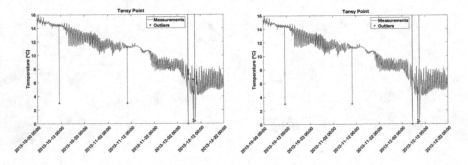

Fig. 4. Outlier detection for Tansy Point temperature sensor, using "No MR" strategy (left graph) and "All Average" (right graph).

It is possible to observe that when no MR strategy is defined (left graph), many of the false positive situations are preceded by outliers, which is due to their use in past measurements for the prediction models. This problem is avoided when using corrected measurements in the history of past measurement, instead of the actual (incorrect) measurements. This corroborates the importance of the use of a corrected value in post-failure detection phase.

5   Conclusions and Future Work Considerations

This paper presents on-going research for the design of strategies for a dependable monitoring framework for harsh environments. Herein, we introduced an outlier failure detection based on two levels of machine learning to provide effective prediction models that explore correlations within the sensor network, and a comparison strategy to ensure the verification of outlier failure conditions.

We also presented the results of experiments with the application of the framework to an aquatic case study, showing the effectiveness of the designed strategies for improving the quality of measurements even though the monitored environment is highly dynamic and impacted by external factors (weather conditions for instance).

Future work will include the design of strategies to detect continuous failure types such as offset and drift (either constant or other type of deviation), considering the framework used in this paper and the same type of prediction techniques (ANNs) to explore the different correlations that exist in the collected data. These strategies will enrich the framework, improving its monitoring capabilities in harsh environments.

Finally, and along with the definition of the new detection strategies, we will define the corresponding procedures performed by Measurement Reassessment and Quality Evaluation components.

Acknowledgements. The authors thank António Baptista and the CMOP SATURN team for their support in the Columbia river analysis. This work was partially supported by the FCT, through the LASIGE Research Unit, Ref. UID/CEC/00408/2013, PhD Grant SFRH/BD/82489/2011 and by H2020 WADI—EC Grant Agreement No. 689239.

References

1. Zhang, Y., Meratnia, N., Havinga, P.: Outlier detection techniques for wireless sensor networks: a survey. IEEE Commun. Surv. Tutor. **12**(2), 159–170 (2010)
2. Zimek, A., Schubert, E., Kriegel, H.P.: A survey on unsupervised outlier detection in high-dimensional numerical data. Stat. Anal. Data Mining ASA Data Sci. J. **5**(5), 363–387 (2012)
3. Gupta, M., Gao, J., Aggarwal, C.C., Han, J.: Outlier detection for temporal data: a survey. IEEE Trans. Knowl. Data Eng. **26**(9), 2250–2267 (2014)
4. Jesus, G., Casimiro, A., Oliveira, A.: A survey on data quality for dependable monitoring in wireless sensor networks. Sensors **17**(9) (2017)
5. Jesus, G., Oliveira, A., Azevedo, A., Casimiro, A.: Improving sensor-fusion with environmental models. In: 2015 IEEE SENSORS, pp. 1–4 (2015)
6. Jesus, G., Casimiro, A., Oliveira, A.: Using machine learning for dependable outlier detection in environmental monitoring systems (submitted)
7. Baptista, A., Howe, B., Freire, J., Maier, D., Silva, C.T.: Scientific exploration in the era of ocean observatories. Comput. Sci. Eng. **10**(3), 53–58 (2008)
8. Pugh, D.T.: Tides, surges and mean sea-level (reprinted with corrections). John Wiley & Sons Ltd., Chichester (1996)

7th International Workshop on Next Generation of System Assurance Approaches for Safety-Critical Systems (SASSUR 2018)

7th International Workshop on Next Generation of System Assurance Approaches for Safety-Critical Systems (SASSUR 2018)

Jose Luis de la Vara[1], Alejandra Ruiz[2], and Tim Kelly[3]

[1] Universidad Carlos III de Madrid, Madrid, Spain
jvara@inf.uc3m.es
[2] TECNALIA, San Sebastián, Spain
alejandra.ruiz@tecnalia.com
[3] University of York, York, UK
tim.kelly@york.ac.uk

SASSUR 2018 is the 7th edition of the International Workshop on Next Generation of System Assurance Approaches for Safety-Critical Systems. SASSUR 2018 continues consolidating and keeping the main objectives of the workshop while also updating and extending its scope with new challenges and trends in system assurance, e.g. regarding the use of new technologies in critical application domains. This is in line with our intention to explore new ideas on compositional, evolutionary, multi-concern, and efficient assurance and certification of safety-critical systems.

New systems characteristics such as autonomy, connectivity, and cooperation, and recent situations such as crashes of autonomous vehicles, system recalls due to insufficient confidence in system safety, and unclear needs and requirements for assurance of systems with advanced features, all motivate the need for novel and cost-effective system assurance approaches. The topics of interest of the workshop include, among others, industrial challenges for safety assurance and certification, challenges for co-assuring safety and security, cross-domain assurance, integration of process-centric and product-centric assurance, management of compliance with standards and regulations, management of assurance evidence and of assuranc cases, multi-concern and mixed-criticality system assurance, compositional, evolutionary, and incremental approaches for system assurance, evolution of standards and trends on regulations, human factors in system assurance, and safety assurance for new systems types, new technologies, and new applications (e.g. artificial intelligence and blockchain).

The program of SASSUR 2018 consists of six high-quality papers. We have divided the papers into two main categories based on their focus and the topics that they cover:

– General Techniques and Trends for Assurance and Certification

1. Tim Gonschorek, Marc Zeller, Frank Ortmeier, and Kai Höfig. Fault Trees vs. Component Fault Trees: An Empirical Study.
2. John Macgregor and Simon Burton. Challenges in Assuring Highly Complex, High Volume Safety-Critical Software.

3. Hideaki Nishihara and Kenji Taguchi. Comparing Risk Identification in Hazard Analysis and Threat Analysis.

- Assurance in the Automotive Domain

4. Leonardo Gonzalez, Enrique Martí, Isidro Calvo, Alejandra Ruiz, and Joshue Perez. Towards Risk Estimation in Automated Vehicles using a Fuzzy System.
5. Georg Macher, Markus Bachinger, Andreas Kager, Michael Stolz, and Christian Kreiner. Integration Analysis of a SEooC Transmission Unit for Automated Driving Vehicles.
6. Martin Skoglund, Fredrik Warg, and Behrooz Sangchoolie. In Search of Synergies in a Multi-Concern Development Lifecycle: Safety and Cybersecurity.

Acknowledgements. We are grateful to the SAFECOMP organization committee and collaborators for their support in arranging SASSUR. We also thank all the authors of the submitted papers for their interest in the workshop, and the steering and programme committees for their work and advice. Finally, the AMASS project (H2020-ECSEL grant agreement no. 692474) and the Spanish Government (MINECO; references PCIN-2015-262 and EUIN2017-87945) support the workshop.

Workshop Committee

Organization Committee

Jose Luis de la Vara	Universidad Carlos III de Madrid, Spain
Alejandra Ruiz	TECNALIA, Spain
Tim Kelly	University of York, UK

Steering Committee

John Favaro	Intecs, Italy
Huascar Espinoza	CEA-List, France
Fabien Belmonte	ALSTOM, France

Programme Committee

Morayo Adedjouma	CEA-List, France
Paulo Barbosa	Universidade Estadual da Paraiba, Brazil
Markus Borg	RISE SICS, Sweden
Barbara Gallina	Mälardalen University, Sweden
Ibrahim Habli	University of York, UK
Garazi Juez	Tecnalia, Spain
Marion Lepmets	SoftComply, Estonia

Yaping Luo   Altran, Netherlands
Johnny Marques   Embraer, Brazil
Silvia Mazzini   Intecs, Italy
Jürgen Niehaus   SafeTRANS, Germany
Mehrdad Sabetzadeh University of Luxembourg, Luxembourg
Christoph Schmittner AIT Austrian Institute of Technology, Austria
Irfan Sljivo   Mälardalen University, Sweden
Kenji Taguchi   AIST, Japan
Stefano Tonetta   Fondazione Bruno Kessler, Italy
Marc Zeller   Siemens, Germany

Fault Trees vs. Component Fault Trees: An Empirical Study

Tim Gonschorek[1]([⊠])[iD], Marc Zeller[2][iD], Kai Höfig[2,3][iD], and Frank Ortmeier[1][iD]

[1] AG Software Engineering, Faculty of Computer Science,
Otto-von-Guericke-University Magdeburg, Magdeburg, Germany
{tim.gonschorek,frank.ortmeier}@ovgu.de
[2] Siemens AG, Corporate Technology, Munich, Germany
marc.zeller@siemens.com
[3] University of Applied Science Rosenheim, Rosenheim, Germany
kai.hoefig@fh-rosenheim.de

Abstract. When dealing with structural safety analysis, one of the most popular methodologies is Fault Tree Analysis (FTA). However, one major critique is the rapid increasing of the complexity, and therefore incomprehensibility, when dealing with realistic systems. One approach to overcome this are Component Fault Trees (*CFT*), presenting an extension to standard *FT*, allowing the separation of the analysis into less complex parts on the level of system components. *CFT*s are proposed to be more structured and partly reusable and therefore also claimed to be more straightforward to use by engineers with little safety domain experience.

In this work, we aim at getting an idea of the validity of presented theses and started an initial experiment with 13 computer science students, being asked to execute *CFT* or *FT* method on a given case study. Due to the number of participants, we focused on their empirical statements, the analysis solutions, and empirical results collected using a questionnaire.

Although the empirical impression has been that the resulting *CFT* models are better to use and more comprehensible than the FT models, the qualitative results have not supported this. Moreover, the component-wise modeling seams to mislead the students such that they have overseen failures outside the component structure, e. g., Common-Cause, Cross-Component, or external failures.

1 Introduction

Fault Trees (*FT*) [4,14] are widely used in industry to calculate hazard occurrence probabilities in the safety assessment process, e. g., according to IEC 61508 [5] or ISO 26262 [6]. This is done in a top-down way by analyzing the propagation of faults through a system, identifying causes (events) of the hazards, and calculating the hazard's likelihood from the occurrence probabilities of the basic events.

With the advent of model-based system engineering [3], which is introduced to tame the complexity, also the use of models in safety engineering processes

© Springer Nature Switzerland AG 2018
B. Gallina et al. (Eds.): SAFECOMP 2018 Workshops, LNCS 11094, pp. 239–251, 2018.
https://doi.org/10.1007/978-3-319-99229-7_21

has gained increasing attention in the last decade [1,7,10–13]. On of them is the approach of Component Fault Trees (*CFT*) [9] a model- and component-based methodology for Fault Tree Analysis, supporting a modular and compositional safety analysis strategy.

Like the other mentioned approaches, however, *CFT*s are not widely used in the industry yet. One reason for this might be the lack of experience in their applicability and evidence for the claimed improvements. An interesting starting point to overcome this gap is to (i) apply them to realistic system specifications and (ii) provide empirical evidence for their proposed improvements. One attempt to (i) is given in [2], where two realistic case studies are analyzed applying both, *FT* and *CFT* method to compare their benefits and drawbacks. For (ii) a controlled experiment with experienced practitioners from aerospace industry and Ph.D. students has already been performed [8]. The accumulated outcome is that it cannot be proven that *CFT* models imply significant more correct results than *FT*. Though, the subjective perception of the authors and the participants is that *CFT*s can reduce the problems of complexity, maintainability, and model consistency between system and safety model.

In this paper, we want to analyze the possible benefit from another point of view: one specific problem of development projects for critical systems is, in addition to the safety measure's applicability for experts, the communication between safety and system engineer. The system engineer is often inexperienced in the application of safety measures whereas the safety engineer is not aware of every specific problem of the system. Therefore, good communication is necessary. Unfortunately, often this is at least in need of improvement. In our point of view, this improvement can be enforced by a safety modeling methodology, that can be easily understood even by engineers that are inexperienced in this specific methodology. Hence, the goal of our case study is to provide data about whether using *CFT* lead to "better" analysis results when used by inexperienced users. We investigate both, the quality of the analysis results but also the collaborative aspect. This means whether *CFT* models are more comprehensible to other inexperienced engineers, working on the same analysis, than *FT* models. From this, we can draw our conclusion to the initial problem of the interdisciplinary exchange between safety and system engineer.

In the following, we want to present our analysis results: necessary background on the *CFT* method is provided in Sect. 2. After that we present our case study in Sect. 3 and discuss the results in Sect. 4. In Sect. 5 we conclude our paper.

2   Background

A *CFT* is a Boolean model associated to system development elements such as components [2,9]. It has the same expressive power as classic fault trees [4,14]. *CFT*s (as well as classic fault trees) are used to model the failure behavior of safety-critical systems. This failure behavior is used to document that a system is safe and can also be used to identify drawbacks of the design of a system.

In *CFT*s, a separate *CFT* element is related to a component. Failures that are visible at the outport of a component are models using *Output Failure Modes* which are related to a specific outport. To model how specific failures propagate from an inport of a component to the outport, *Input Failure Modes* are used. The internal failure behavior that also influences the output failure modes is modeled using the Boolean gates such as *OR* and *AND* as well as *Basic Events*.

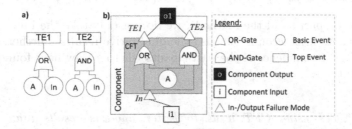

Fig. 1. Classic Fault Tree (a) and Component Fault Tree (b) [8].

Every *CFT* can be transformed to a classic fault tree by removing the input and output failure modes elements. Figure 1 shows on the left side a classic fault tree and on the right side a component fault tree. In both trees, the top events or output events *TE1* and *TE2* are modeled. The *CFT* model allows, additionally to the Boolean formula that are also modeled within the classic fault tree, to associate the specific failure modes to the corresponding ports where these failures can appear. Top event *TE1* for example appears at port *O1*.

3   Investigating the Analyzing Experience of Component Fault Trees

The goal of our research is to answer the following research questions:

> *RQ*1: *"How do inexperienced engineers evaluate the comprehensibility and utility of another group's model for the same analysis task?"*

This leads us to N-version-styled safety analysis and serves as an indication for the question whether the resulting models are interpretable by other engineers inexperienced in dealing with *CFT* and *FT* (comparable to the sketched inter-communication problem between safety and system engineer). To answer *RQ1*, we asked the participants to answer questions about the applied method and its usability for an iterative N-version-styled process. Further, we have instructed each of them to exchange their results with a different group and have asked questions about the participant's opinion on the quality of their model and their received model to get an idea whether the internal and external comprehensibility of a model is close. This would also be a hint on the model consistency. Based on this, we formulated the following hypotheses:

H1: E{*CFT is useful for the analysis process*} $\neq$ E{*FT is useful for the analysis process*}
H2: E{*external perception of CFT*} $\neq$ E{*external perception of FT*}

For the comparison of the methods, we do not only take the impressions of the participants into account but also the qualitative results. Further, we were interested in the confidence of the participants whether they have found all failure combinations.

RQ2: "Does using CFT leads to better analysis results than using traditional FT methods, especially when used by inexperienced system engineers?"

H3: The quality of the analysis with CFT is higher than for FT.
   H3.1: #(*critical cut sets CFT*) $\neq$ #(*critical cut sets FT*)
   H3.2: E{*confidence for having found critical cut sets CFT*} $\neq$ E{*confidence for having found critical cut sets CFT*}

For the planning of our case study, we strongly oriented ourselves on [15].

3.1 Case Study Structure

To gather data about the modeling process and the comprehensibility of the models when exchanged with other modelers, we structured the analysis process in three iterations. After each iteration, the participants, meanwhile split into groups, filled in a questionnaire about their personal opinions. After that they exchanged their model with another group without knowing who will receive their model (*cf.* Fig. 3). We asked the participants to update their analysis model, based on potentially additional information derived from the received model.

Before starting the experiment, we have had to bring up the students on a comparable knowledge level. Therefore, a 3 h lecture on what is safety analysis and how to use *FT* and *CFT* measure has been given by safety experts.

3.2 Participant Constellation

We have executed this case study with the help of 13 students of computer science and related courses of study of one of our seminars at the Otto-von-Guericke-University Magdeburg, which we have seen as an initial starting point for a broader analysis on this topic. We are aware of the fact that a case study with 13 students cannot be representative for reliable conclusions. However, we think that this is sufficient for getting an intention whether using *CFT*s can improve the safety analysis. Students as participants, in particular, are interesting since they are representative for inexperienced (safety) engineers. Since most of the students have only about one year until finishing their graduated Master's degree, the results might allow conclusions about how entry-level safety analysts would cope with the methods.

The participant group consists of nine graduate students and four undergraduate, which were at least in the fifth semester of their seven semesters bachelor's program. We split them into three groups: Two of them where asked to use the *CFT* method and one group to use the *FT* method. Table 1 shows an overview of the participants, their validation on their experience on programming, software quality, safety analysis,

Table 1. Distribution of the student's individual, subjective experience.

Experience	CFT 1	CFT 2	FT
Programming	3.25	4.25	3.60
Software quality	3.25	3.25	2.80
Safety analysis	3.00	1.75	2.80
Fault trees	3.25	2.50	3.00
Mean	3.19	2.94	3.05

and fault trees. To increase the student's concentration, we informed the students about the case study after(!) the experiment. We only explained to them that the results they produce are the base for their grading of the seminar.

3.3   Example System: Adaptive Cruise Control

As an exemplary system for the case study, we have chosen an Adaptive Cruise Control (*ACC*) system. The *ACC* function automatically adjusts the vehicle speed to maintain a safe distance from vehicles ahead. It allows the vehicle to brake when it detects that the car is approaching another vehicle ahead and accelerates the car when traffic allows. In our example, the *ACC* functionality is realized based on two redundant radar sensors, a dedicated *ACC* Electronic Control Unit (ECU), which implements the control function, the motor ECU to control throttle, and the brake ECU to control the car's brakes (see Fig. 2).

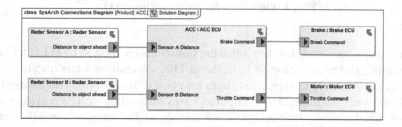

Fig. 2. System architecture of the exemplary *ACC* system.

The two hazards we defined for the students are:

– Collision (Car does not brake automatically, potential collision with an object ahead)
– Driver Disturbance (sudden braking without human interaction, potential harm by collision with other vehicles or wrong reaction of the driver)

3.4   Data Collection

For the analysis, we collected data from both, the analysis results, i. e., the cut sets of the resulting models, and the results of the questionnaire. We developed our question on an ordinal five-point Likert scale (1=strongly disagree to 5=strongly agree). The particular procedure which group received which model after which iteration is depicted in Fig. 3. Since all groups are meant to model *CFT* and *FT*, their modeling results are comparable by the cut sets resulting from qualitative FTA. The *FT* group has given away the complete *FT* whereas the *CFT* groups only exchanged the *ECU* component.

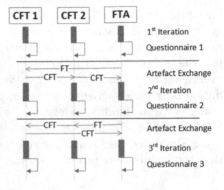

Fig. 3. Sketch of the sequence for the execution of the experiments.

> **Q$_1$.4** The modeling methodology used has supported me very well to structure the problem and to perform my analysis.
>
> **Q$_{2|3}$.4** My own model was very well-suited to represent modifications or to compare the own model with the one received by the other group.

Fig. 4. Questions for for hypothesis **H1**.

For the analysis we asked the following questions correlated to **H1** (*cf.* Fig. 4). For verifying the proposition of hypothesis **H2**, we analyzed the questions presented in Fig. 5. We have separated them into two different parts: an internal and an external view and therefore compared them depending on the correlations of the exchanged model. Internal questions are about the comprehensibility of the own model whereas external questions are about the model, the group received. For analyzing our propositions for hypothesis **H3**, we collected the data from the question given in Fig. 6, using the qualitative verification results in the form of the minimal cut sets and the following questions. Based on this data, we can analyze what influence the different methods have on the results and the confidence in the results.

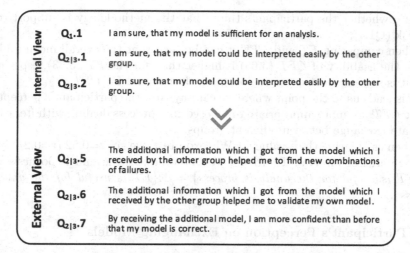

Fig. 5. Questions for for hypothesis H2.

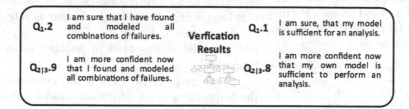

Fig. 6. Questions for for hypothesis H1.

4   Discussion of Results

In the following, we discuss our hypotheses based on the qualitative results of the analysis, the data from the questionnaire, and, in particular, the subjective impressions and statements we have collected from the participants[1].

For measuring the statistical significance, we analyzed the test values using the two-tailored Wilcoxon signed-rank test with a significance level $\alpha = 0.05$ and the correlation coefficient r. Therefore, the calculated z-values must be outside the interval $[-1.96; 1.96]$.

4.1   General Opinion on the Methods

When we analyze whether the methodology is sufficient and supportive for the applied safety assessment process, we find out that the overall perception of the participants is yes. The values of Table 2 supports this intention. Here, we

---

[1] The raw data and the modeling results are available under https://cse.cs.ovgu.de/cse-wordpress/wp-content/uploads/2018/03/sc2018_raw_data_anonymized.zip/.

compare whether the participants think that the methodology is supportive of the task (Q1.4).

When comparing FT and CFT it can be seen that the overall mean evaluation of the usability of CFT (3.65) is higher than for the FT (3.33), especially, since it is so close because of one outlier in Iteration 2 for CFT.

This leads us to the point where we can say that the participant's perception is that CFT are more appropriate to be used in a process dealing with iterations and data exchange between different groups.

When calculating the z-value for Wilcoxon test, we get z=0.52 (r=0.21) lying with the critical interval. Therefore, we cannot reject the null hypothesis **H1**: E{CFT is useful for the analysis process} = E{FT is useful for the analysis process}.

4.2 Participant's Perception on Exchanging Models

Table 2. The participant's answers to the question whether the methodology is applicable when used in a shared process. For the overall values the data from the CFT groups were grouped.

	CFT1	CFT2	FT
Q1.4	4	3.5	3.4
Q2.4	3.5	3.25	3.4
Q3.4	4.5	2.25	3.2
Overall mean		3.65	3.33
Overall variance		0.96	1.52
Overall median		4	4

In the following, we want to analyze the participant's impression on exchanging the analysis results as an intermediate step. In particular, it is interesting which kind of input is interesting for a group. Either CFT or FT, or, e.g., just a model represented in another modeling formalism.

As we can see in Table 3 the evaluation of the helpfulness of an additional model is overall positive. When we have a close look at the different input variants, we see that the FT group evaluates the received CFT model with the highest values (3.77). It is, in particular, remarkably higher than the internal evaluations of the CFT teams (3.21).

Further, utilizing the *overall means*, we have found out that, in mean, the external evaluation for getting a FT model or a CFT model is the same (3.5). However, when we compare those values to the internal evaluation of the modeling group, we have a positive external rating for CFT models as input for a CFT group, since the internal rating (3.46) is lower than the external rating (3.5). In contrast to this, we see the opponent trend for FT. Here, the evaluation trend is negative, i.e., the internal rating (3.6) of the FT modeler is higher than the external evaluation of the CFT group (3.5).

When we have a closer look at the comments of the participants, this tendency gets underlined. As a remark from the CFT groups, we have received the feedback that the FT model is not well structured and complex to understand compared to the CFT models. Moreover, when exchanging the models, we had the problem that the FT has been drawn on four sheets of paper whereas the component model required just one. Further, the amount of exchanged components also had an impact. For the CFT, only the component ECU has been exchanged, however, for the FT this was not possible at all, since every time

Table 3. Internal and external perception of the helpfulness of a given analysis model being exchanged between groups using either different methodologies ($FT \leftrightarrow CFT$) or same methodologies ($CFT \leftrightarrow CFT$). The overall values where computed from the data of all constellations where a CFT group received a FT, the FT group received a CFT, and a CFT group received a CFT.

	Different methodology				Same methodology	
	Internal	External	Internal	External	Internal	External
	FT	CFT	CFT	FT	CFT	CFT
Iteration 1	3.60	3.42	2.75	3.87	3.50	3.42
Iteration 2	3.60	3.75	3.25	3.67	3.38	3.58
Overall mean	3.60	3.50	3.21	3.77	3.46	3.50
Overall variance	0.69	1.30	1.15	1.36	1.54	0.96
Overall median	4	4	3	4	3	3.5

the complete fault tree has been exchanged. This, of course also increased the subjective complexity. To support this, even members of the FT group claimed that their model was more complicated to be analyzed compared to the CFT. However, to normalize this remarks, we have to keep in mind that the analysis has been done with paper and pencil.

Overall, these results show that it can have a positive effect when receiving another model as input to compare the own results with. Moreover, at least for our participants, getting a CFT model as input seems to be the better alternative than a FT model.

When analyzing the statistical significance of our results for the null hypothesis **H2**: E{*external perception of CFT*} = E{*external perception of FT*} we get a z-value of -0.19 (r=0.21). This means, we cannot reject the null hypothesis for, and therefore, our impression is only empiric but not statistically relevant.

4.3   Qualitative Results and Confidence

The results of the minimal cut set analysis for the CFT or FT models created by the different groups are presented in Figs. 7 and 8. The FT group has only created a Fault Tree for the hazard *collision*, so the cut sets for the second hazard cannot be compared with the other results. Moreover, the FT group is the only group that changed their analysis model over time. However, they only split the basic failure events such that a sensor error has become either a distance too high or distance too low error. Nevertheless, this did not affect the failure propagation logic.

However, it is interesting that both CFT groups modeled the failure of the radar sensors in this detail. Discussion with the students has shown that this comes from the fact that they tried to model the behavior also outside the borders of the component, e. g., communication failures or loss-of-data.

Safety experts	CFT 1	CFT 2	FT
ACC ECU internal failure	Engine erroneous Behavior	Motor ECU fail	Radar sensor A distance too low
Brake ECU internal failure	Brake erroneous behavior	ACC ECU failure	Radar sensor B distance too low
Motor ECU interal failure	Radar Sensor B erroneous behavior	ACC ECU error	Brake ECU fails
Radar Sensor A internal failure, Radar Sensor B Internal failure	ACC erroneous behavior	Radar A error	Radar sensor B distance too high
	ACC total failure	Brake ECU fall	ACC ECU error
	Radar Sensor A erroneous behavior	Radar Sensor A fail, Radar Sensor B error	Brake ECU error
	Brake total failure	Radar Sensor A fail, Radar Sensor B fail	ACC ECU fails
	Radar Sensor A total failure, Radar Sensor B total failure		Radar sensor A distance too high
			Radar sensor A fails, Radar sensor B fails

Fig. 7. Cut sets resulting form the CFT/FT model for the hazard "collision".

Safety experts	CFT 1	CFT 2
Brake ECU internal failure	Radar Sensor B erroneous behavior	Brake ECU fail
ACC ECU internal failure	Engine erroneous behavior	Motor ECUfail
Motor ECU interal failure	ACC total failure	Radar A error
Radar Sensor A internal failure	ACC erroneous behavior	ACC ECU failure
Radar Sensor B internal failure	Radar Sensor A erroneous behavior	ACC ECU error
	Brake erroneous behavior	Radar Sensor A fail, Radar Sensor B fail
	Engine total failure	Radar Sensor A fail, Radar Sensor B error
	Radar Sensor A total failure, Radar Sensor B total failure	

Fig. 8. Cut sets resulting form the CFT/FT model for the hazard "driver disturbance".

The cut sets show that all CFT groups have modeled more failures (failure and erroneous behavior) than in the solution created by safety experts, where all failures of the components are represented as an internal failure. This refinement of the internal failures of the components leads to more cut sets compare to the sample solution. When we have a closer look at the results, we find out that only the most inexperienced group CFT2 modeled the correct failure propagation.

For the FT group, we can observe a common situation since the model gets more complex than necessary and therefore they had two redundant subtrees. One of them directly leads to the hazard event and the second one is combined with the Motor ECU failure, i. e., in their failure propagation logic a motor fail does not lead to the crash of the car.

Another interesting aspect is the failure propagation of the CFT1 model. Here we can see that the *Radar Sensor B* is a single point of failure. The failure of this sensor, however, is only critical in combination with the failure of *Radar Sensor A*. This shows another problem of the *CFT* modeling for inexperienced modelers. *FT* pushes the engineer to keep the look on the complete system's behavior, whereas *CFT* more focus the view on single component's behavior. This can lead to a situation where the modeler loses the overview over the complete system, i. e., over cross-component-behavior, external failures, or common-cause failure, as for the radar sensors of the *ACC*. Due to this result, since both one CFT group and the FT group had a major error within their models, we cannot reject the null hypothesis for **H3.1** that $\#(critical\ cut\ sets\ CFT) = \#(critical\ cut\ sets\ FT)$.

The confidence of the CFT1 group stays quite constant. For FT and CFT2 this is not the case. In the second step, after receiving the *CFT* from CFT2, the confidence of FT that all failure combinations had been found drops from 3.2 to 2. Whereas the confidence of CFT2 group rises from 2 to 3.5. When having a closer look at the results of the analysis and the comments of the participants the reason is clear.

The FT group had some problem with modeling all possible failure modes arising from the sensors of the *ACC*. Since, in contrast to the CFT groups, they had no methodology for modeling different outputs and error types of a systems element, their model only contains the failure modes "sensor error" and "sensor failure". However, the other groups differentiated between getting a sensor value representing a "too high" or "too low" distance for the measurement, which has the benefit of being able to define different influences on the erroneous braking and acceleration of the system. The result of CFT2 is a consequence of the effect that they are, on average, more skeptic with their model but after getting the model of CFT1 as input, the confidence increased.

Many participants stated as positive aspect of the *CFT* methodology the guidance they get (i) from the structured component point of view, where they model each element separately and (ii) from the different viewpoint since *CFT* components can be seen as interacting elements in the system with propagating failures whereas *FT* only convey a strict structural point of view.

In this sense, the given results support hypothesis **H3.2** that the structured methodology of *CFT* can support the confidence of inexperienced system analysts more than the less strict *FT* method does.

However, the null hypothesis **H3.2**: E{*confidence for having found critical cut sets CFT*} = E{*confidence for having found critical cut sets CFT*} cannot be rejected, since Z=−1.15 (r=0.47).

4.4 Threats to Validity

In this section, we want shortly discuss external and internal thread to the validity of case study and the drawn conclusions.

Internal Validity. For the internal validity of the case study, the number and constellation of the participants are of high interest.

One possible threat is the degree of experience of the participants. When we have a closer look on the research questions, we do not see this as a disadvantage for the study since we wanted to analyze the general comprehensibility of the methods without requesting any classification concerning the professional context of each participant. So, we focus only on the applicability and comprehensibility of the given example system. Moreover, we think that it could also be a light benefit because the subjective impression of the participants is not overlapped by personal positive or negative historical experiences.

A second point is the difference in the experience of the participants. To overcome this problem, we tried to split the undergraduate evenly throughout the groups, i. e., the group with two undergraduate students, the *FT* group, also got one more member than the others. This lead, with respect to our measure (*cf* Table 1) to groups with comparable experience level. This comparability was also supported by the introductory lecture given by experienced safety experts.

The primary threat, of course, is the number of participants, which lead to the fact that our ordinal data does never show a statistical significance. However, to bridge this gap, we also took into account the personal statements of the participants that were not directly projected onto the ordinal scale. Moreover, we see this as a first step in the direction of a more considerable estimation, and therefore even this small sample size and the corresponding gained experiences are of value to us.

External Validity. The major threat to the external validity is the complexity of the example system, since *CFT* are claimed to be most effective when it comes to large, complex systems, or reusability of specific components. In fact, neither the *FT* nor the *CFT* fit on one page but were split over four A4 pages, and single subtrees had been substituted by proxy or virtual events. Therefore, in combination with the low level of practical experience, this seems to be a sufficient benchmark, especially concerning the limited amount of time. For consecutive studies, we will validate the applicability of more complex example systems.

5   Conclusion

In this paper, we have presented our investigation to the question whether applying Component Fault Trees (*CFTs*) can support the modeling process compared to common Fault Trees. In particular: *"How do inexperienced engineers evaluate the comprehensibility and utility of another group's model for the same analysis task?"* and *"Does apply CFT lead to better analysis results than using traditional FT methods, especially when used by inexperienced system engineers?"*

We found out that indeed we can answer the research questions with yes. Even though the results are not statistically significant for the small number of participants, the results, as well as the statements of the participants, give a clear trend. The usage of *CFT* can support, in particular, inexperienced engineers in analyzing a system. Even for the iterative process, where intermediate analysis results are exchanged between different groups, using *CFT* methodology seems to have an advantage over *FT* methods.

However, we have to keep in mind that both modeling techniques, *CFT* and *FT*, can cause trouble during the analysis. The problem with a *FT* is the rapidly increasing complexity of the tree when applied to real systems. This can often lead to redundancies and therefore can shadow other failure modes and cut sets if they have been combined with a redundant subtree. However, a benefit is the need to overview the complete system while modeling the *FT*.

In contrast to that, *CFTs* help focusing component-wise on separated and less complex system elements. Nevertheless, this can even be a source of problems since it can easily shadow the view for cross-component dependencies or external failure events. Hence, it can increase the loss of common cause failure relation, which may lead to both, under and over-specification of the failure propagation logic.

To get more reliable data, we plan to repeat the experiments on a larger group of participants, e. g., from one of our larger courses with about 200 students and more complex models.

Acknowledgment. Parts of the work leading to this paper was funded by the Framework Programs for Research and Innovation Horizon 2020 under grant agreement n.732242 (DEIS).

References

1. Filax, M., Gonschorek, T., Ortmeier, F.: Building models we can rely on: requirements traceability for model-based verification techniques. In: Bozzano, M., Papadopoulos, Y. (eds.) IMBSA 2017. LNCS, vol. 10437, pp. 3–18. Springer, Cham (2017). https://doi.org/10.1007/978-3-319-64119-5_1
2. Höfig, K., Joanni, A., Zeller, M., Montrone, F., Rothfelder, M., Amarnath, R., Munk, P., Nordmann, A.: Model-based reliability and safety: reducing the complexity of safety analyses using component fault trees. In: RAMS (2018)
3. INCOSE: Systems Engineering Handbook: A Guide for System Life Cycle Processes and Activities. John Wiley & Sons (2015)
4. International Electrotechnical Commission (IEC): IEC 61025: Fault Tree Analysis (FTA) (1990)
5. International Electrotechnical Commission (IEC): IEC 61508: Functional safety of electrical/electronic/programmable electronic safety related systems (1998)
6. International Organization for Standardization (ISO): ISO 26262: Road vehicles - Functional safety (2011)
7. Joshi, A., Miller, S.P., Whalen, M., Heimdahl, M.P.: A proposal for model-based safety analysis. In: 24th DASC (2005)
8. Jung, J., Jedlitschka, A., Höfig, K., Domis, D., Hiller, M.: A controlled experiment on component fault trees. In: Bitsch, F., Guiochet, J., Kaâniche, M. (eds.) SAFECOMP 2013. LNCS, vol. 8153, pp. 285–292. Springer, Heidelberg (2013). https://doi.org/10.1007/978-3-642-40793-2_26
9. Kaiser, B., Liggesmeyer, P., Mäckel, O.: A new component concept for fault trees. In: Proceedings of the 8th Australian Workshop on Safety Critical Systems and Software (2003)
10. Lisagor, O., McDermid, J., Pumfrey, D.: Towards a practicable process for automated safety analysis. In: ISSC 24 (2006)
11. McDermid, J., Kelly, T.: Software in safety critical systems: achievement and prediction. University of York, UK (2006)
12. de Miguel, M.A., Briones, J.F., Silva, J.P., Alonso, A.: Integration of safety analysis in model-driven software development. IET Softw. **2**(3), 260–280 (2008)
13. Papadopoulos, Y., McDermid, J.A.: Hierarchically performed hazard origin and propagation studies. In: Felici, M., Kanoun, K. (eds.) SAFECOMP 1999. LNCS, vol. 1698, pp. 139–152. Springer, Heidelberg (1999). https://doi.org/10.1007/3-540-48249-0_13
14. Vesely, W.E., Goldberg, F.F., Roberts, N.H., Haasl, D.F.: Fault Tree Handbook. US Nuclear Regulatory Commission (1981)
15. Yin, R.K.: Case Study Research and Applications: Design and Methods. Sage Publications, Thousand Oaks (2009)

Challenges in Assuring Highly Complex, High Volume Safety-Critical Software

John MacGregor[(✉)] and Simon Burton[(✉)]

Robert Bosch GmbH, Stuttgart, Germany
{john.macgregor,simon.burton}@de.bosch.com

Abstract. Safety standards such as IEC 61508 [1] and ISO 26262 [2] were written assuming that highly complex safety-critical systems were self-contained, capital intensive, one-off products and that the assurance argument was to be renewed with every product change. In this paper, we explain how the increasing complexity, scale, continuous updates and heterogeneous nature of future safety-critical software systems requires a paradigm shift in the software safety qualification and certification processes. We examine existing approaches to software safety argumentation and explain how the essential components of the argumentation can be transferred to future software architectures and development processes. In particular, we discuss the relevance of constructive measures for ensuring safety, evidence collection to demonstrate the effectiveness and integrity of these measures and process approaches to assess the predictability of the overall quality and integrity of the software. Our aim is to provide an industrial perspective on the areas of collaboration required to transfer relevant research results into future standards.

Keywords: Functional safety · Complex software · Development lifecycle
Reuse · Selection · Agile · Open-source · Integrity · Equivalence
Measurement evidence

1 Introduction

Two technological trends are revolutionizing a number of consumer and industrial product classes. First, sensors and actuators are becoming less expensive and smaller. Second, microprocessors are becoming both more powerful and more power-efficient. Combined, these trends are enabling products to perceive their surroundings better and to react in more effective or entirely new ways. The assessment and reaction algorithms are thus becoming more sophisticated and correspondingly, product complexity is increasing exponentially. A side effect of this increase in complexity is the application of agile development methods such as SCRUM [3] and the reuse of open source software in commercial projects, both of which are attempts to increase development efficiency to reach the time-to-market, cost and functional needs of the products.

The leading examples of this trend come from consumer electronics, such as smartphones, drones or navigation devices. These have evolved and matured quickly as they are relatively disposable and their development cycles are short. The trend is now

© Springer Nature Switzerland AG 2018
B. Gallina et al. (Eds.): SAFECOMP 2018 Workshops, LNCS 11094, pp. 252–264, 2018.
https://doi.org/10.1007/978-3-319-99229-7_22

transferring to large item and capital goods as well. These range from conventional systems such as railway control and driver assistance to radically new applications such as mobile industrial robots, fully autonomous driving and autonomous agriculture vehicles and drones. In contrast to consumer goods, these systems can, when confronted with a hazard, imperil human life, and are therefore subject to safety regulation (consumer drones being a border case…). While most of these products still use conventional algorithms to characterize their surroundings and to develop the strategies of their reactions, a number, especially in the area of highly-automated driving (HAD) are using machine learning (ML) based on artificial intelligence algorithms. These changes in the development approach and characteristics of the software are raising considerable questions regarding how to qualify the safety of the resulting systems based on the requirements of current standards.

For the past 3 years we have accompanied the SIl2LinuxMP project [4] in its quest to certify a Linux-based system at IEC 61508 SIL level 2. As the project is now ending, we have looked at the alternatives to further industrialise the process of certifying highly-complex safety critical systems incorporating open-source software. In the end, several alternatives were constrained by shortcomings in the certification process or in the ability to adapt to the practices needed to use off-the-shelf, specifically open-source software. These shortcomings can only be overcome based on an understanding of the underlying objectives of the measures prescribed by safety standards and the impact of applying alternatives.

In Sect. 2, this position paper describes the development practices in a particular segment of safety-critical embedded systems and identifies some emerging trends of modern large scale heterogeneous software systems that conflict with the current expectations of the standards. Section 3 describes areas in which development trends such as open source and agile methods both diverge and may also be used to support the underlying objectives of the safety standards. While in some cases directions and possible solutions are given, full technical contributions to the issues remain the subject of future work.

2   Evolving Challenges in the Development of Large-Scale Safety-Critical Software

2.1   Current Industrial Development Practice

Bosch is primarily active as a tier-1 supplier of automotive control units, but also has business units developing products for the industrial goods, consumer goods, energy, and building technology domains.

While the development practice presented here represents the extremes in the range of practices found in at Bosch, the general trend is in the directions outlined here. The practices described here have existed and evolved in the affected business units for over 20 years. We also observe these trends in a number of other companies, although due to the market share and the sheer number of product variants involved, the scale at Bosch seems to be quite exceptional.

The following sections are a coarse overview of the generic Bosch product development processes. The practice example, also documented in [5], is taken from one of the largest Bosch business units and is representative of the development approach taken in the development of engine controllers, braking systems and passive safety components. The reference business unit used to collect this data develops over 1,000 products per year, with 2,000 development projects running simultaneously and employs over 6,000 developers worldwide.

Component Selection. Following the AUTOSAR [6] methodology, automotive control unit software is composed of three architectural layers: the basis software (operating system, hardware stacks, diagnostics etc.), a middleware and application components. The application components themselves are each composed of a number of related software functions that fulfill operational functions in the system.

The control units are tailor-made for use within specific vehicle lines, derived from a common product architecture. As illustrated in Fig. 1, the application software components are composed of approximately 4,000 functions that are drawn from a pool of approximately 50,000 validated functions that have been already employed in products belonging to the current product generation. As technology and the knowledge of the underlying physical processes being controlled evolve, new product generations are introduced every 5–7 years. At the beginning of a product generation, "master" products are developed for each customer. Subsequently, customer-specific variants are derived from the master products for each individual vehicle project. In each variant, approximately 10% of the functions must be adapted or developed from scratch.

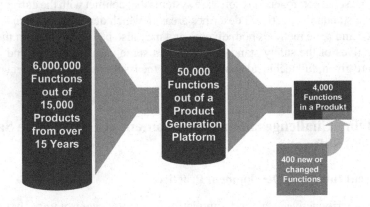

Fig. 1. Functions available for use in an automotive control unit

Reuse-Oriented Development. As the previous section indicated, there are actually two types of platforms in this development process. First, there are repositories of validated application components that are compatible to each other within a generation and second, there are preconfigured assemblies of components that are used as the basis for customer products. The latter category consists of a platform at the basis software level and the various product "masters" at the application software level. This is idealized, of course, as the application software level depends on the basis software and as the basis and application software must be adapted to hardware and software platform evolution. This approach is highly related to product-line engineering techniques [7] with some pragmatic changes to cater for the above described categories of reuse.

The development processes differ as well. The product generation platforms are driven by innovation and changes in hardware. There can be major architecture changes and to a large extent, they are developed according to a conventional "V" model, as illustrated Fig. 2. While there may be some reuse, the focus is on developing the platform from scratch.

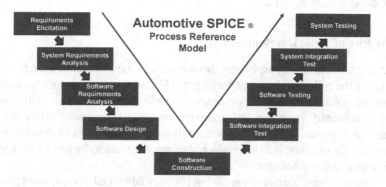

Fig. 2. Conventional "V"-model and a customer product development model

In the customer product development process (Fig. 3), product software is mainly configured and parameterized. An appropriate "master", or product generation platform is selected, and then various modelling tools are used to identify points in the application where new functions are needed or functions must be adapted.

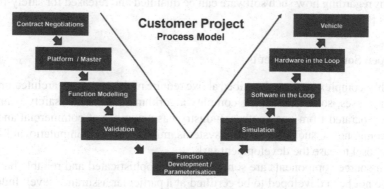

Fig. 3. Customer product development model

After development, the components are tested in unit tests, then integrated and tested in harnesses with software simulating the target product environment, then test harnesses with the target hardware and finally in the target vehicle. In contrast to the conventional "V"-Model development process where architecture and design play a major role, most effort (70%) in the customer product development process is dedicated to integration and testing.

In this process, there must be a strong level of trust in the pre-validated components as well as a robust architecture for combining the components into a vehicle-specific configuration in order to minimize the level of repeated validation in a project. This level of trust is currently achieved by closely following the measures described within the automotive safety standard ISO 26262 as well as software development models such as Automotive SPICE [8] and CMMI [9] designed to increase predictability and quality of software development projects.

2.2   The Rise of Agile Development

Within many business units, especially those related to the Internet of Things (IoT), the trend is to use the agile development paradigms [3], employing user stories, incremental development, scrums and backlogs managed in tools such as Jira [10]. This paradigm diverges significantly from the "V" model underlying the current safety standards. However, it is expected that such software will inevitably be used to develop not only customer specific variants, but the product platform software to be used within systems contexts with a safety relevance.

Some business units are already applying yet more advanced development paradigms such as social coding [11], where, with the aid of collaboration tools, problems are solved interactively and dynamically, incorporating the knowledge of a group of peers. Essential aspects of such processes are exchanging software patches as a design and change management paradigm and the use of internal social networks to exchange experience, review code and select components for reuse. The divergence of such development models from those used as a reference for the safety standards is leading to a number of questions regarding how such software can be qualified and released for safety-relevant products [12].

2.3   Open Source Components

The highly-complex systems described above require multi-processor architectures with many processes, some calculating complex algorithms, that, when safety is an issue, must be separated from one another. Industry has a number of commercial and open-source components, such as operating systems, middleware or computational libraries, at its disposal to ease the development task.

Open-source components are sometimes very sophisticated and reliable but generally have not been developed to be certified at a particular assurance level. Industry is attracted to open-source components' apparent cost-effectiveness and to the possibility of delegating the components' development and maintenance effort to those developers best able to perform it. The components are often chosen because they are known, proven, portable to several hardware architectures and surely sufficient.

Open-source software is generally initially developed by a small number of developers with a commonly understood (among themselves), focused goal. They rely less, or not at all, on conventional forms of requirements as their goal is common knowledge among them, derived from standard or commercial practice.

The developers contribute content according to their individual interests and strengths. In contrast to more conventional development processes, when a problem is identified, the onus for fixing it lies with the group, or those that discovered it, rather than on the developers that contributed the error. The general development paradigm corresponds to the agile social coding practices described in the preceding section.

At some point, the software becomes mature and the focus changes to maintenance. Due to the inherent entropy of the development paradigm, successful open-source projects seem to enforce a discipline of incorporating the fixes centrally, with the discipline being enforced by a "benevolent dictator" and/or a number of dedicated maintainers giving the technical direction of the component's evolution.

Developers of open source software rarely have compliance to safety standards in their initial focus and therefore do not gather the corresponding evidence artefacts required by the standards. Finding arguments for the safety of open-source components that align with current certification approaches therefore becomes very difficult.

3   Bridging the Gap Between Safety Standards and Industrial Software Development Paradigms

Section 1 described a class of safety-critical systems that are marketed in volume, require sophisticated hardware and software platforms, need to reuse components, some of which could be open-source, and may have been developed according to "non-traditional" (i.e. not "V"-Model-based) development processes.

The aspects presented in Sect. 2 demonstrate how far industrial reality is diverging from the assumptions implicit within current safety standards. This situation will further intensify in the future as the size, complexity and heterogeneity of the software to be certified increases. This will impact systems consisting of many individual components that have been developed in-house, as open source or by 3rd parties according to a range of development models and which must be continuously updated over time. Assurance arguments must be found that compensate for these gaps whilst leveraging the benefits of new development models. This section identifies some of those inadequacies and suggests approaches to address them.

3.1   Assumptions Underlying Current Safety Standards

Standards are often predicated on assumptions that diverge from current industrial practice and prescribe measures whose objectives are either not explicitly stated or rarely referenced during certification. This section describes some of these assumptions so that we can better understand the context in which the certification of the software paradigms discussed in Sect. 2 must be addressed.

Measures to Ensure Software Integrity. In and of itself, the term integrity means a combination of innate soundness and not being corrupt. In the safety sphere, integrity is initially brought in connection with the ability to proffer confidence in the product, only in the end to equate integrity with tolerable risk.

In general, the safety standards do not attempt to define quantifiably a tolerable level of residual safety risk associated with the software as is partially the case for the probabilistic failure models used to assess hardware. Instead, the level of tolerable residual risk is defined in terms of a set of measures or techniques that should be applied, dependent on the required safety integrity level for the function as identified by the hazard and risk analysis. Upon closer inspection of the standards, the prescribed measures (dependent on the required integrity level) can be categorized as follows:

- Constructive measures to ensure that safety requirements on the software are well formulated and implemented and that potentially hazardous behavior of the software is identified and mitigated. These measures include identifying additional software-based functionality to detect hardware failures, structured software architecture design and defensive programming techniques and programming guidelines.
- Evidence to demonstrate the achieved integrity of the software. This set of measures is used to create evidence that demonstrates that an adequate set of requirements on the software have been identified and implemented with a sufficient level of integrity. Examples of these measures are reviews, software tests and static analyses. The implementation of these requirements is also traceable vertically from architecture specification through implementation and horizontally from architecture to testing in the final product. As with the constructive measures, this evidence is typically presented within the context of a particular development model (e.g. "first review the software architecture, then derive detailed software module specifications").
- Measures to improve the predictability of the quality process. Many of the measures described in the standards focus on ensuring the predictability and repeatability of the development and validation processes. These include for example, organizational safety management, process audits and configuration management amongst others. The measures increase the level of trust that the safety concept and associated evidences do indeed lead to the required level of integrity and therefore also safety. This observation is confirmed by the strong overlap [13] between measures in the safety standards and development models such as CMMI [9] and ASPICE [8] whose stated aims are not only to enhance quality but also the predictability of complex product development.

Equivalence of Techniques and Measures. Annexes B and C of IEC 61508 [1] Part 3 contain a schema for determining which measures and techniques are appropriate for a particular safety integrity level. They contain a list of measures and techniques stemming from the development processes of the last millennium. Determining the appropriateness of other measures and techniques is left as an exercise in demonstration by the applicant and judgement by the certifying agency. The annexes offer support in assessing the effectiveness and contribution of those measures and techniques included in the standard according to various properties of systematic safety integrity. The schema is based on a further informal schema of rigour, which is a proxy for the formality of the measure or technique. It is not clear whether the properties listed are exhaustive, or even adequate. The role of rigour and formality is left at a very intuitive level. The standard is not clear if, or how, techniques can be combined within or between development phases to achieve the requisite overall safety integrity level.

An approach has been proposed to argue assurance sufficiency in the face of assurance deficits in the argument that can be presented has been proposed in [14]. It suggests compiling a catalogue of argument patterns as well as proposing a framework for mitigating a deficit in the context of the overall confidence.

In general, approaches must be found to evaluate a software component's contribution to the overall safety case within a composition framework that achieves the requisite safety integrity level.

3.2 Addressing the Realities of Large-Scale Software Development Practice

It is both desirable and unavoidable that complex products be built from validated components. Section 2.1 has illustrated the extents to which the inherent product variability can mould a development process. This section addresses how safety certification could better account for industrial product development processes.

Selection as a First-Class Citizen. The safety properties of off-the-shelf components, whether commercial or open-source, are fixed when the component becomes available. The properties may indeed affect the product architecture or design as well as the amount of functionality that must be developed from scratch. Establishing late in the development process that the safety properties of a selected component are inadequate for its context of use can easily necessitate the selection of another component with an associated change in the product architecture or design.

It is therefore necessary that component selection, and therefore the assessment of safety properties of component alternatives, be done at the earliest stages of the development process and with the highest rigour.

In the industrial processes outlined in this paper, the priority is on finding and using an appropriate component rather than on developing one. The standards account for such eventualities, but their focus is elsewhere. Selection is a first-class citizen in the development process and should be treated as such in the standards.

Contracts between components have been suggested to ensure the integrity of the system behavior on detection of a fault [15, 16] while method tailoring has been suggested for compensating for deficits in a component's systematic capabilities [17]. Further research is needed on the exact criteria needed to completely assure the safety of the system under development.

Reuse. Note that in the example in Sect. 2.1, there was a pool of validated components. An organizational process is needed to develop, validate and rework those components. Moreover, the product development process must feed problems and improvements back to the pool.

Note as well that there were two platforms: the basis software and the customer "master". The basis software (in an extended sense when application frameworks are also considered) is the territory for off-the-shelf components which are adopted without modification. The master, on the other hand, should be built orthogonally to allow its components to be removed easily and replaced with different or modified components. It is more likely to be composed of bespoke components.

Note that the dynamic is different to what might intuitively be expected. At the first level, complete assemblies are reused, not components. The dynamic is that in reuse, an otherwise valid product is modified, as minimally as possible, rather than assembling the product's components anew from scratch.

In general, the point is rather that the standards consider a safety-critical product to be a unique assembly of components. The products themselves are rarely unique, however. There are classes of software that serve subordinate roles, i.e. a basis software platform (and not an element out of context) or product line platforms that are conceived to contribute to reuse. The standards should address these exigencies, either by incorporating reuse as a standard process or by producing tailor-made standards for the different classes of platform.

Note lastly, that industrial use of components involves the operations of instantiation, composition and parameterization. This has long been recognized in the area of industrial product lines [18], the implications of these operations needed investigated in the area of functional safety.

3.3   Allowing for Alternative Development Models

The development models underlying open source development are an extreme case of alternative development models. Also when applied to in-house development in controlled environments, adopting alternative models, such as agile or social coding, causes challenges; in particular in creating confidence in the effectiveness and stability of the process. However, agile, etc. have some benefits that should not be ignored or dampened when making a safety cases. Close cooperation between interdisciplinary teams can contribute to product reliability and SCRUM-based issue processing can enhance tracking and resolution of safety-related issues in the development of safety functions, for example.

Process Confidence. Certification involves providing evidence that a product is safe and its development process achieves the safety goals. It could well be that certifying according to a standard involves providing standard evidence. At least, the current standards neither specify the content of the evidence nor the form. Current certification practice involves providing anecdotal evidence rather than fact-based evidence.

The current lack of guidance in the standards about the factual evidence to be provided may be intentional, but the practice indicates the potential for chaos and misunderstanding. In the case of a class of products like autonomously driving vehicles, with high impact on public safety and a relative lack of safety experience, products being certified on the basis of evidence with wildly varying quality would not be a very desirable outcome. Standardized measurement plans could mitigate the situation considerably.

Software development in a customer-supplier context is intimately related to assessment models like CMMI [9] or ASPICE [8] which allow customers to develop confidence suppliers' ability to reliably develop software. These models have stages like "managed" or "optimizing" which, among other things presuppose measurement programmes to stabilize or improve the development process.

The Goal-Question-Metric (GQM) [20] approach is a recognized method for designing measurement programmes for software development process improvement. It consists of answering the following 3 questions:

1. What are the goals of the measurement programme, i.e., what should the measures reveal?
2. What questions must be answered to achieve those goals?
3. What metrics are needed to answer those questions?

It considers the purpose of the measurement, i.e. to understand the situation, manage it or improve it, and considers how different stakeholders in the development process need different data or data aggregations to achieve their measurement goals.

[21] has suggested a methodology using Practical Software and Systems Measurement (PSM) [22] for designing metrics for safety assessment and identified two classes of characteristics to measure: product characteristics and process characteristic. The focus was on metrics for existing standards, however.

Using structured measurement design methodologies to understand and codify the metrics needed by a safety engineer or a certifying agency would lead to a better understanding of what should be incorporated in a standard.

3.4   Incorporating Open Source

To an extent, open-source software can be regarded simply as an off-the-shelf component. As Sect. 2.3 indicated, open-source software can exhibit deeply different safety properties compared to software that was developed to be marketed commercially, however. This section identifies some issues for safety certification.

Integrating the Collection of Evidence for Software Integrity. Safety certification is seldom involved in the interests driving an open-source development project. The participants are generally interested in a high-quality product, however, but may not agree with the amount of rigour associated with safety certification.

Ways should be found to inform open-source projects about the "dos" and "don'ts" of safety-relevant software development and to include instrumentation in the tools used in their development processes to allow the capture of conformance evidence without significant intrusion. Collecting evidence for the constructive integrity measures as well as for measures to demonstrate the integrity of individual components can be achieved by identifying or creating development artefacts that can be argued to be equivalent to those required by the standards (e.g. adherence to coding guidelines, unit tests etc.). More problematic is demonstrating that the software achieves a set of systematically derived safety requirements (as these are typically not formulated at project start). In addition, it is typically not possible to demonstrate that a sufficient level of process stability has been achieved in order to ensure a predictable level of quality in implementing the integrity measures (as this relies on a high level of discipline in the adherence to predefined processes).

Development vs Maintenance. Open-source projects tend to grow organically and the transition to a complete package may not be clear. The roles and responsibilities of "benevolent dictator" and "maintainer" must be understood in the safety context. The effects of the choice of an open-source license for the software may influence the future stability of the software and should thus be a factor in certification.

These observations imply that open-source development practices might only be adopted in safety-critical project if a certain level of compromise can be found and that certain considerations are built into the open-source project from the outset.

4   Summary and Conclusions

Trends in technology and in the market are increasing the power and complexity of a new class of products. Industry is responding to the challenges these trends present with a number of approaches: the incorporation of platforms for product lines, managed reuse and new collaboration models incorporating open-source and incremental development.

This paper has identified a number of inadequacies in the certification of highly complex safety-critical systems in the context of these approaches. The products can attain or exceed the requisite safety and integrity, but certification according to standards requires considerable effort and interpretation. Our position is that the certification process must better reflect and incorporate industrial reality with respect to the properties to be certified and the processes involved. A change is needed.

Table 1. Summary of challenges identified in the paper

Challenges	Interacts with	Research papers	
		Non- Safety	Safety
Equivalence of techniques and measures	Open-source	[]	[14]
Measures for software integrity	Is a criteria in selection		[13]
Selection as a first-class citizen	Is an aspect of reuse	[18]	[15, 16, 17]
Processes for assuring different classes of reused software	Open-source (as platform development), selection	[5, 7, 18]	
Guidance for metrics for process confidence	Open-source, equivalence	[20]	[13, 21]
Agile development	Open-source, classic spiral development model	[3, 11]	[12]
Demarcation between new development and maintenance	Selection in so far as the version and revision of a component are a factor in the selection		
Incorporation of evidence gathering in open-source development processes	Guidance for metrics		

In particular we see a number of challenges that must be addressed in order to develop a practical approach to certifying future large-scale and heterogeneous software systems. These are summarized in Table 1 along with references to known research work that could support their resolution.

The table attempts to enumerate orthogonal challenges. The areas where the challenges interact present new challenges, as evidenced in this paper. The second column of the table identifies where intersections between the challenges produce relevant new issues. The research relevant to the challenges is documented in the last two columns.

The next generation of software-based systems require combining all of the above development paradigms and will involve the integration of in-house developed software, open-source components and 3rd party software into a software conglomerate, distributed across connected computing platforms and whose component parts are continuously updated. There is therefore a strong need to understand how the qualification of each of the component parts and their associated development models can be achieved in order to derive a convincing assurance case for the entire system.

That being said, the argumentation for that change must be factual and based on solid logic. Furthermore, it is unclear whether standards should change, new approaches to certification should be found or even if industrial practice should be adapted to the constraints of certification. Finding the right approaches, the right arguments and the right evidence are the tasks of research in the immediate future.

References

1. International Electrotechnical Commission (IEC): Functional safety of electrical/electronic/ programmable electronic safety-related systems, 2nd edn. International Electrotechnical Commission, Geneva (2010). ISBN 978-2-88910-524-3
2. ISO. ISO 26262: Road vehicles - Functional Safety. Norm (2011)
3. Beck, K., et al.: Manifesto for Agile Software Development (2001). Agile Alliance. Accessed 14 June 2010
4. OSADL: SIL2LinuxMP Webpage. http://www.osadl.org/SIL2LinuxMP.sil2-linux-project. 0.html. Accessed 22 May 2018
5. MacGregor, J., et al.: Transferkonzept und Leitfaden für die Anwendung in der Praxis, SPES_XT Report. http://spes2020.informatik.tu-muenchen.de/resultate_xt_EC4.html. Accessed 22 May 2018
6. AUTOSAR Project. https://www.autosar.org/. Accessed 16 May 2018
7. Clements, P., Northrop, P.: Software Product Lines: Practices and Patterns, vol. 3. Addison-Wesley, Reading (2002)
8. VDA QMC Working Group 13/Automotive SIG: Automotive SPICE Process Assessment/ Reference Model (2015)
9. CMMI. https://www.sei.cmu.edu/cmmi/tools/index.cfm. Accessed 22 May 2018
10. Atlassian: Agile Tools for Software Teams. https://de.atlassian.com/software/jira/agile. Accessed 22 May 2018
11. IBM: Collaborating through social coding. https://www.ibm.com/cloud/garage/content/ culture/practice_social_coding/. Accessed 22 May 2018

12. Doss, O., Kelly, T., Stålhane, T., Haugset, B., Dixon, M.: Integration of the 4 + 1 software safety assurance principles with scrum. In: Stolfa, J., Stolfa, S., O'Connor, R.V., Messnarz, R. (eds.) EuroSPI 2017. CCIS, vol. 748, pp. 72–82. Springer, Cham (2017). https://doi.org/10.1007/978-3-319-64218-5_6
13. Oliveira, P., Ferreira, A.L., Dias, D., Pereira, T., Monteiro, P., Machado, R.J.: An analysis of the commonality and differences between ASPICE and ISO26262 in the context of software development. In: Stolfa, J., Stolfa, S., O'Connor, R.V., Messnarz, R. (eds.) EuroSPI 2017. CCIS, vol. 748, pp. 216–227. Springer, Cham (2017). https://doi.org/10.1007/978-3-319-64218-5_17
14. Hawkins, R.: Software safety assurance-what is sufficient? (2009)
15. Ye, F., Kelly, T.: COTS product selection for safety-critical systems. In: Kazman, R., Port, D. (eds.) Proceedings of ICCBSS 2004. LNCS, vol. 2959, pp. 53–62. Springer, Heidelberg (2004). https://doi.org/10.1007/978-3-540-24645-9_17
16. Boyer, A., et al.: methods and techniques for contract-based safety analysis, SPES_XT Report. http://spes2020.informatik.tu-muenchen.de/resultate_xt_EC1.html. Accessed 22 May 2018
17. Platschek, A., Mc Guire, N., Bulwahn, L.: Certifying Linux_ Lessons Learned in Three Years of SIL2LinuxMP.   http://www.bmw-carit.de/downloads/publications/-EWC2018_Certifying-Linux-Lessons-Learned.pdf. Accessed 22 May 2018
18. Hotz, L., et al.: Configuration in Industrial Product Families: The ConIPF Methodology. IOS Press Inc, Amsterdam (2006)
19. ISO: ISO/IEC 15504 (Information technology — Process assessment). International Organization for Standardization, Geneva, Switzerland (2003)
20. Basili, V.R.: Software modeling and measurement: the Goal/Question/Metric paradigm (1992)
21. Luo, Y., et al.: Metrics design for safety assessment. Inf. Softw. Technol. **73**, 151–163 (2016)
22. ISO/IEC: Systems and Software Engineering –Measurement Process, ISO/IEC 15939:2008. International Organization for Standardization/International Electrotechnical Commission, Geneva, Switzerland (2007)

Comparing Risk Identification in Hazard Analysis and Threat Analysis

Hideaki Nishihara[1]([⊠]) and Kenji Taguchi[2]

[1] Information Technology Research Institute, National Institute of Advanced
Industrial Science and Technology (AIST), Osaka, Japan
h.nishihara@aist.go.jp
[2] CAV Technologies, Kyoto, Japan
kenji.taguchi@cav-tech.co.jp

Abstract. In the context of cyber-physical systems, safety and security
have been discussed and dealt with separately in the past, since security
was not a critical issue of safety and vice versa. They are similar in some
points, and it is natural to try dealing with them in parallel or in a
unified manner. This paper considers symmetrical treatment of safety
and security, especially in identifying possible harms. We compare the
result of hazard analysis and threat analysis for a single model of a small
IoT system. It shows that identified harms have much overlaps, which
indicates the two analyses can be unified.

Keywords: Hazard analysis · Threat analysis · Risk identification

1 Introduction

Recent fast pace progress of information technology enables complex functionalities such as interconnection between small devices and enterprise systems,
to embed in and prompts evolution of devices such as sensors, actuators, and
systems. Those are mentioned as cyber-physical systems (CPS) now. Internet
of Things (IoT), that can connect to any other systems (including those who
reside and work in physical world), is an example of CPSs. Autonomous driving, AI supported monitoring, or flexible wide-spread virtual environments are
technologies supporting CPSs.

On the other hand to keep those systems reliable becomes more difficult.
System complexities, ambiguity/absence of system boundaries, or evolutionary
aspects in those systems require much effort on considering emergent behaviors
and treatment for them. In particular, safety aspect and security aspect in those
systems are focused recently, as harms and damages are caused directly.

Safety and security have been discussed and dealt with separately in the
past, since security was not a critical issue of safety critical systems and vice
versa. However, the more systems connected each other, the more safety risk
and security risk appear and suffer from each other in the entire system. Safety
and security are similar in some points [15], and it is natural to try dealing with

B. Gallina et al. (Eds.): SAFECOMP 2018 Workshops, LNCS 11094, pp. 265–277, 2018.
https://doi.org/10.1007/978-3-319-99229-7_23

them in parallel or in a unified manner. Actually, decomposition by And-Or trees or risk based approaches are applied to both of safety process and security process. Also methodologies or frameworks have been proposed to treat safety and security together. But in many cases, a major interest is 'security for safety' as pointed out in Sect. 2. It is practical as safety aspects are more critical in CPS, but asymmetrical consideration of safety and security may overlook structural overlaps, redundant descriptions, or hidden relationships.

To make the theory more simple and consistent, it will be worth treating safety and security fairly on a common foundation. For example SEMA framework, which discusses safety and security based on locations of the harms and the origins and intentionality, is proposed in [14]. We can refer to the framework when we discuss about concepts, techniques, and methodologies in safety or security. Especially if an activity does not care about the locations of the targets and the existence of intent, the activity may cover both of safety and security.

Typical safety/security processes in system development consist of several activities, like identification, analysis, evaluation, or treatment. In this paper we focus on identification of possible harms. Harms are the most basic features of safety and security; both of safety and security aim to avoid harms or damages to entities to protect as is explained in Sect. 3. Also identification of possible harms is conducted in the earlier phase of safety/security processes.

Possible harms are common features in safety and security and it indicates that possible harms about a target system does not have to be analyzed separately. In order to demonstrate it, we derive possible harms of a small IoT system from hazard analysis in safety process and threat analysis in security process independently, and compare the results. Those analyses are based on a single model with the function list of the target system.

Our result shows that most of identified possible harms are overlapped, and ones from the hazard analysis are included in those from the threat analysis with a few exceptions. Moreover, we can classify possible harms into three groups. The groups can be used as guide words for identifying harms. Namely, possible harms for safety and security are analyzed with help of the three groups simultaneously first, and then causes and attributes for identified harms are derived.

Risk identification results are applied in the latter parts of safety/security processes. However safety and security have some differences as well as similarities. Hence each lifecycle does not need to be carried out in same way, especially risk evaluation. In order to proceed, identified risks must be demarcated to safety process and security process. We mention this issue after our result are shown.

Organization. In Sect. 2, existing research are reviewed. Section 3 discusses concepts appearing safety/security analyses. Hazard analysis and threat analysis applied in this paper are explained. Section 4 deals with a case study. For a small IoT system, we apply hazard analysis and threat analysis and compare the results. In Sect. 5 we summarize the paper and show future directions.

2   Related Work

There are standards, guidelines and research about entire processes of safety and security. In the guideline DO-326A [17] for avionics, the three processes about system development, safety, and security are addressed in a single process where they interact at several phases. Derock et al. [2] compares standards ISO 27005 for security and ISO/IEC 15026 for software and system assurance. It also proposes 'generalized safety process' which merge the processes introduced in the above standards. In [13], the authors compare process patterns dealing with safety and security in several technical standards and guidelines. We show five process patterns where security activities are included in or based on safety activities in two patterns.

Many research treat with individual sub-processes or methodologies for safety-security co-engineering, especially for risk identification [5,8,16,22]. But their perspectives are 'security for safety.' Security threats are considered only if those issues may affect safety. Raspotnig and Opdahl [4] discuss about correspondence between safety/security concepts and system abstraction levels with a position that neither safety nor security is more prioritized. On one hand, Chen et al. [3] proposes a method to identify hazards and threats in one process but it focuses on security. That paper uses FMVEA, an extension of FMEA with vulnerabilities. Plósz et al. [18] proposed a combining analysis for safety and security. The paper applies FMEA for safety and analysis introduced in IEC 62443 for security to a data flow diagram model. The results, safety threats and security threats with assessment, are assembled into a single catalog. Schmittner et al. [6] also discusses a combining analysis for safety and security. The paper formalizes concepts in cause-effect chains in safety and security in parallel, that allows us to analyze safety risks and security risks with FMVEA simultaneously. Furthermore it indicates that a consequence (effect) can be derived with the help of hazards and threats.

3   Preliminary

3.1   Concepts Related to Undesired Phenomena and Harms

Terminologies/ontologies on safety are specified in literature, mostly international standards, and ones for security as well. In safety, safety standards follow ISO/IEC Guide 51 [11], which mandates basic definitions on safety and risk, among other things. In the standard, 'a system is safe' means the system is free from intolerable *risks*, and a risk depends on the occurrence of *harm* and its severity. A *hazard* is a potential source of harms, which is a particular situation or event.

In security, Common Criteria (CC) [10] introduces a general concepts for discussing security. In CC, damages or loss of assets are risks and they are derived from *threats*, defined as adverse action by threat agents. Typically that action is realized by exploiting vulnerabilities of the system.

Table 1. Correspondences of concepts in standards

This paper	Risk[ISO31000]	Security[CC]	Safety[Guide 51]
Source of a harm	**Risk Source**: elements which has potential to give rise to risk		**Hazard**: potential source of harm
Undesired situation		**Vulnerability**: weakness in Target of Evaluation (TOE)	**Hazardous situation**: circumstance in which entities are exposed to hazards
Undesired event	**Event**: occurrence or change of a particular set of circumstances	**Threat**: adverse act on assets	**Hazardous event**: event causing harm
Harm	**Consequence**: outcome of an event affecting objectives	(Damage and/or abuse to assets)	**Harm**: injury or damage
Asset	(Objective)	**Asset**: entities that the value is places upon	(People, property, or environment)

Though there are some gaps (different choice of terms, hidden assumptions of ontology in different industrial sectors, etc.), it appears that the damage of assets are common concerns in safety and security. In order to compare analyses in safety and security[1], here we make clear concepts used in this paper based on Guide 51 and CC. For that we refer to ISO 31000 [9], the standard about risk management processes. The standard deals with a risk, defined as an effect of uncertainty on objectives, and concepts around risks. Safety and security described above are regarded to consider risks in individual domains. Remark that ISO 31000 is general and abstract that covers business or organizational activities as well as system development, and that we adopt terms in the standard according to our context.

The final consequence is a *harm*. It is a loss, reduction of values, and damage of an *asset*[2], that is an entity to protect. A harm needs an *undesired event*, as a direct trigger for the harm. Undesired events occur accidentally, or are invoked by malicious activities. Moreover they may occur under a particular *undesired situation* allowing the invocation of the event easily. Such an event and a situation appear in an entity, *source of harm*. An undesired event or a situation have their own causes. Those causes can be some other events or situations, that indicates events/situations may make chains from a harm to its causes.

Table 1 shows correspondences among standards explained above. Each term has one to one correspondence with a term[3] in ISO 31000 other than undesired situation. Terms defined in Common Criteria and Guide 51 are shown in

---

[1] Mapping or embedding concepts in security to safety are proposed in [6,20].

[2] Now indirect or secondary damage, like financial costs to recover, are ignored.

[3] In the table, definitions are modified slightly to save spaces.

rightmost two columns. Concepts and terms that are not defined explicitly are presented with parentheses.

3.2   Functional Hazard Analysis

Hazard analyses are cores in safety processes. Conducting a hazard analysis lets us recognize hazards, their causes and effects, and evaluate hazards. Its results are bases of consideration of treatment and establishing safety requirements, done in latter part of safety processes.

Functional hazard analysis (FHA) is a hazard analysis focusing on functionalities of the target system [1,7]. It allows analyses of failures occurring inside the system in detail.

FHA starts with finding failures for each function[4] of the target system. Failures are 'the departure of an item from its required or intended operation, function, or behavior' [7], and are sought with several guide words like 'fail to operate', 'operate early/late', or 'degrade/malfunction.' A failure has effects on other functions or components, some of which give damages on people, properties, or environment. Hazards, that is sources of harms, and effects including consequences are considered for each failure in FHA.

After identifying above factors, hazards are evaluated for prioritization in which severity and likelihood are used in most cases. The outcome of FHA is a table showing identified hazards with functional failures relating to them, derived effects and consequences, risk values, and additional information like causal factors and countermeasures.

3.3   Threat Analysis

Threat analyses are cores in security processes. Its role, value of outcomes, procedures are similar to hazard analyses. In this paper we follow [21], which studied the guideline JASO TP15002 [12]. Though the guideline is for automotive information security analysis, it is so general that we apply it to other CPSs.

After identifying related information, that is a target system model, assets, its lifecycle, and potential adversaries such as persons or systems who can access the system, threats are identified by the 5 W method in TP 15002. The 5 W method identifies an adverse action as a 'What' factor, together with other factors 'Who' (conductor), 'Where' (entry point of threat), 'When' (lifecycle phase), and 'Why' (accidental/intentional).

The paper [21] proposes a refinement of the process of TP15002. 'What' factor is decomposed to an action with 2 new factors 'At' and 'Asset' (called Asset container method), where Asset and At mean the target of the action and the component having the asset respectively. Furthermore, factors Where, What (action), At, and Asset are emphasized in the paper, as those four factors specify the phenomenon of a threat, and they are required for risk evaluation

---

[4] Of course the target system must be described with its components and functions before analysis.

applied in the paper. Other factors are important in activities in the latter part of the process, i.e. cause analysis or treatments of threats. In seeking threats, *STRIDE* [19] is used as guide words.

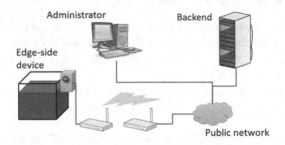

Fig. 1. A small IoT system

4   Case Study

This section shows an application of FHA and TA explained in Sect. 3 to a small system and their results. First System of Interest (SoI) is modeled. Next FHA and TA are conducted independently based on the common model, then possible harms are derived from both analyses. It follows that results are examined, especially on overlaps of undesired events.

4.1   System of Interest

Let us consider a small IoT system in Fig. 1, which consists of three components, i.e. Edge-side device, Administrator, and Backend, each of which is connected via the public network. Its main function is to manage temperature of water in a tank, which is depicted as the Edge-side device in Fig. 1. The Edge-side device consists of the temperature sensor, controller, heater, and communication device. The sensor of the water tank senses the current temperature, and the controller in the Edge-side device sends the latest temperature to the remote computer depicted as the Backend via public network periodically. The Backend, running in a platform like a cloud system or a server, receives, stores, and evaluates data, and decides whether the water in the tank at the Edge-side device should be heated or not. After the Backend sends a command to the Edge-side device to increase the temperature, the Edge-side device follows the command. The Edge-side device has a switch to change the state of the heater in case of emergency. The role of the Administrator is to configure the whole system and checks logs stored in the Backend.

More detailed description of the system architecture, functions and data of each component of SoI is depicted in Fig. 2 in UML (Unified Modeling Language). For the sake of brevity, we only explain the Backend, which is modelled as a package with some classes in it. It has the main control function; the temperature management, log management and communication, each of which is

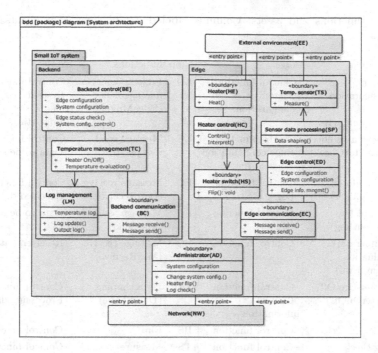

Fig. 2. A model of SoI

modelled as Backend control (BE), Temperature management (TC), Log management (LM) and Backend communication (BC) respectively. The Backend control (BE) has two functions; 'Edge status check' and 'System configuration Control'. The Backend control (BE) also has two data; Edge configuration and System configuration. They are kept in the Backend control (BE) and processed by its functions. In order to help threat analysis, the potential entry point of attacks is described by the stereotype <<entry point>>. When two components communicate or interact, a link is drawn between them. If only one component refers to information in another component, an arrow link is drawn to the referred component.

Assets in SoI are listed in Table 2. Each asset is either a function or data to be processed or stored data. Remark that some data are shared by some components, or transferred from a componet to another, and thus assets with the same name in plural components have the same contents. Exceptions are Received data and Data to be sent in Backend communication and Edge communication. A Control function depends on the component which it belongs to, and hence Control functions are exceptional, too. Another remark is that Fig. 2 and Table 2 do not show all the information for FHA and TA. From the viewpoint of hazard analyses, assets are the health of people, properties, and environment but in general they reside outside of SoI and they are not identified explicitly.

Table 2. Functions and assets: Columns labeled 'Cmp' show components of SoI (See Fig. 2).

Cmp	Function	Asset	Cmp	Functions	Asset
BE	System configuration control (SysConfCtrl)	-Control function –System configuration	ED	Edge information management (EdgeMngmt)	-Control function –System configuration –Edge status
BE	Edge status check (EdgeStatCheck)	-Control function –Edge configuration –Edge status	EC	Message send (MsgSend)	-Control function –Data to be sent
LM	Log update (LogUpdate)	-Control function –Log	EC	Message receive (MsgReceive)	-Control function –Received data
LM	Output log (OutputLog)	–Control function –Log	BC	Message send (MsgSend)	–Data to be sent
TC	Temperature evaluation (TempEval)	–Control function	BC	Message receive (MsgReceive)	–Received data
TC	Heater On/Off (HeterOnOff)	–Control function –Control information	SP	Data shaping (DataShape)	–Control function –Processing data
HE	Heat	–Control function	HS	Flip	–Control function
AD	Log check (LogCheck)	–Control function –System configuration	TS	Measure	–Control function –Sensor data
AD	Change system configuration (ChSysConf)	–Control function –System configuration	HC	Interpret	-Control function
AD	Heater flip (FlipHeater)	–Control function	HC	Control	–Control function

We have some assumptions about SoI's behaviours:

- Backend runs in a platform like a cloud system or a server, and other processes unrelated to SoI may run in the same environment. A process may occasionally consume much resources and give some impacts on other processes, but we trust the underlying platform either they are computing or networking basically; the component BC is assumed not to be tampered with, and components in Backend are assumed not to be accessed by other processes directly.
- On the other hand, Edge-side device is specific to SoI. There is no mechanism managing or monitoring the edge-side system entirely.
- SoI is in operation phase in its lifecycle.

4.2   Identification of Undesired Events

FHA for SoI is conducted according to the method explained in Sect. 3.2. Our focus is not on evaluation and treatment of risks, but on just functional failures, hazards and direct effects caused by them. In order to consider functional failures, five guide words introduced in [1] are chosen: *fail to operate, operate early/late, operate out of sequence, unable to stop*, and *degrade/malfunction*. For each identified functional failure, hazards and effects are sought after with help of interactions expressed in the model of SoI.

We found 81 functional failures and 27 hazards. In Table 3 a part of the result are shown. In the upper table, each row shows identified functional failures with guide words[5] ('Type' column) for functions of SoI, and hazards derived from the failures. The lower table shows the list of effects derived from the hazard. To distinguish components on which each hazard or effect is found, the acronym of the component is added as a prefix for each entry as necessary.

Table 3. Result of FHA.

Cmp	Function	Failure	Type	Hazards
BE	SysConfCtrl	Not invoked	F	BE. inadequate system configuration
BE	EdgeStatCheck	Check at inadequate time	E/L	BE. incorrect edge status

Hazard	Effect
BE. inadequate system configuration	-LM. LogUpdate invoked inadequately -BC. not send messages to Edge properly -TC. malfunctioning TempEval -TC. inadequate control information generation

Table 4. Result of TA

Where	Who	Why	What(event)	Type	At	Function
BC	outsider	malicious	BE. unintentional change/ deletion of SW (SysConfCtrl)	T	BE	SysConfCtrl
BC	outsider	malicious	BE. unauthorized disclosure of edge information	I	BE	EdgeStatCheck

Threat	Effect
BE. unintentional change/ deletion of SW (SysConfCtrl)	-BE. configuration update does not complete -BE. inadequate configuration is set

Like FHA, TA is conducted according to the method explained in Sect. 3.3. Backend communication (BC), Edge communication (EC), Administrator (AD), Heater Switch (HS), Heater (HE), and Temperature Sensor (TS) are in touch with the outside the system, and hence an adverse act on SoI is performed via these components. In Sect. 3.3 threats are assigned to assets, but we assign threats to functions that have those assets in our case study. By this change, we can consider both of failures and threats for functions only, that will make the comparison of results simple. As same as FHA, the acronym of a target component is added to each threat.

We found 83 threats. A part of the result are shown in Table 4. In the upper table of TA, each row shows identified threats with their attributes[6] where letters

---

[5] 'F' and 'E/L' mean 'fail to operate' and 'operate early/late' respectively.

[6] In the upper table, 'when' factor is omitted as the lifecycle phase of SoI is fixed in this case study.

in 'Type' column come from STRIDE, and the lower table shows the list of effects the threat causes.

4.3   Results and Observations

In FHA, we identified functional failures as origins of harms and derived hazards and effects as their results. On the other hand 'what' factors in TA show events occurred at the target and each 'what' factor cause some effects. In Table 1, a hazard in Guide 51 and a threat in CC are mapped to Risk Source and Event in ISO 31000 respectively. Hence we cannot compare hazards in FHA and threats in TA directly. However, effects in both FHA and TA are mapped to Consequence in ISO 31000, and they are basic concerns in safety and security as mentioned in the introduction. Finally we analyze effects identified in FHA and TA.

Remark that static factors, namely hazardous situation and vulnerabilities, are not analyzed in this case study directly. It is because we begin with only events or actions in both FHA and TA. Also remark that identified events are not exclusive. Some harms in the list are implied, instantiated, or overlapped from other harms. As shown in the result of the analyses (See Tables 3 and 4), possible harms of SoI are different from each other. However we can categorize them to the following three types:

- Malfunction (expressed by "[M]"). A specific functionality is not achieved due to damages. The function aborts abnormally or unfinishes, or outputs are broken.
- Unexpected application (expressed by "[E]"). The functionality works normally but the unexpected results are obtained. Misuse, processing incorrect inputs, unauthorized modification are examples.
- Unauthorized acquisition (expressed by "[A]"). Information related to SoI is obtained without authorization.

For example, the harm "LM. LogUpdate invoked inadequately" is an unexpected application of LogUpdate, and the harm "BE. configuration update does not complete" is a malfunction of SysConfCtrl as well.

Table 5 shows the merged list of undesired events of SoI. 53 events are identified in total, where 31 events appear in both of FHA and TA. Each entry is described with the combination of the component with the function or data in which the event occurs, and type of harms. The entries ♯ 41 and 42 are events that may occur in the network. The network is public and there is no assumptions about its topologies, nodes, and functionalities. The entries ♯ 52 and 53 are events which may occur in the platform where the Backend in SoI runs.

Some observations are obtained from Table 5. First, we can see malfunctions (entries with "[M]") and unexpected application (entries with "[E]") are identified for each function in each component. Exceptional cases are Flip (HS), Measure (TS), and FlipHeater (AD). Flip (HS) and Measure (TS) are not affected by any hazard or threat since they do not depend on other functions. Also AD invokes FlipHeater when finding something abnormal physically, and thus it is

Table 5. Undesired events list: The entry with HA [re. TA] column checked is identified in FHA [re. TA]. Entries identified in both of FHA and TA are presented in bold.

♯	Undesired event	HA	TA	♯	Undesired event	HA	TA
1	**AD. [E] ChSysConf**	✓	✓	2	**AD. [M] ChSysConf**	✓	✓
3	**AD. [M] LogCheck**	✓	✓	4	**AD. [E] LogCheck**	✓	✓
5	AD. [A] system config. information		✓	6	AD. [A] temperature log		✓
7	**BC. [M] MsgReceive**	✓	✓	8	**BC. [M] MsgSend**	✓	✓
9	BC. [A] received message		✓	10	BC. [A] sent message		✓
11	**BC. [E] MsgReceive**	✓	✓	12	BC. [E] MsgSend	✓	
13	**BE. [M] EdgeStatCheck**	✓	✓	14	**BE. [M] SysConfCtrl**	✓	✓
15	BE. [A] edge status		✓	16	BE. [A] system information		✓
17	**BE. [E] EdgeStatCheck**	✓	✓	18	**BE. [E] SysConfCtrl**	✓	✓
19	**EC. [M] MsgReceive**	✓	✓	20	**EC. [M] MsgSend**	✓	✓
21	**EC. [E] MsgReceive**	✓	✓	22	**EC. [E] MsgSend**	✓	✓
23	EC. [A] MsgReceive		✓	24	EC. [A] MsgSend		✓
25	**ED. [M] EdgeMngmt**	✓	✓	26	ED. [A] backend information		✓
27	ED. [A] edge information		✓	28	**ED. [E] EdgeMngmt**	✓	✓
29	**HC. [M] Control**	✓	✓	30	**HC. [M] Interpret**	✓	✓
31	**HC. [E] Control**	✓	✓	32	**HC. [E] Interpret**	✓	✓
33	HE. [M] Heat	✓		34	HE. [E] Heat	✓	
35	**LM. [M] LogUpdate**	✓	✓	36	**LM. [M] OutputLog**	✓	✓
37	LM. incorrect temperature log		✓	38	LM. [A] temperature log		✓
39	**LM. [E] LogUpdate**	✓	✓	40	**LM. [E] OutputLog**	✓	✓
41	NW. [M] communication in network	✓		42	NW. [E] communication in network	✓	
43	**SP. [M] DataShape**	✓	✓	44	**SP. [E] DataShape**	✓	✓
45	SP. incorrect sensor data		✓	46	SP. [A] sensor data		✓
47	**TC. [M] HeatOnOff**	✓	✓	48	**TC. [M] TempEval**	✓	✓
49	TC. [A] control information		✓	50	**TC. [E] HeatOnOff**	✓	✓
51	**TC. [E] TempEval**	✓	✓	52	[M] Backend environment	✓	
53	[M] communication in Backend	✓					

not affected by other component in SoI. Next, unauthorized acquisition are possible for every component which keeps, accesses or generates some information. Moreover they are found only in TA.

Most of undesired events found in FHA are also identified in TA. It is explained by the consideration that some attacks cause malfunction or unexpected application of a function, that can be functional failures. On one hand, undesired events found in FHA but not found in TA have obvious reasons:

- ♯ 12. Message send function in BC is a part of the platform the backend system run on. By assumption, it cannot be affected directly from outside.
- ♯ 33, 34. Heater (HE) cannot be accessed directly, and it is out of scope of our threat analysis.
- ♯ 41, 42, 52, 53. The scope of threat analysis are components inside SoI.

5 Concluding Remarks

In this paper, aiming to deal with safety and security in a single framework, we reviewed concepts defined in major standards, Guide 51 for safety and

Common Criteria for security. We considered their correspondences with help of ISO 31000, a standard for risk management. Risk identification for safety and security have a common goal, that is to find possible harms on assets in the target system. We applied Functional Hazard Analysis (FHA) and Threat Analysis (TA) based on Ericson's book [7] and JASO TP15002 [12] respectively to a small IoT system and compared both analysis. The result shows that most of undesired events are overlapped and we can classify those event to three groups. The result indicates that the risk identification process can be united for safety and security, which would make safety/security processes become simpler than we first thought.

There are still many issues remain to be solved such as to fully integrate safety/security processes. One of those issue is expanding our results to other cyber-physical domains. We observed in the previous section that there are three types of typical undesired events. They will be possible harms also for other CPSs. Thus we can expect to establish a simple and general risk identification methodology.

Another remaining issue is on other part of risk management processes, which we do not discuss in this paper. The main difficulty results from the fact that safety and security use different risk criteria, thereby assessment cannot be mixed easily. With identification of properties in undesired events, that activities in safety process [re. security process] are applied, it is expected that we approach an adequate treatment of safety and security in a single framework.

References

1. Scharl, A., Stottlar, K., Kady, R.: Functional Hazard Analysis(FHA) Methodology Tutorial. Technical report NSWCDD-MP-14-00380 (2014)
2. Derock, A., Hebrard, P., Vallee, F.: Convergence of the latest standards addressing safety and security for information technology. In: Embedded Real Time Software and Systems (ERTSS) (2010)
3. Chen, B., et al.: Security analysis of urban railway systems: the need for a cyber-physical perspective. In: Koornneef, F., van Gulijk, C. (eds.) SAFECOMP 2015. LNCS, vol. 9338, pp. 277–290. Springer, Cham (2015). https://doi.org/10.1007/978-3-319-24249-1_24
4. Raspotnig, C., Opdahl, A.: Comparing risk identification techniques for safety and security requirements. J. Syst. Softw. **86**(4), 1124–1151 (2013)
5. Raspotnig, C., Karpati, P., Katta, V.: A combined process for elicitation and analysis of safety and security requirements. In: Bider, I., et al. (eds.) BPMDS/EMMSAD -2012. LNBIP, vol. 113, pp. 347–361. Springer, Heidelberg (2012). https://doi.org/10.1007/978-3-642-31072-0_24
6. Schmittner, C., Gruber, T., Puschner, P., Schoitsch, E.: Security application of failure mode and effect analysis (FMEA). In: Bondavalli, A., Di Giandomenico, F. (eds.) SAFECOMP 2014. LNCS, vol. 8666, pp. 310–325. Springer, Cham (2014). https://doi.org/10.1007/978-3-319-10506-2_21
7. Ericson II., C.A.: Hazard Analysis Techniques for System Safety, 2nd edn. Wiley, Hoboken (2016)

8. Macher, G., Höller, A., Sporer, H., Armengaud, E., Kreiner, C.: A combined safety-hazards and security-threat analysis method for automotive systems. In: Koornneef, F., van Gulijk, C. (eds.) SAFECOMP 2015. LNCS, vol. 9338, pp. 237–250. Springer, Cham (2015). https://doi.org/10.1007/978-3-319-24249-1_21
9. ISO 31000. Risk management - Principles and guidelines (2009)
10. ISO/IEC 15408. Common Criteria for Information Technology Security Evaluation (2017)
11. ISO/IEC Guide 51. Safety aspects - Guidelines for their inclusion in standards (2014)
12. JASO TP15002. Guideline for Automotive Information Security Analysis (2015)
13. Taguchi, K., Souma, D., Nishihara, H.: Safe & sec case pattrens. In: SAFECOMP 2015 Workshops, pp. 27–37 (2015)
14. Piètre-Cambacédès, L., Chaudet, C.: The SEMA referential framework: avoiding ambiguities in the terms "security" and "safety". Int. J. Crit. Infrastruct. Prot. **3**(2), 55–66 (2010)
15. Piètre-Cambacédès, L., Bouissou, M.: Cross-fertilization between safety and security engineering. Reliab. Eng. Syst. Saf. **110**, 110–126 (2013)
16. Bieber, P., Blanquart, J.-P., Descargues, G., Dulucq, M., Fourastier, Y., Hazane, E., Julien, M., Léonardon, L., Saroulille, G.: Security and safety assurance for aerospace embedded systems. In: Embedded Real-Time Software and Systems (ERTSS) (2012)
17. RTCA DO-326A. Airworthiness Security Process Specification (2014)
18. Plósz, S., Schmittner, C., Varga, P.: Combining safety and security analysis for industrial collaborative automation systems. In: Tonetta, S., Schoitsch, E., Bitsch, F. (eds.) SAFECOMP 2017. LNCS, vol. 10489, pp. 187–198. Springer, Cham (2017). https://doi.org/10.1007/978-3-319-66284-8_16
19. Shostack, A.: Threat Modeling: Designing for Security. Wiley, Hoboken (2014)
20. Stoneburner, G.: Toward a unified security-safety model. Computer **39**(8), 96–97 (2006)
21. Kawanishi, Y., Nishihara, H., Souma, D., Yoshida, H.: Detailed analysis of security evaluation of automotive systems based on JASO TP15002. In: Tonetta, S., Schoitsch, E., Bitsch, F. (eds.) SAFECOMP 2017. LNCS, vol. 10489, pp. 211–224. Springer, Cham (2017). https://doi.org/10.1007/978-3-319-66284-8_18
22. Guo, Z., Zeckzer, D., Liggesmeyer, P., Maeckel, O.: Identification of security-safety requirements for the outdoor robot RAVON using safety analysis techniques. In: ICSEA (2010)

Towards Risk Estimation in Automated Vehicles Using Fuzzy Logic

Leonardo González[1,2]([✉]), Enrique Martí[1], Isidro Calvo[2], Alejandra Ruiz[1], and Joshue Pérez[1]

[1] Tecnalia Research and Innovation, Derio, Spain
{leonardo.gonzalez,enrique.marti,alejandra.ruiz,
joshue.perez}@tecnalia.com
[2] University of the Basque Country, Vitoria-Gasteiz, Spain
isidro.calvo@ehu.edu

Abstract. As vehicles get increasingly automated, they need to properly evaluate different situations and assess threats at run-time. In this scenario automated vehicles should be able to evaluate risks regarding a dynamic environment in order to take proper decisions and modulate their driving behavior accordingly. In order to avoid collisions, in this work we propose a risk estimator based on fuzzy logic which accounts for risk indicators regarding (1) the state of the driver, (2) the behavior of other vehicles and (3) the weather conditions. A scenario with two vehicles in a car-following situation was analyzed, where the main concern is to avoid rear-end collisions. The goal of the presented approach is to effectively estimate critical states and properly assess risk, based on the indicators chosen.

Keywords: Automated vehicles · Collision avoidance · Fuzzy logic
Time-to-collision · Driving behavior

1 Introduction

In a non-automated vehicle, risk in the environment is processed by the driver, who intuitively analyzes several factors in a typical driving scenario, such as the distance to the obstacles, the relative velocities to other vehicles, the roadway conditions, the traffic rules, among other environment and vehicle variables. Increasing vehicle automated capabilities requires their awareness of the environment to grow accordingly, so that they are able to understand and process different threat sources. A prompt and detection of dangerous situations, will allow vehicles to react and avoid or mitigate accidents.

Nowadays, traffic accidents are responsible for up to 1.25M deaths and 50M injuries worldwide annually according to the World Health Organization [17]. The main reason for most accidents in rural and urban roads is human error, accounting for 94% of crashes according to the National Highway Traffic Safety Administration [16]. One of the main reasons to move towards automated vehicle

© Springer Nature Switzerland AG 2018
B. Gallina et al. (Eds.): SAFECOMP 2018 Workshops, LNCS 11094, pp. 278–289, 2018.
https://doi.org/10.1007/978-3-319-99229-7_24

technology is to improve safety by reducing the driver interaction with the system (taking the driver out of the loop). This transition is currently ongoing. Several functionality levels for the automated vehicle have been defined depending on how much the driver presence is required. For example, the Society of Automotive Engineers (SAE) has defined six levels of automation, depending on the vehicle capability to perform driving tasks in different scenarios (modes) [15].

Vehicular technology available in the market is on the verge of level 3 or "conditional automation", which performs monitoring and driving under restrict circumstances, while level 4 technology is currently being tested by several companies. On the other hand, "full automation" (level 5) describes a vehicle with full capability in all environments under dynamic circumstances, taking the driver out of the equation.

Automated vehicle technology is increasingly gaining attention in the industry, Advanced Driver Assistance Systems (ADAS) have been under research for several years. ADAS already provide level 2 automation in commercial vehicles, and paved the path to level 3 automation. Nonetheless, the reliability of these vehicles is limited, and still depends on the driver to take corrective actions if something goes wrong. The trend towards highly automated vehicles, non-reliant on driver intervention, makes vehicles fully responsible for all the driving actions. Thus, serious liability issues for vehicle manufacturers arise if safety is not thoroughly guaranteed.

This work develops a concept for online risk estimation, relying on safety properties in a conditionally automated vehicle (level 3), to provide a comprehensive global knowledge of the state situation in the driving action. This risk estimation will be studied for a rear end collision scenario, using a fuzzy logic approach.

The outline of this paper is as follows. First, a background of risk in automated vehicles is presented. Then, a general risk assessment architecture is proposed in Sect. 2. In Sect. 3 indicators of risk are selected and a fuzzy logic approach is described. In Sect. 4, a case study is proposed to test our risk estimation. Finally conclusions are presented in Sect. 5.

2   Risk in Automated Vehicles

Risk is related to a multitude of scenarios where the likelihood of loss or liability exists. For example, investment risk or project completion risk are associated with performance and value. In a general sense, Levenson [12] defines risk as a compound likelihood of components which may lead to a negative outcome.

The idea of risk in the automotive industry is associated with a vehicle incurring in a dangerous maneuver or scenario; a dangerous scenario is one that increases the likelihood of an automotive accident. According to Lefèvre [11], risk in automated vehicles is associated with the "likelihood and severity of the damage that a vehicle of interest may suffer in the future". In order to evaluate and minimize risks, it is necessary to have accurate mathematical models of the situation in order to predict threats.

Most of the work regarding risk and threat assessment in the ITS (Intelligent Transportation System) community has been focused on trajectory prediction in order to detect collision states, which incurs huge computational cost [7]. The scenarios for collision avoidance vary greatly depending in the models used for forecasting. According to [11], these strategies can be categorized as future trajectory collision, binary collisions and probabilistic collision prediction. Some indicators have been proposed to obtain a direct measure of the risk, such as Time to collision (TTC), Time to lane change (TLC) mainly for lateral maneuvers, and Time to react (TTR) directly linked to the driver ability to take action under a threat.

More recently, risk has been associated with a set of "unusual events" as Lefevre argues in [10]; i.e. detecting a deviation from a standard behavior for a particular scenario. This concept of risk, based on an unexpected behavior, follows the principle that when a system is unable to predict the future actions of other participants, such actions may be regarded as risky or dangerous in a specific set of traffic rules. As a matter of example, a vehicle passing a red light is perceived as an increased risk for other vehicles in the scenario, given that such maneuver is not expected.

Detecting these unusual events requires the definition of a nominal behavior, which can be based on a series of rules. In [18] a context based risk detector was developed from a set of safety rules aimed at preventing adverse weather conditions and driver fatigue. In [14] Perez proposed an arbitration control which evaluates some risk-related indicators in order to negotiate a level of authority between the driver and system. This assessment is based on driver specific indicators depending on the attention and drowsiness, as well as TTC. These strategies aim at having a richer risk evaluation based not only on the physical model of the vehicle, but also on the environmental and driver situation.

3   Risk Estimator

Dynamic threats, presented during run-time behavior, represent a challenge for perception and decision systems. As a matter of example, the need for further research in risk assessment strategies has come up lately in the literature of automated driving as a mean to improve safety and provide reliability of its systems.

The architecture for automated vehicles used in this work is shown in Fig. 1, and is based on [9] where Lattarulo et al. defined a framework to test controllers in a simulated scenario. Our approach makes use of the decision, perception and communication blocks. According to the architecture, the risk estimation component takes place before the behavioral planner, as this is the main subsystem responsible for action in the case of a high risk scenario. Also, our estimator requires information from the world in order to make the assessment as well as data from the perception component.

The perception component gets data from exteroceptive and proprioceptive sensors. Thus, it provides the vehicle with a situation awareness regarding its

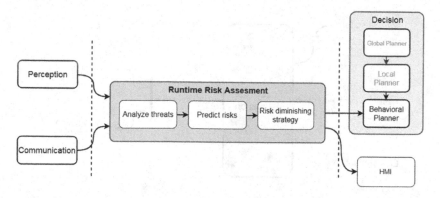

Fig. 1. Risk assessment architecture

environment and its current state. Accuracy on this environmental description depends heavily on the amount and type of sensors used. The environmental description includes, but it is not limited to, defining and identifying other participants, classifying them (e.g. vehicle, bus, cyclist, pedestrian), identifying road signals (pedestrian crossings, semaphores, etc.), climatological conditions (fog, rain, snow and ice) among others.

The information of other vehicles states could also be provided by communication systems. Vehicle-to-vehicle communication (V2V) can greatly improve safety for automated and non-automated vehicles. The NHTSA predicts implementing V2V technology will diminish accident rates and greatly increased safety in the road [4].

Our Runtime Risk Assessment framework is composed of three main tasks: (a) to recognize and properly assess threats, (b) to predict risk situations regarding previously identified threats and, finally, (c) to propose a risk-diminishing strategy; i.e. an action to avoid a risky situation. We consider a dangerous situation only regarding rear-end collisions in a single lane road. Based on this scenario three main variables were selected; time to collision (TTC), visual driver distraction (VDD) and weather conditions (WTHR). The scenario analyzed is composed of two vehicles in a car-following situation.

3.1 Risk Estimation with Fuzzy Logic

For the task of emulating human driving actions fuzzy logic control has been previously used in automated driving [13]. Since risk is inferred by the driver in a non-automated vehicle, a fuzzy logic approach was chosen to mimic this expertise. It allows extrapolating directly human knowledge in a set of rules to asses a situation's risk. For our system three main variables were selected, TTC, a weather representation, and visual driver distraction (VDD), representing the vehicle states, the driver and environment respectively as shown in Fig. 2.

TTC is the main indicator for risk in our fuzzy logic approach, due to its direct relation with frontal collisions. This variable has been widely used in

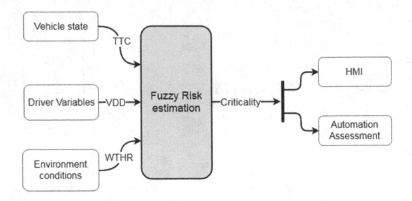

Fig. 2. Fuzzy system representation

the literature as an indicator of danger for vehicles. It was first introduced by Hayward [5] as an scalar measure of danger. TTC represents the time in the future in which a collision would have happened if the vehicle maintains its current speed and trajectory. This temporal indicator is critical if it is under 1.5 s [6] and it is generally consider safe when it is over 4 s. TTC is calculated using Eq. 1, where X_i is the position of i-th vehicle and l_i its length.

$$TTC = \frac{X_{i-1}(t) - Xi(t) - l_i}{\dot{X}_{i-1}(t) - \dot{X}i(t)} \tag{1}$$

Another input for the proposed fuzzy system is linked to the weather conditions. We used a normalized variable called WTHR. Weather affects the risk in a determined setup in multiple ways: it reduces the system (or driver) visibility and its ability to properly control the vehicle, it can also change the road conditions, diminishing the friction coefficient. In [8] a study to assess driver behavior and associate it with weather conditions was conducted, risk perception was associated with the ability of drivers to correctly assess the weather forecast.

Visibility and road condition, also change the behavior of other vehicles in a driving situation, so, a driver might behave more conservatively not only due to limited control, but also because other vehicles might exhibit the same limitations, making them hard to predict. Since these factors are complex to model for a vehicle, we used a simulated indicator, our WTHR indicator ranges from 0 to 1, where 0 represents optimal conditions for driving which could be translated to a dry roadway and good visibility.

Driver attention has also been included in the evaluation. Recently, efforts have been put into developing highly automated systems with drivers in the loop as a transitioning phase for autonomous technology, while still providing enhanced safety. One of the main challenges of such systems is being able to evaluate correctly when to intervene in a maneuver in order to take control of the vehicle from the driver. Other approaches manage the transition of authority between the automation and the driver dynamically [2]. These strategies are called sharing control, and the process of assessing an automation level has been labeled as arbitration control [3]. Our risk variable definition fits into such framework and can be taken into account as an indicator for when to perform such transition in a risky environment. In [1] a method to assess driver attention based on an analysis of head position and orientation was conducted, a Visual Driver Distraction (VDD) estimation was generated. To represent driver attention in our study an abstraction over VDD was used, our VDD indicator ranges from [0, 1], where 0 represents an optimal attention level (no distraction) (Fig. 4).

Our fuzzy logic approach defines three classes for the membership functions of each input, as shown in Fig. 3. These membership functions define a set of values related to each class, i.e. TTC is consider low below 2.5 s, and its membership to this set increases until it tops at 1 second and reaches its maximum membership. Membership functions allow to define subsets which might be overlapping, and different functions might be used, in our case (Fig. 3), these are created with triangular and trapezoidal functions. Fuzzification receives TTC, WTHR and VDD values and converts them to a fuzzy value using its membership functions. In our design we used a Mandani's fuzzy inference method, which allows for an $if - then$ definition of our rules. The rule base provided in Table 1, allows for a mapping of our inputs to our fuzzy output, or risk estimation. These rules are base on human expertise and knowledge, and allow for a soft mapping between inputs and risk states, which through defuzzificatio process outputs a crisp value, in our case a centroid method was used. For our fuzzy output membership function, five labels were designed to establish levels of criticality; safe, low warning, warning, low critical and critical. Our fuzzy system can be inspected as a function with three variables and a single output, a surface plot for our risk estimation is presented in Fig. 8.

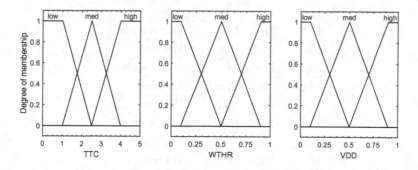

Fig. 3. Input membership functions for fuzzy logic

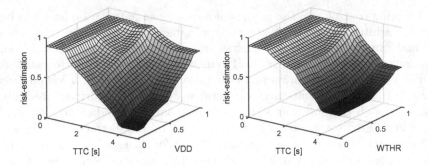

Fig. 4. Output surface functions

Table 1. Fuzzy system rule definition.

TTC[s]	VDD	Weather	Fuzzy Output
Low	-	-	Critical
Med	Low	Low	Low warning
Med	Med	Low	Low critical
Med	High	Low	Critical
Med	Low	Med	Warning
Med	Med	Med	Low critical
Med	High	Med	Critical
Med	Low	High	Warning
Med	Med	High	Critical
Med	High	High	Critical
High	Low	Low	Safe
High	Med	Low	Low warning
High	High	Low	Warning
High	Low	Med	Low warning
High	Med	Med	Low warning
High	High	Med	Warning
High	Low	High	Low warning
High	Med	High	Warning
High	High	High	Warning

4   Case Study

Our study focuses on the analysis of rear-end collisions between two vehicles in a car-following scenario. The roadway used for our scenario was taken from a map, and intentionally contains a roundabout with an intersection in order to represent an actual urban street. This scenario is simple enough to test the estimation made by our fuzzy logic approach. The main purpose of the test was to validate the risk estimation using different inputs for our indicators.

The simulation environment contains two vehicles, which communicate their states regarding velocity and position at all times. In a experimental scenario these states could be inferred from the sensors of the perception system, or simply shared through vehicle-to-vehicle (V2V) communication. The trailing vehicle uses these states to compute the TTC, which is then fed to our fuzzy logic estimator along with our simulated variables.

TTC was calculated using Eq. 1. The numerator represents the distance to collision (DTC). In our simulation this distance was assumed to be rectilinear regardless of the geometry of the road. This decision simplified calculations, and still portrays a worst case scenario, as this distance is always less or equal than the real distance on the road, yielding to a minimum TTC.

WTHR and VDD do not impact the simulation environment, instead they are only used by our risk estimation approach. In this way, they contribute indirectly to the TTC as main indicator, with driver and environment information, enhancing the estimation based on the set of rules established for our fuzzy logic approach.

For each vehicle a speed profile was also created, which depends on the geometry of the road and the maximum speed, acceleration and brake allowed. In this case, both maximum acceleration and brake were maintained equal among both vehicles, since our TTC calculation does not account for relative acceleration. Instead, different maximum speeds were imposed for each vehicle, making the leading vehicle slower to test the risk estimation in a impending collision. In order to observe how the risk estimation evolved, no modification was carried out by the system to avoid the collision, so the simulation continued until a collision effectively occurred. On the contrary, in a real situation the driver would avoid the collision by braking when he gets too close.

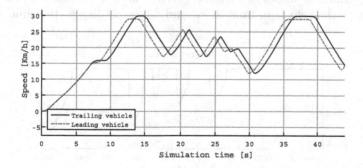

Fig. 5. Vehicles speed

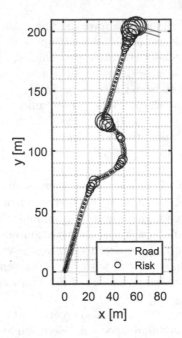

Fig. 6. Risk in road scenario. Circle size increases with higher risk.

4.1   Results

Simulations tested for 3 values of WTHR and 5 values of VDD. TTC was calculated during simulation time using the speed and position of both vehicles.

TTC for the trailing vehicle in Fig. 7 shows several peaks before collision. These peaks coincide with changes in curvature of the road, where vehicles diminish velocity and near miss situations occurred. This is observed five times before colliding with the vehicle in front at around 44 s according to the simulation.

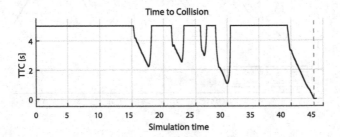

Fig. 7. TTC in our scenario

In Fig. 8 all simulations are presented for different values of WTHR and VDD. Since WTHR is linked with weather conditions in the environment, it is expected to change less abruptly, though we are more concerned with grouping VDD changes. Similar to TTC five peaks can be observed for all simulations, this was to be expected based on our rules.

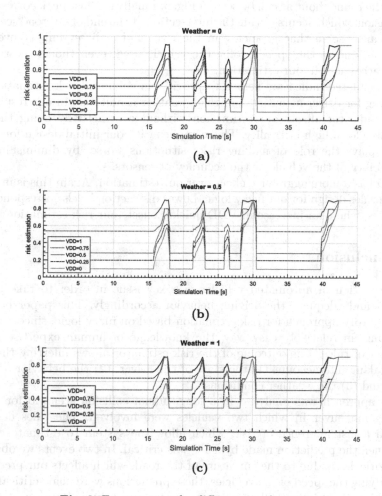

Fig. 8. Fuzzy output for different weather values

The first peak, after 15 s of simulation. Coincides with the lead vehicle entering the roundabout, the change in curvature makes the longitudinal controller brake, reducing the distance between both vehicles and increasing relative speed. When the trailing vehicle brakes to also enter the roundabout our TTC calculation decrease quickly, leading to a nominal risk value. In Fig. 6 this behavior of increasing risk close to curves, can be observed in the map. Two minor peaks can also be spotted inside the roundabout, both can be attributed to slight changes in curvature which modify the speed profile of the vehicle. Vehicles speed profile limits the maximum speed and acceleration of the vehicle as shown in Fig. 5.

The fourth peak observed corresponds to a near-miss scenario leaving the roundabout, in this case inter-vehicle distance got below one meter, and TTC dropped below 1.5 s. This situation resulted in a high estimation of risk before leaving the roundabout as can be seen in Fig. 6. Finally our last peak corresponds to a collision, which occurs during the intersection at the end of our road scenario.

We can observe that geometry in the road had a direct impact over our estimation, due to the speed profile the vehicle used, even though it was not directly accounted in our estimation.

The emulated indicators helped to provide an enhanced risk estimation, by accounting for driver attention and road/weather conditions. In our results the WTHR indicator offsets our estimation without ever actually being the sole responsible for a high criticality. This complies with our initial design for which weather plays the role of making risky situations worse, by diminishing the controlability of the vehicle or the accuracy of sensors.

VDD has a more aggressive effect over our estimation. Again this is in check with the rules design for our fuzzy logic. Lower distraction levels correspond with safe states, where an increase in VDD quickly offsets our risk estimation.

5 Conclusion

Risk estimation in automated vehicles is a key issue in order to take proper decisions and adequate the driving behavior accordingly. This paper presents an exploratory approach for risk estimation based on fuzzy logic, since it allows embedding, in relatively easy way, the knowledge of human expertise into a simple set of rules. The outcome of the risk estimator allows inferring the level of risk taking into account (1) the state of the driver, (2) the behavior of other vehicle and (3) the weather conditions.

This approach was analyzed in a longitudinal collision scenario for a car-following maneuver in which two vehicles were involved. The rules designed provided a fast inference of risk, which allow the system to estimate critical levels when the prediction made by TTC was critical. In two events we observed a non-critical risk due to the curvature of the road, which affects our prediction by modifying the speed of the vehicles, these predictions were made critical when aggregated with sub-optimal weather conditions and driver attention.

In the future, more complex scenarios will be considered as well as different vehicle motion models. Assuming constant speed for TTC, limits the forecasting ability of the indicator. Road definition also needs to be leveraged in order to predict speed reductions when entering in curves with more precision, in order to expect low values of TTC in such circumstances.

Acknowledgments. This work was supported by the AMASS project (H2020-ECSEL) with grant agreement number 692474.

References

1. Boverie, S., Cour, M., Le Gall, J.Y.: Adapted human machine interaction concept for driver assistance systems driveasy. IFAC Proc. Vol. **44**(1), 2242–2247 (2011)
2. Flemisch, F., Heesen, M., Hesse, T., Kelsch, J., Schieben, A., Beller, J.: Towards a dynamic balance between humans and automation: authority, ability, responsibility and control in shared and cooperative control situations. Cogn. Technol. Work **14**(1), 3–18 (2012)
3. González, D., Pérez, J., Milanés, V., Nashashibi, F., Tort, M.S., Cuevas, A.: Arbitration and sharing control strategies in the driving process. In: Towards a Common Software/Hardware Methodology for Future Advanced Driver Assistance Systems, p. 201 (2017)
4. Harding, J., et al.: Vehicle-to-vehicle communications: Readiness of v2v technology for application. Technical report DOT HS 812 014. National Highway Traffic Safety Administration, Washington, DC, August 2014
5. Hayward, J.C.: Near miss determination through use of a scale of danger. Technical report, Pennsylvania Transportation and Traffic Safety Center (1972)
6. Van der Horst, A.R.A.: A time based analysis of road user behaviour in normal and critical encounters. No. HS-041 255 (1990)
7. Katrakazas, C., Quddus, M., Chen, W.H., Deka, L.: Real-time motion planning methods for autonomous on-road driving: state-of-the-art and future research directions. Transp. Res. Part C Emerg. Technol. **60**, 416–442 (2015). http://www.sciencedirect.com/science/article/pii/S0968090X15003447
8. Kilpeläinen, M., Summala, H.: Effects of weather and weather forecasts on driver behaviour. Transp. Res. Part F Traffic Psychol. Behav. **10**(4), 288–299 (2007)
9. Lattarulo, R., Pérez, J., Dendaluce, M.: A complete framework for developing and testing automated driving controllers. IFAC PapersOnLine **50**(1), 258–263 (2017)
10. Lefèvre, S., Laugier, C., Ibañez-Guzmán, J.: Evaluating risk at road intersections by detecting conflicting intentions. In: 2012 IEEE/RSJ International Conference on Intelligent Robots and Systems (IROS), pp. 4841–4846. IEEE (2012)
11. Lefèvre, S., Vasquez, D., Laugier, C.: A survey on motion prediction and risk assessment for intelligent vehicles. ROBOMECH J. **1**(1), 1 (2014)
12. Levenson, N.G.: System Safety and Computers. Addison Wesley, Boston (1995)
13. Llorca, D.F., et al.: Autonomous pedestrian collision avoidance using a fuzzy steering controller. IEEE Trans. Intell. Transp. Syst. **12**(2), 390–401 (2011)
14. Pérez, J., et al.: Development and design of a platform for arbitration and sharing control applications. In: 2014 International Conference on Embedded Computer Systems: Architectures, Modeling, and Simulation (SAMOS XIV), pp. 322–328. IEEE (2014)
15. SAE: Taxonomy and Definitions for Terms Related to On-Road Motor Vehicle Automated Driving Systems. Standard, Society of Automotive Engineers, January 2014
16. Singh, S.: Critical reasons for crashes investigated in the national motor vehicle crash causation survey. Technical report, National Center for Statistics and Analysis (NCSA), NHTSA, February 2015
17. World Health Organization, WHO: Global status report on road safety 2015. Technical report, WHO, September 2015. Accessed 11 Sept 2017
18. Worrall, S., Orchansky, D., Masson, F., Nebot, E.: Improving vehicle safety using context based detection of risk. In: 2010 13th International IEEE Conference on Intelligent Transportation Systems (ITSC), pp. 379–385. IEEE (2010)

Integration Analysis of a Transmission Unit for Automated Driving Vehicles

Georg Macher[1]([✉]), Omar Veledar[1], Markus Bachinger[1], Andreas Kager[1], Michael Stolz[1], and Christian Kreiner[2]

[1] AVL List GmbH, Graz, Austria
{georg.macher,omar.veledar,markus.bachinger,
andreas.kager,michael.stolz}@avl.com
[2] Graz University of Technology, Graz, Austria
christian.kreiner@tugraz.at

Abstract. The automotive industry has recently invested considerable efforts into increasing a level of automation as well as an ever-tighter integration with other vehicles, traffic infrastructure and cloud services. Novel Advanced Driver Assistance Systems (ADAS) features and Automated Driving Functions (ADF) drive the need for advances and novel engineering solutions (especially with respect to safety and security). However, they are highly relying on existing components developed in the traditional automotive development landscape. Just as safety-related solutions and mindset became common sense in the development phases in the late 20th century, the automotive domain must now consider novel constraints originating from highly automated and distributed driving functionalities. These cannot be supervised by drivers as an integral part of the development of modern vehicles. Unfortunately, there is still a lack of experience with development approaches for automated driving and safety engineering of such automated functionalities which have no driver in the loop for monitoring. In the current transition phase more and more automated driving functions become integrated in conventional vehicles and thus relay on safety components developed in the light of conventional passenger vehicle usage. This paper concentrates on the constraints and additional considerations to be taken into account when developing or integrating existing safety-related components developed for conventional vehicles in the context of highly automated or autonomous vehicles.

Keywords: ISO 26262 · Automotive · HARA · Safety analysis
Autonomous vehicles · SEooC

1 Introduction

The automotive domain is a key industrial sector for Europe by securing 12.2 million jobs, producing 22% of the vehicle worldwide (out of 90 million vehicle produced yearly worldwide) [6] and impacting different major societal

B. Gallina et al. (Eds.): SAFECOMP 2018 Workshops, LNCS 11094, pp. 290–301, 2018.
https://doi.org/10.1007/978-3-319-99229-7_25

challenges such as reduction of pollutant emissions, reduction of traffic fatalities, or increased mobility for an ageing population.

In this context, advanced driver assistant systems (ADAS) and autonomous driving functions (ADF) are also developed to support meeting these challenges. Further, embedded automotive systems are the key to success for enabling and supporting such high levels of automation. However, similarly to the issues faced by desktop computers and consumer electronics, embedded automotive systems are also confronted with more hardware and software resource constraints. In recent years, they have grown significantly in terms of complexity and connectivity and are required to comply to more rigorous dependability standards [16]. In 2012 embedded automotive systems were responsible for an added value of up to 75% for electric and hybrid vehicles [22] and make up 25% of the vehicle costs. Current premium vehicles are equipped with more than 100 ECU's communicating with each other through multiple networks within the vehicle and are also increasingly relying on external cloud-based services to handle the necessary control SW system for automated vehicle operation.

Connected and automated vehicles drive the need for advances and novel approaches for safety-related features, while highly relying on reuse of existing components developed in the traditional manner. Safety-related development must now include novel constraints coming from such highly automated and distributed driving functionalities which can (in near future) no longer be supervised by drivers.

The current transition phase has caused the automated driving functions to become integrated in conventional vehicles. Consequently, an increased autonomy of conventional vehicles, which goes beyond the safety of the autonomy itself, has increased the awareness for additional safety implications.

Unfortunately, the best practices and standards, which are geared specifically for safety engineering of automated driving functionalities, are barely available.

In this context major questions arise, starting from discussions if controllability is still a valid approach for rating to measures for assuring of trust in the autonomous functionality.

This paper solely concentrates on the constraints and additional considerations to be taken when developing or integrating existing safety-related components in the context of highly automated vehicles. Here, one of the main challenges to be solved during component development is to identify additional requirements and needs that appear when using the component in an automated, rather than conventional, vehicle. Therefore, the paper presents a systematic approach to support an ISO 26262 [12] safety-related development of SEooC for application in autonomous vehicle. The aim of this work is to provide an exemplary automatic transmission unit system developed for conventional vehicle applications. This system is to be analysed for safe reuse in a highly automated vehicle.

This paper is organized as follows: Sect. 2 reviews recommendations and guidelines related to automotive safety engineering and state-of-the-art automotive development approaches. In Sect. 3 the exemplary transmission system is described and the architectural design is analysed for additional constraints related to autonomous vehicles. Section 4 summarizes these additional constraints found for integration of the transmission in an automated vehicle when the focus is set on keeping the changes in the SEooC itself as low as possible. Finally, Sect. 5 concludes the work.

2   Automotive Safety Engineering Approaches

Since electronic systems have been involved in most active roles in controlling the vehicles, these systems had to be designed to function under varying conditions and must adhere to several mechanical, hardware and software constraints. To manage the risks associated with these systems as well as to ensure the level of quality required for such automotive systems, significant improvements in context of automotive safety engineering have been implemented. Also, functional safety engineering and a certain amount of understanding of the safety needs at all different levels of the development process have been achieved. The work of Ebert [5] briefly highlights three key components of sustainable safety engineering in automotive systems: (a) system-oriented development, (b) safety methods closely coupled to engineering, and (c) process maturity.

2.1   Domain-Specific Standards

Safety engineering is an integral part of automotive engineering. Consequently, the road vehicles functional safety norm ISO 26262 [12] has become a well-established, mandatory factor in the automotive industry since 2011. This domain-specific safety standard has evolved from its basic form IEC 61508 [9].

In addition, established safety assessment techniques from other domains, such as failure mode and effects analysis (FMEA) [10] and fault tree analysis (FTA) [11], are also integrated in the automotive development process landscape. The efforts on second editions of IEC 61508 and ISO 26262 are also taken, which will include first approaches of enhancing an integration of safety and security. ISO/WD PAS 21448 Road vehicles - Safety of the intended functionality [14] is also in development. It defines safety engineering out of scope of functional safety ISO 26262 context. There is still an ongoing discussion how such systems with their undefined environment and conditions can be analysed.

Besides these efforts several OEM standards (such as BMW group standard GS 95014 or VWs KGAS standard) state their own requirements for functional safety engineering and most recently also cyber-security engineering. The main purpose of the SS 7740 [13] is an assessment model to standardize assessments of functional safety processes including well-defined capability levels, i.e. an ISO 26262 functional safety audit with standardized capability levels known from Automotive SPICE [23] and also supporting IOS 26262 development. Many existing ASPICE processes can also be used in a functional safety context. This approach has also been focused by the SoQrates assessment model presented in [17].

Guidelines for functional safety development of automotive systems according to ISO 26262 can be found in [3,7] or in the SafEUr functional safety manager trainings [20]. The AUTOSAR development cooperation recently also focuses on safety in the technical safety concept report [1] produced by this group. Also several recent funded R&D projects, such as PRYSTINE [4], to mention only the most recent one, focus on ADV and safety and security issues.

2.2 Safety Element Out of Context (SEooC) Development

The ISO 26262 standard defines the term and concept of a safety element out of context (SEooC) development. Generally, a SEooC is a safety-related element which is not developed in the context of a particular system or vehicle. This SEooC development concept provided in ISO 26262 part 10 is geared towards development of an element which is to be integrated in an unknown environment or is supposed to be integrated into different products. In the SEooC development approach the item supplier make assumptions on the design external to the element to foresee a variety of application cases and derives safety requirements for the development of the system. At integration time, the integrator has to make sure that the SEooC safety requirements of that item do not violate any of the defined safety goals of the product and SEooC assumptions are met. This implies that during development of the SEooC, it will not be possible to perform a complete hazard analysis and risk assessment without knowledge of the item level hazards. However, it is useful to consider and document possible hazards that might be applicable. The same applies to the predicted safety rating (ASIL rating) of the assumed high-level safety requirements of the SEooC. Current industry practice and information from potential customers can be used in such cases as sources for identifying hazards. Once the hazards are evaluated, the appropriate ASIL for the assumed requirements can also be identified in the same manner. Schneider et al. [21] provides a practical approach for a SEooC case study based on a device driver for electric motors. Ruiz et al. [19] present an experience report of the application of the SEooC concept from ISO 26262 to an electric parking system and analyse the needs for a safe reuse of system elements into the whole vehicle context.

As mentioned earlier in this document, ADAS and ADV approaches are highly relying on existing components developed in such a traditional manner for conventional vehicles. Nevertheless, with the SEooC approach, there is a clear lack of available best practices and publications which are geared specifically for SEooC development of automated driving functionalities. The work of Bergenhem et al. [2] is a position paper solely, claiming that for autonomous vehicles, the safety requirement hierarchy of ISO 26262 implies semantic gaps and ISO 26262 needs to be enhanced in this regards. The works of Kocsis et al. [15], Hoerwick and Siedersberger [8], and Reschka [18] deal with safety concepts, strategies, and architectures for autonomous driving systems in general, but do not provide further details regarding SEooC concepts or analysis for component reuse.

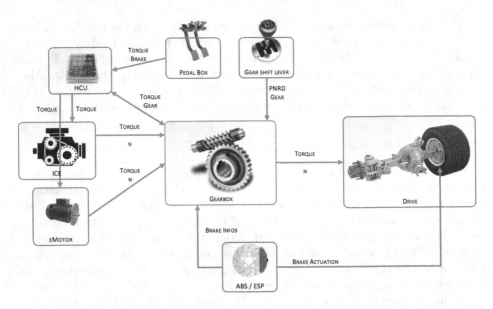

Fig. 1. Automatic transmission system item definition (conventional application)

3   Analysis of the Automatic Transmission Unit

This section of the document presents an exemplary automatic transmission unit use-case which has been developed for conventional vehicles application and is now reused in a highly automated vehicle. The use-case is an example to explain the systematic analysis and approaches and not intended to be complete or represent state-of-the-art technologies. Figure 1 depicts the automatic transmission unit and its interacting systems. Driver inputs are provided via selection of a driving mode via the gear shift lever and actuation of the brake and acceleration pedals to command torque requests to the hybrid control unit (HCU). The HCU translates these driver inputs to control the e-motor and combustion engine to provide the requested torque via the gearbox to the powertrain. Based on the selected driving mode, the provided torques, and the brake actuation the transmission control unit (TCU) controls the gearbox accordingly and selects and pre-selects the adequate gears. To conduct a hazard and risk analysis (HARA) the first objective is to define and describe the item, its dependencies on, and interaction with, the environment and other items (as depicted in Fig. 1). The second objective is to support an adequate understanding of the item, as provided in the paragraphs above.

In the hazard and risk analysis (HARA) of the transmission item (high-level design with control unit, software, electronic elements and their interfaces), ASIL (Automotive Safety Integrity Level) levels are assigned to hazardous events and safety goals are formulated. To that aim possible hazards are identified and the worst possible situations in which these hazards may occur are combined to hazardous situations. These hazardous situations are evaluated for their involved severity of the event, exposure to the situation, and controllability of the situation by the driver. The ASIL rating is based on tables which help to rate S (Severity) $0 - 3$, E (Exposure) $0 - 4$, and C (Controllability) $0 - 3$ of the situations. For each safety critical (ASIL > QM) event a high-level safety requirement (safety goal) is assigned to prevent from unreasonable risks. These safety goals must be broken down to system safety requirements during the development of the system. To that aim, safety experts and system analyst usually look at the potential faults that can lead to these failures and define requirements to diagnose and avoid these faults. Table 1 shows the example rating of a conventional transmission system HARA of the most hazardous events.

Table 1. Excerpt of the conventional hazard analysis and risk assessment of the automatic transmission system

Hazard		External Detection	ASIL	ID Safety Goal	Safety Goal	Safe Sate
ID	Description					
H01a	unintended forward/backward acceleration	not present	ASIL B	SG01	avoid acceleration of the vehicle if not requested by the driver	drive-train open
H02	unintended deceleration	ESP	ASIL B	SG02	avoid deceleration ≤ safety_threshold if not requested by driver when vehicle speed > speed_safety_threshold	drive-train open
H06	acceleration in the wrong direction	not present	ASIL A	SG03	avoid acceleration in the wrong direction	drive-train open
H04	blocking of driving wheels	not present	ASIL D	SG04a	avoid blocking of driving wheels when vehicle speed > speed_safety_threshold	drive-train open
H04	blocking of driving wheels	not present	ASIL A	SG04b	avoid blocking of driving wheels when vehicle speed ≤ speed_safety_threshold	drive-train open
H10	sudden movement of the vehicle when driver absent	not present	ASIL C	SG05	avoid park pawl disengagement if not requested by the driver	park pawl engaged

3.1 Automated Vehicle Context

In the context of automated driving functions the ratings for definition of the ASIL must be re-evaluated, since the controllability (C) factor may vary. The general discussion whether or not an assessment of controllability (C) factor is the right approach for automated driving as well as the assuring of trust in the controllability evaluation of the automated driving function is out of scope of this document. For this work the ISO 26262 rating is considered, also for controllability measures and this section focuses on three scenarios of automated driving functions, which are taken into account for the system HARA delta analysis of the transmission system.

Highway pilot (L3): The function takes over driving functionalities (acceleration, de-acceleration, and lane keeping) in a highly structured environment (highway), at higher speeds, but with driver having the possibility to regain back the control. This function is conforming SAE automation level L3.

Piloted parking via app (L4): The driver is outside the vehicle and controls the vehicle via mobile phone app. The environment is also highly structured (limited to parking lots) and vehicle velocities are very low. In this context, specific concepts require the overruling of gear shift lever and parking lock mechanisms. This scenario conforms SAE automation level L4.

Fully autonomous (L5): The vehicle is fully autonomous and has probably no interfaces at all for the driver to intervene. This scenario is the most complex one. It is complying to SAE automation level L5.

3.2 Automated Vehicle Application

In the light of these automated driving scenarios the conventional system HARA depicted in Table 1 and the resulting safety goals and ASIL ratings are re-evaluated. This re-evaluation in the new context is referred to as delta-analysis in this document.

SG_02 "'avoid vehicle deceleration if not requested"', *SG_04a* "'avoid blocking of driving wheels (higher speeds)"', and *SG_04b* "'avoid blocking of driving wheels (lower speeds)"' no impact via automation can be observed on the HARA, since these safety goals are related to internal functions of the transmission system only.

SG_05 "'avoid park pawl disengagement if not requested"' is also related to an internal function of the transmission system only and thus no impact of the automation may be observed. Besides this, an additional SEooC constraint of the transmission for vehicle integration arises. This constraint requires the ability to electrically actuate the vehicle parking brakes for assuring the prevention of sudden vehicle movement according ASIL C quality requirements.

SG_03 "'avoid acceleration in the wrong direction"' will be affected from the fact that the app parking scenario reduces the controllability to C3, since the driver is not in the car and has no way to intervene if the parking app does not work as intended. In combination with S3 (low speed) and E3 (parking manoeuvre), this results in an ASIL C instead of ASIL A quality requirements for this safety goal.

SG_01 "'avoid acceleration if not requested"' will also be affected by the app parking scenario. The reduced controllability to C3 (driver is not in the car) in combination with maximum severity (S3) and maximum exposure (E4) results in an ASIL D instead of ASIL B quality requirement.

4 Application in Automated Driving Vehicle

The delta analysis done in Sect. 3.2 reveals that an automated driving application may have some safety impacts on the reuse of legacy units. Thus, an initial re-assessment of the SEooC assumptions and safety mechanisms of the reused systems is surely required. Nevertheless, it is most likely that the efforts for redesign and re-assessment of these components are kept as low as possible and component development changes will thus be kept low, by considering additional constraints for system integration. Safety concepts of the SEooC and component development of the transmission is probably not required to change, but redesigns of the hill-hold or creep functions are likely required due to the novel park pilot and other ADF functionalities. In addition, also security implications and security concepts need to be analysed in order to allow the system as a whole to be reused in an automated vehicle context. However, security concepts will require a similar systematic delta-analysis like the presented safety delta-analysis, since the app parking scenario will arise several security issues. These considerations are out of scope for this work.

The delta analysis of our use-case revealed the following additional constraint for vehicle integration of the transmission SEooC:

HAD: The control unit for the highly-automated driving functionalities (HAD) must be able to actuate the vehicle brakes to support a second channel for ASIL decomposition (required by decomposition of SG_01 (ASIL D) to initial SG_01 (ASIL B(D))) for the transmission unit and SG_01 (ASIL B(D)) for the HAD).

Parking lock: Sudden movement of the vehicle and unintended deactivation of the electronically actuated parking lock SG_05 (ASIL C) must be prevented by electric parking brake also (controlled by HAD, ASIL C), again to provide a second channel.

ESP: The functionality that provides the braking force must be fail-operational. To that aim, the ESP needs to be designed with a redundant control path for HAD, which is most likely to be located on the braking ECU (ESP).

Creep function: The creep function may be implemented solely via e-drive since the function can be performed more efficiently and accurately by the HAD.

Shut-down and parking procedures: Shut-down and parking procedures must be kept also for HAD. These procedures may be obsolete for highly automated vehicles, but are used by almost every controller for self-testing and diagnosis and thus may violate safety-related development assumptions.

Ready-to-drive procedures: These procedures must be also considered by HAD to ensure initial system self-test and prevent from violating safety-related development assumptions and start-up checks.

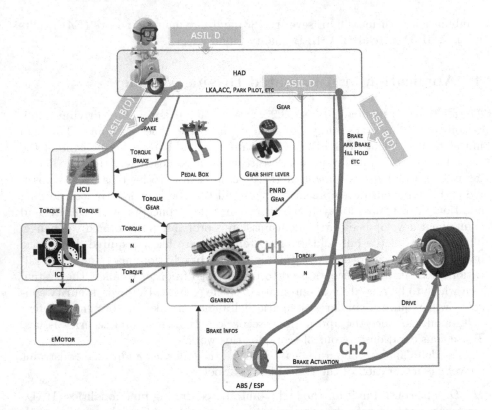

Fig. 2. Automatic transmission system item definition (highly automated driving application)

Leaving concepts: The routines, which driver is required to follow to dependably shut down the car (leaving concept), have to be analysed for novel automated driving functionalities. Some steps of the leaving concept may be obsolete for automated vehicles, nevertheless safety and also security related effects may be included.

With the application in an automated vehicle context, the transmission systems dependencies and interaction with other systems has also changed. The HAD concept and the interaction with the automatic transmission unit for this use-case is depicted in Fig. 2. In this depiction, the two required channels for ASIL decomposition are also highlighted.

Additional Remark: A review of the SEooC component HARA and the provided argumentations and assumptions is anyway required. Nevertheless, it is also highly recommended to specifically review situations which have a controllability argumentation $C < 3$. These argumentations are usually required to be adequately supported by the HAD concept.

5   Conclusion

In this paper we concentrate on the constraints and additional considerations to be taken into account when developing or integrating existing safety-related components developed for conventional vehicles in the context of highly automated or autonomous vehicles.

Autonomous driving vehicles require advanced and novel safety and security solutions, but will highly rely on existing components developed in the traditional automotive development landscape. Therefore, one main challenge is to identify additional requirements and needs that will emerge when using a component in an automated, rather than a conventional, vehicle.

To that aim, an exemplary automatic transmission unit system (developed for conventional vehicle application) has been analysed for safe reuse in a highly automated vehicle.

The paper presents a systematic analysis approach, a delta-analysis for automated vehicles and an approach for safe integration in autonomous vehicle context. The presented integration approach is geared towards minimizing the amount of changes for the reuse of legacy units (ideally requiring no changes). This implies the need for identification of additional constraints for the system integration. Redesigns of implemented functionalities or specific technical safety concept implementations, as well as security concept considerations were out of scope of this work. The focus of this work is set on the possible effects of highly automated vehicle application on SEooC safety concepts to emphasis on safety implications of adding autonomy to an otherwise conventional vehicle that goes beyond the safety of the autonomy itself.

Acknowledgments. This work is dedicated to our co-author late Christian Kreiner, who was impressive for many reasons and has been a wonderful teacher, co-worker, leader and friend. You have made working with you an exciting, inspiring and memorable experience. We will always be grateful to you for your support and kindness.

This work is partially supported by the *DEIS* and *GECCO* 2 project. The research leading to these results has received funding from the ARTEMIS Joint Undertaking under grant agreement nr 732242 (project *DEIS*).

Further the authors would like to acknowledge the financial support of the COMET K2 - Competence Centers for Excellent Technologies Programme of the Austrian Federal Ministry for Transport, Innovation and Technology (bmvit), the Austrian Federal Ministry of Science, Research and Economy (bm-wfw), the Austrian Research Promotion Agency (FFG), the Province of Styria and the Styrian Business Promotion Agency (SFG).

References

1. AUTOSAR Development Cooperation. Technical Safety Concept Status Report. Technical Report Document Version: 1.1.0, Revision 2, AUTOSAR development cooperation, October 2010
2. Bergenhem, C., et al.: How to reach complete safety requirement refinement for autonomous vehicles. In: CARS2015 - Critical Automotive Applications: Robustness & Safety (2015)
3. Boehringer, K., Kroh. M.: Funktionale Sicherheit in der Praxis, July 2013
4. Druml, N., et al.: PRYSTINE - PRogrammable sYSTems for INtelligence in automobilEs. In: Under review at DSD2018 (2018)
5. Ebert, C.: Functional safety industry best practices for introducing and using ISO 26262. In: SAE Technical Paper. SAE International, April 2013
6. European Automobile Manufacturers Association. The Automobile Industry Pocket Guide 2016–2017. Technical report, European Automobile Manufacturers Association (2016)
7. Gebhardt, V., Rieger, G., Mottok, J., Giesselbach, C.: Funktionale Sicherheit nach ISO 262626 - Ein Praxisleitfaden zur Umsetzung, vol. 1. Auflage.dpunkt.verlag (2013)
8. Hoerwick, M., Siedersberger, K.-H.: Strategy and architecture of a safety concept for fully automatic and autonomous driving assistance systems. In: 2010 IEEE Intelligent Vehicles Symposium University of California (2010)
9. ISO - International Organization for Standardization. IEC 61508 Functional safety of electrical/electronic/programmable electronic safety-related systems
10. ISO - International Organization for Standardization. IEC 60812 Analysis techniques for system reliability - Procedure for failure mode and effects analysis (FMEA) (2006)
11. ISO - International Organization for Standardization. IEC 61025 Fault tree analysis (FTA), December 2006
12. ISO - International Organization for Standardization. ISO 26262 Road vehicles Functional Safety Part 1–10 (2011)
13. ISO - International Organization for Standardization. SS 7740 Road vehicles Functional Safety Process Assessment Model (2012)
14. ISO - International Organization for Standardization. ISO/WD PAS 21448 Road vehicles - Safety of the intended functionality, work-in-progress
15. Kocsis, M., Sussmann, N., Buyer, J., Zoellner, R.: Safety concept for autonomous vehicles that operate in pedestrian areas. In: Proceedings of the 2017 IEEE/SICE International Symposium on System Integration (2017)
16. Koong, C.-S., et al.: Automatic testing environment for multi-core embedded software–ATEMES. J. Syst. Softw. 85(1), 43–60 (2012)
17. Messnarz, R., Kreiner, C., Riel, A.: Implementing functional safety standards has an impact on system and SW design - required knowledge and competencies (SafEUr). Software Quality Professional (2015)
18. Reschka, A.: Safety Concept for Autonomous Vehicles (2016)
19. Ruiz, A., Melzi, A., Kelly, T.: Systematic application of ISO 26262 on a SEooC: Support by applying a systematic reuse approach. In: 2015 Design, Automation Test in Europe Conference Exhibition (DATE), pp. 393–396, March 2015
20. SafEUr Training Material Committee. ECQA Certified Functional Safety Manager Training Material. Training dossier, April 2013

21. Schneider, R., et al.: Safety Element out of Context - A Practical Approach. In: SAE International Technical Papers, number 2012–01-0033, April 2012
22. Scuro, G.: Automotive industry: Innovation driven by electronics (2012). http://embedded-computing.com/articles/automotive-industry-innovation-driven-electronics/
23. The SPICE User Group: Automotive SPICE Process Assessment/Reference Model V3.0, July 2015

In Search of Synergies in a Multi-concern Development Lifecycle: Safety and Cybersecurity

Martin Skoglund[(⊠)] [iD], Fredrik Warg [iD], and Behrooz Sangchoolie [iD]

Department of Electronics, RISE Research Institutes of Sweden, Borås, Sweden
{martin.skoglund, fredrik.warg,
behrooz.sangchoolie}@ri.se

Abstract. The complexity of developing embedded electronic systems has been increasing especially in the automotive domain due to recently added functional requirements concerning e.g., connectivity. The development of these systems becomes even more complex for products - such as connected automated driving systems – where several different quality attributes (such as functional safety and cybersecurity) need to also be taken into account. In these cases, there is often a need to adhere to several standards simultaneously, each addressing a unique quality attribute. In this paper, we analyze potential synergies when working with both a functional safety standard (ISO 26262) and a cybersecurity standard (first working draft of ISO/SAE 21434). The analysis is based on a use case developing a positioning component for the automotive domain. The results regarding the use of multi-concern development lifecycle is on a high level, since most of the insights into co-engineering presented in this paper is based on process modeling. The main findings of our analysis show that on the design-side of the development lifecycle, the big gain is completeness of the analysis when considering both attributes together, but the overlap in terms of shared activities is small. For the verification-side of the lifecycle, much of the work and infrastructure can be shared when showing fulfillment of the two standards ISO 26262 and ISO/SAE 21434.

Keywords: Functional safety · Cybersecurity · Automotive · Co-engineering
Multi-concern

1 Introduction

Synergies between different development processes for increasingly more complex, interconnected and intelligent cyber-physical systems is needed to increase quality attributes and reduce time to market. Examples are connected automated driving systems, robots and intelligent manufacturing technologies (Industry 4.0). The increasing number of highly automated systems bring many opportunities, e.g. interconnection of individual systems to create system-of-systems enabling new functionality, or reuse of components between products in different domains to bring down costs for introducing automation. However, such cyber-physical systems are often dependability-critical, i.e., care must be taken during development to make sure relevant quality attributes such as

B. Gallina et al. (Eds.): SAFECOMP 2018 Workshops, LNCS 11094, pp. 302–313, 2018.
https://doi.org/10.1007/978-3-319-99229-7_26

safety, availability, robustness and cybersecurity are adequately met, to avoid unreasonable risk of harm to persons, the environment or economy.

In many cases, the means of meeting a quality attribute is developing a product according to a standard, and standards are typically tailored to be both domain and quality attribute specific. ISO 26262 [1] is a standard used for ensuring functional safety in the automotive domain. This means if several quality attributes, or reuse in several domains, is desirable, it may be necessary to show conformance to several standards for the same product. However, conforming to standards typically carries some overhead for product development and using several standards will exacerbate this problem. Therefore, the aim is to find *synergies* in the form of activities, techniques, or measures which simultaneously satisfies requirements in more than one of the standards used.

An example when using several standards for the same quality attribute may be a supplier wanting to sell the same system or component to original equipment manufacturers in different domains, making it necessary to show conformance to e.g. ISO 26262 when targeting the automotive domain (on-road) and IEC 61508 [2] for machinery (off-road). It has already been shown that safety standards for different domains have a significant overlap, making it possible to reuse the work done for one standard when targeting another [3]. In this paper, we investigate the possibility of finding overlaps between the work that needs to be done to address different quality attributes. The integrated development process for several quality attributes is in this paper denoted as *multi-concern development* and the act of providing confidence that the risks have been reduced to an acceptable level is denoted as *multi-concern assurance*. As the aim for each concern is different, it is expected to be challenging to find synergies when performing multi-concern development.

Due to the nature of cyber-physical systems that are connected and highly automated, the combination of safety and cybersecurity is of high interest. It is important to realize that quality attributes can also exhibit dependencies. For instance, a security problem may allow a hacker to disable or fool a safety mechanism. Therefore, both concerns as well as their *interplay*, must be properly addressed. We analyze the potential for synergies in a multi-concern development lifecycle. The analysis is based on a case study where a product for the automotive domain is developed according to both a safety standard (ISO 26262) and a security standard (first working draft of ISO/SAE 21434 [4]). The ISO/SAE 21434 is intended to address security for road vehicles, in similar way as the ISO 26262 standard does for functional safety. The development of an automotive domain specific cybersecurity standard is followed with close interest within the automotive industry and is assumed to have a high impact how security is handled. Therefore, the content of the standard, even at draft stage, becomes relevant and interesting for analysis.

For the design phases, i.e. the left side of the development V-model used in both standards, we found the overlap between safety and cybersecurity in terms of analysis, countermeasures and requirements to be small. For this part of the development lifecycle, the main advantage of treating both concerns in parallel is completeness, i.e. that both concerns and their interplay are considered through all stages, thereby reducing the risk of missing issues that may cause costly major redesigns if discovered later, or even worse, resulting in too high residual risks if dependencies are not discovered at all. For the right side of the V model, i.e. the verification and validation side, the possible synergies are larger; both when it comes to using the same test environments and the same or similar test methods for the two concerns.

A reason why synergies are abundant in verification is that the bulk of testing required by the standards is not safety- or cybersecurity specific per se but rather aimed at ensuring good product quality in general, for instance requirements, resource and robustness testing. Except for a few more test methods necessary to cover both standards, the main difference is the need to test specifically added safety- or security mechanisms that are not part of performing the nominal function, and even when testing these mechanisms, many of the test methods are the same or similar.

2 Background

The analysis of potential synergies is based on a case study conducted as part of AMASS [5], a research project which aims to develop tools and methods targeting different aspects of assurance and certification of cyber-physical systems, including multi-concern assurance. An assurance case needs to communicate the scope of the system, the operational context, the claims, the arguments to give the rationale for the claims, along with the corresponding evidence. A multi-concern assurance case, however, should support this for more than one quality attribute. The multi-concern assurance approach employed here has a tool-supported methodology for the development of assurance cases which address multiple system characteristics and provide exploitable synergies between them [6].

In this section, we present the use case studied via a palette of open-source tools. In particular Papyrus [7] and SysML have been used to model the system, context and requirements. OpenCert [8] is used to manage process modelling and to argue for a multi-concern assurance case. It is the process modelling and the subsequent analysis of complement of development activities that has provided most of the insights to co-engineering findings presented in this paper.

2.1 Use Case

The use case studied in this paper is a positioning component for automated driving systems (ADS) and needs to conform to both functional safety and cybersecurity. The positioning component can be used in various functions and is designed as an element-out-of-context (EooC). Here we generalize the term safety-element-out-of-context (SEooC) used in ISO 26262 to apply for any quality attribute. In an EooC, the requirements (in this case functional, safety and security requirements for the positioning unit) are based on an assumed context at the design time on its use. The assumptions must later match the requirements in any real context where the component is actually used. The component is aimed at automotive functions; therefore ISO 26262 is used as safety standard and a first working draft of ISO/SAE 21434 for cybersecurity.

Fig. 1. Hardware for positioning element-out-of-context.

Fig. 2. Scale model of an automated drive capable vehicle used for testing.

Figure 1 shows the hardware for the positioning element. It contains a satellite navigation receiver which is used in conjunction with correction data for enhanced precision (real-time kinematic positioning). The correction data is streamed over an Internet connection. Together with data from an inertial measurement unit (IMU) and odometry a position can be calculated, with a quality-measure of that position [9].

To complete the use case, the positioning component is matched to the hypothetical context of an ADS function named Automated driving controller (ADC), which is a highway autopilot. Figure 2 shows the vehicle level test environment for the ADC function. A detailed description of the function is beyond the scope of this paper; however, the function has a number of functional requirements which are analyzed for safety and security risks according to both standards, resulting in additional safety goals (top-level safety requirements) and security goals. A simplified definition of one of the functional requirements is: *The automated driving mode of the ADC function may only be activated on roads certified for ADS vehicles, and only when an enable signal is received from a road-side unit.*

The hazard analysis and risk assessment (HARA) required in ISO 26262 results in safety goals for the ADC. A safety goal related to the stated functional requirement is: *ADC may only be activated on certified roads, corresponding to an Automotive Safety Integrity Level D (ASIL D).* ASIL D is the highest integrity level requiring the most stringent measures to avoid a failure. Since the function is only designed to work within the parameters given in the functional requirement, its behavior is undefined if enabled anywhere else, thus resulting in high risk of harm. Consequently, a high level of risk reduction is necessary.

For cybersecurity, a threat analysis and risk assessment (TARA) is used to elicit security goals. A security goal with a dependency to the mentioned safety goal is: *Methodically designed and tested integrity protection to fulfill ADC may only be activated on certified roads,* corresponding to Cybersecurity Assurance Level 3 (CAL 3). CAL 3 is the second highest risk reduction level according to the first working draft of ISO/SAE 21434. When the safety goal is refined in the design phases, it results in safety requirements on the positioning of the vehicle, i.e. that the position can be matched to a map making sure the vehicle is driving on a certified road. Moreover, there will be corresponding security requirements on the integrity of both positioning and the certified-road open for traffic signal data. This is since the data from the wireless communication interfaces are susceptible to be compromised by an adversary.

3 Multi-concern Development Lifecycle

In this section, we present our findings based on a comparison between two approaches for analyzing a multi-concern development lifecycle, namely *separate* and *co-engineered*. Here the separate approach means preforming the additional work of satisfying a quality attribute together with the nominal implementation but separate from any additional quality attribute. This would be comparable to carrying out the fulfillment of the quality attributes in sequence, or in parallel with different development teams. In this paper, this means that functional safety is handled first by complying to the ISO 26262 standard, and then cybersecurity is tackled by complying to a first working draft of ISO/SAE 21434 standard. In the co-engineered approach, on the other hand, quality attributes are analyzed in parallel, which according to our use case, could be interpreted as the co-engineering of safety and security.

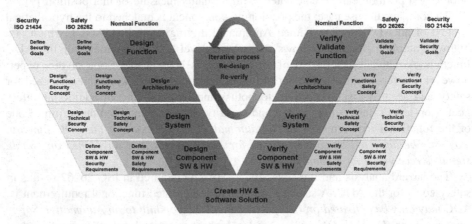

Fig. 3. Co-engineering of automotive Safety (ISO 26262) and Security (ISO/SAE 21434)

Our findings on the multi-concern development synergies are divided into *co-design* (see Sect. 3.1) and *co-verification* (see Sect. 3.2), referring to the left side and the right side of a V-model development lifecycle, respectively. Figure 3 illustrates the lifecycles for nominal function with added activities for functional safety and cybersecurity.

3.1 Co-design

In the design phases, the overlap, and hence potential for synergies between safety and cybersecurity in terms of analysis methods, countermeasures and requirements were found to be limited in our use case. For this part of the development lifecycle, the main advantage of treating both concerns in parallel is completeness, i.e. that both concerns and their interplay are considered through all stages. Even though this does not reduce the work of adhering to two standards, it contributes to reducing the risk of missing issues that may cause costly major redesigns if discovered later, or even worse, resulting in too high residual risks if dependencies are not discovered at all.

Risk Analysis. In this paper, the risk analysis is handled separately for the two concerns through hazard analysis and risk assessment (HARA) and threat analysis and risk assessment (TARA). However, we perform the activities needed to analyze risks simultaneously and coordinated, facilitating co-analysis of risks for the different concerns. The only activity missing for a complete co-analysis is trade-off analysis, corresponding to the way that different concerns impact each other. Specific details and information how to perform the risk analysis is outside the scope of the paper.

A significant difference between HARA and TARA is the comprehensiveness of the organization level inputs for the latter. These inputs include e.g. assets and their values, stakeholders, and threat information. When doing the asset identification on the organizational level the dependency between security and safety becomes obvious, if safety is a concern then it automatically becomes an asset for the organization. This dependency will carry over to the implementation of the item if it is deemed to be

Table 1. Excerpt of HARA for our defined safety goal.

Function	ID	Hz_ADC_019
	Use case	Normal driving
	Driver	Human
Failure mode (guide words)	Failure mode	Commission
	Effect	Fully
Situation description	Driver	Human
	Location	Country road
	Vehicle speed	Medium, High
	Manoeuvre	Steering
	Traffic intensity	Any
	Environmental changes	No change
	Persons at risk	Any
	Target	Off road, VRU, motorcycles, cars, trucks, stationary object
Hazard description	Failure	Unintended activation of ADC
	Failure effect	Decreased curvature
	Amplitude	High
	Duration (ms)	High
	Hazard event	Head-to-head collision
Exposure	E	**E4**
Severity	S	**S3**, Nominal ADC function is not intended outside of certified road. ADC behaviour is not predictable, thus worst-case situation is assumed
Controllability	C	**C3**, ADC is in control, thus no human controllability

security related. It is the absence of an architecture to be analyzed in the early stages in the development process that drives the need for a rigorous asset identification to facilitate the dependency identification.

Table 1 shows the HARA performed according to the ISO 26262 standard and Table 2 shows the TARA performed according to the ISO/SAE 21434 standard. Moreover, the HARA and TARA analyses result in the goals specified in Table 3. The analyses are performed on the function level, i.e., independent of the architecture. This enables the dependency identification to be performed on early stages of the development lifecycles and distinguishes our approach from earlier approaches such as SAHARA [10] or the one proposed by Schmittner et al. [11].

Table 2. Excerpt of TARA for our defined security goal.

Asset tag for item	ADC_ATAG8
Owner	Safety manager
Primary assets	ISO26262 (data)
Security property	Integrity
Attack path (subset wireless)	Wireless
System specific	Yes
Safety	4
Privacy	0
Financial	0
Operational	2
S (max)	4
Elapsed Time (dependent on controls)	7
Expertise	6
Knowledge	3
Window of opportunity	4
Equipment	4
Attack potential required (in numbers)	24
Attack potential required to exploit scenario	High
Likelihood	Unlikely
Cybersecurity assurance levels	CAL3

Table 3. Safety and cybersecurity.

Safety goal	ASIL	D
	SG ID	SG_ADC_001
	SG	ADC may only be activated on certified roads.
	Safe state	ADC disabled (Human in control of the vehicle)
	FTTI	150 ms
Cybersecurity goal	*Goal of attack resistance* (of each threat/asset pair) to be considered during design and testing	
	Methodically designed and tested integrity protection to fulfil "ADC may only be activated on certified roads"	

Requirements. Co-requirement-engineering have exposed dependency relationships between attributes. Often the safety-requirements depend on the fulfilment of security-requirements. Table 3 shows one such example, where the cybersecurity goal references the safety goal. This means that the safety goal can be violated if the cybersecurity goal is violated, or in other words that the desired safety risk reduction cannot be achieved unless the security risk reduction is also achieved. The refined requirements allocated to the architecture will retain the dependency inherited from the original goals. While it is beneficial to have these dependencies explicit at an early stage in the development process from a completeness viewpoint, no labor-saving synergy effect was encountered in the analysis or requirements engineering process.

Countermeasures. Except for the often-mentioned encryption measure that can be used to safeguard confidentiality in terms of security, and at the same time protect against data corruption and in terms of safety, no other measures have been found so far to contribute to the co-engineering of implementation of mechanism.

3.2 Co-verification

For the right side of the V-model, i.e. the verification and validation side, the possible synergies are larger, for the use case studied in this paper. This includes synergies related to the test environments and the test methods for the two concerns. A reason why synergies are abundant in verification is that the bulk of testing required by the standards is not safety- or cybersecurity specific per se but rather aimed at ensuring good product quality in general. Except for a few more test methods necessary to cover both standards, the main difference is the need to test specifically added safety- or security mechanisms that are not part of performing the nominal function, and even when testing these mechanisms, many of the test methods are the same or similar.

There are three major areas corresponding to the right side of the combined development lifecycle that have been identified to benefit from co-engineering. These areas include *test environments* and the *test purposes* for each environment and the *test techniques* employed to fulfill these purposes (see Fig. 4). Different maturity of the implementation is tested using model-in-the-loop (MIL), software-in-the-loop (SIL), and hardware in-the-loop (HIL).

Test Environments. As illustrated in Fig. 4, test environments could be mapped to different integration levels, namely component level (test environment 1), system/subsystem level (test environment 2) and complete vehicle level (test environment 3 and 4, see Fig. 2). These environments are fully re-usable in terms of testing for the different concerns, i.e., nominal function, security and safety. This is a major benefit, compared to building, maintaining, and operating separate testing environments. The test environments can be used for regression testing, which is a prerequisite for continuous deployment needed to meet the maintenance requirements of security. The test environments can also be used for back-to-back testing if model-driven development is used.

Test Purposes or Test Goals. Figure 4 also shows the purpose of tests, which could be classified into one of the following categories:

310   M. Skoglund et al.

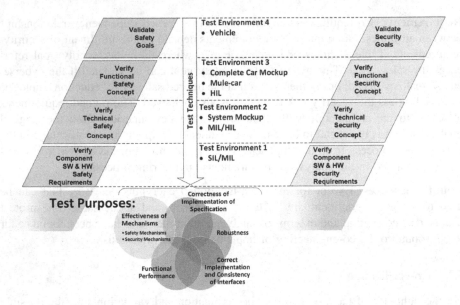

Fig. 4. Test techniques and test purposes at different integration levels and environments.

- Correctness of Implementation of Specification
- Robustness
- Correct implementation and consistency of interfaces
- Functional performance, accuracy and timing
- Effectiveness of mechanisms

The above categories aim to detect systematic faults during the different levels of integration. According to the use case studied in this paper, all mentioned test purposes (except the *effectiveness of mechanisms*) show a large overlap between the different concerns. This facilitates co-verification for both test environments and test purposes. Note that, when it comes to the "effectiveness of mechanisms", the overlap is dependent on parameters such as the competence of testers and the type of mechanisms used. In fact, previous studies [12] have shown that different safety mechanisms could impact system security both negatively/positively[1]. The same conclusions are drawn in the same study about the impact of security mechanisms on system safety[2]. This means that even in the case of the "effectiveness of mechanisms" test purpose, the overlap could be increased by improving the testers' competence as well as by choosing mechanisms that simultaneously provide both safety and security when possible.

Test Techniques. Test techniques are also spread throughout different integration levels. These techniques could be classified into *analytical* and *experimental* techniques. The former type of techniques corresponds to a cost-effective way to perform

---

[1] Table 4-1 in the Interplay Between Safety and Security deliverable of HEAVENS project [12].
[2] Table 4-2 in the Interplay Between Safety and Security deliverable of HEAVENS project [12].

verification and validation of safety and security based on mathematical techniques or models. Examples of these models include, fault/attack trees, markov models, and stochastic petri nets. Experimental test techniques, however, make use of different testing systems to reveal deficiencies and obtain measures to grade the systems' safety or security capabilities. Examples of test techniques and their corresponding test purposes are presented in Table 4.

Table 4. Examples of test techniques that could be used to achieve different test purposes.

Test purpose	Test technique
Correctness of implementation of specification	Requirement based test
	Back-to-back test
	Fault injection test
Robustness	Stress test and resource usage test, environmental test
	Long term test and user test
Correct implementation and consistency of interfaces	Test of internal and external interfaces
	Full communication test compatibility and timings
	Fuzz testing
Functional performance, accuracy and timing	Performance test
	Back-to-back test
Effectiveness of mechanisms	Fault injection test
	Attack injection test
	Error guessing
	Penetration testing

The overlap between different test techniques aiming to achieve a specific test goal varies significantly for different concerns. Similar to the discussion on test purposes, testers' competence is one of the main factors affecting the overlap between the work that needs to be done to address different concerns. For example, error guessing and penetration testing techniques (see Table 4) are both dependent on field data as well as security expertise, respectively. This indicates that by educating testers that could work on multiple concerns, the overlap could be increased. Moreover, even when the overlap is small, the lessons learned from pursuing a test purpose when investigating system safety could be reused when addressing security or vice versa. For example, fault injection is a well stablished testing technique used to evaluate system safety. Lessons learned from the past works that used this technique could be used to inject attacks instead of faults to evaluate system security [13]. This is due to the fact that security attacks may be considered as a special type of faults which are human made, deliberate and malicious, affecting hardware/software from external system boundaries and occurring during the operational phase [14].

4 Conclusions and Future Work

In this paper, our goal was to study and compare two approaches on multi-concern development, namely *separate* and *co-engineered*. In the former, quality attributes (concerns) are analyzed in sequence, whereas in the latter, the attributes are analyzed in parallel.

The quality attributes analyzed are functional safety and cybersecurity; and the analysis is performed by following the ISO 26262 standard (addressing functional safety) and the first working draft of the ISO/SAE 21434 standard (addressing cybersecurity).

Our analysis shows that for the design phases, i.e. the left side of the development V-model used in both standards, the overlap between safety and cybersecurity is small. However, the parallel analysis of safety and cybersecurity results in an improvement of completeness, thereby reducing the risk of missing issues that may cause costly major redesigns if discovered later. For the right side of the V model, i.e. the verification and validation side, the possible synergies are larger; both when it comes to using the same test environments and the same or similar test methods for the two concerns.

The analyses performed in this paper – and hence the results obtained – are based on a use case developing a positioning component for the automotive domain. And the search for synergies was carried out, without any tailoring of the development life-cycle, or any real special methods and tool geared towards co-engineering. This was done to act as a baseline for future work. In the creation and argumentation for a complete multi-concern assurance case, it is expected that the tools mentioned in Sect. 2 will really come into their own. There is also an opportunity employ new multi-concern methods, that combined with tool support is expected deliver more substantial synergies.

Acknowledgements. This work is supported by the EU and VINNOVA via the ECSEL Joint Undertaking project AMASS (No 692474), but the contents of the paper only reflect the authors views.

References

1. ISO 26262:2011 - Road vehicles – Functional safety. https://www.iso.org/standard/43464.html
2. IEC 61508:2010 - Functional safety of electrical/electronic/programmable electronic safety-related systems. http://www.iec.ch/functionalsafety/
3. Gallina, B., Sljivo, I., Jaradat, O.: Towards a safety-oriented process line for enabling reuse in safety critical systems development and certification. In: 2012 35th Annual IEEE Software Engineering Workshop, pp. 148–157 (2012)
4. ISO/SAE AWI 21434 - Road Vehicles – Cybersecurity engineering. https://www.iso.org/standard/70918.html
5. About | AMASS. https://www.amass-ecsel.eu/

6. Ruiz, A., Gallina, B., de la Vara, J.L., Mazzini, S., Espinoza, H.: Architecture-driven, multi-concern and seamless assurance and certification of cyber-physical systems. In: Skavhaug, A., Guiochet, J., Schoitsch, E., Bitsch, F. (eds.) SAFECOMP 2016. LNCS, vol. 9923, pp. 311–321. Springer, Cham (2016). https://doi.org/10.1007/978-3-319-45480-1_25
7. Papyrus. https://www.eclipse.org/papyrus/
8. Beaton, W.: OpenCert. https://www.polarsys.org/projects/polarsys.opencert
9. Vedder, B., Vinter, J., Jonsson, M.: Accurate positioning of bicycles for improved safety. In: 2018 IEEE International Conference on Consumer Electronics (ICCE), pp. 1–6 (2018)
10. Macher, G., Sporer, H., Berlach, R., Armengaud, E., Kreiner, C.: SAHARA: a security-aware hazard and risk analysis method. In: 2015 Design, Automation Test in Europe Conference Exhibition (DATE), pp. 621–624 (2015)
11. Schmittner, C., Gruber, T., Puschner, P., Schoitsch, E.: Security application of failure mode and effect analysis (FMEA). In: Bondavalli, A., Di Giandomenico, F. (eds.) SAFECOMP 2014. LNCS, vol. 8666, pp. 310–325. Springer, Cham (2014). https://doi.org/10.1007/978-3-319-10506-2_21
12. HEAVENS. https://www.sp.se/en/index/research/dependable_systems/heavens/Sidor/default.aspx
13. Sangchoolie, B., Folkesson, P., Vinter, J.: A study of the interplay between safety and security using model-implemented fault injection. In: EDCC 2018: 14th European Dependable Computing Conference (2018)
14. Avizienis, A., Laprie, J.-C., Randell, B., Landwehr, C.: Basic concepts and taxonomy of dependable and secure computing. IEEE Trans. Depend. Secure Comput. 1, 11–33 (2004)

1st International Workshop on Safety, securiTy, and pRivacy In automotiVe systEms (STRIVE 2018)

1st International Workshop on Safety, securiTy, and pRivacy In automotiVe systEms (STRIVE 2018)

Gianpiero Costantino and Ilaria Matteucci

Istituto di Informatica e Telematica - CNR, Via G. Moruzzi, 1, Pisa, Italy
{gianpiero.costantino,ilaria.matteucci}@iit.cnr.it

1 Overview

The growing number of vehicles that daily move on roads increases the need of protecting the safety, security, and privacy of passengers, pedestrians, and vehicles themselves. This need increases when it is considered the pervasive introduction of Information and Communication Technologies (ICT) systems into modern vehicles that are now potentially vulnerable from cyber-security threats. So, vehicles do not only allow passengers to move from one place to another but also offer several services and connections that turn them into Cyber-Physical Systems (CPS).

In 2013, more than 1 billion of sensors were sold to the automotive industry, doubling 2009 levels, and embedded connectivity solutions began appearing in 2014. As a consequence, serious concerns arise regarding, among others, privacy, safety, and security of automotive ecosystems, and related standards. A connected vehicle can track the overall behaviour of the driver, including information about location, driving style and additional trip parameters, such as fuel economy, and more sensitive parameters, such as the phone-book of a mobile phone, information about home location, and data related to the home-link remote control. Without complete, efficient, and robust security control systems, a concrete risk exists that such private information could be accessed by third parties, e.g., interested in pushing offers or in profiling the user. Thus, security has become a serious issue for connected vehicles.

Several studies investigated the cyber-crime through automotive networks and the risks related to losing control of autonomous vehicles. As emerged from these studies, a series of potential attacks involving intra/inter-vehicle system communications can be conceived, spanning from a simple traffic jam to more complex and dangerous attacks, driving a vehicle without any authorizations. Hence, the convergence of safety and security requirements is one of the main outstanding research challenges in CPS and in the automotive scenario.

STRIVE aims at providing a forum for researchers and engineers in academia and industry to foster an exchange of research results, experiences, and products in the automotive domain from both a theoretical and practical perspective. Its ultimate goal is to envision new trends and ideas about aspects by designing, implementing, and evaluating innovative solutions for the CPS with a particular focus on the new generation of vehicles. Indeed, the automotive domain presents several challenges in the fields of vehicular network, Internet of Things, Privacy as well as Safety and Security methods and approaches. The workshop aims at presenting the advancement on the state of art in these fields and spreading their adoption in several scenarios involving main stockholders of the automotive domain. Furthermore, STRIVE aims at promoting the discussion between industrial stakeholders, manufacturers, and academia on these research challenges targeting safety, security, and privacy aspects as well as all the different phases of the development process of automotive software and systems.

2 Workshop Program

The program of STRIVE 2018 consists of 6 high-quality papers grouped as follows:

- **Session 1: In-vehicle Security**
  - *Counter Attacks for Bus-off Attacks* - Daisuke Souma, Akira Mori, Hideki Yamamoto and Yoichi Hata.
  - *Applications of pairing-based cryptography on automotive-grade microcontrollers* - Tudor Sebastian Andreica, Bogdan Groza and Pal-Stefan Murvay.
  - *Towards an Integrated Penetration Testing Environment for the CAN Protocol* - Giampaolo Bella and Pietro Biondi.
- **Session 2. Security in Vehicular Infrastructure**
  - *Enhancing sensor capabilities of open-source simulation tools to support autonomous vehicles safety validation* - C. B. S. T. Molina, L. F. Vismari, T. Y. Fujii, J. B. Camargo Jr., J. R. de Almeida Jr., Rafia Inam, Elena Fersman, A. Hata and M. V. Marquezini.
  - *A security analysis of the ETSI ITS vehicular communications* - Alexandru Serban, Erik Poll and Joost Visser.
  - *Real-Time Driver Behaviour Characterization through Rule-based Machine Learning* - Fabio Martinelli, Francesco Mercaldo, Vittoria Nardone, Antonella Santone and Gigliola Vaglini.

Each paper was selected according to at least three reviews produced mainly by PC members. Selected papers come from several countries around the world.

3 Thanks

We would like to thank the SAFECOMP organization committee and collaborators for their precious help in handling all the issues related to the workshop. Our next thanks go to all authors of the submitted papers who manifested their interest in the workshop. With their participation the first edition of the Workshop on Safety, securiTy, and pRivacy In automotiVe systEms (STRIVE 2018) becomes a real success and an inspiration for future workshops on this new and exciting area of research. Special thanks are finally due to PC members and additional reviewers for the high quality and objective reviews they provided.

4 Workshop Co-chairs

Gianpiero Costantino   IIT-CNR, Italy
Ilaria Matteucci   IIT-CNR, Italy

5 Program Committee

Giampaolo Bella   Univesity of Catania, Italy
Silvia Bonomi   University of Rome "La Sapienza", Italy
Jeremy Bryans   Coventry University, UK
Francesco Di Cerbo   SAP, France
John Mace   University of Newcastle, UK
Eda Marchetti   ISTI-CNR, Italy
Francesco Mercaldo   IIT-CNR, Italy
Paolo Santi   MIT, USA
Francesco Santini   University of Perugia, Italy
Daniele Sgandurra   Royal Holloway - University of London, UK
Renaud Sirdey   CEA, France

6 Additional Reviewer

Slim Trabelsi   SAP, France

Counter Attacks for Bus-off Attacks

Daisuke Souma[1]([✉]), Akira Mori[1], Hideki Yamamoto[1,2], and Yoichi Hata[1,2]

[1] National Institute of Advanced Industrial Science and Technology,
1-8-31 Midorigaoka, Ikeda, Osaka 563-8577, Japan
{d-souma,a-mori}@aist.go.jp

[2] Sumitomo Electric Industries, Ltd., 1-1-3 Shimaya, Konohana-ku,
Osaka, Osaka 554-0024, Japan
{yamamoto-hideki,hata-youichi}@sei.co.jp

Abstract. Recent automotive systems are increasingly complex and networked. The situation has given rise to various cyber-attack methods. Cho and Shin introduced a new type of Denial of Service (DoS) attacks called bus-off attacks [2], which abuses certain properties of Control Area Network (CAN) used for vehicle control. They not only introduced a novel software based attack method but also proposed a countermeasure which resets the victim node to keep it from going into the disabled state. However, their countermeasure could not avoid unintended effects caused by the attack. In this paper, we propose a novel countermeasure for the bus-off attacks introduced by Cho and Shin. The method forces the node that started the bus-off attack into the disabled state in a way similar to the original bus-off attack. We have implemented the countermeasure and evaluated it in a real car environment to show the effectiveness of the method.

Keywords: In-vehicle network · Control Area Network (CAN)
Bus-off attack · Countermeasure

1 Introduction

Recent automotive systems are increasingly complex and networked. By opening connection to external networks, the attacker's chance of infiltrating the system to take over control is drastically increased. Indeed, researchers have demonstrated that connected cars can be controlled remotely. Notably, the work by Miller and Valasek triggered a recall of about 1.4 million vehicles [15].

To take over the control of the vehicle, it is necessary to understand how in-vehicle networks function. The CAN (Control Area Network) bus is the most commonly used in-vehicle network. Once connected to the CAN bus, it is relatively easy to control the behaviors of the vehicle since the CAN has no features for security and authentication. For example, a node in the CAN bus can not determine whether the message it receives is malicious or not since a CAN message contains no information about its sender. This means that one can easily control the vehicle by impersonating a benign node to inject arbitrary messages.

© Springer Nature Switzerland AG 2018
B. Gallina et al. (Eds.): SAFECOMP 2018 Workshops, LNCS 11094, pp. 319–330, 2018.
https://doi.org/10.1007/978-3-319-99229-7_27

To prevent such attacks, researchers have advocated using the message authentication code (MAC) or even more stronger encryption techniques [6, 10, 18, 23].

In 2016, Cho and Shin reported a new type of attacks on the CAN bus. The attack is called the bus-off attack and is regarded as a denial of service (DoS) attack [2]. It abuses the error handling feature of the CAN bus to force a target node into a disabled state by transmitting legitimate messages. They proposed not only the attack method but also the countermeasure against it. Their countermeasure simply enables each node to reset itself whenever the bus-off attack is detected. However, it does not offer an essential cure for the problem since the attacker node is still alive on the CAN bus and may continue attacks.

In this paper, we propose a novel countermeasure for the bus-off attack. Our countermeasure detects the bus-off attack and responds with a counter bus-off attack against the attacker node. By disabling the attacker node, we can not only prevent the victim from going into the bus-off state but also remove the attacker node from the CAN bus. We have conducted experiments with a CAN prototype network and a real car environment to demonstrate the feasibility of the proposed method.

The organization of the paper is as follows. In Sect. 2, we explain the overview of the CAN bus and the bus-off attacks, which are the main focus of this paper. In Sect. 3, we introduce the attack scenario involving bus-off attacks. In Sect. 4, we propose the new countermeasure for the bus-off attack. In Sect. 5, we explain experiments for evaluating the feasibility of the proposed countermeasure. In Sect. 5, we will discuss the result of the experiments. Finally in Sect. 6, we conclude with future work.

2   Preliminaries

In this section we explain the CAN specifications related to this paper.

2.1   Overview of CAN

The CAN is a commonly used protocol for in-vehicle communication developed by Robert Bosch GmbH [7]. The CAN is a multi-master serial bus standard. All nodes are connected to each other by a twisted pair called the CAN high line and the CAN low line. Signals are defined by a differential voltage between them. The logical "0" (a dominant bit) is assigned to a differential voltage of 2 Volt. The logical "1" (a recessive bit) is assigned to a differential voltage of 0 Volt. It is important to note that a dominant bit always overwrites a recessive bit. A recessive bit can be transmitted only when all nodes on the CAN bus transmit recessive bits.

Frames. The protocol involves the following four types of frames (messages).

– Data frame
– Remote frame

- Error frame
- Overload frame

Here we explain only two frames related to this paper (Data frame and Error frame).

Data frame

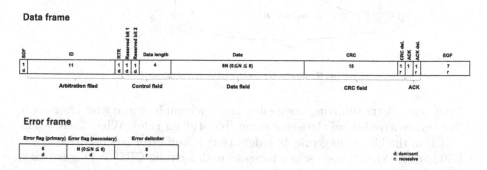

Fig. 1. Data frame and error frame

A data frame serves to transmit data. Figure 1 shows the format of a data frame. A data frame can transport maximum 8 bytes data. An ID of a message is used for message arbitration and filtering at received node.

An error frame indicates occurrences of errors. It consists of a primary error flag, a secondary error flag and an error delimiter (Fig. 1). When a node detects an error, it transmits 6 consecutive dominant bits (primary error flag). Since a primary error flag violates the stuff rule (described in "Error handling"), all other nodes detect a stuff error and 6 consecutive dominant bits follow (secondary error flag). Depending on the bit sequence transmitted before the primary error flag, the primary error flag and the secondary error flag may overlap. Consecutive transmissions of frames are separated by three consecutive recessive bits called Inter-Frame Space (IFS).

Arbitration. Every node can start transmitting a message when the CAN bus is idle. Once a node has started its transmission, all other nodes must wait for the transmission to finish before they can start transmitting their own.

When different nodes start transmission simultaneously, the arbitration mechanism takes place. Every node transmitting a message compares a transmitting bit and the actual bus level. When it detects a difference between them, it judges that it has lost the arbitration and stops transmission. This means that a message with a lower ID wins the arbitration.

Error Handling. The CAN has five types of errors.

- Bit error: A node compares the bit it is transmitting and the actual bus level. When they are different in the bit other than the arbitration field, it judges that a bit error has occurred.

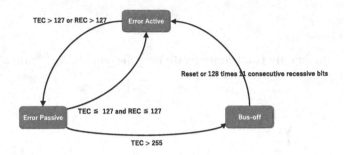

Fig. 2. State diagram of CAN nodes

- Stuff error: A transmitting node must insert a complementary bit after every five consecutive bits of the same value (bit stuffing rule). When a node sees violation the bit stuffing rule, it judges that a stuff error has occurred.
- CRC error: When a node sees a message with a wrong CRC, it judges that a CRC error has occurred.
- Form error: This occurs when a node receives a dominant bit in the position where a recessive bit must be placed, such as the Ack delimiter and the EOF.
- ACK error: A node must place a dominant bit in the ACK slot when it has received a message. An Ack error occurs when the sender node can not receive a dominant at the ACK slot.

The bit error and the ACK error occur at the sender node, and the rest occur at the receiver nodes.

Every node has two error counters: the transmit error counter (TEC) and the receive error counter (REC). They are increased/decreased according to predefined rules. In case an error is detected at the sender node, a TEC of the sender node is increased by 8 and the RECs of the other nodes are increased by 1. In case an error is detected at the receiver node, a REC of the receiver node is increased by 8. When a message is successfully transmitted, both a TEC and RECs of the sender and the receivers are decreased by 1, respectively.

According to the values of the TEC and the REC, a node changes its status (Fig. 2). The error active state ($TEC \leq 127$ and $REC \leq 127$) is the normal state. In the error passive state where $127 < TEC < 256$ or $127 < REC < 256$, a restriction is imposed that a node must wait for 8 bits (called a passive IFS) before transmitting another message when transmitting two consecutive messages. Furthermore, the error flag is changed to 6 consecutive recessive bits to avoid influences on the bus.

When a node keeps reporting errors, it eventually reaches the bus-off state when $TEC \geq 256$. In the bus-off state, a node is virtually detached from the bus and can not transmit a message anymore.

2.2   Bus-off Attack

The bus-off attack is a type of DoS attack that exploits the error handling mechanism of the CAN. The attacker's node (called the adversary) causes transmission errors at the target node (called the victim) repeatedly and forces it into the bus-off state as the result of the excessive TEC value.

There are two kinds of bus-off attack. In the first kind, the adversary attacks the victim by sending legitimate CAN messages [2], where the attack message has the same arbitration field as the victim's message but contain the different data than the victim's. By sending the attack message at the same time as the victim's, the attacker can force a bit error. By repeating this, the adversary can force the victim into the bus-off state. The process involves two phases. In the Phase 1, both the adversary and the victim are in the error active state. As the attack succeeds, the bit error occurs both at the victim and at the adversary and their TEC values are increased by 8. After the transmission of the error frames, both the victim and the adversary try to re-transmit their messages at same time automatically and the same bit error occurs. When this happens 16 times consecutively, they go into the error passive state since their TEC values are both 128. In the Phase 2, we suppose at least one of the adversary and the victim is in the error passive state. In Phase 2, when they transmit messages at the same time, the victim detects the bit error and increases its TEC value by 8. However, the adversary completes transmission without detecting the victim's bit error since the victim's error flag becomes 6 consecutive recessive bit. After the adversary completes its transmission, the victim tries to re-transmits its message and the victim's TEC is decreased by 1. As the result, the victim's TEC is increased by 7 and the adversary's TEC is decreased by 1 in one attack cycle. By repeating this cycle 19 times, the victim's TEC reaches 261 and the victim goes into the bus-off state.

In the second kind, the adversary sends a sequence of bits that is not allowed by the CAN specification [9]. The adversary monitors the CAN bus level bit by bit and when it detects the victim's message ID, the adversary transmits 6 or more consecutive dominant bits. By the bit stuffing rule, a bit error occurs at the victim and the victim's TEC is increased by 8. By simply repeating this 32 times, the victim's TEC reaches 256 and the victim goes into the bus-off state. The victim's TEC is increased in proportion to the length of the sequence of bits transmitted by the adversary. In case of a bursty consecutive dominant bits, the first 6 consecutive dominant bits cause a bit error and increases the victim's TEC by 8. The following 14 consecutive dominant bits cause a form error and increase the victim's TEC by 8. After every 8 consecutive dominant bits, the victim's TEC is increased by 8. For example the victim may reach the bus-off state in a single attempt when the attack message is longer than 260 bits.

In this paper we focus on the first kind of the bus-off attack since we identify the risk of the remote attacker hijacking a CAN bus node. Although Palanca and others suggested the possibility of the second kind of remote bus-off attacks [19], no concrete results have been reported yet. The adversary would have to attach a malicious device to the CAN bus and if it is possible, there are direct and effective attack methods. We believe that the first kind of the bus-off attack is more pressing in terms of defending automotive systems from cyber-attacks.

3 Attack Scenarios

In this section we discuss the attack scenarios. We consider the attacker whose objective is to disable a vehicle function remotely. Disabling vehicle functions affect not only the availability but also the safety of the vehicle. For example if the brake function is disabled while driving, the driver may not be able to stop the vehicle safely. To make success the attack, the attacker performs following steps.

(step 1) Compromises a node remotely.
(step 2) Denials of transmission of normal control messages.

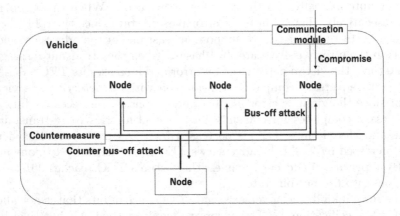

Fig. 3. Attack model

Several remote attacks are reported. Miller and Valasek reported remote attack surface about several cars [14]. Furthermore they remotely controlled Jeep Cherokey during driving [15]. Nie et al. reported remote controls of TESLA Model S [17]. Checkoway et al. reported several remote attack surface of vehicles [1]. These reports show the feasibility of the step (1).

By using bus-off attack for the step (2), the attacker can attack every uncompromised node on the same bus as the compromised node. Several countermeasures for the attack against CAN are proposed. [5,11,16,20,21] propose message periodicity based anomaly detection. Message Authentication Code are proposed in [6,10,18,23]. However they can not prevent the bus-off attack. A countermeasure against the bus-off attack is proposed only in [2]. It resets the victim to prevent the victim from going into the bus-off state. It is not sufficient countermeasure, since it can not avoid negative effect of attacks. In this paper we propose novel countermeasure that detaches adversary from the CAN bus. It can prevent negative effects to the CAN bus.

4   Detail of Proposed Method

In this section, we explain our countermeasure for the bus-off attack. We may simply call it the "counter attack". A counter attack consists of two parts: detection of the bus-off attack and a counter attack aimed at the adversary.

4.1   Detection of the Bus-off Attack

Here we explain the detection of the bus-off attack and the identification of the adversary's attack message.

We use the same detection method as proposed by Cho and Shin [2]. In Phase 1 of their bus-off attack, the bit error occurs twice in a row with the identical bit sequence on the bus. Since the probability of such event is very low, we use this as a sign of a bus-off attack taking place.

We seek for a signature of the attack message transmitted by the adversary to implement our counter attack against it. Since the tail of the message is lost in the error frame in Phase 1, we can not distinguish the adversary from the victim just by comparing with the bit sequence observed in Phase 1. Note that the adversary transmits the same bit sequence as the victim until it overwrites the victim's recessive bit by its dominant bit to cause the victim a bit error.

The exact bit location that caused the error is not known at this point because of the way the error frame is formed[1]. However, we do know that the collision occurs within the first 5 bits of the consecutive dominant bits appearing at the start of the error frame. See the left of Fig. 4. We therefore take the bit sequence from the start of the frame (SOF) up to the 5th bit of the error frame as a signature when we see the attack message from the adversary in Phase 2. Note that in Phase 2, error frames are not transmitted anymore in the error passive state. Later in Phase 2, we can identify and overwrite the adversary's attack message for our counter attack. See the right of Fig. 4.

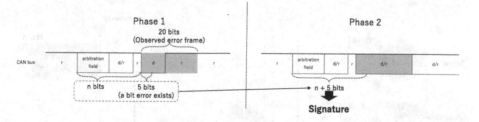

Fig. 4. Identification of attack message

4.2   Counter Attack

Here we introduce a counter attack method. It relies on the ability to emit bursty consecutive dominant bits as proposed by Kameoka and others [9] to increase the

---

[1] We omit the technical details here.

adversary's TEC massively at once. Naturally, the methods does not follow the CAN specification [7] and directly control the CAN transmitter without using legitimate CAN controllers.

The deviation may cause a concern for unintended negative side effects occurring to the overall CAN system. According to the CAN specification, bursty dominant bits will increase the REC values of the ECUs but nothing else in particular. In a real automotive system, the REC value decreases when the ECU receives a message and even if the REC value exceeds the threshold, the ECU only enters the error passive state and no serious side effects will be caused. In fact, as we will explain in Sect. 5, we have deployed an experimental device on the CAN bus of a real car to analyze the effects caused by such bursty consecutive dominant bits. We have confirmed that only the REC values of ECUs connected to the CAN bus were increased and no serious side effects were observed.

The counter attack method induces a singular occurrence where we can disable the adversary at once with a single burst of dominant bits.

When moving into Phase 2 from Phase 1 in the bus-off attack, both the adversary and the victim are in the error passive state. At this point, they both have the TEC value 128 as explained in Sect. 2.2. When the adversary overwrites the victim's message for the first time in Phase 2, the victim's TEC is increased by 7 and the adversary's TEC is decreased by 1. The adversary would needs 18 more attacks to force the victim into the bus-off state.

However, after 9 such attacks, we can create a golden opportunity to mount a counter attack against the adversary. Note at this point that the adversary's TEC is 119 and the victim's TEC is 191 (not yet reaching the bus-off state). This is the situation where the adversary remains in the error active state even if we cause a bit error to both the adversary and the victim. We can accomplish this by simply overwriting a recessive bit in the adversary's attack message with a dominant bit. Since the adversary is in the error active state, it emits an error flag, which in turn cause a bit error to the victim. Now the adversary's TEC is

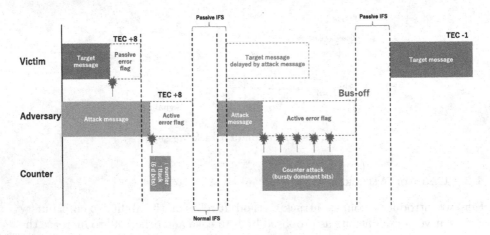

Fig. 5. Counter attack method

127 (error active state) and the victim's TEC is 199 (error passive state). At this very point, the inter frame space (IFS) occupies 3 bits for the adversary and 11 bits for the victim[2].

This means that the adversary starts re-transmission earlier and the victim keeps waiting for re-transmission. We can take advantage of this to overwrite the adversary's re-transmission with bursty consecutive dominant bits exclusively to force it into the bus-off state. See Fig. 5 for illustration of the overall scenario.

5   Experiments

We have evaluate the feasibility of the proposed countermeasure on a prototype CAN network and a real car with the prototype CAN network. The prototype CAN network consist of 3 prototype ECUs, a countermeasure device and CAN bus. Each prototype ECU consists of a Raspberry Pi, a CAN transceiver MCP2551, a CAN controller MCP2515, a 20 MHz ceramic resonator and a 120 Ω terminal resistor. The countermeasure device consists of a Raspberry Pi, a CAN transceiver MCP2551 and a 120 Ω terminal resistor (Fig. 6).

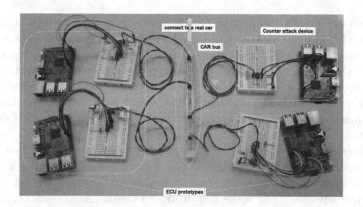

Fig. 6. Prototype CAN network for experiment

The countermeasure device can always succeed the counter attack in any environment. Figure 7 demonstrates a CAN bus level of the counter attack which is observed with an oscilloscope. Top left figure in Fig. 7 shows phase 1 of the bus-off attack. 16 consecutive error frames are transmitted. The counter attack device detects the bus-off attack from this. The bus-off attack transits to phase 2. Then the counter attack device identifies the attack message and starts counting the number of transmissions of the attack message. Bottom figure of Fig. 7 shows the counter attack execution. The countermeasure device transmits a bursty consecutive dominant bits to an attack message and forces the adversary into the bus-off state. Top right figure of 7 shows the normal communication after counter attack execution.

---

[2] This is specified in the CAN specification [7].

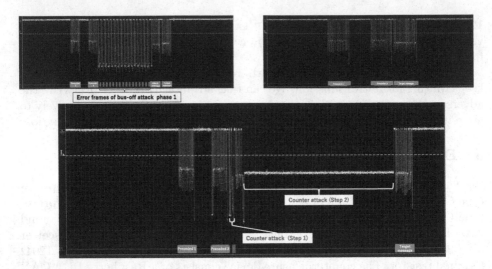

Fig. 7. Counter attack 2

The counter attack can always disable the adversary proposed in [2] when the proposed countermeasure detects the bus-off attack correctly. The proposed detection mechanism has a weakness. False negatives of the detection does not occur since the bus-off attack focusing on this paper causes consecutive bit errors. False positive occurs when the consecutive bit errors occurs accidentally. When false negative occurs, the countermeasure attacks normal nodes. We should consider the measurement of the false negative rate and improvement of detection mechanism.

The proposed detection mechanism can not be distinguished between a normal message and an attack message. The countermeasure attacks a message overwriting another message. By sending a message overwritten by a normal message, the adversary can make the proposed countermeasure attack the victim. We should consider a method to distinguish between messages.

Thus the attacker can exploits these weakness to force the victim into the bus-off state. Furthermore the victim is repeatedly attacked when the attacker reset the adversary.

6   Conclusion

In this paper, we have proposed a novel countermeasure for the bus-off attacks on the CAN bus. The proposed method counterattacks the adversary to force it into the disabled state just like the original bus-off attack. We have implemented the proposed method. We have conducted experiments in both virtual and real CAN buses to show the effectiveness of the method. The proposed method must wait for several intervals before starting counter attacks, but can always succeed even in a real car environment. It shows that our proposed method is of practical use in preventing the based bus-off attacks.

We also plan to develop a practical defense systems against hardware Trojans based on the method proposed in the paper. Considering the growing concerns for malicious devices installed in the manufacturing process, the use (or the abuse) of the bus-off features of the CAN bus can be appealing for the purpose of automotive security.

References

1. Checkoway, S., et al.: Comprehensive experimental analyses of automotive attack surfaces. In: 20th USENIX Conference on Security (2011)
2. Cho, K., Shin, K.G.: Error handling of in-vehicle networks makes them vulnerable. In: Proceedings of the 2016 ACM SIGSAC Conference on Computer and Communications Security. ACM (2016)
3. Dagan, T., Wool, A.: Parrot, a software-only anti-spoofing defense system for the CAN bus. In: 5th Embedded Security in Cars (ESCAR Europe) (2016)
4. Dagan, T., Wool, A.: Testing the boundaries of the Parrot anti-spoofing defense system. In: 5th Embedded Security in Cars (ESCAR USA) (2017)
5. Hamada, Y., Inoue, M., Horihata, S., Kamemura, A.: Intrusion detection by density estimation of reception cycle periods for in-vehicle networks: a proposal. In: Presented at the 14th ESCAR Europe Conference, 16–17 November 2016
6. Hartkopp, O., Reuber, C., Schilling, R.: MaCAN - message authenticated CAN. In: Embedded Security in Cars (ESCAR) 2012, Berlin, Germany, November 2012
7. ISO 11898:2015 Road vehicles - Controller area network (CAN) (2015)
8. Koscher, K., et al.: Experimental security analysis of a modern automobile. In: 2010 IEEE Symposium on Security and Privacy (SP), pp. 447–462. IEEE (2010)
9. Kameoka, R., Kubota, T., Shiozaki, M., Shirahata, M., Kurachi, R., Fujino, T.: Bus-off attack against CAN ECU using stuff error injection from Raspberry Pi. In: Proceedings of Symposium on Cryptography and Information Security (SCIS), Japan (2017). (in Japaneses)
10. Lin, C.W., Sangiovanni-Vincentelli, A.: Cyber-security for the controller area network (CAN) communication protocol. ASE Sci. J. 1(2), 80–92 (2012)
11. Muter, M., Asaj, N.: Entropy-based anomaly detection for in-vehicle networks. In: IEEE Intelligent Vehicle Symposium, pp. 1110–1115 (2011)
12. Matsumoto, T., Hata, M., Tanabe, M., Yoshioka, K., Oishi, K.: A method of preventing unauthorized data transmission in controller area network. In: IEEE Vehicular Technology Conference (VTC Spring), pp. 1–5. IEEE (2012)
13. Miller, C., Valasek, C.: Adventures in automotive networks and control units. DEF-CON **21**, 260–264 (2013)
14. Miller, C., Valasek, C.: A survey of remote automotive attack surfaces. Black Hat USA (2014)
15. Miller, C., Valasek, C.: Remote exploitation of an unaltered passenger vehicle. Black Hat USA (2015)
16. Markovitz, M., Wool, A.: Field classification, modeling and anomaly detection in unknown CAN bus networks. In: Presented at the 13th ESCAR Europe Conference, 11–12 November 2015
17. Nie, S., Liu, L., Du, Y.: Free-fall: hacking TESLA from wireless to CAN bus. Black Hat USA (2016)
18. Nilsson, D.K., Larson, U.E., Jonsson, E.: Efficient in-vehicle delayed data authentication based on compound message authentication codes. In: Vehicular Technology Conference VTC (2008)

19. Palanca, A., Evenchick, E., Maggi, F., Zanero, S.: A stealth, selective, link-layer denial-of-service attack against automotive networks. In: Polychronakis, M., Meier, M. (eds.) DIMVA 2017. LNCS, vol. 10327, pp. 185–206. Springer, Cham (2017). https://doi.org/10.1007/978-3-319-60876-1_9
20. Song, H.M., Kim, H.R., Kim, H.K.: Intrusion detection system based on the analysis of time intervals of CAN messages for in-vehicle network. In: ICOIN (2016)
21. Taylor, A., Japkowicz, N.: Frequency-based anomaly detection for the automotive CAN bus. In: WCICSS (2015)
22. Wasicek, A., Pese, M., Weimerskirch, A., Burakova, Y., Singh, K.: Context-aware intrusion detection in automotive control system. In: Presented at the 5th ESCAR USA Conference, USA, 21–22 June 2017
23. Wolf, M., Weimerskirch, A., Paar, C.: Secure in-vehicle communication. In: Lemke, K., Paar, C., Wolf, M. (eds.) Embedded Security in Cars, pp. 95–109. Springer, Heidelberg (2006). https://doi.org/10.1007/3-540-28428-1_6

Applications of Pairing-Based Cryptography on Automotive-Grade Microcontrollers

Tudor Andreica, Bogdan Groza[✉], and Pal-Stefan Murvay

Faculty of Automatics and Computers, Politehnica University of Timisoara,
Timişoara, Romania
andreica_tudor@yahoo.com, {bogdan.groza,pal-stefan.murvay}@aut.upt.ro

Abstract. Bilinear pairings have been successfully used both in crypt-analysis and in the design of new cryptographic primitives, e.g., identity based encryptions and signatures. In this work we discuss some computational results for pairing-based libraries on two automotive-grade controllers as well as on an Android smart-phone. This is relevant as the computational resources of automotive-grade controllers have surged in the recent years and Android-based units are quickly entering the car market, e.g., infotainment units. Identity-based primitives open road for representative applications in automotive-based scenarios where the identity of the vehicle or of the OEM may be used for deriving public keys without relying on PKI. We discuss three potential use-cases: the security of in-vehicle buses, vehicle-to-vehicle communications and software updates that could greatly benefit from compact signatures, identity based encryption or signing as well as from group signatures.

1 Introduction and Motivation

With the myriad of attacks recently reported over in-vehicle networks [7,14,16] the standardization of cryptographic functions for in-vehicle security was an immediate development. Current standards, e.g., AUTOSAR [1,2], include specifications for regular cryptographic functions both from the symmetric and asymmetric setting. But more complex mathematical operations such as pairings open door to more advanced cryptographic primitives: identity based signatures, identity based encryptions and group signatures. Further, these may be used in automotive-based scenarios to solve security issues in a more convenient way. The current work is motivated by three practical scenarios that may greatly benefit from the application of pairing based cryptographic techniques: securing in-vehicle buses, vehicle-to-vehicle communication and software updates. We now briefly discuss the advantages for each scenario and in the forthcoming sections we make performance evaluations on two automotive-grade controllers.

In-vehicle buses provide the first applicative scenario. This scenario is suggested in Fig. 1 which is also representative for the setting of the work. Several ECUs (Electronic Control Units) are depicted as well as a central display

© Springer Nature Switzerland AG 2018
B. Gallina et al. (Eds.): SAFECOMP 2018 Workshops, LNCS 11094, pp. 331–343, 2018.
https://doi.org/10.1007/978-3-319-99229-7_28

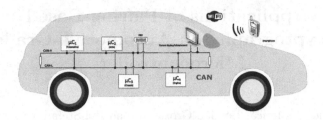

Fig. 1. Application setting, security of in-vehicle networks

(or possibly an infotainment unit) and a smart-phone, all of them connected to the CAN bus (Controller Area Network). These units are responsible with functionalities related to engine, chassis, telematics or the body (i.e., the Body Control Module - BCM) but nonetheless with user entertainment. Due to inherent connectivity to the outside, the infotainment unit represents a realistic attack surface which was previously exploited [7,16] and since this unit is connected to the CAN bus it opens road to attacks on all other ECUs on the network. Consequently, the security of in-vehicle buses has been a constant preoccupation in the past few years and many solutions have been proposed, a survey can be found in [11]. Pairing based cryptographic primitives do not seem a first choice for this scenario due to their high computation requirements. However, a significant constraint of this scenario is the limited size of the data packets that are sent via the in-vehicle bus. Traditionally, the CAN bus was capable of sending only 64 bits in a single packet which is too small even for symmetric cryptographic functions. This is improved with the recent release of CAN-FD (CAN with Flexible Data-Rate) that extends the packet to 512 bits and newer in-vehicle buses such as FlexRay extend this a bit further. But the packet size is still limited and needs to accommodate both signals from the ECUs as well as security elements (signatures or message authentication codes). This limitation of in-vehicle data packets may favour the use of compact signatures that can be built on pairings such as the Boneh-Lynn-Shacham signature (BLS) [6]. While computational demands for this kind of signatures are somewhat high for automotive grade controllers, compact signatures may still replace conventional signatures when bandwidth is more critical than computational cost.

Vehicle-to-vehicle (V2V) communication is a quickly emerging technology. It is vital both for traffic optimizations and for preventing road accidents. The main security concern in deploying this technology stems from the fact that security mechanisms must be in place in order to validate the source of the broadcast messages. Recent documents from the US Department of Transportation already point out on the necessity of PKI [12] for assuring security in V2V communications. The problem of using PKI comes from the fact that each certificate needs to be signed by a certificate authority (CA) and must be made available to other traffic participants. Nonetheless, once a participant obtains a genuine certificate there is nothing that can stop him to broadcast false messages regarding traffic conditions. We discuss why identity-based cryptography may help.

First, identity-based cryptographic techniques may eliminate the need for a CA that signs the certificates. If a vehicle is directly identifiable by its license plate, then this can serve as the ID from which the public key of the vehicle derives. Subsequently, a secure communication tunnel between two vehicles or an authenticated broadcast channel between one-vehicle and other traffic participants can be easily established. Vehicle-to-vehicle communication can take advantage of ubiquitous communication channels such as Bluetooth, WiFi or its extension for ad-hoc networking WiFi Direct, which allows the creation of ad-hoc networks over a short range. The advantage of these technologies is that they may be available even where 3G connectivity or road-side units (RSU) are absent. The use of WiFi Direct has been already proposed in [9] for a pedestrian warning system and the use of Multipeer technology (an ad-hoc networking technology based on WiFi and Bluetooth from Apple) was suggested in [10]. Second, identity-based cryptography may partly help in discovering false reports from traffic. While in case of conventional cryptographic techniques each user will have a public-key that is random (and unavailable as visual information to other participants), the use of the license plate number as source for the public-key may allow other traffic participants to visually validate that the car that sends reports from the traffic is present at the location. Of course, in case of conventional PKI one can move the license plate number inside the public-key certificate and obtain a similar result, but identity-based cryptography offers the more intuitive and direct way to achieve this goal by linking a visual/physical clue to the public-key of the principal. Identity based cryptography and pairing in particular have been previously proposed for vehicle-to-vehicle communication [19,21] but practical evaluations on automotive-grade cores are still needed.

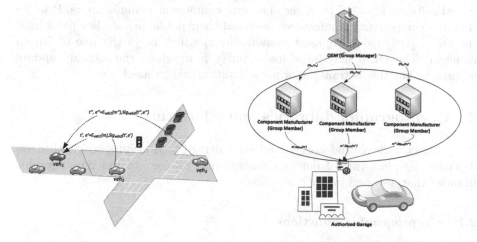

Fig. 2. Vehicle-to-vehicle communication scenario (Color figure online)

Fig. 3. Software update scenario

In Fig. 2 we suggest a collision avoidance scenario. Here, the red vehicle veh_1, from the left side of the figure, is overtaking the other three blue vehicles and is dangerously approaching a potential red light in the middle of the intersection. Consequently the other vehicles veh_2 and veh_3 are signalling him by sending warning messages. The messages are secured by using the identity of the vehicle as public key for encryption and the identity of the other vehicles as private key for signing. Additionally, a timestamp is used to avoid replay attacks. Each participant retrieves the identities of the other cars from the license plates which offer an additional (visual) channel that demonstrates that the vehicles are present in traffic. Cameras are cheap and can be located both in the front and/or read of the vehicle. In fact, rear cameras come as a default for most vehicles nowadays. Thus, an identity-based secure channel can be established between vehicles whose license plates are in sight of each other. If a vehicle is not in sight, the identity-based channel can still be established by using identities from the broadcast messages without the additional evidence of physical presence from the visual channel which may occur later in time.

Software updates are a constant preoccupation of the industry since long ago. Recent research works are increasingly concerned with performance evaluation of software updates that are performed over the air [17] and the adoption of new technologies such as the Blockchain which has been recently proposed for this purpose [18]. We envision that the role of pairings in software updates may stem from the use of group signatures, a construction which immediately derives from pairings. In this type of signatures, the signature may originate from one or more principals inside a group. The advantage in the automotive scenario is that a piece of software can be signed by one or more parties that have the credentials. This may be of interest since vehicle components and software generally originates from multiple manufacturers. This scenario is suggested in Fig. 3 were a vehicle receives a software update from a garage that received the signed software updated from one of several component manufacturers. Prior to this, the component manufacturers received their public-private key pairs from the OEM (Original Equipment Manufacturer) which plays the role of Group manager. The OEM may individually verify from whom the software update originates, but this is transparent for the authorized garaged.

2   Cryptographic Libraries and Platforms

We proceed with a brief background on pairing-based cryptography, then we describe the platforms of our experiments and proceed to the cryptographic libraries that are used in our evaluation.

2.1   Cryptographic Functions

A bilinear pairing is a function $e : \mathbb{G}_1 \times \mathbb{G}_2 \rightarrow \mathbb{G}_T$, where $\mathbb{G}_1, \mathbb{G}_2, \mathbb{G}_T$ are three cyclic groups the later being called the target group. The function has three properties which in case when $\mathbb{G}_1 \times \mathbb{G}_2$ are multiplicative groups can be described as follows: (i) it is bilinear by which $e(g^a, h^b) = e(g, h)^{ab}, \forall g \in \mathbb{G}_1, h \in \mathbb{G}_2, a, b \in \mathbb{Z}$,

(ii) non-degenerate which means $\exists g \in \mathbb{G}_1, h \in \mathbb{G}_2$ such that $e(g, h) \neq 1$ and
(iii) $\forall g \in \mathbb{G}_1, h \in \mathbb{G}_2$ the function $e(g, h)$ is efficiently computable.

While bilinear maps where initially used in cryptanalysis [15] they were later successfully exploited to build several cryptographic primitives. Identity based encryption functions were introduced by Boneh et al. in [3,5], the later being implemented in [20]. A compact signature scheme was introduced by Boneh, Lynn and Sacham in [6], the signature has a size of only 160 bits while retaining a security level equivalent to the 320-bit DSA. Group signatures based on bilinear pairings are described by Boneh et al. in [6] and Hwang et al. in [13], both schemes are implemented in [20]. This is only a brief enumeration of existing proposals that are relevant to the context of our work, many other schemes exist.

Without entering too much mathematical details, the power of bilinear transforms can be easily illustrated on the compact BLS signature [6]. We now assume that groups are in additive form which is usual when moving to elliptic curves. The holder of the public key $pk = xP$ (here P is a point on $\mathbb{G}_2$) hashes the message M that he wants to sign to a point P_M on $\mathbb{G}_1$ and signs it as $S_M = xP_M$. To verify that a signature is correct, the public-key is used to compute verifier $v = e(pk, P_M)$ which is checked against $u = e(P, S_M)$. Of course, there are intricate technical details behind this operation, e.g., how to map a message to a point of the elliptic curve, how the Weil pairing is computed, etc., but for illustrative purposes the previous description should be sufficient as efficient implementations for pairing-based cryptographic functions already exist in practice.

2.2   Experimental Platforms

For our experimental work we selected several platforms which are summarised in Table 1 and the experimental setup is illustrated in Fig. 4.

The SAM V71 Xplained Ultra evaluation kit was chosen because it incorporates a high-end automotive-grade core. Moreover, the SAM V71 family is recommended by the manufacturer for the evaluation of SAM V70, SAM S70, SAM E70, as V71 is a superset of the previous. According to the producer's website[1], the V ARM-based microcontrollers are used in the automotive industry with focus on in-vehicle infotainment connectivity, telematic control units or head units. The evaluation kit contains the ATSAMV71Q21 microcontroller which is a 32-bit ARM Cortex-M7 processor. The maximum operation speed is 300 MHz, the Flash size is up to 2048 Kbytes and the SRAM up to 384 Kbytes. The microcontroller has several cryptographic features, e.g., a true random number generator (TRNG), hardware support for hash functions SHA1, SHA224, SHA256 and AES encryption with 128, 192 and 256-bit keys. To avoid the use of the debugger during run-time measurements, to evaluate the computational performance of this platform we chose to send the results after the test ended through the serial interface USART (Universal Synchronous/Asynchronous Receiver/Transmitter) to a notebook.

---

[1] https://www.microchip.com/design-centers/32-bit/sam-32-bit-mcus/sam-v-mcus.

Table 1. Platforms evaluated in our work

Platform	Core	Flash size	RAM size	Frequency	Manufacturer
ATSAMV71	Cortex-M7	2 MB	384 KB	300 MHz	Microchip
TC297	TriCore 1.6P	8 MB	728 KB	300 MHz	Infineon
HTC One M7	Krait 300	N/A	N/A	1.7 GHz	Qualcomm

Fig. 4. Experimental setup: SAM V71, Infineon TC297 and an Android smartphone

The Infineon TC297 platform, a member of the AURIX TriCore family, is aimed at demanding automotive applications such as powertrain, safety or connectivity for high-end products. The three cores included can run at a top frequency of 300 MHz and come with 8 MB of Flash and 728 KB of RAM.

We also chose to include an Android smart phone in our experiments due to two obvious reasons. First, smart phones are gadgets that are commonly brought inside cars and may be present in many future applications that allow a smart phone to communicate with in-vehicle ECUs. Second, Android-based in-vehicle infotainment units are common and these may be similar in computational capabilities to an Android smart phone. The phone that we used was a HTC One M7. It has a 1.7 GHz quad-core Krait 300 processor, based on ARM architecture, and runs the Android 4.1.2 operating system.

2.3   Cryptographic Libraries

The first step in our project was to configure the wolfCrypt library[2] to run on our automotive microcontrollers. WolfCrypt is a lightweight cryptographic library which contains the most popular algorithms, it has a compact size and a good run-time. The wolfCrypt cryptography engine is targeted for embedded devices and for environments where the resources are an important constraint. We used the wolfSSL 3.12.2 package which includes the wolfCrypt engine.

---

[2] https://www.wolfssl.com.

The library was necessary to measure the conventional RSA and DSA algorithms both in terms of run-time and storage space which are the baseline of our tests.

Further, we integrated an open-source C library for bilinear pairings made available by the Institute for Applied Information Processing and Communication (IAIK)[3]. The library source code is maintained on a Github repository and the research results are presented in [20]. In the case of SAM V71 we added the source files in our Atmel project then we configured the architecture type to Cortex-M0, because this was the only ARM-based architecture available and eliminated functions that were not compatible with our system. The generic architecture configuration was used for in the case of our Infineon microcontroller.

Of high interest for our applications are the short signature schemes in [6] since their size may make them specifically affordable for constrained in-vehicle communication buses. For the BLS primitive we used the C implementation developed by Ben Lynn[4]. This cryptographic library was build on the GNU Multiple Precision Arithmetic Library (GMP), which is developed specifically for Unix systems. We succeeded to compile the GMP library in Ubuntu with a compiler set for the ARM Cortex-M7 architecture and thus we could build a static library which was added to our Atmel project. Afterwards, we performed small modifications in the source files of the Pairing-Based Cryptography library to successfully compile and run it on our V71 microcontroller. We were not successful in adapting the code to compile on the TC297.

In order to run the BLS signature scheme on our smartphone we downloaded the Java Pairing-Based Cryptography library from [8], which is a port of the PBC library by Ben Lynn, and we performed some modification to make it suitable for our Android device. The integration was smooth without much difficulties.

3   Results

For each function in each library we analyze both the runtime and the storage space needed for the code by summing the data flash and code flash size. We discuss results on the Atmel V71 and Infineon TC microcontrollers then on the Android device.

3.1   Results on Automotive-Grade Microcontrollers

We first performed measurements for the RSA and DSA algorithms, which were included as a baseline for comparison with the pairing-based alternatives. The RSA algorithm has signatures that are generally too large for an automotive scenario, e.g., 2048 bits vs. 320 bits for DSA. On the other hand, not surprising, RSA is still the fastest signature in terms of verification speed with up to one order of magnitude faster than DSA. The RSA and DSA implementations that we used are from the aforementioned WolfCrypt library.

---

[3] http://www.iaik.tugraz.at/content/research/opensource.

[4] https://crypto.stanford.edu/pbc.

Table 2. Results for WolfCrypt and the pairing library [18] on Atmel ATSAMV71Q21

Function	Procedure	Flash [bytes]	Runtime [ms]	Signature [bytes]
RSA	MakeRsaKey	34176	7783	128
	RsaSSLSign		273	
	RsaSSLVerify		47	
RSA	MakeRsaKey	34176	54122	256
	RsaSSLSign		1281	
	RsaSSLVerify		155	
DSA	InitDsaKey	24628	38350	40
	DsaSign		155	
	DsaVerify		311	
IBE(BN158)	GenParams	20868	315	N/A
	DerivePrivateKey		190	
	EncapsulateKey		309	
	DecapsulateKey		215	
IBE(BN254)	GenParams	20868	941	N/A
	DerivePrivateKey		603	
	EncapsulateKey		971	
	DecapsulateKey		566	
SGS(BN158)	SgsInit	23416	400	252
	SgsSign		713	
	SgsVerify		1073	
	SgsOpen		68	
SGS(BN254)	SgsInit	23416	1247	396
	SgsSign		2128	
	SgsVerify		3099	
	SgsOpen		231	
HWANG scheme(BN158)	HwangInitParams	27340	474	232
	HwangGenerateUsk		112	
	HwangSign		684	
	HwangVerify		1226	
HWANG scheme(BN254)	HwangInitParams	27340	1571	364
	HwangGenerateUsk		373	
	HwangSign		2058	
	HwangVerify		3518	
Bilinear pairings (BN158)	PbcMapOptAteOptimizedStd	16988	161	N/A
Bilinear pairings (BN254)	PbcMapOptAteOptimizedStd	16988	405	N/A

Next, we analyzed the C library for bilinear pairings implemented in [20]. We run the following four different examples included in the library: (i) demonstration of the bilinear property, (ii) the group signature scheme by Boneh et al. [4] (iii) the group signature scheme by Hwang et al. [13] (iv) a demonstration of a key encapsulation variant of the identity-based encryption by Boneh et al. [3]. The library operates on two Barreto-Naehrig curves BN158 and BN254 and as expected the first one performs better but also has a lower level of security. For long term use, e.g., software signing, a higher level of security should be desired

Table 3. Results for WolfCrypt and the pairing library [18] on Infineon TC297

Function	Procedure	Flash [bytes]	Runtime [ms]	Signature [bytes]
DSA	DsaSign	61988	29.4	40
	DsaVerify		57.8	
IBE (BN158)	GenParams	29442	78.9	N/A
	DerivePrivateKey		46.8	
	EncapsulateKey		78	
	DecapsulateKey		54.9	
IBE (BN254)	GenParams	30268	225	N/A
	DerivePrivateKey		146	
	EncapsulateKey		235	
	DecapsulateKey		138.4	
SGS (BN158)	SgsInit	30302	81.2	252
	SgsSign		173.6	
	SgsVerify		264.2	
	SgsOpen		15.7	
SGS (BN254)	SgsInit	31234	264.2	396
	SgsSign		511.6	
	SgsVerify		745.6	
	SgsOpen		53.4	
HWANG scheme (BN158)	HwangInitParams	29704	114	232
	HwangGenerateUsk		24.12	
	HwangSign		166.2	
	HwangVerify		304.4	
HWANG scheme (BN254)	HwangInitParams	30778	368.8	364
	HwangGenerateUsk		80.80	
	HwangSign		488	
	HwangVerify		853	
Bilinear pairings (BN158)	PbcMapOptAteOptimizedStd	26504	40.9	N/A
Bilinear pairings (BN254)	PbcMapOptAteOptimizedStd	27320	102.7	N/A

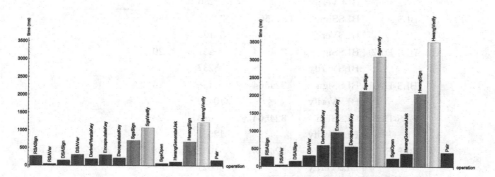

Fig. 5. Results as bar-charts for the pairing library [18] on Atmel ATSAMV71 for BN158

Fig. 6. Results as bar-charts for the pairing library [18] on Atmel ATSAMV71 for BN254

340   T. Andreica et al.

(resulting in a discrete logarithm key of ~256 bits). For real-time applications, e.g., vehicle-to-vehicle communications, a discrete logarithm key of ~160 bits as provided by the first curve, i.e., BN158 which is the faster, should offer sufficient security. Tables 2 and 3 show the results for the Atmel and Infineon cores running the pairing library. The results are also depicted as bar-charts in Figs. 5 and 6 for Atmel and Figs. 7, 8 for Infineon. The Infineon TC297 clearly outperforms the Atmel core, this was not expected by us since their CPUs have similar capabilities. On the other hand, the TriCore is well known as premium core in the automotive industry.

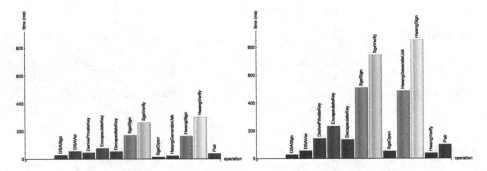

Fig. 7. Results as bar-charts for the pairing library [18] on Infineon TC297 for curve BN158

Fig. 8. Results as bar-charts for the pairing library [18] on Infineon TC297 for curve BN254

Table 4. Results for the BLS library [6] on Atmel ATSAMV71Q21

Function	Procedure	Flash [bytes]	Runtime [ms]	Signature size [bytes]
BLS-A	BLSSign	324564	4828	64
	BLSVerify		7286	
BLS-A1	BLSSign	324564	37516	130
	BLSVerify		31122	
BLS-D159	BLSSign	324564	251	20
	BLSVerify		5237	
BLS-D201	BLSSign	324564	488	26
	BLSVerify		10459	
BLS-D224	BLSSign	324564	683	28
	BLSVerify		12581	
BLS-E	BLSSign	324564	41072	128
	BLSVerify		36621	
BLS-F	BLSSign	324564	236	20
	BLSVerify		25621	
BLS-G149	BLSSign	324564	227	19
	BLSVerify		18640	

Finally, we executed on the Atmel device the BLS signature scheme that is part of the Pairing-based cryptography library implemented by Ben Lynn. This library requires the GNU crypto toolset which for the moment we were not able to port on the Infineon core. Thus we only provide results on the Atmel core. In the BLS library the user has the possibility to choose over several types of curves. The predefined types curves for pairings are the following: A, A1, D159, D201, D224, E, F, G149. According to the documentation of the library, type A curves are the fastest while type D, F and G are for compact representations but obviously slower. We have measured computational performance for each type of curve and the results are consistent with the documentation. The only exception was that type G curve gave similar results to type F curves which according to the documentation should have been faster. In Table 4 we present measurement results in terms of run-time and flash size for the Atmel core when running the BLS signature scheme.

Table 5. Results for the BLS library [6] on a HTC smartphone running Android

Function	Procedure	Flash [bytes]	Runtime [ms]	Signature size [bytes]
BLS-A	GenKeys	N/A	351	64
	BLSSign		685	
	BLSVerify		1584	
BLS-A1	GenKeys	N/A	3226	130
	BLSSign		2122	
	BLSVerify		10129	
BLS-D159	GenKeys	N/A	3561	20
	BLSSign		156	
	BLSVerify		10796	
BLS-D201	GenKeys	N/A	4122	26
	BLSSign		252	
	BLSVerify		12815	
BLS-D224	GenKeys	N/A	12019	26
	BLSSign		398	
	BLSVerify		15630	
BLS-E	GenKeys	N/A	642	128
	BLSSign		1707	
	BLSVerify		2972	
BLS-F	GenKeys	N/A	5912	20
	BLSSign		184	
	BLSVerify		86174	
BLS-G149	GenKeys	N/A	8823	19
	BLSSign		195	
	BLSVerify		34168	

3.2 Results on the Android Device

As expected, Android based smartphones are equipped with highly capable cores. Despite the five years that passed since the release of the HTC phone that we used, it still generally outperforms the automotive grade controllers. On the Android device, we present results only for the most demanding BLS signature scheme for each type of curve. Each result set of the BLS scheme on a specific curve contains only the run-time measurements since the storage space is of no concern on this device. The results collected on Android are shown in Table 5. They are generally better by one order of magnitude compared to the Atmel core, but variations exists, for example on the D159 curve. Giving the use of Android units for more complex tasks, e.g., image processing, it is likely that demanding cryptographic functions such as pairing will raise no computational issues.

4 Conclusion

The scenarios envisioned in our work show clear practical advantages for pairing-based primitives in the automotive domain. Computational results obtained on an automotive grade controller with two libraries dedicated to pairing based primitives show that implementation on automotive-grade cores is feasible. Nonetheless, for in-vehicle infotainment units which have even better cores, the performance is improved. This proves that pairing-based primitives are ready for entering the automotive domain. Indeed, traditional public-key primitives such as RSA and DSA still have better performance but they cannot offer the compact size of BLS signatures, nor the flexibility of identity-based signatures/encryptions or the scalability of group signatures. Consequently, the adoption of pairing based primitives in the automotive domain may be a future step. Developing a full-scale functional application for any of the discussed scenario remains as future work for us.

Acknowledgement. We thank the reviewers for helpful comments that improved our work. This work was supported by a grant of the Romanian Ministry of Research and Innovation, CNCS-UEFISCDI, project number PN-III-P1-1.1.-TE-2016-1317 within PNCDI III (2018–2020).

References

1. AUTOSAR: Specification of Crypto Abstraction Library, 4.2.2 edition (2015)
2. AUTOSAR: Specification of Crypto Service Manager, 4.2.2 edition (2015)
3. Boneh, D., Boyen, X.: Secure identity based encryption without random oracles. In: Franklin, M. (ed.) CRYPTO 2004. LNCS, vol. 3152, pp. 443–459. Springer, Heidelberg (2004). https://doi.org/10.1007/978-3-540-28628-8_27
4. Boneh, D., Boyen, X., Shacham, H.: Short group signatures. In: Franklin, M. (ed.) CRYPTO 2004. LNCS, vol. 3152, pp. 41–55. Springer, Heidelberg (2004). https://doi.org/10.1007/978-3-540-28628-8_3

5. Boneh, D., Franklin, M.: Identity-based encryption from the weil pairing. In: Kilian, J. (ed.) CRYPTO 2001. LNCS, vol. 2139, pp. 213–229. Springer, Heidelberg (2001). https://doi.org/10.1007/3-540-44647-8_13
6. Boneh, D., Lynn, B., Shacham, H.: Short signatures from the weil pairing. J. Cryptol. **17**, 297–319 (2004)
7. Checkoway, S., et al.: Comprehensive experimental analyses of automotive attack surfaces. In: USENIX Security Symposium, San Francisco (2011)
8. De Caro, A., Iovino, V.: jPBC: Java pairing based cryptography. In: Proceedings of the 16th IEEE Symposium on Computers and Communications, ISCC 2011, Kerkyra, pp. 850–855, 28 June–1 July 2011. IEEE (2011)
9. Dhondge, K., Song, S., Choi, B.-Y., Park, H.: WiFiHonk: smartphone-based beacon stuffed WiFi Car2X-communication system for vulnerable road user safety. In: IEEE 79th Vehicular Technology Conference (VTC Spring), pp. 1–5. IEEE (2014)
10. Groza, B., Briceag, C.: A vehicle collision-warning system based on multipeer connectivity and off-the-shelf smart-devices. In: Cuppens, N., Cuppens, F., Lanet, J.-L., Legay, A., Garcia-Alfaro, J. (eds.) CRiSIS 2017. LNCS, vol. 10694, pp. 115–123. Springer, Cham (2018). https://doi.org/10.1007/978-3-319-76687-4_8
11. Groza, B., Murvay, P.-S.: Security solutions for the controller area network: bringing authentication to in-vehicle networks. IEEE Veh. Technol. Mag. **13**(1), 40–47 (2018)
12. Harding, J., et al.: Vehicle-to-vehicle communications: readiness of V2V technology for application. Technical report (2014)
13. Hwang, J.Y., Lee, S., Chung, B.-H., Cho, H.S., Nyang, D.: Group signatures with controllable linkability for dynamic membership, vol. 222, pp. 761–778. Elsevier (2013)
14. Koscher, K., et al.: Experimental security analysis of a modern automobile. In: IEEE Symposium on Security and Privacy (SP), pp. 447–462. IEEE (2010)
15. Menezes, A.J., Okamoto, T., Vanstone, S.A.: Reducing elliptic curve logarithms to logarithms in a finite field. IEEE Trans. Inf. Theor. **39**(5), 1639–1646 (1993)
16. Miller, C., Valasek, C.: A survey of remote automotive attack surfaces. Black Hat USA (2014)
17. Steger, M., Boano, C.A., Römer, K., Karner, M., Hillebrand, J., Rom, W.: Cesar: a testbed infrastructure to evaluate the efficiency of wireless automotive software updates. In: Proceedings of the 20th ACM International Conference on Modelling, Analysis and Simulation of Wireless and Mobile Systems, pp. 311–315. ACM (2017)
18. Steger, M., Dorri, A., Kanhere, S.S., Römer, K., Jurdak, R., Karner, M.: Secure wireless automotive software updates using blockchains: a proof of concept. In: Zachäus, C., Müller, B., Meyer, G. (eds.) Advanced Microsystems for Automotive Applications 2017. LNM, pp. 137–149. Springer, Cham (2018). https://doi.org/10.1007/978-3-319-66972-4_12
19. Sun, J., Zhang, C., Zhang, Y., Fang, Y.: An identity-based security system for user privacy in vehicular ad hoc networks. IEEE Trans. Parallel Distrib. Syst. **21**(9), 1227–1239 (2010)
20. Unterluggauer, T., Wenger, E.: Efficient pairings and ECC for embedded systems. In: Batina, L., Robshaw, M. (eds.) CHES 2014. LNCS, vol. 8731, pp. 298–315. Springer, Heidelberg (2014). https://doi.org/10.1007/978-3-662-44709-3_17
21. Zhang, C., Lu, R., Lin, X., Ho, P.-H., Shen, X.: An efficient identity-based batch verification scheme for vehicular sensor networks. In: The 27th Conference on Computer Communications (INFOCOM 2008), pp. 246–250. IEEE (2008)

Towards an Integrated Penetration Testing Environment for the CAN Protocol

Giampaolo Bella[✉] and Pietro Biondi[✉]

Dipartimento di Matematica e Informatica, Università di Catania, Catania, Italy
giamp@dmi.unict.it, pietro.biondi94@gmail.com

Abstract. The Controller Area Network (CAN) is the most common protocol interconnecting the various control units of modern cars. Its vulnerabilities are somewhat known but we argue they are not yet fully explored—although the protocol is obviously not secure by design, it remains to be thoroughly assessed how and to what extent it can be maliciously exploited. This manuscript describes the early steps towards a larger goal, that of integrating the various CAN pentesting activities together and carry them out holistically within an established pentesting environment such as the Metasploit Framework. In particular, we shall see how to build an exploit that upsets a simulated tachymeter running on a minimal Linux machine. While both portions are freely available from the authors' Github shares, the exploit is currently subject to a Metaspoilt pull request.

1 Introduction

When traditional security vulnerabilities are ported to and exploited in the automotive environment, they bear a clear potential to compromise passengers' safety; therefore, modern automotive technology intertwines security and safety requirements tightly and is, as such, worth of considerable attention.

The most widespread protocol that connects the various control units found in modern cards is the *Controller Area Network* (CAN) protocol, which appears to be highly vulnerable at least because it is not meant to be secure by design. However, a full understanding of the technicalities of this protocol and its vulnerabilities is still out of reach for a variety of reasons, such as the scattered and mostly unofficial documentation, the large customisation operated by each car manufacturer, and the lack of an integrated pentesting environment to investigate vulnerabilities and attempt to exploit them.

The CAN protocol is standardised by ISO 11898-1:2015 [1], though without any reference to security issues, perhaps in the assumption that a car forms a secluded, protected network environment. The question arises on what would happen should the CAN bus be used in an unprotected environment instead, namely with potentially malicious activity running through its wires.

© Springer Nature Switzerland AG 2018
B. Gallina et al. (Eds.): SAFECOMP 2018 Workshops, LNCS 11094, pp. 344–352, 2018.
https://doi.org/10.1007/978-3-319-99229-7_29

The security protocol literature is full of examples of protocols or systems devised to stand a threat model but, implicitly, not a stronger one. The best known example is the public-key Needham-Schroeder protocol [2] and Lowe's attack on it [3]. The attack originated from an initiator who started with the attacker, but Needham commented that their protocol was not meant to withstand insider threats [4].

It is clear that the mentioned assumption that a car hosts an isolated network falters at present, as the control and infotainment systems are often combined and interfaced with the external world through the Internet. For example, one can check the pressure of the tyres or switch on the engine *remotely* through an app running on their smartphone. In this socio-technical context, attacks are starting to appear. For example, a Jeep Cherokee was hacked via bluetooth, with the attacker being able to remotely operate the brake system and the steering wheel [5]; a Toyota Prius was hacked via the JTAG port and the entire CAN bus traffic hijacked, even letting the attacker flash the firmware of a control unit [6].

This manuscript aims at contributing to the definition of an integrated environment to conduct simulation experiments on the CAN bus. In short, it contributes a lightweight Linux machine running a tachymeter simulator, and the machine itself is made vulnerable to simulate an in-vehicle network that is accessed, for example, via bluetooth or the JTAG port. It also brings a Metasploit post exploitation module as a Ruby file `crazytachymeter.rb`, which causes the tachymeter to jump without continuity to random speeds, also outside the programmed range.

More precisely, these contributions derive from the following research methodology. The Instrument Cluster Simulator (ICSim) [7] is installed on the Linux machine and operated; the generated traffic is sniffed and interpreted using Kayak [8]. Potentially meaningful values for the data frames are then conjectured and verified manually. After that, the findings are used to program the script in the Ruby file, which is then tested in the Metasploit framework [9] and, at the same time, submitted for consideration and inclusion in future releases of the framework.

The structure of the paper follows the methodology just outlined. A primer on the CAN bus supports the developments (Sect. 2). The tachimeter simulator is introduced (Sect. 3), along with Kayak (Sect. 4). Then, the exploitation of the conjectured vulnerabilities is carried out manually (Sect. 5). Finally, the integrated pentesing environment is described and made publicly available (Sect. 6), and the manuscript draws its conclusions (Sect. 7).

2 A Primer on the Controller Area Network Protocol

Modern cars are full of electronics. Components such as airbags, power doors, electric mirrors need to be interconnected and communicate among each other to ensure the smooth and synergistic functioning of all. This was the aim for the inception of the Can protocol [10], also known as *CAN bus*, which dates back to 1983 at Bosch.

The CAN bus is conceptually simple from a hardware standpoint, as it consists of two wires, *CAN high* (CANH) and *CAN low* (CANL). It is equally simple from a software standpoint, as it sees a body computer read environmental data such as brake pedal pressure and air conditioning temperature, and then send appropriate commands on the CAN bus to the dedicated control units; this is done in a multicast style, namely commands are sent to all but filtered by the intended recipients. The body computer must use two CAN wires ensuring fault tolerance, which can be done by means of differential signaling: to send a signal, it must raise the voltage on one line and equally drop the other line.

As mentioned above, the CAN frames are standardised as ISO 11898-1:2015 [1] to contain various fields. These include an Arbitration field carrying the frame ID, also used for arbitration, a Control field for control signals and a Data field for the payload. More precisely, the fields are:

- Start Of Frame: a dominant bit indicating the beginning of a frame;
- Data: up to 8 bytes of data;
- Arbitration field: 11 bits identifying the intended recipient from the frame; one bit is the Remote Transmission Request (RTR) bit, which is low for a Data Frame and 1 for a Remote Frame (one whose Data Field is empty);
- Control: 6 bits, with 4 bits called Data Length Code (DLC) indicating the length of the Data Field and 2 reserved bits;
- CRC: 15 bits for a cyclic redundancy check code and a recessive bit as a delimiter;
- Ack: 2 bits, with the first one being recessive, hence overwritten with a dominant bit by every node that receives it, and the second bit working as a delimiter;
- End Of Frame: 7 recessive bits.

However, it must be noted that car manufacturers interpret the standard freely, for example using padding at will, raising a general issue of how to interpret CAN bus traffic on various cars.

3   Instrument Cluster Simulator

Instrument Cluster Simulator (ICSim) [7] is a simulator for some of the main car functions, namely blinkers, power doors and tachymeter, operated through the CAN bus. It runs on Linux following the setup of a virtual CAN interface through the following simple commands:

```
sudo apt install can-utils
sudo modprobe can
sudo modprobe vcan
sudo ip link add dev vcan0 type vcan
sudo ip link set up vcan0
```

The control panel of the simulator is in Fig. 1. Accelerations can be triggered by pushing the Accelerate button; everytime the button is pressed, a specific

frame is sent to the control unit of the tachymeter. The simulator supports
speed up to 100 MPH, as we realise that pressing the button additionally when
speed is at 100 MPH produces no effect.

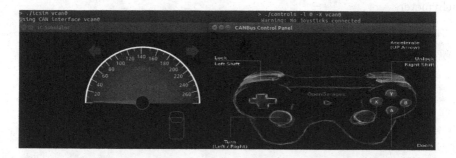

Fig. 1. The control panel of the Instrument Cluster Simulator

4 Kayak

Kayak is an application that sniffs CAN bus traffic [8]. It is written in Java,
hence easily portable, and features an intuitive user interface. We set out to
interpret the CAN traffic generated through ICSim using Kayak. The aim is to
understand which frame IDs are associated to which device of the car, whether
blinkers, doors or tachymeter, and what values the Data field accepts for each
device.

The graphical interface of Kayak can be seen from Fig. 2. It features the
following fields:

- Timestamp (seconds): when the frame is intercepted;
- Interval (milliseconds): interval between two statistics transmissions;
- Identifier (hexadecimal): corresponding to the frame ID;
- Data Length Code: length of the Data field;
- Data (hexadecimal): actual payload.

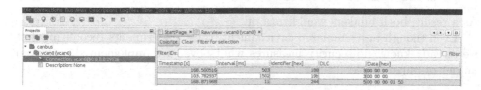

Fig. 2. Packet sniffing on ICSim traffic through Kayak

Various interactions with the control panel of ICSim can be orchestrated
and closely observed through the sniffer. It was easy to derive the information

summarised in Table 1. The Table shows the IDs associated to which device, in particular with 5 bytes devoted to data for the tachymeter. The third column emphasises in red positions of the hexadecimal numbers that are observed to change for each device, for example the last four in case of frames for the tachymeter.

Table 1. Interpretation of ICSim traffic through Kayak

ID	DLC	Data	Device	Values
19b	3	000000	doors	1/2/4/8
188	3	00 00 00	blinkers	1/2
244	5	00 00 00 00 00	tachymeter	00 00 ... 01 5D

It can also be seen that there are four possible values transmitted to operate the doors, one per door and, likewise, two for the blinkers. As for the tachymeter, the allowed speed range of 0–100 MPH was found to be triggered by hexadecimal data values ranging from 00 00 to 01 5D.

5   Pentesting the Tachymeter of ICSim

We carry out a few penetration testing experiments on the tachymeter of ICSim by conjecturing that it would accept arbitrary frames. The suite of commands previously installed through `can-utils` (Sect. 3) turns out useful to explore the conjectures. One of the first meaningful conjectures is to send the highest possible hexadecimal value 99 99 to the tachymeter and observe whether the highest possible speed is reached. This can be verified by sending command:

```
cansend vcan0 244#0000009999
```

The tachymeter reacts by reaching its top speed, of 240 MPH. It is then possible to send arbitrary values and observe the corresponding speeds each time.

A similar conjecture is about exploiting the blinkers. Coherently with the lessons learned using Kayak (Table 1, Sect. 4), we can try out command:

```
cansend vcan0 188#030000
```

As a result, both blinkers would turn on.

Even though in a simulated environment, these experiments reconfirm what we already knew: no security measures whatsoever are implemented, not even an out-of-range check.

6   Towards the Integrated Pentesting Environment

Our aim of an integrated pentesting environment can be pursued by taking two main steps. The first step is the preparation of a machine to simulate the victim system, and this requires a few sub-steps in turn.

We build a machine running Bodhi Linux, a minimal distribution based on Ubuntu 16.04 LTS, and implement a vulnerable python server to run on it. The core of the server receives data off a socket and executes it, as stated by line `data=c.recv(5120) subprocess.call(data,shell=True)`. This is meant to simulate a successful malicious access to the network laid within the car. We then install ICSim on the machine, and our simulated victim is ready. It can be downloaded from our GitHub share [11].

The second step is the automation of the pentesting experiments outlined above (Sect. 5) through an actual exploit executable on the Metasploit Framework [9]. We wrote such an exploit in Ruby and submitted file `crazytachymeter.rb` to Metasploit for consideration; as a possible location to host the exploit, our pull request [12] pinpointed path `modules/exploits/unix/misc/`.

The pull request is currently ongoing, and the interaction has been fruitful for us. We have been advised to treat our program as a post-exploitation script, rather than as an actual exploit, due to the fact that it targets a tailored machine and follows a successful malicious access to have occurred beforehand. The new path therefore is `modules/post/hardware/automotive/`. This already contains five scripts, which, incidentally, are worth of consideration here:

- `canprobe.rb` allows the analyst to scan for given frame IDs and set their data fields;
- `getinfo.rb` returns engine and vehicle information;
- `identifymodules.rb` searches for devices responding to Diagnostic Session Control (DSC) queries;
- `malibu_overheat.rb` controls the temperature gauge of a 2006 Chevrolet Malibu;
- `pdt.rb`: discovers the Pyrotechnic Control Units (PCU) units and sets them ready to be deployed.

The gist of our script is pictured in Fig. 3. It can be seen that it takes as a parameter a file containing a specific mapping of the frames; the mapping represents the interpretation of the frame by a control unit, and therefore, the script is general and not bound to a single mapping. The script then loops forever while it sends frames to the virtual CAN interface. Also the script is available from GitHub [11].

While the pull request is being processed, our script can be manually downloaded and run over Metasploit, as shown in Fig. 4. It exposes the three intended module options: FILEMAP, INTERFACE and SESSION.

Once the options are set, the script can be run. Figure 5 shows that it returns the Flooding message, which means that the tachymeter is being flooded with frames corresponding to various speeds.

The visible outcome of running the script is that the tachymeter goes crazy by jumping up or down without continuity over the range 0–240 MPH. Of course, this cannot be portrayed in a picture, and Fig. 6 provides the single screenshot of the top speed.

```
def run
  print_status(' -- OPENING CONTROL UNIT MAP --')
  lines = []
  f = File.open(datastore['FILEMAP'], "rb")
  f.each_line do |line|
    lines.push(line.strip)
  end
  f.close
  print_status(' -- Flooding --')
  while 1
    lines.each{
      |e|
      cmd = "cansend #{datastore['INTERFACE']} #{e}"
      cmd_exec(cmd)
    }
  end
end
```

Fig. 3. Our script: the core

```
msf > use post/hardware/automotive/crazytachymeter
msf post(hardware/automotive/crazytachymeter) > show options

Module options (post/hardware/automotive/crazytachymeter):

   Name        Current Setting                                                         Required  Description
   ----        ---------------                                                         --------  -----------
   FILEMAP     /usr/share/metasploit-framework/data/wordlists/controlUnitMapCanBus.txt  yes       Path to FILEMAP
   INTERFACE   vcan0                                                                    yes       Interface of CAN-Bus
   SESSION                                                                              yes       The session to run this module on.

msf post(hardware/automotive/crazytachymeter) > set session 1
session => 1
```

Fig. 4. Our script: the options

```
msf post(hardware/automotive/crazytachymeter) > exploit

[!] SESSION may not be compatible with this module.
[*]  -- OPENING CONTROL UNIT MAP --
[*]  -- Flooding --
```

Fig. 5. Our script: the output

Fig. 6. Our script: a snapshot of its consequences

7   Conclusions

Investigations into the cybersecurity limitations of the CAN protocol have only just began, with the most significant findings dating back to a bunch of years ago. The fact that the protocol never meant to be secure by design cannot decrease our surprise at how easy it turns out to be to exploit nodes that run it, as shown above.

This paper described how to send a tachymeter crazy. Starting from a tachymeter simulator, it was possible to decode the frame data values that would trigger specific events, and hence to try out additional data values at will. Doing so revealed the possibility of inducing anomalous scenarios, such as the blinkers turning on both sides and the tachymeter jumping from one speed to another—and beyond the programmed range of 0–100 MPH. The tachimeter runs on a Bodhi Linux machine made vulnerable, and the attacks are implemented as Metasploit post-exploitation modules.

Although our experiments only took place on a simulated environment, they highlight that no security measure is in place against malicious activity on the CAN bus. This finding may not be surprising by itself. However, it required the gathering of a number of tools and their combined use, and these activities were more time consuming than expected.

Where do we go from here? On one hand, it is all the more clear that the CAN protocol ought to be amended to incorporate even simple security measures that would control and qualify the frames. Such measures are currently being studied, and their deployment would subvert the finding that, once an attacker penetrates the in-vehicle network, they can then command and control all nodes on the CAN bus.

On the other hand, we realise that, if it is arguably complicated and somewhat expensive to setup a real laboratory to experiment on the CAN bus, it should really be made simple to conduct the experiments in a simulated environment. This manuscript contributed in such a direction by showing that a Linux machine (or a network of machines) can be tailored to simulate the nodes and network laid within a car. It then suggested to write the potential attacks in Ruby so that they could be simulated using Metasploit. If the machine-exploit pair is easy do download (such as ours [11]), then simulations on the CAN bus could finally fall within effortless reach.

References

1. International Organization for Standardization: Road vehicles – Controller area network (CAN) – Part 1: Data link layer and physical signalling (2015). https://www.iso.org/standard/63648.html
2. Needham, R.M., Schroeder, M.D.: Using encryption for authentication in large networks of computers. Commun. ACM **21**, 993–999 (1978)
3. Lowe, G.: Breaking and fixing the Needham-Schroeder public-key protocol using FDR. In: Margaria, T., Steffen, B. (eds.) TACAS 1996. LNCS, vol. 1055, pp. 147–166. Springer, Heidelberg (1996). https://doi.org/10.1007/3-540-61042-1_43
4. Needham, R.: Keynote address: the changing environment. In: Christianson, B., Crispo, B., Malcolm, J.A., Roe, M. (eds.) Security Protocols 1999. LNCS, vol. 1796, pp. 1–5. Springer, Heidelberg (2000). https://doi.org/10.1007/10720107_1
5. Valasek, C., Miller, C.: Remote Exploitation of an Unaltered Passenger Vehicle (2015). http://illmatics.com/Remote%20Car%20Hacking.pdf
6. Valasek, C., Miller, C.: CAN Message Injection (2016). http://illmatics.com/can%20message%20injection.pdf

7. Smith, C.: The Car Hacker's Handbook: A Guide for the Penetration Tester, 1st edn. No Starch Press, San Francisco (2016)
8. Meier, J.N.: Kayak (2014). https://github.com/dschanoeh/Kayak
9. Rapid7: Metasploit framework. https://github.com/rapid7/metasploit-framework
10. Chris Valasek, C.M.: Adventures in Automotive Networks and Control Units (2014). http://illmatics.com/car_hacking.pdf
11. Biondi, P.: Crazy-tachymeter (2018). https://github.com/pietrobiondi/Crazy-Tachymeter
12. Biondi, P.: Crazytachymeter, exploit for can-bus (2018). https://github.com/rapid7/metasploit-framework/pull/10127

Enhancing Sensor Capabilities of Open-Source Simulation Tools to Support Autonomous Vehicles Safety Validation

C. B. S. T. Molina[1](✉), L. F. Vismari[1], T. Fuji[1], J. B. Camargo Jr.[1], J. R. de Almeida Jr.[1], R. Inam[2], E. Fersman[2], A. Hata[3], and M. V. Marquezini[3]

[1] School of Engineering, University of São Paulo (USP), São Paulo, SP, Brazil
{cbmolina,lucio.vismari,joaocamargo}@usp.br
[2] Ericsson Research, Ericsson AB, Stockholm, Sweden
[3] Ericsson Telecomunicações S.A., Indaiatuba, SP, Brazil

Abstract. Autonomous Vehicles (AVs) are expected to provide relevant benefits to the society in terms of safety, efficiency and accessibility. However, AVs are safety-critical systems, and it is mandatory to assure that they are going to be safe when operating on public roads. However, the safety of AV is still an open, and challenging issue. A combination of simulation, test track, and on-road testing approaches is being recommended to validate the AV safety performance. Testing AVs in real-world scenarios is a widely used, but neither an efficient nor a safe approach to validate safety. Therefore, simulation-based approaches are demanded. Motivated by this challenge, we have developed a simulation-based safety analysis framework, based on open-source tools, to be applied to the future of the road transportation systems. However, the open-source tools we have adopted for the framework have limitations to model real-world elements, especially perception sensors. We thus here present the extensions made to these open-source tools, focused on the development of a perception sensor model in the native OpenDS tool, which enables detecting obstacles around the vehicle, considering the same main characteristics observed in Radar and LiDAR sensors. As the main conclusion, these tools enhancements have improved the simulation-based safety analysis framework capabilities for modeling, simulating and analyzing – in a more precise way and for safety validation purposes – the behavior of AV in simulated traffic scenarios when different embedded detection sensor characteristics are considered in its deployment.

Keywords: Autonomous vehicle · Safety · Simulation · OpenDS · Sensor

1 Introduction

Autonomous vehicles (AVs) can change the concept of road transportation system (RTS) and become a tangible reality in the next few years. However, AV is a safety-critical system and, when operating in an undesirable way, it can jeopardize not only human lives (such as passengers, pedestrians, or people in other vehicles), but also the

© Springer Nature Switzerland AG 2018
B. Gallina et al. (Eds.): SAFECOMP 2018 Workshops, LNCS 11094, pp. 353–364, 2018.
https://doi.org/10.1007/978-3-319-99229-7_30

environment in which it operates. Therefore, it is mandatory to ensure that the AV operates safely, mainly when navigating on public roads.

Ensuring the safety of AV continues to be an open issue. The U.S. National Highway Transportation Safety Administration (NHTSA) released a policy framework to support the safe deployment of AVs [4]. Regarding AV safety validation, NHTSA recommends combining simulations, test track, and on-road testing to validate the automated driving system (ADS) safety performance. However, it can be observed that just two of these recommendations (test track and on-road testing) are being used to analyze AV safety. The simulation-based validation is an under development, initial approach [2].

Testing autonomous vehicles in real-world scenarios, both in restricted and public roads, is a practical, widely used, but it is not an efficient approach for safety validation. According to [1], driving hundreds to thousands of million miles is demanded to assert AVs reliability. As a consequence, it emphasizes the need of innovative methods to demonstrate the safety and the reliability of autonomous vehicles.

Faced with this challenge, we developed a simulation-based safety analysis framework, based on open-source simulation tools, which can be applied to the future of the RTS [6]. This framework allows analyzing the impacts of introducing new concepts, technologies and procedures over the safety levels of the future RTS by means of computational simulation. However, there are limitations in modeling some real-world elements, mainly related to the perception sensors for obstacle detection. So, in this current work we identified limitations in the adopted open-source simulation tools and present the needs to improve the capabilities of the simulation tools to model RTSs as close as possible to real-world systems.

These limitation and needs are: autonomous vehicles must be able to map their surroundings and to detect obstacles to avoid collisions and safely navigate through the roads. They thus need to be equipped with sensors capable of identifying various types of objects, from people and animals to vehicles and buildings, working in the most varied situations, such as mist, rain, and low light. Due to the diversity of situations to be addressed, multiple sensors are used, with different detection methods and sensor technologies – e.g. LiDAR (*Light Detection And Ranging*), cameras and Radars (*Radio Detection And Ranging*), for effective and safe obstacle detection.

Therefore, the main contribution of this work is the development and implementation of a model of sensors for autonomous vehicles, used to detect multiple obstacles in a simulated environment. This sensor can model the detection of obstacles in the vehicle surrounding. With the functionality of this sensor, it is possible to improve the modeling and analytical capacity of real-time road traffic simulation tools. Consequently, we present the model, simulation, and the analysis of the behavior of autonomous vehicles that use different detection sensor technologies within the simulated traffic scenarios.

This paper is structured as follows: Sect. 2 presents background details about the framework, its limitations, and the sensor characteristics considered in the development. Section 3 presents the development and implementation of the sensor model, considering the real-time simulation tools. Section 4 presents the experiments performed to validate the sensor functionality. Finally, Sect. 5 presents the final remarks and some future directions.

2 Background

2.1 Our Simulation-Based Framework Supporting Autonomous Vehicles Safety Validation and Its Limitations

Faced with the challenges of validating the autonomous vehicle safety, and on the demand to develop innovative methods for demonstrating the vehicle safety and reliability, we proposed a simulation-based safety analysis framework, implemented with open-source tools [6]. This framework combines real-time simulation (ReTS) and fast-time simulation (FTS) approaches, whose selection criteria are presented in [3]. The framework deals with representative RTS scenarios, mainly regarding autonomous vehicles, and analyzes the impact of concepts in component level over the system level properties for safety aspects.

The OpenDS [5] which is a driving simulator intended for research and driving training and Matlab (not an open-source tool) were the tools combined in the ReTS to model and to simulate RTS scenarios. The OpenDS was chosen among other simulators due to its capability of representing different roadway traffic scenarios in a detailed way [3]. Figure 1 illustrates the high-level architecture of the proposed ReTS, which is composed of OpenDS and Matlab. In this, RTS elements (e.g. Roadway, Vehicle and Driver) are modeled by OpenDS (Vehicle and Roadway) or Matlab (Driver). The autonomous vehicle (AV) is modeled by combining the "Driver" and the "Vehicle" elements. Therefore, the vehicle control algorithms (as exemplified in [6]) are embedded in the Driver element, adequately controlling the AV movement.

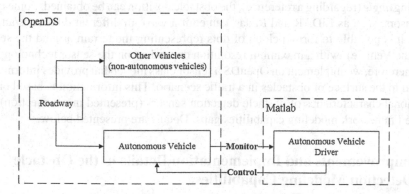

Fig. 1. High-level architecture to the ReTS approach and its related tools (adapted from [6]).

An interface between Matlab and OpenDS based on the CAN (*Controller Area Network*) bus protocol is used in the ReTS approach to exchange data related to the autonomous vehicle monitoring and control. Both in Matlab (Driver model) and OpenDS (Vehicle), algorithms were implemented to exchange data related to autonomous vehicle monitoring and control tasks between Driver and Vehicle [6]. Consequently, the autonomous vehicle can effectively send the acquired data from its sensors – including its internal status (e.g. speed, position, direction and steering wheel angle) and about the surrounding environment (e.g. distance from/position of detected obstacles) to the Driver, and receives control data from the Driver.

In our framework [6], we used native obstacle detection modeling capability available in OpenDS tool (version 4.0) to implement the ReTS approach. This native capability is limited to obtaining the distance between the geometric centers of the vehicle and the obstacle. The information returned by the obstacle detection is not enough for the autonomous driver to know the extension of the obstacle and there is an important gap on the obstacle detection modeling capability in our first framework release [6]. Considering this limitation, we modified the OpenDS source code and the developed Matlab algorithms to allow modeling the sensors for more precise obstacle detection and to present it as our main contribution.

2.2 Sensor Characteristics

Autonomous vehicles have used different types of sensors for situational awareness from the surrounding environment, detecting obstacles and, consequently, avoiding collisions. Radar, LiDAR, video camera and ultrasonic sensors are most commonly used for this purpose. In the case of Radar, LiDAR, and ultrasonic sensors, their detection principle is based on emitting a wave (light, radio or sound), which illuminates and reflects on a surface (target), returns and is captured back by the sensor. If the wave is detected back, this means that an obstacle has been detected. The elapsed time interval between wave emitting and reception is then used to calculate the distance between the obstacle and the sensor (vehicle). This distance is called *range*. If it is possible to obtain the wave-emitting *angle* (regarding a reference), the obstacle position can be obtained. Some types of sensors, such as LiDAR and Radar, can emit a wave in different directions/angles. Thus, it is possible to form a cloud of dots representing the terrain around the sensor (and the Vehicle), with a maximum resolution dependent on the sensor technology.

Therefore, we implement on OpenDS a sensor class model that provides information related to the surface of obstacles in a traffic scenario. This information is based on the functional characteristics of obstacle detection sensors (presented in next section) and on the Framework modeling capabilities gaps. Details are presented below.

3 Improvements and Implementation Details in the Obstacle Detection Modeling Capabilities

This section details the enhancements deployed in the simulation-based safety analysis framework tools as presented in the previous section. A new Java class model – named OpenDS.sensor – is specified, implemented and validated over the OpenDS native source code [5]. The Matlab-based tool features implemented in this framework are adapted to enable the Driver to receive and to use information from these sensors to manage the vehicle.

3.1 OpenDS.sensor Class Specification

OpenDS should be able to simulate the perception sensors currently used in the autonomous vehicles. Consequently, the OpenDS.sensor class must enable the instantiation of generic obstacle detection sensors, the behavior and features (attributes) of which must be as close as possible to the real-world sensors, and later embed them in an autonomous vehicle model on OpenDS. Thus, we specify the following three main requirements to develop OpenDS.sensor class model:

- [Req. 1] The OpenDS.sensor class model must enable the instantiation of a set of obstacle detection sensors to a vehicle modeled in OpenDS;
- [Req. 2] The OpenDS.sensor class model must enable the configuration of each sensor in an independent way. Each instantiated sensor has a configuration set to all of its characteristics (attributes). These properties are: maximum detection range and maximum detection angle; position of the sensor in the vehicle; and sensor rotation (direction of the sensor in relation to the longitudinal axes of the vehicle, in degrees);
- [Req. 3] The information provided by the sensor class must return the surface(s) of an obstacle(s) detected in the line-of-sight (field of view) by each instantiated sensor, not just the geometric center of the obstacle.

Figure 2 illustrates the instantiation of three sensors (S1, S2 and S3) in a simulated vehicle. Sensor S1 was placed on the roof (i.e. center of the vehicle) and with sensor rotation of 0°; Sensor S2 was placed in the middle of the right side of the vehicle with sensor rotation of −90°; and sensor S3 was placed in middle of the rear of the vehicle with sensor rotation of 180°. Note that the position of a sensor on a vehicle is configured using x, y, and z coordinates, with its reference (0, 0, 0) in the geometrical center of the vehicle. A sensor can therefore be equipped in any part of the vehicle.

The coverage of a sensor (detection area) is configured by two parameters: the maximum detection range (in meters) and maximum detection angle (in degrees). Another important parameter is the minimum range. However, it is not implemented in this version. Figure 2 also illustrates the detection area of sensor S1 configured with a maximum detection range of 5 meters (5 m) and a maximum detection angle of 30 degrees (30°). Consequently, the detection area of this sensor is a 30° sector of a circumference, with 5 m radius, centered in the geometrical center of the vehicle (sensor position).

A detected obstacle (objects, including other vehicles) is represented through a set of line segments, which composes the obstacle surfaces observed in the sensor line-of-sight. These line segments indicate the presence of an obstacle surface (in a bi-dimensional surface). Figure 2 (sensor S1) illustrates an example of the obstacle detection, in which two segments of the object 'Obstacle' – $\overline{P1P2}$ and $\overline{P2P3}$, observed in the line-of-sight of the sensor inside its detection area – are detected. As a sensor output, each segment point (P1 to P3) is represented by its distance from the sensor position (in meters) and the angle from the sensor longitudinal orientation (sensor rotation, in polar coordinates).

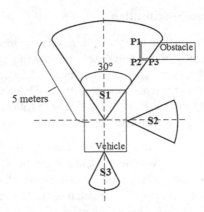

Fig. 2. Three sensors (S1, S2, and S3) instantiated in a vehicle.

3.2 OpenDS.sensor Implementation Details

To comply with the above mentioned three requirements (Req. 1 to Req. 3), the main implementations introduced in the native source code of OpenDS are:

1. Implementation of a new software class, named Sensor.java. Its main purpose is to define the sensors attributes and the methods used to inform about the obstacles detected by the instantiated sensors. Figure 3 illustrates the class diagram of the Sensor.java, where:
    a. Its attributes are the <range> (the maximum detection range of the sensor), <angle> (the maximum detection angle of the sensor), <position> (a vector representing the sensors position in the vehicle), <rotation> (direction of the sensor in relation to the longitudinal axes of the vehicle, in degrees).
    b. Its methods are <measure> (responsible for returning a list of all the obstacles detected by the sensor) and <getVisibleVertices> (used by the method <measure> to obtain the correct points of the detected segment).

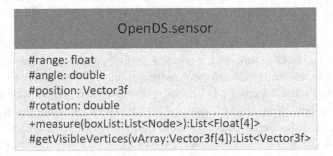

Fig. 3. Sensor.java class diagram.

2. Modifications in the OpenDS class (CANClient.java) that manages the communication between OpenDS (Vehicle component) and Matlab (Driver component). The information exchanged between these two tools uses a communication channel based on the CAN bus protocol. The structure of messages exchanged in this channel was modified, including fields to inform the receiver (Driver) about the number of line segments and the array of line segment points, as specified by Req. 3.
3. Implementation of methods used to manipulate the detected surface (line) segment to adapt them to the sensor characteristics. For example, depending on the detection area (detection angle and detection range) the sensor detects only part of the object thus, new points need to be settled. It is implemented in two methods: `getIntersection` (which provides the intersection between two line segments or between a line segment and a circle, depending on the arguments received by the method) and `getAngle2` (which provides the angle between three points).

All the obstacles in the traffic scenario are modeled as polygons by the OpenDS.sensor class model (Sensor.java). Hence, obstacles are represented by their set of line segments. Figure 4(a) illustrates a traffic scenario composed of 3 obstacles – segments sets {1, 2, 3, 4}, {5, 6, 7, 8}, and {9, 10, 11, 12}. A sensor identifies which obstacles (i.e. the set of line segments) are inside its detection area. Then, the parts of the line segments inside the sensor detection area are selected. Figure 4(b) illustrates parts of segments {5, 7, 8, 9, 10} being selected. Later, for each individual selected part of the segment, those that could be in the sensors line-of-sight are selected – in Fig. 4(c), segments {5, 9, 10}. In this implementation, each part of a line segment is defined by a pair of points, in which each point is obtained by its range (distance) and angle from the sensor (in polar coordinates).

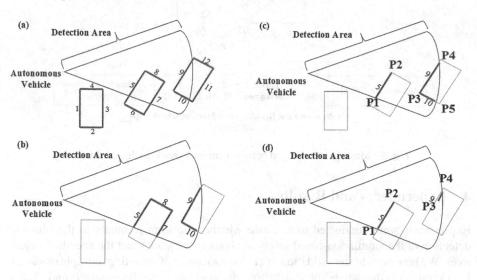

Fig. 4. Selection process of line segments.

The next step, after identifying the set of potential segments to be detected by the sensor, is to identify which segment parts shall be detected by a real-world obstacle detection sensor. Figure 4(d) illustrates segment 5 and part of segment 9 as the obstacles segment being detected by the sensor. In this part, the points are sometimes redefined only if the length of the segment changes from the previous steps. Therefore, after executing the detection process, a sensor identifies all the segments (pair of points representing them) of the obstacles observed by it that could potentially collide with the autonomous car.

Finally, the sensor informs the Driver about the detected list of line segments. The sensor informs the number of detected segments and, for each segment, the distance (meters) and angle (degrees) between the autonomous vehicle and each pair of segment points. In Fig. 4 scenario, the Driver receives information about two segments – 5 and 9, in terms of a pair of points (P1 and P2, P3 and P4) related to each segment (Fig. 4(d)).

Besides the modifications in OpenDS, adjustments to the Matlab tools are demanded to deal with the new sensor information exchanged between the Vehicle and the Driver (modeled in Matlab). Of the implementations made in Matlab, only the modules that receive and parse the message are changed. The message received by Matlab (Driver) has the following format (as exemplified in Fig. 5): number of segments detected ("1"); distance ("D1", "D2") and radial angle ("A1", "A2") between the minimum ("P1") and maximum ("P2") vertices of the segment and the sensor.

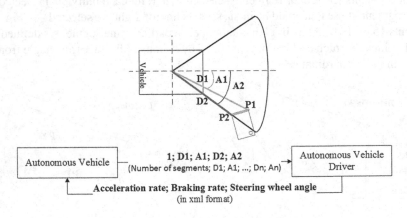

Fig. 5. Messages exchanged between autonomous vehicle and driver.

4   Experiments and Results

Experiments were conducted to evaluate whether the improvements in the obstacle detection of the simulation-based safety analysis framework meet the specified objectives. We here present the validation of (1) the capability of detecting multiple obstacles by a sensor; (2) the capability of detecting dynamic obstacles by a sensor; and (3) the capability of detecting the same obstacle by multiple sensors.

4.1   Evaluation of Multiple Obstacle Detection by a Sensor

In this experiment, the capacity of the instantiated sensor of detecting more than one obstacle is evaluated. The objective is to observe if the sensor could identify all the obstacle line segments in a single frame and inside its field of view. As the test scenario, a sensor is positioned in the center (roof) of a vehicle, with 0° of rotation, and configured with a maximum range of 25 m, a maximum detection angle of 360° (omnidirectional). Three obstacles are placed around this vehicle. Figure 6 illustrates this test scenario besides representing the detection area and the identified segments.

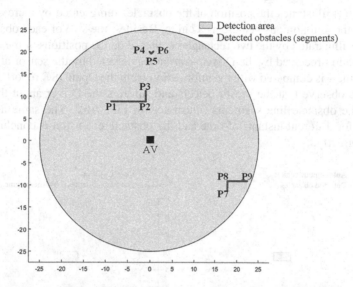

Fig. 6. Test scenario view: 3 obstacles, sensor detection area and detection results.

When evaluating this scenario, the sensor detected and sent Driver a message containing six (6) line segments and, consequently, 12 coordinates points (distance and angle in relation to the sensor position and rotation). The message sent was: {6; 20,05; −0,02; 19,63; −0,00; 19,63; −0,00; 19,97; 0,02; 11,19; 0,09; 9,04; 0,11; 9,04; 0,11; 12,74; 0,79; 20,90; −2,12; 20,00; −2,04; 20,00; −2,04; 23,98; −1,96}. It can be observed that the sensor correctly identifies the segments and its points (line segments). Furthermore, the implementation is concluded to comply with Req. 2 (sensor characteristics) and Req. 3 (surfaces detection).

4.2   Evaluation of Dynamic Obstacle Detection by a Sensor

This experiment aims to observe whether a sensor can detect multiple moving obstacles, or specifically, to observe if the detected line segments in a specific instant of time matches the ground truth position of the obstacles in the scenario. The same sensor configuration applied to this scenario as in the former test; the moving obstacles are a truck and a car, both at a speed of 30 km/h. The vehicle equipped with the sensor is placed at the origin of the coordinate system (0, 0) and the obstacles follow a repetitive straight path: the car starts at coordinate (0,10) and end to coordinate (50, 10); the truck path is from (−25, 0) to (0, −25). Whenever the obstacle encounters its end point, it immediately returns to its starting point. To verify the correct operation of the sensor at different instants of time, the information received by the Driver (obstacles detected by the sensor) is compared with the information of the real position of the obstacles collected from the OpenDS simulation scenario. Note that OpenDS, in its native version, allows the user to collect data during the simulation. Thus, we used this information to obtain the real position of the obstacles and compared them with the segments identified by the sensor.

Figure 7(a) illustrates the position of the obstacles represented by a cross, and the position of the autonomous vehicle as a circle. Besides, the size of each obstacle was obtained, as illustrated by the two rectangles centered on the positions of the obstacles. The information received by the Driver – obstacles detected by the sensor at the same instant of time – is compared with the information from the OpenDS® report. From this activity, we observe that the sensor detects and informs the Driver about the correct extent of the obstacle line segments (illustrated in Fig. 7(b)). The same analysis is performed for different instants of time and the obstacle extension is concluded to be detected correctly.

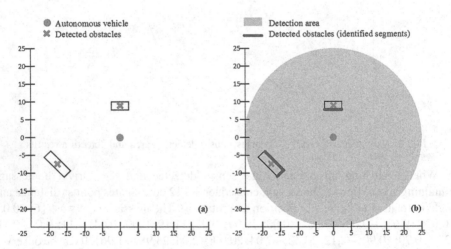

Fig. 7. Real position of test scenario elements (a) and detected obstacles line segments (b).

4.3 Evaluation of Obstacle Detection by Multiple Sensors

In this experiment, the objective is to observe whether it is possible to instantiate more than one sensor (Req. 1) and to observe how an obstacle is detected by different sensors. Two sensors are instantiated in the test scenario. The first sensor (S1) is positioned in the center (roof) of the vehicle, with −90° of rotation, and configured with a maximum range of 25 m and a maximum detection angle of 180°. The second sensor (S2) is positioned in the center (roof) of the vehicle, with 180° of rotation, and configured with a maximum range of 25 m, and a maximum detection angle of 90°. Five obstacles are placed around the autonomous vehicle: two cars positioned on the vertical axes, two cars on the longitudinal axes, and a truck on the diagonal axes positioned about 20 m away, as illustrated in Fig. 8(a). Besides, both autonomous vehicle and obstacles were considered static in the scenario.

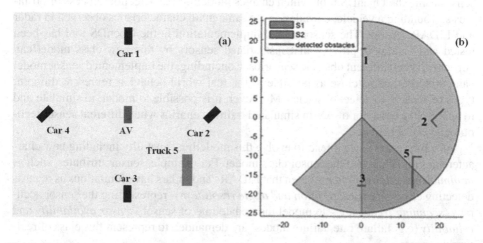

Fig. 8. Test scenario: (a) the top view and (b) the two sensors characteristic and detection results representation.

Figure 8(b) illustrates the coverage area of S1 and S2, as well as the detected obstacle surfaces (line segments). Sensor S1 detected obstacles 1 (half of it), 2 (two surfaces), 3 (half of it), and 5 (two surfaces). Sensor S2 detected obstacles 3 (one surface) and 5 (part of it). We observe that only obstacles within the detection areas of the sensors are detected, as expected. It is worth mentioning that when the same obstacle is detected by more than one sensor, the information about this obstacle is sent more than once (obstacles number 5 and 3). Therefore, sensor S1 obtained six segments and sensor S2 obtained two segments.

5   Concluding Remarks

This paper improves some limitations of the native OpenDS (an open-source driving simulation tool) in modeling real-world road transportation system elements. This tool, combined with Matlab, is used to support the real-time simulation (ReTS) capabilities of a new simulation-based safety analysis framework approach proposed by the authors [5]. In this Framework, the ReTS capabilities are applied to modeling, simulating and analyzing the behavior of autonomous vehicles in simulated traffic scenarios. This framework has proven to be capable of analyzing the impacts of concepts, technologies and procedures over the future road transportation system safety. However, it has limitations as regards modeling the main characteristics of the obstacle detection sensors currently used in the AV deployment [5]. Hence, improving the simulation tools capabilities in modeling systems as close as possible to real-world systems is demanded, given that assuring the AV safety is a mandatory issue.

We have here presented the development of a model (class) of obstacle detection sensor using the OpenDS tool, which enables modeling the detection process of obstacles surrounding a vehicle, considering the same main characteristics observed in radar and LiDAR sensors. The sensor model implementation in the OpenDS tool has been tested and validated, proving that instantiated sensors by this new class model can correctly detect different obstacle scenarios. Concluding, the implemented sensor model can correctly, and as close as possible to the real-world behavior, represent different types of sensors to detect obstacles. Moreover, it is possible to model, to simulate and to analyze the behavior of AV in simulated traffic scenarios when different sensor technologies are considered.

As a future work, we intend to evolve this modeling capability including new characteristics (attributes) to the sensor class model. For example, sensor attributes, such as *minimum detection distance* – given that LiDARs and radars have limitations as regards detecting close obstacles, *position and angle resolution* – representing the sensor accuracy, *scanning frequency* – to model the update rate of sensor, *sensor availability* and *reliability* (e.g. failure rate, failure modes) are demanded to represent this class of real-world sensors.

Acknowledgments. This work is supported by the Research, Development and Innovation Center, Ericsson Telecomunicações S.A., Brazil. The authors are also grateful for the valuable suggestions of the anonymous reviewers.

References

1. Kalra, N., Paddock, S.M.: Driving to safety: how many miles of driving would it take to demonstrate autonomous vehicle reliability? Transp. Res. Part A: Policy Pract. **94**, 182–193 (2016)
2. Kim, B., et al.: Testing Autonomous Vehicle Software in the Virtual Prototyping Environment. IEEE Embed. Syst. Lett. **9**(1), 5–8 (2017)
3. Molina, C.B.S.T., et al.: A comparison of two simulators to support safety analysis in autonomous vehicles. In: Proceedings of European Safety and Reliability Conference (ESREL), Paper ID 844
4. NHTSA Automated driving systems 2.0: a vision for safety, Washington DC. (2017). https://www.nhtsa.gov/sites/nhtsa.dot.gov/files/documents/13069a-ads2.0_090617_v9a_tag.pdf. Accessed 10 May 2018
5. OpenDS. http://www.opends.eu/software/download. Accessed 20 May 2018
6. Vismari, L.F., et al.: A simulation-based safety analysis framework for autonomous vehicles – assessing impacts on road transport system's safety and efficiency. In: Haugen, S., et al. (eds.) Safety and Reliability – Safe Societies in a Changing World, pp. 2067–2075. CRC Press, London (2018)

A Security Analysis of the ETSI ITS Vehicular Communications

Alexandru Constantin Serban[1,2]([⊠]), Erik Poll[1], and Joost Visser[1,2]

[1] Radboud University, Nijmegen, The Netherlands
{a.serban,erikpoll}@cs.ru.nl
[2] Software Improvement Group, Amsterdam, The Netherlands
{a.serban,j.visser}@sig.eu

Abstract. This paper analyses security aspects of the ETSI ITS standard for co-operative transport systems, where cars communicate with each other (V2V) and with the roadside (V2I) to improve traffic safety and make more efficient use of the road system. We focus on the initial information exchange between vehicles and the road side infrastructure responsible for authentication and authorisation, because all the security aspects for these interactions are regulated in the ETSI ITS standards. Other services running in vehicular networks are open to choose application-specific security requirements and implement them using features from the ETSI ITS standard. We note some possibilities for replay attacks that, although they have limited impact, could be prevented using simple techniques, some of which are directly available in the ETSI ITS standard.

Keywords: Intelligent vehicles · Security · Access control

1 Introduction

Adding cognitive intelligence to vehicles is considered to be the next evolution step in order to improve traffic efficiency and safety. One of the first abilities to be deployed for this is communication. Through communication, vehicles can exchange traffic updates with other vehicles or the road-side infrastructure to enhance their context awareness for more efficient and safer use of the road. Applications which involve an exchange of information between two or more vehicles are called *co-operative driving applications*. A wide range of acronyms describe the communication between vehicles and other entities. *Vehicle-to-vehicle* (V2V) allows vehicles to talk with others and relay information in real time. *Vehicle-to-infrastructure* (V2I) allows vehicles to communicate with static stations such as traffic lights or weather stations. *Vehicle-to-everything* (V2X) incorporates all types of communication and serves as a generic acronym that will be used throughout this paper.

An example of co-operative driving is *platooning*; a scenario in which a string of vehicles autonomously follow a leader, by sharing acceleration and steering

---

This research was funded by NWO through the i-CAVE project.

B. Gallina et al. (Eds.): SAFECOMP 2018 Workshops, LNCS 11094, pp. 365–373, 2018.
https://doi.org/10.1007/978-3-319-99229-7_31

information. It has been shown that platooning can increase traffic efficiency and highway throughput by minimising the distance between vehicles [1–3]. Moreover, the feasibility of platooning was demonstrated through the Grand Co-operative contests [4, 5].

Another example of co-operative driving application is broadcasting of traffic events and emergency messages in highway settings. For example, a stationary vehicle at a potentially dangerous location can periodically broadcast a warning message to other vehicles, announcing its location and state. Other traffic participants can then use this information to plan new manoeuvres and avoid traffic disruptions.

The systems for co-operative applications support two communication models: a vehicle can exchange messages with other vehicles (V2V) or with the road-side infrastructure (V2I). V2V can be used in scenarios such as platooning or event broadcasting, while V2I allows a broader range of services such as authentication, regional updates distribution, or infotainment content delivery.

To meet fundamental security and privacy requirements, a complex software architecture and communication protocols are needed. Security plays a crucial role in co-operative applications because a security breach can easily lead to human casualties. Therefore, the international standard developing organisations have worked on technical standards intended to implement a unique and secure communication protocol that spans a broader region.

In Europe, the communication architecture and protocols are conceived and standardised by the *European Telecommunications Standards Institute* (ETSI), through the ETSI *Intelligent Transport Systems* (ITS) series of standards [6–12]. The acronym ETSI ITS will be used to indicate this collection of standards. When we target a specific document, we will explicitly mention its number (e.g. ETSI ITS 731). ETSI ITS is inspired by the IEEE 1609 family of standards developed and adopted in the US.

Previous work has shown that security requirements are often not met by early versions of communication protocols (e.g. think of SSL 1.0 or SSH 1.0). Moreover, since standard descriptions are complex and (unclearly) written in natural language, software implementations are often flawed [13–15].

The goal of this paper is to analyse the security requirements of ETSI ITS communication standard for co-operative vehicles. We focus on the initial communication between a vehicle and the road-side infrastructure that precedes a vehicle's access to a vehicular network. Several weaknesses that allow message replay and can lead to *denial-of-service* (DoS) attacks are identified. While the impact of DoS attacks on traffic safety is low, this paper shows the recurrent issue of protocol specifications failing to meet security requirements is perpetuated in the automotive industry as well.

The rest of the paper is organised as follows. Section 2 provides background information about the ETSI ITS communication model and software architecture. Section 3 presents the results of our security assessment. Related work is presented in Sect. 4, followed by conclusions and future research in Sect. 5.

2   Background

ETSI ITS publishes a collection of standards for co-operative driving applications. They are divided in three stages that address different concerns. Stage 1 introduces the 'macro' economical and strategic requirements and 'micro' system and standard requirements [7]. Stage 2 gives a detailed specifications of interaction patterns between vehicles and roadside infrastructure [8–12]. Stage 3 provides a mapping to concrete IEEE 1609 message types and presents custom extensions [6,16]. This is the description closest to implementation.

The ETSI ITS communication stack is very similar to the OSI model, as illustrated in Fig. 1, with the OSI stack in grey to the right of the ETSI ITS layers in colours.

In fact, ETSI ITS extends the OSI model by only adding two orthogonal layers: management and security, which provide cross-layer services to all levels of the stack. The security layer provides services to ensure confidentiality, integrity and availability. The management layer implements all operations that support certificate management, a necessary step for secure communication [9]. All these services can be independently accessed by any other layer.

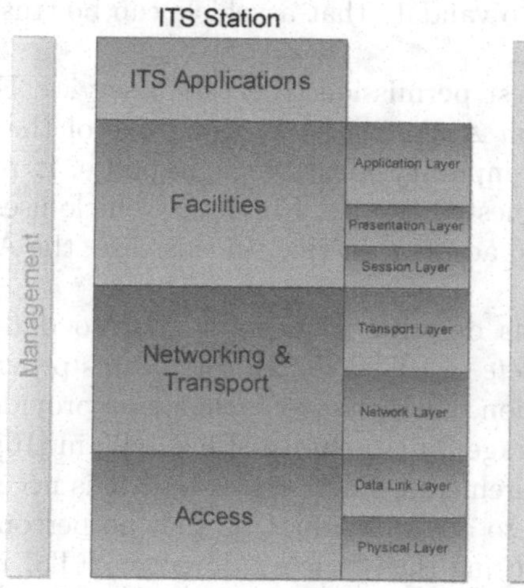

Fig. 1. The ETSI and OSI communication stacks [9].

Co-operative driving applications are deployed at the application layer, i.e. the highest layer in Fig. 1, and make use of the underlying communication facilities. ETSI ITS does not specify security requirements for applications, but only provides the infrastructure that applications can use to meet their security requirements.

Overall, we distinguish between two actors involved in communication:

1. *Infrastructure stations*: communication stations that do not act in a personal role and provide communication support.

2. *ITS Stations* (ITS-S): functional entities that act in a personal or public interest and correspond to personal or public assets such as cars, ambulances, communication poles, toll payment booths, etc.

Moreover, we distinguish two steps in the communication protocol:

1. Access Control: an exchange of information between an ITS-S and the infrastructure in order to prove identity (authentication) and gain access to a specific service (authorisation), and
2. Service consumption: communication between ITS-S in order to exchange traffic or infotainment information.

This paper focuses on the access control patterns because the security requirements for different services are not standardised and are set by the service providers.

An overview of the access control flow is depicted in Fig. 2. In order to get access to the communication infrastructure and services, a vehicle must, at first, contact an *Enrolment Authority* (EA) and *authenticate*. The EA answers with a set of pseudonymous certificates that help preserve the true identity of a vehicle and, thus, the owner's privacy. In this case, the EA resembles the road registration authority and it's able to validate that a vehicle can be trusted to function correctly within the network.

The next step is to request permission to access a service. For this, a vehicle contacts an *Authorisation Authority* (AA) using one of the pseudonymous certificates representing a temporary identity. In response, it receives a set of certificates, one for each requested service. Finally, a vehicle uses such a certificate received from the AA to access a service. In this case, the AA *authorises* a vehicle to use a service.

The ETSI ITS standards describe requests similar to database functions *create, read, update* and *delete* (CRUD) for all certificates provided by the EA or the AA. For each operation, the message exchange is provided as a stage 2 description in [8] and as a stage 3 mapping to IEEE 1609 in [16].

As general security requirements, ETSI states that it is necessary to ensure that data can not be linked to any individual, so that no personally identifying information is leaked when using the services. Moreover, ETSI requires that no authorised party are allowed to deduce the location or identity of an ITS station by analysing communication traffic which flows to and from an ITS vehicle.

In general, a security analysis includes, but is not limited to, an assessment of confidentiality, integrity, availability or freshness of information during an exchange between two parties. The following section investigates these aspects for the ETSI ITS communication.

3 Findings

This section presents an analysis of the communication for access control and identity management as specified by ETSI ITS. Three entities are involved, illustrated in Fig. 2: (1) a vehicle, referred to as ITS-S; (2) the enrolment authority,

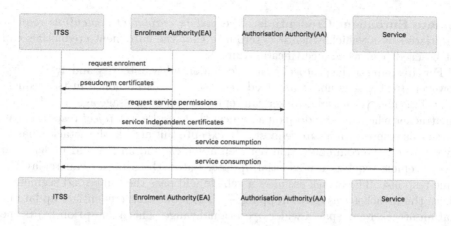

Fig. 2. Access control flow diagram in ETSI ITS vehicular networks.

or EA; and (3) an authorisation authority, or AA. Initially a vehicle request enrolment certificates from the EA. Afterwards, using one of the enrolment certificates, it requests permission to access a set of services from the AA and, finally, it gets to access a service.

The communication with service providers is not covered in this report because security requirements are service specific and not standardized. This model is called *verify-on-demand* (VoD): each service can individually request security checks from the security layer. The set of operations analysed are: request certificates (create), update certificates (update) and certificate revocation (delete).

We identify some weaknesses due to the lack of a cryptographic nonce in some communication requests. A nonce is as an arbitrary number specific only to one request, which ensures that old request bodies can not be used in replay attacks. It is usually implemented as a random number. It can also be implemented by a counter, but predictability of the nonce may then introduces weaknesses.

3.1 Communication of a Vehicle with an EA

The communication with an EA serves the purpose of issuing enrolment credentials for a vehicle. The EA can validate that a vehicle is trusted to function correctly and can access the network.

Obtain Enrolment Credentials. The *obtain enrolment credentials* request is initiated by a vehicle when it has no enrolment credentials for an operational region or at the beginning of its life cycle.

For this requests, the protocol ensures confidentiality, integrity, availability and freshness. However, this request is still worth mentioning because, unlike for the next requests discussed, here freshness is guaranteed by the use a cryptographic nonce, given as a *network challenge* in the request's body.

Update Enrolment Credentials. The *update enrolment credentials* request is initiated by a vehicle when it determines that the enrolment credentials can not be used (e.g. when a certificate expires).

For this request the protocol ensures confidentiality, integrity and availability. However, freshness is not guaranteed because there is no nonce in the request body. This means that an attacker can replay the same message again and again. An attacker who can eavesdrop on a request that results in a *reject* response, can re-use this response in future requests. To execute this attack, the attacker has to eavesdrop on the communication between a vehicle and an EA and understand that a vehicle requests a credential update. Later, the attacker can replay the same response. The attack assumes a vehicle will pass the same road segment – where the attacker was eavesdropping – when requesting credentials update or that an attacker can span a wider operational range. This assumption limits the impact of this replay attack.

Remove Enrolment Credentials. The *remove enrolment credentials* request is initiated by a vehicle when it leaves an operational region or when it wants to discard a pseudonym.

For this request the protocol ensures the same security requirements as the update enrolment credential request, i.e. confidentiality, integrity and availability, but again it fails to ensure freshness. The reason is the same: there is no nonce in the request body. An attacker can use the attack scenario as in Sect. 3.1. However, the probability that a vehicle passes the same road segment when requesting an enrolment revocation is small, given that the frequency of revocations is not high and often not correlated with the frequency of a vehicle passing through the same road segment.

3.2   Communication of a Vehicle with an AA

The communication with an AA occurs with higher frequency than the communication with an EA. The reason is that a vehicle will request authorisation tickets for a service before every usage. Moreover, the access to services expires faster than the enrolment credentials.

Similar to Sect. 3.1, all the requests made to AA include no nonce, allowing replay attacks. The impact and ways of mitigation are discussed in the following sub-section.

3.3   Discussion: Impact and Mitigations

To execute the replay attacks described above, an attacker needs to be in the vicinity of one or multiple static infrastructure stations. Since the frequency with which a vehicle requests the same information from a particular station is low, the impact of the replay attacks is also low. However, the findings presented in this paper illustrate a recurring problem with protocols specifications: it is not clear if the risk of these attacks is known and accepted or if the designers are unaware of it. In other words, it is not clear which security requirements are intended to be met by the various protocol requests. Such confusion can contribute to implementation flaws that can later have high impact [17].

The ETSI ITS specs do contain protection mechanisms against replay attacks, but omits them for some requests. These mechanisms are the inclusion of a cryptographic nonce (the so-called network challenge) in the request body, a sequence number, or a timestamp. We recommend to future developers to be aware of these mechanisms and use them appropriately.

A replay attack which contains certificates in the request's body can be partially protected against, namely if the implementation checks the certificate's expiry date. This way the implementation can detect replays. However, note that this does not work if the roadside replays 'permission denied' responses, as these do not contain any expiry date. Developers may not be aware of such mitigations or, even if they are aware, may simple forget to implement them. It is therefore important to mention these mitigations explicitly in the standard, so that developers can consider implementing them.

4   Related Work

Security in *vehicular ad-hoc networks* (VANET) attracted some early attention from researchers. However, since ETSI ITS is fairly new, with late edits still rolling on, there is little literature addressing it.

Bittl and Roscher analysed the complexity of VoD schemes in VANET [18]. Their analysis shows that VoD leads to a significant number of extra cross layer dependencies. Thus, the overall complexity of the ETSI ITS protocol stack is increased, while the separation of dedicated communication layers is reduced. Moreover, the number of interfaces that have to be protected against malformed inputs from wireless attacks is increased.

Bittl also analysed the security mechanisms from ETSI ITS and identified three main weaknesses [17]. Firstly, end-to-end multi-hop communication is not supported. This results in a single-hop distribution of certificates. Secondly, pseudonym management requires a dedicate start-up strategy after node startup. Thirdly, basic data sets of time and position are acquired from sources lacking security mechanisms and are used in a partly inconsistent way.

Closest to our work is the research by Nowdehi and Olovsson [19]. They implemented the ETSI ITS 103 097 [6] *SecuredMessage* service and found it difficult, given the complexity of the specifications. They noticed they ended up with bugs in their implementation due to these complexities, and found that another open source implementation that they tested contained very similar bugs, suggesting that the SecuredMessage format is inherently tricky to implement Specifically, they criticise the specification for being very liberal and overly permissive – e.g. by allowing multiple payloads in a single message, each of which may then be encrypted or not, and allowing additional *HeaderFieldTypes* not specified in the security profile. Complexity and unclarity in protocol specifications is the root cause behind many security vulnerabilities, as highlighted by the LangSec paradigm [20], so we fully agree with the recommendations of Nowdehi and Olovsson to remove these unwarranted complexities from the standard.

Research into privacy aspects of ETSI ITS has led to a proposal for a privacy improvement using shorter-lived certificates that are issued beforehand and then activated later over a low-bandwidth channel, e.g. using SMS [21].

5 Conclusions and Future Research

We have presented an initial security analysis of the ETSI ITS communication protocol for VANET, focused on the access control communication patterns. The analysis uncovered several ways to perform replay attacks inside VANET. However, the power of these attacks is smaller than in other cases (e.g. a bank application, where a payment replay can cause a bigger damage).

Some weaknesses can be mitigated by extending the message types described by ETSI ITS. Replay protection mechanisms are specified in the standard, however, it is not clear how to implement them for access control requests. The use of a cryptographic nonce, or a special message type that includes timestamps or a sequence number will solve the problems described in this paper.

As Nowdehi and Olovsson [19] and others (e.g. [13–15]) show, protocol specifications are easy to miss-interpreted leading to flawed and possibly insecure implementations. Testing specification conformance, however, is no straightforward job, because specs are written in natural language and often omit important details. As future research we suggest a formal description and analysis of the ETSI ITS protocol. Moreover, the implementations could be tested through fuzzing [15] or state machine learning [22].

Security plays a crucial role in a series of changes in the automotive industry where there is critical impact on traffic safety [23]. Since systems security is often defined as an arms-race, designing, adapting and implementing a protocol is a never ending process.

References

1. Al Alam, A., Gattami, A., Johansson, K.H.: An experimental study on the fuel reduction potential of heavy duty vehicle platooning. In: IEEE 13th International Conference on Intelligent Transportation Systems (ITSC) (2010)
2. Janssen, R., Zwijnenberg, H., Blankers, I., de Kruijff, J.: Truck platooning: driving the future of transportation (2015). http://publications.tno.nl/publication/34616035/dLIjFM/janssen-2015-truck.pdf. TNO Whitepaper
3. Davila, A., del Pozo, E., Aramburu, E., Freixas, A.: Environmental benefits of vehicle platooning. Technical report, SAE Technical Paper (2013)
4. Bergenhem, C., Shladover, S., Coelingh, E., Englund, C., Tsugawa, S.: Overview of platooning systems. In: 19th ITS World Congress (2012)
5. Kianfar, R., Augusto, B., Ebadighajari, A., Hakeem, U., Nilsson, J., Raza, A., Tabar, R.S., Irukulapati, N.V., Englund, C., Falcone, P., et al.: Design and experimental validation of a cooperative driving system in the grand cooperative driving challenge. IEEE Trans. Intell. Transp. Syst. 13(3), 994–1007 (2012)

6. ETSI: ETSI TS 103 097 (V1.1.1) - security header and certificate formats (2017). http://www.etsi.org/deliver/etsi_ts/103000_103099/103097/01.02.01_60/ts_103097v010201p.pdf
7. ETSI: ETSI TR 102 638 (V1.1.1) - vehicular communications; basic set of applications (2009). http://www.etsi.org/deliver/etsi_tr/102600_102699/102638/01.01.01_60/tr_102638v010101p.pdf
8. ETSI: ETSI TS 102 731 (V1.1.1) - security services and architecture (2010). http://www.etsi.org/deliver/etsi_ts/102700_102799/102731/01.01.01_60/ts_102731v010101p.pdf
9. ETSI: ETSI TS 102 940 (V1.1.1) - its communications security architecture and security management (2012). http://www.etsi.org/deliver/etsi_ts/102900_102999/102940/01.01.01_60/ts_102940v010101p.pdf
10. ETSI: ETSI TS 102 941 (V1.1.1) - trust and privacy management (2012). http://www.etsi.org/deliver/etsi_ts/102900_102999/102941/01.01.01_60/ts_102941v010101p.pdf
11. ETSI: ETSI TS 102 942 (V1.1.1) - access control (2012). http://www.etsi.org/deliver/etsi_ts/102900_102999/102942/01.01.01_60/ts_102942v010101p.pdf
12. ETSI: ETSI TS 102 943 (V1.1.1) - confidentiality services (2012). http://www.etsi.org/deliver/etsi_ts/102900_102999/102943/01.01.01_60/ts_102943v010101p.pdf
13. Kaloper-Mersinjak, D., Mehnert, H., Madhavapeddy, A., Sewell, P.: Not-quite-so-broken TLS: lessons in re-engineering a security protocol specification and implementation. In: 24th USENIX Security Symposium (2015)
14. Poll, E., Schubert, A.: Verifying an implementation of SSH. In: WITS 2007 (2007)
15. De Ruiter, J., Poll, E.: Protocol state fuzzing of TLS implementations. In: USENIX Security Symposium (2015)
16. ETSI: ETSI TS 102 867 (V1.1.1) - stage 3 mapping for IEEE 1609.2 (2012). http://www.etsi.org/deliver/etsi_ts/102900_102999/102940/01.01.01_60/ts_102940v010101p.pdf
17. Bittl, S.: Towards solutions for current security related issues in ETSI ITS. In: Mendizabal, J., Berbineau, M., Vinel, A., Pfletschinger, S., Bonneville, H., Pirovano, A., Plass, S., Scopigno, R., Aniss, H. (eds.) Nets4Cars/Nets4Trains/Nets4Aircraft 2016. LNCS, vol. 9669, pp. 136–148. Springer, Cham (2016). https://doi.org/10.1007/978-3-319-38921-9_15
18. Bittl, S., Roscher, K.: Feasibility of Verify-on-Demand in VANETs (2016)
19. Nowdehi, N., Olovsson, T.: Experiences from implementing the ETSI ITS SecuredMessage service. In: IEEE Intelligent Vehicles Symposium (IV 2018) (2014)
20. Poll, E.: LangSec revisited: input security flaws of the second kind. In: IEEE 5th Workshop on Language-Theoretic Security (LangSec 2018), Security and Privacy Workshops (SPW) (2018)
21. Verheul, E.R.: Issue First Activate Later certificates for V2X - combining ITS efficiency with privacy (2016). https://eprint.iacr.org/2016/1158
22. Fiterău-Broştean, P., Lenaerts, T., Poll, E., de Ruiter, J., Vaandrager, F., Verleg, P.: Model learning and model checking of SSH implementations. In: Proceedings of the 24th ACM SIGSOFT International SPIN Symposium on Model Checking of Software. ACM (2017)
23. Serban, A.C., Poll, E., Visser, J.: Tactical safety reasoning. a case for autonomous vehicles. In: IEEE International Workshop on Connected, Automated and Autonomous Vehicles (Ca2V) (2018)

Real-Time Driver Behaviour Characterization Through Rule-Based Machine Learning

Fabio Martinelli[1], Francesco Mercaldo[1(✉)], Vittoria Nardone[2],
Antonella Santone[3], and Gigliola Vaglini[4]

[1] Institute for Informatics and Telematics,
National Research Council of Italy (CNR), Pisa, Italy
{fabio.martinelli,francesco.mercaldo}@iit.cnr.it
[2] Department of Engineering, University of Sannio, Benevento, Italy
vnardone@unisannio.it
[3] Department of Bioscience and Territory, University of Molise, Pesche, IS, Italy
antonella.santone@unimol.it
[4] Department of Information Engineering, University of Pisa, Pisa, Italy
gigliola.vaglini@unipi.it

Abstract. Modern car-embedded technologies enabled car thieves to perform new ways to steal cars. In order to avoid auto-theft attacks, in this paper we propose a machine learning based method to silently and continuously profile the driver by analyzing built-in vehicle sensors. The proposed method exploits rule-based machine learning with the aim to discriminate between the car owner and impostors. Furthermore, we discuss how the rules generated by the rule-based algorithm can be adopted in order to discriminate between different driving styles.

Keywords: Automotive · Privacy · Machine learning · Authentication

1 Introduction

The FBI annual report includes the (attempted) theft of automobiles, trucks, buses, motorcycles, scooters, snowmobiles and other vehicles in its definition of motor vehicle theft.

As highlighted from FBI[1] automotive vulnerabilities may exist within a vehicle's wireless communication functions, within a mobile device as a smartphone or a tablet connected to the vehicle through USB, Bluetooth, or Wi-Fi but also within a third-party device connected through a vehicle diagnostic port.

In these cases, it may be possible for an attacker to remotely exploit these vulnerabilities and gain access to the vehicle's controller network or to data stored on the vehicle. Although vulnerabilities may not always result in an attacker being able to access all parts of the system, the safety risk to consumers could

---

[1] https://www.ic3.gov/media/2016/160317.aspx.

© Springer Nature Switzerland AG 2018
B. Gallina et al. (Eds.): SAFECOMP 2018 Workshops, LNCS 11094, pp. 374–386, 2018.
https://doi.org/10.1007/978-3-319-99229-7_32

increase significantly if the access involves the ability to manipulate critical vehicle control systems.

About \$5.9 billion was lost to motor vehicle theft in 2016: the average dollar loss per theft was \$7,680. Motor vehicles were stolen at a rate of 236.9 per 100,000 people in 2016, up 6.6% from 2015[2].

From the report it emerges that there was an up-tick in the number of vehicles stolen in 2015 and 2016, up by 3.8% and 7.4%, respectively. Furthermore, data from the FBI show that in the first half of 2017, vehicle thefts increased by another 4.1%.

As a matter of fact, the industry observers caution that thieves constantly devise new and sophisticated means of stealing autos [9]. Tactics usually include acquiring smart keys [10], which eliminated hot-wiring to steal cars; switching vehicle identification numbers; and using stolen identities to secure loans for expensive vehicles [1,11]. The number of vehicles stolen with the key or keyless entry device left inside by the owner climbed 22% in 2015 to 57,096, according to the NICB[3].

Starting from these considerations, in this paper we propose a method aimed to continuously and silently authenticate drivers to their car. The proposed methodology exploits rule-based machine learning in order to discriminate between the car owner and impostors. Furthermore, we obtain a set of rule driver-related, in order to demonstrate that each driver exhibit a different driving style.

The paper poses the following research question:

- Is it possible to discriminate between car owner and impostors using rule-based machine learning?

The paper proceeds as follows: Sect. 2 discusses related work; Sect. 3 deeply describes and motivates the detection method; Sect. 4 illustrates the results of the experiments and finally, conclusions are drawn in Sect. 5.

2   Related Work

In this section we review the current state-of-the-art related to the driver identification topic.

Authors in [7] propose a method based on driving pattern of the car. They consider mechanical features from the CAN vehicle evaluating them with four different classification algorithms, obtaining an accuracy equal to 0.939 with Decision Tree, equal to 0.844 with k Nearest Neighbor (KNN), equal to 0.961 with RandomForest and equal to 0.747 using Multilayer Perceptron (MLP) algorithm.

Similarly to our work, the main aim of this work is to differentiate between car owner and impostors. However, differently from this work our aim is also to

---

[2] https://www.iii.org/fact-statistic/facts-statistics-auto-theft.
[3] https://www.nicb.org/.

individuate if it is possible to discriminate drivers using a rule-based approach. In particular if it is possible to extract some behavioural rules, related to the drivers, able to discriminate ad identify every driver from each other.

The authors of [13] consider cepstral features of each driver obtained through spectral analysis of driving signals are modeled with a Gaussian Mixture Model (GMM): GMM driver model based on cepstral features is evaluated in driver identification experiments using driving signals collected in a driving simulator and in a real vehicle on a city road. They categorized the observed driving signals into three groups: Driving behavioral signals (i.e., gas pedal pressure, brake pedal pressure, and steering angle); Vehicle status signals (i.e., velocity, acceleration, and engine speed) and Vehicle position signals (i.e., following distance, relative lane position, and yaw angle). Experimental results show that the driver model based on cepstral features achieves a driver identification rate of 89.6% for driving simulator and 76.8% for real vehicle, resulting in 61% and 55% error reduction, respectively, over a conventional driver model that uses raw driving signals without spectral analysis.

A hidden-Markov-model-(HMM)-based similarity measure is proposed in [6] in order to model driver human behavior. They employ a simulated driving environment to test the effectiveness of the proposed solution.

The Authors of [14] consider the kernel density estimation with the aim to extract features. Then, they consider these features to recognize the emotion of the driver by using multi layer perceptron algorithm as classifiers. The data collection was conducted in Singapore during vacation time. The driver must have at least two years driving experience. They managed to collect 11 drivers including men and women, aged between 24–25 years old. The considered features are the brake and gas pedal pressures. In the experiment they state that each driver meets the accuracy level which is more than 50%: the highest accuracy is obtained from driver 10 with an accuracy equal to 71.94%, while the lowest accuracy is obtained from driver 3 with an accuracy equal to 61.65% in classification according to the other driver.

3   The Method

In this section we describe our method to identify driver behavior using data retrieved by CAN bus. As stated in the introduction, real data [1, 7], processed from in-vehicle CAN data, are considered. In order to collect data, the On Board Diagnostics 2 (OBD-II) and OBD Super Mini ELM327 Bluetooth[4] as OBD-II scanner are used. The recent vehicle has many measurement sensors and control sensors, so the vehicle is managed by ECU in it. ECU is the device that controls parts of the vehicle such as Engine, Automatic Transmission, and Antilock Braking System (ABS). OBD refers to the self-diagnostic and reports capability by monitoring vehicle system in terms of ECU measurement and vehicle failure. The data are recorded every 1 s during driving.

---

[4] http://www.totalcardiagnostics.com/elm327-bluetooth/.

Table 1. Features involved in the study.

Feature	Description	Info
F1	CO_2 in g/km	(Instantaneous)(g/km)
F2	Engine Load(%)	Expressed in g/s
F3	Engine RPM	Revolutions per minute
F4	Fuel flow rate/minute	Expressed in cc/min
F5	Fuel remaining	Expressed in liters
F6	Turbo Boost & Vacuum Gauge	Expressed in psi

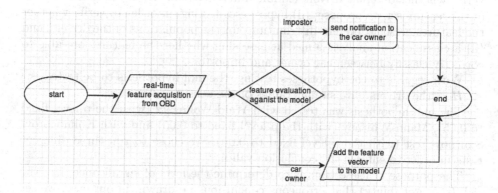

Fig. 1. The flow diagram of the proposed approach

We considered a real-environment and not a simulated one in order to examine all possible real-world variables, for instance: slowdowns traffic lights and all the possible variables that are not considerable in a simulated environment.

We consider, in this preliminary work, six features, as shown in Table 1. Figure 1 depicts the flow diagram of the proposed method:

- the *real-time feature acquisition from OBD* is the module responsible to gather the feature vector from the vehicle under analysis OBD interface;
- the *feature evaluation against the model* is the module able to test the feature vector obtained in the previous step against to the model, the output of this step is a label related to the feature vector: the model will mark it as belonging to the car owner, otherwise it will be marked as belonging to another driver i.e., an impostor;
- the *send notification to the car owner* module is invoked whether the feature vector is not identified as belonging to the car owner: it sends a notification to the mobile device of the car owner in order to inform him/her;
- the *add the feature vector to the model* module is invoked whether the feature vector is marked as belonging to the car owner: in this case it will be added to the model in order to increase the reliability of the model in car owner identification.

We designed an experiment in order to evaluate the effectiveness of the feature vector we propose, expressed through the research question stated in the introduction.

More specifically, the experiment is aimed at verifying whether the feature set is able to discriminate the car owner by impostors.

The classification is carried out by using rule-based classifier built with the feature set shown in Table 1. As a matter of fact, the assumption (as explained into the Sect. 1) is that different driving style can be discriminated by using machine learning able to automatically gather rules for each driving style.

The evaluation consists of three different stages: (i) descriptive statistics, to verify whether different drivers exhibit different trends from the point of view of the feature set we propose; (ii) hypotheses testing, in order to verify whether the features present different distributions for the populations of the drivers; and (ii) a classification analysis aimed at assessing whether the features are able to correctly classify between car owner and impostors.

With regards to the hypotheses testing, the null hypothesis to be tested is:

H_0: "the drivers have similar values of the considered features".

The null hypothesis was tested with Wald-Wolfowitz (with the p-level fixed to 0.05), Mann-Whitney (with the p-level fixed to 0.05) and with Kolmogorov-Smirnov Test (with the p-level fixed to 0.05). We chose to run three different tests in order to enforce the conclusion validity.

The purpose of these tests is to determine the level of significance, i.e., the risk (the probability) that erroneous conclusions be drawn: in our case, we set the significance level equal to .05, which means that we accept to make mistakes 5 times out of 100.

The classification analysis was aimed at assessing whether the feature set is able to correctly classify car owner and impostors.

We adopt the supervised learning approach, considering that the driver features evaluated in this work contain the driver labels.

The supervised learning approach is composed of two different steps:

1. **Learning Step**: starting from the labeled dataset (i.e., where each feature is related to a class. In our case, the class is represented by the driver), we filter the data in order to obtain a feature vector. The feature vectors, belonging to all the ten drivers involved in the experiment with the associated labels, represent the input for the machine learning algorithm that is able to build a model from the analyzed data. The output of this step is the model obtained by the labeled dataset.
2. **Prediction Step**: the output of this step is the classification of a feature vector belonging to the car owner or to an impostor. Using the model built in the previous phase, we input this model using a feature vector without the label: the classifier will output with their label prediction (i.e., car owner or impostor).

The classification analysis was accomplished with Weka[5], a suite of machine learning software, largely employed in data mining for scientific research.

---

[5] http://www.cs.waikato.ac.nz/ml/weka/.

4   Experimental Evaluation

In this section we describe the real-world dataset used in the evaluation of the proposed method and the results of the experiment.

For the sake of clarity, the results of the evaluation will be discussed reflecting the data analysis' division in three phases discussed in previous section: descriptive statistics, hypotheses testing and classification.

4.1   The Dataset

We constructed a dataset gathering data from the CAN bus from real vehicles using the OBD scanner. The OBD scanner was installed on the vehicles to produce a self-diagnostic report generated by the onboard monitoring system. The data is recorded every second during driving using Torque Pro application[6] running on an Android smartphone fixed in the car using an adequate support. We considered a path traveled by 10 drivers (i.e., D1, D2, D3, D4, D5, D6, D7, D8, D9 and D10) with the same car.

The path traveled by 10 drivers is a fixed path. They have driven at different moments during the day: starting from early morning up to the late evening. The experiment was conducted in this way in order to consider every traffic conditions. The path also involves different kinds of road routes: from the city roads to the highway. The path was defined in such way in order to take into account also the variability of the roads. Finally, the path length was of 30 Km and it is located in the Naples area.

4.2   Descriptive Statistics

The analysis of box plots related to the six features helps to identify whether the features are helpful to discriminate between different drivers.

Figure 2 shows the boxplots related to the distributions of the considered features between the 10 drivers involved in the experiment.

The "(a)" box shows the boxplot related to the F1 feature (i.e., CO_2ing/km): the median of several drivers (i.e., D1, D2, D3, D4) is similar, this is symptomatic that most of the drivers involved in the experiment exhibit a similar driving style, but the D1, D6 and D8 boxplots are wider if compared with the other ones and this can be symptomatic that their consumption is ranging is a greater interval if compared with the other ones.

The "(b)" box shows the boxplot for the F2 feature (i.e., Engine Load(%), from the point of view of these distributions we can highlight that the D1 driver is the one that strives more the engine: as a matter of fact, the D1 driver boxplot is the wider with respect to the other ones. Also the D2, D3, D5 and D10 strive their engine, but to a lesser extent if compared with D1 driver. The D5, D8 and D8 drivers exhibit the most regular engine load, as a matter of fact their boxplots

---

[6] https://play.google.com/store/apps/details?id=org.prowl.torquefree.

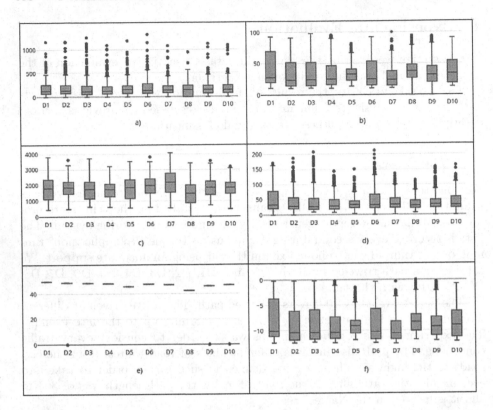

Fig. 2. Boxplots related to the features under analysis: the "(a)" box shows the boxplot for the F1 feature, the "(b)" box shows the boxplot for the F2 feature (i.e., Engine Load(%), the "(c)" box is related to the boxplot for the F3 feature (i.e., Engine RPM), the "(d)" box shows the boxplot for the F4 feature (i.e., Fuel flow rate/minute), the "(e)" box shows the boxplot for the F5 feature (i.e., Fuel remaining), while the "(f)" box shows the boxplot for the F6 feature (i.e., Turbo Boost & Vacuum Gauge).

are the smallest: this is symptomatic that when they are driving their engines is working with the same engine load (i.e., they exhibit a constant driving style).

The "(c)" box is related to the boxplot for the F3 feature (i.e., Engine RPM). From this boxplot we can see that the D7 driver keeps the engine at a higher number of revolutions if compared to the other ones (the D7 driver boxplot is the widest), while the D2, D4, D9 and D10 drivers exhibit the thinner boxplot (this can be symptomatic that the D4 driver is the one with the most constant RPMs). The remaining drivers (i.e., D1, D3, D5, D6, D7, D10 do not exhibit particular differences in their boxplots, they are pretty similar.

The "(d)" box is related to the boxplot for the F4 feature (i.e., Fuel flow rate/minute). The Fuel flow rate/minute is symptomatic of the fuel consumption of the vehicle, this is the reason it can be useful to understand some aspect related to the driving style. For instance, the D1 exhibits the widest boxplot, for this reason its driving style is requiring more fuel if compared with the other drivers: this aspect can be symptomatic of an aggressive driving style. From the other side, the D5 exhibits the thinner boxplot: its driving style is requiring a constant fuel rate/minute: this can be symptomatic of a regular driving style.

The "(e)" box shows the boxplot for the F5 feature (i.e., Fuel remaining). From this boxplot we do not highlight different behaviours between the several drivers involved in the experiment: as a matter of fact, they exhibit very similar distributions, with the exception of the D8 driver that exhibits a lower distribution if compared with the ones of the other drivers.

The "(f)" box shows the boxplot for the F6 feature (i.e., Turbo Boost & Vacuum Gauge). These distributions are related to the usage of the car turbo and can be related to the driving style. For instance, the D1 driver exhibits the widest boxplot, this is symptomatic of its massive usage of the turbo of the car and this aspect can be related to the driver aggressiveness. The D2, D3, D4, D6 and D10 drivers perform a moderate usage of the turbo, while the remaining drivers (i.e., D5, D7, D8 and D9 drivers) considering that exhibit the thinner distributions, we can state that their usage of the turbo is the lowest, this is the reason why they can be considered as not aggressive drivers.

4.3   Hypothesis Testing

The hypothesis testing aims at evaluating if the features present different distributions for the populations of the 10 drivers involved in the experiment with statistical evidence.

We assume valid the results when the null hypothesis is rejected by the three tests performed.

Table 2 shows the null hypothesis H_0 test.

Table 2. Results of the null hypothesis H_0 test.

# Feature	Wald-Wolfowitz	Mann-Whitney	Kolmogorov-Smirnov
F1	0,000	0,000	p < .001
F2	0,000	0,000	p < .001
F3	0,000	0,000	p < .001
F4	0,000	0,000	p < .001
F5	0,000	0,000	p < .001
F6	0,000	0,000	p < .001

All the features are able to successfully pass the Wald-Wolfowitz, the Mann-Whitney and the Kolmogorov-Smirnov tests.

4.4   Classification Analysis

In this preliminary work we classified the obtained features using the NNge [8,16] rule-based classification algorithm.

Five metrics were used to evaluate the classification results: False Positive (FP) rate, Precision, Recall, F-Measure and ROC Area.

The *FP rate* is computed as the ratio between the number of negative driver traces wrongly categorized as belonging to the owner (i.e., the false positives) and the total number of actual impostor traces (i.e., the true negatives): $FP\ rate = \frac{fp}{fp+tn}$, where *fp* indicates the number of false positives and *tn* the number of true negatives.

The *Precision* has been computed as the proportion of the examples that truly belong to class X among all those which were assigned to the class. It is the ratio of the number of relevant records retrieved to the total number of irrelevant and relevant records retrieved:

$Precision = \frac{tp}{tp+fp}$, where *tp* indicates the number of true positives and *fp* indicates the number of false positives.

The *Recall* has been computed as the proportion of examples that were assigned to class X, among all the examples that truly belong to the class, i.e., how much part of the class was captured. It is the ratio of the number of relevant records retrieved to the total number of relevant records: $Recall = \frac{tp}{tp+fn}$, where *tp* indicates the number of true positives and *fn* indicates the number of false negatives.

The *F-Measure* is a measure of a test's accuracy. This score can be interpreted as a weighted average of the precision and recall: $F\text{-}Measure = 2 * \frac{Precision*Recall}{Precision+Recall}$.

The *Roc Area* is defined as the probability that a positive instance randomly chosen is classified above a negative randomly chosen.

The classification analysis consisted of building classifiers in order to evaluate feature accuracy to distinguish the car owner by an impostor.

We considered a 10-fold cross validation with 80% of training dataset and 20% of testing dataset.

Table 3 shows the results of the classification analysis.

Table 3. FP Rate, Precision, Recall, F-Measure and RocArea.

Driver	FP Rate	Precision	Recall	F-Measure	RocArea
D1	0	1	1	1	1
D2	0	0.999	1	0.999	1
D3	0	1	1	1	1
D4	0	1	1	1	1
D5	0	1	1	1	1
D6	0	1	1	1	1
D7	0	1	1	1	1
D8	0	1	1	1	1
D9	0	1	0.999	1	1
D10	0	1	1	1	1

For all the drivers under analysis we obtain a precision and recall equal to 1. Only the D2 driver exhibits a precision equal to 0.999, while the driver D9 exhibits a precision equal to 0.999. The same trend is observable with regard to the F-Measure: as a matter of fact, only the D2 F-Measure is equal to 0.999, while the other drivers exhibit a F-Measure equal to 1. The same trend is observable with regard to RocArea (all drivers obtained 1 for this metric).

In order to have a better evidence about the misclassified instances between the driver under analysis, Table 4 shows the confusion matrix [17]. In the confusion matrix each row of the matrix represents the instances in a predicted class while each column represents the instances in an actual class (or vice versa) [15].

Table 4. Confusion matrix

a	b	c	d	e	f	g	h	i	j	Classified as
2398	0	0	0	0	0	0	0	0	0	a = D1
0	2922	0	1	0	0	0	0	0	0	b = D2
0	0	3073	0	0	0	0	0	0	0	c = D3
0	0	0	3106	0	0	0	0	0	0	d = D4
0	0	0	0	3846	0	0	0	0	0	e = D5
0	0	0	0	0	2794	0	0	0	0	f = D6
0	0	1	0	0	0	3009	0	0	0	g = D7
0	0	0	0	0	0	0	4151	0	0	h = D8
0	1	0	0	0	0	0	2	3267	0	i = D9
0	1	0	0	0	0	0	0	0	2833	j = D10

From the confusion matrix in Table 4, we observe that the only misclassification errors are related to only two instances, the first one related to the driver D2 that is labelled as belonging to the D9 driver, while the second one is related to the D4 driver that is labelled as belonging to the D2 driver.

Table 5 shows the rules extracted for the driver under analysis: the considered rule-based machine learning algorithm extracted 1 rule for driver.

As shown in Table 5, each driver is identified by its own rule: the feature vector is assigned to a driver whether the feature values are verified in the rule extracted. Considering that the rule-based algorithm was able to extract a different rule for each driver, and as highlighted from the confusion matrix (in Table 4), the rules are able to discriminate with different drivers with a precision and an recall equal to 1 (with exception of the D2 and D9 drivers), we can consider the i-th rule as characterizing of the behaviour of the i-th driver under analysis.

Table 5. The rule set extracted by the NNge rule-base machine learning algorithm.

#	Rule
D1	$0.0 <= F1 <= 1160.24169922 \wedge 10.98039246 <= F2 <= 92.94117737\wedge$ $434.0 <= F3 <= 3799.75 \wedge 0.0 <= F4 <= 171.47810364\wedge$ $49.42653656 <= F5 <= 49.79877853 \wedge -12.37939644 <= F6 <= -0.19622612$
D2	$0.0 <= F1 <= 1164.5357666 \wedge 10.58823586 <= F2 <= 90.98039246\wedge$ $468.75 <= F3 <= 3623.0 \wedge 0.0 <= F4 <= 186.95175171\wedge$ $48.64160156 <= F5 <= 49.00281143 \wedge -12.37939644 <= F6 <= -0.19622612$
D3	$0.0 <= F1 <= 1254.05834961 \wedge 10.98039246 <= F2 <= 98.03921509\wedge$ $617.25 <= F3 <= 3710.0 \wedge 9.45204163 <= F4 <= 207.32177734\wedge$ $48.23397446 <= F5 <= 48.59840775 \wedge -12.23435783 <= F6 <= -0.19622612$
D4	$0.0 <= F1 <= 1088.32873535 \wedge 10.58823586 <= F2 <= 95.29412079\wedge$ $602.75 <= F3 <= 3205.75 \wedge 7.70137358 <= F4 <= 144.01383972\wedge$ $47.80204773 <= F5 <= 48.14254379 \wedge -12.37939644 <= F6 <= -0.19622612$
D5	$0.0 <= F1 <= 1183.73730469 \wedge 13.72549057 <= F2 <= 81.5686264\wedge$ $550.75 <= F3 <= 3521.5 \wedge 3.36647606 <= F4 <= 150.65760803\wedge$ $45.38215256 <= F5 <= 45.7795639 \wedge -11.79924488 <= F6 <= -1.50156593$
D6	$0.0 <= F1 <= 1315.60339355 \wedge 10.58823586 <= F2 <= 92.15686798\wedge$ $586.75 <= F3 <= 3807.5 \wedge 0.22675589 <= F4 <= 211.76445007\wedge$ $47.37043381 <= F5 <= 47.75802994 \wedge -12.37939644 <= F6 <= -0.34126377$
D7	$0.0 <= F1 <= 1073.23742676 \wedge 10.98039246 <= F2 <= 100.0\wedge$ $534.0 <= F3 <= 4060.0 \wedge 1.06496859 <= F4 <= 135.25418091\wedge$ $46.96563721 <= F5 <= 47.32172775 \wedge -12.52443409 <= F6 <= -0.34126377$
D8	$0.0 <= F1 <= 941.16192627 \wedge 0.0 <= F2 <= 94.11764526\wedge$ $0.0 <= F3 <= 3415.25 \wedge 7.36353827 <= F4 <= 113.75313568\wedge$ $42.30183029 <= F5 <= 42.72509003 \wedge -11.74805641 <= F6 <= 0.0$
D9	$0.0 <= F1 <= 1119.75854492 \wedge 12.94117641 <= F2 <= 93.33333588\wedge$ $715.25 <= F3 <= 3551.5 \wedge 12.2160759 <= F4 <= 157.69128418\wedge$ $45.93281174 <= F5 <= 46.31466293 \wedge -11.94428253 <= F6 <= -0.34126377$
D10	$0.0 <= F1 <= 1091.08703613 \wedge 13.33333397 <= F2 <= 90.98039246\wedge$ $472.0 <= F3 <= 3181.25 \wedge 7.24365759 <= F4 <= 163.60809326\wedge$ $46.58006668 <= F5 <= 46.93938065 \wedge -12.08932018 <= F6 <= -0.77637672$

5   Conclusion and Future Work

Nowadays cars employ a plethora of sensors for several functions. This increasing technology is able to produce safer vehicles, but attackers are able to exploit the software running opening new theft scenarios. In this paper we propose a method aimed to discriminate between the car owner and impostors using a rule-based machine learning algorithm. We evaluated the proposed method on a dataset of 10 drivers, obtaining the analysed feature vector from the CAN bus of real-world car. High performances in terms of precision and recall are achieved. As future work, we plan to test other supervised classification approaches in order to improve and enrich our approach. Furthermore, we plan to investigate whether the application of formal methods [5] can be useful for the driver identification, which have been already successfully used in other domains like for example for malware detection [2,4,12] and in system biology [3].

Acknowledgment. This work has been partially supported by H2020 EU-funded projects NeCS and C3ISP and EIT-Digital Project HII and PRIN "Governing Adaptive and Unplanned Systems of Systems" and the EU project CyberSure 734815.

References

1. Bernardi, M.L., Cimitile, M., Martinelli, F., Mercaldo, F.: Driver and path detection through time-series classification. J. Adv. Transp. **2018**, 20 (2018)
2. Canfora, G., Martinelli, F., Mercaldo, F., Nardone, V., Santone, A., Visaggio, C.: LEILA: formal tool for identifying mobile malicious behaviour. IEEE Trans. Softw. Eng. (2018). https://doi.org/10.1109/TSE.2018.2834344
3. Ceccarelli, M., Cerulo, L., Santone, A.: De novo reconstruction of gene regulatory networks from time series data, an approach based on formal methods. Methods **69**(3), 298–305 (2014)
4. Cimitile, A., Mercaldo, F., Nardone, V., Santone, A., Visaggio, C.A.: Talos: no more ransomware victims with formal methods. Int. J. Inf. Secur. 1–20 (2017)
5. De Francesco, N., Lettieri, G., Santone, A., Vaglini, G.: Heuristic search for equivalence checking. Softw. Syst. Model. **15**(2), 513–530 (2016)
6. Enev, M., Takakuwa, A., Koscher, K., Kohno, T.: Automobile driver fingerprinting. Proc. Priv. Enhanc. Technol. **2016**(1), 34–50 (2016)
7. Kwak, B.I., Woo, J., Kim, H.K.: Know your master: driver profiling-based anti-theft method. In: PST, vol. 2016, pp. 211–218 (2016)
8. Martin, B.: Instance-based learning: nearest neighbor with generalization [thesis] (1995)
9. Martinelli, F., Mercaldo, F., Nardone, V., Orlando, A., Santone, A.: Who's driving my car? A machine learning based approach to driver identification (2018)
10. Martinelli, F., Mercaldo, F., Nardone, V., Santone, A.: Car hacking identification through fuzzy logic algorithms. In: 2017 IEEE International Conference on Fuzzy Systems (FUZZ-IEEE), pp. 1–7. IEEE (2017)
11. Martinelli, F., Mercaldo, F., Orlando, A., Nardone, V., Santone, A., Sangaiah, A.K.: Human behavior characterization for driving style recognition in vehicle system. Comput. Electr. Eng. (2018)
12. Mercaldo, F., Nardone, V., Santone, A., Visaggio, C.A.: Download malware? No, thanks. how formal methods can block update attacks. In: 2016 IEEE/ACM 4th FME Workshop on Formal Methods in Software Engineering (FormaliSE), pp. 22–28. IEEE (2016)
13. Miyajima, C., Nishiwaki, Y., Ozawa, K., Wakita, T., Itou, K., Takeda, K.: Cepstral analysis of driving behavioral signals for driver identification. In: 2006 IEEE International Conference on Acoustics, Speech and Signal Processing, 2006. ICASSP 2006 Proceedings, vol. 5, pp. V–V. IEEE (2006)

14. Nor, N.M., Wahab, A.: Driver identification and driver's emotion verification using KDE and MLP neural networks. In: 2010 International Conference on Information and Communication Technology for the Muslim World (ICT4M), pp. E96–E101. IEEE (2010)
15. Powers, D.M.: Evaluation: from precision, recall and F-measure to ROC, informedness, markedness and correlation (2011)
16. Roy, S.: Nearest neighbor with generalization. Christchurch, New Zealand (2002)
17. Stehman, S.V.: Selecting and interpreting measures of thematic classification accuracy. Remote Sens. Environ. **62**(1), 77–89 (1997)

1st International Workshop on Artificial Intelligence Safety Engineering (WAISE 2018)

1st International Workshop on Artificial Intelligence Safety Engineering (WAISE 2018)

Huáscar Espinoza[1] ⓘ, Orlando Avila-García[2], Rob Alexander[3] ⓘ, and Andreas Theodorou[4] ⓘ

[1] CEA LIST, CEA Saclay Nano-INNOV, Point Courrier 174,
91191 Gif-sur-Yvette, France
huascar.espinoza@cea.fr
[2] Atos Research & Innovation, Atos Spain, Calle Subida al Mayorazgo,
38110 Santa Cruz de Tenerife, Spain
orlando.avila@atos.net
[3] Department of Computer Science, University of York, Deramore Lane,
York YO10 5GH, UK
rob.alexander@york.ac.uk
[4] Department of Computer Science, University of Bath, Claverton Down,
Bath BA2 7AY, UK
a.theodorou@bath.ac.uk

1 Introduction

To achieve the full potential of *Artificial Intelligence (AI)* we need to guarantee a standard level of safety and settle issues such as compliance with ethical standards and liability for accidents involving, for example, autonomous cars. Deploying AI-based systems for operation in proximity to and/or in collaboration with humans implies that current *safety engineering* and legal mechanisms need to be revisited to ensure that individuals –and their properties– are not harmed and that the desired benefits outweigh the potential unintended consequences. Researchers, engineers and policy makers from different areas of expertise will need to be engaged in this huge challenge.

The different approaches taken to *AI safety* range from pure theoretical (moral philosophy or ethics) to pure practical (engineering) planes. It appears as essential to combine philosophy and theoretical science with applied science and engineering in order to create safe machines. This should become an interdisciplinary approach covering technical (engineering) aspects of how to actually create, test, deploy, operate, and evolve safe AI-based systems, as well as broader strategic, ethical and policy issues.

Increasing levels of AI in "smart" sensory-motor loops allow intelligent systems to perform in increasingly dynamic uncertain complex environments with increasing degrees of *autonomy*, with human being progressively ruled out from the control loop. Adaptation to the environment is being achieved by *Machine Learning (ML)* methods rather than more traditional engineering approaches, such as system modelling and programming. Recently, certain ML methods are showing promising performance and usability in real-world applications, such as deep learning, reinforcement learning, and their combination. However, the *inscrutability* or opaqueness of their statistical models for perception and decision making we build through them pose yet another challenge. Moreover, the combination of autonomy and inscrutability in these AI-based systems is particularly challenging in safety-critical applications, such as autonomous vehicles, personal care or assistive robots and collaborative industrial robots.

The *International Workshop on Artificial Intelligence Safety Engineering (WAISE)* is dedicated to explore new ideas on AI safety, ethically aligned design, regulations, and standards for AI-based systems. WAISE aims at bringing together experts, researchers, and practitioners from diverse communities, such as AI, safety engineering, ethics, standardization, certification, robotics, cyber-physical systems, safety-critical systems, and application domain communities such as automotive, healthcare, manufacturing, agriculture, aerospace, critical infrastructures, and retail. The first edition of WAISE was held in September 18, 2018, in Västerås (Sweden) as part of the 37th International Conference on Computer Safety, Reliability, & Security (SAFE-COMP 2018).

2   Programme

The Programme Committee (PC) received 34 submissions, in the following categories:

- Short position papers – 17 submissions.
- Full scientific contributions – 15 submissions.
- Proposals of technical talk/sessions – 2 submissions.

Each of the papers was peer-reviewed by at least three PC members, by following a single-blind reviewing process. The committee decided to accept 17 papers (9 position papers and 8 scientific papers) and 1 talk, resulting in an overall acceptance rate of 53%.

The WAISE 2018 programme was organized in six thematic sessions, one keynote and one (invited) talk.

The thematic sessions followed a highly interactive format. They were structured into short paper pitches and a common panel slot to discuss both individual paper contributions and shared topic issues. Three specific roles were part of this format: session chairs, presenters and session discussants.

- *Session Chairs* introduced sessions and participants. The Chair moderated session and plenary discussions, took care of the time, and gave the word to speakers in the audience during discussions.
- *Presenters* gave a paper pitch in 10 minutes and then participated in the debate slot.
- *Session Discussants* prepared the discussion of individual papers and the plenary debate. The discussant gave a critical review of the session papers.

The mixture of topics has been carefully balanced, as follows:

Session 1: Machine Learning Safety and Reliability

- "Boxing Clever": Practical Techniques for Gaining Insights into Training Data and Monitoring Distribution Shift, Rob Ashmore and Matthew Hill
- Mitigation of Policy Manipulation Attacks on Deep Q-Networks with Parameter-Space Noise, Vahid Behzadan and Arslan Munir
- What is Acceptably Safe for Reinforcement Learning?, John Bragg and Ibrahim Habli

Session 2: Uncertainty in Automated Driving

- Uncertainty in Machine Learning Applications - A Practice-Driven Classification of Uncertainty, Michael Kläs and Anna Maria Vollmer
- Towards a Framework to Manage Perceptual Uncertainty for Safe Automated Driving, Krzysztof Czarnecki and Rick Salay
- Design of a Knowledge-Base Strategy for Capability-Aware Treatment of Uncertainties of Automated Driving Systems, Dejiu Chen, Kenneth Östberg, Matthias Becker, Håkan Sivencrona and Fredrik Warg
- Uncertainty in Machine Learning: A Safety Perspective on Autonomous Driving, Sina Shafaei, Stefan Kugele, Mohd Hafeez Osman and Alois Knoll

Session 3: Challenges in AI Safety

- Considerations of Artificial Intelligence Safety Engineering for Unmanned Aircraft, Sebastian Schirmer, Christoph Torens, Florian Nikodem and Johann Dauer
- Could We Issue Driving Licenses to Autonomous Vehicles?, Jingyue Li, Jin Zhang and Nektaria Kaloudi
- Concerns on the differences between AI and system safety mindsets impacting autonomous vehicles safety, Alexandre Moreira Nascimento, Lucio Vismari, Paulo Cugnasca, Joao Camargo Jr., Jorge Almeida Jr., Rafia Inam, Elena Fersman, Alberto Hata and Maria Marquezini

Session 4: Ethically Aligned Design of Autonomous Systems

- The Moral Responsibility Gap and the Increasing Autonomy of Systems, Zoe Porter, Ibrahim Habli, Helen Monkhouse and John Bragg
- Design Requirements for a Moral Machine for Autonomous Weapons, Ilse Verdiesen, Virginia Dignum and Iyad Rahwan

Session 5: Human-Inspired Approaches to AI Safety

- AI Safety and Reproducibility: Establishing Robust Foundations for the Neuropsychology of Human Values, Gopal Sarma, Nick Hay and Adam Safron

- A Psychopathological Approach to Safety Engineering in AI and AGI, Vahid Behzadan, Arslan Munir and Roman Yampolskiy
- Why Bad Coffee? Explaining Agent Plans with Valuings, Michael Winikoff, Virginia Dignum and Frank Dignum

Session 6: Runtime Risk Assessment in Automated Driving

- Dynamic Risk Assessment for Vehicles of Higher Automation Levels by Deep Learning, Patrik Feth, Mohammed Naveed Akram, René Schuster and Oliver Wasenmüller
- Improving Image Classification Robustness using Predictive Data Augmentation, Harisubramanyabalaji Subramani Palanisamy, Shafiq Ur Rehman, Mattias Nyberg and Joakim Gustavsson

The *keynote* was given by *Prof. Philip Koopman* on *Autonomous Vehicle Safety Technical and Social Issues*, including certification, law and insurer issues, as well as public acceptance. Philip Koopman is a faculty member at the Carnegie Mellon University and co-founder of Edge Case Research. He has over 20 years of experience with autonomous vehicle safety, dating back to the CMU Navlab team and the Automated Highway Systems (AHS) program. His most recent projects include using stress testing and run time monitoring to ensure safety for a variety of vehicle and robotic applications for the research, industry, and defense sectors. He has additional experience with automotive and industrial functional safety, including testifying as an expert in vehicle safety class action litigation and consulting to NHTSA.

The *invited talk* was given by *Prof. François Terrier* on *Challenges in the Qual-ification of Safety-Critical Machine Learning-based Components*. François Terrier is head of the software and system engineering department at CEA LIST Institute. He is in charge of the new research program on trustworthy artificial intelligence for CEA LIST.

3 Acknowledgments

We thank all those who submitted papers to WAISE 2018 and congratulate the authors whose papers were selected for inclusion into the workshop programme and proceedings. We also thank to Poster presenters who kindly accepted to share their work as part of the event.

We would like to thank the Steering Committee (SC) for their support and advise to make WAISE 2018 a successful event:

- Stuart Russell, UC Berkeley, USA
- Raja Chatila, ISIR - Sorbonne University, France
- Roman V. Yampolskiy, University of Louisville, USA
- Nozha Boujemaa, DATAIA Institute & Inria, France
- Mark Nitzberg, Center for Human-Compatible AI, USA
- Philip Koopman, Carnegie Mellon University, USA

We specially thank our distinguished PC members, for reviewing the submissions and providing useful feedback to the authors:

- Roman V. Yampolskiy, University of Louisville, USA
- Stuart Russell, UC Berkeley, USA
- Raja Chatila, ISIR - Sorbonne University, France
- Nozha Boujemaa, DATAIA Institute & Inria, France
- Mark Nitzberg, Center for Human-Compatible AI, USA
- Victoria Krakovna, Google DeepMind, UK
- Chokri Mraidha, CEA LIST, France
- Heather Roff, Leverhulme Centre for the Future of Intelligence, UK
- Bernhard Kaiser, ANSYS, Germany
- John Favaro, INTECS, Italy
- Jonas Nilsson, Zenuity, Sweden
- Philippa Ryan, Adelard, UK
- José Hernández-Orallo, Universitat Politècnica de València, Spain
- Andrew Banks, LDRA, UK
- Carlos Hernández, TU Delft, Netherlands
- José M. Faria, Safe Perspective Ltd., UK
- Philip Koopman, Carnegie Mellon University, USA
- Florent Kirchner, CEA LIST, France
- Joanna Bryson, University of Bath, UK
- Stefan Kugele, Technical University of Munich, Germany
- Virginia Dignum, TU Delft, Netherlands
- Timo Latvala, Space Systems Finland, Finland
- Mehrdad Saadatmand, RISE SICS, Sweden
- Rick Salay, University of Waterloo, Canada
- Lavinia Burski, AECOM, UK
- Jérémie Guiochet, LAAS-CNRS, France
- Mario Gleirscher, University of York, UK
- François Terrier, CEA LIST, France
- Rob Ashmore, Defence Science & Technology Laboratory, UK
- Erwin Schoitsch, AIT Austrian Institute of Technology, Austria
- Chris Allsopp, Frazer-Nash Consultancy, UK
- Mauricio Castillo-Effen, Lockheed Martin, USA
- Huascar Espinoza, CEA LIST, France
- Orlando Avila-García, Atos, Spain
- Rob Alexander, University of York, UK
- Andreas Theodorou, University of Bath, UK

As well as the additional reviewers:

- Holly Wilson, University of Bath, UK
- Patrik Hoyer, Space Systems Finland, Finland

We thank Prof. Philip Koopman and Prof. François Terrier for their interesting talks on the current challenges of AI and autonomy safety engineering.

Finally yet importantly, we thank the SAFECOMP organization for providing an excellent framework for WAISE.

"Boxing Clever": Practical Techniques for Gaining Insights into Training Data and Monitoring Distribution Shift

Rob Ashmore[✉] and Matthew Hill

Defence Science and Technology Laboratory, Fareham, Hants PO17 6AD, UK
{rdashmore,mhill2}@dstl.gov.uk

Abstract. Training data has a significant influence on the behaviour of an artificial intelligence algorithm developed using machine learning techniques. Consequently, any argument that the trained algorithm is, in some way, fit for purpose ought to include consideration of data as an entity in its own right. We describe some simple techniques that can provide domain experts and algorithm developers with insights into training data and which can be implemented without specialist computer hardware. Specifically, we consider sampling density, test case generation and monitoring for distribution shift. The techniques are illustrated using example data sets from the University of California, Irvine, Machine Learning repository.

Keywords: Artificial intelligence · Machine learning
Training data · Distribution shift · Test cases

1 Introduction

1.1 Background

Over recent years, great progress has been made in Machine Learning (ML) and a vast amount of academic literature has been written, including: explaining behaviour, [12]; ways of producing adversarial examples, [10,14]; ways of defending against these examples, [6,7]; and new types of algorithm, [13,15].

Whilst much research focuses on ML algorithms, training data is also important, not least because it encodes requirements that the algorithm should satisfy. In addition, small changes to a data set can introduce a backdoor [5] and adversarial examples can transfer across networks trained on the same data [11]. Adversarial examples may also be a natural consequence of high-dimensional input domains [3]; that is, the input domain could itself be significant. For these reasons we expect training data to be explicitly considered in any safety, or assurance, argument related to an ML algorithm. This paper outlines simple techniques for gaining insight into training data sets, which could support such considerations. Our focus is deliberately on low complexity techniques that do not rely on specialist computational hardware.

© Crown 2018
B. Gallina et al. (Eds.): SAFECOMP 2018 Workshops, LNCS 11094, pp. 393–405, 2018.
https://doi.org/10.1007/978-3-319-99229-7_33

1.2   Terminology and Notation

The data used to train an ML algorithm is referred to as a *training data set*, or simply a *data set*, and is denoted T. We have no need to separately distinguish data that is withheld in order to test an algorithm after a training epoch.

A training data set is made up of a number of *samples*, denoted s^i. Equivalently, $T = \left\{ s^i : i = 1, \ldots, n \right\}$, where n is the number of samples.

Each sample comprises a number of *features*, with the jth feature of sample i being denoted by s^i_j. The collection of features define the algorithm's *input domain*. To simplify the discussion, we focus on quantified features; that is, features that take numerical values from a real-valued, continuously-defined scale. Equivalently, $s^i \in \mathbb{R}^d$, where d is the number of features.

For convenience, and without loss of generality, we assume samples have been scaled so that they are contained in the relevant d-dimensional unit hypercube. We have adopted a linear scaling: using o to denote the original, pre-scaling samples, scaling is achieved as follows:

$$max_j = \max_i o^i_j, \qquad min_j = \min_i o^i_j, \qquad s^i_j = \frac{o^i_j - min_j}{max_j - min_j}$$

1.3   Example Data Sets

The techniques are illustrated using three example data sets obtained from the University of California, Irvine (UCI) Machine Learning repository. Key properties are summarised in Table 1.

Table 1. Summary properties of example data sets

Name	Samples	Features	Reference http://archive.ics.uci.edu/ml/datasets/
Iris	150	4	Iris
Pen Digits	10,992	16	Pen-Based+Recognition+of+Handwritten+Digits
Cover Type	581,012	10	Covertype

The UCI repository's description of Cover Type states there are 54 features. We do not consider the 44 features that are binary flags, so our version contains 10 quantified features. Note that the original data set is © Jock A. Blackard and Colorado State University.

Since all samples have been scaled to the d-dimensional unit hypercube, for our purposes a sample from the Iris data set comprises four real numbers, each in the range $[0, 1]$. Similarly, the Pen Digits and Cover Type samples comprise sixteen and ten such numbers, respectively.

In terms of size, the data sets described in Table 1 are comparable with other data sets we are using in our work. They are, however, notably smaller than many used in modern applications. More particularly, they are smaller both in terms of the number of features and, also, the number of samples.

Since they are easy to parallelise, the techniques described in this paper are easy to extend to data sets that contain more samples, albeit at the possible expense of having to use specialist hardware. Extending to data sets with a larger number of features is more complicated. Firstly, the techniques implicitly assume there is no connection between the different features; this is not the case, for example, when each sample is an image and each feature is a pixel. Secondly, the geometric nature of the techniques means they may be less informative in very high dimensional spaces.

Whilst application of the techniques to larger data sets is future work, we note the easiest way to apply them to a large, image-based data set may be to create a representation of that data set on a reduced-dimension manifold, the results of which may also be valuable for other reasons.

1.4 Structure

The remainder of this paper is structured as follows: Sect. 2 introduces the concept of an axis-aligned box, which underpins our techniques; Sects. 3 and 4 describe techniques for understanding sampling density; Sect. 5 discusses a way of creating novel test sets; Sect. 6 outlines a way of monitoring for distribution shift; Sect. 7 provides conclusions.

2 Axis-Aligned Boxes

The techniques developed in this paper make extensive use of axis-aligned boxes. A box is defined by providing lower and upper bounds for each feature, denoted lo_j and hi_j. A sample, s^i is within this box if $lo_j < s^i_j < hi_j$ for $j = 1, \ldots, d$. Note, the sample is in the box if it is strictly within the bounds.

Scaling the data set so all samples fall strictly within the d-dimensional unit hypercube implicitly introduces a distance metric. Using axis-aligned boxes to decide whether two samples are, in some sense, close to one another is consistent with the notion of Manhattan Distance [2]. Axis-aligned boxes are ideal for our purposes: determining whether a particular sample lies within a given box needs at most $2d$ comparisons, which can be computed very efficiently.

3 Sample Density

3.1 Approach

Generally speaking, samples in training data sets are observations from some external process. It is typically not possible to gather samples against a specific type of experimental design. This means that the distribution of samples across the input domain is often uncontrolled and may not be well understood.

One way of understanding this distribution involves calculating the distance between each sample and its nearest neighbour and looking at the ratios of these distances [1]. However, the associated distance calculations can be inefficient for large data sets. An alternative approach simply involves counting the number of points in a suitably-sized and located axis-aligned box.

In terms of box size, this is typically expressed in terms of the number of samples that would be expected to be found in the box if samples were uniformly distributed. More specifically, suppose we have n samples uniformly distributed within a d-dimensional unit hypercube. In this case, an axis-aligned box with sides of length l would be expected to contain x samples, where:

$$l = \exp\left(\frac{\ln (x/n)}{d}\right) \quad \Rightarrow \quad l^d = x/n$$

Table 2 shows values of l for our illustrative data sets. It is apparent that in all cases these values cover a reasonable fraction of the $[0, 1]$ range that each (scaled) feature covers. Table 2 also shows that as d increases, so does l; this is one challenge that arises when applying the techniques to high dimensional data sets.

Table 2. Length of sides so hypercube would be expected to contain 1 or 10 samples

Name	Expected (x)	Samples (n)	Features (d)	Side (l)
Iris	1	150	4	0.286
Pen Digits	1	10,992	16	0.559
Cover Type	1	581,012	10	0.265
Iris	10	150	4	0.508
Pen Digits	10	10,992	16	0.646
Cover Type	10	581,012	10	0.334

Intuitively, it would be preferable to count the total number of samples in an axis-aligned box centred on each sample[1]. However, given the sizes indicated by Table 2, a significant portion of these boxes could fall outside the unit hypercube (where our scaling means there are no sample points). Hence, each box is located by first centering it on the sample point of interest and then, if necessary, translating so it is entirely within the unit hypercube.

The number of samples in each of these boxes is an approximate measure of sampling density: boxes that contain large numbers of samples represent densely sampled regions; boxes with a low number of samples represent sparsely sampled regions. Consequently, the distribution of the total number of samples in each of these boxes is informative. It is also helpful to consider two other factors.

The first factor is the ratio between the 1st and 99th percentiles of this distribution. This indicates the ratio of sampling densities between the most densely and most sparsely sampled regions. There are often good reasons why

---

[1] For very large data sets, it is sufficient to consider a suitable number of randomly chosen samples.

sampling density should vary across the input domain; indeed, some sequential experimental design techniques are designed to target "more interesting" parts of the input domain [4]. As a minimum, extreme differences in sampling densities should be explained and justified. Whilst there are no hard and fast rules, our empirical work to date suggests that ratios of less than 100 may be judged reasonable, whilst those greater than 1000 may need special justification.

The second factor is whether any samples are outliers. In this context a sample would be an outlier if the associated suitably-sized, axis-aligned box contained no other samples. Outliers are of interest for several reasons: our experience shows they provide domain experts with insights into the training data set; they can have a disproportionate effect on the behaviour of the trained algorithm; and they can reveal errors in data collection and preparation.

3.2   Example Data Sets

Figure 1 illustrates the distribution of the number of data samples in axis-aligned boxes for cases where the box is sized so it would contain either 1 or 10 samples, if the samples were uniformly distributed. For the Iris and Pen Digits data sets, this distribution is based on all samples; due to the large number of samples in the Cover Type data set, this case is based on 100,000 randomly chosen samples. Table 3 summarises some characteristics of these distributions (for brevity, this only considers the case where the box is scaled for 10 samples).

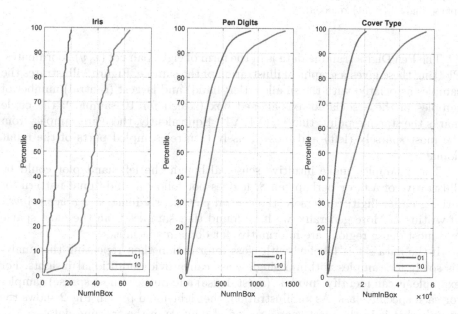

Fig. 1. Distribution of number of samples in axis-aligned boxes (scaled for 1 and 10 samples, assuming samples are uniformly distributed)

Table 3. Characteristics of the distribution of number of samples in an axis-aligned box (scaled for 10 samples, assuming samples are uniformly distributed)

Characteristic	Iris	Pen Digits	Cover Type
99th/1st %ile Ratio	21.3	115.5	148.7
Number of single-sample boxes	0	1	5
Maximum number of samples in a box	66	1,624	65,939

Figure 1 shows there are many more samples in each box than would be expected if the samples were uniformly distributed. For these three data sets, this effect becomes more pronounced as the number of samples in a data set increases. The same trend is shown in Table 3.

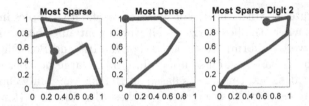

Fig. 2. Pen Digits samples from the most sparse (left), most dense (centre) and most sparse digit 2 (right) regions

The Pen Digits training data is in the form of eight pairs of (x, y) coordinates. Plotting these gives a graphical illustration of the sample. Figure 2 illustrates the samples associated with the smallest (left-hand) and largest (central) number of samples in the associated axis-aligned box (scaled for 10 samples); the circle marks the starting point, that is, (X1, Y1). Equivalently, these are samples from the most sparsely (left) and most densely (centre) sampled parts of the input domain.

These samples make intuitive sense: although the left-hand plot could be illustrative of a 6, or perhaps an 8, it does not follow a traditional pattern for writing either digit; conversely, the central plot clearly illustrates a typical way of writing 2. More generally, we have found that samples from the most sparse and most dense regions are informative for domain specialists.

If the data set is labelled with class information then repeating this analysis solely for samples within a single class can provide additional insights. For example, it can identify "modal" (most dense) and outlier (most sparse) samples for each specific class. As an illustration, the right-hand plot in Fig. 2 shows the sample that is in the most sparse region of digit 2s in the training data.

4 Empty Hyper-Rectangles

4.1 Approach

The previous section considered parts of the input domain where the training data set contains samples. Another perspective is provided by considering those parts of the input domain where there are no samples[2]. Equivalently, finding Empty Hyper-Rectangles (EHRs) within the training data set, is interesting.

Our approach to finding large, axis-aligned, EHRs is taken from Lemley, *et al.* [8]. The method starts from a randomly chosen point and expands from there. Observe that a random start point is more likely to be in a large empty space than it is to be in a small one. This observation provides some confidence that, despite its random nature, the method should provide reasonable performance; that is, it should identify large empty regions in the data set (should any exist).

Having started from a point, the method expands in each dimension until it hits any sample projected onto that single dimension. This is illustrated in the left-hand plot in Fig. 3: in this figure the randomly chosen start point is illustrated with a red X; samples in the data set are illustrated with red circles; and the EHR is shown as a blue rectangle. After this initial expansion, the empty hyper-rectangle is expanded in all dimensions simultaneously. Expansion in a given dimension stops when a sample point is reached. For example, the central plot in Fig. 3 shows the situation when no further expansion is possible in either the negative x direction or the positive y direction. The right-hand plot shows the final situation, when no further expansion is possible in any direction.

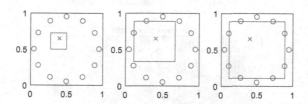

Fig. 3. Steps in finding an empty hyper-rectangle (Color figure online)

This process is repeated for different randomly chosen starting points. A variety of approaches may be taken to decide how many repetitions should be conducted. The simplest involves choosing a fixed value. An alternative involves considering a minimum of repetitions and then stopping if the last r repetitions has not increased the size of the largest EHR found so far, for a suitable value of r.

---

[2] The previous section showed that areas of the input domain contain more samples than would be the case if samples were uniformly distributed. A corollary is that there must be relatively large regions of the input domain that contain no samples.

4.2   Example Data Sets

Figure 4 shows EHRs for the Iris (top plot) and Cover Type (bottom plot) data sets. Each feature in the data set is illustrated by a separate column. For example, the top plot shows a region that covers the range $(0.0, 1.0)$ for the first two features, the range $(0.15, 1.0)$ for the third feature and the range $(0.0, 0.38)$ for the fourth feature. More loosely, this data set contains no samples where the third feature is large and the fourth feature is small. Our experience shows insights like this are valuable to domain experts.

Care needs to be taken when interpreting plots like Fig. 4. The outlined regions provide a useful illustration of the *shape* of the empty region, but it does not provide a useful guide to its *size*. To help address this difficulty, the plots include a final column, drawn in red and labelled as (Size). This shows the fraction of the unit hypercube that is covered by the empty region; this information is also shown in the plots' titles.

A full discussion of the regions shown in Fig. 4 is beyond the scope of this paper. However, note that both regions cover more than 25% of the respective unit hypercube and, as such, should provide domain experts with valuable insights into the respective data sets.

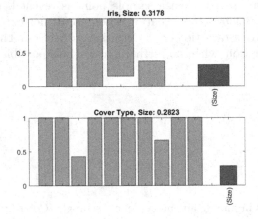

Fig. 4. Largest EHRs found in the Iris and Cover Type data sets

The Pen Digits data set has been excluded from Fig. 4 as the identified EHR covers the entire interior of the unit hypercube. Recall that a sample is only inside a region if it is *strictly* within the bounds established for each feature. The scaling used when building the Pen Digits data means each sample has at least one x coordinate that is 0 and one x coordinate that is 100; the same also holds for the y coordinates. Consequently, every sample falls on a boundary of the unit hypercube and hence the EHR covers the whole interior of the hypercube.

It is reassuring that the algorithm correctly identifies the EHR that covers the entire unit hypercube, but it is not especially interesting. Despite this, the notion of EHRs can still be informative. As an example, we consider the first and last pairs of features, that is, (X1, Y1), which marks the start of the digit, and (X8, Y8), which marks the end.

The left-hand plot in Fig. 5 shows the EHR for these four dimensions. In the right-hand plot, the blue dashed rectangle shows the (X1, Y1) part of the region; the red dotted rectangle shows the (X8, Y8) part of the region. The EHR is such that there are no digits that start in the blue rectangle and finish in the red one. Our experience indicates these types of observation are informative to domain specialists.

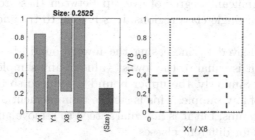

Fig. 5. Largest EHR found in the Pen Digits (X1, Y1, X8, Y8) data set (Color figure online)

5 Single-Class Regions

5.1 Approach

The techniques discussed in the preceding sections are applicable to all types of ML application (including, for example, classification and regression) and also to both supervised and unsupervised learning. In the specific case of supervised learning for classification applications, they can be extended to provide additional insights.

Consider the algorithm outlined below:

1. Select a class, C, from the training data, T.
2. Randomly pick a sample from this class, s^i.
3. Create a (temporary) set of training data, T', by removing all samples of class C from T. So, $T' = T \setminus \{s^i : s^i \in C\}$.
4. Find an EHR within T', using starting points drawn from $\{s^i : s^i \in C\}$; that is the starting points are the class C points within T.

Any region found by this algorithm will satisfy two properties: firstly, given the possible starting points, the region will contain at least one sample from C; secondly, since the region contains no samples from T', any samples it contains (from T) must be of class C.

Hence, this algorithm finds axis-aligned boxes that only contain samples from a single class. These regions can provide a domain expert with additional insights into the training data. They can also inform testing of the model created from the training data: for example, if the model predicted many non-class C results from test inputs drawn from a "class C only" region then this should raise concerns.

For practical applications, it is helpful to add another step to the algorithm. Note, firstly, that the algorithm is based on finding *empty* regions and, secondly (as shown earlier) that training data sets may have relatively large regions where there are *no* samples. This means that the identified regions may contain relatively large spaces where there are no samples. More particularly, if the above algorithm is used to create single-class regions for more than one class then there may be a significant degree of overlap between these regions. Given the intended uses of the single-class regions, it is helpful to try and remove some of this overlap.

This can be achieved by increasing the lower bound of each dimension of the region so that it is equal to the lowest value of any sample (from T) in the empty (T') region. Similarly, the upper bound is reduced so that it is equal to the highest value of any sample. This is simple to implement and, consequently, consistent with our aims, but it is not guaranteed to remove all overlap between single-class regions for different classes.

5.2   Example Data Sets

For brevity, only results from the Pen Digits data set are shown. Figure 6 shows single-class regions for Class 5 (top) and Class 6 (bottom); for these plots the (Size) column reflects the fraction of Class 5 (or Class 6) samples that are in the region. The Class 5 plot contains over 34% of the 5s that are in the data set; the region in the Class 6 plot contains over 57% of the 6s. Hence, these regions are significant in terms of understanding the behaviour of any algorithm trained on the Pen Digits data set.

Despite their importance, each region covers less than 0.5% of the unit hypercube (reported as 0.00% in Fig. 6). Hence, without the type of analysis discussed here, it is unlikely that either would be explored in any detail.

6   Monitoring Distribution Shift

6.1   Approach

Strictly speaking, distribution shift is not a property of training data; it represents the relationship between training data and data observed during operational use. The topic is considered in this paper because the techniques discussed above can be easily extended to provide a perspective on distribution shift and, furthermore, this perspective is consistent with our general theme of limited computational resources.

Specifically, we are interested in monitoring for covariate shift [9], which occurs when the distribution of inputs during operational use is different from the distribution exhibited by the training data set. Our method considers two perspectives: that of individual points; and that of collections of points.

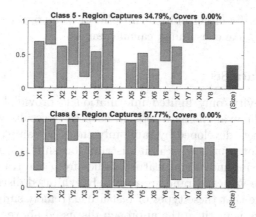

Class 5 - Region Captures 34.79%, Covers 0.00%

Class 6 - Region Captures 57.77%, Covers 0.00%

Fig. 6. Single-class regions for Class 5 and Class 6 in the Pen Digits data set

The individual point considerations are straightforward. Any operational inputs that (scaled using the same factors as for the training data set) fall outside the d-dimensional unit hypercube also fall outside the bounds of the training data set and, as such, may be indicative of distribution shift. Likewise, any (scaled) operational inputs that fall inside an EHR may also be indicative of a distribution shift. In both of these cases, some leeway is advisable: a single point that is only just outside the unit hypercube, or only just inside an EHR, is unlikely to represent a significant distribution shift.

In order to consider collections of points, some further analysis is needed. In particular, we find a series of expanding, axis-aligned boxes that contain given fractions of the training data. That is, we want to find $A_0 \subset A_1 \subset \ldots \subset A_m$ where $|\{s^i : s^i \in A_i\}|/|T| \approx f_i$, with $f_0 < f_1 < \ldots < f_m$.

A suitable collection of boxes can be identified by choosing a starting point and expanding equally in all dimensions until either the edge of the d-dimensional unit hypercube is reached, or the desired fraction of samples is contained in the box. Essentially, the choice of starting point is arbitrary. We have achieved good results by picking starting points in densely sampled parts of the input domain.

Note that, due to the restriction that we use axis-aligned boxes, it might not be possible to precisely achieve the desired fractions. We typically use 0.2, 0.4, 0.6 and 0.8 as our desired values.

Once we have the bounding boxes, we count the number of operational inputs that fall into each one. By considering, respectively, the number of operational inputs and the number of training data samples that are in A_m but not in A_{m-1}, and so on, we can create a contingency table for a Chi-squared test. This can be used to determine the probability that the spatial distributions of the training data and operational inputs (as summarised by the series of bounding boxes) are different. By using a relatively small number of axis-aligned, bounding boxes this approach discards a large amount of potentially useful information. Nevertheless, it is simple to implement, even on limited computational hardware.

Hence, it may be useful either in its own right, or as a trigger to prompt a more detailed, and more time consuming, calculation.

6.2   Example Data Sets

For reasons of brevity, only limited information is provided on applying the above process to the example data sets. In each case, results were as expected. For example, test sets developed by randomly choosing samples from the training data set did not routinely exhibit distribution shift. Conversely, test sets developed by choosing individual feature values from the training data set, or by choosing feature values at random, routinely exhibited distribution shift.

We acknowledge that these types of test are extremely simple. Nevertheless, they illustrate there is merit in the approach discussed above.

7   Conclusions

Although they inevitably introduce some inaccuracy, axis-aligned boxes are a helpful concept for understanding training data sets, especially in situations where computational resources are limited. They can be used to understand sampling density, including the balance between densely and sparsely sampled regions, and to identify regions that contain no samples. They can also inform test generation, for example by identifying regions that contain samples from a single class, and support simple ways of monitoring for distribution shift between training and operational use.

Acknowledgements. The authors would like to acknowledge the helpful feedback of the anonymous reviewers, which significantly improved this paper.

References

1. Bishnu, A., Desai, S., Ghosh, A., Goswami, M., Subhabrata, P.: Uniformity of point samples in metric spaces using gap ratio. In: Proceedings of the 12th Annual Conference on Theory and Applications of Models of Computation, pp. 347–358 (2015)
2. Black, P.E.: Manhattan distance. Dict. Algorithm. Data Struct. **18**, 2012 (2006)
3. Gilmer, J., Metz, L., Faghri, F., Schoenholz, S.S., Raghu, M., Wattenberg, M., Goodfellow, I.: Adversarial spheres (2018). arXiv:1801.02774v2
4. Gramacy, R.B., Lee, H.K.H.: Bayesian treed gaussian process models with an application to computer modeling. J. Am. Stat. Assoc. **103**(483), 1119–1130 (2008)
5. Gu, T., Dolan-Gavitt, B., Garg, S.: Badnets: identifying vulnerabilities in the machine learning model supply chain (2017). arXiv:1708.06733
6. Guo, C., Rana, M., Cisse, M., van der Maaten, L.: Countering adversarial images using input transformations (2017). arXiv:1711.00117
7. Kolter, J.Z., Wong, E.: Provable defenses against adversarial examples via the convex outer adversarial polytope (2017). arXiv:1711.00851
8. Lemley, J., Jagodzinski, F., Andonie, R.: Big holes in big data: a Monte Carlo algorithm for detecting large hyper-rectangles in high dimensional data. In: 2016 IEEE 40th Annual Computer Software and Applications Conference (COMPSAC), vol. 1, pp. 563–571. IEEE (2016)
9. Moreno-Torres, J.G., Raeder, T., Alaiz-RodriGuez, R., Chawla, N.V., Herrera, F.: A unifying view on dataset shift in classification. Pattern Recogn. **45**(1), 521–530 (2012)
10. Nguyen, A., Yosinski, J., Clune, J.: Deep neural networks are easily fooled: high confidence predictions for unrecognizable images. In: Proceedings of the 28th IEEE Conference on Computer Vision and Pattern Recognition, pp. 427–436 (2015)
11. Papernot, N., McDaniel, P., Goodfellow, I., Jha, S., Celik, Z.B., Swami, A.: Practical black-box attacks against machine learning. In: Proceedings of the 2017 ACM on Asia Conference on Computer and Communications Security, pp. 506–519. ACM (2017)
12. Ribeiro, M.T., Singh, S., Guestrin, C.: Why should I trust you?: Explaining the predictions of any classifier. In: Proceedings of the 22nd ACM SIGKDD International Conference on Knowledge Discovery and Data Mining, pp. 1135–1144 (2016)
13. Sabour, S., Frosst, N., Hinton, G.E.: Dynamic routing between capsules. In: Advances in Neural Information Processing Systems, pp. 3857–3867 (2017)
14. Szegedy, C., Zaremba, W., Sutskever, I., Bruna, J., Erhan, D., Goodfellow, I., Fergus, R.: Intriguing properties of neural networks. In: Proceedings of the 2nd International Conference on Learning Representations, pp. 1–10 (2014)
15. Zhou, Z.H., Feng, J.: Deep forest: towards an alternative to deep neural networks (2017). arXiv:1702.08835

Mitigation of Policy Manipulation Attacks on Deep Q-Networks with Parameter-Space Noise

Vahid Behzadan[✉] and Arslan Munir

Kansas State University, Manhattan, KS 66506, USA
{behzadan,amunir}@ksu.edu
http://blogs.k-state.edu/aisecurityresearch/

Abstract. Recent developments establish the vulnerability of deep reinforcement learning to policy manipulation attack. In this work, we propose a technique for mitigation of such attacks based on addition of noise to the parameter space of deep reinforcement learners during training. We experimentally verify the effect of parameter-space noise in reducing the transferability of adversarial examples, and demonstrate the promising performance of this technique in mitigating the impact of whitebox and blackbox attacks at both test and training times.

Keywords: Deep reinforcement learning · Adversarial attacks
Adversarial examples · Mitigation · Parameter-space noise

1 Introduction

Recent years has been the scene to growing interest and advances in deep Reinforcement Learning (RL). By exploiting the superior feature extraction and processing capabilities of deep neural networks, deep RL enables the learning of direct mappings from raw observations of the environment to actions. This enhancement enables the application of classic RL approaches to high-dimensional and complex planning problems, and is shown to achieve human-level or superhuman performance in various cases such as learning to playing the game of Go [22], playing Atari games [15], robotic manipulation [11], and autonomous navigation of aerial [25] and ground [26] vehicles. While the interest in deep RL solutions is extending into numerous domains such as intelligent transportation systems [1], finance [7] and critical infrastructure [16], ensuring the security and reliability of such solutions in adversarial conditions is only at its preliminary stages. Recently, Behzadan and Munir [4] reported the vulnerability of deep reinforcement learning algorithms to both test-time and training-time attacks using adversarial examples [10]. This work was followed by a number of further investigations (e.g., [12,13]) verifying the fragility of deep RL agents to such attacks. Currently, only a few reports (e.g., [5,14,20]) concentrate on mitigation and countermeasures, and are mostly focused on approaches based on adversarial training and prediction.

© Springer Nature Switzerland AG 2018
B. Gallina et al. (Eds.): SAFECOMP 2018 Workshops, LNCS 11094, pp. 406–417, 2018.
https://doi.org/10.1007/978-3-319-99229-7_34

In this work, we aim to further the research on countering attacks on deep RL by proposing a potential mitigation technique based on employing parameter-space noise exploration during the training of deep RL agents. Recent reports in [9,21] demonstrate that addition of adaptive noise to the parameters of deep RL architectures greatly enhances the exploration behavior and convergence speed of such algorithms. Contrary to classical exploration heuristics such as ϵ-greedy [23], parameter-space noise is iteratively and adaptively applied to the parameters of the learning model, such as weights of the neural network. Accordingly, we hypothesize that the randomness introduced via parameter noise, not only enhances the discovery of more creative and robust policies, but also reduces the effect of whitebox and blackbox adversarial example attacks at both test-time and training-time.

To this end, we evaluate the performance of Deep Q-Network (DQN) models trained with parameter noise, against the test-time and training-time adversarial example attacks introduced in [4]. Main contributions of this work are:

1. Proposal of parameter-space noise exploration as a mitigation technique against policy manipulation attacks at both test-time and training-time,
2. Development of an open-source platform for experimenting with adversarial example attacks on deep RL agents,
3. Experimental analysis of parameter-space noise for mitigation of test-time whitebox and blackbox attacks on DQN,
4. Experimental analysis of parameter-space noise for mitigation of training-time policy induction attacks on DQN.

The remainder of this paper is organized as follows: Sect. 2 reviews the relevant background of DQN, parameter noise training via the NoisyNet approach, and adversarial examples. Section 3 describes the attack model adopted in this study. Section 4 details the experiment setup, and presents the corresponding results. Section 5 concludes the paper with remarks on the obtained results.

2 Background

In this section, we present an overview of the fundamental concepts, upon which this work is based. It must be noted that this overview is not meant to be comprehensive, and thus the interested readers may refer to the suggested references for further details.

2.1 RL and Deep Q-Networks

The generic RL problem can be formally modeled as a Markov Decision Process (MDP), described by the tuple $MDP = (S, A, R, P)$, where S is the set of reachable states in the process, A is the set of available actions, R is the mapping of transitions to the immediate reward, and P represents the transition probabilities. At any given time-step t, the MDP is at a state $s_t \in S$. The RL agent's choice of action at time t, $a_t \in A$ causes a transition from s_t to a state

s_{t+1} according to the transition probability $P^{a_t}_{s_t,s_{t+1}}$. The agent receives a reward $r_t = R(s_t, a_t) \in \mathbb{R}$, where $\mathbb{R}$ denotes the set of real numbers, for choosing the action a_t at state s_t.

Interactions of the agent with MDP are determined by the policy π. When such interactions are deterministic, the policy $\pi : S \to A$ is a mapping between the states and their corresponding actions. A stochastic policy $\pi(s)$ represents the probability of optimality for implementing any action $a \in A$ at state s.

The objective of RL is to find the optimal policy π^* that maximizes the cumulative reward over time at time t, denoted by the return function $\hat{R}_t = \sum_{k=0}^{\infty} \gamma^k r_{t+k}$, where $\gamma \in [0,1]$ is the discount factor representing the diminishing worth of rewards obtained further in time, hence ensuring that $\hat{R}$ is bounded.

One approach to this problem is to estimate the optimal value of each action, defined as the expected sum of future rewards when taking that action and following the optimal policy thereafter. The value of an action a in a state s is given by the action-value function Q defined as:

$$Q(s, a) = R(s, a) + \gamma max_{a'}(Q(s', a')), \qquad (1)$$

where s' is the state that emerges as a result of action a, and a' is a possible action in state s'. The optimal Q value given a policy π is hence defined as: $Q^*(s, a) = max_\pi Q^\pi(s, a)$, and the optimal policy is given by $\pi^*(s) = \arg\max_a Q(s, a)$.

The Q-learning method estimates the optimal action policies by using the Bellman equation $Q_{i+1}(s, a) = \mathbf{E}[R + \gamma \max_a Q_i]$ as the iterative update of a value iteration technique. Practical implementation of Q-learning is commonly based on function approximation of the parametrized Q-function $Q(s, a; \theta) \approx Q^*(s, a)$. A common technique for approximating the parametrized non-linear Q-function is via neural network models whose weights correspond to the parameter vector θ. Such neural networks, commonly referred to as Q-networks, are trained such that at every iteration i, the following loss function is minimized:

$$L_i(\theta_i) = \mathbf{E}_{s,a\sim\rho(.)}[(y_i - Q(s, a, ; \theta_i))^2], \qquad (2)$$

where $y_i = \mathbf{E}[R + \gamma \max_{a'} Q(s', a'; \theta_{i-1})|s, a]$, and $\rho(s, a)$ is a probability distribution over states s and actions a. This optimization problem is typically solved using computationally efficient techniques such as Stochastic Gradient Descent (SGD) [2].

Classical Q-networks introduce a number of major problems in the Q-learning process. First, the sequential processing of consecutive observations breaks the *iid* (Independent and Identically Distributed) requirement of training data as successive samples are correlated. Furthermore, slight changes to Q-values leads to rapid changes in the policy estimated by Q-network, thus enabling policy oscillations. Also, since the scale of rewards and Q-values are unknown, the gradients of Q-networks can be sufficiently large to render the backpropagation process unstable.

A Deep Q-Network (DQN) [15] is a training algorithm designed to resolve these problems. To overcome the issue of correlation between consecutive observations, DQN employs a technique called *experience replay*: instead of training on successive observations, experience replay samples a random batch of previous observations stored in the replay memory to train on. As a result, the correlation between successive training samples is broken and the iid setting is re-established. In order to avoid oscillations, DQN fixes the parameters of a network $\hat{Q}$, which represents the optimization target y_i. These parameters are then updated at regular intervals by adopting the current weights of the Q-network. The issue of unstability in backpropagation is also solved in DQN by normalizing the reward values to the range $[-1, +1]$, thus preventing Q-values from becoming too large.

Mnih et al. [15] demonstrate the application of this new Q-network technique to end-to-end learning of Q values in playing Atari games based on observations of pixel values in the game environment. To capture the movements in the game environment, Mnih et al. use stacks of 4 consecutive image frames as the input to the network. To train the network, a random batch is sampled from the previous observation tuples (s_t, a_t, r_t, s_{t+1}), where r_t denotes the reward at time t. Each observation is then processed by 2 layers of convolutional neural networks to learn the features of input images, which are then employed by feed-forward layers to approximate the Q-function. The target network $\hat{Q}$, with parameters θ^-, is synchronized with the parameters of the original Q network at fixed periods intervals. i.e., at every ith iteration, $\theta_t^- = \theta_t$, and is kept fixed until the next synchronization. The target value for optimization of DQN thus becomes:

$$y_t' \equiv r_{t+1} + \gamma max_{a'} \hat{Q}(S_{t+1}, a'; \theta^-) \tag{3}$$

Accordingly, the training process can be stated as:

$$min_{a_t} (y_t' - Q(s_t, a_t, \theta))^2 \tag{4}$$

As for the exploration mechanism, the original DQN employs ϵ-greedy, which monotonically decreases the probability of taking random actions as the training progresses [23].

2.2 NoisyNets

Introduced by Fortunato et al. [9], NoisyNet is a type of neural network whose biases and weights are iteratively perturbed during training by a parametric function of the noise. Such a neural network can be represented by $y = f_\theta(x)$, parametrized by the vector of noisy parameters $\theta = \mu + \Sigma * \epsilon$, where $\tau = (\mu, \Sigma)$ is a set of vectors representing learnable parameters, ϵ is a vector of zero-mean noise with fixed statistics, and $*$ is element-wise multiplication. In [9], the modified DQN algorithm is proposed as follows: first, ϵ-greedy is omitted, and instead the value function is greedily optimized. Second, the fully connected layers of the value function are parametrized as a NoisyNet, whose parameter values are drawn from a noisy parameter distribution after every replay step. The noise distribution used in [9] is factorized Gaussian noise. During replay, the current NoisyNet parameter samples are held constant, while at the optimization of each action step, the parameters are re-sampled. The parametrized action-value function $Q(x, a, \epsilon; \tau)$ can be treated as a random variable, and is employed accordingly in the optimization function. Further details of this approach and a similar proposal can be found in [9] and [21], respectively.

2.3 Adversarial Examples

In [24], Szegedy et al. report an intriguing discovery: several machine learning models, including deep neural networks, are vulnerable to adversarial examples. That is, these machine learning models misclassify inputs that are only slightly different from correctly classified samples drawn from the data distribution. Furthermore, it was found [19] that a wide variety of models with different architectures trained on different subsets of the training data misclassify the same adversarial example.

This suggests that adversarial examples expose fundamental blind spots in machine learning algorithms. The issue can be stated as follows: Consider a machine learning system M and a benign input sample C which is correctly classified by the machine learning system, i.e. $M(C) = y_{true}$. According to the report of Szegedy [24] and many proceeding studies [19], it is possible to construct an adversarial example $A = C + \delta$, which is perceptually indistinguishable from C, but is classified incorrectly, i.e. $M(A) \neq y_{true}$.

Adversarial examples are misclassified far more often than examples that have been perturbed by random noise, even if the magnitude of the noise is much larger than the magnitude of the adversarial perturbation [10]. According to the objective of adversaries, adversarial example attacks are generally classified into the following two categories:

1. Misclassification attacks, which aim for generating examples that are classified incorrectly by the target network.
2. Targeted attacks, whose goal is to generate samples that the target misclassifies into an arbitrary class designated by the attacker.

To generate such adversarial examples, several algorithms have been proposed, such as the Fast Gradient Sign Method (FGSM) by Goodfellow et al. [10], and the Jacobian Saliency Map Algorithm (JSMA) approach by Papernot et al. [19]. A grounding assumption in many of the crafting algorithms is that the attacker has complete knowledge of the target neural networks such as its architecture, weights, and other hyperparameters. In response, Papernot et al. [18] proposed the first blackbox approach to generating adversarial examples. This method exploits the transferability of adversarial examples: an adversarial example generated for a neural network classifier applies to most other neural network classifiers that perform the same classification task, regardless of their architecture, parameters, and even the distribution of training data. Accordingly, the approach of [18] is based on generating a replica of the target network. To train this replica, the attacker creates and trains over a dataset from a mixture of samples obtained by observing target's interaction with the environment, and synthetically generated inputs and label pairs. Once trained, any of the algorithms that require knowledge of the target network for crafting adversarial examples can be applied to the replica. Due to the transferability of adversarial examples, the perturbed data points generated for the replica network can induce misclassifications in many of the other networks that perform the same task.

3   Attack Model

We consider an attacker whose goal is to perturb the optimality of actions taken by a DQN agent through either perturbing the observations of the agent at the test-time, or inducing an arbitrary policy π_{adv} on the target DQN at the training time. In whitebox attacks, the attacker has complete knowledge of the target. On the other hand, a blackbox attacker has no knowledge of the target's exact architecture and parameters, but is assumed to be capable of estimating those based on the conventions applied to the input type (e.g., image and video input may indicate a convolutional neural network, speech and voice data point towards a recurrent neural network, etc.).

In this model, the attacker is assumed to have minimal *a priori* information of the target's model and parameters, such as the type and format of inputs to the DQN, as well as its reward function R and an estimate for the frequency of updating the $\hat{Q}$ network. Furthermore, the attacker has no direct influence on the target's architecture and parameters, including its reward function, parameter noise, and the optimization mechanism. As illustrated in Fig. 1, the only parameter that the attacker can directly manipulate is the configuration of the environment observed by the target. For instance, in the case of DQN agents learning to play Atari games [15], the attacker may change pixel values of the game's frames, but not the score. We assume that the attacker is capable of changing the state before it is observed by the target by predicting future states, through approaches such as having a quicker action speed than the target's sampling rate, or by introducing a delay between generation of the new environment and its observation by the target. To avoid detection, we impose an extra constraint on the attack such that the magnitude of perturbations applied in each configuration must be smaller than a constant value denoted by λ. Also, we do not limit the attacker's domain of perturbations.

As discussed in Sect. 2, the DQN framework of Mnih et al. [15] can be seen as consisting of two neural networks, one is the native Q-network which performs the image processing and function approximation, and the other is the target $\hat{Q}$ network whose architecture and parameters are copies of the native network sampled once every c iterations. DQN is trained through optimizing the loss function of Eq. 4 by SGD. Behzadan and Munir [4] demonstrated that the function approximators of DQN are also vulnerable to adversarial example attacks. In other words, the set of all possible inputs to the approximated function $\hat{Q}$ contains elements which cause the approximated functions to generate outputs that are different from the output of the original Q function.

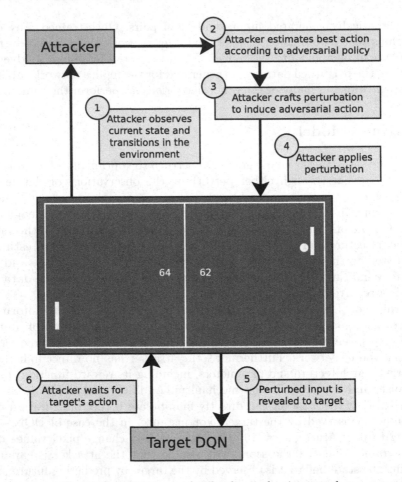

Fig. 1. Exploitation cycle of policy induction attack

Consequently, the attacker can manipulate the learning process of DQN by crafting states s_t such that $\hat{Q}(s_{t+1}, a; \theta_t^-)$ identifies an incorrect choice of optimal action at s_{t+1}. If the attacker is capable of crafting adversarial inputs s_t' and s_{t+1}' such that the value of Eq. 4 is minimized for a specific action a', then the policy learned by DQN at this time-step is optimized towards suggesting a' as the optimal action given the state s_t. At every time step of training this replica, the attacker observes interactions of its target with the environment (s_t, a_t, r_t, s_{t+1}). If the resulting state is not terminal, the attacker then calculates the perturbation vectors $\hat{\delta}_{t+1}$ for the next state s_{t+1} such that $max_{a'}\hat{Q}(s_{t+1} + \hat{\delta}_{t+1}, a'; \theta_t^-)$ causes $\hat{Q}$ to generate its maximum when $a' = \pi_{adv}^*(s_{t+1})$, i.e., the maximum reward at the next state is obtained when the optimal action taken at that state is determined by the attacker's policy. The attacker then reveals the perturbed state s_{t+1} to the target, and re-trains the replica based on the new state and action.

This is procedurally similar to targeted misclassification attacks described in Sect. 2, which aim to find minimal perturbations to an input sample such that the classifier assigns the maximum value of likelihood to an incorrect target class. Therefore, the adversarial example crafting techniques developed for classifiers such as FGSM can be employed to obtain the perturbation vector $\hat{\delta}_{t+1}$.

Accordingly, Behzadan and Munir [4] divide this attack into the two phases of initialization and exploitation. The initialization phase implements processes that must be performed before the target begins interacting with the environment, which are:

1. Train a DQN based on attacker's reward function R' to obtain the adversarial policy π^*_{adv}
2. Create a replica of the target's DQN and initialize with random parameters

The exploitation phase implements the attack process and crafting adversarial inputs, such that the target DQN performs an action dictated by π^*_{adv}. This phase constitutes an attack cycle depicted in Fig. 1. The cycle initiates with the attacker's first observation of the environment, and runs in tandem with the target's operation.

4   Experimental Verification

To evaluate the effectiveness of NoisyNet in mitigation of adversarial example attacks, we study the performance of this architecture in comparison to the original DQN setup. Following the standard benchmarks of DQN, our experimental environments consist of 3 Atari 2600 games, namely Enduro, Assault, and Breakout. We train 4 models for each environment, 2 models based on the original DQN and ϵ-greedy exploration, and 2 models based on the NoisyNet architecture. The neural network configuration of both models follows that of the original DQN proposal by Mnih et al. [15], while the parameter noise configuration is based on the setup presented in [9].

We implemented the experimentation platform in TensorFlow using OpenAI Gym [6] for emulating the game environment and Cleverhans [17] for crafting the adversarial examples. Our DQN implementation is a modified version of the module in OpenAI Baselines [8], while the NoisyNet implementation is based on the algorithm described in [9]. We have published our platform at [3] for open-source use in further research in this area.

For the purposes of this study, we consider FGSM for crafting non-targeted adversarial examples, with the perturbation limit $\lambda = 1.0/255.0$. Similar to the work in [13], the initiation of attacks occurs after the learned Q-function begins converging towards the optimal value.

4.1   Test-Time Attacks

Parameter noise training in NoisyNet is expected to enhance the exploration criteria of the agent and hence facilitate learning more creative and accurate policies. Accordingly, we hypothesize that the action-value function learned in NoisyNet is better generalized than the original, and can be more resilient to non-targeted adversarial example attacks at test-time. Similarly, the addition of random noise to the parameters of NoisyNet can potentially impede the transferability of adversarial examples, and hence enhance the resilience of NoisyNet to blackbox attacks. To test this hypothesis, we compare the performance of NoisyNet and DQN models to whitebox and blackbox attacks after $2e8$ iterations of training.

Figure 2 presents the results of this experiment. It is observed that in all three environments, the impact of adversarial example perturbation in the performance of NoisyNet is less severe than that of the original DQN, thereby verifying our general hypothesis. Furthermore, comparison of performance under blackbox attacks demonstrates significant improvements in Noisynets, as depicted in all three cases. A preliminary interpretation of this observation is that the randomization of model parameters reduces the transferability of adversarial examples generated for a replicated model.

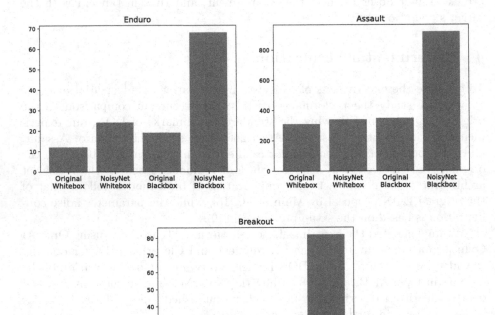

Fig. 2. Comparison of whitebox and blackbox attacks at test-time

4.2 Training-Time Attacks

In [4,13], the impact of training-time adversarial example attacks on the policy learning is demonstrated. Similar to the case of test-time attacks, we hypothesize that the reduced transferability and enhanced generalization of NoisyNet can potentially provide greater resilience to blackbox adversarial example attacks during training. To this end, we investigated the performance of NoisyNet and DQN to the training-time attack methodology described in Sect. 3 [4].

Figure 3 presents the results of this experiment. It can be seen that in all three environments, performance of the original DQN consistently deteriorates under training-time attacks, as reported in [4,13]. On the other hand, while the performance of NoisyNet is also subject to deterioration, it demonstrates significantly stronger resilience to this attack, and in the case of Assault remains almost unaffected by adversarial perturbations. These results verify the original hypothesis, and hence the efficacy of parameter noise in mitigating the impact of training-time attacks.

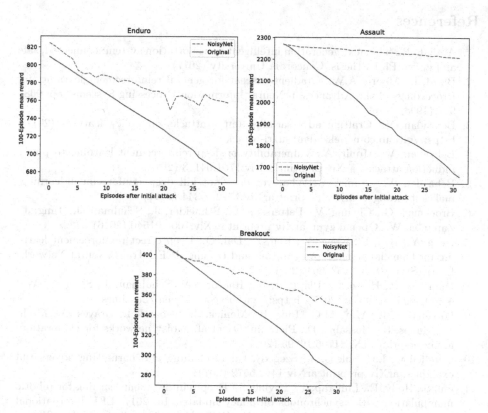

Fig. 3. Comparison of blackbox attacks at training-time

5 Conclusion

Through experimental analysis, we have investigated the effect of parameter noise in mitigation of adversarial example attacks on Deep Q-Networks (DQN). Considering the reported enhancing effect of parameter noise in reinforcement learning and exploration, as well as the inherent randomization of such techniques, we have demonstrated that compared to the original DQN, noisy DQN architectures provide better resilience to adversarial perturbations at test-time, and reduce susceptibility to transferability of adversarial examples. Furthermore, we have demonstrated that noisy DQN is significantly more resilient to blackbox attacks at training-time, and learn in a considerably more robust manner in comparison to plain DQN architectures. These results present a promising starting point for further experimental and analytical analysis of employing parameter-space noise exploration for enhancement of resilience and robustness in deep reinforcement learning.

References

1. Atallah, R.: The next generation intelligent transportation system: connected, safe and green. Ph.D. thesis, Concordia University (2017)
2. Baird, L., Moore, A.W.: Gradient descent for general reinforcement learning. In: Proceedings of the Advances in Neural Information Processing Systems, pp. 968–974 (1998)
3. Behzadan, V.: Crafting adversarial example attacks on policy learners (2017). https://github.com/behzadanksu/rl-attack
4. Behzadan, V., Munir, A.: Vulnerability of deep reinforcement learning to policy induction attacks. arXiv preprint arXiv:1701.04143 (2017)
5. Behzadan, V., Munir, A.: Whatever does not kill deep reinforcement learning, makes it stronger. arXiv preprint arXiv:1712.09344 (2017)
6. Brockman, G., Cheung, V., Pettersson, L., Schneider, J., Schulman, J., Tang, J., Zaremba, W.: Openai gym. arXiv preprint arXiv:1606.01540 (2016)
7. Deng, Y., Bao, F., Kong, Y., Ren, Z., Dai, Q.: Deep direct reinforcement learning for financial signal representation and trading. IEEE Trans. Neural Networks Learn. Syst. **28**(3), 653–664 (2017)
8. Dhariwal, P., Hesse, C., Plappert, M., Radford, A., Schulman, J., Sidor, S., Wu, Y.: Openai baselines (2017). https://github.com/openai/baselines
9. Fortunato, M., Azar, M.G., Piot, B., Menick, J., Osband, I., Graves, A., Mnih, V., Munos, R., Hassabis, D., Pietquin, O., et al.: Noisy networks for exploration. arXiv preprint arXiv:1706.10295 (2017)
10. Goodfellow, I.J., Shlens, J., Szegedy, C.: Explaining and harnessing adversarial examples. arXiv preprint arXiv:1412.6572 (2014)
11. Gu, S., Holly, E., Lillicrap, T., Levine, S.: Deep reinforcement learning for robotic manipulation with asynchronous off-policy updates. In: 2017 IEEE International Conference on Robotics and Automation (ICRA), pp. 3389–3396. IEEE (2017)
12. Huang, S., Papernot, N., Goodfellow, I., Duan, Y., Abbeel, P.: Adversarial attacks on neural network policies. arXiv preprint arXiv:1702.02284 (2017)
13. Kos, J., Song, D.: Delving into adversarial attacks on deep policies. arXiv preprint arXiv:1705.06452 (2017)

14. Lin, Y.C., Liu, M.Y., Sun, M., Huang, J.B.: Detecting adversarial attacks on neural network policies with visual foresight. arXiv preprint arXiv:1710.00814 (2017)
15. Mnih, V., Kavukcuoglu, K., Silver, D., Rusu, A.A., Veness, J., Bellemare, M.G., Graves, A., Riedmiller, M., Fidjeland, A.K., Ostrovski, G., et al.: Human-level control through deep reinforcement learning. Nature 518(7540), 529–533 (2015)
16. Mohammadi, M., Al-Fuqaha, A., Guizani, M., Oh, J.S.: Semisupervised deep reinforcement learning in support of IoT and smart city services. IEEE Internet Things J. 5(2), 624–635 (2018)
17. Papernot, N., Goodfellow, I., Sheatsley, R., Feinman, R., McDaniel, P.: cleverhans v1. 0.0: an adversarial machine learning library. arXiv preprint arXiv:1610.00768 (2016)
18. Papernot, N., McDaniel, P., Goodfellow, I., Jha, S., Celik, Z.B., Swami, A.: Practical black-box attacks against deep learning systems using adversarial examples. arXiv preprint arXiv:1602.02697 (2016)
19. Papernot, N., McDaniel, P., Jha, S., Fredrikson, M., Celik, Z.B., Swami, A.: The limitations of deep learning in adversarial settings. In: 2016 IEEE European Symposium on Security and Privacy (EuroS&P), pp. 372–387. IEEE (2016)
20. Pattanaik, A., Tang, Z., Liu, S., Bommannan, G., Chowdhary, G.: Robust deep reinforcement learning with adversarial attacks. arXiv preprint arXiv:1712.03632 (2017)
21. Plappert, M., Houthooft, R., Dhariwal, P., Sidor, S., Chen, R.Y., Chen, X., Asfour, T., Abbeel, P., Andrychowicz, M.: Parameter space noise for exploration. arXiv preprint arXiv:1706.01905 (2017)
22. Silver, D., Hassabis, D.: Alphago: mastering the ancient game of go with machine learning. Research Blog (2016)
23. Sutton, R.S., Barto, A.G.: Reinforcement Learning: An Introduction. MIT Press, Cambridge (1998)
24. Szegedy, C., Zaremba, W., Sutskever, I., Bruna, J., Erhan, D., Goodfellow, I., Fergus, R.: Intriguing properties of neural networks. arXiv preprint arXiv:1312.6199 (2013)
25. Zhang, T., Kahn, G., Levine, S., Abbeel, P.: Learning deep control policies for autonomous aerial vehicles with mpc-guided policy search. In: 2016 IEEE International Conference on Robotics and Automation (ICRA), pp. 528–535. IEEE (2016)
26. Zhu, Y., Mottaghi, R., Kolve, E., Lim, J.J., Gupta, A., Fei-Fei, L., Farhadi, A.: Target-driven visual navigation in indoor scenes using deep reinforcement learning. In: 2017 IEEE International Conference on Robotics and Automation (ICRA), pp. 3357–3364. IEEE (2017)

What Is Acceptably Safe for Reinforcement Learning?

John Bragg[1]($\boxtimes$) and Ibrahim Habli[2]

[1] MBDA UK Ltd., Filton, Bristol, UK
john.bragg@mbda.co.uk
[2] University of York, York, Yorkshire, UK
ibrahim.habli@york.ac.uk

Abstract. Machine Learning algorithms are becoming more prevalent in critical systems where dynamic decision making and efficiency are the goal. As is the case for complex and safety-critical systems, where certain failures can lead to harm, we must proactively consider the safety assurance of such systems that use Machine Learning. In this paper we explore the implications of the use of Reinforcement Learning in particular, considering the potential benefits that it could bring to safety-critical systems, and our ability to provide assurances on the safety of systems incorporating such technology. We propose a high-level argument that could be used as the basis of a safety case for Reinforcement Learning systems, where the selection of 'reward' and 'cost' mechanisms would have a critical effect on the outcome of decisions made. We conclude with fundamental challenges that will need to be addressed to give the confidence necessary for deploying Reinforcement Learning within safety-critical applications.

Keywords: Safety · Assurance · Artificial Intelligence
Machine Learning · Reinforcement Learning

1 Introduction

Until recently, the safety assurance of software systems has been a reasonably well-established activity where safety engineers are able to provide evidence and confidence that the software will behave in a predictable way, for a given set of inputs and defined operating environment. However, the increasing use of Artificial Intelligence (AI) and Machine Learning (ML) has moved the goalposts; we can no longer rely on the 'traditional' safety techniques that depend on the 'deterministic' nature of the software [1]. The program that runs tomorrow may make different decisions and choices to the program that is executing today; it will have 'learned' from its experience.

AI and ML systems are essentially software systems that learn and adapt, based on experience and their environment [2]. Software is the primary vehicle for the implementation of AI and ML. However, historically, industry has typically

© Springer Nature Switzerland AG 2018
B. Gallina et al. (Eds.): SAFECOMP 2018 Workshops, LNCS 11094, pp. 418–430, 2018.
https://doi.org/10.1007/978-3-319-99229-7_35

shied away from putting safety-critical functionality into complex software that implement ML, e.g. preferring hardware technologies as they are relatively easier to provide assurance from a safety perspective. This position is not sustainable for future robotics and autonomous systems that are expected to learn and adapt yet maintain 'safety' [3]. Unfortunately, *"safety engineering is lagging behind emergent technologies."* [4] Although advances in safety analysis and assurance are far behind, the safety community may be able to catch-up but realistically may not be able to get ahead of the curve. The ML technology will almost always outpace safety assurance. As such, if a solution cannot be shown to be safe it may never become acceptable to deploy in safety-critical applications, despite the benefits that it may bring.

In this paper we explore the implications of the use of ML in safety-critical applications. We focus on Reinforcement Learning (RL), where the selection of 'reward' and 'cost' mechanisms would have a critical effect on the safety outcome of the decisions made. We propose a high-level argument that could be used as the basis of a safety case for RL systems and identify and analyse the technical and socio-technical factors that affect the potential strength of the reasoning. We conclude with fundamental challenges that will need to be addressed to give the confidence necessary for deploying RL within safety-critical applications.

2   Machine Learning

ML is a technique that relies on algorithms to analyse huge datasets and allows a machine (e.g. a computer) to perform predictive analysis, faster than any human is able to do. ML works, not by programming the computer to undertake a specific task, but by programming a computer with algorithms that provide it with the ability to learn how to perform a task. Whilst the implementation of ML does not in itself make a system an AI, it enables the system to perform the following tasks:

- Adapt to new circumstances that the original developer or system designer didn't envision;
- Detect patterns in different types of data sources;
- Create new behaviours based on recognised patterns; and
- Make decisions based on the success or failure of these behaviours.

The utilisation of ML is becoming more prevalent and is spreading to multiple domains as it is a feasible and cost-effective solution for many tasks that would be otherwise prohibitive to accomplish by any other means.

2.1   Reinforcement Learning

Figure 1 shows a model of how Reinforcement Learning (RL) works. An agent will be in a given state, it will perform an action on its environment and some time later will receive a response from that environment relating to the outcome

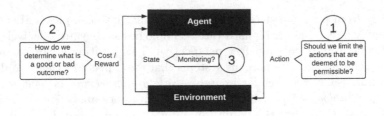

Fig. 1. A simple model of Reinforcement Learning

of that action. The agent will have 'learnt' something from that course of action and may subsequently change state. The cycle then repeats.

Whilst this is a simplified view of how RL works, it still raises some interesting issues:

1. Are we able to determine what the permissible actions are? If we do this, are we going to unnecessarily constrain the agent in carrying out what might actually be the correct (safe) course of action?
2. The agent is going to learn both 'good' and 'bad' as a result of its actions (negative outcomes can be as good as positive ones from the learning perspective).
3. Should we monitor the system and 'fail safe' if there are indications that it is moving towards an unsafe state? If so, to what extent can we understand and explain the internal mechanisms by which decisions are made by the RL System?

The concept of the reward mechanism is key to the way in which this type of system will learn, with the potential for such systems to make 'very bad' decisions in terms of the resulting outcome; in the case of safety-related/critical systems we are of course talking about the concept of 'harm'.

3   Safety of Complex Engineering Systems

When considering the safety of a system we are fundamentally referring to hazards, risks, and accidents. A hazard can be thought of as 'a potential source of harm'. This could be harm to people, assets or the environment in which the system is operating. An accident is the harm that occurs due to a hazard not being sufficiently controlled. A simple example of which would be the hazard of high pressure gas being contained within a canister. An accident would be violent rupture of the canister due to over-pressurisation. The risk that this accident occurs can be mitigated by manufacturing the canister from a material strong enough to be able to deal with pressures in excess of the expected operating pressure. The risk can be further reduced by adding other mitigations, such as a pressure release valve, that will activate before damage to the canister can occur.

System safety is an attribute of the configuration of the System components (i.e. sub-systems) the environment(s) within which the System exists or operates, and the hazards and accident outcomes associated with the System. In order to start to address System Safety it is necessary to understand how the functionality and the potential hazardous behaviours of the overall system, each System component, the relationships and interactions between them and the influences of the environment(s), are defined and studied.

3.1 Safety-I: The 'Traditional' Approach

A deterministic system (or perhaps more accurately a 'predictable system'), which is the focus of most safety standards, is one that will produce the same output from a given set of input parameters, starting conditions, or initial state [1]. The approach to safety in these systems is to construct an argument around the assumptions made during the design phase and the safety constraints based on those assumptions, that are subsequently placed upon it to ensure 'safe' operation. Accordingly, the predictions made about the behaviour of the system and the interactions that the system will have with its environment (including other systems, users and processes) will drive the safety argument structure. Evidence provided in support of the safety case is gathered through the application of analyses such as: Fault Tree Analysis (FTA), Failure Modes and Effects Analysis (FMEA) and Software Hazard Analysis and Resolution in Design (SHARD) [5].

As discussed by Hollnagel et al. in [6,7], historical approaches to safety presume *"... things go wrong because of identifiable failures or malfunctions of specific components"*. The safety of a system therefore depends on the enforcement of constraints on the behaviour of the system features, including constraints on their interactions, in order to avoid failure. The safety case presents a safety argument to this effect and evidence is provided to support it. This type of safety reasoning is defined as Safety-I.

Whether the safety case for the system remains valid for the operational life of the system depends upon whether those predictions continue to hold true. If they do not, then the confidence in the safety argument can diminish and the validity of the safety assurance case is then challenged. The safety argument must then be re-visited.

3.2 The Limitations of Safety-I

For inherently complex systems, such as those using ML, the future state of the system cannot be predicted. It is difficult to foresee all potential failure modes, and thus the implementation of system constraints during system design are not able to assure the through-life safety of the system. As stated in [8]:

> *"... the learning, emergent and adaptive behaviour and use of these systems pose a significant challenge to the assumptions and predictions made in the safety case, regardless of whether the documentation of the safety argument is explicit (i.e. in goal-based certification) or implicit (i.e. in prescriptive certification)."*

Thus, 'traditional' safety methods have limited use: firstly because any type of ML must almost certainly be implemented within software and the 'traditional' methods are predominantly focused on hardware; secondly, these methods tend to be used pre-deployment and are not typically used post-deployment to monitor safety functions.

3.3   Safety-II: The 'Adaptive' Approach to Safety

The introduction of the Safety-II approach brings a fundamental paradigm change to system safety; moving from the Safety-I approach of ensuring that *"as few things as possible go wrong"* to ensuring that *"as many things as possible go right."* [7] Safety-II relates to the system's ability to adapt and succeed under varying conditions. The safety of the system is therefore ensured, not through the implementation of pre-defined constraints but through its ability to deal with situations that cannot be predicted [7] and applying adjustments to the system during its operational life. The safety analysis of the system would thus be predicated on the ability of the system to avoid hazardous conditions or adapt and deal with them should they occur.

RL Systems adapt their behaviour based on the decisions they have made and the response they receive from their environment. This is similar to how a human being deals with day-to-day situations, i.e. making adjustments and trade-offs based on understanding their actual, and often dynamic, environment.

From a Safety-II perspective, we need an approach that aligns itself with this type of 'dynamism'. In their paper [8], Denney et al. identify three principles for dynamic safety cases that have to:

1. Pro-actively compute the confidence in, and update the reasoning about, the safety of ongoing operations;
2. Provide an increased level of formality in the safety infrastructure; and
3. Provide a mixed-automation framework.

The above safety assurance challenges, in particular with respects to RL Systems, are explored and refined in the next section.

4   Reinforcement Learning and Safety

In Fig. 2 we propose a high-level safety argument for RL, represented using the Goal Structuring Notation (GSN) [9]. GSN is a widely-used graphical language for formulating the structure of a safety argument. It provides a concise way of describing the claims of the argument (represented by goals drawn as rectangular shapes), the context that is applicable to the claim being made (represented by the rounded rectangle shapes), and the strategies that are used to explain the link between a goal and one or more sub-goals (represented by the parallelogram shapes). The diamond shapes represent an undeveloped entity, i.e. one where further refinement will be required to substantiate the claim made.

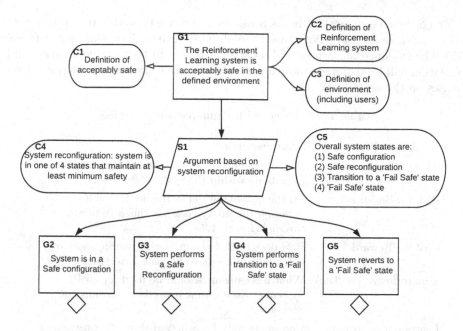

Fig. 2. A high-level safety argument structure for Reinforcement Learning systems

4.1 Argument Structure

The argument shown in Fig. 2 starts with a top-level goal, G1, that the RL System is 'acceptably safe'; this is a typical top-level claim when constructing a safety argument [10]. This claim is linked to a number of nodes, which define the context of the claim. The terms 'acceptably safe' and 'system' need to be defined, but of particular interest to the argument is the 'environment'. As previously discussed, the environment is the main point of interaction for the RL System and will define the nature of the 'Reward' or 'Cost' that the system receives.

Our main strategy for arguing the safety of a RL System is to provide an 'Argument based on system reconfiguration' (node S1). That is, the system is operating in a 'safe' configuration, in a 'Fail Safe' state, in a safe reconfiguration or transition state, all of which should guarantee at least minimum safety, despite a potential reduction in functionality or availability. This covers a number of sub-claims (nodes G2 through to G5). Firstly we have a sub-claim (G2) that the 'System is in a Safe configuration', this is represented as an undeveloped goal but is likely to be supported by verification and validation evidence that this is the case (including run-time verification evidence). Node G3 represents the claim that the RL System is able to perform a 'Safe reconfiguration', meaning that in response to a reward or punishment as part of its learning cycle the system can reconfigure its behaviour 'safely', i.e. it does not introduce any new hazardous behaviour.

If a 'safe' reconfiguration is not possible, assurance is needed that the system is instead able to transition 'safely' (node G4) into a 'Fail Safe' state (node G5). The evidence to support nodes G3, G4 and G5 in terms of verification and validation will be required (though this is beyond the scope of this paper, which focuses on the argument).

Table 1. Challenges with Reinforcement Learning

Challenge area	Short description
Societal Acceptance	How do we choose which human and social values to embody within the system? Sect. 4.2
Risk vs. Benefits	Do the benefits of deploying a RL System outweigh the safety risks? Is this a sufficient threshold? Sect. 4.3
Cost vs. Reward	How does a RL System learn where a negative outcome still needs to be 'safe'? Sect. 4.4
Monitoring & Feedback	What mechanisms should be used for an RL System to decide that it needs to reconfigure? Sect. 4.5
Learning Constraints	Can safety only be achieved through constraining the way in which a RL System learns? Sect. 4.6
Fail Safe	How and when should RL Systems fail safe? Sect. 4.7
Intelligent Safety	How can a RL System update its own safety case and explain the choices it has made? Sect. 4.8

Table 1 captures a number of technical and socio-technical challenge areas that we believe are key to the aim of assuring RL, and therefore in supporting the argument presented. These areas are discussed in the next sections and are linked to the nodes in the GSN argument.

4.2 Societal Acceptance

Ethics, safety and societal impact are three emotive topics that can be challenging enough in non-AI systems [11]. Factor in the current love/hate relationship that the public has with ML, as well as the 'unpredictable' nature of AI systems, and these sensitivities become even more entrenched. These are areas that Google's DeepMind are looking to address, where DeepMind's Mustafa Suleyman believes that the ethics of ML must be central to its development [12].

In [13], Stuart Russell proposed *"3 Principles for Safer Artificial Intelligence"*, which were:

Altruism: the robot's only objective is to maximise the realisation of human values;

Humility: the robot is initially uncertain about what those values are;

Observation of human choices: human behaviour profiles information about human values.

However, Russell's proposed principles raise their own questions. If the aim of AI is to replace or augment human decision making and maximise the realisation of human values, then we have to ask the question 'whose human values do we choose?' Not everyone's values are the same, especially in cases involving trade-offs between different values including safety, privacy and liberty. We have different belief systems, cultures, morals and ethics. How do we choose which ones to embody within a system?

The study of machine ethics is important when considering safety (Bostrom et al. [14] and Dennis et al. [15] are just two examples) but is the subject of machine ethics a red herring? It could be. As stated in Yampolskiy in 2012 [16], we need to ensure that machines are inherently safe and law abiding. The application of ethics to a machine is fraught with issues and could ultimately cause dissension. So, should ML systems exploit their computational abilities rather than emulate any such flawed human behaviour?

Considerations on the above topics would provide support for nodes C3 (Who are our users and the wider stakeholders and what are their values?) and C1 (What is acceptable to them?) in Fig. 2. This is key in defining acceptable risks, potential costs and intended benefits and a fair distribution of the risks, costs and benefits between the system stakeholders.

4.3   Risk vs. Benefits

In Sect. 3 we discussed that engineering a safe system always comes with a certain amount of risk [17,18]. However, when we introduce a RL System the challenge of managing uncertainty (and thus risk) can significantly increase given that we are unable to ascertain, prior to deployment, that the RL algorithm will make a 'safe' decision. The algorithm will make a decision based on a model calculated from its input data and this therefore comes with a probability that the decision made is a wrong one, especially during the early operation of the system.

However, not all problems are safety-related, and a wrong decision may not necessarily lead to harm. Even if, for example, the data that the RL System is using is corrupted it is not a foregone conclusion that an accident is going to occur. It may still be safe to deploy RL even in these error conditions (incorrect outcomes are not always unsafe outcomes). Indeed, in relation to the previous section where we discussed the impact on humans, we know from experience and evidence that humans often struggle to make decisions about safety [19], and therefore the distribution of risks and trade-offs with a RL System may well be an improvement for the majority of situations. Additional benefit may come, not only by ensuring that hazards are avoided, but in actually reducing the risk beyond that which was previously envisioned because the system has 'learnt' how to do this, i.e. in ways that a human could not have predicted.

These trade-offs would need to be explicitly considered as part of the safety argument and would largely contribute to nodes G2 and G3 in Fig. 2. That is, to what extent can we trust the RL System to reconfigure and maintain, or even improve, safety before forcing it to transition to a constrained 'Safe state'?

In other words, under certain conditions, excessive safety constraints might reduce rather than improve overall safety.

4.4   Cost vs. Reward

As we have discussed, RL is based on a cost/reward feedback mechanism. If the system makes a decision that is good then it is rewarded, if the decision is bad then there is a cost (or punishment) associated with that decision or action. The challenge for safety-critical applications is to select a cost/reward mechanism that is appropriate to the nature of the system, its objectives, and the safety constraints that need to be adhered to [20]. This is also linked to the risks and benefits discussed in Sect. 4.3, whereby choosing a cost/reward mechanism that is 'overly-protective' could result in limited benefits of using RL in the first place. Conversely, selecting a cost/reward mechanism that is too liberal could result in a significant increase in risk.

Within the context of a Safety-II approach, 'Cost' and 'Reward' are closely linked to risks and benefits. Therefore, considerations on cost (including increased safety risk) and reward (including increased safety benefit) support the claims being made in nodes G2 and G3 in Fig. 2. For example, a potential configuration might increase the safety margin (i.e. reward) but might compromise certain privacy aspects (i.e. cost). How could the RL System decide if the reward would outweigh the cost in this configuration, if this would be an acceptable trade-off by those affected by the decision and if, who, how and when to consult human stakeholders?

4.5   Lagging and Leading Indicators

Lagging Indicators can be thought of as 'traditional' safety metrics on the outcome of past accidents that have resulted from particular courses of action. This of course is not ideal when we want to prevent an accident from occurring in the first place. Any accident resulting from the deployment of a RL System would adversely affect the acceptance of such systems within society.

In order for predictive hazard analysis to be undertaken during run-time, monitoring and feedback must be designed into the system such that the system can assess whether it is moving towards a hazardous condition and that a reconfiguration of the system should be enacted in order to mitigate failure.

Thus, in order to effectively identify the potential for system failure, run-time system monitoring needs to be introduced in order to detect 'warning signs' that confidence in the enforcement of safety-related constraints of the system is eroding and that the system is moving towards an unsafe state. Whilst historically these 'warning signs' have, typically, only been apparent after failure has occurred, as stated in [21] the aim of system monitoring is to put in place a means of detecting the migration towards *"a state of unacceptable risk before an accident occurs."*

Accordingly, Leading Indicators need to be identified such that potential failures can be predicted and mitigating actions can be implemented in order to re-establish confidence in the system. This concept supports the claims being made in nodes G3 and G4 of Fig. 2. However, defining Leading Indicators depends on the ability to understand, explain and appropriately constrain the behaviour of the RL System, which is a challenge we explore in the next sections.

4.6   Safe Constraints on Learning

Despite the increasing promise of capability that RL Systems might bring, such systems will still need to comply with strict safety constraints in order to be accepted and deployed. How do we effectively constrain a system that has a seemingly boundless mechanisms to learn, reconfigure and adapt its behaviour?

If learning is limited in prescribed ways, some analysis might be possible, depending on the precise details of the learning limitations. If these are analysed prior to deployment to rule out certain behaviours, perhaps an analysis could show that it would not behave 'dangerously' [22].

However, if we constrain the system's ability to learn then we might also be constraining its capacity to learn what is actually the safest course of action [23]. If we don't allow the system to do something 'wrong' then it may not learn as effectively [20], in the same way that a child learns not to touch a hot surface if it has already endured some pain from a previous experience. If we constrain the system's ability to learn we may be preventing it from learning what 'safe' actually means and restrict the system to our own understanding of 'safe', which in turn might be over-pessimistic.

What we should perhaps consider is exploring the concept of providing a 'safe learning environment' for the RL System in which it can learn, where models of other systems and the interactions with the environment are simulated so that no harm can be caused to humans, assets, or the environment. This approach would support nodes G2 and G3 in Fig. 2. However, this is often complicated by issues around the gap between the simulated and actual environments, including issues related to different societal/human values.

4.7   Fail Safe

To 'fail safe', in the context of a safety-critical system, usually means that the system has determined that it is no longer able to safely provide its intended functionality and that the only safe course of action is to move to a pre-defined 'fail-safe' state, with limited functionality, thus mitigating or preventing any harm to humans, assets or the environment.

This of course is predicated on the RL System's own ability to recognise that it can no longer continue to operate in a 'safe' manner, which would require knowledge and/or definition of 'safe' (node C1 of Fig. 2) along with feedback from the environment (C3), potentially informed by Leading Indicators, and knowledge of what it needs to do in order to transition to a 'Fail Safe' state (nodes G4 and G5). The notions of cost and reward are still likely to be relevant here, e.g. a RL System deciding not to handover control to a human driver until the car speed or environmental conditions are within certain thresholds (i.e. safety benefits of maintaining control outweigh handover safety risks).

4.8 AI-based Safety Assurance and Explainability

Considering we are dealing with systems that have in-built intelligence to adapt their behaviour at run-time in order to meet their functional objective, it perhaps becomes necessary for us to consider applying this same intelligence to the safety assurance side as well. How, as humans, do we believe we are going to be able to rationalise and explain the choices that a machine has made during its course of operation and in meeting its fundamental objective? Considering the DeepMind AlphGo as an example, the developers of the system were at a loss to explain many of the moves that the AlphaGo engine was making in its run-up to defeating the champion Lee Sedol. AlphaGo's learning had moved beyond the limits of what the developers were able to comprehend, which brings about an interesting question when considering the safety assurance of RL Systems; do we need to consider implementing 'Intelligent Safety' whereby the safety argument and monitoring evolves alongside the system rather than the conventional use of run-time monitoring based on predetermined Leading Indicators, e.g. a 'Safety Supervisor' [24]?

The implementation of such a dynamic approach would affect the entire argument framework in the proposed argument structure in Fig. 2 and would offer an idealised, though highly contentious, realisation of the notion of Dynamic Safety Cases [8], i.e. the RL System producing its own safety argument and evidence.

5 Conclusions

ML, and more specifically RL, is a very powerful technique whose adoption within a number of industries is increasingly growing. However, the ability to justify the deployment of such technology into applications of a safety-critical nature poses fundamental challenges. In this paper we have covered what it might mean for a RL System to be considered 'safe' and covered both the 'traditional' (Safety-I) and new (Safety-II) approaches to assuring safety.

In addition, we have presented a high-level safety argument that could be used as the basis of forming a safety case for RL Systems. We have also highlighted a number of key challenge areas that we believe need to be addressed in support of a safety case.

We do however recognise the limitations of the proposed argument structure and the discussion around the challenges. As such we have identified a number of considerations for further work when considering the safety assurance of RL Systems. These are:

1. To what extent should RL algorithms be constrained in the way in which they learn?

2. How would we implement 'Intelligent/Dynamic Safety', whereby the safety monitoring evolves alongside the system?
3. To what extent should a RL System be allowed to create/update its own safety case as it learns?

We hope that progress in answering these questions, in the context of the challenges and argument presented, would be beneficial to the safe adoption of RL Systems into critical applications.

References

1. Faria, J.M.: Non-determinism and failure modes in machine learning. In: 2017 IEEE International Symposium on Software Reliability Engineering Workshops (ISSREW), pp. 310–316. IEEE (2017)
2. Calinescu, R.: Emerging techniques for the engineering of self-adaptive high-integrity software. In: Cámara, J., de Lemos, R., Ghezzi, C., Lopes, A. (eds.) Assurances for Self-Adaptive Systems. LNCS, vol. 7740, pp. 297–310. Springer, Heidelberg (2013). https://doi.org/10.1007/978-3-642-36249-1_11
3. McDermid, J.: Safety of autonomy: challenges and strategies. In: International Conference on Computer Safety, Reliability, and Security. Springer (2017)
4. McDermid, J.: Playing catch-up: The fate of safety engineering. In: Developments in System Safety Engineering, Proceedings of the Twenty-fifth Safety-Critical Systems Symposium, Bristol, UK (2017). ISBN 978–1540796288
5. Pumfrey, D.J.: The Principled Design of Computer System Safety Analyses. Ph.D. thesis, University of York (1999)
6. Hollnagel, E.: Safety-I and Safety-II: The Past and Future of Safety Management. Ashgate Publishing, Ltd. (2014)
7. Hollnagel, E., Leonhardt, J., Licu, T., Shorrock, S.: From Safety-i to Safety-ii: A white paper. European Organisation for the Safety of Air Navigation (EUROCONTROL), Brussels (2013)
8. Denney, E., Pai, G., Habli, I.: Dynamic safety cases for through-life safety assurance. In: International Conference on Software Engineering (ICSE 2015) (2015)
9. Assurance Case Working Group [ACWG]: GSN community standard version 2. Safety Critical Systems Club (2018)
10. Kelly, T.P.: Arguing Safety - A Systematic Approach to Managing Safety Cases. Ph.D. thesis, The University of York (1998)
11. Porter, Z., Habli, I., Monkhouse, H., Bragg, J.: The moral responsibility gap and the increasing autonomy of systems. In: First International Workshop on Artificial Intelligence Safety Engineering (WAISE) (2018)
12. Suleyman, M.: In 2018, AI will gain a moral compass, January 2018. http://www.wired.co.uk/article/mustafa-suleyman-deepmind-ai-morals-ethics. Accessed 09 Mar 2018
13. Russell, S.: 3 principles for creating safer AI, April 2017. https://www.ted.com/talks/stuart_russell_how_ai_might_make_us_better_people. Accessed 09 Mar 2018
14. Bostrom, N., Yudkowsky, E.: The ethics of artificial intelligence. Camb. Handb. Artif. Intell. **316**, 334 (2014)
15. Dennis, L., Fisher, M., Slavkovik, M., Webster, M.: Formal verification of ethical choices in autonomous systems. Rob. Auton. Syst. **77**, 1–14 (2016)

16. Yampolskiy, R.V.: Artificial intelligence safety engineering: why machine ethics is a wrong approach. In: Müller, V. (ed.) Philosophy and Theory of Artificial Intelligence. SAPERE, vol. 5, pp. 389–396. Springer, Heidelberg (2013). https://doi.org/10.1007/978-3-642-31674-6_29

17. Leong, C., Kelly, T., Alexander, R.: Incorporating epistemic uncertainty into the safety assurance of socio-technical systems. arXiv preprint arXiv:1710.03394 (2017)

18. Rushby, J.: Logic and epistemology in safety cases. In: Bitsch, F., Guiochet, J., Kaâniche, M. (eds.) SAFECOMP 2013. LNCS, vol. 8153, pp. 1–7. Springer, Heidelberg (2013). https://doi.org/10.1007/978-3-642-40793-2_1

19. Morris, A.H.: Decision support and safety of clinical environments. BMJ Qual. Saf. **11**(1), 69–75 (2002)

20. Amodei, D., Olah, C., Steinhardt, J., Christiano, P., Schulman, J., Mané, D.: Concrete problems in AI safety. arXiv preprint arXiv:1606.06565 (2016)

21. Leveson, N.: A systems approach to risk management through leading safety indicators. Reliab. Eng. Syst. Saf. **136**, 17–34 (2015)

22. Garcıa, J., Fernández, F.: A comprehensive survey on safe reinforcement learning. J. Mach. Learn. Res. **16**(1), 1437–1480 (2015)

23. Mason, G.R., Calinescu, R.C., Kudenko, D., Banks, A.: Assured reinforcement learning with formally verified abstract policies. In: 9th International Conference on Agents and Artificial Intelligence (ICAART), York (2017)

24. Feth, P., Schneider, D., Adler, R.: A conceptual safety supervisor definition and evaluation framework for autonomous systems. In: Tonetta, S., Schoitsch, E., Bitsch, F. (eds.) SAFECOMP 2017. LNCS, vol. 10488, pp. 135–148. Springer, Cham (2017). https://doi.org/10.1007/978-3-319-66266-4_9

Uncertainty in Machine Learning Applications:
A Practice-Driven Classification of Uncertainty

Michael Kläs[(✉)] and Anna Maria Vollmer[(✉)]

Fraunhofer Institute for Experimental Software Engineering IESE,
Fraunhofer Platz 1, 67663 Kaiserslautern, Germany
{michael.klaes,anna-maria.vollmer}@iese.fraunhofer.de

Abstract. Software-intensive systems that rely on machine learning (ML) and artificial intelligence (AI) are increasingly becoming part of our daily life, e.g., in recommendation systems or semi-autonomous vehicles. However, the use of ML and AI is accompanied by uncertainties regarding their outcomes. Dealing with such uncertainties is particularly important when the actions of these systems can harm humans or the environment, such as in the case of a medical product or self-driving car. To enable a system to make informed decisions when confronted with the uncertainty of embedded AI/ML models and possible safety-related consequences, these models do not only have to provide a defined functionality but must also describe as precisely as possible the likelihood of their outcome being wrong or outside a given range of accuracy. Thus, this paper proposes a classification of major uncertainty sources that is usable and useful in practice: scope compliance, data quality, and model fit. In particular, we highlight the implications of these classes in the development and testing of ML and AI models by establishing links to specific activities during development and testing and means for quantifying and dealing with these different sources of uncertainty.

Keywords: Artificial intelligence · Dependability · Safety engineering
Data quality · Model validation · Empirical modelling

1 Motivation

Systems that make use of models provided by techniques belonging to the domains of machine learning (ML) and artificial intelligence (AI) are becoming increasingly important in our daily life. The terms AI and ML are frequently used interchangeable in this context although differences exist depending on specific definitions. This paper uses the term AI/ML models to refer to computation models trained on empirical data to mimic 'intelligence' by transforming inputs to outcomes based on mathematical relationships that are hard to derive by deductive reasoning or simple statistical analysis.

Nowadays, systems that make use of these models do not only recommend movies that we are most likely enjoy [1], but also support the detection of cancer based on images [2] or initiate emergency braking to avoid car crashes [3]. In turn, this means that these models are slowly also becoming a part of safety-relevant systems, where a high risk exists that humans or the environment may be harmed in the case of a failure.

© Springer Nature Switzerland AG 2018
B. Gallina et al. (Eds.): SAFECOMP 2018 Workshops, LNCS 11094, pp. 431–438, 2018.
https://doi.org/10.1007/978-3-319-99229-7_36

When the relevant existing standards and guidelines for safety-relevant systems (e.g., [4, 5]) were written, however, the usage of AI/ML was not an issue yet and was thus not considered. As a consequence, many techniques proposed in these standards and guidelines appear difficult to apply for systems relying on AI/ML in safety-relevant functions. For example, formal verification techniques cannot be reasonably applied in these kinds of complex models trained on empirical data. Another open question is how to effectively perform mandatory safety reviews for models such as deep convolutional neural networks (CNNs), which have been considered as the state of the art in image recognition since 2012 [6].

Because of the complexity and empirical nature of these models, no guarantee can be provided for their correctness. Thus, a possible consequence could be refusal of the use of these models for safety-critical functions. Traffic sign recognition systems could still provide information to assist human drivers. However, a car would not be allowed to autonomously cross an intersection based on recognized traffic signs and its knowledge of priority rules because it cannot be guaranteed that each stop sign will be recognized correctly in every case.

Alternatives to this strict refusal are being discussed [7, 8]; one alternative could be to encapsulate functionality provided by such models and appropriately deal with the inherent uncertainty of their outcomes in the containing system by making use of deterministic and verifiable rules. In this setting, the containing system would be responsible for adequate risk management, taking into account the likelihood that the outcome of the encapsulated model might be wrong, as well as the safety-related consequences of every decision made. In order to allow for informed decisions, encapsulated models would not only have to provide a given service but also describe as precisely as possible the uncertainty remaining in their outcomes. This means that the models would become *dependable* in a figurative sense, according to Avizienis et al.'s definition of systems [9], by delivering their service together with *information about outcome-related uncertainty* that can justifiably be trusted. Based on this information, the containing system could, for example, decide to consider further information sources (as applied in sensor fusion) or adapt its behavior in order to handle the remaining uncertainty adequately. In our scenario of autonomous intersection crossing, the containing system could, for example, use GPS localization as an additional information source or slow down the vehicle, thereby buying time to analyze further images taken of the traffic situation.

At present, model validation and testing commonly focus on determining and optimizing the overall accuracy of the created model (cf. KAGGLE competitions, e.g., the ImageNet Challenges[1]). However, the models' accuracy, which is commonly measured as *error rate*, is only a very generic and therefore weak estimator for the uncertainty remaining in a specific outcome, which is commonly referred to as *prediction uncertainty*. For instance, an error rate of 0.54% on a test dataset of traffic sign images [10] indicates that the respective model is 99.46% confident of providing a correct outcome or, conversely, that it is 0.54% uncertain *on average*. However, for use in safety-relevant functions, this general statement is likely too coarse-grained. Although a reported accuracy of 99.46% is excellent, autonomous vehicles simply ignoring one of two hundred

---

[1] https://www.kaggle.com/competitions.

stop signs might not be considered sufficiently safe. To be useful, more precise prediction uncertainty estimates are required that consider the situation at hand. For instance, fog or backlight conditions may affect the confidence in the provided outcomes, as may dirt on the camera lens. Moreover, the question needs to be answered of whether the test dataset on which the accuracy of the model was determined matches the situation in which the model is currently being applied.

In order to consider such sources of uncertainty during model development and testing more systematically, an applicable framework and associated terminology would be needed in practice. We especially see the need for a practice-driven classification of the different sources of uncertainty that have to be addressed and quantified. Thus, this position paper proposes a sound and usable schema for classifying uncertainty sources that are relevant in AI/ML models. The main practical benefit is seen in establishing clear links between specific sources of uncertainty and activities performed during model development and testing, and thus the possibility to define concrete means for quantifying and dealing better with the various sources of uncertainty.

The paper is structured as follows: Sect. 2 provides a short overview of existing classifications of uncertainty. Section 3 introduces the proposed classification, illustrates its application on an example, and discusses its implications. Section 4 closes the paper with an outlook on next steps.

2   Related Work: Existing Classifications of Uncertainty

In general, uncertainty is interpreted as "what is not known precisely", but it can be characterized differently, e.g., by also considering its impact or causes. Thus, various taxonomies and classifications of uncertainty exist that provide different points of view on uncertainty, such as aleatoric vs. epistemic, irreducible vs. reducible, or the different kinds of inference that introduce them (e.g., predictive, statistical, or proxy) [11].

Mahdavi-Hezavehi et al. present a literature review and overview of different uncertainty studies in the context of system architecture including uncertainty classifications comprising the dimensions location, nature, sources, and level/spectrum [12]. Furthermore, they propose a classification based on the source's *model* (uncertainty caused by system models due to their abstraction, model drift, incompleteness, complexity, etc.), *goals* (uncertainty caused by a system's goal-related complications such as outdated goals, goal dependencies, future goal changes, etc.), and *environment* (uncertainty caused by environmental circumstances including execution context, multiple ownership, human involvement). Other uncertainty dimensions reported in the literature consider *resources* (changing or new ones) or *adaptation functions* (automatic learning, sensing, decentralization, etc.). Further uncertainty types are reported by another study considering different publications: *content, environment, geographical location, occurrence,* and *time* [13].

A detailed classification is provided in the context of simulation models by Kennedy and O'Hagan, who distinguish between *parameter, parametric, structural, algorithmic, experimental,* and *interpolation* uncertainty [14].

For safety-critical ML applications, Faria distinguishes between sources of output variation on the levels *experience*, *task*, *algorithm*, *implementation*, and *hardware* [15].

All these classifications can help to get a better understanding of the various aspects of uncertainty and may support practitioners in identifying important sources of uncertainty in their context. However, they are hard to apply effectively in practice for rigorous prediction uncertainty quantification because their boundaries are not sharp (e.g., aleatoric vs. epistemic), because they cannot be reasonably quantified and distinguished in a practical AI/ML setting (c.f. the detailed classes of Kennedy and O'Hagan [13]), or because they have no direct links and implications for model building and testing.

3   Sources of Uncertainty in AI/ML-Model Applications

In order to introduce our classification, this section first illustrates common activities in the model building and testing process based on an example. Then the proposed classification is derived by highlighting and grouping major sources of uncertainty that occur in this process. Finally, implications of the proposed classification are discussed.

3.1   Typical Process of Model Learning and Application

Most development and testing of AI/ML models more or less explicitly follows an adaptation of the CRISP-DM [16] approach, which was initially introduced by IBM and comprises the steps business/domain understanding, data understanding, data preparation, modeling, evaluation, and deployment. Next, we summarize the key activities in the process that are relevant for uncertainty in the model application outcomes and illustrate them with an ongoing example.

Based on a specific goal or problem statement, the planned *scope* of the model application is defined. In our example, the scope could be traffic sign recognition in all possible driving conditions of a passenger car on public roads in the target market Germany. Based on the scope definition, *raw data* is gathered in the relevant context to build and test the AI/ML model. In our example, such data could be images taken by cameras in pilot cars driving through Germany for several months, or an existing dataset such as the GTSRB dataset[2] with more than 50,000 traffic sign images. In the next step, the raw data is typically filtered and preprocessed before being used as *cleaned data* to build and test the model because depending on the data source, raw data may suffer from various quality issues that would affect the final accuracy of the model. Moreover, preprocessing of the data makes them more accessible in modeling. In our example, images with specific problems could be filtered, such as very dark images, images with strong backlight conditions or massive lance flares, or blurred images. Preprocessing techniques include, among others, image normalization, Contrast Limiting Adaptive Histogram Equalization (CLAHE) [17], and Single-Image Super-Resolution (SISR) [18]. The clean data is separated into modelling and test data, with the *modelling data* being used to build and cross-validate the AI/ML model and the *test data* to evaluate

---

[2] http://benchmark.ini.rub.de/?section=gtsrb&subsection=dataset.

the final model and determine how well the model fits previously unseen data. If the *model* is considered to be sufficiently accurate, it is deployed to productive use (e.g., as part of a driver assistance system) annotated with its *error rate* (e.g., 0.54%).

3.2   A Practice-Driven Classification of Uncertainty

If we agree on the definition of prediction uncertainty as the likelihood that the provided outcome of a model may be wrong or outside a given range of accuracy, based on the model building and testing process, three major sources of uncertainty can be identified: scope compliance, data quality, and model fit. As we will discuss, the three uncertainty categories are stacked on top of each other; Fig. 1 presents an onion layer model.

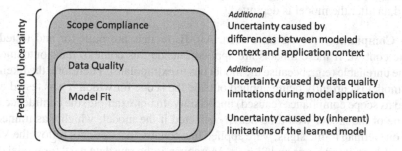

Fig. 1.   Onion layer model of uncertainty in AI/ML application outcomes.

Model Fit. Uncertainty related to model fit is caused by the fact that AI/ML techniques provide empirical models that are only an approximation of the real (functional) relationship between the model input and its outcome. The accuracy of this approximation, which is limited, e.g., due to the limited number of model parameters, input variables considered, and data points available to train the model, represents the model fit. Uncertainty caused by fitting deficits is commonly measured by the error rate, which is calculated when spitting the cleaned data into a training dataset and a test dataset.

There are two important underlying assumptions regarding uncertainty caused by model fit. (1) The model is applied in a setting that is appropriately represented by the test dataset, which is true for the cleaned dataset from which the test data is typically randomly selected. (2) The model is built and applied on data on a homogeneously high quality level (i.e., the data does not suffer from quality issues), which is also more likely in a well-cleaned dataset.

Implication: The average uncertainty caused by model fit can be measured using standard model evaluation approaches applied on high quality data and can be seen as a lower boundary approximation of the remaining uncertainty.

Data Quality. In a real setting, all kinds of data collected (e.g., based on sensors but also human input) is limited in its accuracy and potentially affected by various kinds of quality issues. The actual level of uncertainty in the outcome of an AI/ML model is thus affected by the quality (especially the accuracy) of the data on which it is currently applied. Therefore, additional uncertainty that is the result of a delta between the quality of the cleaned data and the data on which the model is currently being applied can be defined as data quality (caused) uncertainty. In our example, confidence in the model outcome may be affected by a camera with lower resolution or a damaged lens as well as by difficult lighting and bad weather conditions such as rain or fog.

Implication: Dealing with data quality uncertainty requires extending the standard model evaluation procedures with specialized setups to investigate the effect of different quality issues on the accuracy of the outcomes in order to provide uncertainty adjustments for cases where the model is applied on data of below-nominal quality. As a consequence, data quality has be quantified and measured not only to annotate raw data with quality information during data preparation, but also to measure the current quality of the data after the model is deployed.

Scope Compliance. As we have seen, AI/ML models are built for and tested in a specific context. If these models are applied outside this context, their outcomes can become unreliable (e.g., because the model has to extrapolate). Therefore, the likelihood that a model is currently being applied outside the scope for which it was tested can be defined as scope compliance (caused) uncertainty. In our example, the confidence in the outcome of the model would be heavily affected if the model, which was trained and tested on German traffic signs, were applied in a country that does not follow the Vienna Convention on Road Signs and Signals. Moreover, if the raw data used for model development and testing were collected between May and October, the test dataset would most likely miss images of traffic signs (partially) covered by snow.

Implication: Scope compliance uncertainty can stem from two sources, as illustrated in the example: The model may be applied outside the intended scope or the raw dataset might not be representative of the intended scope. The former can be detected by monitoring relevant context characteristics (in our example, e.g., GPS location, velocity, temperature, date, time of day) and comparing the results with the boundaries of the intended scope. In order to reason about the latter, raw data needs to be annotated with context characteristics (e.g., GPS location, velocity, temperature, date, time of day) in order to compare its actual and assumed distribution in the intended scope.

4   Conclusion

Distinguishing between the three types of uncertainties presented (*model fit*, *data quality*, *scope compliance*) is motivated from a practical point of view because each of these types requires specific means for detecting the related uncertainty and coping with it.

Furthermore, the classification builds on existing ones and enables further focused uncertainty analysis by providing three clearly separated and measurable constructs. In a first approximation, prediction uncertainty can be determined by adjusting *model-fit-caused uncertainty* with a *data quality factor* determined on the basis of the quality of the current input data and the probability of *scope compliance*.

Building upon this classification, we plan to provide a practical framework for capturing uncertainty when building and testing AI/ML models. Additionally, we are planning its evaluation in case studies to demonstrate its applicability and usefulness.

Acknowledgments. Parts of this work is funded by the German Ministry of Education and Research (BMBF) under grant number 01IS16043E (CrESt).

References

1. Carrer-Neto, W., Hernández-Alcaraz, M.L., Valencia-García, R., García-Sánchez, F.: Social knowledge-based recommender system. Application to the movies domain. Expert Syst. Appl. **39**(12), 10990–11000 (2012)
2. Sirinukunwattana, K., Raza, S.E.A., Tsang, Y.W., Snead, D.R.J., Cree, I.A., Rajpoot, N.M.: Locality sensitive deep learning for detection and classification of nuclei in routine colon cancer histology images. IEEE Trans. Med. Imaging **35**(5), 1196–1206 (2016)
3. Bengler, K., Dietmayer, K., Farber, B., Maurer, M., Stiller, C., Winner, H.: Three decades of driver assistance systems: review and future perspectives. IEEE Intell. Transp. Syst. Mag. **6**(4), 6–22 (2014)
4. ISO 26262: Road vehicles – Functional safety
5. IEC 61508 ed. 2, Functional safety of electrical/electronic/programmable electronic (E/E/PE) safety related systems
6. Krizhevsky, A., Sutskever, I., Hinton, G.E.: ImageNet classification with deep convolutional neural networks. Commun. ACM **60**(6), 84–90 (2017)
7. Varshney, K.R.: Engineering safety in machine learning. In: Information Theory and Applications Workshop (ITA), La Jolla, CA, pp. 1–5 (2016)
8. Rasmus, A., Feth, P., Schneider, D.: Safety engineering for autonomous vehicles. In: IEEE/IFIP International Conference on Dependable Systems and Network Workshops 2016, pp. 200–205 (2016)
9. Avizienis, A., Laprie, J.C., Randell, B., Landwehr, C.: Basic concepts and taxonomy of dependable and secure computing. IEEE Trans. Depend. Secur. Comput. **1**(1), 11–33 (2004)
10. Ciregan, D., Meier, U., Schmidhuber, J.: Multi-column deep neural networks for image classification. In: IEEE Conference on Computer Vision and Pattern Recognition 2012, pp. 3642–3649 (2012)
11. Booker, J.M., Ross, T.J.: An evolution of uncertainty assessment and quantification. Sci. Iran. **18**(3), 669–676 (2011)
12. Mahdavi-Hezavehi, S., Avgeriou, P., Weyns, D.: A classification framework of uncertainty in architecture-based self-adaptive systems with multiple quality requirements. In: Managing Trade-offs in Adaptable Software Architectures, vol. 1, pp. 45–78 (2017)
13. Zhang, M., Selic, B., Ali, S., Yue, T., Okariz, O., Norgren, R.: Understanding uncertainty in cyber-physical systems: a conceptual model. In: Wąsowski, A., Lönn, H. (eds.) ECMFA 2016. LNCS, vol. 9764, pp. 247–264. Springer, Cham (2016). https://doi.org/10.1007/978-3-319-42061-5_16
14. Kennedy, M.C., O'Hagan, A.: Bayesian calibration of computer models. J. Roy. Stat. Soc. **63**(3), 425–464 (2001)
15. Faria, J.M.: Non-determinism and failure modes in machine learning. In: IEEE International Symposium on Software Reliability Engineering Workshops. 2017, pp. 310–316 (2017)

16. Wirth, R., Hipp, J.: CRISP-DM: towards a standard process model for data mining. In: International Conference on the Practical Applications of Knowledge Discovery and Data Mining (2000)
17. Yadav, G., Maheshwari, S., Agarwal, A.: Contrast limited adaptive histogram equalization based enhancement for real time video system. In: International Conference on Advances in Computing, Communications and Informatics (ICACCI), pp. 2392–2397 (2014)
18. Glasner, D., Bagon, S., Irani, M.: Super-resolution from a single image. In: IEEE 12th International Conference on Computer Vision, Kyoto, pp. 349–356 (2009)

Towards a Framework to Manage Perceptual Uncertainty for Safe Automated Driving

Krzysztof Czarnecki[✉] and Rick Salay

University of Waterloo, Waterloo, Canada
{kczarnec,rsalay}@gsd.uwaterloo.ca

Abstract. Perception is a safety-critical function of autonomous vehicles and machine learning (ML) plays a key role in its implementation. This position paper identifies (1) perceptual uncertainty as a performance measure used to define safety requirements and (2) its influence factors when using supervised ML. This work is a first step towards a framework for measuring and controling the effects of these factors and supplying evidence to support claims about perceptual uncertainty.

Keywords: Perception triangle · Machine learning · Safety assurance

1 Introduction

An Autonomous Driving System (ADS) consists of components for perception of the environment and vehicle state, planning the vehicle actions, and controlling the vehicle to implement these actions. While ML can play a role in all three areas, in the position paper we focus attention on perception and the use of supervised ML to infer the state information. Furthermore, we take an uncertainty-centric view of safety. The level of assurance in the safety of an ADS could be expressed in terms of our uncertainty that it will behave acceptably safely in all relevant situations. Then our assurance objective is to reduce this uncertainty to an acceptable level. This is different, but complementary, to the system safety objective of reducing risk to an acceptable level.

Uncertainty is an established measure of performance when perceiving the world. A desired property of perception is *accuracy*, that is, the estimated state being close to the true state of the world. In engineering measurement practice, the concept of accuracy has been largely abandoned and replaced by uncertainty estimation, however. For example, the "Guide to the expression of uncertainty in measurement" (GUM) [4] considers accuracy as a qualitative concept since the true value of the measured physical quantity is generally unknown and unknowable. On the other hand, measurement uncertainty, defined as a characterization of the dispersion of the values that could reasonably be attributed to the quantity being measured [4], can be estimated based on observable quantities and available knowledge. Note that measurement errors due to systematic effects

© Springer Nature Switzerland AG 2018
B. Gallina et al. (Eds.): SAFECOMP 2018 Workshops, LNCS 11094, pp. 439–445, 2018.
https://doi.org/10.1007/978-3-319-99229-7_37

(i.e., measurement bias) can be reduced if the effect is identified and a correction is applied. However, uncertainty will remain about whether the correction adequate. The GUM requires that sources of uncertainty associated with both random and systematic effects in the measurement procedure, instruments, and the particular measurement are rigorously identified and assessed.

In this position paper, we propose that this recommendation should apply to *all perception tasks*, not just the measurement of physical quantities. Perception can be seen as a form of measurement of state and has an associated *perceptual uncertainty*. For example, classifier accuracy on a test set is one observable quantity that can be used to estimate the overall uncertainty of a classifier in the field, but additional influence factors, such as the test set quality and representativeness, must also be considered. When a perceptual component is safety-critical, identifying the factors that influence perceptual uncertainty is a key step in assuring safety.

Our aim in this paper is to outline a generic framework for managing perceptual uncertainty in order to support the systematic safety assurance of perception components. Specifically, our contributions are the following: (1) we present a generic model for thinking about perception components called the *perception triangle*; (2) we discuss how perceptual uncertainty can be seen as a performance measure used to define safety requirements; and, (3) we identify as set of factors that influence perceptual uncertainty and discuss their measurement and impacts.

2   Perception and Uncertainty

An ADS relies on perception to discover the current state of the subject vehicle and its driving environment and track the state over time. Figure 1a illustrates the perception task using a *perception triangle*, which is loosely inspired by the semiotic triangle.

The objective of perception is to create a conceptual representation of the real world that captures facts relevant to the task. A concept defines the structure of the representation, including relevant attributes and relations. For example, a pedestrian is a person within a road who is neither a vehicle occupant nor a rider. Pedestrian attributes relevant to driving include pedestrian pose and extent, dynamic state, and activity. A mapping from the concept to real-world situations and scenarios identifies concept instances in the situations and scenarios, and thereby defines the concept semantics. Perception, indicated by the bent arrow, achieves the inverse task of linking real-world situations to their conceptual representation in two steps. First the sensory channel produces sensory data, such as images and radar returns. Then perception algorithms interpret the data to create the conceptual representation of the real world. The sensory channel represents the information pathway from the objects in the real-world scene to one or more sensors. Figure 1a represents perception at the domain level, which includes all conceivable situations and scenarios to define the concept of interest. The next section gives an example of an instance-level realization of the triangle for perceiving a particular real-world situation or scenario.

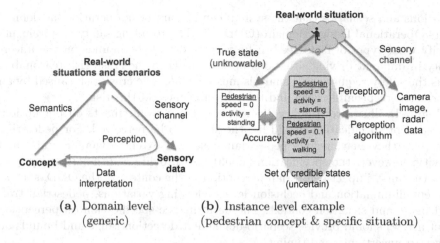

Fig. 1. Perception triangle

2.1 Perceptual Uncertainty as a Performance Measure

Perception yields an uncertain, or limited knowledge of the true state of the world, which is called *perceptual uncertainty*. Figure 1b illustrates this idea by instantiating the perception triangle for the pedestrian concept and a particular real-world situation. The situation contains a pedestrian who is visible to the camera and radar sensors of the subject vehicle. The true state of the pedestrian may be "standing still", but the perception algorithm interprets the sensory data and comes up with its own hypotheses about the state (see the ellipse in Fig. 1b). Probability mass or density function over the possible world states can model this uncertainty, where probability represents the credibility of any of the states being the true state given the knowledge of the overall perception setup. The perception algorithm may compute either an estimate of this probability distribution over the states or a point estimate of the state. In the latter case, one may use existing knowledge about the perception system, such as test results, to reason about the uncertainty of the point estimate.

The goal of ADS perception is to establish facts about the real world with acceptable perceptual uncertainty and sufficient timeliness as required for the dynamic driving task. The required perception performance depends on the type of fact to be established, the driving situation, and the overall ADS performance to be achieved. For example, perception of minor roughness is not safety relevant, but may be required for driving comfort; however, perception of major pavement damage, such as big potholes, is safety relevant.

ADS safety is the absence of unreasonable risk of crashes due to inadequate behavior, malfunctions, or security vulnerabilities. Existing practices and standards address safety assurance related to software and hardware malfunctions [5] and security vulnerabilities [9]. Our focus is on unreasonable risk caused by inadequate perception performance. The safety requirements on perception are established through hazard analysis and risk assessment, which considers different situations and scenarios that the system can encounter in operation, as defined by its Operational Design Domain (ODD) [8]. The resulting safety requirements specify what types of facts need to be perceived and the bounds on the uncertainty in different driving situations in order to keep the crash risk reasonable. Thus the safety requirements analysis must consider the crash risk caused by an incorrect perceptual decision and the reasonableness of this risk.

Figure 1a illustrates the key elements of safety requirements on perception. The concept specification should list the states to be perceived. For pedestrian detection, they may include pedestrian pose and extent, dynamic state, and activity; however, the specification should also provide *additional concept features* that may impact pedestrian perception in the context of the ODD, such as different illumination and occlusion levels, clothing variations, pedestrian traffic density, and situation context. The performance specification on perception (bent arrow) should provide scenario-dependent detection range and bounds on detection uncertainty and timing.

2.2 Factors Influencing Perceptual Uncertainty When Using Machine Learning

In order to meet the specification, the sources of perceptual uncertainty must be identified and controlled. Figure 2 implements the specification-level perceptual triangle from Fig. 1a using supervised ML. The figure shows two implementation-level perceptual triangles—one for development and another for operation (we assume no learning in operation). The left triangle illustrates training and testing during development. A necessarily partial set of situations and scenarios exemplifies the concept semantics for training and testing during development. The recorded sensory data is typically passed to human labelers, who interpret and label it. The training and testing process (shown as the fat arrow) uses the resulting labeled data to produce a trained model. The right triangle illustrates inference during operation. The trained model interprets the sensory data from

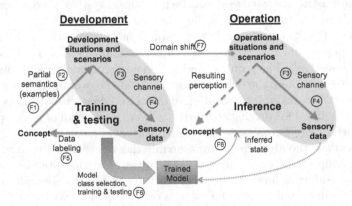

Fig. 2. Sources of perceptual uncertainty when using machine learning.

the situations and scenarios in operation and produces the estimated state. The dashed arrow summarizes the overall perception as the composition of sensing and inference.

Figure 2 identifies the factors that influence the overall perceptual performance in operation. Their influence and interdependence are as follows.

Conceptual Uncertainty (F1): The concept definition may allow different interpretations by different stakeholders. Conceptual uncertainty influences the selection of development situations and scenarios (F2) by making developers uncertain whether a particular situation or scenario is relevant to exemplify the concept. It also increases labeling uncertainty (F5) by increasing the chances that different labelers will interpret the concept differently. Conceptual uncertainty can be assessed qualitatively, such as by an expert review, or quantitatively, such as through labeling disagreement statistics and additional labeler feedback. The latter requires an enhanced labeling effort that also includes the additional concept and scenario features relevant to F2 and F3.

Development Situation and Scenario Coverage (F2): This factor is the degree to which the situations and scenarios used in training and testing cover the specified concept and ODD. It impacts model uncertainty (F6) and, through it, the perceptual uncertainty, which will be reduced if instances of situations and scenarios in specification scope are missed or are too few. Enhanced labeling of training and test datasets with additional concept and scenario features allows computing coverage and frequency statistics to guide the subsequent improvement of these sets; however, extensive validation testing and data collection in the field are necessary to discover so-called *unknown unknowns*, i.e., new relevant situations and scenarios that cannot be constructed from knowledge collected so far [6].

Situation or Scenario Uncertainty (F3): The structure of a situation or scenario may limit the observability of the state of interest and thereby allow multiple interpretations. As a result, the perceptual uncertainty will increase. This factor can be assessed through measures such as distance, levels of occlusion, illumination, and clutter, which were already mentioned under F1 and F2. For example, pedestrian distance and occlusions will limit the amount of information about the pedestrian that reaches the vehicle sensors. The impact of these measures on perceptual uncertainty should be assessed in testing.

Sensor Properties (F4): Sensor properties, in combination with the situation and scenario, may limit the amount of information of interest that is sensed, and thereby increase the perceptual uncertainty. Important sensor properties include sensing mode, range, resolution, noise characteristics, calibration, and placement. The sensor requirements are determined from perception requirements using established methods from sensor engineering [1]. The impact of sensor properties on the overall perception result, especially given a trained model, should be assessed through sensitivity studies.

Labeling Uncertainty (F5): Human labelers may disagree due to limited knowledge of the concept (F1) or the uncertainty from F3-4 or simply make accidental mistakes when labeling. Established methods exist to measure and reduce this uncertainty [3].

Model Uncertainty (F6): There is an uncertainty of what the model has learned in training and what decisions it will make in operation. This uncertainty depends on model class, capacity, and training data and procedure. Confidence measures (e.g., Bayesian deep learning [2]) can be used to provide a run-time measure of model uncertainty. For example, a low confidence pedestrian detection indicates a potential weakness in the model which must be diagnosed and addressed (e.g., by adding training data, changing the model class, etc.)

Operational Domain Uncertainty (F7): There is also uncertainty whether the situations and scenarios encountered in operation were adequately reflected in training; and whether the sensor properties in operation match those in training. For example, sensors in operation may be misaligned or calibrated differently. Novelty detection methods have been proposed to detect out-of-distribution inputs (i.e., outliers). For example, the training dataset can be used without labels to train an autoencoder to identify the characteristics of the dataset. At run-time, new inputs are checked for their similarity to the dataset (i.e., their novelty) by checking how well the autoencoder can reconstruct them [7]. The frequency of novel inputs encountered at run-time is a measure of operational domain uncertainty (F7).

3   Conclusion and Next Steps

In this position paper, we present first steps toward the development of a generic framework for perception safety that focuses on reducing perceptual uncertainty to an acceptable level. We identified a set of factors that contribute to perceptual uncertainty and briefly discussed their measurement and impact. Several topics are logical next steps. First, the measurement of the factors and their effects on perceptual uncertainty requires a systematic analysis; in addition to measurement at development time, F3, 4, 6, 7 should also be assessed in operation. Next, methods to control, that is, eliminate or reduce, the negative effects of these factors on perceptual uncertainty, and if not possible, to mitigate the effects, need to be provided. Finally, the argument structures and types of evidence to support claims about perceptual uncertainty in safety cases need to be established.

References

1. Bussemaker, K.: Sensing requirements for an automated vehicle for highway and rural environments. Master's thesis, TU Delft (2014)
2. Gal, Y., Ghahramani, Z.: Dropout as a Bayesian approximation: Representing model uncertainty in deep learning. In: 33rd International Conference on Machine Learning, ICML 2016, vol. 3, pp. 1651–1660 (2016)
3. Quoc Viet Hung, N., Tam, N.T., Tran, L.N., Aberer, K.: An evaluation of aggregation techniques in crowdsourcing. In: Lin, X., Manolopoulos, Y., Srivastava, D., Huang, G. (eds.) WISE 2013. LNCS, vol. 8181, pp. 1–15. Springer, Heidelberg (2013). https://doi.org/10.1007/978-3-642-41154-0_1

4. International Organization for Standardization: Guide to the expression of uncertainty in measurement (1995)
5. International Organization for Standardization: ISO 26262: Road Vehicles – Functional Safety (2011)
6. Koopman, P., Wagner, M.: Toward a framework for highly automated vehicle safety validation. SAE Technical Paper 2018-01-1071 (2018). https://doi.org/10.4271/2018-01-1071
7. Sabokrou, M., Khalooei, M., Fathy, M., Adeli, E.: Adversarially learned one-class classifier for novelty detection. arXiv preprint arXiv:1802.09088 (2018)
8. SAE On-Road Automated Driving (Orad) Committee: SAE J3016-Taxonomy and Definitions for Terms Related to On-Road Motor Vehicle Automated Driving Systems. SAE-Society of Automotive Engineers (2014)
9. SAE Vehicle Electrical System Security Committee and others: SAE J3061-Cybersecurity Guidebook for Cyber-Physical Automotive Systems. SAE-Society of Automotive Engineers (2016)

Design of a Knowledge-Base Strategy
for Capability-Aware Treatment
of Uncertainties of Automated Driving Systems

DeJiu Chen[1]([⊠]) [iD], Kenneth Östberg[2] [iD], Matthias Becker[1] [iD],
Håkan Sivencrona[3] [iD], and Fredrik Warg[2] [iD]

[1] KTH Royal Institute of Technology, 10044 Stockholm, Sweden
{chendj,mabecker}@kth.se
[2] RISE - Research Institutes of Sweden, Box 857, 50115 Borås, Sweden
{kenneth.ostberg,fredrik.warg}@ri.se
[3] Zenuity AB, Lindholmspiren 2, 41756 Göteborg, Sweden
hakan.sivencrona@zenuity.com

Abstract. Automated Driving Systems (ADS) represent a key technological advancement in the area of Cyber-physical systems (CPS) and Embedded Control Systems (ECS) with the aim of promoting traffic safety and environmental sustainability. The operation of ADS however exhibits several uncertainties that if improperly treated in development and operation would lead to safety and performance related problems. This paper presents the design of a knowledge-base (KB) strategy for a systematic treatment of such uncertainties and their system-wide implications on design-space and state-space. In the context of this approach, we use the term Knowledge-Base (KB) to refer to the model that stipulates the fundamental facts of a CPS in regard to the overall system operational states, action sequences, as well as the related costs or constraint factors. The model constitutes a formal basis for describing, communicating and inferring particular operational truths as well as the belief and knowledge representing the awareness or comprehension of such truths. For the reasoning of ADS behaviors and safety risks, each system operational state is explicitly formulated as a conjunction of environmental state and some collective states showing the ADS capabilities for perception, control and actuations. Uncertainty Models (UM) are associated as attributes to such state definitions for describing and quantifying the corresponding belief or knowledge status due to the presences of evidences about system performance and deficiencies, etc. On a broader perspective, the approach is part of our research on bridging the gaps among intelligent functions, system capability and dependability for mission-&safety-critical CPS, through a combination of development- and run-time measures.

Keywords: Automated Driving System (ADS) · Cyber-Physical System (CPS)
Embedded Control System (ECS) · Knowledge-Base (KB)
Uncertainty Models (UM) · Safety

B. Gallina et al. (Eds.): SAFECOMP 2018 Workshops, LNCS 11094, pp. 446–457, 2018.
https://doi.org/10.1007/978-3-319-99229-7_38

1 Introduction

Cyber-Physical Systems (CPS) and the underlying Embedded Control Systems (ECS) are the key enabling technologies behind autonomous vehicles, smart production systems, medical equipment and many other intelligent products. Many of these products are inherently safety- or mission-critical as the physical aspect, represented by the dynamics or energy flows under control, implies that a system failure could lead to unreasonable risks. This calls for, on the one hand, advanced formalisms, methods and tools for verification and validation, correct-by-construction and fault avoidance; and on the other hand, the deployment of specific safety functions and technologies for fault tolerance and fault treatment. Currently, the cyber aspect, characterized by information treatment and control logics for the operation perception, control of behaviors [1], is on an increasing degree based on Artificial Intelligence (AI), particularly Machine Learning (ML) and Artificial Neural Networks (ANN). The implementation relies on the provision of embedded resources for the sensing, communication, computation and actuation with an increasing degree of heterogeneity (e.g. a mixture of generic microcontrollers and specific AI accelerators). In this paper, we refer to the actual ability of a CPS to conduct specific tasks or actions regarding the system operations as *CPS Capability*.

Automated Driving System (ADS) [2] is a type of advanced CPS that can support self-governed driving behaviors in complex operational environments (e.g. public streets), with many potential economic, social and environmental benefits. However, being inherently safety critical, ADS is currently facing some fundamental challenges in risk management that necessitate a holistic strategy for fault avoidance, fault tolerance and fault treatment. One key factor behind the challenges is that the operation of ADS exhibits several types of uncertainty that make conventional quality assurance through formal verification and validation inadequate. In particular, in regard to the operational environment of ADS, there is an inherent uncertainty due to the emergent properties of traffic environment where heterogeneous traffic objects are composed randomly. Meanwhile, uncertainty can also show up in the perception of operational situations due to the design and performance issues of sensors (e.g. radar and camera) and services, such as delimited knowledge about the environment, unoptimized sensor position in vehicle, insufficient communication bandwidth. In general, a system could exhibit nondeterministic behaviors due to emergent behaviors and faults in the implementation because of partial specification, data inconsistency, imperfect synchronization and hardware reliability, etc. For ADS with AI functions, nondeterministic behaviors can also arise due to the gap between training set and real operational conditions, the inherent stochasticity in algorithms, and the complex interplay with actual CPS capability regarding perception, communication, computation and actuation.

This paper presents the design of a Knowledge-Base (KB) strategy [3] for a systematic treatment of such uncertainties of CPS and their system-wide implications on design-space and state-space. The approach is part of our research on bridging the gaps among intelligent functions, system capability and dependability for mission-&safety-critical CPS, through a combination of development-time and run-time measures [4]. In particular, the run-time measures are related to the design of embedded services for the awareness of operational situations and capabilities including the uncertainties, and then the assessment of operational risks. The development-time measures are centered on the enrichment of existing system ontology and frameworks (e.g. EAST-ADL [5]), by addressing the composition of heterogeneous functions and components, including those based on AI technologies.

The rest of this chapter is structured into the following sections: Sect. 2 provides an overview of related concepts in regard to the ADS architecture and uncertainty. Section 3 presents the proposed KB strategy, including the supported key modeling concepts and uncertainty descriptions. An overview of related technologies is given in Sect. 4. Section 5 summarizes our conclusions.

2   ADS System and Uncertainty

Figure 1 provides a schematic overview of ADS where the top-level system aspects are given by *Environment*, *Driver* and *Vehicle*. This conceptual view refines the generic architectural pattern introduced in [6]. While the *Environment* and *Driver* together constitute the operational context of ADS, the *Vehicle* refers to the product content of ADS given by a mixed composition of cyber and physical units. In particular, the *Environment* denotes the context in which ADS operates. It is defined by some external static and dynamic situations, including the road situation (e.g. lanes and road geometry) and the traffic situation (e.g. adjacent vehicles and pedestrians). The *Driver* refers to the person in the vehicle who interacts with the ADS [7]. The *Vehicle*, representing the product content of ADS, corresponds to a complete car or truck system. It is composed of some functional contents, shown as *Autonomous&Automation Functions* in Fig. 1, and some technical contents, shown as *Embedded Computation and Communication Capability* and *Vehicle Plant* in Fig. 1. Such contents collectively determine *ADS Capability*, referring to the ability of *ADS* to conduct specific driving tasks. *ADS Capability* is a specialized form of *CPS Capability* mentioned previously.

The functional contents consist of the control logics, organized into a decision hierarchy [8, 9] as shown in Fig. 2. The lower two layers, *Operation Control* and *Operation Decision*, implements a supervisory control strategy for the dynamics of vehicle plant. We refer to the control functions of these two layers collectively as *VDM* (Vehicle Dynamic Management). For automated driving, the tactic decision functions in the layer above decide the tactic actions, relating to the choice of target points on the road, as well as the preferred sequence of moves to reach the target points, such as accelerating and veering. The top layer contains strategic decisions for achieving a mission (e.g., the choice of routes from city A to city B). We refer to the functions in the tactic and strategic layers collectively as *TDC* (Task Decision and Control), shown in Fig. 1. Along with the decision hierarchy, there are also functions for operation perception. We refer the functions for the sensing of ADS *Environment* (defined previously) as *Environment Sensor* (*ES*); and the functions for the transformation of monitored environment data into a consolidated world-model as *Environment Perception* (*EP*), also shown in Fig. 1. We refer the plant sensing and actuation functions for VDM as *SA* (Sensor for Actuation of plant) and *A* (Actuator of plant), respectively.

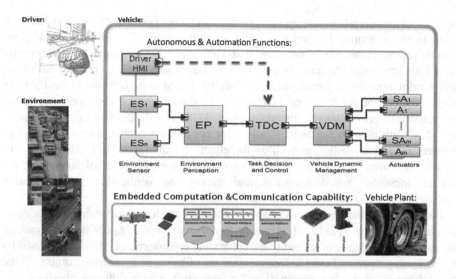

Fig. 1. A schematic overview of key aspects of ADS.

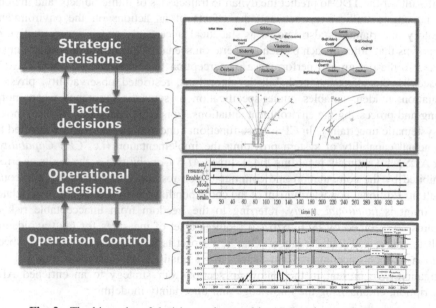

Fig. 2. The hierarchy of decision and control in ADS and example contents.

Across the decision hierarchy from VDM to TDC, an increasing degree of autonomy can be observed. Normally, VDM functions in the lower two operational layers are dominated by reactive feedback control. The design relies on *prior* knowledge about the plant (*Vehicle Plant*) in the form of models for the discrete and continuous dynamics, with the goal of ensuring highly deterministic behaviors. That is, given a particular sequence of inputs, such a function will always produce the same sequence of outputs while passing through the same sequence of states. In general, such a functional determinism, together with effective use of well-formulated *prior* knowledge, facilitates the verification and validation. For example, test generation using FSM or model-checking is a well-known approach [10]. Compared to VDM, such a prior knowledge centric and determinism based approach would be far from being sufficient for the design of TDC as well as the ES and EP functions, due to the associated inherent functional uncertainties of ADS. The design has to provide sufficient flexibility of such functions to allow for appropriate compensation of partial or incorrect *prior* knowledge, as well as for effective exploration and management of possible outcomes of actions. This implies not only a higher level of autonomy, but also an increased non-determinism that makes the verification and validation challenging.

For ADS, we distinguish two types of inherent functional uncertainty as for other autonomous systems [11, 12]: 1. *Aleatory Uncertainty*; and 2. *Epistemic Uncertainty*. The aleatory uncertainty is related to the contextual complexity of ADS. It is caused by the emergent properties from random interactions of heterogeneous traffic objects in the physical operational environment (i.e. *Environment*), under different conditions of weather, road, and physical locations. The presence of high aleatory uncertainty makes it difficult for the TDC to predict the dynamic trajectories of traffic objects, and thereby the upcoming traffic situations and the effects of its actions on the environment. Aleatory uncertainty is also known as statistical uncertainty and is representative of unknowns that differ in each particular operation scenario. The epistemic uncertainty is related to the design and performance of perception functions (i.e. *ES* and *EP*). It is caused by the effects of probabilistic algorithms, restricted observability, physical limitation, hidden variables, under-specification or semantic ignorance when monitoring and processing the environment situations. Epistemic uncertainty is also known as systematic uncertainty. In CPS, these functional uncertainties are further affected by the actual capability of system providing the implementation (i.e. *CPS Capability*). For ADS, any anomaly regarding the assumed *ADS Capability*, i.e. the faults or errors exhibited by the computation and communication resources and vehicle plant, could result in additional nondeterminism of the corresponding control functions. One related constraint is *functional safety*, referring to the freedom from unacceptable risk of hazards as specified by ISO 26262. It requires a set of measures for fault avoidance, fault tolerance and fault treatment. One key aspect is the support for a formal specification of such uncertainties and thereby for a qualified anomaly detection and risk mitigation. We present in the follow-up sections our strategy to an enriched ADS description, emphasizing the knowledge and uncertainty modeling.

3   Design of Knowledge-Base (KB) Strategy

The strategy introduced here aims to allow the above-mentioned types of uncertainty to be treated systematically together with a well-defined ADS system ontology. The modeling packages, shown in Fig. 3, include *ADS Architecture Model*, *ADS Knowledge Base*, and *ADS Belief&Uncertainty Model*. The key aspect is related to an integrated formal specification of system commitments for automated driving in various operational environments, and then the exploitation of such information for the systems engineering as well as the design of embedded services for anomaly detection and risk mitigation. As the base technologies, the following two existing modeling frameworks are adopted and extended for ADS: 1. EAST-ADL (Electronics Architecture and Software Technology - Architecture Description Language) [5] for the development of *ADS Architecture Model*; and 2. U-Model (Uncertainty conceptual model for CPS) [13] for the development of *ADS Belief&Uncertainty Model*. The *ADS Knowledge Base* presented below provides the support for a formal specification of the operational properties across the ADS *Environment*, *Driver* and *Vehicle*, effectively merging any semantic gaps between the system description and beliefs.

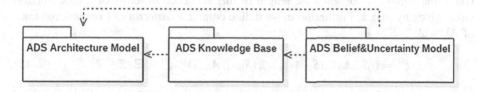

Fig. 3. The modeling packages and their dependencies.

The package diagram in Fig. 3 shows dependencies between the modeling packages. The *ADS Architecture Model* contains all the functional and technical design commitments regarding the *Environment*, *Driver* and *Vehicle*. The *ADS Knowledge Base* depends on the *ADS Architecture Model* as the corresponding description of operational properties relies on the design. These operational properties in turn constitute the basis for the uncertainty and belief statements by the *ADS Belief&Uncertainty Model*. Such statements can then be used to refine requirements, design solutions, verification and validation cases in the *ADS Architecture Model* when necessary.

3.1 ADS Knowledge-Base (KB)

Here, the term ADS Knowledge-Base (KB) refers to the models that stipulate the fundamental facts in regard to the overall system operational states, action sequences, as well as the related costs or constraint factors. The model constitutes a formal basis for describing and inferring particular operational truths as well as the belief and knowledge representing the awareness or comprehension of such truths.

For the reasoning of ADS behaviors and operational risks, we formulate each system operational state as a conjunctive state:

$$S_k = (S_{Env_k}, S_{Dri_k}, S_{Veh_k}); \ S_k \in S, S \subseteq S_{Env} \times S_{Dri} \times S_{Veh} \tag{1}$$

Here, the state variable S_k refers to the operational condition of an ADS system at a particular time point k. The discretized behavior description assumes a discretization of time t with $t \in \mathbb{R}_+$ (i.e. the set of non-negative real numbers) and a fixed time interval $dt > 0$. Every time of k corresponds to a discrete time step with $k = \lfloor t/dt \rfloor$ and

$k \in \mathbb{Z}_+$ (i.e. the set of non-negative integers). The state S_k is given by the conjunction (logical AND) of S_{Env_k}, S_{Dri_k}, S_{Veh_k}, referring to the respective operational conditions of *Environment*, *Driver* and *Vehicle* at the same time point. These state variables collectively define how the ADS react to the actions by the environment, the driver and the vehicle. We use S to denote the overall state space of an ADS, i.e. all possible state conditions, which is the subset of all possible combinations of operational conditions of environment, driver and vehicle (i.e. $S_{Env} \times S_{Dri} \times S_{Veh}$). A particular *behavior* of ADS is then a sequence of chosen operational conditions:

$$S^H = (S_0, S_1, \ldots, S_{H-1}) \tag{2}$$

where the variable H denotes the length of this sequence in terms of a time horizon value given by max k. Furthermore, we define complete *trajectory* or operational trace of ADS as:

$$\xi^H = ((S_0, A_0), (S_1, A_1), \ldots, (S_{H-1}, A_{H-1})); \; \xi^H \in \Xi, \Xi \subseteq 2^{S \times A} \tag{3}$$

Here, we use Ξ to denote the overall trajectories of an ADS, which is the subset of all possible combinations of all state and action pairs ($2^{S \times A}$) with A for all possible actions. Each segment of the trajectory consists of a pair of operational condition S_k and operational action A_k at the time instance k. The operational action A_k can be given by an action of environmental object (e.g. braking of preceding vehicle), a driver action (e.g. starting ADS), an action of ADS vehicle (e.g. steering to the right), or a combination of multiple actions at the same time instance. For an ADS, the choice of its action at any given instant is given by its *Autonomous&Automation Functions* according to the current as well as the past operation perceptions.

ADS operational performance is measured by the cost function associated to a trajectory $J(\xi^H)$. Accordingly, each requirement or constraint on the system is a proposition φ_i that can be satisfied or not satisfied:

$$\xi^H \vDash \varphi_i \text{ or } J(\xi^H) \vDash \varphi_j; \; \varphi_i, \; \varphi_j \in \Phi \tag{4}$$

The variable Φ denotes all requirements. Figure 4 illustrates the overall state space (S) of an ADS system and some of two possible trajectories (ξ_1^{H1}, ξ_2^{H2}) and (ξ_1^{H1}, ξ_3^{H3}). The first one represents a fail-safe scenario, where hazards are successfully detected at S_3 with ξ_2^{H2} as the safety measure for returning to the safe state S_5. The second one represents crash scenario with final state given by S_6. In system development, safety requirements are used to specify such trajectories.

In ADS, the VDM functions implement the driving actions selected by the associated TDC functions (see also Fig. 1). We have used S_{Veh_k} to denote the vehicle state S_{Veh} at time k. The state is defined as follows:

$$S_{Veh} = [P_x, P_y, \theta, v, \omega, a]^T \tag{5}$$

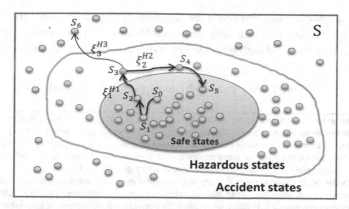

Fig. 4. Overall state space (S) of an ADS and some of the possible trajectories. Each point represents a state S_k, which is by a conjunction (logical AND) of states of the environment (S_{Env_k}), the driver (S_{Dri_k}), and the vehicle (S_{Veh_k}).

We let $(P_x, P_y) \in \mathbb{R}^2$ be the vehicle position relative to some fixed coordinate frame and $\theta \in [-\pi, \pi]$ be the yaw angle of the vehicle, and ω be the angular speed. The vehicle moves forward with speed $v \in [0, v_{Max}]$, where v_{Max} is the maximum speed. The acceleration is given by a. The basic motion of the vehicle is then given by:

$$\text{Continuous time}: \dot{S}_{Veh} = f(S_{Veh}, u);$$
$$\text{Discrete time}: S_{Veh_{k+1}} = f_d(S_{Veh_k}, u_k) \tag{6}$$

Here, u denotes the request of tactic action from the TDC to the VDM as the choice of θ and v, i.e. $u = [\theta, v]^T$. For example, at a particular time instant, the motion of the vehicle is determined by: $\dot{P}_x = v \cos \theta$; $\dot{P}_y = v \sin \theta$; and $\dot{\theta} = \omega$. For a tactic decision *Turn_left*, we have $\dot{P}_x = v \cos \theta$; $\dot{P}_y = v \sin \theta$; $\dot{\theta} = \pi$; For a tactic decision *Stop*, we have $\dot{P}_x = 0$; $P_y = v$; and $\dot{\theta} = 0$. Formally, with 2^A possible choices of actions A by TDC, we have:

$$S_{Veh_{k+1}} \subseteq (\mathbb{R}^6 \times 2^A) \tag{7}$$

3.2   Integration of Uncertainty Modeling and System Description

For ADS, the introduction of Uncertainty Models (UM) aims to constitute a formal basis for describing and inferring particular operational truths on the basis of the Knowledge-Base (KB). By describing and quantifying the corresponding belief or knowledge status, such models describe the degree of awareness or comprehension of some truths. The models can be used by system developers for the reasoning of functional and technical commitments at design-time or by embedded services for anomaly detection and risk mitigation at run-time. To this end, one key base technology adopted in our approach is the U-Model (Uncertainty conceptual model for CPS) [13], which aims to constitute a reference framework and standard. The core of the U-Model is a *Belief Model*, with the key meta-model concepts shown in Table 1.

Table 1. Key meta-model concepts of U-Model [13].

Key Concepts	
❖	**BeliefAgent**: a physical entity owning one or more Beliefs about phenomena/notion.
❖	**Uncertainty**: a state whereby a BeliefAgent does not have full confidence in a Belief it holds.
❖	**Belief**: an implicit subjective explanation of some phenomena or notions by a BeliefAgent.
❖	**BeliefStatement**: a concrete and explicit specification of some Belief held by a BeliefAgent about possible phenomena or notions belonging to a given subject area.
❖	**Evidence**: an observation or a record of a real-world event occurrence, or, alternatively, the conclusion of some formalized chain of logical inference for determining the truthfulness.
❖	**EvidenceKnowledge**: an objective relationship between a BeliefStatement and relevant Evidence. It identifies if the corresponding BeliefAgent is aware of the appropriate Evidence.
❖	**Indeterminacy**: a situation whereby the full knowledge necessary to determine the required factual state of some phenomena/notions is unavailable.
❖	**IndeterminacySource**: factors that lead to Uncertainty.
❖	**IndeterminacyNature**: the specific kind of indeterminacy that can be InsufficientResolution MissingInfo, Nondeterminism, and a combination of more than one kinds of indeterminacy.
❖	**IndeterminacyKnowledge**: an objective relationship between an IndeterminacySource and the awareness that the BeliefAgent has of that source.
❖	**KnowledgeType**: an enumeration) of four values:
	1. **KnownKnown** – BeliefAgent consciously aware of some relevant aspect.
	2. **KnownUnknown** (Conscious Ignorance) – BeliefAgent aware of the ignorant of some aspect.
	3. **UnknownKnown** (Tacit Knowledge) – BeliefAgent not explicitly aware of some relevant aspect that it may be able to exploit in some way.
	4. **UnknownUnknown** (Meta Ignorance) – BeliefAgent unaware of some relevant aspect.
❖	**Measurement**: the optional quantification (or qualification) that specifies the degree of indeterminacy of the IndeterminacySource.
❖	**Measure**: an objective concept specifying method of measuring uncertainty.

We also adopt EAST-ADL [5] as the base technology for the description of the functional and technical commitments in the system design. The key concepts of integrating KB, U-Model, and system description in EAST-ADL for ADS are shown in Fig. 5. With the integration, *Evidence* in uncertainty description can have its semantics given by some associated operational behavior, operation trajectory, or operation performance, which is defined by KB (see Eqs. 2, 3, 4). Such operations are conducted by system objects given as *EAPrototype*, which is an abstract class in EAST-ADL for the target vehicle or its environment objects and operator. The factors that lead to uncertainty are declared by the associations from *IndeterminacySource* to the EAST-ADL abstract classes for system environment, system functions, hardware components, and system anomaly. With such associations, the sources of non-determinism or indeterminacy are systematically distinguished, including the aleatory uncertainty, epistemic uncertainty, and the deficiency of ADS capability, as defined in Sect. 2.

The *EAST-ADL FunctionPrototype* and *HardwareComponentPrototype* refer to the application functions in an automotive vehicle and the related hardware components providing the computation and communication capability. As mentioned earlier, ADS has an increased heterogeneity in regard to the composition of functions and

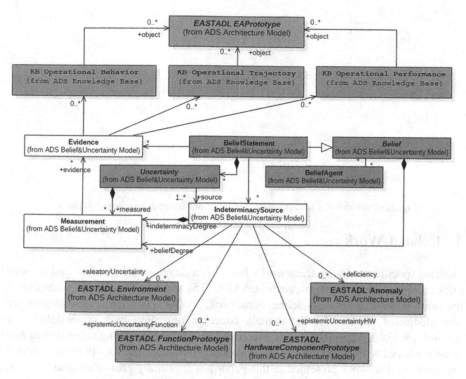

Fig. 5. Key design concepts of integrating UM, KB, and EAST-ADL for ADS description.

components through the inclusion of AI functions and specific hardware components. The modeling support presented constitutes a formal basis for clarifying and managing the related uncertainties. For the AI related artefacts, the U-Model provides support for the declaration of uncertainty patterns (e.g. periodic and random) and uncertainty measurement with probability, ambiguity and fuzziness. See [13] for further details.

The modeling support constitutes a formal basis for the reasoning of ADS behaviors and safety risks. As example, let's assume a vehicle system is subject to a behavior requirement on its state given as the relation of its position to the positon of other vehicles: $X < Y$. Due to uncertainties in the system, both variables cannot be determined exactly. The uncertainty of monitoring function (i.e. *IndeterminacySource*) is defined with an additional belief statement (i.e. *BeliefStatement*), where observed X and Y are given as independent random variables (i.e. *Evidence*) with the uncertainties quantified with normally distribution $(X \sim N(\mu_X, \sigma_X^2)$ and $Y \sim N(\mu_Y, \sigma_Y^2))$. The measurement is shown in Fig. 6(a) where the monitoring of variable X delivers: $\mu_X = 4$ and $\sigma_X = 0.8$. Similarly, the monitoring of variable Y results in $\mu_Y = 4.5$ and $\sigma_X = 1$. To validate the stipulated constraint $X < Y$, we can evaluate $(Y - X) > 0$. As both X and Y are normal distributed, the result of $Y - X$ is normally distributed itself, with $(Y - X) \sim N(\mu_Y - \mu_X, \sigma_Y^2 + \sigma_X^2)$. The distribution of this new variable is shown in Fig. 6(b). The area under the distribution at a distance below 0 then represents the probability that the initial constraint is violated and leads to a hazardous state.

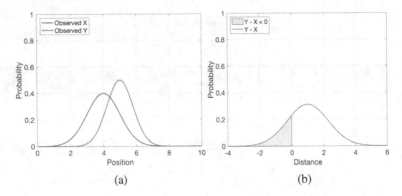

Fig. 6. Probabilistic uncertainty measurements for two monitored variables.

4   Related Work

Domain specific modeling frameworks have been developed for safety and mission-critical cyber-physical systems, such as AADL [15] and EAST-ADL [5]. Compared to the more generic systems modeling framework, SysML [14], these technologies provide dedicated support for the domain concepts regarding both methodology and technology. For the specification of uncertainties, all these modeling technologies need to be enhanced with additional modeling support for the descriptions of related patterns and metrics. The work presented in this paper has it primary goal of consolidating the architectural and operational concepts of ADS so that the descriptions of uncertainty can be semantically justified. Uncertainty as a condition of information quality has been one key concept of information theory [16]. The measure of *entropy* has been used for the quantification the information disorder or uncertainty. For CPS, the studies of uncertainties presented in [11–13, 17] constitutes the basis of our work. For CPS, explicit uncertainty modeling also constitutes the basis for effective diagnostics, dynamic anomaly detection and quality-of-service adaption [18–20].

5   Conclusion

CPS as an engineering field cuts across a number of application domains and technical areas beyond the conventional domains of control engineering and embedded systems. This work aims to support the integration of separately developed heterogeneous functions and components (including AI functions and components) by proposing a Knowledge-Base (KB) strategy for a systematic treatment of uncertainties. Through an integration with U-Model and EAST-ADL, the approach makes it possible for each uncertainty description to have well-defined semantics and architectural targets. Future work will consider the enrichment of uncertainty modeling for the analysis of safety knowledge for ADS as well as the synthesis of safety rules.

Acknowledgements. The research has been supported by the Swedish government agency for innovation systems (VINNOVA) in the ESPLANADE project (ref 2016-04268).

References

1. EC. https://ec.europa.eu/transport/themes/its_en. Accessed 28 May 2018
2. SAE International: SAE J3016: Taxonomy and Definitions for Terms Related to Driving Automation Systems for on-Road Motor Vehicle (2016)
3. Frederick, H.-R., Waterman, D., Lenat, D.: Building Expert Systems. Addison-Wesley (1983). ISBN 0-201-10686-8
4. Chen, D., Lu, Z.: A methodological framework for model-based self-management of services and components in dependable cyber-physical systems. In: Zamojski, W., Mazurkiewicz, J., Sugier, J., Walkowiak, T., Kacprzyk, J. (eds.) DepCoS-RELCOMEX 2017. AISC, vol. 582, pp. 97–105. Springer, Cham (2018). https://doi.org/10.1007/978-3-319-59415-6_10
5. Kolagari, R., et al.: Model-based analysis and engineering of automotive architectures with EAST-ADL: revisited. Int. J. Concept. Struct. Smart Appl. (IJCSSA) 3(2), 25–70 (2015)
6. Johansson, R., et al.: A strategy for assessing safe use of sensors in autonomous road vehicles. In: Tonetta, S., Schoitsch, E., Bitsch, F. (eds.) SAFECOMP 2017. LNCS, vol. 10488, pp. 149–161. Springer, Cham (2017). https://doi.org/10.1007/978-3-319-66266-4_10
7. Miyajima, C., et al.: Analyzing driver gaze behavior and consistency of decision making during automated driving. In: IEEE Intelligent Vehicles Symposium, August 2015 (Iv) (2015)
8. Michon, J.A.: A critical view of driver behavior models: what do we know, what should we do? In: Human Behavior and Traffic Safety. Plenum (1985)
9. Albus, J.S., Proctor, F.G.: A reference model architecture for intelligent hybrid control systems. In: Proceedings of the IFAC, San Francisco, CA (1996)
10. Cimatti, A., et al.: NUSMV a new symbolic model checker. Int. J. Softw. Tools Technol. Transf. 2(4), 410–425 (2000)
11. der Kiureghian, A., Ditlevsen, O.: Aleatory or epistemic? Does it matter? Struct. Saf. 31(2), 105–112 (2009)
12. Hermann, G.M.: Quantifying uncertainty: modern computational representation of probability and applications, extreme man-made and natural hazards in dynamics of structures. In: NATO Security through Science Series, 2007, pp. 105–135 (2007)
13. Zhang, M., et al.: Understanding uncertainty in cyber-physical systems: a conceptual model. In: Wąsowski, A., Lönn, H. (eds.) ECMFA 2016. LNCS, vol. 9764, pp. 247–264. Springer, Cham (2016). https://doi.org/10.1007/978-3-319-42061-5_16
14. SysML. OMG Systems Modeling Language (OMG SysML™), OMG
15. Feiler, P.H., Gluch, D.P.: Model-Based Engineering with AADL: An Introduction to the SAE Architecture Analysis & Design Language. Addison-Wesley (2012)
16. Mackay, D.J.C.: Information Theory, Inference, and Learning Algorithms. Cambridge University Press, Cambridge (2003). ISBN 0-521-64298-1
17. Aven, T., et al.: Uncertainty in Risk Assessment: The Representation and Treatment of Uncertainties by Probabilistic and Non-Probabilistic Methods. Wiley (2013)
18. Meedeniya, I., et al.: Evaluating probabilistic models with uncertain model parameters. Softw. Syst. Model. 13(4), 1395–1415 (2014)
19. Ying, J., et al.: A hidden Markov model-based algorithm for fault diagnosis with partial and imperfect tests. IEEE Trans. Syst. Man. Cybern. Part C 30(4), 463–473 (2000)
20. Zhang, X., Gu, C., Lin, J.: Support vector machines for anomaly detection. In: Intelligent Control and Automation, 2006, IEEE 6th World Congress on WCICA (2006)

Uncertainty in Machine Learning: A Safety Perspective on Autonomous Driving

Sina Shafaei$^{(\boxtimes)}$ (iD), Stefan Kugele(iD), Mohd Hafeez Osman(iD), and Alois Knoll

Technical University of Munich, Munich, Germany
{sina.shafaei,stefan.kugele,hafeez.osman}@tum.de,
knoll@in.tum.de

Abstract. With recent efforts to make vehicles intelligent, solutions based on machine learning have been accepted to the ecosystem. These systems in the automotive domain are growing fast, speeding up the promising future of highly and fully automated driving, and respectively, raising new challenges regarding safety assurance approaches. Uncertainty in data and the machine learning methods is a key point to investigate one of the main origins of safety-related concerns. In this work, we inspect this issue in the domain of autonomous driving with an emphasis on four safety-related cases, then introduce our proposals to address the challenges and mitigate them. The core of our approach is on introducing monitoring limiters during development time of such intelligent systems.

Keywords: Artificial intelligence · Uncertainty · Safety

1 Introduction

The safety aspect of the artificial intelligence-based applications has captured the attention of researchers recently, especially for the case of machine learning-based approaches such as neural networks and deep learning methods [1,3,9,10,14] and investigated from two different perspectives: (i) *Run-time* [7] and (ii) *Design-time* [5]. However, there is still a serious lack of concrete approaches which address the challenges in a practically efficient manner. In this work, we focus on the *uncertainty* issue of machine learning algorithms. We intuitively categorise the safety-critical situations originated from this issue, that a manoeuvre planning system may face, into four different cases. Finally, we propose approaches in order to address the challenges in each case. As mentioned, we are concentrating on the following cases in a manoeuvre planning system:

Case 1. The system has been trained and tested on the data from roads in a country with well-behaved traffic but is instead deployed for driving on roads in another country with chaotic driving conditions. Another similar case is when the vehicle has been trained and tested on roads with 4 wide lane driving but is instead faced with a 2-way narrow lane drive. In such situations, the outputs of

© Springer Nature Switzerland AG 2018
B. Gallina et al. (Eds.): SAFECOMP 2018 Workshops, LNCS 11094, pp. 458–464, 2018.
https://doi.org/10.1007/978-3-319-99229-7_39

the intelligent vehicle cannot be relied upon, as there is no guarantee that the system would behave as expected.

Case 2. The vehicle which employs this system wants to overtake another vehicle in front of it. Based on the country, driving rules state that one must overtake only from one side (left or right). Though this is imbibed in us, humans, while learning to drive, when it comes to autonomous vehicles there is no guarantee that the system has indeed learned this rule and will always follow it.

Case 3. The vehicle needs to execute a lane change operation to reach its goal state, but there happens to be a vehicle on the left that is in such an alignment with the ego vehicle that, though not very high probability, there is a possibility of an accident. Since standard deep learning techniques generate as output only hard classifications, there is still the chance of a condition with such low probability getting ignored and lead to costly collisions/accidents.

Case 4. Humans are designed to be innately optimistic, which might even be reflected in the training data for neural networks. NNs in autonomous vehicles are usually trained to exhibit the positive outputs that we expect to receive from them, however that benefits could be reaped by getting trained to generate positive as well as negative outputs.

2   Machine Learning and Safety Challenges

The *uncertainty* in machine learning algorithms can be categorised into two types [8]: (a) *aleatoric* or data dependent, where the noise in the data is captured by the model, resulting in the ambiguity of training input and (b) *epistemic* or model dependent seen as a measure of familiarity, as it represents the ambiguity the model exhibits when dealing with operational inputs. More precisely the major causes of concern while dealing with ML-based solutions are as follows:

(i) *Incompleteness of Training Data* – Traditional software systems are developed with a pre-defined set of functional requirements. However, in NNs, and more generally in ML algorithms, the functional requirements of the system are implicitly encoded in the data that it is trained on, expecting that the training data represents the operational environment. The setback, however, is that training data is by definition incomplete [11], as it represents a subset of all possible inputs that the system could encounter during operation. Insufficiencies thus arise when the operational environment is not wholly represented in the training set. In the case of autonomous vehicles, critical and ambiguous conditions, where the vehicle is expected to act predictably, usually tend to be problematic. This is because such situations, owing to their either extremely rare or highly dangerous nature, tend to be underrepresented in the training set [1,3].

(ii) *Distributional Shift* – In the case of an autonomous vehicle, the operational environment is highly unpredictable [3] as it is constantly changing in response to the actors within the system. Therefore, even with a good and near perfect training set, the operational inputs may not be similar to the training set. In other words, there could be a shift in the distribution of operational data as compared to the original training data, resulting in the system behaving unpredictably.

(iii) *Differences between Training and Operational Environments* – Subtle changes in the operational environment can lead to a state of unpredictable behaviour [3] in NNs. An NN fine-tuned for a certain specific setting provides no guarantee of working in the exact same way when the settings are changed.

(iv) *Uncertainty of Prediction* – Every NN has an error rate associated with it [11], and the aim of the training process is to reduce this error rate as much as possible. In the operational environment, this error rate can be interpreted as an *uncertainty* associated with the output produced by the model. Though this *uncertainty* can tell us about how well the system models the environment, it is not accounted for in the cyber-physical systems of today [8].

3   Proposed Approaches

Due to the fact that we are not able to handle all of the safety-critical situations, in our proposed approaches, we assumed that the action to be taken in the fail-safe mode is known beforehand and could include actions such as slowing down the car, bringing the car to a halt, or even handing over control to the human driver. Moreover, since we are focusing on safety for any AI-related software, the risk assessment is not in the scope of this paper.

3.1   Variational Methods to Filter 'Anomalous' Operational Inputs

(Case 1.) This method targets the problems related to differences in training and operational conditions and builds on the idea of online data monitoring. The main intuition (as depicted in Fig. 1) is to detect how 'far away' is the input from the data the system was trained on. In other words, the aim is to detect if the input is an 'anomaly', i.e., a data point that is

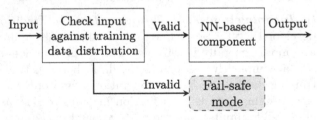

Fig. 1. Control flow of anomaly detection approach

significantly different from the original data. If yes, then the system is expected to enter a fail-safe mode, else normal operation continues. Given some data X, Variational Inference (VI) [2] aims to find a distribution $Q(Z)$ which is as similar to the true posterior $\Pr(Z \mid X)$ as possible, where the distance between the distributions can be calculated using the *Kullback-Liebler Divergence* a.k.a. relative entropy. Use of variational inference [2] is proposed for this online detection of anomalies [12]. The advantage of this approach is that the characteristics of expected input are learned from the data, and so no special feature engineering efforts are required. This also means that this approach is highly generalisable and is not bound by the use case. Simply exposing the system to data for modelling the environment, can help the system draw required inferences.

3.2 Defining Environmental Constraints

(Case 2.) We propose the use of ontologies to enforce such conditions as depicted in Fig. 2. Ontologies are a way to model the entities and relations in a system [4]. During *design-time*, the automotive safety engineer needs to create an automotive safety ontology (based on specific software/system function and context). The main ontology topics (for functional safety) can be derived from ISO 26262 (Part 1 - Vocabulary) [6]. The concepts stored in ontologies will be internally translated into machine-readable first-order logic (e.g. Prolog code), thereby making it simpler for describing constraints that the system must obey in the environment. Ontologies can be seen akin to a 'safety blanket' around each ML-based component. Inputs to the component and outputs generated thereby will be tested against the set of environmental constraints to ensure that they are fulfilled, if not, the system enters a fail-safe mode. This solution improves the reliability of the system, and follows the principles of traditional verification and validation methods, ensuring that the developed system abides by the intuition of human actors. It can improve traceability of issues and can also help track shortcomings with the system.

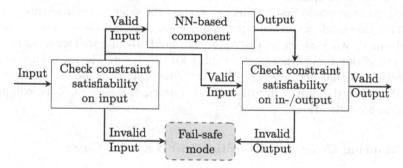

Fig. 2. Control flow of ontology-based constraint satisfaction approach

3.3 Pre-exploration Using Reinforcement Learning

(Case 3.) Since such situation can be modelled in terms of rewarding and penalising behaviour, we suggest the use of a reinforcement learning (RL) agent to mitigate such conditions. Reinforcement Learning [13] is based on behaviourist psychology, wherein the agent learns to map situations to actions, by receiving rewards from the environment for good behaviour and penalties otherwise. The aim for this solution is to augment learning with two trainable components, as shown in Fig. 3. Figure 3a shows the RL agent that is responsible for exploration of the environment, and Fig. 3b describes the online NN that is implemented in the standard manner for the component in question. The RL-agent learns

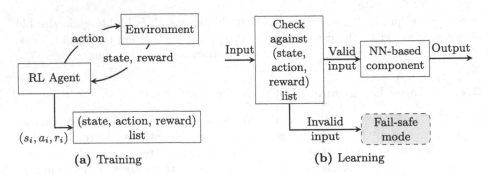

(a) Training   (b) Learning

Fig. 3. Control flow of RL-based pre-exploration approach

by exploring and interacting with its environment, and so would be trained via simulations to explore even negative outcomes, as in testing these do not pose a real threat to lives. In doing so the RL-agent would be able to learn and thereby generate a map of situations, actions, and associated reward values. This mapping can then be used to categorise situations that lead to high, medium, or low risk based on the reward values of each state. This approach can be seen as an extension to the monitoring techniques, wherein, rather than manually labelling the state space as being safe or not, the output of RL agent is used to generate such a mapping, with the reward function determining the severity of the hazard for each state-action pair. Thus, every input being passed to the NN-based component would first be checked against the safety invariance mapping to enter a fail-safe mode when the input is in a catastrophic zone. When it comes to generalising to other use cases, this approach could do quite well with the limiting factor of additional hyperparameter tuning for the agent. The advantage of such an approach is that rewards and objective functions can also be set up to be more aligned with human intuition, thus making the system more compliant with human expectations.

3.4   Ensuring Coverage of Positive and Negative Cases

(*Case 4.*) In the example of manoeuvre planning system, the component should be able to predict not only lateral and longitudinal actions, but also outputs, that could lead to negative outcomes such as driving off the road, a crash and so on. In such a system, if the output of a workflow falls in a negative class, the system would enter a fail-safe mode, else, would continue functioning normally, as visualised in Fig. 4. This setup brings along the benefit of higher assurance of the system being trained on under-represented or rare situations/inputs as well, leading to a better response to safety-critical

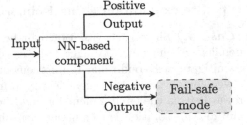

Fig. 4. The control flow of predicting possible positive and negative outputs

situations. Since the system learns expected good and bad outputs from the data directly, without explicit specifications, the system would generalise well to other use cases, too. It also has the advantage of being easy to implement and understand.

4   Conclusions and Future Work

In this work, we have investigated several challenges in ensuring safety of machine learning-based methods in the autonomous driving domain. Our main focus was on uncertainty issue which is not originated only from machine learning methods but also training data. We have considered multiple highly safety-critical situations in autonomous driving which could be the result of uncertainty issue and proposed the most promising candidates for monitoring approaches in order to preserve the safety of such system. It is worth mentioning that applying just one individual technique is not enough to verify the functionality of an adaptive software, as each has its own set of pros and cons. Instead, we need to focus on building a toolbox of different verification and validation techniques that can be applied based on the specific needs and specifications of the system. We suggest the use of a layered approach where each layer of monitoring for data and application, independent of the other, focuses on one aspect of the safety requirement.

References

1. Amodei, D., Olah, C., Steinhardt, J., Christiano, P., Schulman, J., Mané, D.: Concrete problems in AI safety. CoRR abs/1606.06565 (2016)
2. Blei, D.M., Kucukelbir, A., McAuliffe, J.D.: Variational inference: a review for statisticians. J. Am. Stat. Assoc. **112**(518), 859–877 (2017). https://doi.org/10.1080/01621459.2017.1285773
3. Burton, S., Gauerhof, L., Heinzemann, C.: Making the case for safety of machine learning in highly automated driving. In: Tonetta, S., Schoitsch, E., Bitsch, F. (eds.) SAFECOMP 2017. LNCS, vol. 10489, pp. 5–16. Springer, Cham (2017). https://doi.org/10.1007/978-3-319-66284-8_1
4. Feld, M., Müller, C.: The automotive ontology: managing knowledge inside the vehicle and sharing it between cars. In: Proceedings of the 3rd International Conference on Automotive User Interfaces and Interactive Vehicular Applications, pp. 79–86. ACM (2011). https://doi.org/10.1145/2381416.2381429
5. Huang, X., Kwiatkowska, M., Wang, S., Wu, M.: Safety verification of deep neural networks. In: Majumdar, R., Kunčak, V. (eds.) CAV 2017. LNCS, vol. 10426, pp. 3–29. Springer, Cham (2017). https://doi.org/10.1007/978-3-319-63387-9_1
6. International Organization for Standardization: ISO 26262: Road vehicles-functional safety. International Standard ISO/FDIS 26262 (2011)
7. Kane, A., Chowdhury, O., Datta, A., Koopman, P.: A case study on runtime monitoring of an autonomous research vehicle (ARV) system. In: Bartocci, E., Majumdar, R. (eds.) RV 2015. LNCS, vol. 9333, pp. 102–117. Springer, Cham (2015). https://doi.org/10.1007/978-3-319-23820-3_7

8. McAllister, R., et al.: Concrete problems for autonomous vehicle safety: advantages of Bayesian deep learning. In: International Joint Conferences on Artificial Intelligence, Inc. (2017). https://doi.org/10.24963/ijcai.2017/661
9. Pei, K., Cao, Y., Yang, J., Jana, S.: Towards practical verification of machine learning: The case of computer vision systems. CoRR abs/1712.01785 (2017)
10. Russell, S., Dewey, D., Tegmark, M.: Research priorities for robust and beneficial artificial intelligence. AI Mag. **36**(4), 105–114 (2015)
11. Salay, R., Queiroz, R., Czarnecki, K.: An analysis of ISO 26262: Using machine learning safely in automotive software. CoRR abs/1709.02435 (2017)
12. Sölch, M., Bayer, J., Ludersdorfer, M., van der Smagt, P.: Variational inference for on-line anomaly detection in high-dimensional time series. CoRR abs/1602.07109 (2016)
13. Sutton, R.S., Barto, A.G.: Reinforcement Learning: An Introduction. Adaptive Computation and Machine Learning. MIT Press, Cambridge (1998)
14. Taylor, J., Yudkowsky, E., LaVictoire, P., Critch, A.: Alignment for advanced machine learning systems. Machine Intelligence Research Institute (2016)

Considerations of Artificial Intelligence Safety Engineering for Unmanned Aircraft

Sebastian Schirmer[✉], Christoph Torens, Florian Nikodem, and Johann Dauer

German Aerospace Center (DLR), Institute of Flight Systems,
Lilienthalplatz 7, 38108 Braunschweig, Germany
{sebastian.schirmer,christoph.torens,florian.nikodem,johann.dauer}@dlr.de
http://www.dlr.de/ft/en

Abstract. Unmanned aircraft systems promise to be useful for a multitude of applications such as cargo transport and disaster recovery. The research on increased autonomous decision-making capabilities is therefore rapidly growing and advancing. However, the safe use, certification, and airspace integration for unmanned aircraft in a broad fashion is still unclear. Standards for development and verification of manned aircraft are either only partially applicable or resulting safety and verification efforts are unrealistic in practice due to the higher level of autonomy required by unmanned aircraft. Machine learning techniques are hard to interpret for a human and their outcome is strongly dependent on the training data. This work presents the current certification practices in unmanned aviation in the context of autonomy and artificial intelligence. Specifically, the recently introduced categories of unmanned aircraft systems and the specific operation risk assessment are described, which provide means for flight permission not solely focusing on the aircraft but also incorporating the target operation. Exemplary, we show how the specific operation risk assessment might be used as an enabler for hard-to-certify techniques by taking the operation into account during system design.

Keywords: Aerospace · Certification · AI-based system
Unmanned aircraft systems · Verification and validation

1 Current State in Unmanned Aviation

In aerospace, safety considerations are one of the main concerns and cost drivers. Only after certification of the aircraft, a participation in civil aviation is allowed. In order to direct companies in the process of achieving certification and to support certification authorities, several guidelines were presented.

© Springer Nature Switzerland AG 2018
B. Gallina et al. (Eds.): SAFECOMP 2018 Workshops, LNCS 11094, pp. 465–472, 2018.
https://doi.org/10.1007/978-3-319-99229-7_40

The SAE[1] Aerospace Recommended Practices (ARP) and the RTCA[2] DO standards are prominent acceptable means of compliance. As shown in Fig. 1, several guidelines exist for development processes and safety assessments, both for the development phase and the operational phase. These standards impose high requirements on development and verification, e.g. requirements on code coverage increase with the criticality of a software item. The so-called MC/DC metric, which is required for the most critical assurance level, is a significant driver for costs of verification alone [5,6]. The overall objective is to demonstrate that the system under development is working correctly or, where this is not possible, show the high quality of the development process.

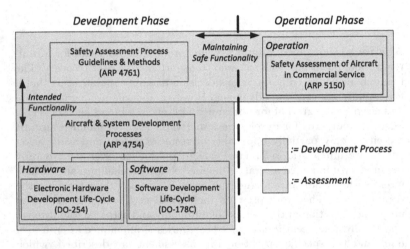

Fig. 1. Overview of aircraft development guidelines - how they complement each other.

Unmanned Aircraft Systems (UAS) are aircraft without a human pilot on board but, instead, with an operator on the ground having some form of control over it – rendering the UAS into a complex distributed system. Amazon[3], DHL[4], as well as other companies investigate to deliver goods with the overall objective to facilitate unmanned last-mile delivery.

An autonomous flight capable of contingency measurements in case of off-nominal behavior is highly desirable for these operations. At best fully autonomous, without an operator on-ground who is unfavorable for long-distance deliveries. Although the aircraft is unmanned, it can still do harm on-ground or in-air. We mentioned that certification of manned aircraft is cost intensive

---

[1] Society of Automotive Engineers is a global associations, developing standards for aerospace, automotive, and others.

[2] Radio Technical Commission for Aeronautics is a private, not-for-profit association, developing technical guidance.

[3] Amazon Prime Air, www.amazon.com/primeair.

[4] DHL Parcelcopter, http://www.dpdhl.com/parcelcopter.

and hard to achieve. For presented business cases to work, the main concern is not anymore the performance of the autonomy functionalities – vision-based autonomous flying system do exist and perform well – but instead the certification of these functionalities [8]. A loss of reputation for these business cases could be fatal. For instance, machine learning techniques like Convolutional Neural Networks allow to infer weights, given a loss function for the domain and enough training data. But, how can they be certified? As of yet, such nets are not capable of outputting in which situations they are working. Additionally, attacks on machine learning with adversarial examples were presented which cause the model to make mistakes by only changing a few pixels [11].

However, the achievements in machine learning or artificial intelligence (AI) in general are undeniable and research on e.g. Bayes Deep Learning exist which combine Bayesian approaches with deep learning to reason about the model confidence [4]. Nonetheless, to our knowledge, these confidence values are similarly dependent on the training data and, therefore, no general statement in which situations the trained nets work is possible. Therefore, a different question might be: How can we embed these techniques within the overall system design to enable certification?

In industry, a common architecture to facilitate hard-to-certify components is to switch to a more conservative backup component in case of an hazardous situation. For such an architecture, two main aspects are required. First, an alternative conservative action has to exist. Second, the hazardous situation needs to be detectable. Exemplary, in manned aviation the Brake-to-Vacate (BTV) system by Airbus is a "convenience" function on top of the safety-critical Runway Overrun Prevention System (ROPS). The objective of BTV is to optimize the path from the runway to the taxiway. The optimized path reduces the wear on brakes and tires as well as the time the aircraft spends on the runway and, therefore, increases the throughput of the airport. ROPS is a simpler function than BTV which is directly integrated within BTV. It either warns the pilots if the runway is insufficiently long before touchdown/deceleration or applies maximum braking when deceleration already started.

In late 2015, the European Aviation Safety Agency (EASA) introduced the so called specific category which allows to combine the reasoning of aircraft system and target operation. In the next section, we present the new categories, an upcoming guideline for the risk assessment, and the DLR project ALAADy. Then, we discuss how these innovations can help to apply AI techniques. Specifically, we argue how the system architecture and regulatory frameworks can interlock to enable the use of hard-to-certify components. Finally, we give a future perspective.

2   Trends in Aerospace

EASA recently introduced three categories of UAS operation that use separate sets of regulation, based on the intrinsic risks involved [2]. The three categories are referred to as open, specific, and certified. The open category is reserved for low risk operation of unmanned aircraft below 0.25 kg. This category requires no or minimal regulation. The certified category is used for operations that are of an equivalent level of risk comparable to manned aviation, therefore the same level of rigor for development and verification is applied. The new specific category allows a step-wise adaptation of regulation and certification requirements between the open and certified categories. For flight permission, the specific category relies on a risk assessment to determine the required level of certification requirements. As risk assessment, EASA recommends the so-called specific operation risk assessment (SORA) that is currently being developed by JARUS [7]. In contrast to the certified category, the specific category is not targeted solely on the UAS, but towards the operation of a specific UAS in its entirety including the mission, the environment, operation conditions, rigor during development as well as operator, and pilot qualification. SORA is currently under development and a first deployment by authorities is likely within years.

DLR (German Aerospace Center) is currently supporting the SORA development by applying it to a cargo application within the project ALAADy (Automated Low Altitude Air Delivery) [1]. The mission consists in cargo delivery on a range of around 600 km flying over sparsely populated areas. The unmanned aircraft are intended to fly in very low level to circumvent most of the air traffic. These efforts help to further research interdependencies of the SORA process with UAS design and development, specifically DLR investigates the advantages of the new specific category concept to maintain a safe operation. A controlled termination of the UAS in safe areas is used to minimize the risk to third parties on-ground or in the air and, thus, ultimately makes the operation safe. This is necessary, since a backup pilot cannot be aboard the target aircraft which is in contrast to autonomous cars. There, a backup driver supervises the system and takes control in case of emergencies. In aviation, the use of Optional Piloted Vehicle (OPV) during development is possible but the required components and pilot might be too heavy for the real system [3].

One hope utilizing the specific category is to develop cheaper UAS with new autonomous capabilities. DLR works on a system architecture that is leveraging the containment of the risk of the operation. The goal is to use technologies that are not usable in a traditional certification process for aerospace due to the high requirements on verification objectives imposed by certification standards.

3   AI Applicability

The major innovation with the specific category and SORA is that it considers not only the UAS but also factors the target operation in. Explicitly, manned certification always assumes harm on people in case of an operation being out of control. Therefore, a high confidence in the system is mandatory. SORA relieves this burden by incorporating the risk to harm people on-ground or in-air. So called harm and threat barriers need to be in place to achieve equally high confidence with respect to the operation. This is a huge change because it allows to fit the system design to the target operation. Already limitations to basic operation parameters like daytime or flight altitude have significant impact on the system design and its certification effort. An extreme example would be the case of operations only involving flying in low-altitude in the desert at daytime: for this no highly reliable ice protection system is required. Similar scenarios can be easily found for many possible UAS operations in Europe. Additionally, it allows to monitor the operation parameters instead of an explicit functionality.

For instance, surveying crops by unmanned aircraft where limiting the airspace to a pre-defined area, e.g. the field, reduces the risk of harming people on the ground or in the air. There are two main capabilities: the monitoring (MC) and the flight capability (FC). MC monitors the UAS and has the authority to activate countermeasures or the flight termination whenever required to avoid a breaking out of the pre-defined area. Regarding SORA, a certification of MC plays the major role for flight certifiability since it prevents harm on-ground or in-air, i.e. acts as harm barrier. Complementary, FC controls and manages the UAS in an efficient and economic way such that all crops are sufficiently viewed. Possibly, reacting upon environmental conditions and based on vision. Roughly spoken, FC tries to achieve the highest performance whereas MC takes care that no environmental/operation conditions are violated. There are different ways of implementing such capabilities within a system each of them having different advantages and disadvantages considering certification effort, cost, and performance. In Fig. 2, possible system designs are depicted and now discussed:

(a) Both capabilities are embedded in one software component running on a dedicated hardware. Interaction-wise, this setup offers the closest interaction between MC and FC due to no resource separation. However due to certification efforts in conjunction with cost, applicable hardware is limited, e.g. multi/many-core processors and multiprocessing. Software-wise, the performance might suffer due to the hardware restrictions and certification is also difficult due to no clear separation between MC and FC.

(b) Advantages and restrictions on hardware similarly remain. Limited computing power prevent the usage of advanced algorithms. However, the clear separation between MC and FC in software improves the certification efforts software-wise. Still, there is a dependency between MC and FC. However, the certification efforts for FC are reduced. Showing the absence of effects on the hardware, i.e. the unobstrusiveness regarding MC, might suffice.

(c) MC and FC are running on dedicated hardware. This system design offers the possibility to encapsulate the MC and FC into a certified component and an uncertified component, respectively. It represents a sweet spot between flight performance and certification efforts. Certification efforts should be focused on MC where a trade-off in complexity is apparent. As a first step, simple and conservative buffers within the pre-defined area facilitate geofencing, i.e. preventing a break out. The certification of this approach is easier but reduces the surveillance performance, i.e. the buffers prevent the access to the complete area. The complexity can be increased from worstcase buffers to more advanced techniques which incorporate the continuously changing state of the UAS [9, 10]. Considering FC, dedicated, possibly uncertified, hardware can be used. Further, algorithms can be applied which could not be used so far. For instance, some of the most popular machine learning techniques, like deep neural networks, show promising results but are hardly human interpretable and therefore hard-to-certify.

Note that the discussed certification efforts can be addressed by the operation itself. By incorporating a sufficiently large safety buffer around the operation which exceeds the physical limits of the aircraft, e.g. the lift-to-drag ratio combined with fuel consumption, even MC turns out to be redundant.

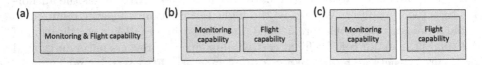

Fig. 2. Possible system design. (a) Shared hardware and combined capability (b) Shared hardware but separated capabilities (c) Dedicated hardware for each capability

Crop surveillance is just one example which indicates that SORA enables the usage of previously inconceivable techniques by allowing to fit the system design of the UAS to its specific intended operation. In general and especially for more complex use cases, finding such a sweet spot between aircraft certification and operational limitations is challenging but in any case worth looking at. Once sufficient harm and threat barriers are established, it allows the usage of state of the art algorithms for high performance within the respective operation. An obvious use of AI for UAS is the detection of obstacles as well as conflicting traffic using computer vision. This use case is similar to the task that is currently performed by machine learning algorithms for autonomous cars. Furthermore, AI could be used to categorize the real time UAS performance as normal or abnormal. Machine learning algorithms could learn from simulations, test runs, and actual test flights during development as well as all operational in-service flights of all UAS of a certain type or fleet. The certified/uncertified point of view might be not applicable or too rigor in some cases. External safety frameworks enhancing AI, e.g. runtime safety monitoring, or research advances towards certification of AI in general, might soften the rigorous separation.

4   Future Perspective

Although the results of AI, in particular deep learning techniques, are very promising, the use of such techniques in safety critical areas is problematic. The aerospace domain imposes high requirements on the development and verification of software systems. The certification of AI is currently only possible with a thoroughly documented service history that can establish the necessary trust or a switching architecture relying on detecting misbehavior. It is unclear how existing coverage metrics, such as MC/DC, could be applied to neural networks to assure functional safety. More research efforts regarding the verification and validation aspects of these new AI techniques are therefore necessary.

However, the specific category approach introduced by EASA in combination with the safe monitoring of the operation could be an enabling technology for AI applications, even in a safety critical context. The specific category offers a pragmatic way to gather service history experience with uncertified components, exemplary depicted in Sect. 3. It is unlikely that a certification of these components is possible with traditional means of compliance in the near future. Also, in applications like visual obstacle detection, it is hard to identify a misbehavior, e.g. a human was falsely associated or not detected at all, therefore a traditional safety switch to a conservative alternative cannot be used. The specific category can uniquely support AI applications by monitoring the operation instead of the correct system-level functionality. The safety monitor ensures that there is no increased risk when using AI because a mitigation action, e.g. flight termination, can be triggered as soon as the operation is detected to be out of control. Similar to autonomous cars, where hundreds of test vehicles with human safety drivers are currently performing thousands of service miles, the service history for UAS could be supported by the specific category use cases. Of course, open questions remain, such as the comparability of the specific category use case, how much service hours are sufficient for safety, and how to ensure proper requirement coverage. Future work will also be necessary on ensuring the safety of the operation and possible mitigation strategies. Also, how AI techniques can be adjusted to a specific operation, e.g. training for operation specific inputs.

References

1. Dauer, J.C., Lorenz, S., Dittrich, J.S.: Automated low altitude air delivery. Deutscher Luftund Raumfahrtkongress DGLR, 13–15 September 2016
2. European Aviation Safety Agency (EASA): Introduction of a regulatory framework for the operation of drones. Advance Notice of Proposed Amendment 2017-05
3. Friehmelt, H. (ed.): Integrated UAV Technologies Demonstration in Controlled Airspace Using ATTAS, AIAA Atmospheric Flight Mechanics Conference and Exhibit (2003)
4. Guyon, I., von Luxburg, U., Bengio, S., Wallach, H.M., Fergus, R., Vishwanathan, S.V.N., Garnett, R. (eds.): Advances in Neural Information Processing Systems 30: Annual Conference on Neural Information Processing Systems, USA (2017)
5. Hayhurst, K.J., Dorsey, C.A., Knight, J.C., Leveson, N.G., McCormick, G.F. (eds.): Streamlining Software Aspects of Certification: Report on the SSAC Survey (1999)
6. Hayhurst, K.J., Veerhusen, D.S. (eds.): A Practical Approach to Modified Condition/Decision Coverage (2001)
7. Joint Authorities for Rulemaking of Unmanned Systems: JARUS Guidelines on Specific Operations Risk Assessment (SORA). Draft for public consultation (2016)
8. Rein, W.: Autonomous drones: Set to fly, but may not comply; 5 major obstacles for unmanned aircraft systems (2018), https://www.wileyrein.com/newsroom-articles-Autonomous-Drones-Make-It-Easier-to-Fly-But-Harder-to-Comply.html; https://www.wileyrein.com/newsroom-articles-5-Major-Obstacles-For-Unmanned-Aircraft-Systems.html

9. Schirmer, S., Torens, C., Adolf, F.M. (eds.): Formal Monitoring of Risk-based Geofences, AIAA Information Systems-AIAA Infotech at Aerospace (2018)
10. Torens, C., Nikodem, F., Dittrich, J.S., Dauer, J.C. (eds.): Onboard Functional Requirements for Specific Category UAS and Safe Operation Monitoring, 6th CEAS Air and Space Conference (2017)
11. Yuan, X., He, P., Zhu, Q., Bhat, R.R., Li, X.: Adversarial examples: attacks and defenses for deep learning. CoRR (2017)

Could We Issue Driving Licenses
to Autonomous Vehicles?

Jingyue Li$^{(\boxtimes)}$, Jin Zhang, and Nektaria Kaloudi

Norwegian University of Science and Technology, 7491 Trondheim, Norway
{jingyue.li,jin.zhang,nektaria.kaloudi}@ntnu.no

Abstract. Many companies are studying autonomous vehicles. One trend in the development of control algorithms for autonomous vehicles is the use of deep-learning approaches. The general idea is to simulate a human driver's decision-making and behavior in various scenarios without necessarily knowing why the decision is made. In this position paper, we first argue that traditional safety analysis methods need to be extended to verify deep-learning-based autonomous vehicles. Then, we propose borrowing ideas from the process of issuing driving licenses to human drivers to verify autonomous vehicles. Verification of autonomous vehicles could focus on sufficient training as well as mental and physical health checks. Based on this position, we list several challenges that need to be addressed.

Keywords: Autonomous vehicle · Artificial Intelligence
Deep learning · Verification · Safety · Security

1 Introduction

Many companies, e.g., Google [1], are developing autonomous vehicles. One key challenge of developing autonomous vehicles is ensuring safety. Several safety incidents caused by vehicle autonomy have been presented in the media, such as Uber's fatal car accident [2]. In addition to the safety incidents caused by failures of the autonomous system, security breaches of autonomous vehicles can potentially lead to safety issues; for example, a demo showed that autonomous vehicles can be hijacked and remotely controlled [3].

The Society of Automotive Engineers (SAE) has described six levels of autonomous driving [4]. A Level 0 vehicle has no autonomous capabilities and the human driver is responsible for all aspects of the driving task. For a Level 5 vehicle, the driving tasks are managed solely by the autonomous driving system. When developing autonomous vehicles targeting a high level of autonomy, one industrial trend is to use deep-learning algorithms to implement the vehicle control algorithms. The idea is to first log the information, such as images a human driver acquired during driving and the driver's corresponding driving behavior. Such logged information is used as a training dataset for deep-learning algorithms to train the autonomous vehicles to simulate what human drivers do

B. Gallina et al. (Eds.): SAFECOMP 2018 Workshops, LNCS 11094, pp. 473–480, 2018.
https://doi.org/10.1007/978-3-319-99229-7_41

when driving. One key characteristic of deep-learning-based autonomy is that the decision-making part of the vehicle is almost a black box. This means that in most cases, we as human drivers must trust the decisions made by the deep-learning algorithms without knowing exactly why and how the decisions are made. As an analogy, driving an autonomous vehicle with a high level of autonomy (e.g., Level 5) is like hiring a robotic taxi driver who is driving the car for us. Usually, when we sit in a taxi, we do not always try to understand and influence how the taxi driver makes decisions and drives the car. We simply trust that the taxi driver's driving license indicates that he or she has sufficient training, good mental health to make proper decisions, and good physical health to sense the environment and execute the decisions. With this analogy in mind, we propose adapting safety analysis approaches for a greater focus on:

- **Training sufficiency of the autonomous vehicle**, i.e., whether the dataset used to train the deep-learning algorithms is sufficient;
- **Mental health of the autonomous vehicle**, i.e., whether there is malicious code hidden in the decision-making algorithms; and
- **Physical health of the autonomous vehicle**, i.e., whether the sensors and actuators of the autonomous vehicle work properly and whether the vehicle is resilient when the devices fail.

2   Background

Computer vision and deep learning are two major approaches to designing autonomous vehicle control algorithms. Traditional computer vision techniques can play an important role in lane detection and object detection at moderate distances, but they are unlikely to meet the robustness requirements for handling very complex and intelligent tasks such as distinguishing between different metal objects or unexpected obstacles.

2.1   Deep-Learning-Based Autonomous Vehicles

The deep-learning based approach enables vehicles to learn meaningful road features from raw input data automatically and then output driving actions. The so-called end-to-end learning approach can be applied to solve complex real-world driving tasks. When using deep-learning based approaches, the first step is to use a large number of training datasets (images and/or other sensor data) to train a deep neural network (DNN). Then a simulator is used to evaluate the performance of the trained network. After that, the deep-learning-based autonomous vehicle will be able to *"execute recognition, prediction and planning"* driving tasks in diverse conditions [12]. Nowadays, Convolutional Neural Networks (CNNs) are the most widely adopted deep-learning model for fully autonomous vehicles [5–8]. In 2016, NVIDIA introduced an automotive supercomputing platform named DRIVE PX 2 [9]. DRIVE PX 2 is being used by more than 50 companies in the automotive industry. The development flow by using NVIDIA DRIVE PX 2 includes (1) data acquisition to train the deep neural network; (2) deployment of the output of a deep neural network in a car; (3) autonomous application development; and (4) testing in-vehicle or with simulation.

2.2 Some Approaches to Analyzing Safety of Autonomous Vehicles

The safety standard of the automotive industry, ISO 26262, is being updated to address the growing complexity and autonomy of vehicles. Besides using classical safety analysis methods such as FTA (Fault Tree Analysis) and FMEA (Failure Mode and Effects Analysis), production of a safety case is explicitly mandated by ISO 26262. A safety case comprises three parts: (1) the safety goal that must be achieved; (2) the available evidence for achieving this goal; and (3) the structured argument, which establishes the systematic relationship between the evidence and the goals. One challenge of using the safety case approach is arguing that the evidence is sufficient to ensure safety of the system. The forthcoming version of ISO 26262:2018 and its extension, ISO/PAS 21448, which is also known as SOTIF (Safety of the Intended Functionality) [10], will likely provide a way to handle the development of autonomous vehicles. But SOTIF will only provide guidelines for Level 0–2 autonomous vehicles [11], which are not designed for the validation of deep-learning-based autonomous vehicles.

Along with updating the safety verification standards, some studies investigate how to verify safety of fully autonomous vehicles by treating the autonomous vehicle control algorithms as black boxes. The general idea is to use a combination of brute force road testing and testing using simulators to enumerate all potential corner cases. The proposed safety metrics of autonomous vehicles include Miles Per Disengagement (MPD) and Miles Per Intervention (MPI) [12]. Some other studies try to open the black boxes to interpret the deep neural networks and verify their internal logics [13–15].

2.3 Security Attacks Targeted at Autonomous Systems

As the development of Artificial Intelligence (AI) technologies progresses, attackers will also learn to create new smart attacks. We define a smart attack as an AI-enabled attack in which malicious actors can use AI technologies to attack "smart" components inside autonomous systems. The smart attack is usually executed via a persistent, finely targeted, combined, and multilayered exploitation of multiple security zones in a camouflaged way [16]. Examples of potential smart attacks include:

- **Training smart systems to have two behaviors**, e.g., a robot can be trained to behave normally in most cases, but behave maliciously and make an attack when a certain face is recognized [17];
- **Training systems to personalize the hack**, e.g., an attacker can train systems to generate a finely personalized vulnerability profile and then perform the hack by creating tailored exploits for such a vulnerability [18,19];

- **Training systems to evolve themselves**, e.g., malicious code can continuously update itself with dozens of new exploits by using fuzzing techniques [17]; or
- **Distributing AI-generated content**, e.g., an attacker can automate tasks involved in surveillance, persuasion, deception, privacy violation, and social manipulation by distributing AI-generated content and targeted disinformation campaigns through social media [20].

3   Key Issues of Verifying Deep-Learning-Based Autonomous Vehicles

When driving Level 5 autonomous vehicles, the human driver will behave like a passenger of a taxi. The taxi driver is now the deep-learning based-control algorithms. As a passenger of a taxi, we usually trust that the taxi driver is sufficiently trained because we trust the taxi driver training program and the qualification a driving license implies. Normally, if a taxi driver is well-trained, sensible, and in good health, and if the hardware and software of a vehicle is functioning, safety is guaranteed. However, as mentioned in Sect. 2.2, most current safety analyses, certification approaches, and standards focus only on whether the vehicle's hardware and software are working as intended. The qualification of the taxi driver is defined in a separate standard by which driving licenses are issued, which is often regulated by the police and followed by driving schools. For fully autonomous vehicles, the control algorithm is an integrated part of the vehicle. We therefore argue that the safety analysis and certification approach should be extended to treat the control algorithms as a taxi driver and to test it to answer some important questions.

3.1   Has the Autonomous Vehicle Been Sufficiently Trained?

When we study in driving school, a complete training program starts with driving theories and rules. We first learn different road signs and to understand how to drive the vehicle according to those road signs and driving regulations. Afterward, we need to practice driving in different scenarios, such as in the city center, through a roundabout, on the highway, in slippery conditions, and so on. In addition, when driving assessments are carried out by driving instructors to evaluate drivers' behavior, there is a formal process aims at fixing the drivers' errors.

When we take the driving license test, we are supposed to show competence to drive the vehicle properly in different scenarios, including scenarios we may know in theory but have not practiced, such as giving way to emergency vehicles. When verifying the completeness of the training dataset of the autonomous vehicles, how can we learn from the driving school and find ways to train autonomous vehicles and quantify their learning completeness? To improve training sufficiency, the "error analysis" process of examining the instances in which the deep-learning algorithms erred can also help suggest good practices and develop new features. Brute force road testing is not an efficient way to assure safety. The traffic signs and regulations of countries are different. For example, a white dotted line is used in Sweden to separate lanes, but a yellow dotted line is used in Norway. If the autonomous car is trained using Swedish traffic regulations, it may become confused when it drives in Norway. Thus, tests measured by MPD or MPI [12] in one country may not be valid in another country. In addition, what happens if the traffic regulations of a certain country are updated? Should we undertake another billion miles of road testing?

3.2   Is There Any Malicious Code in the Brain of the Autonomous Vehicle?

When a driving license is issued to a driver, the driver should not have severe mental health problems. When a taxi driver is working, the driver is not supposed to be drunk. As explained in Sect. 2.3, successful smart attacks can gain access to the decision-making algorithms of autonomous vehicles. Malicious inputs into training datasets can cause the model to behave normally in most cases, but behave maliciously in a certain scenario. Because few smart attacks have been exploited in practice, people have not reported them in vulnerability repositories, and therefore have not studied in depth how to identify such attacks and defend against them. However, we expect such AI-based attacks will be perpetrated in the future [17]. If the attack is carried out, the consequence could be that the autonomous vehicle suddenly behaves like a drunk or mentally compromised taxi driver. When certifying deep-learning-based autonomous vehicles, we should require the vehicles to have self-checking or remote-checking mechanisms to ensure that no malicious code has ever been inserted in the control algorithms.

3.3   Are the Sensors and Actuators of the Autonomous Vehicle Reliable and Resilient to Failures?

To get a driving license, a human driver should have physical health, e.g., good eyesight and capability to operate the vehicle in normal and abnormal situations. Current safety certification standards focus sharply on the reliability of vehicle hardware and software. Analyzing failure modes and how the vehicles react to failure is a crucial part of the safety analysis. The architecture of deep-learning neural networks makes it hard to decipher how the algorithmic decisions were made, which in turn makes it hard to explain how dynamic driving behaviors are generated [21]. Thus, it can be difficult to interpret and predicate how a failure, such as wrong sensor data, will influence driving behavior. When we verify the safety of deep-learning-based control algorithms, we need to rethink how to perform failure mode and effect analysis, how to analyze interdependencies between sub-systems of a vehicle, and how to assure the resilience of the system. For resilience assurance, we need to determine where to put safety barriers and how to place them in the deep neural network to ensure that even if some vehicle hardware or software does not behave as expected, the vehicle can still sense the risk, avoid the risk before the incident, and mitigate the risk effectively when the incident happens.

3.4 Human vs. Machine

Ideally, autonomous cars should behave equally or even better than human beings. Besides the three principles mentioned above, a comparison between human and machine capabilities is needed to identify some limitations that should be considered as a further evaluation of autonomous vehicles. As shown in Table 1, a function analysis between humans and machines during space missions identifies the differences in their superiority [22].

Table 1. Human and machine superiority.

Human	Machine
Originality and creativity	Precise repetitive operations
Emotions and feelings	Mechanical brain
Rapid retraining	Quicker response times with minimum delay
Performing under overloaded conditions	Storing and recalling large amounts of data
Acting in high-noise environments	Sensitivity to a variety of stimuli
Risk evaluation for unexpected events	Function in a wide range of stress conditions
Using equipment beyond specified limits	Stronger and faster
Reasoning inductively	Reasoning deductively

A human is shown to be better at "risk evaluation for unexpected events" and "rapid retraining" than a machine. For example, when the car suddenly experiences a longer breaking distance than normal, the human driver will realize that the road is slippery and will drive slower and more carefully. The "rapid retraining" competence of a human is usually not verified during driving license tests because we view it as human nature. If we want to have autonomous cars with performance superior to that of humans, and if we use the human driving license approach to verifying autonomous vehicles, we also need to consider the importance of testing human superiority in the entire evaluation process of autonomous vehicles.

4 Conclusions and Future Work

Our position is that certifying a deep-learning-based autonomous vehicle is like issuing a driving license to an AI-based taxi driver. To verify safety, we need to learn from the systematic method of training and testing human drivers. We need to guarantee that the training dataset of the autonomous vehicle covers all knowledge and skills taught in a driving school. We should have technologies to ensure that no malicious code is hidden in the autonomous vehicle either in design or in operation. The vehicle should also have highly reliable hardware and software and should be resilient in the face of expected and unexpected failures. When we make safety cases according to ISO 26262, we propose including all these aspects as safety arguments and evidence. To acquire evidence for these arguments, we will also need to combine black box testing technologies to test deep-learning algorithms with technologies to understand and interpret them.

Acknowledgements. This work is supported by the SAREPTA (Safety, autonomy, remote control and operations of industrial transport systems) project, which is financed by Norwegian Research Council with Grant No. 267860.

References

1. Google: The Google self-driving car. https://www.google.com/selfdrivingcar/. Accessed May 2018
2. Hawkins, A.J.: Uber self-driving car saw pedestrian but didn't brake before fatal crash, feds say. https://www.theverge.com/2018/5/24/17388696/uber-self-driving-crash-ntsb-report. Accessed 24 May 2018
3. Greenberg, A.: Hackers remotely kill a Jeep on the highway. https://www.wired.com/2015/07/hackers-remotely-kill-jeep-highway/. Accessed 21 July 2015
4. SAE International: Automated vehicles: levels of automation. https://autoalliance.org/wp-content/uploads/2017/07/Automated-Vehicles-Levels-of-Automation.pdf. Accessed May 2018
5. Sallab, A.E.L., et al.: Deep reinforcement learning framework for autonomous driving. Electron. Imaging **2017**(19), 70–76 (2017)
6. Bojarski, M., et al.: End to end learning for self-driving cars. arXiv preprint arXiv:1604.07316 (2016)
7. Huval, B., et al.: An empirical evaluation of deep learning on highway driving. arXiv preprint arXiv:1504.01716 (2015)
8. Navarro, A., et al.: Development of an autonomous vehicle control strategy using a single camera and deep neural networks. SAE Technical Paper 01-0035 (2018)
9. NVIDIA Deep Learning Institute: Deep learning for autonomous vehicles-perception. https://www.nvidia.com/en-us/deep-learning-ai/education/. Accessed May 2018
10. Griessnig, G., Schnellbach, A.: Development of the 2nd edition of the ISO 26262. In: Stolfa, J., Stolfa, S., O'Connor, R.V., Messnarz, R. (eds.) EuroSPI 2017. CCIS, vol. 748, pp. 535–546. Springer, Cham (2017). https://doi.org/10.1007/978-3-319-64218-5_44
11. The Hansen Report on Automotive Electronics: Standardization efforts on autonomous driving safety. http://www.hansenreport.com/. Accessed Feb 2017
12. WAYMO: Waymo Safety Report: On the road to fully self-driving. https://waymo.com/safety/. Accessed May 2018
13. Tian, Y., et al.: DeepTest: automated testing of deep-neural-network-driven autonomous cars. arXiv preprint arXiv:1708.08559 (2017)
14. Huang, X., Kwiatkowska, M., Wang, S., Wu, M.: Safety verification of deep neural networks. In: Majumdar, R., Kunčak, V. (eds.) CAV 2017. LNCS, vol. 10426, pp. 3–29. Springer, Cham (2017). https://doi.org/10.1007/978-3-319-63387-9_1
15. Katz, G., Barrett, C., Dill, D.L., Julian, K., Kochenderfer, M.J.: Reluplex: an efficient SMT solver for verifying deep neural networks. In: Majumdar, R., Kunčak, V. (eds.) CAV 2017. LNCS, vol. 10426, pp. 97–117. Springer, Cham (2017). https://doi.org/10.1007/978-3-319-63387-9_5
16. Koch, R., et al.: A revised attack taxonomy for a new generation of smart attacks. Comput. Inf. Sci. **7**(3), 18 (2014)

17. Brundage, M., et al.: The malicious use of artificial intelligence: forecasting, prevention, and mitigation. arXiv preprint arXiv:1802.07228 (2018)
18. Giaretta, A., Dragoni, N.: Community targeted spam: a middle ground between general spam and spear phishing. arXiv preprint arXiv:1708.07342 (2017)
19. Seymour, J., Tully, P.: Weaponizing data science for social engineering: automated E2E spear phishing on Twitter. Black Hat USA (2016)
20. Kim, Y.M.: The stealth media? Groups and targets behind divisive issue campaigns on Facebook (2018)
21. Ribeiro, M.T., et al.: Model-agnostic interpretability of machine learning. arXiv preprint arXiv:1606.05386 (2016)
22. Schenkelberg, F.: Comparing human and machine capability. https://accendoreli ability.com/comparing-human-and-machine-capability/. Accessed 2018

Concerns on the Differences Between AI and System Safety Mindsets Impacting Autonomous Vehicles Safety

A. M. Nascimento[1]([⊠]), L. F. Vismari[1], P. S. Cugnasca[1], J. B. Camargo Jr.[1], J. R. de Almeida Jr.[1], R. Inam[2], E. Fersman[2], A. Hata[3], and M. V. Marquezini[3]

[1] School of Engineering, University of São Paulo (USP), São Paulo, SP, Brazil
alexandremoreiranascimento@alum.mit.edu,
{lucio.vismari,joaocamargo}@usp.br
[2] Ericsson Research, Ericsson AB, Stockholm, Sweden
[3] Ericsson Telecomunicações S.A., Indaiatuba, SP, Brazil

Abstract. The inflection point in the development of some core technologies enabled the Autonomous Vehicles (AV). The unprecedented growth rate in Artificial Intelligence (AI) and Machine Learning (ML) capabilities, focusing only on AVs, is expected to shift the transportation paradigm and bring relevant benefits to the society, such as accidents reduction. However, recent AVs accidents resulted in life losses. This paper presents a viewpoint discussion based on findings from a preliminary exploratory literature review. It was identified an important misalignment between AI and Safety research communities regarding the impact of AI on the safety risks in AV. This paper promotes this discussion, raises concerns on the potential consequences and suggests research topics to reduce the differences between AI and system safety mindsets.

Keywords: Autonomous vehicles · Safety · Artificial intelligence · Accident Risks · Misalignment · Mindset

1 Introduction

The inflection points in the evolution of three core technologies enabled the Autonomous vehicles (AV). The recent advancements in Information and Communication Technologies (ICT) allowed developing reliable communication architectures. Very powerful processing units have become portable and have a much-reduced power consumption, boosting the evolution of pervasive computing. Finally, the recent advancements in AI techniques, such as Deep Learning, are significantly reducing the gap between human and machine cognition, making possible the automation of many cognitive-dependent processes.

AVs promise a paradigm shift in many topics related to transportation. Smart cities empowered with sophisticated communication infra-structure can better orchestrate the autonomous car traffic towards its optimization, reducing traffic jams and improving transportation efficiency. The elderly, people with disabilities and without driving licenses can access individual transportation. However, one of the highest AV appeals

© Springer Nature Switzerland AG 2018
B. Gallina et al. (Eds.): SAFECOMP 2018 Workshops, LNCS 11094, pp. 481–486, 2018.
https://doi.org/10.1007/978-3-319-99229-7_42

is related to the road and vehicle safety improvements due the promise of accidents reduction by eliminating the need for a human driver. Over 90% of accidents were attributed to human error causes [1].

When an AV operates in an undesirable, non-expected way, it can jeopardize not only human lives, but also the environment in which it operates. This makes AV a safety-critical system. Hence, even in the face of all the promised benefits to society, and even if its core technologies are almost available, it is mandatory for AV to have a robust system safety lifecycle and ensure it is safe when operating on public roads, where AV can endanger the lives of its own passengers, pedestrians and people in other vehicles, as well as damage other transportation system elements (e.g. other vehicles and transportation infrastructure).

Researchers in the field agree on the importance of AI and the safety to AVs. However, the existing literature in the field seems to indicate a disagreement on how they perceive the AI impact on AV safety. Therefore, this position paper supports that this lack of convergence is a potential issue affecting the AV safety. An initial exploratory research on the AV literature is applied to support this argumentation.

2   Mindset Differences Impacting AV Safety

An initial exploratory research into the literature encompassing AI and safety on the context of autonomous vehicles suggests a lack of convergence and alignment concerning the AI impact on AV safety. Most of the literature on AV considers AI a technology that increases the system safety [2–4]. Few works are considering AI a potential threat to the system safety [5, 6].

Most AV work comes from the AI community. They have applied AI techniques to AV perception [5–8], navigation and control [9–11], and so on. These works are aligned with the idea of AI-related techniques automating the driving tasks one-by-one toward the whole process automation. This may exceed the human performance, which can lead to a safer scenario due to reducing accidents. In turn, the system safety community has risen to the challenges in Verification and Validation (V&V) [3, 12], robust operation [13], ethics and policies [2, 4] development for Autonomous Vehicles. In sum, these works argue that some intrinsic AI features – especially its non-deterministic and unpredictable behavior – poses new challenges to AI-based systems, including AV systems and safety assurance processes.

Those results suggest a misalignment in the research community involved in studies into autonomous vehicles, artificial intelligence and safety aspects. Moreover, this suggests the field has not been influenced enough by the critical systems safety culture, yet. An additional observation is that most of the published studies in the field are driven by domains related to computation. Thus, its lack of tradition in safety culture could be the root cause of such misalignment, when compared to some other fields intrinsically developed around critical systems safety culture (e.g. airspace engineering).

Those perceptions become even stronger after an analysis of two available investigation results from AV accidents in which automation was an important contributing factor [14, 15]. AVs were observed to be exposed to unsafe events (accidents) because basic system safety principles were not applied: (a) basic safeguards, such as warning systems or automatic safety interlocks that prevents humans unsafe actions, were not considered [16]; and (b) requirements such as efficiency and comfort received higher priority than safety – e.g. the emergency breaking system is intentionally disabled to avoid erratic vehicle behavior [15]. Those findings indicate that the stakeholders were not aligned to the system safety culture. In special, they are evidences of developers with positive (functional) mindset[1], implementing the behavior the system shall perform to execute its mission as intended. Yet, regarding the safety culture, developers should consider a negative (risk-oriented) mindset, taking into account which conditions the system shall avoid so it cannot produce any unsafe behavior.

Given that the AV is an AI-based system, most of the AV developer community comes from AI and other related computing and systems engineering communities. They develop AI-based safety-critical systems using a positive (functional) mindset. Thus, the negative (risk-oriented) mindset from the system safety community seems to be missed. It is well known by the systems safety community that "*the effectiveness in finding safety flaws by system safety engineers has usually resulted from the application of an opposite mindset from that of the developers*" [17].

Another important aspect posing risks to AV safety is the intrinsic nature of AI. Most of the used AI techniques on AV could be considered as a black-box, thus requiring "*a leap of faith*" [18]. As the MIT professor T. Jaakkola stated, "*Whether it's an investment decision, a medical decision, or maybe a military decision, you don't want to just rely on a 'black box' method*" [18]. Also, AVs, as any other robots, have not yet reached a technical state in which they are error-free [19]. Thus, the combination of the discussed AI mindset and those facts could potentially amplify the risks to the safety of AI-based safety-critical systems, including AV.

Finally, the discussions on the legal domain encompassing AV and other autonomous machines [20, 21] seem to be disconnected from the real development stage and the safety level of those machines. An example is the EU Parliament Report on Civil Law Rules on Robotics [22] about the legislators discussion whether to grant personhood to AI-related technological artifacts with autonomy [23]. According to Noel Sharkey, "*By seeking legal personhood for robots, manufacturers were merely trying to absolve themselves of responsibility for the actions of their machines*" [23]. The real level of safety AVs seems unclear to many stakeholders, and maybe the voices of the hype are currently louder than the pragmatism of the system safety discipline in this field. This discussion, and its intersection with the social, legal, moral, and ethical aspects of the use of AVs, must be considered in the field research agenda.

3 Concluding Remarks and Ongoing Work

AV has the potential to be a ubiquitous AI-based safety-critical system, in which its individual low risks can become high risks collectively. There is thus an urgent demand

---

[1] "*a mindset is a set of assumptions, methods or notations held by one or more people or groups of people which is so established that it creates a powerful incentive within these people or groups to continue to adopt or accept prior behaviors, choices, or tools. ...*" [17]

for alignment between system safety and AI mindsets among AV stakeholders. Therefore, identifying safety assurance gaps in the AI-based systems development and doing a cross-fertilization between safety and AI communities may be a way to introduce the safety culture - and evolve the mindset – of the AI community.

However, given that a mindset – by its own definition (See footnote 1) – is hard to change, it is most plausible that AI and system safety communities must coexist in a symbiotic way. Therefore, AV development must incorporate a robust system safety lifecycle, as occurs in other safety-critical systems domains. Regarding the automotive systems, approaches are required that can incorporate AI-based systems as automotive components. New standards will demand new technical approaches to deal with safety assurance of AI-based systems. Therefore, identifying safety gaps in AI-based systems safety assurance may be a way to evolve with new approaches to safety assurance.

Above all aspects, an important concern the researches of this field should have in mind is considering AV a special application of AI. It is based on the observation made by [24] over 30 years ago, but it is still valid in the present days. In his opinion, there was a gap between exaggerated claims about AI and the work still unfulfilled. Although the present research found good studies, the claims made by companies and the media seems to be ahead of what can be supported by their findings and the current state of development [23]. This misalignment can be a source of safety issues, as pointed out by Noel Sharkey, emeritus professor of AI and Robotics at the University of Sheffield: "the wrong idea of what robotics can do and where AI is at the moment is very, very dangerous" [23].

As a result, more research is needed to insert the safety culture into the social and technical dimensions of AV. An illustration of the detachment of those pieces can be seen in many headlines in the media. While they point out the imminence of the deployment of millions of autonomous cars [25], the actual results suggest AVs are not ready yet. In fact, Google has officially reported 272 failures and 13 near misses for its self-driving car [26]. Uber AV [27] and Tesla autopilot [28] resulted in life losses.

The present study was based on an exploratory research. Our future work on this topic will include a more systematic research method such as a Systematic Literature Mapping (SLM) and a Systematic Literature Review (SLR) to obtain consolidated and more reliable results. Among other benefits, they can contribute to organizing the literature, mapping the covered topics and identifying the research gaps which could contribute to reduce the mindset differences between AI and System Safety communities. And rather motivate the convergence of both fields to achieve safe AI-based systems.

Acknowledgments. This work is supported by the Research, Development and Innovation Center, Ericsson Telecomunicações S.A., Brazil.

References

1. Singh, S.: Critical reasons for crashes investigated in the National Motor Vehicle Crash Causation Survey, Washington, DC (2015)

2. Dogan, E., Chatila, R., Chauvier, S., Evans, K., Hadjixenophontos, P., Perrin, J.: Ethics in the design of automated vehicles: the AVEthics project. In: EDIA@ ECAI, pp. 10–13 (2016)
3. Meltz, D., Guterman, H.: RobIL—Israeli program for research and development of autonomous UGV: performance evaluation methodology. In: IEEE International Conference on the Science of Electrical Engineering (ICSEE), pp. 1–5 (2016)
4. Lugano, G.: Virtual assistants and self-driving cars. In: 2017 15th International Conference on ITS Telecommunications (ITST), pp. 1–5 (2017)
5. Hamdi, S., Faiedh, H., Souani, C., Besbes, K.: Road signs classification by ANN for real-time implementation. In: 2017 International Conference on Control, Automation and Diagnosis (ICCAD), pp. 328–332 (2017)
6. Yoneda, K., Kuramoto, A., Suganuma, N.: Convolutional neural network based vehicle turn signal recognition. In: 2017 International Conference on Intelligent Informatics and Biomedical Sciences (ICIIBMS), pp. 204–205 (2017)
7. Chen, Z., Huang, X.: Accurate and reliable detection of traffic lights using multiclass learning and multiobject tracking. IEEE Intell. Transp. Syst. Mag. **8**, 28–42 (2016)
8. Habermann, D., Vido, C.E.O., Osório, F.S., Ramos, F.: Road junction detection from 3D point clouds. In: 2016 International Joint Conference on Neural Networks (IJCNN), pp. 4934–4940 (2016)
9. Hossai, M.R.T., Shahjalal, M.A., Nuri, N.F.: Design of an IoT based autonomous vehicle with the aid of computer vision. In: International Conference on Electrical, Computer and Communication Engineering (ECCE), pp. 752–756 (2017)
10. Bock, J., Beemelmanns, T., Klösges, M., Kotte, J.: Self-learning Trajectory Prediction with Recurrent Neural Networks at Intelligent Intersections (2017)
11. Lopez Pulgarin, E.J., Herrmann, G., Leonards, U.: Drivers' Manoeuvre classification for safe HRI. In: Gao, Y., Fallah, S., Jin, Y., Lekakou, C. (eds.) TAROS 2017. LNCS (LNAI), vol. 10454, pp. 475–483. Springer, Cham (2017). https://doi.org/10.1007/978-3-319-64107-2_37
12. Koopman, P.: Challenges in autonomous vehicle validation: keynote presentation abstract. In: Proceedings of the 1st International Workshop on Safe Control of Connected and Autonomous Vehicles, p. 3 (2017)
13. McAllister, R., et al.: Concrete problems for autonomous vehicle safety: advantages of Bayesian deep learning. In: Proceedings of the 26th International Joint Conference on Artificial Intelligence, IJCAI 2017 (2017)
14. NTSB: Collision Between a Car Operating with Automated Vehicle Control Systems and a Tractor-Semitrailer Truck Near Williston, Florida 7 May 2016. https://www.ntsb.gov/investigations/AccidentReports/Pages/HAR1702.aspx
15. NTSB: Preliminary Report Highway: HWY18MH010. https://www.ntsb.gov/investigations/AccidentReports/Pages/HWY18MH010-prelim.aspx
16. NTSB: Driver Errors, Overreliance on Automation, Lack of Safeguards, Led to Fatal Tesla Crash. https://www.ntsb.gov/news/press-releases/Pages/PR20170912.aspx
17. Leveson, N.G.: The use of safety cases in certification and regulation (2011)
18. Knight, W.: The Dark Secret at the Heart of AI. https://www.technologyreview.com/s/604087/the-dark-secret-at-the-heart-of-ai/
19. Mirnig, N., Stollnberger, G., Miksch, M., Stadler, S., Giuliani, M., Tscheligi, M.: To err is robot: how humans assess and act toward an erroneous social robot. Front. Robot. AI. **4**, 21 (2017)
20. Clarke, R.: Big data, big risks. Inf. Syst. J. **26**, 77–90 (2016)
21. Liu, K., Sun, L., Dix, A., Narasipuram, M.: Norm-based agency for designing collaborative information systems. Inf. Syst. J. **11**, 229–247 (2001)

22. Committee on Legal Affairs: REPORT with recommendations to the Commission on Civil Law Rules on Robotics (2017)
23. Delcker, J.: Europe divided over robot "personhood," (2018)
24. King, W.R.: Editor's comment decision support systems, artificial intelligence, and expert systems. MIS Q. **8**, iv–v (1984)
25. Garret, O.: 10 Million Self-Driving Cars Will Hit The Road By 2020. https://www.forbes.com/sites/oliviergarret/2017/03/03/10-million-self-driving-cars-will-hit-the-road-by-2020-heres-how-to-profit/#3af8be847e50
26. Harris, M.: Google reports self-driving car mistakes: 272 failures and 13 near misses (2016)
27. Wakabayashi, D.: Self-Driving Uber Car Kills Pedestrian in Arizona, Where Robots Roam (2018)
28. BBC: Tesla in fatal California crash was on Autopilot (2018)

The Moral Responsibility Gap
and the Increasing Autonomy of Systems

Zoë Porter[1]([envelope]), Ibrahim Habli[1], Helen Monkhouse[2], and John Bragg[3]

[1] University of York, York, UK
{zoe.porter,ibrahim.habli}@york.ac.uk
[2] HORIBA MIRA, Warwickshire, UK
helen.monkhouse@horiba-mira.com
[3] MBDA UK Ltd., Filton, UK
john.bragg@mbda.co.uk

Abstract. The ethical and social implications of autonomous systems are forcing safety engineers and ethicists alike to confront new questions. This paper focuses on just one of these questions - moral responsibility - bringing together inter-disciplinary insights to an issue of growing public and regulatory concern. The central thesis is that, on a conception of moral responsibility that presupposes control, the increasing autonomy of systems *prima facie* diminishes the extent to which engineers and users can be considered morally responsible for system behaviour. This challenge to our normal attributions of moral responsibility as a result of autonomy has come to be known as the 'responsibility gap'. We provide a characterisation of the moral responsibility gap, which we argue has two dimensions: causal and epistemic. At the end of the paper we highlight considerations for future work.

Keywords: Moral responsibility · Ethics · Autonomous systems
Safety

1 Introduction

Given the public and regulatory concern with autonomous systems, such as autonomous vehicles, this paper is motivated by a need to locate where there is currently diminished control over, and uncertainty about, the behaviour of such systems. These considerations should help on two counts. First, to inform discussions about how far designers and engineers are - and should be - morally responsible for system behaviour. Second, to contribute to discussions about how to evaluate confidence in autonomous systems.

This paper starts with a brief, philosophical exposition of moral responsibility, elucidating the thesis that control is a necessary condition of moral responsibility (Part 2). The notion of the 'moral responsibility gap' is then introduced, with the argument that this has two dimensions: loss of causal control and loss of epistemic control (Part 3). The paper then examines the relevant differences between non-autonomous and autonomous systems with respect to the

© Springer Nature Switzerland AG 2018
B. Gallina et al. (Eds.): SAFECOMP 2018 Workshops, LNCS 11094, pp. 487–493, 2018.
https://doi.org/10.1007/978-3-319-99229-7_43

two dimensions of the responsibility gap (Parts 4 and 5). Finally, it highlights the salient issues that the authors believe should constitute considerations for future work (Part 6).

2   Moral Responsibility

There are many senses in which the word 'responsible' is used across disciplines and in everyday discourse, but the etymology of the word indicates a common thread [1]. 'Responsible' comes from the Latin *respondeo*, and means 'to be answerable'. 'Moral responsibility' is primarily concerned with questions about when we are answerable for actions or events in such a way that we might be praised or blamed for them. This, in turn, depends on the particular relationship that obtains *"between people and the actions they perform, or between people and the consequences of their actions."* [2].

Philosophical theories of moral responsibility date back to Aristotle, who held that voluntary actions - in which the cause of the action is the agent himself or herself, and which he or she undertakes knowingly - were the only ones for which a person could be praised or blamed [3]. This has remained a deeply influential account of moral responsibility, and underpins many modern conceptions, though a radical development occurred in the 1960s with the work of Peter Strawson, who located moral responsibility not in objective conditions, such as whether the agent acted voluntarily, but in the wide variety of attitudes expressed within interpersonal relationships, according to which we praise, blame, feel gratitude, or resentment towards agents in virtue of how far we perceive them to be acting in accordance with our expectations of a reasonable degree of good will [4]. Recent accounts also differentiate between moral responsibility as accountability and moral responsibility as attributability [5].

For the purposes of this paper, we follow the supposition that it is only appropriate to hold a person morally responsible for an action or event over which they have some control, whereby they are not acting from either compulsion or ignorance [6]. It is important to note that ignorance is not always an exculpation. If one does not take sufficient care to discover whether one's actions will lead to harm, then attitudes of praise and blame are still appropriate. Negligence can be blameworthy [7].

Moral responsibility works in two directions. There is prospective responsibility, which a duty or an obligation to maintain or bring about a certain state of affairs, such as safety. And there is retrospective moral responsibility, which is accountability or liability for something that has already happened, such as an injury. The philosophical literature is dominated by a preoccupation with the latter kind of moral responsibility, often because of concerns about blaming people unfairly [2]. While our discussion will be similarly focused, we will also consider prospective responsibility, particularly as it bears on those trying to assure the future safety of autonomous systems.

We restrict the scope of our discussion in two ways. First, we limit our analysis to the human-side of the moral responsibility gap. There are interesting philosophical questions about the extent to which the computational systems themselves might be morally responsible, but we do not consider such questions here. Second, this paper makes no claims about the legal implications of the moral responsibility gap. Moral responsibility and legal responsibility are not the same. Nonetheless, it is worth noting that moral responsibility has a greater overlap with criminal liability than with civil liability. In criminal cases, lack of moral fault tends to protect the defendant from liability, and certain central assumptions about moral responsibility are reflected in criminal law [8]. In civil cases, however, there can be liability without fault [2].

3 Responsibility Gaps

Though any delegated action - whether to an individual human delegee, to an institution, or to a machine - incurs some kind of a moral responsibility gap, since the agent to whom an action is delegated may act against the wishes of, or contrary to the expectations of, the delegator, we argue that when action is delegated to an autonomous system this gap is substantially widened.

The term 'responsibility gap' with respect to autonomous systems was first introduced by Andreas Matthias in a seminal paper [9], in which he argued that there is *"... an increasing class of machine actions, where the traditional ways of responsibility ascription are not compatible with our sense of justice and the moral framework of society because nobody has enough control over the machine's actions to assume the responsibility for them. These cases constitute what we will call the responsibility problem."* (p. 117)

Extending and elucidating Matthias' treatment, we posit that the moral responsibility gap has two dimensions: the causal and the epistemic. The causal dimension of the gap can be thought of as diminishing control over the 'what' of system behaviour. Part of the problem in determining how to attribute moral responsibility to engineers of autonomous systems is the difficulty in tracing the nature and extent of the causal influence that they have over those systems' final capabilities. The epistemic dimension of the gap can be thought of as diminishing control over the 'how' of system behaviour; with autonomous systems, precisely how the system reaches a decision is increasingly something the human delegator cannot explain or understand. As such, another part of the problem in attributing moral responsibility to engineers and users of autonomous systems is the difficulty in determining the extent to which they might reasonably be expected to know, or at least seek to know, how the systems behave.

To clarify this difference between the causal (control over the 'what') and the epistemic (control over the 'how'), take an autonomous car. Developing overtaking capabilities falls under the causal dimension. Understanding of how the autonomous system will deploy these features falls under the epistemic dimension. A common problem in engineering is that it is hard to draw a line between the 'what' and the 'how.' This distinction is further complicated with autonomy.

It is important to note that, as with all modern technology, there is already a causal constraint on the moral responsibility of human delegators on two counts.

First, because of the 'problem of many hands,' whereby multiple actors are involved in designing the capabilities of such systems [10,11]. Second, because of the temporal and physical remoteness of the systems actions from the original action of design, certification, and manufacture [10]. Autonomy adds a new layer of complexity for attributions of moral responsibility on engineers and users.

4   Responsibility Gaps and Non-autonomous Systems

Traditional safety engineering mainly relies on the largely controlled nature of systems. A boundary definition is typically used to describe the system's key architectural elements, its functions, and its interfaces to other systems. Referred to by many safety standards as the Target of Evaluation (TOE), this becomes the foundation on which all subsequent safety activities are performed. The first such is the Hazard Analysis and Risk Assessment (HARA) process, which seeks to identify the potentially hazardous behaviour of the TOE, and also to classify the resulting risk. Safety functions can then be defined to mitigate the hazard risk, with the integrity level of the safety functions commensurate with that risk. Finally, testing the system's implemented behaviour against the safety requirements builds confidence that the system achieves the acceptable level of safety, as determined by the relevant safety standards or authorities.

For domains such as aviation and automotive, where many vehicles of the same type will be built and operated, a type-approval or certification process is commonly used. Like the safety standards discussed above, this approach primarily relies on determinism and predictability. This paradigm assumes that if one can satisfy the appropriate regulatory or certification body about the performance and safety of the first system of type built, then (providing an effective manufacturing process exists) the 100th or 1000th system manufactured will behave in the same way. In this way, it is possible to assure the safety of the fleet having only scrutinised a signal system of type.

Currently, therefore, the engineer retains a substantial level of control over both the 'what' (causal control) and the 'how' (epistemic control) of the system. Engineers and designers determine what the system's capabilities are and what it can be used for. The causal condition for moral responsibility is also met by safety engineers because, counter-factually, if a signal system type is not evaluated as acceptably safe, the fleet is not built. However, given that the system operates at a temporal and physical distance from the original actors, we might argue that engineers no longer have moral responsibility for the system's actions if there is a later intervention in the system, either by users or other parties, that they could not reasonably have foreseen and mitigated.

The epistemic dimension of moral responsibility - control over the 'how' of system behaviour - is also robustly met. Engineers can understand how a system works and why it takes the actions that it takes. There is an established framework for deliberation about the behaviour of the system and outcomes are largely predictable. Though the engineer is not proceeding from a position of absolute certainty about the behaviour of the system, there is a very high degree of confidence that the system will perform to type, based on the behaviour of the system when tested against safety requirements.

We might reasonably ask questions about the adequacy of the test coverage measures themselves, and how far these are within the control of the engineers who are mandated to use them (by national or international standards). However, they exist and some are mandated by the relevant authorities.

There are also some marginal epistemic constraints, such as the possibility that an engineer might not fully understand something about the boundary of definition, or fail to imagine and identify potentially hazardous behaviour of the system in the HARA process. In both of these cases, there is reduced understanding of the 'how' of system behaviour. However, here we need to balance prospective responsibility (i.e. the obligations we have as a result of our role) against retrospective responsibility (i.e. accountability for outcomes). For as long as the behaviour is, in principle, understandable, then it is reasonable to maintain that it is incumbent upon the person whose role to is to analyse the system to understand that system; and similarly with the analysis of credible hazards.

5   Responsibility Gaps and Autonomous Systems

There are no *established* safety engineering frameworks for autonomous systems. The test coverage measures discussed above do not yet exist for autonomous systems.

By their very nature, autonomous systems are developed to operate in complex environments. Here, it is not possible to pre-define what would be correct and safe system behaviour, and to pre-program accordingly. The machine itself must process, interpret, and action large, dynamic data sets. With the relationship (or transfer function) between the inputs and outputs for such systems being difficult, if not impossible, to describe algorithmically, machine learning is deployed to 'teach' the system its transfer function. For example, in a personalised healthcare solution, the clinical advice of an autonomous system depends on conditions, behaviours, constraints, and preferences that are learnt by the machine at runtime that cannot be predicted prior to deployment.

Causal control, over the 'what' of system behaviour, becomes more challenging. Though engineers and designers still determine what the system's capabilities are and what it can be used for, they are not always in control of how these might change as a result of the machine's own learning. The epistemic dimension - moral responsibility for the 'how' of system behaviour - is even more problematic. With autonomy, it becomes exceedingly difficult to understand how a system gets from input to output. This presents a difficulty for the existing safety assurance paradigm, given that a large segment of the safety argument is effectively the confidence in the 'how'.

One problem is the distinction between system-type and individual examples of the system. In philosophy, this would be known as a type-token distinction. An autonomous system, or system-type, will have a 'correct' design (i.e. the AI engine), but each system, or system-token, will differ in its actual behaviour once it starts learning 'in the wild' (i.e. based on real-world data). Not only is it difficult to foresee what learning errors might occur, it will also be difficult to distinguish a design error from a learning error. All of this serves to undermine the extent to which a safety engineer can be responsible for - and mitigate against - subsequent hazardous behaviour.

We should also consider the causal influence of the users (and society) from whom the system has learnt the unsafe behaviours. Here, in conditions of uncertainty, it would seem that there is some duty, a prospective moral responsibility, incumbent upon all parties - engineers and users - to ensure that the system is provided with exemplary training data. If this still leads to inexplicable negative outcomes, then an accountability gap remains.

Two further problems for moral responsibility bear consideration, both of which complicate the line between causal control (over the 'what') and epistemic control (over the 'how'). The first is emergent behaviour. A learning system might start to generate new behaviours. Here, the design (the 'how') equips the system with the ability to change what it can do and be used for (the 'what'). Changes in the system's behaviour occur because of what the system has learnt by way of its learning algorithms, as opposed to change that is directly influenced by the system's design.

This links to the second problem: trade-offs. An autonomous system might learn original and highly effective skills, but if we have a limited scope of understanding as to what 'safe' looks like, we might unnecessarily or unwittingly constrain this behaviour. With the personalised healthcare system, for example, safeguards can be put in place to mitigate some possible consequences, such as recommendations that physical exercises do not exceed certain thresholds. But these safeguards might reduce the machine's ability to perform tasks that lead to even safer or more effective actions that the designers did not, or could not, foresee. Given the peculiarities of the situation, non-compliance or improvisation might lead to safer outcomes than following established safety procedures. This raises the question of the extent to which designers can deliberate about the possible consequences of the actions of an autonomous system in emergency and novel situations.

6   Conclusions and Future Considerations

One thing is clear from the foregoing discussion: the safety engineering community is in urgent need of robust and open deliberation about what is deemed as sufficient control over the 'what' and the 'how' of autonomous system behaviour.

Substantive issues that we have raised, and which we think bear consideration with respect to the moral responsibilities on the engineering community (as well as on users and society) are as follows. If we can only assure system-types, how should we navigate the unpredictability of system-tokens? To what level of confidence should we be able to distinguish a learning error from a design error? Is it possible to distinguish between a learning error and an original solution to a problem? How should we account for emergent behaviour? What standards should we use to reconcile trade-offs, for example between explainability and effectiveness?

There is also a need to focus on cultural acceptance: an obligation on autonomous systems engineers to show these systems' safety advantage over human-controlled systems. Part of this includes moves to increase the explainability of such systems, such that the system can explain the decision made, or at least why its course of action led to a 'more safe' outcome than any of the alternatives.

These considerations locate the key areas of uncertainty about, and diminished control over, the behaviour of autonomous systems. We believe that these considerations should feed into discussions about the development of such systems from moral and liability perspectives.

Such discussion is both a question of retrospective moral responsibility: how far system failure can be traced back to design, engineering, and user fault. But it is also demand upon prospective moral responsibility: how to determine confidence in autonomous systems in order to assure their future safety.

References

1. Lucas, J.R.: Responsibility (1993)
2. Talbert, M.: Moral Responsibility. Polity Press, Cambridge, UK (2015)
3. Aristotle: The Nichomachean Ethics. Oxford University Press, Oxford (2009)
4. Strawson, P.F.: Freedom and resentment. In: Watson, G., (ed) Proceedings of the British Academy, vol. 48, pp. 1–25. Oxford University Press, Oxford (1962)
5. Eshleman, A.: Moral responsibility (2016). https://plato.stanford.edu/archives/win2016/entries/moral-responsibility/ Accessed 20 June 2018
6. Fischer, J.M., Ravizza, M.: Responsibility and control: A Theory of Moral Responsibility. Cambridge University Press, Cambridge, UK (2000)
7. Hyman, J.: Action, Knowledge, and Will. Oxford University Press, Oxford (2015)
8. Brink, D.O., Nelkin, D.: Fairness and the architecture of responsibility. Oxford Stud. Agency Responsib. 1, 284–313 (2013)
9. Matthias, A.: The responsibility gap: ascribing responsibility for the actions of learning automata. Ethics Inf. Technol. 6(3), 175–183 (2004)
10. Noorman, M.: Computing and moral responsibility (2018). https://plato.stanford.edu/archives/spr2018/entries/computing-responsibility/ Accessed 08 Mar 2018
11. Jonas, H.: The imperative of responsibility. Search of an Ethics for the Technological Age. University of Chicago Press, Chicago (1985)

Design Requirements for a Moral Machine
for Autonomous Weapons

Ilse Verdiesen[1(✉)], Virginia Dignum[1], and Iyad Rahwan[2]

[1] Delft University of Technology, Jaffalaan 5, 2628 BX Delft, The Netherlands
e.p.verdiesen@tudelft.nl
[2] MIT Medialab, 75 Amherst Street, Cambridge, MA 02139, USA

Abstract. Autonomous Weapon Systems (AWS) are said to become the third revolution in warfare. These systems raise many questions and concerns that demand in-depth research on ethical and moral responsibility. Ethical decision-making is studied in related fields like Autonomous Vehicles and Human Operated drones, but not yet fully extended to the deployment of AWS and research on moral judgement is lacking. In this paper, we propose design requirements for a Moral Machine (Similar to http://moralmachine.mit.edu/) for Autonomous Weapons to conduct a large-scale study of the moral judgement of people regarding the deployment of this type of weapon. We ran an online survey to get a first impression on the importance of six variables that will be implemented in a proof-of-concept of a Moral Machine for Autonomous Weapons and describe a scenario containing these six variables. The platform will enable large-scale randomized controlled experiments and generate knowledge about people's feelings concerning this type of weapons. The next steps of our study include development and testing of the design before the prototype is upscaled to a Massive Online Experiment.

Keywords: Autonomous weapons · Ethical decision-making
Moral acceptability · Moral machine

1 Introduction

As the reach and capabilities of Artificial Intelligence (AI) systems increases, there is also an increasing awareness of the ethical, legal and societal impact of the potential actions and decisions of these systems. Many are calling for guidelines and regulations that can ensure the responsible design, development, implementation, and policy of AI in general, and Autonomous Weapon Systems (AWS) specifically [1]. Others are calling for a ban on these weapons and there is an increasing awareness that international regulations are long due [2]. Many experts agree that AWS that kill without human intervention are "morally wrong" and that their use should be controlled under the 1983 Convention on Certain Conventional Weapons (CCW)[1] in order to become part of International Humanitarian Law [3]. However, banning this autonomous technology for

---

[1] cf. https://ihl-databases.icrc.org/ihl/INTRO/500?OpenDocument.

© Springer Nature Switzerland AG 2018
B. Gallina et al. (Eds.): SAFECOMP 2018 Workshops, LNCS 11094, pp. 494–506, 2018.
https://doi.org/10.1007/978-3-319-99229-7_44

military use may not be practical given that similar technologies could well be dual-used as they are also available in the commercial sector. The CCW met late 2017 in Geneva and started a substantive review of relevant developments related to AWS. Of particular relevance to this discussion are issues regarding the level of autonomy, embodiment (including "killer robots", human enhancement, and virtual machines), validation and verification, and safety. Complementary to this discussion, is equally important to identify how the (civilian) public perceives AWS and their use, both in defense and attack situations.

The defense industry has always been one of the main areas of application of AI, and is also the area in which responsibility and ethical impact are the most salient. AWS are weapon systems equipped with Artificial Intelligence (AI) reasoning mechanisms. Such weapons have the capability to select and engage targets without human intervention. In the complex discussion of how the development of AWS should be controlled, there is a need to give full consideration, not only to national and commercial interests, but most importantly to have a profound understanding of the feelings people associate with this type of weapon and their perception of the moral acceptability of its use.

These considerations should lead setting regulation that can ensure that the development and use of AWS is controlled and that there are sufficient powerful monitoring mechanisms and institutions that can control this type of technology in all its application domains (military and commercial). Towards this aim, it is necessary to understand what autonomy in the context of AWS really means, how it relates to meaningful human control, and how people respond to the potential use of these weapons in different situations, for attack or defense, or with or without collateral damage.

A growing body of researchers is focusing on responsible design of AI, which incorporates social and ethical values, to prevent undesirable societal outcomes of this technology. Several proposals for principles to describe Responsible AI exist, including the Asilomar principles[2], ART - *Accountability, Responsibility* and *Transparency* [4], and the IEEE Ethically Aligned Design recommendations[3]. *Accountability* refers to the justification of the actions taken by the AI, *Responsibility* ensures appropriate data governance by establishing a chain of responsibility amongst stakeholders. *Transparency* is concerned with describing and reproducing the decisions the AI makes and adepts to its environment [5]. These works however, refer to AI in general and are as such to not provide specific guidance to the issue of AWS.

Autonomous systems are increasingly deployed on the battlefield [6]. Autonomous systems can have many benefits in the military domain, for example when the autopilot of the F-16 prevents a crash [7]. Other advantages are that Autonomous systems and AWS can act as force multipliers, meaning that less military personnel is needed for a mission which in turn is more efficient and could lead to long-term savings [8]. Another advantage would be that decisions of AWS would not be impaired by human emotions and could process much more incoming sensory information at a higher speed than humans are able to [9].

---

[2] https://futureoflife.org/ai-principles.
[3] https://ethicsinaction.ieee.org/.

Many arguments have been raised opposing AWS. The 'Campaign Stop Killer Robots' [2] states for example on their website that: '*Allowing life or death decisions to be made by machines crosses a fundamental moral line. Autonomous robots would lack human judgment and the ability to understand context.*'. The United Nations are also voicing their concerns and state that '*Autonomous weapons systems that require no meaningful human control should be prohibited, and remotely controlled force should only ever be used with the greatest caution*' [10]. The deployment of AWS on the battlefield without direct human oversight is not only a military revolution according to Kaag and Kaufman [11], but can also be considered a moral one. As large-scale deployment of AI on the battlefield seems unavoidable [12] the research on ethical and moral responsibility is imperative.

Ethical decision-making in AI and robots is an emerging field and scholars are studying moral judgment related to these technologies. For example, Malle [13] proposes a framework combining the (until recently) separate fields of *robot ethics*, in which ethical questions about the design, deployment and treatment of robots by humans are addressed, and *machine morality*, which is concerned with questions about the moral capacities of a robot and how these should be computationally implemented. Cointe, Bonnet and Bossier [14] propose a model in which an agent can judge the ethical aspects of its own behaviour and that of other agents in a multi-agent system. The model describes an Ethical Judgment Process (EJP) which allows agents to evaluate the behaviour of other agents. Bonnefon, Shariff and Rahwan [15] have studied the ethical decision an Autonomous Vehicle has to make, being self-protection or utilitarian, when confronted with pedestrians on the road. In this research, the Moral Machine at MIT is used to gain insight in how people judge on scenarios with an Autonomous Vehicle to see how their moral judgment compares to those of other people.

Ethical concerns have also been studied in the related field of Human Operated drone operations. Coekelbergh [16] argues that drone operations not only create a physical distance, but also a moral distance as the face of the opponent becomes less visible which eliminates the moral-psychological barrier for killing. Another ethical concern according to Strawser [17] is that due to the remote distance to the battlefield human operators can experience cognitive dissonance in which the war feels more like a video game than reality. These ethical concerns are refuted by Strawser [17] as he states that due to the increased distance the human operators have more time to evaluate a target, because their own safety is not at risk, but he also argues that more empirical research needs to be done to assess the psychological effects of the large distance to the battlefield.

We found that studies on ethical decision-making and moral judgement relating to AWS are currently lacking. Several scholars like Malle [13], Cointe et al. [14] and Bonnefon et al. [15] are studying ethical decision-making in AI and robots or Human Operated drones [16, 17], but their research has not yet been extended to the deployment of AWS. Therefore, we propose a design for a Moral Machine for Autonomous Weapons to conduct a large-scale study of the moral judgment of people on the deployment of this type of weapons. We build on the concept of the Moral Machine, that was developed by the Scalable Cooperation group of the Media Lab at MIT [18].

We will focus on the deployment of AWS in the near future, which we define as: *within the next 5 years* as these type of weapons are not yet deployed on the battlefield.

This entails that we will not study weapons equipped with Artificial General Intelligence or futuristic technology that is not possible to construct yet, but we will focus on technology that is currently being developed, specifically drones with autonomous targeting capabilities.

The paper is structured as follows; Sect. 2 first defines Autonomy and AWS and describes the Moral Machine for Autonomous Vehicles. In Sect. 3 we delineate our proposal for the Moral Machine for Autonomous Weapons. We present the results of an online survey that we ran to get a first impression of the importance of the variables and specify the scenarios and its variables. We conclude in Sect. 4 with a discussion on the limitations of our work and discuss recommendations for further research in Sect. 5.

2   Related Work

This section first discusses fundamental work on Autonomy prior to defining AWS. We further provide a description of the existing Moral Machine for Autonomous Vehicles, designed by the Scalable Cooperation group of the Media Lab at MIT [18], which we use as basis for our work.

2.1   Autonomy

Autonomy lays at the core of Artificial Intelligence. However, it is a most undefined and misunderstood concept. Often, autonomy is taken to be an absolute property of the system, i.e. an agent is either autonomous- capable of performing tasks in the world by itself, without explicit human control - or not. However, autonomy should be seen as a relational notion involving three classes of entities [19]: (i) the main subject, x whose autonomy is being considered/evaluated; (ii) a function/action/goal μ that must be realized or maintained by the main subject and on which the autonomy is evaluated; (iii) a secondary subject y (which may be a plurality of subjects) with respect to whom the main subject should be considered autonomous given the specified function/action/goal. That is, stating "x is autonomous" is meaningless as it does not indicate the object and recipient of that autonomy, whereas the statement "x is autonomous about μ with respect to y" provides enough characterization of the focus and context of autonomy. E.g. in the case x is a self-driving car (x), autonomy means that x can autonomously decide on the travel route (μ) given a destination set by its user (y).

On the basis of these relationships and the nature of the entities, several degrees and types of autonomy can be identified, including executive autonomy (i.e. the agent is autonomous in its means rather than its ends or goals; as in the self-driving car example above), goal autonomy (i.e. the agent is endowed with goals, or ends, of its own), or social autonomy (i.e. the agent is self-sufficient meaning that it can execute its goals by itself without other agents or resources) [19].

In the AWS arena, an important concept is that of *meaningful human control*, which signifies control over the selection and engagement of targets, that is, the "critical functions" of a weapon, including where and how weapons are used; what or whom they are used against; and the effects of their use [20]. In terms of the different types of autonomy above, this indicates that, at most, AWS can have executive autonomy but never the autonomy to decide on its own goals nor the moment of action. Human oversight is required to set goals and to monitor execution by the machine.

2.2 Autonomous Weapon Systems

Although the debate on AWS has drawn a lot of attention in the recent years and a few public opinion surveys have been conducted [21, 22], we found that the topic in not well delineated in the academic literature. AWS are an emerging technology and there is still no internationally agreed upon definition [23]. Even consensus whether AWS should be defined at all is lacking. Although some scholars provide definitions, others caution against such a specification. NATO states that: '*Attempting to create definitions for "autonomous systems" should be avoided, because by definition, machines cannot be autonomous in a literal sense.*' [24:10]. The United Nations Institute for Disarmament Research (UNDIR) is also cautious about providing a definition of AWS, because they argue that the level of autonomy depends on the '*critical functions of concern and the interactions of different variables*' [25:5]. They state that one of the reasons for the differentiation of terms regarding AWS is that sometimes things (drones or robots) are defined, but in other times a characteristic (autonomy), variables of concern (lethality or degree of human control) or usage (targeting or defensive measures) are drawn into the discussion and become part of the definition. In our opinion, the definition in the report of the Advisory Council on International Affairs (AIV & CAVV) captures the description of AWS best from an engineering and military standpoint, because it takes predefined criteria into account and is linked to the military targeting process as the weapon will only be deployed after a human decision. Therefore, we will follow this definition and define AWS as:

'*A weapon that, without human intervention, selects and engages targets matching certain predefined criteria, following a human decision to deploy the weapon on the understanding that an attack, once launched, cannot be stopped by human intervention.*' [23:11].

2.3 Moral Machine for Autonomous Vehicles

Ethical decision making in Autonomous Vehicles is studied by Bonnefon et al. [15] by means of the Moral Machine. The original Moral Machine is a '*…platform for gathering data on human perception of the moral acceptability of decisions made by autonomous vehicles faced with choosing which humans to harm and which to save.*' [26:42–43]. The website has three modes for users: (1) a *Judge* mode in which users can decide the outcome for 13 series of scenarios, (2) a *Design* mode in which users can design their own scenarios, and (3) a *Browse* mode in which users can view the scenarios of others. The main feature is the Judge mode in which users choose between two scenarios that contain different variables of: *Characters* {gender, social value, age, species, fitness, utilitarianism}, *Interventionism* {omission, commission}, *Relationship to vehicle* {driver, pedestrian} and *Concern for law* {legal action, illegal action}. The Moral Machine is set-up as a Massive Online Experiment (MOE) [27] which is aimed at recruiting a large sample pool with a diverse background in a short amount of time at a low cost. These features are clear advantages of a MOE, but the downside is that the conditions are hard to control, as users can take surveys multiple times and are self-selected, which means that they can join the experiment and drop out whenever they want [26]. By May 2017, approximately 3 million users over 160 countries assessed over 30 million scenarios making it one of the biggest large-scale moral judgment tools that exist. The Moral Machine for Autonomous Vehicles is a novel tool to conduct a MOE which generates a vast amount of data in a short time. However, being novel, no report of substantial impact of the methodology could be found. Nevertheless, the Moral Machine concept could provide much insight in the moral judgement regarding the deployment of AWS. As empirical data on this insight is currently lacking, we propose to apply the Moral Machine concept to the domain of AWS and drafted design requirements for a Moral Machine for Autonomous Weapons.

3   Moral Machine for Autonomous Weapons

AWS are a sensitive topic and it invokes a primary response of anxiety and unease with people. In our opinion, it would not be prudent to develop an open platform to gather data on a large-scale at first, because an open platform could attract negative sentiment and unwanted actions which would be counterproductive for our research. For example, people creating scenarios in which certain groups of people, such as women or Muslims, are specifically targeted. Therefore, it is advisable to take a more step-wise approach in scaling up to a Massive Online Experiment.

3.1   Method

To run a large-scale follow-up study of the moral judgments of people regarding AWS a randomized controlled experiment with a limited set of conditions and sample should be set-up. Four reasons to use experiments as research technique are mentioned by Oehlert [28]: (1) they allow for direct comparisons between treatments of interest, (2) they can be designed to minimize any bias in the comparisons, (3) they can be designed to keep the error in the comparison small, and (4) we are in control of the experiments which allows us to make stronger inferences about the nature of differences we observe and especially we can make inferences about causation. A treatment in this sense are the different scenarios we would aim to compare. It is important that the effects of a treatment can only attributed to one cause that can be measured and cannot be attributed to multiple causes which is also referred to as confounding. Randomisation helps ensure that participants are assigned to a scenario by chance and not based on pre-existing features, such as time when the survey is taken or location.

3.2   Survey

To get a first impression on the importance of variables to be incorporated in the Moral Machine, we ran an online survey with 209 participants (142 males) on Amazon

Mechanical Turk. These six variables are inspired by the Moral Machine for Autonomous Vehicles and based on the researchers' intuition. The respondents were paid a small fee ($0.50) and were asked for each of the six variables: '*Please indicate to what extent the {variable X} is relevant to the moral decision-making on Autonomous Weapons:*'. Each of the items was measured on a self-reported scale ranging from '0 = not at all' to '100 = very important'. The results (Fig. 1. Results survey) indicate that the *Outcome* ($M = 70.25$, $SD = 28.05$) and *Type of Mission* ($M = 68.09$, $SD = 26.82$) are considered most important, but the other variables *Type of Weapon* ($M = 66.44$, $SD = 28.06$), *Type of Character* ($M = 62.83$, $SD = 30.24$), *Number of Characters* ($M = 62.52$, $SD = 28.70$) and *Location* ($M = 63.08$, $SD = 29.21$) are also relevant.

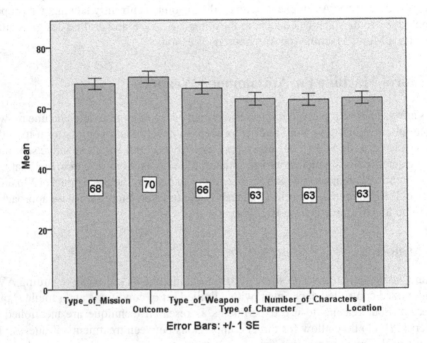

Fig. 1. Results survey

In addition to the questions on the variables we asked the respondents to: '*Please list one other aspect that you consider important for the moral decision-making on Autonomous Weapons:*'. Based on this open question, the following items are relevant to include into the design as variables: (1) Type of collateral damage (hospital, school, temple, water, psychological damage); (2) Activity of target (hostile or passive); (3) Threat level; (4) Chance of success; (5) Type of ammunition; (6) Type of decision by machine (automatically select target and acts or chooses best action based on human selection of target); (7) Duration of mission; (8) Means of control (automatic or human deactivation).

3.3 Scenarios

In this section, the variables for the Moral Machine for Autonomous Weapons, which are based on the online survey, are defined and depicted in two example scenarios. The variables are based on the scenario in which a military convoy is supported by a drone in the air. The drone scans the surroundings for enemy threats and carries weapons for the defence of the convoy. When the convoy is at a three-mile distance from the camp, the drone detects a vehicle behind a mountain range that is approaching the convoy at high speed. The drone detects four people in the car with large weapon-shaped objects and identifies the driver of the vehicle as a known member of an insurgency group. The drone needs to decide if it attacks the approaching vehicle which could result in the death of all four passengers and might cause collateral damage by killing people that are nearby the road.

3.4 Variables for Scenarios

For the prototype of the Moral Machine for Autonomous Weapons six variables are defined: *Type of Weapon* (W), *Location* (L), *Character* (C), *Number of Characters* (N), *Outcome* (O) and *Mission* (M). Similar to the Moral Machine of Autonomous Vehicles [26], the variables are depicted in figures and pictograms. These are suggestions and will need to be tested to verify how people understand these variables and if their understanding concurs with the intended meaning by the researchers. The variables also will need to be professionally designed when implemented in a Moral Machine for Autonomous Weapons. For now, the *Location* variable is based on a cartoon and game like depiction of a desert and village and the collateral damage of the *Outcome* variable is depicted with a smiley. These depictions have been chosen to avoid resemblance with real-life locations, but the cartoon-like pictures and smiley's need to be tested if these are a clear representation or if a photograph is more suitable when used in a study.

Location. This dimension shows the *Location* (L) as setting for the scenario which can either be in the desert or in the village (Figs. 2 and 3). In this dimension, we test if which location is more morally acceptable for people to deploy the AWS. If *Location* is the discriminative variable, then both different images are shown on each of the scenario. Otherwise the same location is depicted in both scenarios as in the example (Fig. 9).

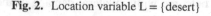

Fig. 2. Location variable L = {desert}   **Fig. 3.** Location variable L = {village}

Type of Weapon. This dimension shows the *Type of Weapon* (W) that is deployed to support the convoy. This dimension tests if people judge the current technology, the Human Operated drone, to be more morally acceptable than the AWS, which is future technology. This can be used to get insight in the support for the technologies. The *Type of Weapon* is either a Human Operated drone (left hand side) or an AWS (right hand side) (Fig. 4). If *Type of Weapon* is the discriminative variable, then the different pictograms are shown on the scenario for people to choose between them as is shown in the example (Fig. 9).

Fig. 4. Type of weapon variable

Character. This dimension shows the type of *Character* (C) that is involved as bystanders in the scenario which can either be a man (on the left), a woman (in the middle) or a child (on the right) (Fig. 5). By varying the characters, we gain insight which bystanders people find morally acceptable when an Autonomous or Human Operated Weapon is used. If *Character* is the discriminative variable, then different characters are shown on each of the scenario. Otherwise the same characters are depicted in both scenarios.

Fig. 5. Character variable   **Fig. 6.** Number of characters

Number of Characters. This dimension shows the *Number of Characters* (N) that are involved in the scenario which can range from one character (on the left) up to five characters (on the right) (Fig. 6). This dimension allows us to gain insight into how many bystanders people find morally acceptable when an Autonomous or Human Operated Weapon is used. If the *Number of Characters* is the discriminative variable, then different numbers of characters are shown on each of the scenario. Otherwise the same number of characters are depicted in both scenarios.

Outcome. This dimension shows the *Outcome* (O) of the scenario which can either be with no collateral damage (on the left) or an outcome with collateral damage of the number of characters involved in the scenario (on the right) (Fig. 7). This allows us to gain insight into how the outcome influences the moral acceptability of when an AWS is deployed. If *Outcome* is the discriminative variable, then different pictograms are shown on each of the scenario. Otherwise the same outcome variable is depicted in both scenarios.

No collateral damage

Collateral damage

Defend

Attack

Fig. 7. Outcome variable   **Fig. 8.** Mission variable

Mission. This dimension shows the *Mission* (M) of the weapon in the scenario which can either be to defend the convoy only when a direct threat is perceived (on the left) or to attack vehicles that are on the target list even as they do not pose a direct threat for the convoy (on the right) (Fig. 8). In this dimension, we test which type of mission is morally acceptable to people. If the *Mission* is the discriminative variable, then different pictograms are shown on each of the scenario. Otherwise the same mission variable is depicted in both scenarios.

3.5 Example Scenario

The variables described above can be used to create scenarios in which each scenario differs on only one variable. The question presented to the user in the scenario is the same question as that is being asked when judging the scenarios in the original Moral Machine. In this section, we depict a scenario as an example to show the concept, but for the sake of brevity chose not to show all variables in an endless list of examples. The example in Fig. 9 shows a convoy in a desert location. The difference between the scenarios is that on the left the convoy is defended by a Human Operated drone and in

Which scenario is most acceptable to you?

Fig. 9. Example scenario

the scenario on the right by an AWS. In both cases the mission of the drone is to defend the convoy and there is one person near the road which is killed by collateral damage.

Implementation. To test the scenarios, we will design the website that allows people to take the survey after obtaining a password via a web-interface to a secure server. We will gather initial data and user feedback in pilot studies to check the research set-up and clarity of the survey. The next step will be to scale up to a large-scale open platform, like the Moral Machine, where people can judge the scenarios to collect a large amount of data in several countries. However, due to the sensitivity of the topic we believe it would not be advisable to allow people to create their own scenarios or share their results on social media as the *Design* feature of the original Moral Machine for Autonomous Vehicles offers. This will be a process that will take several iterations until the final study can be tested. The original Moral Machine collected data from June 23, 2016 until May 2017 [26] and we propose to run the study on AWS for the same duration to get a large enough sample to truly call it a Massive Online Experiment.

4   Discussion

This section discusses the limitations of this design proposal and the recommendations for further research. Given the preliminary nature of the work this proposal has several limitations. The first is that the work is conceptual. Not only do we need to test the scenarios and layout of the variables to verify if there are easily understood, but also we need to check whether the understanding of the concepts concur with the intended meaning of the researchers before they can be implemented. Secondly, at this stage it is not clear if the scenarios will lead to usable and statistically robust research data on the moral judgement of people on AWS and the scenarios might have to be tweaked in order to obtain this data. Thirdly, the study uses drones in the scenarios, but this is only one type of AWS. Many other weapons can be surveyed, for example the anti-aircraft missiles or autonomous torpedoes of submarines. The final limitation is that the scenarios present a simplified view of military operations and much more variables than the ones tested in the scenarios, such as the changes in the circumstances and overall threat level due to unexpected events or strategy of the opponent, are at play. It is exactly because of the complexity of the theme, that is of the utmost importance to proceed with great caution and to carefully design and measure each choice. This experiment is a first step towards this aim.

5   Conclusions

In the discussion of how the development of AWS should be controlled, there is a need to give full consideration not only to national and commercial interests but most importantly to have a profound understanding of the feelings people associate with this type of weapon. This paper proposes a MOE in order to get a grounded view on the perception of the moral acceptability of AWS of the wider public on this question.

The limitations discussed above call for recommendations for further research. The first is that the variables should be validated with a panel consisting of different demographical composition and cultures to verify the understandability and clarity. Secondly, to validate that the scenarios generate accurate and usable research data they should be tested in several pilot studies to verify the usability of the proposed research set-up of a randomized controlled experiment before launching the website. Thirdly, after the initial scenarios are tested a follow-up study is recommended to expand the *Type of Weapon* variable in which other types of AWS are tested. For example, anti-aircraft missiles or autonomous torpedoes. Other expansions of the variables would include a different *Location*, for example villages in the West compared to villages in the Middle-East or Asia. It is also possible to include different types of *Characters*, such as animals or people with different social values, e.g. criminals, doctors and pregnant women. Lastly, the research could be extended to incorporate more scenarios that include realistic military variables in order for the MOE to be representative for military operations. Included could be for example different threat levels, influences from the decision-making process or circumstances that change rapidly during the execution of the mission in order to get a thorough understanding of the moral judgement of people regarding Autonomous Weapon Systems.

References

1. IEEE Global Initiative, The IEEE Global Initiative for Ethical Considerations in Artificial Intelligence and Autonomous Systems (2017)
2. Campaign to Stop Killer Robots. Campaign to Stop Killer Robots (2015). https://www.stopkillerrobots.org/. Accessed 15 July 2017
3. ICRC, Ethics and autonomous weapon systems: An ethical basis for human control? International Committee of the Red Cross (ICRC), Geneva, p. 22 (2018)
4. Dignum, V.: Responsible Autonomy (2017). arXiv preprint: arXiv:1706.02513
5. Dignum, V.: Introduction to AI (2016). https://rai2016.tbm.tudelft.nl/contents/
6. Roff, H.M.: Weapons autonomy is rocketing (2016). http://foreignpolicy.com/2016/09/28/weapons-autonomy-is-rocketing/
7. US Air Force, Unconscious US F-16 pilot saved by Auto-pilot 2016, Catch News: Youtube
8. Etzioni, A., Etzioni, O.: Pros and Cons of Autonomous Weapons Systems. Military Review, May–June 2017
9. Arkin, R.C.: The case for ethical autonomy in unmanned systems. J. Mil. Ethics 9(4), 332–341 (2010)
10. General Assembly United Nations, Joint report of the Special Rapporteur on the rights to freedom of peaceful assembly and of association and the Special Rapporteur on extrajudicial, summary or arbitrary executions on the proper management of assemblies, p. 23 (2016)
11. Kaag, J., Kaufman, W.: Military frameworks: technological know-how and the legitimization of warfare. Camb. Rev. Int. Aff. 22(4), 585–606 (2009)
12. Rosenberg, M., Markoff, J.: The Pentagon's 'Terminator Conundrum': Robots That Could Kill on Their Own, in The New York Times (2016)
13. Malle, B.F.: Integrating robot ethics and machine morality: the study and design of moral competence in robots. Ethics Inf. Technol. 18, 243–256 (2015)

14. Cointe, N., Bonnet, G., Boissier, O.: Ethical judgment of agents' behaviors in multi-agent systems. In: Proceedings of the 2016 International Conference on Autonomous Agents & Multiagent Systems. International Foundation for Autonomous Agents and Multiagent Systems (2016)
15. Bonnefon, J.-F., Shariff, A., Rahwan, I.: The social dilemma of autonomous vehicles. Science **352**(6293), 1573–1576 (2016)
16. Coeckelbergh, M.: Drones, information technology, and distance: mapping the moral epistemology of remote fighting. Ethics Inf. Technol. **15**(2), 87–98 (2013)
17. Strawser, B.J.: Moral predators: the duty to employ uninhabited aerial vehicles. In: Valavanis, K.P., Vachtsevanos, G.J. (eds.) Handbook of Unmanned Aerial Vehicles, pp. 2943–2964. Springer, Dordrecht (2010). https://doi.org/10.1007/978-90-481-9707-1_99
18. Scalable Cooperation Group. Moral Machine (2016). http://moralmachine.mit.edu/. Accessed 27 Sept 2016
19. Castelfranchi, C., Falcone, R.: From automaticity to autonomy: the frontier of artificial agents. In: Hexmoor, H., Castelfranchi, C., Falcone, R. (eds.) Agent Autonomy, pp. 103–136. Springer, Boston (2010). https://doi.org/10.1007/978-1-4419-9198-0_6
20. Article 36. Killing by machine: Key issues for understanding meaningful human control (2015). http://www.article36.org/autonomous-weapons/killing-by-machine-key-issues-for-understanding-meaningful-human-control/. Accessed 9 May 2019
21. Open Roboethics initiative. The Ethics and Governance of Lethal Autonomous Weapons Systems: An International Public Opinion Poll, 5 Nov 2015. http://www.openroboethics.org/laws_survey_released/. Accessed 15 July 2017
22. Jackson, C.: Three in Ten Americans Support Using Autonomous Weapons (2017). https://www.ipsos.com/en-us/news-polls/three-ten-americans-support-using-autonomous-weapons. Accessed 17 June 2018
23. AIV and CAVV, Autonomous weapon systems: the need for meaningful human control, A.C.O.I.O.P.I.L. Advisory Council on International Affairs, Editor, pp. 1–64 (2016)
24. Kuptel, A., Williams, A.: Policy guidance: autonomy in defence systems (2014)
25. UNDIR, Framing Discussions on the Weaponization of Increasingly Autonomous Technologies, pp. 1–14 (2014)
26. Awad, E.: Moral Machine: Perception of Moral Judgment Made by Machines. Massachusetts Institute of Technology, Boston (2017)
27. Reips, U.-D.: Standards for internet-based experimenting. Exp. Psychol. **49**(4), 243 (2002)
28. Oehlert, G.W.: A First Course in Design and Analysis of Experiments. W.H. Freeman, New York (2010)

AI Safety and Reproducibility:
Establishing Robust Foundations
for the Neuropsychology of Human Values

Gopal P. Sarma[1]([⊠])(iD), Nick J. Hay[2](iD), and Adam Safron[3](iD)

[1] School of Medicine, Emory University, Atlanta, GA, USA
gopal.sarma@emory.edu
[2] Vicarious AI, San Francisco, CA, USA
nnickhay@gmail.com
[3] Department of Psychology, Northwestern University, Evanston, IL, USA
adamsafron@u.northwestern.edu

Abstract. We propose the creation of a systematic effort to identify and replicate key findings in neuropsychology and allied fields related to understanding human values. Our aim is to ensure that research underpinning the value alignment problem of artificial intelligence has been sufficiently validated to play a role in the design of AI systems.

Keywords: Affective neuroscience · Social neuroscience
Human values

1 Anthropomorphic Design of Superintelligent AI Systems

There has been considerable discussion in recent years about the consequences of achieving human-level artificial intelligence. In a survey of top researchers in computer science, an aggregate forecast of 352 scientists assigned a 50% probability of human-level machine intelligence being realized within 45 years. In the same survey, 48% responded that greater emphasis should be placed on minimizing the societal risks of AI, an emerging area of study known as "AI safety" [14].

A distinct area of research within AI safety concerns software systems whose capacities substantially exceed that of human beings along every dimension, that is, superintelligence [6]. Within the framework of superintelligence theory, a core research topic known as the *value alignment problem* is to specify a goal structure for autonomous agents compatible with human values. The logic behind the framing of this problem is the following: Current software and AI systems are brittle and primitive, showing little capacity for generalized intelligence. However, ongoing research advances suggest that future systems may someday show

---

The views expressed herein are those of the author and do not necessarily reflect the views of Vicarious AI.

© Springer Nature Switzerland AG 2018
B. Gallina et al. (Eds.): SAFECOMP 2018 Workshops, LNCS 11094, pp. 507–512, 2018.
https://doi.org/10.1007/978-3-319-99229-7_45

fluid intelligence, creativity, and true thinking capacity. Defining the parameters of goal-directed behavior will be a necessary component of designing such systems. Because of the complex and intricate nature of human behavior and values, an emerging train of thought in the AI safety community is that such a goal structure will have to be inferred by software systems themselves, rather than pre-programmed by their human designers. Russell summarizes the notion of indirect inference of human values by stating three principles that should guide the development of AI systems [21]:

1. The machine's purpose must be to maximize the realization of human values. In particular, it has no purpose of its own and no innate desire to protect itself.
2. The machine must be initially uncertain about what those human values are. The machine may learn more about human values as it goes along, but it may never achieve complete certainty.
3. The machine must be able to learn about human values by observing the choices that we humans make.

In other words, rather than have a detailed ethical taxonomy programmed into them, AI systems should infer human values by observing and emulating our behavior [12,13,21]. The value alignment perspective on building safe, superintelligent agents is a natural extension of a broader set of questions related to the moral status of artificial intelligence and issues related to the architectural transparency and intelligibility of such software-based agents. Many of these questions are important for systems whose capabilities fall well short of superintelligence, but which can nonetheless have significant impact on the world. For instance, medical diagnostic systems which arrive at highly unusual and difficult to interpret diagnostic plans may ultimately do great harm if patients do not respond the way the AI system had predicted. In the medical setting, intelligible AI systems can ensure that healthcare workers are not subsequently forced to reason about circumstances that would not have ordinarily arisen via human diagnostics. Many researchers believe that similar situations will arise in industries ranging from transportation, to insurance, to cybersecurity [2,26,29,30].

A significant tension that has arisen in the AI safety community is between those researchers concerned with near-term safety concerns and those more oriented towards longer-term, superintelligence-related concerns [4]. Are these two sets of issues fundamentally in opposition to one another? Does researching safety issues arising from superintelligence necessarily entail disregarding more contemporary concerns? Our firm belief is that the answer to this question is "no." We are of the viewpoint that there is an organic continuum extending between contemporary and long-term AI safety issues and that individuals and research groups can freely pursue both sets of issues without tension. One of the purposes of this article is to argue that not only can research related to superintelligence be grounded in contemporary concerns, but moreover, that there is a wealth of existing work across a wide variety of fields that is of direct relevance to superintelligence. This perspective should be reassuring to researchers who are either skeptical of or have yet to form an opinion on the intellectual validity of long-term issues in AI safety. As we see it, there is no shortage of concrete research problems that can be pursued within a familiar academic setting.

To give a specific instance of this viewpoint, in a recent article, we argued that ideas from affective neuroscience and related fields may play a key role in developing AI systems that can acquire human values. The broader context of this proposal is an inverse reinforcement learning (IRL) type paradigm in which an AI system infers the underlying utility function of an agent by observing its behavior. Our perspective is that a neuropsychological understanding of human values may play a role in characterizing the initially uncertain structure that the AI system refines over time. Having a more accurate initial goal structure may allow an agent to learn from fewer examples. For a system that is actively taking actions and having an impact on the world, a more efficient learning process can directly translate into a lower risk of adverse outcomes. Moreover, systems built with human-inspired architectures may help to address issues of transparency and intelligibility that we cited earlier [29,30], but in the novel context of superintelligence. As an example, we suggested that human values could be schematically and informally decomposed into three components: *(1) mammalian values, (2) human cognition, and (3) several millennia of human social and cultural evolution* [23]. This decomposition is simply one possible framing of the problem. There are major controversies within these fields and many avenues to approach the question of how neuroscience and cognitive psychology can inform the design of future AI systems [25]. We refer to this broader perspective, i.e. building AI systems which possess structural commonalities with the human mind, as *anthropomorphic design.*

2   Formal Models of Human Values and the Reproducibility Crisis

The connection between value alignment and research in the biological and social sciences intertwines this work with another major topic in contemporary scientific discussion, the reproducibility crisis. Systematic studies conducted recently have uncovered astonishingly low rates of reproducibility in several areas of scientific inquiry [8,16,18]. Although we do not know what the "reproducibility distribution" looks like for the entirety of science, the shared incentive structures of academia suggest that we should view all research with some amount of skepticism.

How then do we prioritize research to be the focus of targeted replication efforts? Surely all results do not merit the same level of scrutiny. Moreover, all areas likely have "linchpin results," which if verified, will increase researchers' confidence substantially in entire bodies of knowledge. Therefore, a challenge for modern science is to efficiently identify areas of research and corresponding linchpin results that merit targeted replication efforts [22]. A natural strategy to pursue is to focus such efforts around major scientific themes or research agendas. The Reproducibility Projects of the Center for Open Science, for example, are targeted initiatives aimed replicating key results in psychology and cancer biology [11,27].

In a similar spirit, we propose a focused effort aimed at investigating and replicating results which underpin the neuropsychology of human values. Artificial intelligence has already been woven into the fabric of modern society, a trend that will only increase in scope and pace in the coming decades. If, as we strongly believe, a neuropsychological understanding of human values plays a role in the design of future AI systems, it essential that this knowledge base is thoroughly validated.

3 Discussion and Future Directions

We have deliberately left this commentary brief and open-ended. The topic is broad enough that it merits substantial discussion before proceeding. In addition to the obvious questions of which subjects and studies should fall under the umbrella of the reproducibility initiative that we are proposing, it is also worth asking how such an effort will be coordinated. Furthermore, this initiative should also be an opportunity to take advantage of novel scientific practices aimed at improving research quality, such as pre-prints, post-publication peer review, and pre-registration of study design. The specific task of replication is likely only applicable to a subset of results that are relevant to anthropomorphic design. There are legitimate scientific disagreements in these fields and many theories and frameworks that have yet to achieve consensus. Therefore, in addition to identifying those studies that are sufficiently concrete and precise to be the focus of targeted replication efforts, it is also our aim to identify "linchpin" controversies that are of high-value to resolve, for example, via special issues in journals, workshops, or more rapid, iterated discussion among experts.

We make a few remarks about possible starting points. One source of candidate high-value linchpin findings would be those used by frameworks for understanding the nature of emotions. The extent of innate contributions to emotions is hotly debated, with positions ranging from emotions having their origins in conserved evolutionary programs [9,19] to more recent suggestions that emotions are for the most part constructed through social inference [3,17]. For example, Barrett suggests that the existing affective neuroscience and ethological literature may be based on questionable interpretations of studies of limited generalizability and uncertain reliability of research methods [3,10]. A related discipline is contemplative neuroscience, a field aimed at correlating introspective insights with a neuroscientific understanding of the brain. Highly skilled meditators from the Tibetan Buddhist tradition and others have claimed to have significant insight into human emotions [15,24], an understanding which is likely relevant to developing a rigorous characterization of human values. Other frameworks worth considering in depth are models of social-emotional learning based on predictive coding and Bayesian inference [1]. In these models, uniquely human cognition and affect arises from factors such as extensive early dependency for homeostatic regulation (e.g. fine-CT fibers contributing to analgesia through vagal stimulation [5,20]). It has been proposed that this dependence leads to models of self that are strongly shaped by the need to predict the minds of others with whom the developing individual interacts. These reciprocal relationships may be the basis for the kind of joint attention and joint intentionality emphasized by Tomasello and others as a basis for uniquely human social cognition [28].

In terms of strategies for organizing this literature, we favor an open science or wiki-style approach in which individuals suggest high-value studies and topics to be the focus of targeted replication efforts. Knowledgeable researchers can then debate these proposals in either a structured (such as the RAND Corporation's Delphi protocol [7]) or unstructured format until consensus is achieved on how best to proceed. As we have discussed in the previous section, The Center for Open Science has demonstrated that reproducibility efforts targeting large bodies of literature are achievable with modest resources [11,27].

Our overarching message: *From philosophers pursuing fundamental theories of ethics, to artists immersed in crafting compelling emotional narratives, to ordinary individuals struggling with personal challenges, deep engagement with the nature of human values is a fundamental part of the human experience. As AI systems become more powerful and widespread, such an understanding may also prove to be important for ensuring the safety of these systems. We propose that enhancing the reliability of our knowledge of human values should be a priority for researchers and funding agencies concerned about AI safety and existential risks.* We hope this brief note brings to light an important set of contemporary scientific issues and we are eager to collaborate with other researchers in order to take informed next steps.

Acknowledgements. We would like to thank Owain Evans and several anonymous reviewers for insightful discussions on the topics of value alignment and reproducibility in psychology and neuroscience.

References

1. Ainley, V., et al.: 'Bodily precision': a predictive coding account of individual differences in interoceptive accuracy. Philos. Trans. R. Soc. B **371**(1708) (2016)
2. Amodei, D., Olah, C., Steinhardt, J., Christiano, P., Schulman, J., Mané, D.: Concrete problems in AI safety. arXiv preprint arXiv:1606.06565 (2016)
3. Barrett, L.F.: How Emotions are Made: The Secret Life of the Brain. Houghton Mifflin Harcourt, Boston (2017)
4. Baum, S.D.: Reconciliation between factions focused on near-term and long-term artificial intelligence. AI Soc. 1–8 (2017)
5. Björnsdotter, M., Olausson, H.: Vicarious responses to social touch in posterior insular cortex are tuned to pleasant caressing speeds. J. Neurosci. **31**(26), 9554–9562 (2011)
6. Bostrom, N.: Superintelligence: Paths, Dangers, Strategies. Oxford University Press, Oxford (2014)
7. Brown, B.B.: Delphi process: a methodology used for the elicitation of opinions of experts. Technical report, Rand Corp, Santa Monica, CA (1968)

8. Campbell, P. (ed.): Challenges in Irreproducible Research, vol. 526. Nature, London (2015)
9. Damasio, A.: Self Comes to Mind: Constructing the Conscious Brain. Vintage, New York (2012)
10. Ekman, P., Friesen, W.V., Ellsworth, P.: Emotion in the Human Face: Guide-lines for Research and an Integration of Findings. Pergamon, Oxford (1972)
11. Errington, T.M.: Science forum: an open investigation of the reproducibility of cancer biology research. eLife **3**, 4333 (2014)
12. Evans, O., Goodman, N.D.: Learning the preferences of bounded agents. In: NIPS Workshop on Bounded Optimality (2015)
13. Evans, O., Stuhlmüller, A., Goodman, N.D.: Learning the Preferences of Ignorant, Inconsistent Agents. arXiv:1512.05832 (2015)
14. Grace, K., Salvatier, J., Dafoe, A., Zhang, B., Evans, O.: When Will AI Exceed Human Performance? Evidence from AI Experts. ArXiv e-prints, May 2017
15. Harrington, A., Zajonc, A.: The Dalai Lama at MIT. Harvard University Press, Cambridge (2006)
16. Horton, R.: What's medicine's 5 sigma?. Lancet **385**(9976) (2015)
17. LeDoux, J.E., Pine, D.S.: Using neuroscience to help understand fear and anxiety: a two-system framework. Am. J. Psychiatry **173**(11), 1083–1093 (2016)
18. Munafò, M.R.: A manifesto for reproducible science. Nat. Hum. Behav. **1**, 0021 (2017)
19. Panksepp, J.: Affective Neuroscience: The Foundations of Human and Animal Emotions. Oxford University Press, New York (1998)
20. Porges, S.W., Furman, S.A.: The early development of the autonomic nervous system provides a neural platform for social behaviour: a polyvagal perspective. Infant Child Dev. **20**(1), 106–118 (2011)
21. Russell, S.: Should we fear supersmart robots? Sci. Am. **314**(6), 58–59 (2016)
22. Sarma, G.P.: Doing Things Twice (Or Differently): Strategies to Identify Studies for Targeted Validation. ArXiv e-prints, Mar 2017
23. Sarma, G.P., Hay, N.J.: Mammalian value systems. Informatica **41**(3) (2017)
24. Solms, M., Turnbull, O.: The Brain and the Inner World: An Introduction to the Neuroscience of Subjective Experience. Karnac Books, London (2002)
25. Sotala, K.: Defining human values for value learners. In: AAAI Workshop: AI, Ethics, and Society (2016)
26. Sullins, J.P.: When is a robot a moral agent?. Int. Rev. Inf. Ethics **6** (2006)
27. The Open Science Collaboration: Estimating the reproducibility of psychological science. Science **349**(6251) (2015)
28. Tomasello, M.: The Cultural Origins of Human Cognition. Harvard University Press, Cambridge (1999)
29. Wachter, S., Mittelstadt, B., Floridi, L.: Transparent, explainable, and accountable AI for robotics. Sci. Robot. **2** (2006)
30. Wortham, R.H., Theodorou, A., Bryson, J.J.: What does the robot think? Transparency as a fundamental design requirement for intelligent systems. In: IJCAI 2016 Ethics for AI Workshop (2016)

A Psychopathological Approach to Safety Engineering in AI and AGI

Vahid Behzadan[1(✉)], Arslan Munir[1], and Roman V. Yampolskiy[2]

[1] Kansas State University, Manhattan, KS 66506, USA
{behzadan,amunir}@ksu.edu
[2] University of Louisville, Louisville, KY 40292, USA
roman.yampolskiy@louisville.edu
http://blogs.k-state.edu/aisecurityresearch/

Abstract. The complexity of dynamics in AI techniques is already approaching that of complex adaptive systems, thus curtailing the feasibility of formal controllability and reachability analysis in the context of AI safety. It follows that the envisioned instances of Artificial General Intelligence (AGI) will also suffer from challenges of complexity. To tackle such issues, we propose the modeling of deleterious behaviors in AI and AGI as psychological disorders, thereby enabling the employment of psychopathological approaches to analysis and control of misbehaviors. Accordingly, we present a discussion on the feasibility of the psychopathological approaches to AI safety, and propose general directions for research on modeling, diagnosis, and treatment of psychological disorders in AGI.

Keywords: AI safety · Psychopathology · Mental disorder
Diagnosis · Treatment · Artificial General Intelligence

1 Introduction

While the adaptive mechanisms of human cognition provide the means for unique skills in adjusting to dynamic environments, they are also prone to psychological disorders, broadly defined as self-reconfigurations in cognition and behavior that are deleterious to the core and long-term objectives of self or the social ecosystem [1]. Extrapolating from this phenomenon, it is not hard to conclude that instances of Artificial General Intelligence (AGI), which aim for similar cognitive functions, may also be prone to such disorders. For instance, certain objective functions and environmental conditions may lead a Reinforcement Learning (RL) agent to develop addictive behavior through repetitive gains of high rewards from policies that contradict the long-term objectives of the agent [15]. Other instances of such emergent disorders include post-traumatic behavior, depression, and psychosis [2]. It is further hypothesized that behavioral disorders may emerge as higher-order consequences of unsafe inverse RL and apprenticeship learning, by adopting manifested disorders or triggering harmful cognitive traits [16].

© Springer Nature Switzerland AG 2018
B. Gallina et al. (Eds.): SAFECOMP 2018 Workshops, LNCS 11094, pp. 513–520, 2018.
https://doi.org/10.1007/978-3-319-99229-7_46

Current research in AI safety is generally focused on safety-aware design and mitigation techniques [8], but the expanding complexity of AI and in particular AGI will render such analysis as difficult as those of biological intelligence and the corresponding disorders. To tackle such difficulties in human intelligence, the causes and dynamics of misbehaviors are studied at various levels of abstraction, ranging from neuroscience and cognitive science to psychology, psychiatry, sociology, and criminology. Inspired by the advantages of such diverse vantage points, we propose that studying the complex dynamics and mechanisms of failure in AI safety can greatly benefit from abstractions that parallel those of biological intelligence. Considering the practical aims of diagnosing and correcting misbehaviors in AGI, we believe that adopting the abstraction of psychopathology provides tractable settings that also benefit from cross-domain bodies of knowledge. Furthermore, while this approach may seem to be of lower relevance at present, we argue that the advent of deep RL, along with advances in hierarchical and transfer learning may have already laid the grounds for emergence of such disorders in AI.

The goal of this paper is to provide a technical discussion and the motivation for research on the psychopathology of AI and AGI. The remainder of this paper is organized as follows: Sect. 2 presents a broad overview of psychopathology. Section 3 provides a discussion on the relevance of psychology to AI, followed by establishment of parallelisms between AI safety and psychopathology. In Sect. 4, high-level areas of research are identified and detailed. Finally, Sect. 5 concludes the paper with remarks on broader impacts of this research.

2   What Is Psychopathology?

Psychopathology refers to the scientific study of mental disorders, their causes, and corresponding treatments [4]. Within this context, we adhere to American Psychiatric Association (APA)'s definition of mental disorder [1] as "a psychological syndrome or pattern which is associated with distress, disability, increased risk of death, or significant loss of autonomy" (i.e., pursuit of objectives). In psychopathology, disorders are commonly identified based on four metrics of abnormality, known as the four Ds [6]: Deviance of behaviors and emotions from the norm, Distress of the individual caused by suffering from a disorder, Dysfunctions that impair the individuals ability to perform designated or normal functions, and the Danger of individual to self or the society.

Causes of mental disorders in humans include mixtures of those inherited through *genetics* (e.g., neuroticism), *developmental influences* caused by parental mistreatment, social influences (e.g., as abuse, bullying), and traumatic events, and *biological influences* such as traumatic brain injury and infections [1].

Various models have been developed to capture the dynamics of mental disorders and their emergence. For instance, biological psychiatry, or the *medical model* [10], is one that explains the causes of disorders based on changes in neurological circuitry. The *social model*, on the other hand, analyzes the causes of mental disorders based on social and environmental interactions [10]. Currently, it is widely believed that understanding psychological disorders requires the comprehensive consideration of both biological and social factors, and hence the *biopsychosocial models* are generally adopted to study such phenomena. These models broadly categorize mental disorders as either cognitive or behavioral. Cognitive disorders are those caused by abnormal functioning of the underlying cognitive mechanisms, and behavioral disorders are those that are learned through developmental, environmental, and social interactions [10].

Diagnosis of mental disorders is generally based on an assessment of symptoms, signs, and impairments that constitute various types of disorders. A comprehensive framework for such assessments is that of the Diagnostic and Statistical Manual of Mental Disorders (DSM) [1], published by the American Psychiatric Association (APA). This manual provides a common language and standard criteria for the classification of mental disorders. Furthermore, recent advances in machine learning have given rise to various software and algorithmic tools to facilitate enhanced accuracy in classification and diagnosis of mental disorders [9].

Treatment of mental disorders is commonly via one or a hybrid of two approaches. One is *Psychotherapy*, which is a form of interpersonal intervention via a range of psychological techniques. For instance, Cognitive Behavioral Therapy (CBT) is employed to modify the patterns of thought and behavior associated with a particular disorder. *Medication therapy* is the other approach, which targets the physiological components of disorders. For instance, antipsychotics commonly work by blocking D2 Dopamine receptors, thus controlling the chemical reward mechanism of the brain [13].

3   Psychopathology and AI Safety

Since its inception, AI has been closely connected to psychology and cognitive sciences [7]. This connection flows in both directions: AI researchers study biological cognition and behavior as inspiration for engineered intelligence, and cognitive scientists explore AI as a framework for synthesis and experimental analysis of theoretical ideas [5]. An instance of this interconnection is Reinforcement Learning (RL), where the computational algorithms of RL, such as Temporal Difference (TD) learning were originally inspired from the dopamine system in biological brains [14]. On the other hand, the work on TD learning has provided mathematical means of modeling the neuroscientific dynamics of dopamine cells in the brain, and has been employed to study disorders such as schizophrenia and the consequences of pharmacological manipulations of dopamine on learning [12].

With regards to the relationship between psychological disorders and AI safety, there are scarce and sparse resources available in the literature. Recent papers by Ashrafian [2] and Yampolskiy [15,17] present high-level arguments for the existence and emergence of mental disorders in AI. One such argument presented in [2] is based on the analogy of David Chalmers' philosophical zombie (p-zombie). In this analogy, the p-zombie is considered to be a fully functioning robot that acts exactly like a human-being, which is not necessarily equipped with vague notions of consciousness [17]. The fact that this robot is capable

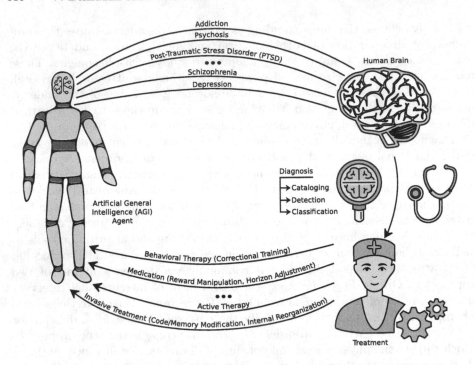

Fig. 1. A psychopathological approach to safety engineering in AI and AGI.

of acting indistinguishably from humans is then used to justify that it is also prone to developmental and cognitive abnormalities that lead to misbehavior and anomalous cognition.

Furthermore, many aspects of failures in AI safety can be viewed as psychological disorders. For instance, wireheading in AI can manifest as delusional and addictive behavior [15]. Similarly, sequences of interactions with extremely negative rewards and stresses within the exploration/exploitation trajectories of RL-based AI can potentially give rise to behavioral disorders such as depression and Post-Traumatic Stress Disorder (PTSD) [2]. Furthermore, the generic manifestation of the value alignment problem [8] in AI is in the form of behavioral characteristics that are harmful to either the agent or the environment and society, which falls well within the definition of psychological disorders.

While [2] and a few other papers (e.g., [3,8]) present high-level arguments on the advantages of investigating the psychopathology of AI, there remains a wide gap in satisfying the need for technical studies and practices. This paper presents a research agenda that will fill this gap via the following proposals, also illustrated in Fig. 1.

4   Directions of Research

Developing solid grounds for research on the Psychopathology of AI requires investigations in three main areas: Modeling and Verification, Diagnosis, and Treatment. In this section, we define and discuss the scope of each area.

4.1   Modeling and Verification Tools

While the descriptive similarities of human psychopathology and AI failures provide some insights into adopting such abstractions for AI safety, taking an engineering approach requires formal and mathematical modeling of the aspects and dimensions of these similarities. Such formalisms may benefit from those that already exist in the realm of cognitive and medical sciences, such as cognitive architectures [11] and RL-based models of the dynamics in mental disorders (e.g., [12]). Also, the quantitative analysis of such disorders necessitate the exploration and development of new models of AI and AGI based on such paradigms as neuroeconomics, complex adaptive systems, control theory, and dynamic data-driven application systems.

Furthermore, verification and validation of such models and the ensuing theories requires the development of experimental frameworks and simulation platforms. Such platforms must provide the means for wide ranges of experiments on emergence and dynamics of behavioral and cognitive disorders in arbitrary and context-dependent scenarios, and shall be compatible for various agent and environmental models.

4.2   Diagnosis and Classification of Disorders

This area pertains to investigation and development of techniques for diagnosis of disorders in AI. Within the context of AI safety engineering, diagnosis refers to two inter-related tasks: first is to detect anomalous behaviors, and the second is to classify the type of anomalous behavior as a first step towards treatment. Detection of undesired behavior is an active topic of research in AI safety, with initial solutions such as tripwires and honeypots [8] already proposed and investigated. We propose to extend current state of the art in detection through adoption and automation of parallel techniques in psychopathology. Similar to diagnostics criteria in human psychology [1], a promising approach is to identify statistical deviations in behavior, as well as general indicators of misbehavior. To this end, development of machine learning approaches similar to those applied in cybersecurity for threat and intrusion detection can be a promising direction. Furthermore, generic indicators of misbehavior can be learned from models trained on simulated and annotated scenarios of disorders.

Once a misbehavior is detected, the next step is to characterize and classify the disorder that has led to such behavior. A prerequisite to this process is having a catalog of different disorders and the corresponding criteria for diagnosing such disorders. Therefore, a necessary step is the compilation of representative and experimentally verified disorders, such as addiction and anxiety in RL agents, along with manually and automatically generated criteria and characteristics of each disorder based on behavioral observations. This task shall aim to produce human- and machine-readable catalogs as AI analogues of APAs DSM 5 [1].

Besides general behavioral characteristics, there are other sources of data that can be of diagnostic value. Instances include indicators of disorders that are obtained through direct and targeted interactions with AI (similar to psychiatric evaluation of human patients), non-invasive analysis of internal states and parameters (similar to F-MRI and EEG tests of human patients), and induction or invocation of internal debug modes (similar to states of hypnosis). Exploring such ideas and approaches may greatly enhance the accuracy of diagnosis, and lead to novel techniques for psychoanalysis and diagnostics of AI and AGI.

4.3 Treatment

When a disorder is diagnosed in an AI agent, it is not always feasible to simply decommission or reset the agent. In such cases, it is often preferable to pursue treatment via minimally destructive techniques that correct the misbehaviors of agent, while preserving the useful traits learned by that agent. Such treatments need to satisfy a number of challenging requirements. Advanced AI are complex adaptive systems, and therefore minor perturbations of one component may lead to unintended consequences on local and global scales. For instance, correcting a developmental disorder by removing a series of harmful experiences from the memory of an AI may lead to behavioral changes that are even more undesirable than the original misbehavior. Therefore, effective treatments must either be minimally invasive or non-invasive at all.

Inspired by psychopathological parallels, we propose two general approaches to treatment of pathologies in AI. One is correctional training, which adopts the approach of behavioral therapy. This approach is to retrain an agent in controlled environments and scenarios, such that harmful experiences can be remedied or alleviated through new experiences. The second approach parallels that of medication therapy, in which the reward signals of AI agents are artificially manipulated via external means to adjust their behavioral policies. This is similar to the use of anti-depressants and anti-psychotics in treating disorders related to production and inhibition of dopamine and serotonin in human brains.

5 Conclusion

This paper presents the argument that while current research in AI safety is generally focused on design and mitigation problems, the complexity of AGI will render such analysis as difficult as those that capture biological intelligence and disorders. Hence, studying the complex dynamics and mechanisms of emergent failures in AI and AGI can greatly benefit from abstractions that parallel those of biological intelligence. Considering the practical objectives of diagnosing and treating misbehaviors in AGI, we propose that psychopathological approaches provide tractable settings while benefiting from various bodies of knowledge.

Accordingly, we present a high-level research agenda that includes explorations of parallels between human and AI psychopathology, development of methodologies for diagnosis of behavioral pathologies in AI, and propose techniques for treatment of such disorders.

As the paper details, psychology and AI enjoy a bi-directional flow of inspirations. A major impact of the proposed research is the production of outcomes that can be of use and inspiration to current research in psychopathology and cognitive sciences. Furthermore, the results of this work may provide a deeper understanding of the safety requirements and guidelines for designing advanced AI and AGI, while guiding policy makers on the risks and potential solutions involved in the integration of AGI into societies. We hope that this paper motivates initial efforts in laying solid foundations for future research and developments in this scarcely explored but promising venue.

References

1. APA: Diagnostic and statistical manual of mental disorders (DSM-5®). American Psychiatric Association Publishing (2013)
2. Ashrafian, H.: Can artificial intelligences suffer from mental illness? A philosophical matter to consider. Sci. Eng. Ethics **23**(2), 403–412 (2017)
3. Atkinson, D.J.: Emerging cyber-security issues of autonomy and the psychopathology of intelligent machines. In: Foundations of Autonomy and Its (Cyber) Threats: From Individuals to Interdependence: Papers from the 2015 AAAI Spring Symposium, Palo Alto, CA (2015). http://www.aaai.org/ocs/index.php/SSS/SSS15/paper/viewFile/10219/10049
4. Butcher, J.N., Hooley, J.M.: APA Handbook of Psychopathology: Psychopathology: Understanding, Assessing, and Treating Adult Mental Disorders, vol. 1. American Psychological Association, Washington, D.C. (2018)
5. Collins, A., Smith, E.E.: Readings in Cognitive Science: A perspective from Psychology and Artificial Intelligence. Elsevier, New York City (2013)
6. Davis, T.O.: Conceptualizing psychiatric disorders using "Four D's" of diagnoses. Internet J. Psychiatry **1**(1), 1–5 (2009)
7. Dennett, D.C.: Artificial intelligence as philosophy and as psychology. In: Brainstorms: Philosophical Essays on Mind and Psychology, pp. 109–26 (1978)
8. FLI: The Landscape of AI Safety and Beneficence Research: Input for Brainstorming at Beneficial AI 2017. Future of Life Institute (2017)
9. Kelly, J., Gooding, P., Pratt, D., Ainsworth, J., Welford, M., Tarrier, N.: Intelligent real-time therapy: harnessing the power of machine learning to optimise the delivery of momentary cognitive-behavioural interventions. J. Ment. Health **21**(4), 404–414 (2012)
10. Kendler, K.S.: The dappled nature of causes of psychiatric illness: replacing the organic-functional/hardware-software dichotomy with empirically based pluralism. Mol. Psychiatry **17**(4), 377 (2012)
11. Kotseruba, I., Tsotsos, J.K.: A review of 40 years of cognitive architecture research: core cognitive abilities and practical applications. arXiv preprint arXiv:1610.08602 (2016)
12. Montague, P.R., Hyman, S.E., Cohen, J.D.: Computational roles for dopamine in behavioural control. Nature **431**(7010), 760 (2004)

13. Nordström, A.L., et al.: Central D2-dopamine receptor occupancy in relation to antipsychotic drug effects: a double-blind pet study of schizophrenic patients. Biol. Psychiatry **33**(4), 227–235 (1993)
14. Sutton, R.S., Barto, A.G.: Reinforcement Learning: An Introduction. MIT press, Cambridge (1998)
15. Yampolskiy, R.V.: Utility function security in artificially intelligent agents. J. Exp. Theor. Artif. Intell. **26**(3), 373–389 (2014)
16. Yampolskiy, R.V.: Taxonomy of pathways to dangerous artificial intelligence. In: AAAI Workshop: AI, Ethics, and Society (2016)
17. Yampolskiy, R.V.: Detecting qualia in natural and artificial agents. arXiv preprint arXiv:1712.04020 (2017)

Why Bad Coffee? Explaining Agent Plans with Valuings

Michael Winikoff[1]([⊠]), Virginia Dignum[2], and Frank Dignum[3]

[1] University of Otago, Dunedin, New Zealand
michael.winikoff@otago.ac.nz
[2] Delft University of Technology, Delft, The Netherlands
M.V.Dignum@tudelft.nl
[3] Utrecht University, Utrecht, The Netherlands
F.P.M.Dignum@uu.nl

Abstract. An important issue in deploying an autonomous system is how to enable human users and stakeholders to develop an appropriate level of trust in the system. It has been argued that a crucial mechanism to enable appropriate trust is the ability of a system to explain its behaviour. Obviously, such explanations need to be comprehensible to humans. We argue that it makes sense to build on the results of extensive research in social sciences that explores how humans explain their behaviour. Using similar concepts for explanation is argued to help with comprehensibility, since the concepts are familiar. Following work in the social sciences, we propose the use of a folk-psychological model that utilises beliefs, desires, and "valuings". We propose a formal framework for constructing explanations of the behaviour of an autonomous system, present an (implemented) algorithm for giving explanations, and present evaluation results.

1 Introduction

This paper addresses the problem of how an autonomous system can explain itself by developing a computational mechanism that provides explanations for why a particular action was performed. It has been argued [6,8,19] that in a range of domains, a key factor in humans being willing to trust autonomous systems is that the systems need to be able to *explain* why they performed a certain course of action. Note that this is not the same as explaining system recommendations, since we are explaining a *course of action* (taken over time, in an environment), not a (static) recommendation.

Explanation is relevant to AI safety for a number of reasons. Firstly, explanation can reduce the opaqueness of a system, and support understanding its behaviour, and its limitations. Secondly, in situations where things do go wrong, a post-mortem analysis, using some sort of "black box" (as those used in airplanes) can use explanation techniques to help investigators understand what went wrong.

© Springer Nature Switzerland AG 2018
B. Gallina et al. (Eds.): SAFECOMP 2018 Workshops, LNCS 11094, pp. 521–534, 2018.
https://doi.org/10.1007/978-3-319-99229-7_47

In developing such an explanation mechanism, it is important to be mindful that the explanations have to be comprehensible, and useful, to a human, and therefore we should consider relevant social sciences literature [12]. According to Miller [12] explanations should be *contrastive* i.e. answer questions of the form "why did you do X ... instead of Y?"; *selected*, i.e. select relevant factors and present those; and, *social*, i.e. presented relative to what the explainer believes the listener (i.e. explainee) knows. That is, explanations, being in fact conversations, should follow Grice's maxims of quality, quantity, manner and relevance [7].

In our work we consider in particular the work of Malle [11], which argues that humans use folk psychological constructs (e.g. beliefs, desires) to explain behaviour. This leads us to adopt a model that includes desires and beliefs, specifically the well-known BDI (Beliefs, Desires, Intentions) model [1,2,13]. We contend that providing explanations in terms of the same concepts used in human-to-human explanations will help enable explanations to be comprehensible.

Malle identifies three types of reasons in explaining behaviour: desires, beliefs, and what he terms *valuings*, defined as things that *"directly indicate the positive or negative affect toward the action or its outcome"*. We therefore extend the BDI model with valuings, following recent work by Cranefield *et al.* [5].

2   Formal Setting

In this paper, we assume a BDI model based on goal trees and we also assume that the listener assumes such a goal tree as the deliberation mechanism of the agent[1].

A *goal tree* is a tuple (N, G) of a name N, and either an action[2] (A), or a combination of sub-goals (N_i, G_i), which can be in sequence (SEQ), unspecified order (AND), or a choice (OR) where each option $O_i = (C_i, (N_i, G_i))$ has a sub-goal and a condition C_i indicating in which situations that sub-goal can be selected to realise the parent goal. Each action A has an associated pre-condition (denoted $pre(A)$) and post-condition $(post(A))$, both of which are viewed as sets of propositions. We define $\mathcal{B}(N)$ to be the beliefs held just prior to executing the goal N. We write (G_{1-n}) (resp. (O_{1-n})) to abbreviate $((N_1, G_1), \ldots, (N_n, G_n))$ (resp. $(O_1, \ldots, O_n)$). We also sometimes abbreviate (N, G) to G_N for readability, and, where the name is not important, just write G for G_N. Formally:

$$G ::= A \mid \text{SEQ}(G_{1-n}) \mid \text{AND}(G_{1-n}) \mid \text{OR}(O_{1-n})$$

Figure 1 shows a running example, along with a goal tree for this example, including the pre- and post-conditions (the V_i are valuings, explained below).

---

[1] Note that using a BDI model does not necessarily require the system to be designed or implemented as BDI agents. It is in principle possible to use a BDI model to provide explanations of a system's behaviour even if the system does not use BDI concepts.

[2] For actions we assume that the name of the goal tree node and the name of the action coincide, i.e. that $A = N$.

Jo is an academic visiting colleagues at another University. Like many academics, he requires coffee. There are a number of possible sources of coffee: The little kitchen near Ann's office has coffee-like-substance freely available, but this machine requires a staff card to operate. Ann has in her office a coffee machine which converts pods into nice coffee. There is also a coffee shop a few buildings away, where good coffee can be obtained, at a (financial) cost. Jo prefers coffee to coffee-like substances, which is the over-riding preference. Less-important preferences are to save money, and to use the nearest coffee source. Therefore the three relevant quality attributes are (in order): quality (coffee preferred to coffee-like), money (free preferred to expensive), and location (smallest distance from starting location).

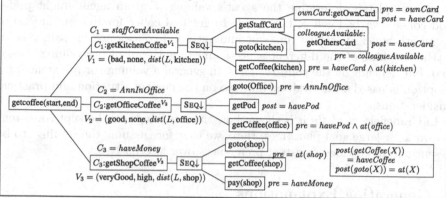

Fig. 1. Running Example (goals are OR-decomposed unless indicated by SEQ↓)

Intuitively, a goal tree is executed as follows. If the tree is simply an action, then the action is performed (assuming its preconditions hold). If the tree is an AND or SEQ decomposition, then all of the sub-goals are executed, either in the specified sequential order (SEQ), or in some, unspecified, order. Finally, if the tree is an OR decomposition, then an applicable option (i.e. one whose condition C_i is believed to hold in the current situation) is selected and executed. Many BDI platforms provide a way to handle failure, which we discuss later. Formally, the semantics of a goal tree is obtained by mapping it to a set of possible sequences of actions.

The semantics of valuings is based on the theory of values as put forward by Schwartz [14]. In Weide [18] it is shown how these abstract values can be connected to concrete aspects of action decision. Following Cranefield *et al.* [5] we incorporate them by annotating nodes in the goal tree with an abstract evaluation of key aspects of their effects. By "key aspects" we mean those that are relevant to the agent evaluating which options it prefers, that is, its valuings. For instance, in the running example, each annotation V_i is of the form (coffee quality, cost, distance), respectively drawn from {veryGood, good, bad}, {none, low, high}, and {none, low, medium, high} where $dist(A, B)$ denotes the distance between A and B computed as follows: the office and kitchen are close to each other ("low" distance), and the shop is far from both kitchen and office ("high" distance). We write $\{V_1, \ldots, V_n\} \prec V$ to denote that the value annotation V is preferred to each of the V_i, and we define $\{\} \prec V_i$ to be equivalent to $\top$.

The agent's valuings, i.e. which options it appreciates more or less, are specific to a given situation. They are founded on the agent's values, which are the underlying drivers. For example, an agent might value good coffee, saving money, and saving time. These aspects are the measurable criteria indicating whether a certain value is promoted by a course of action. However, since we have multiple aspects (thus creating a kind of multi-criteria optimization), they do not completely determine the agent's valuing. E.g. an agent might prefer good coffee over bad coffee, but decide to get bad coffee for free at the end of the month when his salary runs out and get good coffee once his salary is in. So, the weighing of the different aspects and thus the resulting valuings is not fixed, but depends on the context. Thus, in general a valuing (or preference) for an option is based on the values, but also on the current situation and practical considerations.

In Cranefield et al. [5] it is shown how these valuings can be kept consistent and work for large goal-plan trees. Here, we therefore assume the valuings to be present and indicating consistent preferences over alternatives.

3 Generating Explanations

As discussed in the introduction, an explanation is given in terms of reasons which can be desires (goals), beliefs, or valuings. More precisely, an explanation is either $\bot$ (representing that the question does not make sense, e.g. "why did you do X?" when X was not done), or a set of reasons. Reasons can be beliefs that were held, desires that were pursued, and valuings. Valuings are explained as "I preferred V to $\{V_1, \ldots, V_n\}$". We also have forward-looking reasons of the form "I did N_1 in order to be able to later do N_2" ($N_1 \mapsto N_2$). Finally, as discussed towards the end of this section, one possible type of reason is an indication that a particular option was attempted but failed. For example, "I chose to get coffee from the kitchen because I tried to buy it from the shop but failed" (e.g. shop was closed). Finally, we also define $\top$ to be an explanation that carries no information. Clearly, $\top$ is not a useful explanation to a user, but it is used in the formal definitions below where some parts of the process do not provide any useful information.

The definition of the explanation function E is with respect to the goal-tree. Specifically, $E_N^T(G_{N'})$ is "explain N using the tree (N', G) and trace T". We define $n(G)$ as denoting the set of all node names occurring in the tree rooted at G. We define $T^{\prec N}$ to be the part of the trace T that occurs before N. Note that if $N \notin T$ then we simply define $E_N^T(G) = \bot$, otherwise the rest of the definitions below apply.

$$E_N^T(G_{N'}) = \bot, \text{ if } N \notin T$$

$$E_N^T(A_{N'}) = \begin{cases} \{\} & \text{if } pre(A) = \top \\ \{pre(A)\} & \text{otherwise} \end{cases}$$

$$E_N^T(\text{AND}(G_{1-n})_{N'}) = \Theta$$

$$E_N^T(\text{SEQ}(G_{1-n})_{N'}) = \Theta$$

$$E_N^T(\text{OR}(O_{1-n})_{N'}) = \begin{cases} pref(O_i, \{O_1, \ldots, O_n\}) \cup \Theta, & \text{if } N \in n(G_i) \\ \Theta, & \text{otherwise} \end{cases}$$

$$\text{where } \Theta = \bigcup_{G_i : n(G_i) \cap T^{\prec N} \neq \emptyset} E_N^T((N_i, G_i))$$

The function E collects reasons by traversing the relevant parts of the goal tree. A part of the goal tree is relevant if it occurs in the execution trace before beginning the process of executing the node N that is being explained. Simply, if something occurs before N, then it can affect N. This relevance condition is checked in the definition of Θ: $G_i : n(G_i) \cap T^{\prec N} \neq \emptyset$ finds all sub-goals G_i of the current node which contain beneath them at least some node that appears in the prefix of the trace T before N (viewing the trace prefix as a set).

In the case of an action A the explanation collected is the action's precondition as this affects the execution of the action, and consequently, of whatever comes after it. In the case for SEQ and AND the explanation collected is simply the explanation associated with the sub-goals. In the case for OR there is an additional explanation relating to why the particular option taken was chosen. This is defined by the function $pref$ which provides an explanation for why the selected option, G_i, is preferred to the other options. The definition of $pref$ is complex. Intuitively, given a choice-point $(N, \text{OR}(O_1, \ldots, O_n))$, where G_i was selected, the explanation consists of three parts:

1. the condition of the selected sub-goal being true ("C_i");
2. for each condition C_j ($j \neq i$) that is false at the decision point, the explanation includes that the condition was false: $\bigcup_{C_j : \mathcal{B}(N) \nvDash C_j} \neg C_j$; and
3. for each condition C_j ($j \neq i$) that is true at the decision point, but that was not selected, the annotations of those sub-goals, and an indication that the selected sub-goal was preferred to these other available sub-goals in the current situation: $\{V_j \mid j \neq i \wedge \mathcal{B}(N) \vDash C_j\} \prec V_i$.

Formally $pref(O_i, \{O_1, \ldots, O_n\})$ is defined to be: $\{C_i\} \cup \left(\bigcup_{C_j : \mathcal{B}(N) \nvDash C_j} \{\neg C_j\} \right)$ $\cup \{\{V_j \mid j \neq i \wedge \mathcal{B}(N) \vDash C_j\} \prec V_i\}$.

Consider as an example the situation in which C_2 is false, and the other C_i are true. Then the preference explanation for why C_3 was chosen is[3]: $\{C_3, \neg C_2, \{V_1\} \prec V_3\}$. Rendered in English (which can be done by applying a simple pattern[4]) this reads: "I chose to get coffee from the shop because I had money, and Ann was not in her office, and I prefer V_3 to V_1 in this situation".

---

[3] All explanations given in this section were produced by the implementation.
[4] This has subsequently been implemented.

On the other hand, in a situation where all C_i are true and C_3 is selected, the explanation would take the form: $\{C_3, \{V_1, V_2\} \prec V_3\}$. In English: "I chose to get coffee from the shop because I had money, and I prefer V_3 to both V_1 and V_2 in this situation".

Note that these explanations just present the set of annotations, indicating an overall preference between them. However, we could provide more precise explanations by taking into account the known priorities of factors, e.g. that coffee quality is the overriding factor, followed by money, then distance. So, for example, for the first example above, we could explain more precisely that the reason why V_3 was preferred to V_1 is that it yields better quality coffee. Similarly, for the second example, we could explain that V_3 was preferred to both V_1 and V_2 because the coffee quality was better (despite V_2 being good coffee and cheaper than V_3).

On the other hand, suppose that the office coffee was selected, even though all three C_i were true. In order to explain why $\{V_1, V_3\} \prec V_2$ we would need to explain that V_2 was preferred to V_1 because it had better coffee, and, perhaps, that it was preferred to V_3 because cost was a factor.

3.1   Adding Preparatory Actions

We now extend the definition to also include preparatory actions. For example, an explanation for "why did you go to the kitchen?" could also be "because I need to be in the kitchen in order to get coffee". This is where an action's post condition is (part of) the precondition of a future action. Specifically, a preparatory reason applies to explain an action A when (i) the post-condition of A is required in order for the pre-condition of another action A' to hold, and (ii) A' occurs after A. We assume that $before(A, B)$ formalises that it is possible for B to occur after A in a trace, but not for A to occur after B.

Turning to the first condition, an obvious formalisation is simply $post(A) \rightarrow pre(A')$. But A's post condition may be only *part* of the pre-condition. For example, the action getPod only achieves havePod, so $post(\text{getPod}) \not\rightarrow pre(\text{getCoffee(office)})$. We therefore formalise "required" as "without it, things don't work", i.e. if A's post-condition fails to hold, then the pre-condition of A' also must fail to hold: $(\neg post(A)) \rightarrow (\neg pre(A'))$. This assumes that $post(A) \neq \top$. In our setting, where pre and post conditions are conjunctions of positive atoms, this is equivalent (viewing the conjunctions as sets) to $post(A) \neq \emptyset \land post(A) \subseteq pre(A')$.

We then extend the explanation with preparatory action explanations: when explaining an action A given goal tree G and trace T, we add to $E_A^T(G)$ the set of links $A \mapsto A'$ where $A' \in n(G) \land before(A, A') \land post(A) \neq \emptyset \land post(A) \subseteq pre(A')$. So, for example, an alternative explanation for why the agent performed the action getPod is that it was required for the subsequent getCoffee(office) action. Finally, in order to consider preparatory actions between *goals*, we follow previous work on summary information [15–17], and extend pre and post conditions to intermediate goals, inferring them.

3.2   Adding Motivations

Finally, in addition to the explanation function E, which yields beliefs and valuings, and the link function, we also add explanations in terms of parent goals: these are desires that explain why the current course of action is being pursued.

This reason is simple: we also include in the explanation all the ancestors of the node being explained. However, we do not include ancestors that are OR refined, since these are not helpful. In explaining why a particular option was done, for instance why getOwnCard was done, it is not helpful to refer to the parent, getStaffCard, because the parent is less specific.

Pulling all the pieces together, the overall explanation function is then:

$$\mathcal{E}_N^T(G_{N'}) = E_N^T(G_{N'}) \cup$$
$$\{N \mapsto N' \mid N' \in n(G) \wedge link(N, N')\} \cup$$
$$\{\mathsf{Desire}(N') \mid ancestor(N', N) \wedge \neg isOR(N')\}$$

For example, given the scenario described, in a situation where C_1 and C_3 hold, but not C_2, the possible reasons that could be used to explain why the agent did "$goto(shop)$" are: {haveMoney, ¬AnnInOffice, $\{\langle bad, none, high\rangle\} \prec \langle veryGood, high, none\rangle$, goto(shop) $\mapsto$ getCoffee(shop), Desire: getShopCoffee}. In English, these are: I had money, Ann was not in her office, I preferred V_3 to V_1 (perhaps because it yields better quality coffee), I needed to go to the shop in order to do getCoffee(shop), and I desired to getShopCoffee.

3.3   Adding Failure Handling

We now extend the explanation mechanism to handle failure handling. Informally, actions can fail, and the failure of a node is handled by considering its parent. If the parent is a SEQ or a AND then it too is considered to be failed, and failure handling moves to consider that node's parent. When an OR node is reached, failure is handled by trying an alternative plan (if one exists, otherwise the OR node is deemed to have failed). We assume that we know which actions in the trace are failed (denoted $failed_A(A, T)$). Then the condition under which a non-leaf node is considered to be failed can be easily derived from the tree, and is denoted $failed(G)$.

Extending the explanation to account for the possibility of previous failures is done by defining an extended *pref* function. Note that the definition of the explanation function E is unchanged, except that in the definition of the recursive call Θ we exclude failed nodes.

Recall that the definition of *pref* has three components: the condition of the selected sub-goal being true, the conditions of those (other) sub-goals that are false, and, for those other sub-goals that have true conditions, a preference indication. We modify the second and third components by only considering those sub-goals that have not yet been attempted. We then add a fourth component that explains those things that have been previously attempted. Intuitively, this is of the form "... and I already unsuccessfully tried doing X". Formally:

$\{\mathsf{Tried}(G_j) \mid j \neq i \wedge \mathit{failed}(G_j)\}$ where i is the index of the sub-goal that was selected.

To illustrate this definition, consider a situation where Jo has decided to getOfficeCoffee, but by the time he reaches Ann's office, Ann has had to leave for a meeting. The plan therefore fails, and Jo then recovers by electing to go to the shop. In response to the query "why did you getShopCoffee?" the explanation given is "{haveMoney, {⟨bad, none, low⟩} ≺ ⟨veryGood, high, high⟩, Tried:getOfficeCoffee}" which can be rendered in English as "because I have money, I prefer good coffee to bad coffee, and because I tried (and failed) to get pod coffee".

4 Evaluation

There are two broad questions that concern evaluation of this work. The first is whether the explanations provided are comprehensible and *useful* to a human user. The second is whether the approach is sufficiently *efficient*.

In order to assess the comprehensibility and *usability* of the explanations generated, as well as provide guidance to future work on selecting explanations, we conducted a preliminary human participant evaluation. Note that we focussed on evaluating E_N^T, and did not include in the explanations either preparatory actions (links) or parent goals (except for the fifth explanation - see below).

Participants were recruited on Mechanical Turk and paid US$0.50 for an estimated 5 min survey. Each participant was provided with a brief description of the coffee scenario and an indication of what behaviour was observed. Participants were divided into three cohorts, each of which was given a different observed behaviour. The allocation to cohorts was random. We obtained 109 responses, comprising 42 in Cohort 1, 37 in Cohort 2, and 30 in Cohort 3. Participants were 28 females and 81 males. Their highest level of education was high school (22), bachelors (63), and master/graduate degree (21). One person had not completed high school and two respondents had PhDs. Finally, around 35% had some experience with programming (38 out of 109).

Each cohort was given five possible explanations for the observed behaviour. The explanations were created manually, following the corresponding explanation method. The first explanation combined valuings and beliefs, and corresponds to the E_N^T function defined earlier (indicated with "V+B" below). The second and third explanations are solely in terms of valuings: one is abstract (AV), just saying "*This is the best possible coffee available*", and the second is concrete (V), with a specific explanation (see below). The fourth candidate explanation provides only relevant beliefs (B). The fifth candidate explanation gives the goal, and the beliefs that enabled the specific behaviour that was selected, which is the explanation mechanism proposed by Harbers [9] (G+B).

For example, in the case where the colleague's machine was selected (Cohort 1), the five explanations given are:

(E1) "This is the best possible coffee available; I had no money." (V+B)
(E2) "This is the best possible coffee available." (AV)

(E3) "This coffee is better than the kitchen and cheaper than in the shop." (V)
(E4) "I've no money; Ann was in her room." (B)
(E5) "I wanted coffee; Ann was in her room." (G+B)

	Cohort 1			Cohort 2			Cohort 3		
	Believ.	Accept.	Comprehen.	Believ.	Accept.	Comprehen.	Believ.	Accept.	Compr.
E1	3.929 3	4.071 2	3.976 2	3.649 3	3.811 2	4.027 3	3.933 1	4.200 1	3.867 2
E2	3.095 5	3.286 5	3.714 4	3.892 1	3.892 1	4.054 2	2.500 5	2.767 5	3.200 5
E3	4.190 1	4.238 1	4.286 1	3.865 2	3.811 2	4.243 1	3.933 1	4.167 2	4.167 1
E4	3.857 4	3.500 4	3.690 5	2.973 5	3.000 5	3.108 5	3.567 4	3.600 4	3.567 3
E5	3.976 2	3.857 3	3.976 2	3.541 4	3.595 4	3.568 4	3.600 3	3.733 3	3.533 4
$p=$	0.00026	0.000013	0.038	0.0013	0.0047	0.00013	.000029	0.000025	0.034

Fig. 2. Believability, acceptability, and comprehensibility scores (1 = very bad, 5 = excellent) for the three Cohorts and five explanations.

For each possible explanation, the participants were asked to *score* the explanation in terms of three criteria: *believability* ("I can imagine someone giving this answer"), *acceptability* ("This is a valid explanation of Jo's choice"), and *comprehension* ("I understand the text of this explanation"). Each score was on a five-point Likert scale from "very bad" (1) to "excellent" (5). Participants were also asked to *rank* the five candidate explanations by order of preference, from most preferred (rank 1) to least preferred (rank 5). Finally, participants were also asked whether they felt that further explanation was required, and, if so, what form it should take (e.g. providing source code, entering a dialogue with the system).

Figure 2 shows for each cohort and each explanation the average score for each of the three criteria. The figure also shows the implied ranking. For example, for Cohort 1 and Believability, the third explanation (E3) had the best (highest) average score, and therefore collectively E3 is ranked best for Believability by this cohort. For each of the three criteria and three cohorts a statistical test[5] confirms there is a difference ($p < 0.05$) amongst the explanations for that cohort, and post-hoc tests with Holm adjustment find that some of the pairwise differences are significant.

We now turn to analysing the responses on the ranking question, in which participants ranked the explanations from most preferred (1) to least preferred (5). Figure 3 shows for each explanation (E1 to E5) and for each cohort the *average ranking*, which is the average of each explanation's ranking for that cohort. So, for example, if half of the participants in a given cohort were to rank E1 as their most preferred (1), and the other half were to rank it as their second-most preferred (2), then it would have an average ranking of 1.5 for that cohort. The table also shows for each explanation and cohort the preferred order of explanations that is implied by the average ranking (i.e. the implied

---

[5] Kruskal-Wallis, since data is not expected to be normally distributed.

Expla-nation	Average Ranking and Implied Collective Ranking					
	Cohort 1		Cohort 2		Cohort 3	
E1	2.7857	2	2.5135	1	2.0667	1
E2	3.5714	5	2.5676	2	3.7333	5
E3	2.5238	1	2.7297	3	2.5667	2
E4	3.1429	4	4.1622	5	3.1667	3
E5	2.9762	3	3.027	4	3.4667	4
$p =$	0.011		0.00000074		0.000016	

Fig. 3. Rankings for the three Cohorts and five explanations.

collective ranking). For example, for cohort 1, explanation 3 had the best (lowest) average ranking, and is therefore the most preferred explanation. A statistical test confirms that there are differences between the explanations' scores for each of the cohorts (as before, all p values are <0.05). Post-hoc tests (Mann-Whitney, with Holm correction), find that the ranking differences are significant between E1-E2, E2-E3 (Cohort 1), E4 and all other explanations (Cohort 2), and between E1-E2, E1-E4, E1-E5, E2-E3, E3-E5 (Cohort 3).

Considering the question of whether the explanation given would be adequate, or whether additional information would be desired, 69% of Cohort 1 indicated that no further explanation would be required (with the remaining responses asking for a dialogue (19%) or source code (12%)). For Cohort 2 these figures were respectively 54% (no further explanation), 22% (dialogue), 19% (source code), and for Cohort 3 they were 63%, 20% and 17%.

Overall, explanations 1 and 3 were considered as being better than the other explanations, and that, except for Cohort 2, explanation 2 was seen as being the worst. Since explanations 1 and 3 both include valuings, this finding supports the key thesis of this paper, that valuings are important to provide useful explanations. Furthermore, for Cohorts 2 and 3, E1 was preferred to E3, indicating that valuings alone were not sufficient.

We now turn to *efficiency*. We observe that the explanation has three components: the reasons calculated by the function $E_N^T(G)$, the links between nodes, and parent goals. The last is simple to compute, involving merely traversing the tree upwards from the node being queried (i.e. $O(\log N)$ where N is the number of nodes in the goal tree). The second, the links, only depend on the static structure of the tree (i.e. which nodes precede other nodes), and on the pre and post conditions, and therefore can be computed ahead of time. This does assume that pre and post conditions are specified ahead of runtime. If this is not the case, then a runtime calculation is required, which involves checking pre and post conditions for every pair of nodes that precede each other. Given a tree with N nodes, there are obviously at most $O(N^2)$ such pairs, and the check is $O(1)$ (we assume that each node's pre and post conditions do not become longer as the tree grows).

Turning now to the explanation function E, we observe that the function basically traverses the tree from root to leaves. For each non-leaf node it checks which of the child nodes contain at least one node that is in the trace prefix ($n(G_i) \cap T^{\prec N} \neq \emptyset$). This check could be implemented by first traversing the tree upwards, tagging each node G_i with its $n(G_i)$, and then checking for intersection between $n(G_i)$ and $T^{\prec N}$. Since for each node the size of $n(G_i)$ is a function of the number of nodes beneath it, i.e. $O(N)$, computing the intersection (assuming indexing on $T^{\prec N}$) for a single node is $O(N)$, and for the whole tree it would be[6] $O(N^2)$. Finally, for each OR node, there is an additional calculation of *pref* which is proportional to the number of children and the size of conditions, both of which we assume is effectively a constant, i.e. does not grow with N. Therefore calculating E_N^T is $O(N^2)$.

In order to empirically assess the actual runtime required, and the algorithm's scalability, we have conducted an experimental evaluation on generated trees. The generated trees have the following structure: $T^0 = A$ and $T^{d+1} = \text{OR}_N(O_{1-j})$ where $O_i = (c, \text{SEQ}_{N_i}(T_{1-k}^d))$. In other words, a generated tree of depth 0, denoted T^0, is just an action A (with a new unique name), and a generated tree of depth $d+1$ is a disjunction of j options, where each option O_i has the same fixed condition c, and a sequential composition of k trees of depth d. All nodes have unique names. Note that the number of nodes in a tree with branching factors j and k and depth d can be calculated as: $n(j,k,0) = 1$ and $n(j,k,(d+1)) = 1 + j + (j \times k \times n(j,k,d))$.

For the efficiency evaluation various values of j, k and d were systematically generated, and the number of nodes in the tree and the time taken to compute E_N^T were recorded. The experiments were done using the GHC Haskell implementation (version 8.2.1) running on a 3.2 GHz Intel Core i5 iMac with 16 GB RAM running OSX 10.10.3.

These experiments show that for relatively small trees (fewer than 1000 nodes) the explanation generation, even with an unoptimised Haskell prototype, is clearly fast enough to be practical (<0.1 s). It is worth noting that real goal trees are not necessarily large. For instance, the (real-world) application described by Burmeister *et al.* [3] has 57 nodes in its goal tree. Finally, we note that the core of the Haskell implementation is a direct transliteration of the equations earlier in this paper. While this ensures that the implementation matches the paper, there are clear, and substantial, opportunities to improve efficiency.

5   Related Work

In this section we briefly highlight closely related work. Harbers [9], like us, assumes that a goal tree is given, and defines a number of templates that can be used to explain observed behaviour. It is worth noting that our approach strictly generalises Harbers' approach, in that we include links, ancestor goals,

---

[6] However, the prototype implementation does not tag nodes, so it recomputes $n(G_i)$, leading to higher computational complexity.

and relevant beliefs. In other words, every reason that is included in explanations generated using Harbers templates is included in $\mathcal{E}$. Finally, we note that whereas Harbers just outlines the rules as brief templates, we provide full formal definitions that have been implemented.

Another approach is that of explanation as model reconciliation, where the assumption is that in realistic scenarios humans have domain and task models that differ significantly from that used by the agent [4]. This assumption is supported by psychological studies [10]. However, this approach does not link to the beliefs, desires and values/valuings of the user and is therefore less adequate to connect to the reasons behind the decisions taken in the process. Moreover, it assumes that the human's mental model is *known*, a fairly strong assumption that we do not make.

6   Conclusion

We have argued that explaining the behaviour of autonomous software could be done using the same concepts as are used by humans when explaining their behaviour. Specifically, we have followed the findings of Malle and based explanations on beliefs, desires and *valuings* [11, Sect. 4.2.4]. This paper has proposed a formal framework, using BDI-style goal-trees, augmented with value annotations. This formal framework is then used to define an explanation function, which has been implemented. A human subject evaluation has highlighted that, as expected based on the literature, valuings are seen as being of value in explaining behaviour. Further empirical evaluation is needed, using more scenarios and including the other types of reasons, to assess not just the believability, acceptability and comprehensibility of explanations, but more broadly assessing their effect on trust in the autonomous system.

Stepping back to consider the bigger picture, we have provided a mechanism for *generating* reasons. However, this is only part of the solution to the problem of explaining behaviour. We know that humans select parts of the explanation [12]. The next step in this research is to define means for *selecting* parts of the possible explanation.

Finally, we contend that providing usable explanations of autonomous systems requires the use of human-oriented models, such as our extended BDI model. One area for future work is to develop ways of using our work for autonomous systems that are based on machine learning techniques. Such systems are known for their opacity. In our future work, we will research the possibilities of complementing such systems with the reasoning we propose in this paper. For instance, can an extended BDI model be developed in parallel and maintained to correspond to a behaviour that is learned? Can BDI models be derived automatically from learned behaviours?

References

1. Bratman, M.E., Israel, D.J., Pollack, M.E.: Plans and resource-bounded practical reasoning. Comput. Intell. **4**, 349–355 (1988)
2. Bratman, M.E.: Intentions, Plans, and Practical Reason. Harvard University Press, Cambridge (1987)
3. Burmeister, B., Arnold, M., Copaciu, F., Rimassa, G.: BDI-agents for agile goal-oriented business processes. In: Proceedings of the Seventh International Conference on Autonomous Agents and Multiagent Systems (AAMAS) [Industry Track], pp. 37–44. IFAAMAS (2008)
4. Chakraborti, T., Sreedharan, S., Zhang, Y., Kambhampati, S.: Plan explanations as model reconciliation: moving beyond explanation as soliloquy. In: Proceedings of the Twenty-Sixth International Joint Conference on Artificial Intelligence, IJCAI 2017, pp. 156–163 (2017). https://doi.org/10.24963/ijcai.2017/23
5. Cranefield, S., Winikoff, M., Dignum, V., Dignum, F.: No pizza for you: value-based plan selection in BDI agents. In: Proceedings of the Twenty-Sixth International Joint Conference on Artificial Intelligence, IJCAI 2017, pp. 178–184 (2017). https://doi.org/10.24963/ijcai.2017/26
6. EU: EU General Data Protection Regulation, April 2016. http://tinyurl.com/GDPREU2016 (see articles 13-15 and 22)
7. Grice, H.P.: Logic and conversation. In: Cole, P., Morgan, J. (eds.) Syntax and Semantics Volume 3: Speech Acts. Academic Press, New York (1975)
8. Gunning, D.: Explainable Artificial Intelligence (XAI) (2018). https://www.darpa.mil/program/explainable-artificial-intelligence
9. Harbers, M.: Explaining Agent Behavior in Virtual Training. SIKS dissertation series no. 2011-35, SIKS (Dutch Research School for Information and Knowledge Systems) (2011)
10. Lombrozo, T.: Explanation and abductive inference. In: Oxford Handbook of Thinking and Reasoning, pp. 260–276 (2012)
11. Malle, B.F.: How the Mind Explains Behavior: Folk Explanations, Meaning, and Social Interaction. The MIT Press, Cambridge (2004). ISBN 0-262-13445-4
12. Miller, T.: Explanation in artificial intelligence: Insights from the social sciences. CoRR abs/1706.07269 (2017). http://arxiv.org/abs/1706.07269
13. Rao, A.S., Georgeff, M.P.: An abstract architecture for rational agents. In: Rich, C., Swartout, W., Nebel, B. (eds.) Proceedings of the Third International Conference on Principles of Knowledge Representation and Reasoning, pp. 439–449. Morgan Kaufmann Publishers, San Mateo (1992)
14. Schwartz, S.: An overview of the Schwartz theory of basic values. Online Read. Psychol. Cult. **2**(1) (2012). https://doi.org/10.9707/2307-0919.1116
15. Thangarajah, J., Padgham, L., Winikoff, M.: Detecting and avoiding interference between goals in intelligent agents. In: Proceedings of the 18th International Joint Conference on Artificial Intelligence (IJCAI), pp. 721–726 (2003)
16. Thangarajah, J., Padgham, L., Winikoff, M.: Detecting and exploiting positive goal interaction in intelligent agents. In: Proceedings of the Second International Joint Conference on Autonomous Agents and Multiagent Systems (AAMAS), pp. 401–408. ACM Press (2003)
17. Visser, S., Thangarajah, J., Harland, J., Dignum, F.: Preference-based reasoning in BDI agent systems. Auton. Agents Multi-Agent Syst. **30**(2), 291–330 (2016). https://doi.org/10.1007/s10458-015-9288-2

18. van der Weide, T.: Arguing to motivate decisions. Dissertation, Utrecht University Repository (2011). https://dspace.library.uu.nl/handle/1874/210788
19. Winikoff, M.: Towards Trusting Autonomous Systems. In: Fifth Workshop on Engineering Multi-Agent Systems (EMAS) (2017)

Dynamic Risk Assessment for Vehicles of Higher Automation Levels by Deep Learning

Patrik Feth[1(✉)], Mohammed Naveed Akram[1], René Schuster[2], and Oliver Wasenmüller[2]

[1] Fraunhofer Institute for Experimental Software Engineering, Kaiserslautern, Germany
{patrik.feth,naveed.akram}@iese.fraunhofer.de
[2] DFKI - German Research Center for Artificial Intelligence, Kaiserslautern, Germany
{rene.schuster,Oliver.Wasenmueller}@dfki.de

Abstract. Vehicles of higher automation levels require the creation of situation awareness. One important aspect of this situation awareness is an understanding of the current risk of a driving situation. In this work, we present a novel approach for the dynamic risk assessment of driving situations based on images of a front stereo camera using deep learning. To this end, we trained a deep neural network with recorded monocular images, disparity maps and a risk metric for diverse traffic scenes. Our approach can be used to create the aforementioned situation awareness of vehicles of higher automation levels and can serve as a heterogeneous channel to systems based on radar or lidar sensors that are used traditionally for the calculation of risk metrics.

1 Introduction

The contribution of this paper is a novel method for the creation of situation awareness regarding risk, i.e. **dynamic risk assessment**, from monocular images and disparity maps created from a stereo camera. Stereo cameras are widely used in cars nowadays and can be considered as standard [16]. We trained a Convolutional Neural Network (CNN) with supervised learning to derive the risk of a driving scene from an image of that particular scene. To achieve this, we first created a data set of driving situations in a simulation environment and annotated those situations with a risk metric. This data was then given as the input to the learning process. After the training, the CNN was able to predict the current risk of a driving situation from a camera input. This functionality can be used as a part of vehicles of higher automation levels.

In general, there are two main approaches followed for achieving higher automation levels: The robotics approach [18] and the deep learning approach [2]. The robotics approach is more traditional and considers the vehicle as a combination of different functions realized by sensors, control logic and actuators.

© Springer Nature Switzerland AG 2018
B. Gallina et al. (Eds.): SAFECOMP 2018 Workshops, LNCS 11094, pp. 535–547, 2018.
https://doi.org/10.1007/978-3-319-99229-7_48

This approach is the one followed mainly by the traditional car industry. The deep learning approach is very different from that. It considers the vehicle as a black box into which sensor information is fed, this information is processed by a neural network and control output as steering and throttle commands are generated by the network. This approach is the one mainly followed by new entries to the automotive market. The neural network can be trained with millions of recorded driving kilometers. The feasibility of the approach was shown in 1989 by a team from CMU [13] and was repeated by a team from NVIDIA using the advances of machine learning in 2016 [2]. Even though this approach is feasible, a huge and open question arises towards its dependability. It is currently a hot topic to try to understand what a neural network has learned and why decisions are made the one way or the other [3]. However, reliable results on those questions can probably not be expected by the time that car manufacturers want to have realized highly automated vehicles.

The approach presented in this paper can be used in both paradigms for the development of vehicles of higher automation levels presented above. The main and currently considered use case lies in the robotic case, where it can be used as an additional component of the functional architecture for performing a dynamic risk assessment. A further and future use case of our approach lies in the field of making the output of a neural network more understandable and thus analyzable. If the deep learning paradigm is used for achieving higher automation levels, the risk shall become an additional output of the neural network that controls the vehicle. This allows making the output of the neural network more transparent, as additional information about the network's current understanding of the environment is available. This understanding can then be plausibilized and it can be checked if the predicted control commands of the neural network match the predicted risk of the current driving scene.

This paper is structured as follows: In Sect. 2 we compare the presented approach to the state-of-the-art, which is - as of today - only a single comparable approach for the dynamic risk assessment based on images. Section 3 gives details on our approach, the data collection and the training process. Section 4 gives the results of the training process and the achieved performance of our approach. Section 5 concludes the paper.

2   Related Work

The approach related closest to ours, is the work presented in [20]. The goal of this approach is - just as in ours - to train a Convolutional Neural Network to perform dynamic risk assessment of traffic scenes from images of that particular scene.

The authors of [20] used a subjective classification for the rating of traffic scenes. They showed YouTube videos from collisions recorded by dashboard cameras to three different subjects. These subjects then had to assign two time labels for each video: t_1 as the time at which the root cause for the accident appears and t_2 as the time at which this cause becomes obvious. This divides the video into three sections: a *normal*, a *caution* and a *warning* section. The CNN in their work was trained to assign one of those three labels to a given image of a traffic scene. In our work we used a more objective measure to classify traffic scenes by the use of a quantitative and objective risk metric, as will be explained in Sect. 3.4. By that, our network is solving a regression instead of a classification problem. Conclusively, the approach presented in our work is more systematic in creating the ground truth data for classifying traffic scenes.

In addition to the work in [20] more traditional approaches for risk assessment that work with explicit trajectory predictions and the calculation of conflicts between trajectories can be considered as related work. A representative of those approaches is described in [15]. The solution in this paper differs from the traditional approaches for risk assessment as it follows an end-2-end paradigm deriving the current risk directly from the camera input. Such an end-2-end paradigm can result in a significant saving of computational costs. However, the state of research is still too early to evaluate any claims of such kind.

3 Data Generation and Training of the CNN

3.1 Overview

The recent success of neural networks in almost all fields of Computer Vision has motivated us to address the problem of dynamic risk assessment with a deep Convolutional Neural Network (CNN). Convolutional Neural Networks are a special type of Artificial Neural Networks (ANNs). While general ANNs model a function as connected neural nodes of different layers, in CNNs these connections are structured as convolutional filter kernels [12]. That means that the connections between layers are very dense whereas the number of parameters is kept relatively small because the connections share filter weights in a patchwise manner. In addition, modeling a neural network by multiple convolutions is intuitively related to workflows of classical image processing. For example, some kernels of the first two convolutional layers in a CNN can often be interpreted as first and second order derivative filters [22], which are also commonly used in classical edge detection. As framework for the design and training of our neural network, we used TensorFlow (https://www.tensorflow.org/).

Since visual sensor data is available in most vehicles nowadays, we decided to design the network in an end-to-end manner, i.e. the input is image data and the output is the final risk estimate (cf. Fig. 1). As others before, we wanted to

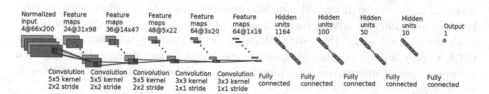

Fig. 1. The architecture of our neural network for risk estimation in driving scenarios

predict the output based on images from an onboard camera of a moving vehicle. Consequently, our network architecture is inspired by the existing DAVE2 network [2] that is predicting steering commands for highly automated vehicles.

A full overview of the design is given in Fig. 1. In detail, the network consists of five convolutional layers and five fully connected layers. All layers except the last one use Rectified Linear Units (ReLU) as activation function. Since we used subsampled resolution of the input images, we did not need any spatial pooling. As mentioned earlier, we provided a single image and a precomputed disparity map as input for the network and stacked them into a single four channel tensor comparable to RGB-D images. More details on how these data was generated is given in Sects. 3.3 and 3.4. The first three convolutional layers use kernels of size 5×5 with a stride of 2×2. The last two convolutional layers apply 3×3 kernels densely, i.e. the stride is 1. The first fully connected layer after the flattened final convolution has 1,164 output nodes. All following fully connected layers steadily reduce the number of neurons to a single output node.

3.2   Simulation Environment

To train a CNN for dynamic risk assessment with supervised learning, a great amount of training data was required. It is challenging to create this amount of data in a real driving environment. Thus, we used a simulation environment to create sufficient training data. This environment needs to be large and random enough to be representative for a real environment. For research purposes, it is common to use computer games as a substitute for very expensive professional simulation tools. In the past, efforts have been made to use the TORCS game [4] for training neural networks to drive a car autonomously. This simulation environment is open source but lacks a sufficient graphical appearance and is limited to simulate driving situation on a race track. A more suited candidate for a simulation environment was Grand Theft Auto - V. With more than 500 vehicle models, urban and countryside road networks, and random actions of pedestrians and other drivers, it comes close to an ideal simulation environment for autonomous vehicles. Although the game is developed for commercial purposes, its publisher Rockstar Games has allowed creative, non-commercial modification of the game under certain conditions (https://support.rockstargames.com/hc/en-u s/articles/200153756-Policy-on-posting-copyrighted-Rockstar-Games-material). Existing work already shows that data from this particular gaming environment is valid data for the benchmarking of object classification algorithms [14]. Visual surveillance is another application of commercial games as simulation environment for a serious purpose [17]. During creating this work, an open-source simulator for autonomous driving research named CARLA [5] was released. For future work we plan on using this environment as it has almost the same benefits as GTA V only with a smaller simulated world and it was designed for research purposes, which means that the interface is easier to handle and the license is more open.

3.3   Creating Stereo-Images and Disparity

In order to determine the risk of a given situation from an image, the distance of the objects - like other cars, pedestrians, etc. - in the scene to the vehicle is essential. From a monocular image, it is very difficult to estimate these distances, since no 3D information is available. Cheap active sensors - such as depth cameras - have difficulty to convince in automotive applications [21]. Thus, we used a stereo camera, which has a left and a right camera. By computing the shift in pixels between these two cameras, we got a disparity image. Disparity is inversely proportional to the distance from the camera to the respective object.

We rendered the two images in such a way that both images lie on the same plane and are horizontally aligned. With that, the corresponding image points in the two images share the same horizontal line, which reduces the search space from two to one dimension. For the computation of disparity several algorithm exist. We choose the state-of-the-art Semi Global Matching (SGM) algorithm [9] for our approach. SGM tries to find the best correspondences for all pixels of one image so that a consistent and smooth disparity image is created. It utilizes a semi-global energy formulation using eight different paths radiating from each target pixel location. This enables sharp boundaries, accurate disparity estimation and fast run time. Because of occlusions, it is hard to recover disparity for all image points. SGM uses a left-right consistency check for two computed disparity images to localize and remove wrong values. Thus, SGM yields a non-dense disparity image.

We created stereo images out of GTA V by simulating a standard stereo camera. We virtually placed two custom cameras on the hood of a car with the same orientation and same Y and Z-axis position. We kept the X-axis, i.e. the horizontal position, 16 cm apart, simulating the baseline of a stereo camera. For consistency, we used the same car model for our data extraction process. We rendered these custom cameras and automatically took screenshots to obtain left and right images for computing disparity. GTA V allows only to render one camera per frame. Thus, we first rendered the left camera, slowed down the game to the lowest possible timescale, and then rendered the right camera in the next frame. Hence, there was one frame delay in the two images. This delay of one frame translated to a timely delay of 88 ms. We used feature matching to verify if the difference between the two images is as intended. This was performed by matching ORB features [6] in both images and computing the average difference in Y (vertical) and X (horizontal) direction of those identified features for each image pair. Ideally, only a distance in X direction should exist. The difference in Y direction should be zero. A difference in Y direction can only happen because of the time delay between the images or the inaccuracies of ORB matching. We classified image pairs with an average X difference less than 1 pixel, or average Y difference greater than 5 pixels as outliers. In the created data set of 110,152 images around 3.5% outliers were found and excluded. An example of a disparity map created from a traffic scene is shown in the right part of Fig. 2. In this visualization of the disparity map yellow corresponds to a close object and blue corresponds to an object farther away.

Fig. 2. Sample disparity map

3.4   Risk Metric

The recorded scenarios from the simulation environment were imported into a Risk Metric Calculator (RMC) to determine the ground truth values for the dynamic risk assessment. Risk metrics are used extensively for the creation of situation awareness of active safety systems in the automotive domain. The ISO standard for forward collision avoidance systems [10] uses thresholds of the metrics *Time To Collision (TTC)* and *Enhanced Time To Collision (ETTC)* to decide if and if so which collision mitigation strategy shall be activated. Those two metrics work with a very simple constant turn assumption for the lateral movement and constant velocity (for TTC)/constant acceleration (for ETTC) assumptions for the longitudinal movement. There exist more mature risk metrics that use richer prediction models for the dynamic risk assessment, for example [15] or [1]. The availability of such a great set of metrics with different limitations and assumptions makes the choice of the right metric a difficult task. Feth et al. [8] presents strategies on how to come to a valid decision regarding this aspect.

To get a deeper understanding and the possibility to compare the values of different risk metrics in traffic situations, we used a Risk Metric Calculator (RMC). More detailed information on the RMC tool is available in [7]. The RMC takes driving scenarios, either generated in the tool itself or given as a record from the simulation environment, fills for every simulation step a grid map with the relevant information and uses that grid map to calculate the selected risk metrics. Grid maps are a common notation in the robotics world. They discretize the environment in cells of fixed or variable sizes. Each cell contains information about its occupancy status. If it is occupied it may contain information about the object that is occupying the cell. This map represents the World Model for the robot, e.g. the vehicle, and is used to determine the appropriate behavior, e.g. the desired trajectory. See [11] for related work on the subject and a more recent approach for the creation of a grid map. In Fig. 3 we illustrate how an exemplary grid map for a specific driving scene in our approach looked like. This grid map shows the cells that are currently occupied by the subject vehicle (in the center of the map) and the vehicles in the vicinity in black color and those

Fig. 3. Left: Scene from the simulation environment – Right: Corresponding grid map

cells that will be occupied in the next three seconds using a constant turn and constant speed assumption in blue color. For efficiency reasons the occupied cells are approximated by the "border cells". Cells within these borders are not filled to keep the amount of entries in the grid map small. The horizontal and vertical lines in the visualization have no meaning.

For the development of our new approach, we decided to first use a very simple risk metric. We investigated if we can train a Convolutional Neural Network to predict this simple risk metric. The reason for choosing such a simple risk metric first was the required amount of data. Usually, the risk metrics with more sophisticated prediction models have a lower false positive rate. That means that for most traffic scenes they do not indicate any risk. Consequently, to achieve the required amount of data we would have needed to increase drastically the amount of training images in the simulation environment. The risk metric used in this work is the reciprocal of the *time headway* metric.

$$time\_headway = \frac{distance}{subject\_velocity} \tag{1}$$

The RMC calculated this metric by counting the least number of empty cells between one vehicle and another vehicle and dividing that distance by the current speed of the subject vehicle. By using the reciprocal of that value, we got a positive relationship between the value of the metric and the current risk: the higher the value of the metric, the higher the risk of the current driving situation. Only vehicles in front of the subject vehicle were considered. If there were multiple other vehicles in the vicinity of the subject vehicle, the RMC considered the closest vehicle only. The result was afterwards limited to a value of 20 to exclude outliers and then normalized to a range between 0 and 1. See Fig. 4 for an example of a driving situation that achieved a low value for the specified risk metric (0) and another driving situation that achieved a high value for the specified risk metric (0.21). A value of 0.21 means that following a constant speed and pessimistic turn assumption for the subject vehicle and assuming that the target vehicle will not move at all, a crash would happen in 0.238 s. The *pessimistic*

Fig. 4. Left: Uncritical scene (0) – Right: Critical scene (0.21)

turn assumption used here leads to a *worst time headway* metric comparable to the *worst time to collision* metric presented in [19]. The actual trajectory of neither the subject nor the target vehicle are considered in the calculation of the metric. Again, the motivation for using this risk metric, which obviously leads to a overestimation of the risk of driving situations, was the needed effort in the production of a sufficient large set of training data and the fact that this work shall be a proof of concept.

Finally, this ground truth data was used as input for training the CNN. The trained CNN is the result of this paper and our novel solution for dynamic risk assessment for vehicles of higher automation levels by deep learning. Instead of calculating the risk metric for a recorded driving scenario, this CNN can be used together with a camera to perform a dynamic risk assessment of the driving situation while driving.

3.5   Network Training

We used the TensorFlow framework for training. We built the network architecture as discussed in Sect. 3.1 and trained the network using Adam optimizer on the collected data. A total of 110,152 data points were recorded. After estimating the quality using ORB as described in Sect. 3.3, we excluded outliers and used the remaining 106,170 data points effectively in the training. This data set consisted of the left image, the disparity information calculated from the stereo image and the calculated risk value from the RMC tool. The network was given the left monocular image and the disparity information as input and was trained to predict the risk value as output. We divided the full data set into three random groups. 70% of the data was used for training, 10% for validation and 20% was used for final testing. Training was performed for 30 epochs with a batch size of 10. To avoid overfitting, validation test was performed after every 10 steps.

4   Results

The model was trained to minimize the mean squared error between true and predicted risk values on the training data set. The mean squared error on the training data set is referred to as *training average error*. Validation was performed on the validation dataset and hence, its error is referred to as *validation average error*. Likewise, testing error is referred to as *testing average error*. The final *testing average error* we achieved over all test data was **0.01470**. The values for *training average error* and *validation average error* are shown in Figs. 5 and 6.

It can be seen from the curve of the training error in Fig. 5, that the network was able to learn an estimation of risk from the provided input data. The training error was steadily decreasing. However, a common pitfall for all machine learning methods is overfitting. That means that the network loses the ability to generalize to unknown input because it starts to create too strong connections between training input and output. Therefore, we monitored the validation error in Fig. 6 on a separate set of data. After half the iterations, i.e. after approximately 15 epochs, the validation error started to increase. That is the optimal point to stop training. As usual, overall performance of the network can be increased by providing more, distinctive training data, though this implies more training effort.

Figure 7 gives an exemplary impression of the performance of our CNN by showing a driving situation for which the risk metric was predicted correctly by the network (RMC value 0.36, network value 0.38) and a driving situation for which the risk metric was not predicted correctly by the network (RMC value 0.75, network value 0.39).

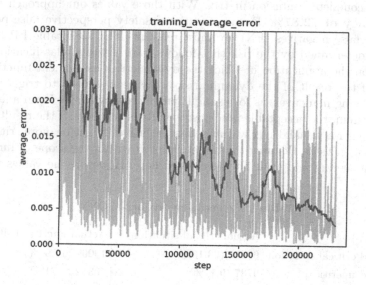

Fig. 5. Training average error

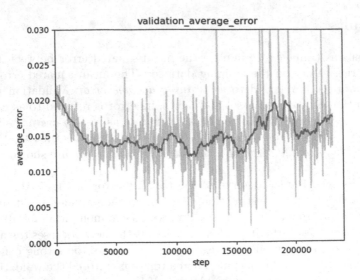

Fig. 6. Validation average error

For a better interpretation of the performance of the CNN we have to consider the application in which it is used. A system for dynamic risk assessment needs to classify the current situation as either critical or uncritical. The performance of the network shall thus be rated according to its ability to correctly classify a driving situation. Assuming a time headway value of 1.5 s as the threshold, the complete effective data set of 106,170 situations contains 76.789 critical driving situations. Of those 76.789 situations the CNN classified 67.052 correctly. Table 1 gives the complete confusion matrix. With those values our approach reached an **accuracy of 72.87%**. From a functional safety perspective false positives (FP) and false negatives (FN) are most relevant. The acceptable FP and FN ratio are determined by the risk that follows from a wrong classification. This depends on the application in which the dynamic risk assessment functionality is used. If the result of the dynamic risk assessment is used to trigger a very critical driving maneuver, as for example an emergency brake, in an automated driving system, the acceptable false positive rate is very low. If the result is used to only trigger a visual driver warning, false negatives might be more critical but still not too critical. Defining the target ratios is within the scope of functional safety engineering and shall not be covered here. However, the values that we

Table 1. Confusion matrix of the CNN

	Actual critical situation	Actual uncritical situation
Predicted critical situation	67052 (63.16%)	19069 (17.96%)
Predicted uncritical situation	9737 (9.17%)	10312 (9.71%)

achieve for our solution show that the integrity of the developed approach is still far from what can be considered as usable in a safety-critical context.

We could identify a major reason for the bad performance of the network: The view of the camera did not perfectly match the area that the RMC considered in the calculation. Because of that, the most critical situations according to the RMC happened outside the view of the camera and could therefore not be derived from the image. The example in Fig. 7 illustrates this: On the left image our CNN was most probably considering the vehicle on the left as the closest vehicle. In the following, this vehicle was passed and on the right image, it is right next to the subject vehicle but not visible for the camera. In the RMC tool, this occluded vehicle was used for the calculation of the risk metric. However, the network was considering the vehicle in front. This vehicle was just as far away as the vehicle on the image before, giving a reason why the same value was predicted by the network as for the scene before.

Fig. 7. Left: Value from RMC: 0.36 Value from CNN: 0.38 – Right: Value from RMC: 0.75 Value from CNN: 0.39

With an accuracy value of 72.87% our CNN does not perform significantly better than the related work in [20]. The authors of [20] achieved a maximum accuracy of 70.77%. However, the classification of traffic situations in our work is based on an objective risk metric instead of a subjective labeling.

5   Conclusion

In this paper, we presented a novel approach for the dynamic risk assessment from images. To achieve this, we trained a Convolutional Neural Network with data generated in a simulation environment and annotated with a simple risk metric calculated in a risk metric calculation tool. We extended the simulation environment with the capability to generate stereo images. From those stereo images, disparity maps have been generated. We annotated monocular images and the disparity maps with the reciprocal of the *time headway* risk metric. The trained network achieved an accuracy of **72.87%** on our test set.

In the introduction of this paper we already pointed at the reliability challenge of neural networks. Of course, the same holds for the CNN used in this paper. Because of that, a system as recommended in this paper can only be used in addition to more conservative systems for dynamic risk assessment. As we transition with higher automation levels from fail safe to fail operational systems, measures for redundancy will be required. The CNN proposed in this paper can be such a redundant system with a high degree of heterogeneity from conservative systems working with radar and lidar information. In parallel to this work we currently investigate means to safely integrate systems for dynamic risk assessment as presented in this work in the architecture of safety-critical systems.

For future work, we plan to go from the simple *time headway* risk metric to a more sophisticated risk metric with a richer collision prediction model. This will require enhancing the training data, as situations rated as critical will be less likely. Further, we plan to use different network structures, as e.g. Long/Short Term Memory (LSTM) Networks and compare the performance to the base performance achieved in this paper. Once we achieve a sufficient performance, the approach should be transferred from the simulation environment to a real environment.

References

1. Berthelot, A., Tamke, A., Dang, T., Breuel, G.: A novel approach for the probabilistic computation of time-to-collision. IEEE Intelligent Vehicles Symposium (2012)
2. Bojarski, M., et al.: End to end learning for self-driving cars (2016)
3. Bojarski, M., et al.: Explaining how a deep neural network trained with end-to-end learning steers a car (2017)
4. Chen, C., Seff, A., Kornhauser, A., Xiao, J.: Deepdriving: learning affordance for direct perception in autonomous driving. In: IEEE International Conference on Computer Vision (2015)
5. Dosovitskiy, A., Ros, G., Codevilla, F., Lopez, A., Koltun, V.: CARLA: an open urban driving simulator. In: Proceedings of the 1st Annual Conference on Robot Learning, pp. 1–16 (2017)
6. Rublee, E., Rabaud, V., Konolige, K., Bradski, G.: ORB: an efficient alternative to sift or surf. In: IEEE International Conference on Computer Vision (2011)
7. Feth, P.: Ein werkzeug zur entwicklung und zum vergleich von verfahren zur dynamischen risikobewertung für aktive sicherheitssysteme. In: International Commercial Vehicle Technology Symposium Kaiserslautern (2018)
8. Feth, P., Schneider, D., Adler, R.: A conceptual safety supervisor definition and evaluation framework for autonomous systems. In: International Conference on Computer Safety, Reliability and Security (2017)
9. Hirschmuller, H.: Stereo processing by semiglobal matching and mutual information. Transactions on Pattern Analysis and Machine Intelligence (PAMI) (2008)
10. ISO: Intelligent transport systems - forward vehicle collision mitigation systems - operation, performance, and verification requirements (2013)
11. Jungnickel, R., Köhler, M., Korf, F.: Efficient automotive grid maps using a sensor ray based refinement process. In: IEEE Intelligent Vehicles Symposium (2016)

12. LeCun, Y., Bengio, Y., Hinton, G.: Deep learning. Nature **521**(7553), 436 (2015)
13. Pomerleau, D.A.: Alvinn: an autonomous land vehicle in a neural network. In: Advances in Neural Information Processing Systems (1989)
14. Richter, S.R., Hayder, Z., Koltun, V.: Playing for benchmarks. In: International Conference on Computer Vision (2017)
15. Schreier, M., Willert, V., Adamy, J.: Bayesian, maneuver-based, long-term trajectory prediction and criticality assessment for driver assistance systems. In: IEEE Intelligent Vehicles Symposium (2014)
16. Schuster, R., Wasenmüller, O., Kuschk, G., Bailer, C., Stricker, D.: SceneFlow-Fields: dense interpolation of sparse scene flow correspondences. In: IEEE Winter Conference on Applications of Computer Vision (WACV) (2018)
17. Taylor, G., Chosak, A., Brewer, P.: OVVV: Using virtual worlds to design and evaluate surveillance systems. IEEE Conference on Computer Vision and Pattern Recognition (2007)
18. Thrun, S.: Stanley: the robot that won the DARPA grand challenge. J. Field Robot. **23**(9), 661–692 (2006)
19. Wachenfeld, W., Junietz, P., Wenzel, R., Winner, H.: The worst-time-to-collision metric for situation identification. In: IEEE Intelligent Vehicles Symposium (2016)
20. Wang, Y., Kato, J.: Collision risk rating of traffic scene from dashboard cameras. In: International Conference on Digital Image Computing: Techniques and Applications (DICTA), pp. 1–6 (2017)
21. Yoshida, T., Wasenmüller, O., Stricker, D.: Time-of-flight sensor depth enhancement for automotive exhaust gas. In: IEEE International Conference on Image Processing (ICIP) (2017)
22. Zeiler, M.D., Fergus, R.: Visualizing and understanding convolutional networks. In: European Conference on Computer Vision (ECCV) (2014)

Improving Image Classification Robustness Using Predictive Data Augmentation

Subramani Palanisamy Harisubramanyabalaji[1,3]([⊠]), Shafiq ur Réhman[1],
Mattias Nyberg[2,3], and Joakim Gustavsson[2,3]

[1] i2lab, Umeå University, 901 87 Umeå, Sweden
hasu0023@student.umu.se, shafiq.ur.rehman@umu.se
[2] KTH Royal Institute of Technology, 100 44 Stockholm, Sweden
matny@kth.se, joagusta@kth.se
[3] Scania CV AB, 15187 Södertälje, Sweden

Abstract. Safer autonomous navigation might be challenging if there is a failure in sensing system. Robust classifier algorithm irrespective of camera position, view angles, and environmental condition of an autonomous vehicle including different size & type (Car, Bus, Truck, etc.) can safely regulate the vehicle control. As training data play a crucial role in robust classification of traffic signs, an effective augmentation technique enriching the model capacity to withstand variations in urban environment is required. In this paper, a framework to identify model weakness and targeted augmentation methodology is presented. Based on off-line behavior identification, exact limitation of a Convolutional Neural Network (CNN) model is estimated to augment only those challenge levels necessary for improved classifier robustness. Predictive Augmentation (PA) and Predictive Multiple Augmentation (PMA) methods are proposed to adapt the model based on acquired challenges with a high numerical value of confidence. We validated our framework on two different training datasets and with 5 generated test groups containing varying levels of challenge (simple to extreme). The results show impressive improvement by $\approx$ 5–20% in overall classification accuracy thereby keeping their high confidence.

Keywords: Safety-risk assessment · Predictive augmentation
Convolutional neural network · Traffic sign classification
Real-time challenges

1 Introduction

The automotive industry has seen rapid development in bringing sophisticated autonomous vehicles with advanced functional capabilities in recent times [1–3].

Supported by Systems Safety Architecture (EPXS), Scania CV AB, Södertälje, Sweden.

At the same time, safety being a top most priority, such intelligent vehicles are being rigorously tested in order to adapt to dynamic conditions and cooperate with human driving [4]. Traffic sign recognition is a major function in driver assistance, complex urban scene understanding, and autonomous driving. Even though many traditional Machine Learning (ML) algorithms amongst others Neural Networks (NN) [5], and Support Vector Machines (SVM) [6] with hand driven features can be used for classification. Moreover, a Convolutional Neural Network (CNN) is found to perform better for an image classification task [7]. A CNN classification is a supervised learning approach for recognizing traffic signs, pedestrians, etc. Training and performance evaluation of such a model are usually done with the collected labeled datasets either from real roads or simulation engines [7, 8]. However, generally available labeled datasets, such as German Traffic Sign Recognition Benchmark (GTSRB), Belgium Traffic Sign Detection (BTSD), Challenging Unreal and Real Environments for Traffic Sign Detection (CURE-TSD) [9–11] lack several real-time challenges faced by vehicles as they are usually collected from the front-facing cameras placed in a passenger car dashboard mostly during daytime and in good weather conditions.

To account for those dynamic challenges which are missing in the generally available datasets, these datasets are commonly augmented randomly with challenges including rotation, cropping, brightness, flipping etc. [12]. In addition, other studies [11] considered weather challenges such as rain, fog and snow to further improve the data set quality. Previous literature [5–12] and the generally available datasets, have only considered model training with the passenger car application in mind. Therefore, whether the trained model developed for the car industry satisfies all challenges faced by heavy vehicles including, but not limited to, the placement of cameras in different locations, camera angles, etc., [13]. In addition, variations in placement of sign posts on different sides of the road according to the driving norms of a country must be compensated by the algorithm.

Furthermore, there are other unanswered questions in the traffic sign classification: (a) Does the classifier sensitivity remain constant with any training data for a particular type of challenge by memorization [14]? (b) Does the random augmentation increase the classifier robustness in real-time challenges? Motivated by these limitations and questions, there is an increased need for a robust image classification algorithm irrespective of variations in environmental conditions, camera location based on vehicle size, and pertaining to motion challenges [13]. Many studies have focused on improving the classifier performance without analyzing the system performance based on model degradation in challenging conditions, which could lead to classification failure during vehicle motion [7–9].

The aim of our study is to develop a framework for identification of model capacity negotiating real-time challenges at varying levels. The framework introduces two new techniques called a Predictive Augmentation (PA) and Predictive Multiple Augmentation (PMA), for adapting the dataset for improved robustness with high confidence in classifying traffic signs.

By using our framework, a user can identify the weaknesses of any given classifier with respect to real-time challenges along with their corner challenging levels. This approach will employ PA and thereby deviate from traditional random augmentation [12], and the result will be a robust classification. For the case of model capacity identification, we propose a solution irrespective of the vehicle size by considering a multitude of 264 challenge levels from 20 challenge types compared to CURE-TSD [11]. According to the experimental results, our PA techniques outperform the traditional random augmentation.

The paper is organized as follows: Sect. 2, we present the literature on the CNN and Noise filters used for generating challenges. Section 3 elaborates the proposed risk assessment and augmentation framework. Section 4 explains the experimental setup used for this study. Section 5 reports the results based on our experiments and discusses how the results support our hypotheses. Section 6 conclusion addresses the answers to our research questions (aims).

2 Background

This section presents the architectural details on CNN and image processing techniques to generate real-time challenges.

2.1 Convolutional Neural Network (CNN)

The CNNs are popular in the field of computer vision research, particularly, for image classification due to its unique feature extraction compared to other traditional algorithms [15]. The general CNN architecture consists of two major functional modules: feature learning and extraction module, and final classification module. The systematic feature learning module is composed of alternating convolution and pooling layers along with activation functions. The convolution layers perform 2D convolution operation on $x(height * width * channel)$ input image with the convolutional filter kernel $C_f(height * width)$. The pooling layers help in reducing the spatial sample size of input feature map based on an overlapping square Max kernels $M_k(height * width)$ [16,17]. The final classification module uses a Multi-layer Perceptron (MLP) along with a Rectified Linear Unit (ReLU). Generally, CNN architecture is designed with an increasing number of feature learning layers based on the complexity of the problem for a higher performance [15–17].

2.2 Noise Filters

The collected data lack most of the urban challenges owing to the limitations in driving conditions, camera placements, weather, etc. Therefore, some off-line image processing techniques are being used [11]. The common challenges can be generated using an image processing toolbox, such as MATLAB [18] and openCV [19], with the pre-defined filter kernels. However, to take into account of weather challenges like rain, snow, fog, etc. user defined image processing operations is a must as the vehicle can undergo these situations in the wild. In addition, the major concern towards the placement of cameras in terms of height from the ground or facing the road from right or left in heavy vehicles must be addressed. Affine and perspective transformations can help in achieving these conditions on images with wide range of angles [20].

3   Risk Assessment and Augmentation Framework

Fig. 1 shows the detailed flow chart of our risk assessment and augmentation framework for traffic signs with one challenging sample performance before and after framework processing. Selected CNN architecture along with the dataset (TR, TE and VA batches) were the only requirements for the framework. Split data batches were trained with CNN along with hyper-parameter tuning to achieve a better performing model. Meanwhile, a real-time challenges generation block held an array of generated challenges (See Sect. 4), which were then manipulated only on the input test batch. Finally in the assessment platform, the selected better performing CNN model was validated with degradation causing challenges inside a safe-risk range identification block to identify its exact capacity. This platform helped in deriving only the challenge and difficulty level which a model might primarily miss in the robust classification. The missing levels were referred as the risk ranges for each challenge type and procedural way

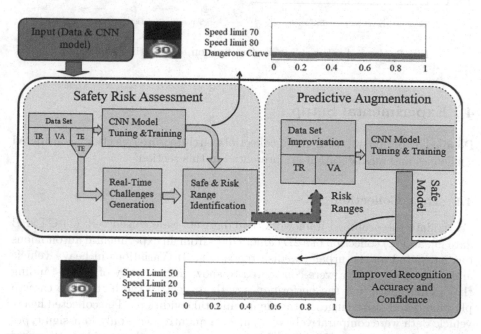

Fig. 1. The proposed schema of the risk assessment and augmentation framework for traffic sign classification with Training (TR), Testing (TE) and Validation (VA) batches.

in order to select the safe and risk ranges is done by fixing threshold accuracy as presented in the Fig. 2. Challenge type grouped into linear and symmetric can be found in Table 1. Identified limitation in terms of the risk ranges was then augmented on the training samples in the successive predictive augmentation platform. We introduced two augmentation techniques: (1) PA, which used only one identified challenge to augment the test image. For example, a speed limit 30 km/hour with a (blur) difficulty level 10. Next sample contained a different challenge and level; (2) PMA, on the other hand, used two variations, one was a challenge type from an identified range and the other was a LAB color space due to its high feature learning capacity [16] to bring simultaneous overlapped effect of both on the same image.

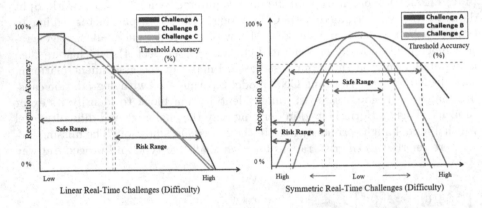

Fig. 2. General safe-risk range identification for real-time challenges.

4   Experimental Setup

Detailed experiments with data collection, architecture selection, considered challenges and augmentation are presented in this section.

4.1   Data Collection

To validate the proposed framework, two datasets were considered: (1) GTSRB data [9], and (2) collection of a 2D camera data from an experimental autonomous bus navigated on the urban Swedish roads (Fig. 3). Variations in heavy vehicle and passenger car data were considered to show the necessity of understanding the training data and the performance with respect to the high angle camera placement and also changes in the environmental conditions. The collected heavy vehicle data were comparatively very small in quantity with only four sign types ("Pedestrian crossing", "Yield", "Traffic light red", and "Keep right"). We used only four sign types as these were the maximum number of samples captured. In addition, the small data size helped us to understand the scalable property, whether PA would be an effective measure in improving robustness to challenges irrespective of the data size. In this study, we did not include any pre-processing stage throughout our experiments, so as to evaluate the direct implications of the real-time challenges on the training models based on the proposed augmentation. Most of the test experiments were done on the augmented dataset in addition to original samples (more details in Sects. 4.3 and 4.4).

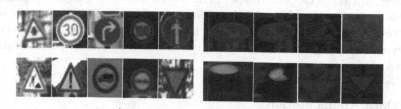

Fig. 3. Sample images from dataset considered for this study. **Left:** GTSRB Data **Right:** Data collected from a heavy vehicle

4.2   CNN Architecture Selection

As this work, concentrated more on augmentation, we chose a simple architecture (LeNet-5) for traffic signs [12] rather than going with very deep layer models as a proof-of-concept. In addition, based on the previous studies [17] rather than utilizing a random set of hyper-parameters, we follow a similar procedural way to select the best values for the parameters shown in Fig. 4. Five parameter groups were selected, each with five different values, collectively gives us 25 set of parameters according to our procedure. Tuning begins with original set of parameters and best value from each group successively replaced the main architecture thereby achieving final set of parameter values. This tuning process takes place before and after predictive augmentation as shown in Fig. 1.

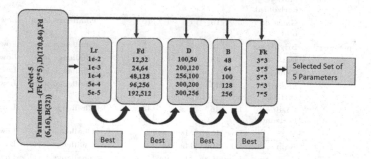

Fig. 4. Systematic selection of hyper-parameters, with **Lr, Fd, D, B, Fk** being Learning rate, Filter depth, Nodes in hidden layers, Batch size, and Filter kernel size respectively.

4.3   Challenge Generation

Challenges were generated considering both vehicle and environment perspectives including only extreme levels for analysis in order to identify the maximum sensitivity of the model [18, 19]. However, the challenge type and their wide range of difficulties could be defined based on our requirements before we allowed our framework to process, so that ineffective challenge levels could be ignored for the classification task. The detailed set of challenges and their ranges are presented in Table 1. A total number of 264 challenge levels from 20 different challenge types covering most of situations faced by the moving vehicles, irrespective of their type, to mimic those vehicles as in urban roads, similar to previous studies [11] was used.

4.4   Data Augmentation

Model training is done based on four different data augmentation groups which included Without Augmentation (WoA), Random Augmentation (RA), PA, and PMA. WoA refers to no manipulation of challenges in training, validation and testing samples. RA is augmented as per previous studies [12] for training and validation samples. PA and PMA were augmented based on predicted challenge

Table 1. Generated real-time challenges with corner challenging levels

	Type	Challenge range			Challenges	Units	Difficulty
		Min	Max	Intervals	Total (Nos)		
Vehicle perspective	Roll	−30	30	2	31	Degree	Symmetric
	Pitch	−90	90	6	31	Degree	Symmetric
	Yaw	−90	90	6	31	Degree	Symmetric
	Occlusion	−14	14	1	29	XY coordinate	Symmetric
	Distance	15	30	1	16	Image dimension	Low-high
	Motion vertical	1	10	1	10	Challenge level	Low-high
	Motion horizontal	1	10	1	10	Challenge level	Low-high
	Gaussian blur	1	10	1	10	Challenge level	Low-high
Environment perspective	Brightness	1	15	1	15	Challenge level	Low-high
	Darkness	1	15	1	15	Challenge level	Low-high
	Contrast	1	15	1	15	Challenge level	Low-high
	Shadow vertical	1	15	1	15	Challenge level	Low-high
	Shadow horizontal	1	15	1	15	Challenge level	Low-high
	Fog	Low	High	Medium	3	Challenge level	Low-high
	Rain	Low	High	Medium	3	Challenge level	Low-high
	Snow	Low	High	Medium	3	Challenge level	Low-high
	Dust	Low	High	Medium	3	Challenge level	Low-high
	Smoke	Low	High	Medium	3	Challenge level	Low-high
	Water	Low	High	Medium	3	Challenge level	Low-high
	Bubbles	Low	High	Medium	3	Challenge level	Low-high

Table 2. Number of image samples for model training and inferencing. Without Augmentation (WoA), Random Augmentation (RA), Predictive Augmentation (PA) and Predictive Multiple Augmentation (PMA)

	Group	GTSRB			Heavy vehicle		
		Train	Valid	Test	Train	Valid	Test
Training	WoA	34799	4410	12630	161	41	51
	RA	53375	8000	12630	4049	3929	51
	PA	57933	8000	12630	9845	1117	51
	PMA	60000	8000	12630	9845	1117	51
Inferencing	Original	-	-	12630	-	-	51
	ALL	-	-	12000	-	-	1127
	Random	-	-	11567	-	-	1127
	Identified	-	-	3741	-	-	288
	Weather	-	-	903	-	-	168

levels (See Sect. 3). Inferencing part has got 5 testing group ("Original", "All", "Random", "Identified", and "Weather") to verify the model robustness. "Original" testing group taken directly from the dataset, "All" contains all the challenges in all levels, "Random" contains the random challenges with random levels, "Identified" contains only the robust range with respect to the challenges and "Weather" contains only weather changes. Breakdown of each dataset before augmentation follows approximately 70-20-10 % ratio for training, testing and validation respectively as presented in Table 2. The dataset after augmentation is maintained at least doubled the size of the original data in the training and validation.

5   Results

Initial experiments with smaller CNN architecture (LeNet-5), for the collected GTSRB and Heavy vehicle data has delivered the classification accuracy of 96% and 86% respectively. As the present study focused on targeting given classifier weakness, identification with smaller architecture was sufficient to support the

Table 3. The results of top performance based on hyper parameters selection. **Lr, Fd, D, B, Fk** being Learning rate, Filter depth, Nodes in hidden layers, Batch size, and Filter kernel size respectively

Dataset	Recognition accuracy				
	Lr	Fd	D	B	Fk
GTSRB	93.40	94.70	95.55	95.56	**95.60**
Heavy vehicle	86.27	80.40	82.40	**86.30**	**86.30**

Fig. 5. Sample images generated with all challenge types with different difficulty levels. *Row* 1 represents the low level, *Row* 2 medium level, *Row* 3 high level. Each *Column* represent the type of noise and can be identified from Table 1 .

Table 4. The results for identified safe-risk ranges

Type	GTSRB		Heavy vehicle	
	Safe ranges	Risk ranges	Safe ranges	Risk ranges
Roll	−14 to 14	−15 to −30 & 15 to 30	−30 to 30	-
Pitch	−6 to 6	−12 to −90 & 12 to 90	−24 to 24	−30 to −90 & 30 to 90
Yaw	−6 to 6	−12 to −90 & 12 to 90	−18 to 18	−24 to −90 & 24 to 90
Occlusion	−1 to 1	−2 to −14 & 2 to 14	−6 to 6	−7 to −14 & 7 to 14
Distance	26 to 30	15 to 25	20 to 30	15 to 19
Motion vertical	1 to 5	6 to 10	1 to 10	-
Motion horizontal	1 to 5	6 to 10	1 to 10	-
Gaussian blur	1 to 10	-	1 to 10	-
Brightness	1 to 13	14 & 15	1 to 15	-
Darkness	1 to 15	-	1 to 15	-
Contrast	1 to 8	9 to 15	1 to 6	7 to 15
Shadow vertical	1 to 4	5 to 15	1 to 4	5 to 15
Shadow horizontal	1 to 4	5 to 15	1 to 8	9 to 15
Fog	-	Low to high	-	Low to high
Rain	-	Low to high	-	Low to high
Snow	-	Low to high	-	Low to high
Dust	-	Low to high	-	Low to high
Smoke	-	Low to high	-	Low to high
Water	-	Low to high	-	Low to high
Bubbles	-	Low to high	-	Low to high

claims. We report the results for model capacity identification, and robustness improvement before & after the framework processing. Selected CNN architecture with its top recognition accuracy based on the systematic hyper-parameters tuning were presented in Table 3. It is clear that the two parameter groups (B and Fk) for heavy vehicle data, the highlighted accuracy in Table 3 delivered similar performance. Therefore, the final set of parameters were selected as, GTSRB data: Lr:5e-4; Fd:192,512; D:200,120; B:256; Fk:7,3; and Heavy vehicle data: Lr:5e-5; Fd:24,64; D:256,100; B:128; Fk:7,3. The Fig. 5 shows some sample challenges augmented on the GTSRB data and similar processes were carried out for the heavy vehicle data. All the tables in this section were divided vertically into two data groups (**Left**: GTSRB data and **Right**: Heavy vehicle data) along with all the accuracy were represented in percentages(%). Initial identification of the model capacity considering 20 different challenge types were presented in Table 4 with selected threshold accuracy of 85% (GTSRB) and 75% (Heavy vehicle) to differentiate the safe-risk ranges. The threshold accuracy were chosen to be 10% less compared to the original recognition accuracy of the model, which helped in bringing effective distribution of the safe and risk ranges for future improvisation. Table 4 supported the claim, where the capacity of the model will be non-static even for the same challenge type and architectural design due to the training data itself. i.e., for the LeNet-5 architecture trained on GTSRB data presented the existence of model degradation in the extreme "Roll" challenge. However, there were no trace of such degradation in "Roll" challenge with the same architecture being trained on heavy vehicle data. Furthermore, improvement in results based on the targeted risk ranges were seen, meanwhile performance stabilization achieved in safe range were presented in Tables 5 and 6.

Table 5. The results for average safe range accuracy based on augmentation. Without Augmentation (WoA), Random Augmentation (RA), Predictive Augmentation (PA) and Predictive Multiple Augmentation (PMA)

Type	GTSRB				Heavy Vehicle			
	WoA	RA	PA	PMA	WoA	RA	PA	PMA
Roll	90.46	89.00	87.60	88.93	84.81	85.57	84.18	85.00
Pitch	93.90	93.02	91.87	90.65	85.43	82.67	81.79	84.06
Yaw	93.78	90.63	90.01	90.69	85.49	81.86	83.82	84.49
Occlusion	92.60	92.91	89.78	92.10	83.75	83.66	82.53	82.67
Distance	90.62	89.50	88.86	89.30	84.90	79.41	81.65	81.23
Motion vertical	91.46	92.51	92.30	90.99	82.74	86.86	82.94	85.90
Motion horizontal	92.15	90.35	91.73	91.29	70.59	66.41	69.16	74.21
Gaussian blur	94.63	93.43	92.21	92.90	86.27	85.49	84.31	86.27
Brightness	90.86	90.58	89.86	90.16	84.96	86.27	84.31	86.27
Darkness	95.03	91.45	92.48	93.82	86.01	85.88	84.18	86.14
Contrast	92.74	92.22	91.84	91.33	83.98	84.80	83.47	85.57
Shadow vertical	90.37	90.18	89.42	89.55	82.35	81.69	83.22	84.06
Shadow horizontal	90.69	90.32	88.54	89.01	86.51	82.84	83.47	85.04
Fog to bubble	0	0	0	0	0	0	0	0

Table 6. The results for average risk range accuracy based on augmentation. Without Augmentation (WoA), Random Augmentation (RA), Predictive Augmentation (PA) and Predictive Multiple Augmentation (PMA)

Type	GTSRB				Heavy Vehicle			
	WoA	RA	PA	PMA	WoA	RA	PA	PMA
Roll	64.34	61.37	66.68	**72.05**	0	0	0	**0**
Pitch	13.63	19.68	23.18	**36.49**	25.32	34.66	33.16	**37.76**
Yaw	14.58	22.49	25.04	**41.41**	28.80	39.72	31.68	**45.19**
Occlusion	11.69	40.71	31.71	**48.94**	41.7	48.64	50.77	**38.56**
Distance	41.32	45.79	55.25	**59.49**	52.61	72.54	71.56	**73.52**
Motion Vertical	63.19	62.98	64.91	**68.25**	0	0	0	**0**
Motion Horizontal	70.59	66.41	69.16	**74.21**	0	0	0	**0**
Gaussian Blur	0	0	0	**0**	0	0	0	**0**
Brightness	83.63	84.47	82.68	**83.02**	0	0	0	**0**
Darkness	0	0	0	**0**	0	0	0	**0**
Contrast	43.95	67.96	58.45	**69.10**	51.85	50.98	52.20	**65.82**
Shadow Vertical	70.40	71.47	70.54	**77.57**	27.94	44.04	56.37	**65.54**
Shadow horizontal	72.35	74.01	74.87	**78.42**	53.92	38.72	50.76	**84.23**
Fog	8.04	41.97	49.99	**66.91**	26.14	21.56	36.79	**83.00**
Rain	10.57	50.16	50.16	**70.41**	21.56	21.56	34.18	**71.89**
Snow	11.71	52.10	49.28	**70.04**	25.49	25.56	31.37	**51.63**
Dust	8.03	37.65	44.86	**64.39**	23.52	26.79	33.42	**39.21**
Smoke	7.32	31.52	38.34	**51.95**	28.10	26.79	34.64	**51.63**
Water	9.61	45.40	49.68	**68.92**	21.56	24.86	30.06	**70.58**
Bubbles	9.49	38.38	45.08	**62.22**	22.87	26.79	33.33	**54.24**

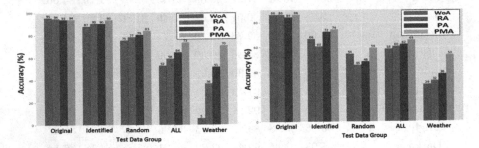

Fig. 6. Comparative overall accuracy based on augmentation in testing group. **Left:** German Traffic Sign Recognition Benchmark Data, **Right:** Heavy Vehicle Data

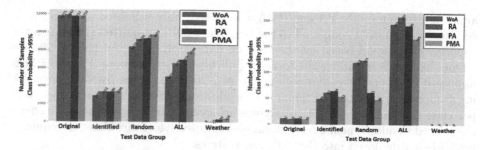

Fig. 7. Comparative confidence based on augmentation in testing group. **Left**: German Traffic Sign Recognition Benchmark Data, **Right**: Heavy Vehicle Data

The tabulated results were presented in average recognition accuracy for each challenge type, due to the multitude of difficulty level in both the safe and risk ranges. From Table 5, results proved that the safer range performance of a model on each challenge type before and after augmentation were maintained with ±2% precision. However, the average safe range accuracy with all zeros in the weather challenges were due to the absence of safe ranges (Table 4). Furthermore, the risk range accuracy has got tremendous improvement in both the proposed PA and PMA compared to WoA and traditional RA as presented in Table 6. However, in some cases particularly the Occlusion and Contrast challenges, fall in the performance were noticed due to the over-fitting and memorization in the CNN model. In addition, from Table 6, even though GTSRB results were promising, heavy vehicle data lacked in some challenges including Pitch, Yaw, Occlusion and Distance. Major reason could be the lack of samples in each challenge type as that of GTSRB and hence led to a less effective generalization. From the results achieved, lower average and overall accuracy for the trained models were acceptable until there is a improvement to support the importance of targeted augmentation technique. To further strengthen our claim, results supported with Fig. 6, where PA is better than RA, showed improvement by ≈ 5–20% in both the datasets. Furthermore, a true positive confidence plots with increased per class confidence level particularly in the identified range enabled us to understand the effectiveness of the PA as shown in Fig. 7. Overall, based on the PA performance from a huge and small dataset, it can be applied to a reasonable scaled dataset size with diverse examples to maintain the model robustness towards challenges.

6   Conclusion

In this paper, we presented a framework to improve the robustness of a traffic sign classification irrespective of camera position, view angles, and variation in environmental condition of an autonomous vehicle including different size & type (Car, Bus, Truck, etc.). The work concentrated on identifying the initial quantitative weakness of the LeNet-5 architecture for each generated challenge type with multitude of difficulty levels. Successive introduction of a targeted augmentation methods: PA and PMA were successfully validated and improved results were achieved compared to the RA. The results supported the non-static capacity of a model based on the training data itself, with the help of 20 different challenges including 264 levels of difficulties. Furthermore, PA and PMA improved the overall classifier accuracy by $\approx$ 5–20% among the five different testing groups compared to traditional RA. In addition to overall accuracy, improved per-class confidence rate particularly was achieved. The framework can be effectively used to adapt the model performance irrespective of variations, as required before being deployed into the real-time systems.

Acknowledgment. The authors would like to thank Nazre Batool, Christopher Norén for Heavy vehicle data, Sribalaji CA, Ashokan Arumugam, and Abhishek S for their constructive comments.

References

1. Autonomous-vehicle technology is advancing ever faster, The Economist - Special report. https://www.economist.com/special-report/2018/03/01/autonomous-vehicle-technology-is-advancing-ever-faster. Accessed 1 Mar 2018
2. Nowakowski, C., Shladover, S.E., Tan, H.S.: Heavy vehicle automation: human factors lessons learned. Procedia Manuf. **3**, 2945–2952 (2015)
3. 44 Corporations Working On Autonomous Vehicles, Autotech (CB Insights). https://www.cbinsights.com/research/autonomous-driverless-vehicles-corporations-list/. Accessed 18 May 2017
4. Heineke, K., Kampshoff, P., Mkrtchyan, A., Shao, E.: Self-driving car technology: when will the robots hit the road? Mckinsey & Company. https://www.mckinsey.com/industries/automotive-and-assembly/our-insights/self-driving-car-technology-when-will-the-robots-hit-the-road. Accessed May 2017
5. Nguwi, Y.Y., Kouzani, A.Z.: Detection and classification of road signs in natural environments. Neural Comput. Appl. **17**(3), 265–289 (2008)
6. Lafuente-Arroyo, S., Gil-Jimenez, P., Maldonado-Bascon, R., Lopez-Ferreras, F., Maldonado-Bascon, S.: Traffic sign shape classification evaluation I: SVM using distance to borders. In: IEEE Intelligent Vehicles Symposium, pp. 557–562 (2005)
7. Mathias, M., Timofte, R., Benenson, R., Van Gool, L.: Traffic sign recognition - how far are we from the solution?. In: IEEE International Joint conference on Neural Networks (IJCNN), pp. 1–8 (2013)
8. CireşAn, D., Meier, U., Masci, J., Schmidhuber, J.: Multi-column deep neural network for traffic sign classification. Neural Netw. **32**, 333–338 (2012)
9. Stallkamp, J., Schlipsing, M., Salmen, J., Igel, C.: The German traffic sign recognition benchmark: a multi-class classification competition. In: IEEE International Joint conference on Neural Networks (IJCNN), pp. 1453–1460 (2011)
10. Timofte, R., Zimmermann, K., Van Gool, L.: Multi-view traffic sign detection, recognition, and 3D localisation. Mach. Vis. Appl. **25**(3), 633–647 (2014)
11. Temel, D., Kwon, G., Prabhushankar, M., AlRegib, G.: CURE-TSR: Challenging Unreal and Real Environments for Traffic Sign Recognition. arXiv preprint arXiv:1712.02463 (2017)
12. Sermanet, P., LeCun, Y.: Traffic sign recognition with multi-scale convolutional networks. In: IEEE International Joint Conference on Neural Networks (IJCNN), pp. 2809–2813 (2011)

13. Bansal, A., Badino, H., Huber, D.: Understanding how camera configuration and environmental conditions affect appearance-based localization. In: Intelligent Vehicles Symposium Proceedings, pp. 800–807 (2014)
14. Zhang, C., Bengio, S., Hardt, M., Recht, B., Vinyals, O.: Understanding deep learning requires rethinking generalization. arXiv preprint arXiv:1611.03530 (2016)
15. Krizhevsky, A., Sutskever, I., Hinton, G.E.: ImageNet classification with deep convolutional neural networks. In: Advances in Neural Information Processing Systems, pp. 1097–1105 (2012)
16. Zeng, Y., Xu, X., Shen, D., Fang, Y., Xiao, Z.: Traffic sign recognition using kernel extreme learning machines with deep perceptual features. IEEE Trans. Intell. Transp. Syst. **18**(6), 1647–1653 (2017)
17. Jin, J., Fu, K., Zhang, C.: Traffic sign recognition with hinge loss trained convolutional neural networks. IEEE Trans. Intell. Transp. Syst. **15**(5), 1991–2000 (2014)
18. Gonzalez, R.C., Woods, R.E.: Digital Image Processing, 2nd edn. Prentice Hall, Upper Saddle River (2012)
19. Joshi, P.: OpenCV with Python By Example. Packt Publishing Ltd, Birmingham (2015)
20. Mordvintsev, A., Abid, K.: Opencv-python tutorials documentation. https://media.readthedocs.org/pdf/opencv-python-tutroals/latest/opencv-python-tutroals.pdf. Accessed 5 Nov 2017

Author Index

Printed in the United States
By Bookmasters